PANDORA

WOMEN IN CLASSICAL GREECE

PANDORA

WOMEN IN CLASSICAL GREECE

ELLEN D. REEDER

WITH ESSAYS BY SALLY C. HUMPHREYS, MARY R. LEFKOWITZ,
FRANÇOIS LISSARRAGUE, JOHN H. OAKLEY, MARGOT SCHMIDT,
H. A. SHAPIRO, CHRISTIANE SOURVINOU-INWOOD,
ANDREW STEWART, FROMA I. ZEITLIN, AND CAROL BENSON

PUBLISHED BY THE TRUSTEES OF

THE WALTERS ART GALLERY
BALTIMORE, MARYLAND

IN ASSOCIATION WITH

PRINCETON UNIVERSITY PRESS
PRINCETON, NEW JERSEY

1995

The Walters Art Gallery acknowledges
with grateful appreciation the sponsors of the exhibition:

PANDORA'S BOX
WOMEN IN CLASSICAL GREECE

National Endowment for the Humanities

Ciba

National Endowment for the Arts

Federal Council on the Arts and the Humanities

Published on the occasion of
Pandora's Box: Women in Classical Greece,
an exhibition conceived, organized, and circulated by
the Walters Art Gallery.

© Copyright 1995 by The Trustees of
The Walters Art Gallery
600 North Charles Street
Baltimore, Maryland 21201

Walters Art Gallery (Baltimore, MD)
    Pandora: Women in Classical Greece
    "In association with Princeton University Press, Princeton."
Library of Congress Catalog Card Number: 95-060831

ISBN: 0-691-01124-9 (softcover)
ISBN: 0-691-01125-7 (hardcover)

Designed by CASTRO/ARTS, Baltimore
Printed by Amilcare Pizzi, S.p.A. - arti grafiche, Milan

THE WALTERS ART GALLERY
Baltimore, Maryland
November 5, 1995 – January 7, 1996

THE DALLAS MUSEUM OF ART
Dallas, Texas
February 4 – March 31, 1996

ANTIKENMUSEUM BASEL UND SAMMLUNG LUDWIG
Basel, Switzerland
April 28 – June 23, 1996

Cover: Head of a Goddess, Athens, Agora Museum, inv. no. S 2094.
Courtesy Agora Museum and the Ephoreia of the Acropolis, photo
Craig Mauzy. Cat. no. 11.

Back cover: Hydria with Danae, by the Danae Painter, Boston, Museum
of Fine Arts, Francis Bartlett Collection, inv. no. 03.792. Courtesy
Museum of the Fine Arts, Boston. Cat. no. 77.

TABLE OF CONTENTS

PREFACE

Over the last few decades, we have acquired a new lens with which to look at Classical Greece. Fueled by advances in anthropology, psychology, social history, and even socio-biology, we ask different questions, and we are better able to identify and interpret the answers. We are now ever more cognizant that Classical Greece was not only a foundation of Western civilization, but also a bridge to prehistoric times, and we are ever more mindful that the Classical period transmitted and rearticulated stories, rituals, motifs, metaphors, and images that were already tens of thousands of years old. We now realize that ways of thinking traditionally identified with Classical Greece have actually characterized human thought for much of human existence.

This exhibition looks at two age-old metaphors for women that pervade Greek myth, ritual, and custom. The first metaphor likens a woman to a container and dominates the stories of Pandora, Danae, Persephone, and Erichthonios. The image aligns women with the earth as a womb and brings to women other properties that a container may suggest, including concealment, withholding, mystery, and treasure. The second metaphor likens a woman to an animal of the wild; the most prominent examples are Thetis, Atalanta, and even Artemis. As the equivalency of an untamed animal, a woman was believed to be instinctively knowledgeable about biological processes and the nurturing of young, but in need of socialization to adapt to man-made institutions of community life; like a domesticated animal, she was regarded as ever harboring impulses to revert, and therewith subvert, society. Mythical articulations of this concept include the Maenads and the Thracian Women; the most graphic ritualistic expression of the idea is the wedding ceremony.

In Classical Greece, the concentration of these ways of thinking about women center on the parthenos, the physically mature young woman who had not yet married. In Greek culture, this girl was between the ages of about eleven and fourteen and was characterized then, as today, as exuberant, spirited, and independent-minded to the point of being uncontrollable. Mythical heroines are invariably parthenoi, as are the unmarried, virgin goddesses, Athena and Artemis. Profound awe and anxiety surrounded this sexually available and fertile young woman, whose commitment was essential to the survival of the community. Numerous myths and rituals address the apprehension that a parthenos will explore her sexual curiosity prematurely (Aglauros), resist marriage (Amazons), or undermine marriage and motherhood (Maenads). Some mythical parthenoi are killed in sacrifice (Iphigenia).

Myths have survived for many thousands of years because, at the same time as they speak vividly and directly of fundamental truths, they also speak on different levels and have multiple, even contradictory, meanings. Like the rituals with which they were often closely aligned, myths have traditionally provided to both adults and children affirmation, instruction, relief, and amusement. As organic entities, myths change with time and with the telling, whether the narration be through words or artistic depictions; thus the myths and rituals depicted in Classical art offer particular insight into the values and concerns that surrounded woman in Classical Greece. At the same time, the representations help us to understand the charged meaning behind everyday customs and behavior, not only in Classical Greece, but even in our own times.

Athens, ACROPOLIS MUSEUM

Athens, AGORA MUSEUM

Athens, NATIONAL ARCHAEOLOGICAL MUSEUM

Baltimore, BALTIMORE MUSEUM OF ART

Baltimore, WALTERS ART GALLERY

Basel, ANTIKENMUSEUM BASEL UND SAMMLUNG LUDWIG

Basel, COLLECTION OF HERBERT A. CAHN

Berlin, STAATLICHE MUSEEN ZU BERLIN PREUSSISCHER
    KULTURBESITZ, ANTIKENSAMMLUNG

Bologna, MUSEO CIVICO ARCHEOLOGICO DI BOLOGNA

Boston, MUSEUM OF FINE ARTS

Brussels, MUSÉES ROYAUX D'ART ET D'HISTOIRE

Cambridge, ARTHUR M. SACKLER MUSEUM, HARVARD
    UNIVERSITY ART MUSEUMS

Cincinnati, CINCINNATI ART MUSEUM

Copenhagen, THE NATIONAL MUSEUM OF DENMARK

Dallas, DALLAS MUSEUM OF ART

Ferrara, MUSEO ARCHEOLOGICO NAZIONALE DI FERRARA

Fulda, SCHLOSS FASANERIE, HESSISCHE HAUSSTIFTUNG

Geneva, COLLECTION OF GEORGE ORTIZ

Hamburg, MUSEUM FÜR KUNST UND GEWERBE

Houston, HOUSTON MUSEUM OF FINE ARTS

Houston, THE MENIL COLLECTION

Jerusalem, COLLECTION OF BATYA AND ELIE BOROWSKI

Kansas City, THE WILLIAM ROCKHILL NELSON AND ATKINS
    MUSEUM OF FINE ARTS

Karlsruhe, BADISCHE LANDESMUSEUM

Kassel, STAATLICHE MUSEEN KASSEL, ANTIKENSAMMLUNG

Leiden, RIJKSMUSEUM VAN OUDHEDEN

London, THE BRITISH MUSEUM

London, COLLECTION OF MR. CLAUDE HANKES-DRIELSMA

Malibu, THE J. PAUL GETTY MUSEUM

Munich, STAATLICHE ANTIKENSAMMLUNGEN MÜNCHEN

Naples, MUSEO ARCHEOLOGICO NAZIONALE DI NAPOLI

New Haven, YALE UNIVERSITY ART GALLERY

New York, COLLECTION OF MR. AND MRS. LAWRENCE A.
    FLEISCHMAN

New York, COLLECTION OF SHELBY WHITE AND LEON LEVY

New York, METROPOLITAN MUSEUM OF ART

New York, THE SOLOW ART AND ARCHITECTURE
    FOUNDATION

Oxford, ASHMOLEAN MUSEUM, UNIVERSITY OF OXFORD

Palermo, MUSEO ARCHEOLOGICO REGIONALE DI PALERMO

Paris, MUSÉE DU LOUVRE

Paris, MUSÉE DU PETIT PALAIS

Princeton, THE ART MUSEUM, PRINCETON UNIVERSITY

Richmond, VIRGINIA MUSEUM OF FINE ARTS

Rome, MUSEO NAZIONALE DI VILLA GIULIA

Saint Louis, THE SAINT LOUIS ART MUSEUM

Saint Petersburg, THE STATE HERMITAGE MUSEUM

San Antonio, SAN ANTONIO MUSEUM OF ART

Syracuse, MUSEO ARCHEOLOGICO REGIONALE DI SIRACUSA

Toledo, THE TOLEDO MUSEUM OF ART

Toronto, ROYAL ONTARIO MUSEUM

University, Mississippi, UNIVERSITY MUSEUMS,
    THE UNIVERSITY OF MISSISSIPPI

Warsaw, THE NATIONAL MUSEUM IN WARSAW

Worcester, WORCESTER ART MUSEUM

Würzburg, MARTIN-VON-WAGNER-MUSEUM DER
    UNIVERSITÄT WÜRZBURG

Zürich, COLLECTION OF MR. HANSJÜRG AND MRS.
    FRANZISKA SAAGER

FOREWORD

The publication of Ellen D. Reeder's landmark volume, *Pandora: Women in Classical Greece*, marks the culmination of nearly a century of devotion to classical art at The Walters, first by Henry Walters (1848-1931), and then by the scholar-curators of the museum he founded. Upon the death in 1894 of his father, William T. Walters, Henry inherited a collection of importance, though of limited scope, which included no classical antiquities. However, by the turn of the century Henry had embarked on an ambitious plan to collect comprehensively from the entire spectrum of the world's artistic heritage, including the art of ancient Greece and Rome.

What began modestly in June 1899, with the acquisition through Sotheby's in London of a few bronzes out of the Forman Collection, had already taken on epic proportions by the spring of 1902, with Henry's bold purchase of the vast collection of Don Marcello Massarenti, a Vatican priest who served as under almoner in the Apostolic Aumbry. Unprecedented in the history of American collecting, this single acquisition brought more than 1,700 works of art to America, including a stellar "Museum" of ancient marbles and bronzes assembled from many parts of Italy, as well as ancient imports from Greece. On July 16, 1902, the chartered steamer *S.S. Minterne* docked in New York with 275 crates of art, some which were not to be opened and catalogued until after Henry Walters' death in 1931, when his entire collection was bequeathed to the City of Baltimore "for the benefit of the people."

Henry Walters' three decades of art acquisition in the classical field were followed by an even longer period of collection cataloguing and object research, mostly associated with the name of Dorothy Hill, who from the mid-1930s to the mid-1970s was Walters' Curator of Ancient Art. With the arrival of Ellen Reeder in that position a decade ago, and especially now with *Pandora*, a new plateau of ancient art scholarship has been reached, characterized by a ground-breaking multidiciplinary approach that explores classical art for what it reveals of the people and culture that gave it birth.

Much as the exhibition can be appreciated on several levels, from the purely aesthetic through the art-historically didactic, to the deeper, anthropological level that invites us to contemplate comparisons with our own culture, so this catalogue is multilevel, from meticulous documentation of individual works in the catalogue proper, to the broadest and most innovative forms of synthesizing interpretation in the essays.

This catalogue and the exhibition it accompanies would not have been possible without the generous collaboration of institutions and individuals worldwide. More than fifty lenders from fourteen countries are cited on their own page in this volume, whose Table of Contents reveals Ellen Reeder's stellar international cast of scholarly collaborators. Special thanks go to the Dallas Museum of Art, under Director Jay Gates, and to the Antikenmuseum und Sammlung Ludwig in Basel, under Dr. Peter Blome, which will present *Pandora* to a national and then an international audience after its departure from Baltimore. We are also especially grateful to Princeton University Press, for collaborating with us in the publication and distribution of this volume.

The catalogue and exhibition were made possible in part by grants from the National Endowment for the Humanities (NEH) and the National Endowment for the Arts (NEA), federal agencies. The exhibition was supported by an indemnity from the Federal Council on the Arts and the Humanities. International sponsorship for the exhibition has been generously provided by Ciba. Our thanks also go to Hillary Rodham Clinton, First Lady of the United States, for agreeing to serve as Honorary Chair of the Exhibition Committee.

Indeed, it was the NEH Implementation Grant for *Pandora*, awarded in 1993, that allowed the transformation of a curator's brilliant idea into reality. Ellen Reeder has masterfully conceived, organized, and now executed what is the most ambitious exhibition that The Walters has undertaken in nearly fifty years. With *Pandora*, Ellen Reeder has set a curatorial standard for the 21st century.

GARY VIKAN
Director, Walters Art Gallery

ACKNOWLEDGMENTS

This exhibition was born in a coffeeshop in 1988, when Andy Stewart remarked to me that it was time for an exhibition about women. His suggestion triggered a memory I had harbored since 1967, when Mary Lefkowitz, in her course on Greek myth at Wellesley, facetiously remarked that a mythical heroine admired by a god could either acquiesce or become a tree. Mary's comment stayed with me longer than I was aware, and in no small way this exhibition is a tribute to her charismatic teaching. This exhibition owes its existence to two other individuals: Bob Bergman as Director of the Walters until 1993 and Gary Vikan, Assistant Director of Curatorial Affairs until 1994, when he assumed the directorship. I salute them both for their willingness to believe in a project that was conceived at a time when an exhibition about women still held overtones of controversy. And I thank Gary profoundly for giving me complete intellectual freedom to carry out this project exactly as I envisioned it. An exhibition becomes a phenomenal outpouring of both hard cash and an institution's human resources, and Gary's willingness to make so sizable a commitment to one person's vision is a gift of extraordinary generosity. That the exhibition was carried out at all is due to the penetrating intelligence, faultless efficiency, and exhaustive assistance of Carol Benson, Assistant Curator of Ancient Art. The exhibition could not have come into being without her, and I am enormously grateful to her.

To Marsha Semmel, Director of Public Programs at the National Endowment for the Humanities. I am deeply appreciative, because her belief in, and enthusiasm for, the exhibition provided the impetus that launched it on its path to realization. Also extremely helpful has been Virginia Wagner in the division of Museums and Historical Organizations at the NEH. At the National Endowment for the Arts, I particularly want to thank Ben Glenn, II, and David Bancroft, Program Specialists in the Museum Program at the NEA. At the Maryland Humanities Council I have appreciated the enthusiasm and support of Barbara Wells Sarudy and Judy Dobbs. I am particularly delighted that my Wellesley classmate, The First Lady Hillary Rodham Clinton, has served as Honorary Chair of our Exhibition Committee.

At the Antikenmuseum Basel und Sammlung Ludwig in Basel, I want to thank Dr. Peter Blome and Dr. Margot Schmidt. Margot's helpfulness, wisdom, encouragement, sympathy, and alacrity in responding to my queries have been invaluable to me throughout this project. At the Dallas Museum of Art, I thank Dr. Anne Bromberg and Jay Gates, whose enthusiasm and commitment were forthcoming from the earliest stages of the project.

International loan exhibitions owe their existence to the goodwill of museum colleagues, and this exhibition represents a particularly extraordinary generosity for which I am very grateful. Colleagues repeatedly gave the very best of their collections and maintained their solid support for the project through several years' worth of endless paperwork and requests for transparencies. I thank Dr. Yannis Tzedakis, Director, Department of Prehistorical and Classical Antiquities, Department of Antiquities, Hellenic Republic; Dr. Peter G. Calligas and Mrs. Ismene Trianti, Acropolis Museum; Mrs. Olga Alexandri, Mrs. Eos Zervoudaki, and Mrs. K. Demakopoulou, National Museum, Athens; Sona Johnston, Baltimore Museum of Art; Herbert Cahn, Basel; Dr. Wolf-Dieter Heilmeyer and Dr. Gertrud Platz, Staatliche Museeen Preussischer Kulturbesitz, Antikensammlung, Berlin; Mrs. Cristiana Morigi Govi and Mrs. Gioia Meconcelli, Museo Civico Archeologico, Commune di Bologna; Dr. Cornelius C. Vermeule, III, and Dr. John Herrmann, Museum of Fine Arts, Boston; Professor F. van Noten, Dr. J. Ch. Balty, and Dr. Christiane Tytgat, Musées royaux d'art et d'histoire, Brussels; Dr. David Mitten and Amy Brauer, Harvard University Art Museums, Arthur M. Sackler Museum, Cambridge; Dr. Glenn Markoe, Cincinnati Museum of Art; Dr. Bodil Bundgaard Rasmussen, Nationalmuseet, Copenhagen; Mrs. Fede Berti and Mrs. Tiziana Giuberti, Museo Archeologico Nazionale di Ferrara, Ferrara; Dr. Meinolf Siemer, Museum Schloss Fasanerie, Hessische Hausstiftung, Fulda; George Ortiz, Geneva; Dr. Wilhelm Hornbostel and Dr. Cornelia Ewigleben, Museum für Kunst und Gewerbe, Hamburg; Dr. Peter Marzio and Anne-Louise Schaffer, Museum of Fine Arts, Houston; Mr. Paul Winkler, Dr. Bertrand Davezac, and Dr. Susan Barnes, The Menil Collection, Houston; Batya and Elie Borowski, Jerusalem; Dr. Robert Cohon, William Rockhill Nelson and Atkins Museum of Fine Arts, Kansas City; Dr. Michael Maass, Badisches Landesmuseum, Karlsruhe; Dr. Peter Gercke, Staatliche Museen Kassel, Antikensammlung; Dr. G. J. Verwers and Dr. R. Halbertsma, Rijksmuseum van Oudheden, Leiden;

Dr. Dyfri Williams, British Museum; Mr. Claude Hankes-Drielsma, London; Dr. Marion True, J. Paul Getty Museum, Malibu; Dr. Raimund Wünsche and Dr. Friedrich W. Hamdorf, Staatliche Antikensammlungen und Glyptothek, Munich; Dr. Stefano de Caro and Mrs. Maria Rosaria Borriello, Museo Archeologico Nazionale, Naples; Susan Matheson, Yale University Art Gallery, New Haven; Mr. and Mrs. Lawrence Fleischman, New York; Shelby White and Leon Levy, New York; Dr. Carlos Picón and Dr. Joan Mertens, Metropolitan Museum of Art, New York; Sheldon Solow and Rosalie S. Wolff, New York; Dr. Michael Vickers, Ashmolean Museum, Oxford; Mrs. Carmela Angela di Stefano and Mrs. Agata Villa, Museo Regionale di Palermo; Dr. Alain Pasquier and Dr. Martine Denoyelle, Musée du Louvre; Mme. Paulette Hornby, Musée du Petit Palais; Dr. Michael Padgett, Princeton University Art Museum; Dr. Margaret Ellen Mayo, Virginia Museum of Fine Arts, Richmond; Dott. Giovanni Scichilone, Dott. Marco Sala, and Dr. ssa Maria Antonietta Rizzo, Museo Nazionale di Villa Giulia, Rome; Dr. Gerry D. Scott, San Antonio Museum of Art; Dr. Sidney Goldstein, St. Louis Art Museum; Dr. Michael Pietrovsky, Dr. V. Matveyev, Dr. S.P. Boriskovskaya, and Mrs. Lyubov 'M Utkina, The State Hermitage Museum, St. Petersburg; Dott. Giuseppe Voza and Mrs. Amalia Curcio, Museo Archeologico Regionale, Syracuse; Dr. Kurt Luckner, Toledo Museum of Art; Dr. Neda Leipen and Mrs. Alison Harle Easson, Royal Ontario Museum, Toronto; William Griffith, University Museums, the University of Mississippi; Dr. W. Godlewski, Dr. Andrew Stoga, and Dr. Witold Dobrowolski, National Museum, Warsaw; Dr. Susan E. Strickler and Dr. David Acton, Worcester Museum of Art; Dr. Irma Wehgartner and Dr. Erika Simon, Martin-von-Wagner-Museum der Universität Würzburg; Mr. Hansjürg and Mrs. Franziska Saager, Zürich.

I owe special thanks to the catalogue essayists, whose enthusiasm, goodwill, and solid advice immeasurably enhanced the volume. In addition to Dr. Margot Schmidt, Dr. Andrew Stewart, and Carol Benson, I thank Sally Humphreys, Dr. Mary Lefkowitz, Dr. François Lissarrague, Dr. John Oakley, Dr. H. A. Shapiro, Dr. Christiane Sourvinou-Inwood, and Dr. Froma Zeitlin. Every one of these colleagues provided references, thoughtful responses to my ideas, and unflagging support. At times, John Oakley functioned as a daily consultant.

A tremendous number of individuals have lent their assistance and advice, and to all of them I am extremely grateful: Dr. William Coulson, Maria Pilali, Dr. John Camp, Craig Mauzy, and Jan Jordan, all of the American School of Classical Studies in Athens, Elizabeth Barber, Hugo Meyer, Angelos Delivorrias, A. Kauffmann-Samaras, Eva Stehle, Allaire Brumfield, Antonio Addari and Katy Spurrell of Propileo Transport; Ambassador Loucas Tsilas and Dionysios Zois of the Greek Embassy in Washington, Roberto Stinelli of the Italian Embassy in Washington, Elaine Fantham, Marcel Detienne, Giulia Sissa, Dick Keresey and Seth Bright of Sotheby's, Ian Jenkins, Tom Swope, Gloria Pinney, Guy Hedreen, Evelyn Harrison, Lilly Kahil, Norma Blumberg, Hadley Kruczek,

Lawrence Seastrum, Laura Freedlander, Marilyn Goldberg, Joe Basile, Kim Hartswick, Beth Cohen, Robert Sutton, Homer Thompson, Marjorie Venit, Getzel and Sheila Cohen, and Linda Roccos and Penny Small of the *LIMC*. Dr. Jerome Eisenberg provided special assistance with arrangements for the exhibition. For the audiovisual, I am indebted to the talents and enthusiasm of Mike Gibbons, Sharon Jackson of Spicer Productions, John Dean, and Bob Dorsey.

An exhibition at the Walters eventually absorbs the energies of every single member of the museum's staff, and I thank all of my colleagues for giving so unstintingly to a project that was not of their choosing. I would particularly like to thank: Beth Howell for her superb grant-writing expertise and for her unflagging support; Susan Tobin for her uncompromising standards in photography; Theresa Segreti, Julia Evins, and Judy Lenehan for their incomparable creativity in graphics; Diane Stillman for her imaginative educational programing; Terry Drayman-Weisser, Eric Gordon, and Julie Lauffenburger for their omnipresent conservation assistance; Harold Stephens for his unending patience in financial details; Joy Heyrman and Donna Wilson for their contagious optimism; Beth Dietrick for her helpful ideas in public relations; Shreve Simpson for her expertise and guidance; John Klink, Charles Mack, Mike McKee, Paul Daniels, Doug Hoagg, Wayne Johnson, Matthew Geneczko, and Susan Wallace for their precision and eye in installation; Will Lowry for going out of his way repeatedly in order to solve my computer problems; and Leopoldine Prosperetti, Kathleen Emerson-Dell, Joan-Elizabeth Reid, and Barbara Fegley for their skillful registrarial management.

The magic force that shaped this volume was Alex Castro, whose talents as a designer are equalled only by his perfectionism and generosity of spirit. I am extremely grateful to him. As copy editor, Carla Brenner effortlessly polished the manuscript, and, as classicist, she unfailingly caught my errors and made suggestions that honed my reasoning. Sara Lycett appeared as if sent from above to add her marvelous proofreading skills. Barbara Sadick and Pamela Schechter of American Pizzi Offset Corporation supplied remarkable capability and calm. And from the beginning, Elizabeth Powers of the Princeton University Press has been an on-going source of encouragement and empathy, a welcome pillar of support that I had the privilege of enjoying during our earlier collaboration in 1988.

Finally, I thank close friends, Martie Sanger, Pat Krongard, Rebecca Hoffberger, and Isabel and Laurance Roberts, who have heard more about *Pandora* than they could ever have wanted. And I thank my parents, who never failed to understand for almost two years that there really never was any time left over for them.

E.D.R.
May, 1995

INTRODUCTION: AN OVERVIEW

This volume has its roots in two important developments that have taken place in the study of Greek civilization over the last two decades. First is the widespread acceptance of a multidisciplinary approach, whereby the traditional methods of Classical scholarship have been enriched by findings from anthropology,[1] psychology, and social history. The second landmark has been the publication of the *Lexicon Iconographicum Mythologiae Classicae*, an unprecedented and comprehensive compilation of mythological representations that has at last made it possible to scrutinize and compare the changing visual presentation of myth throughout the Greek and Roman eras. It is most fitting that the exhibition this volume accompanies is being presented in Basel, the international headquarters of the *LIMC*.

Recent advances in our understanding of human behavior and the human mind have enabled us to appreciate the relevance to Classical scholarship of anthropological analyses of other societies, traditional and advanced. We are also now more attentive to myth and fairy tales[2] as expressive of individual and social concerns, and we know that the human mind not only has a predisposition to work in metaphor and ambiguous visual imagery, but is often at its most insightful and revealing when doing so. We are now more fully cognizant that most of human existence was passed in a hunter-gatherer way of life and that many more of our ways of thinking than was previously assumed almost certainly have their origins in that era.[3] We now realize that, while Classical Greek civilization gives us an unprecedented clarity of thought and a wealth of compelling imagery, many of these patterns of thinking and even forms of their expression, whether myth, ritual, metaphor, or charged imagery, have much older roots in preliterate times. Indeed, the two metaphors explored here, woman as a container and as an untamed animal, very probably go back to an age-old identification of women with what were perceived as the two critically important sources of sustenance in early communities: the womb of the earth and a Mistress of Wild Beasts who provided game.

Today we view myth as a traditional story that can express individual and collective apprehensions and that can communicate social values.[4] The myths addressed in this volume were chosen because they center on anxieties surrounding the mature but unmarried maiden (parthenos) and the transition, even sacrifice, she must undergo in order for the community to survive. As an organic entity, myth changes with the telling, and one of the most exciting recent developments in the study of Classical vase-painting is the realization that, in presenting his interpretation of a myth, a painter could call on as subtle and complex a vocabulary of imagery as was available to his literary counterpart.

Where myth can provide an often graphic exploration of apprehension, ritual can process, if not totally resolve, these dilemmas.[5] As a form of communication, ritual enables participants to affirm social expectations, as, for example, in the wedding ceremony.[6] Sometimes, ritual demonstrates what is socially desirable by acting out its opposite; in the Adonis festival women willingly destroyed young seedlings,[7] and, in some rituals relating to transitions to manhood youths dressed in women's garments.[8]

We also now realize that although Greek poets and artists were male, we can very definitely hear the voice of ancient Greek women. We have objects that women dedicated in sanctuaries, and we have works of art that were intentionally created to please women, especially as wedding gifts. We know a great deal about rituals that were observed exclusively by women and that were thus perpetuated voluntarily by women because these rituals spoke directly to their needs.[9] We also have myths that so specifically address female dilemmas that women surely transmitted and drew comfort from these stories. The most prominent example is the story of Demeter's loss and recovery of Persephone, which explores the theme of a mother's loss of her daughter in marriage.[10] The intensity of Demeter's and Persephone's love, unrivalled in Greek myth as the prototypical bond of affection between two individuals, could not have attained such credibility without female endorsement. Similarly, the many myths that take up the process of resistance and reconciliation as a maturing girl moves to marriage and motherhood would not have survived had they not spoken poignantly to the painful and widespread dilemma of a young woman's forfeiture of individuality and freedom before what was perceived as the greater need of the group.[11] It was a fundamental principle of Greek thought that the community's survival depended upon the integration into it of young adults, even though that integration might well result in death to women in childbirth.

To the argument that women were socialized to believe what they did, we can reply that so, also, were men. What is noteworthy

Fig. 1. Detail, Lekythos by the Phiale Painter, New York, Metropolitan Museum of Art, Rogers Fund, 1917, inv. no. 17.230.35 (Catalogue no. 113).

tasks, young girls must have been perpetually regaled with tales of the recalcitrant Atalanta or descriptions of the splendid wedding of the once hesitant Thetis.

In recent years we have gained a deeper understanding into the strength and age of Greek goddesses. It is now widely agreed that, in the ancestral civilization from which Classical Greek culture is descended, the pre-eminent divinities were female.[14] It has been persuasively argued that a primeval female goddess was originally worshipped as a spontaneous giver of earth's bounty and that only subsequently was the male role acknowledged.[15] It is thought that an accentuation of a male contribution coincided with the introduction of agriculture, because the comparison of male impregnation with the plow was a fundamental conceit in Greek thought, even figuring prominently in the wedding ceremony. Female divinities remained prominent throughout the Bronze Age, and it is fairly certain that the dedication of ritual cloths by women to goddesses was an important part of Bronze Age cult.[16] Similarly, the fairly recent discovery of the Saffron-Gatherer fresco from Thera has provided compelling evidence for the prominence of a female puberty ritual involving saffron.[17] Compelling echoes of these rituals and beliefs resonate in Classical culture,[18] where there is reason to recognize a correlation between women's lessened social stature and her ever more diminished contribution to the economy of the polis.[19]

It is not difficult to understand why Greek culture placed such a focus upon the parthenos, who was a physically mature but unmarried young woman, aged between eleven and fourteen.[20] As has been true is other societies past and present, the young maiden was regarded with awe and wonder for her spirit and exuberance, as she traveled the fascinating pathway from girlhood to womanhood. Because the parthenos was not yet fully integrated into the fabric of society, she seemed to be temporarily, tantalizingly, suspended, even as her fertility symbolized the community's future and survival. What is provocative about Greek attitudes toward the parthenos is not, therefore, that she figured prominently in Greek thought, but rather that the parthenos was thought to harbor a curious and ominous ambiguity. At the same time as she was viewed as the imminent embodiment of family, home, and community, she was also regarded as a potential source of social subversion, an essentially uncontrollable force. The parthenos, and the married woman she became, were believed capable of reverting to her unsocialized origins, causing men to revert with her, and therewith destroying the entire social order.

The far-reaching implications of this attitude toward women explains all levels of sexual tension in Greek thought. These range from the sexual undercurrents of the metaphor of courtship as the pursuit of a female by an armed male,[21] to the sexual electricity that draws bride and groom together in the wedding ceremony,[22] to the outbursts of misogynous violence that color depictions of symposium scenes and combats between Greeks and Amazons.[23] It is widely recognized that one of the most basic tenets of Greek culture

and thought-provoking about this socialization process is not, therefore, that it existed, but how methodical it was. A young girl's steps to womanhood were defined through specific ritual roles (as Little Bears, the Arrephoroi, the kanephoros) and dramatic stories of goddesses and mythical heroines, all of which clarified expected patterns of behavior.[12] Although deprived of a public life, women received support and guidance within a community of women, and they found affirmation and self-confidence in the belief that they enjoyed the special protection of all-powerful female divinities.[13] Women's lives afforded countless opportunities for the transmission to maturing girls of traditional stories that carried didactic subtexts. While spinning, weaving, and performing household

Fig. 2. Greece and the Mediterranean. Map by Judy Lenehan/Alex Castro.

was a belief in the equilibrium of forces. At the same time, however, the Greeks also recognized the validity, even need, to test the edge between balance and imbalance, a compulsion that finds expression in the alignment of a woman's sexuality and fertility with the animal side of her femaleness.[24] Plato Comicus' celebrated comment to a young bridegroom was surely as much of a challenge as a warning when he commented that if the husband relaxed too much, the wife would get out of control.[25]

The gratification derived from experimenting with a balance of sexual tensions does not completely explain why the Greeks envisioned such an extreme polarization of the sexes and why we so often detect a paranoid anxiety toward women that occasionally erupts as misogynous hostility.[26] It has often been pointed out that the Greek tendency to think in antitheses, as evidenced by the grammatical structure of their language, probably accounts for some of their polarization of male and female characteristics. Another explanation is probably the age-old strategy, observed in many other societies, of encouraging boys to embrace qualities

designated as manly by assigning to women characteristics, such as timidity, passivity, and irrationality, considered undesirable in a man. It has also been argued that anxieties about women in Classical Athens were surely related to a well documented awareness that women did not have a direct investment in the democratic system and that subversion of a system is always to be feared from those who have the least to lose if that system is overthrown. One should also keep in mind that Classical Athens was extraordinarily aggressive and competitive. An exaltation of masculinity in the first decades of the fifth century was prompted both by the exhilarating defeat of the Persians[27] and by the development of a democratic form of government that equated all male citizens on the grounds that each of them headed a household in which women, children, and slaves were subordinate. Emphasis upon manliness can translate into intense pressures to attain a demanding standard of manhood, and not all the resulting aggression could be channeled into warfare.[28] It is interesting to note the change in mood in late fifth-century vase-painting, where a celebration of

15

family and romance coincided with a well-attested growing aversion to war and public life.

Just as an undomesticated animal served as a metaphor for a woman, so could one argue that the Greek view of women functioned as a metaphor for an aspect of the human condition that the Greeks believed was intrinsic to both men and women. The image of women as only temporarily socialized, harboring the seeds of social subversion, mirrors the Greek view that irrationality was innate to humanity and that settled community life was fragile, precariously balanced, and ever vulnerable to destabilization.

Structure of the Volume

This volume has five sections.

In the first part of the book, lengthy essays explore specific aspects of female mythical figures, rituals, imagery, and customs in Classical Greek culture. The first essay, "Women and Men in Classical Greece," is intended to provide a general background for the reader and constitutes a synthesis of current scholarship. Special attention is given to the attitudes toward women that underlay the legal and social codes.

The nine other essayists take up more specific topics and demonstrate that, whatever the formal training of these scholars may have been, their current methodology is multidisciplinary, incorporating approaches drawn from art historical and literary analysis, anthropology, cultural history, and psychology.

In her essay "The Last Hours of the Parthenos," Mary Lefkowitz considers the parthenos particularly as she is presented in Athenian drama. Lefkowitz shows that this maiden of approximately the age of fourteen was regarded with wonder and respect as suspended for a brief and glorious moment before becoming integrated into society as wife and mother. A parthenos, Lefkowitz observes, was considered to be beautiful, intelligent, articulate, and courageous, capable of daring action. She was also thought to be reckless and susceptible to errors of judgment; as Lefkowitz notes, a parthenos was not so different from real-life young women. Lefkowitz also focuses on such acts of heroism as self-sacrifice, especially as portrayed in Euripides.

In his essay "The Cult of Heroines: Kekrops' Daughters," Alan Shapiro investigates the Kekropidai, the three daughters of Kekrops who were honored with sanctuaries on the slopes of the Acropolis. Shapiro argues for the considerable antiquity of the heroines and, by means of literary and artistic evidence, he explores the strength and character of their cult. Commenting on the rarity of heroine cults in Greece, he remarks on the exceptionally strong presence of young unmarried women in sanctuaries on and around the Acropolis. Shapiro demonstrates the extent to which the Kekropidai (also called Aglaurides) were linked both with the Arrephoroi and

Athena's peplos, and he specifically explores the association of the Kekropidai with the story of Erichthonios (see **Erichthonios**).

Froma Zeitlin, in "The Economics of Hesiod's Pandora," examines in depth the story of Pandora and shows that Hesiod frames the creation of woman in economic terms. Hesiod, Zeitlin points out, does not view husband-and-wife interaction as one of a shared existence and responsibility but rather regards woman as an economic liability, who depletes man of his worldly assets and consumes him sexually, at the same time as she possesses a power over him that leaves him unable to retaliate. Emphasizing the degree to which Hesiod obscures the physicality between men and women, Zeitlin correlates the Elpis in Pandora's pithos with the child in its mother's womb; to open the pithos, Zeitlin observes, is to breach virginity, while closing the pithos on Elpis marks the beginning of pregnancy. Zeitlin contrasts the story of Pandora with that of Adam and Eve and finds that the key point of differentiation is Hesiod's assumption of woman's unambiguous inferiority to man, in tandem with her irresistible power over him (see **Pandora**).

In her essay "Sorceresses," Margot Schmidt examines two other mythical women, Medea and Circe. Schmidt points out that these women had the ability to destroy men (Medea) or to diminish or enhance their masculinity (Circe); ironically, she notes, these sorceresses represented the antithesis of Athenian customs, because magical incantations in real life were used exclusively by men. Schmidt also observes that in contrast to their descendants—the witches of modern European history—both Medea and Circe were attractive young women. Schmidt further notes that classical vase-painters chose to depict the moment of Circe's defeat, when male supremacy in the social order is re-established (see **Circe** and **Medea**).

John Oakley, author of "Nuptial Nuances: Wedding Images in Non-Wedding Scenes of Myth," examines wedding imagery. This includes: the dressing of the bride; the bridal veil; the wedding wreaths; the bride's gesture of unveiling; the bridegroom's clasp of the bride's wrist; and the bridal procession. Oakley finds that nuptial imagery frequently appears in non-wedding contexts as a means of foreshadowing and of introducing overtones of irony, metaphor, and ambiguity, with the result that the multiple aspects of a scene or subject become accentuated. Oakley urges us to regard red-figure vase-painting as possessing as rich and complex a language of imagery as that which we have long acknowledged and scrutinized in literature (see **The Wedding**).

In his essay, "Rape?," Andrew Stewart examines the many depictions in Greek vase-painting of pursuit scenes in which women flee before gods, heroes, and mortal men, whose pursuit will culminate in sexual intercourse and occasionally marriage. Stewart finds an explanation for the popularity of the scenes in pressures upon men imposed by Athenian society's emphasis upon male supremacy. Stewart points out that the scenes of female flight and resistance express male anxieties about marrying well, and, once married, of achieving the simultaneous orgasm that was thought necessary for conception. Stewart also believes that the early fifth-century popularity of pursuit scenes reflects the emphasis on masculinity, male bonding, and male superiority over women institutionalized by the newly introduced democratic system. The diminution of pursuit scenes in late fifth-century vase-painting is explained by Stewart as a manifestation of a widely internalized self-control, *sophrosyne*, which now classified depictions of male fantasies as distasteful displays of excess, comparable with gluttony and alcoholism (see **Pursuit Scenes**).

In his essay "Women, Boxes, Containers: Some Signs and Metaphors," François Lissarrague addresses one of the key themes of the exhibition: images of containers and their relationship with women. Lissarrague points out that boxes, baskets, and many types of vases were so intimately linked with women as to constitute pivotal motifs in the stories of Danae and the Aglaurides. He further notes that vase-painters used the presence of these receptacles to define women's interior domestic space, and even to reinforce the femaleness of an old woman's inebriation. There was no Classical male equivalent, Lissarrague notes, to the female head vases that dramatically objectified women. Lissarrague also points out that containers, and their contents of toiletries and jewelry, were so closely associated with women's power of seduction that the reverse, an artist's placement of a container in the hands of a man, intimated a corresponding inversion in the story: a man's impending seduction of a woman (see **Women as Containers**, **Danae**, and **Erichthonios**).

Fig. 4. Detail of Side A, Kantharos by Douris, Brussels, Musées Royaux d'Art et d'Histoire, inv. no. A 718 (Catalogue no. 120).

Sally Humphreys, author of "Women's Stories," challenges the traditional point of view that women were completely powerless in Athenian society. She asks whether women's separate, secluded lives were really as pitiable as the modern scholar often assumes. Humphreys points out that women's status outside the system gave them a considerable freedom, especially as priestesses and suppliants. She compares Athenian women's lives with those of women in Islamic societies, in which male and female spheres are separate, but where women, within their own sphere, enjoy a considerable freedom from which male hierarchy is absent. Humphreys asks whether woman's role as a herd animal in the Islamic social system is any less desirable or respectable than that of the domestic pet that, she argues, has characterized the role of the housewife in Western industrialized society. Above all, Humphreys argues that the multiple intentions and interpretations of a custom or a representation warn us not to embrace too simplistic an analysis of Athenian mores.

In her essay, "Male and Female, Public and Private, Ancient and Modern," Christiane Sourvinou-Inwood challenges the long-standing thesis that women had no presence in the public world of the polis. She points out that, whereas in the household women were subjected to their husbands even in religious matters, in the sphere of public religion, such priestesses as those of Athena Polias and Artemis Brauronia were complementary and equal to men. Gender hierarchy, Sourvinou-Inwood comments, asserted itself only where religion interfaced with the political sphere; a woman priestess, for example, was not permitted to address a public assembly. Sourvinou-Inwood also finds a public persona for women within the context of grave monuments which, she argues, were public statements in keeping with the social dimension of cemeteries. Sourvinou-Inwood observes that a woman's representation on

Fig. 3. Detail of Side A, Pelike by Polygnotos, New York, Metropolitan Museum of Art, Rogers Fund, 1945, inv. no. 45.11.1 (Catalogue no. 136).

a grave monument, especially in tandem with a complementary inscription, was intended to secure the survival of her memory beyond the confines of the family. Above all, Sourvinou-Inwood warns against the current eagerness to compare ancient Athenian society with "Mediterranean societies," including modern Greece.

The catalogue proper is divided into four sections. Section One looks at the development of the portrayal of women over the course of the fifth century, with special attention to an evolving vocabulary of pose, gesture, and gaze. The demeanor of the respectable women is contrasted with the conduct expected from the hetaira (prostitute). The works of art show clearly that the Greek sense of femaleness embraced a woman's body, face, clothing, ornament, hair, movement, and gesture. No less important, although least captured in art, were a woman's voice and mind.

Section Two explores the container as a metaphor for a woman, who is viewed as a generative force, bestower of the life cycle that embraces death as well as birth. As the myths of Danae, Pandora, Persephone, and Athena's care of Erichthonios demonstrate, the metaphor of containment carries additional connotations of concealment, treasure, secrecy, deception, and withholding.[29] Also explored is the imagery of textiles, which were regarded in Greek thought as, if not precisely a metaphor for a woman, then as an extension of her being.

Section Three explores the metaphor of a woman as an untamed animal who grows to adulthood under Artemis' supervision, then undergoes the process of socialization symbolized by marriage and motherhood. Mythical heroines such as Iphigenia, Thetis, Amymone, and Atalanta epitomize the difficulty, even impossibility, of this transition.

Section Four explores the catastrophic mythical ramifications of the on-going anxiety that the taming process of women would not work and that innate female impulses would ultimately reassert themselves. Evoking visceral fears, which have survived into modern times, were such perceived female behavior as uncontrollable frenzies that impelled women to murder men (**Orpheus and the Thracian Women**, **Maenads**); utter rejection of a man-centered social structure (**Amazons**); the ability to enervate men, depleting them of their masculinity (**Eos and Kephalos**); and the intangible and irresistible powers of gaze (**Gorgons**), voice (**Sirens**), and mastery over poisonous substances (**Medea** and **Circe**).[30]

A focus upon women inevitably spotlights men and, more specifically, Greek ideas of manhood, against which women, and, indeed, all manifestations of the "other" were defined. The richness of recent anthropological investigations into manhood in traditional and Western industrialized societies[31] promises to lend much needed insight into our understanding of Greek men. Classical scholarship has given us innumerable studies of the Greek hero, but perhaps it is time now to give attention to the almost unattainable ideal of Greek manhood, and to the myths, rituals, and customs that evolved as a response to it.

ELLEN D. REEDER

1. For a good overview, see Kuper (1994).

2 Bettelheim (1975); Tatar (1987); Tatar (1992), especially 98-110.

3. See Wilson (1978); Burkert (1983), especially 16-18, 80; **Aktaeon**.

4. Burkert (1979) 2-23.

5. Burkert (1979) 35-55; Caldwell (1990) 62.

6. See **The Wedding**.

7. See No. 61.

8. See "Women and Men in Classical Greece;" **Maenads**.

9. See the discussion of the Thesmophoria in **Women as Containers**.

10. See **Persephone and Demeter**.

11. See **Thetis and Peleus, Amymone and Poseidon, Atalanta**.

12. See **Little Bears, Plynteria and Arrephoroi**; no. 60.

13. For women's roles as priestesses, see "Male and Female, Public and Private, Ancient and Modern" by C. Sourvinou-Inwood; for a discussion of a community of females, see "Women's Stories," by S. Humphreys.

14. Burkert (1985) 218. See also **Athena, Artemis, Demeter and Persephone**.

15. Cantarella (1987) 11-15; Dubois (1988) 28; see **Demeter and Persephone, The Wedding**.

16. See **Textiles, Athena**.

17. See Doumas (1992) 127-75 and Marinatos (1984) 62-68; see also **Textiles**.

18. For the cult of the Aglaurides, see "The Cult of Heroines: Kekrops' Daughters" by H. A. Shapiro.

19. See **Textiles**; Barber (1994) 283.

20. See "The Last Hours of the Parthenos" by M. Lefkowitz.

21. See **Pursuit Scenes**; see also "Rape?" by A. Stewart.

22 See **The Wedding**; see also "Nuptial Nuances: Wedding Images in Non-Wedding Scenes of Myth" by J. Oakley.

23. See no. 120 and fig. 10 in the essay by S. Humphreys.

24. See **Bears, Women as Animals**.

25. Plato Comicus, 18K.

26. See "Women and Men in Classical Greece."

27. See Castriota (1992) 150 regarding the imagery of the Amazons.

28. See remarks by A. Stewart in "Rape?"

29. See "The Economics of Hesiod's Pandora" by F. Zeitlin and "Women, Boxes, Containers: Some Signs and Metaphors" by F. Lissarrague.

30. See "Sorceresses" by M. Schmidt.

31. Gilmore (1990), esp. 39, 107, 113-14, 224; Rotundo (1993); Strauss (1993).

ESSAYS

Young women, in my opinion, have the sweetest existence known to mortals in their fathers' homes,
for their innocence always keeps children safe and happy.
But when we reach puberty and can understand, we are thrust out and sold away....

Sophokles, *Tereus* frag. 583 (trans. Lefkowitz and Fant, 1982)

Desire conquers, bright, from the eyes of a happily wed bride.

Sophokles, *Antigone* 795-801

We are women, a tribe sympathetic to each other
and most reliable in preserving our common interests.

Euripides, *Iphigenia in Tauris* 1061-62

The Ideal Woman

Greek writers, overwhelmingly male, are quite definite about their conception of the ideal woman. She was beautiful, with a beautiful voice, sexy, intelligent (necessary to run a household well), tall, industrious, well-born, and fertile. She was also virtuous, modest, passive, submissive, silent, and invisible. These latter qualities were the complete antithesis of those considered desirable in the ideal male.[1]

The qualities envisioned for the ideal female were also almost diametrically opposed to the perception of her true nature. A woman was considered incapable of restraining her insatiable sexual appetites, and her sensuality was believed to have the potential to subvert men, the family, and society. To transcend her innate nature was the goal every woman was supposed to strive for with the help of learned behavior, such as modest dress and downcast eyes, and such institutions as marriage. Complicating this effort was the message, clearly expressed in Greek myth and ritual, that men found sexually alluring a young woman who was not yet subdued (see **Women as Animals**, **Atalanta**, and **Peleus and Thetis**). Studies within this century of traditional Greek village life have observed a similar emphasis upon this subtle and complex balance of tensions; the adolescent beauty chosen to lead the girls' dances is expected to be spirited and alluring without giving the impression of being promiscuous.[2] Only a carefully reared young woman could master this formula.

A Woman's Life

A baby girl's first hurdle was to be allowed to live.[3] It was her father's decision whether to rear her or expose her in an unpopulated area to die, because a girl was an expensive addition to a household, requiring a dowry, but not carrying on the family name. The custom of exposing baby girls continued into Hellenistic times and was surely of ancient origin; in one of the versions of Atalanta's childhood, the heroine had been exposed as an unwanted daughter (see **Atalanta**).

In the home of an Athenian citizen, a little girl grew up in the care of a nurse, who was probably a slave, and passed a great deal of time in the women's quarters of the house, which seem most often to have been on an upper floor, and which were entered through doors that in vase-painting signify the quarters themselves. In the *gynaikon*, mothers nursed their children and engaged in textile production, both spinning thread and weaving. Together with childbearing, the time-consuming fabrication of cloth was the principal responsibility of a woman, and was indelibly associated with her (see **Textiles**). Women also passed their leisure time in the *gynaikon*, busying themselves with cosmetics and musical instruments. Here they entertained their female friends. The *gynaikon* was the quintessential female space, and women were closely identified with the concept of enclosure that it represented (see **Women as Containers**).

Although the women's quarters of the house were the private domain of the mistress and mother, she was also inextricably associated with the entire household, manager of its storeroom and receptacles, such as pithoi, and closely identified with the wealth these safeguarded (see **Women as Containers**). As a Hesiod noted, a wife's efficiency was the factor that determined whether a household should prosper,[4] and several centuries later Aristotle compared a marriage to an economic partnership.[5] The sentiment has survived into modern times, because in traditional Greek villages of the twentieth century it is said that a woman makes a house bloom, like a garden.[6] Whereas the dining room (*andron*, literally "man's room") was where a man entertained his drinking friends

Fig. 1. The Acropolis in Athens. Photograph John Dean.

with symposia, a husband and father was most at home in the public spaces of the city where he carried out his primary role as a politically active citizen.

The degree to which a married woman, aged about fourteen and above, could move freely around the city has been a topic of lively debate over the past century.[7] Opinions have consistently reflected the mores of the period in which the scholar was writing, and the current attitude is that women did have a certain amount of mobility. Obtaining water from the fountain house was always a woman's task, as well as a highly sociable activity, although well-to-do houses could send slaves for that purpose and to carry out the basic shopping. Women probably attended dramatic performances, and we know that it was women's responsibility to visit the tombs of family members, bringing offerings and tying sashes around the stelai. We also know that women attended public speeches, such as the funerary oration of Perikles, and they certainly visited such sanctuaries as those of Artemis at Brauron and the Sanctuary of the Nymph at the foot of the Acropolis. Plutarch tells of the gossip that Pheidias arranged assignations for Perikles with Athenian women who came to the Acropolis on the pretext of admiring the works of art,[8] and Euripides refers to female visitors who admired the monuments at Delphi.[9] In all movement outside the home, a woman was supposed to be inconspicuous to the point of invisibility, and although use of the veil is not yet well understood, she was probably expected upon leaving her house to wrap her mantle or a veil about her head so that it obscured part of her face and neck.

Women beyond child-bearing age were given much greater freedom, so much so that we read in a fragment of Hyperides that a woman who travels outside of the house should be of an age that onlookers should ask whose mother she is, not whose wife.[10] Older women served as midwives and dispensers of herbal medicines, including the potions that brought on abortions. Due to their mobility, these women were the vehicle for lively gossip, and, not surprisingly, Greek poets mock their meddlesomeness and imply that they were constantly inebriated.

There was one other context in which women of all ages moved regularly outside their homes and that was to partake in the many religious festivals that dotted the Attic calendar; Demosthenes commented wryly that there was only one day a year without a festival and that these events were organized with military precision.[11] Many of the festivals invited the participation of both men and women, such as the Panathenaia in honor of Athena, the Eleusinian Mysteries that honored Demeter and Persephone, and the Anthesteria sacred to Dionysos. Other festivals were restricted to women alone and were of enough significance that in the case of the Thesmophoria, for example, funding was provided at government expense (see **Women as Containers**).[12] Moreover, the Thesmophoria's observance was publicly recognized by the temporary transferral of meetings of the Assembly to the theater from the Areopagus, the hill at the foot of the Acropolis where the festival was celebrated.

The festivals were the one outlet women had to break free of daily chores and they afforded women an opportunity to socialize with other women, but their significance went far beyond this. The rituals in the all-female festivals (the Thesmophoria, the Haloa, and the Skira) and even in the festivals open to men and women (the Anthesteria, the Lenaia, and the Greater Mysteries) exhibit a striking consistency in underlining the correlation of women's generative capabilities with the renewal of the annual cycle of vegetation, and, by extension, with the survival of the community. The rituals also share much of the same imagery, such that containers and underground chambers underscore the analogies between women's bodies as vessels for babies and Earth as a womb that nourishes new life (see **Women as Containers**). The frequency of these rituals assured that both the mature inhabitants of the polis and the younger, more malleable generation were kept ever mindful of the message.

A young girl, then, would grow up in a household where her mother was mostly in the women's quarters of the house, busied largely with textile production, or involved with the rituals that sustained the spiritual life of the community. Both activities involved story-telling. Girls listened to myths as their mothers taught them to spin and weave, and, when festivals approached, the stories behind these traditions would be told and retold. A girl's education was probably not much more than this practical instruction in wool-working and the type of behavioral guidance provided by allusion to recalcitrant (Atalanta) or disobedient (Aglauros) heroines, and many girls probably knew only the rudiments of reading and writing. Such innocence was considered desirable; Socrates poses to Critobulos a rhetorical question that required no answer: when he married his wife "was she a very young child who had seen and heard virtually nothing in the world?"[13]

A tremendous influence on young girls must have been the special roles reserved exclusively in certain festivals for them and unmarried maidens. The experience of participating in a ritual that was highly honored by the polis and witnessed by all the community would have had an immeasurable ability to inculcate within these girls the values and mores of the society, which they realized would soon be their responsibility and privilege to sustain. We know that in the Greater Panathenaia, sacred to Athena, girls took part in the choruses and ground the sacred grain.[14] Those girls designated Arrephoroi lived on the Acropolis while a new peplos was being woven for the Athena, and at the conclusion of their period of service the girls were given unidentified objects in covered containers to carry to a sanctuary of Aphrodite, where different objects were given the girls for their return. The sexual undercurrents of the ritual are unmistakable (see **Plynteria and Arrephoroi**). Girls were also invited to take part in processions honoring Artemis and Apollo in the temple of Delphinus.[15] Here they carried branches of sacred olive wrapped in wool, which symbolized the industries that traditionally sustained the community's economy, olive oil and textile production. Between the ages of perhaps five and puberty,

selected girls served Artemis in her sanctuary at Brauron (see **Artemis** and **Little Bears**). As Little Bears, the girls acted out the role of untamed animals that would be domesticated and socialized through marriage. At puberty, a maiden might have the honor or good birth to be chosen to be a kanephoros, literally "basket carrier" in sacred processions (no. 60). The basket held sacred grain as well as the knife with which the sacrificial animal would be killed; because women were not allowed to shed blood, the basket with the knife would be handed over to the priest at the altar. The basket was a highly charged image that referred to the mature female's ability both to generate new life and to assure the perpetuation of the entire cycle of death and renewal (see **Women as Containers**). A young maiden, viewed as blossoming in puberty, was the ideal bearer of such a symbol.

The self-perception of a young girl was, therefore, carefully molded through manual and behavioral instruction in the home, through the narration of myths that reiterated social values and concerns, and through participation in rituals that reinforced the messages of those myths. The culmination of her socialization, and her formal entry into the adult community, was her wedding day, which occurred when she was about fourteen or fifteen (see **The Wedding**). Her groom, with whom she had certainly had little contact and may well not even have met before her wedding day, was about thirty years old, far more experienced than she was in every category from sex to education to exposure to the outside world.[16] Her wedding was the single most important event that would ever occur in a woman's life, and its ramifications were enormous. The young bride left her home and the supervision of her mother to enter the house of her mother-in-law who would now be the most central female figure in her life. Marriage was a moment of severe crisis in a girl's life, as she abandoned childhood and her mother's care to enter a physically new world fraught with the anxiety of sexuality, the apprehension of coexistence with a mother-in-law, and the terror of the life-threatening peril of childbirth (see **Iphigenia** and **Persephone and Demeter**). The consummation of her marriage signalled the end to her status as a *kore*, but she would retain the classification of a *nymphe*, or bride, until the birth of her first child when she became a *gyne*, or woman. Children, as many as four or five, seem to have been born at intervals of every few years, such that at the age of twenty-seven, the mother of still another newborn baby would prepare to lose her oldest daughter in marriage. Many scholars believe that the average woman died when she was about forty years old.

Despite the absence of women in public life, both a growing girl and her mother had before them independent and powerful female figures who were unavailable in the Christian era. No mortal female would have mistaken a goddess' privilege for her own; Demeter was able to have her daughter returned to her, Artemis could send a fatal arrow wherever she chose, and Athena could successfully resist marriage and dispense advice to respectful heroes (see **Persephone and Demeter**, **Artemis**, and **Athena**). Nonetheless, the honored position of these goddesses, to the point that their presence had almost a tangible quality, was an ever-present reminder to both men and women of the degree to which society valued female strengths. Athena was the principal deity of Athens, and initiation into the Eleusinian Mysteries, the most profound religious experience of ancient Greece, centered around Demeter and her daughter Persephone. Aphrodite, Hera, Hestia, and Hekate were also powerful goddesses who were intently honored and admired.

To what extent women internalized such self-possession into their own lives and marriages is an interesting question. Publicly and legally, the husband's will prevailed, but there are intimations of compromise. In Euripides' *Trojan Women*, Andromache comments that she "knew when my will must have its way, knew also to give way to him in turn."[17] And both Homer and Pindar equate marital happiness with *homophrosyne*, a union of hearts and minds. The happiest married, though longest separated, couple in Greek literature were Odysseus and Penelope, who were described by Homer as *ekluon*; they listened and heard and paid attention to each other.[18]

What women thought about men can be somewhat inferred. Young girls soon to be brides romanticized the strangers who would be their husbands, and, at the Thesmophoria, married women tossed into pits male genitals made of dough while they exchanged ribald sexual jokes (see **Women as Containers**). Commentary at the all-female Adonia was probably no less earthy (no. 61). Women may have had no illusions about their secondary social status, but, at the same time, myths, rituals, traditions, and contemporary art gave them an equally clear-eyed assessment of the degree to which they held a fascination for men. It is likely, however, that most women did not spend a great deal of time thinking about men. They worried about surviving childbirth, keeping their young children alive, anticipating their daughters' marriages, and worrying about the pregnancies of their daughters and daughters-in-law. In addition to caring for children, women managed their households and tended family graves. They found peace in the rhythm of spinning and weaving and enjoyed informal gatherings of female friends and relatives. They excitedly took part in preparations for weddings and festivals and delighted in the rituals exclusive to women. They appreciated the feeling of a special closeness to female deities, and they found satisfaction in visits to sanctuaries of Artemis and Athena in particular. The world these women inhabited may have been smaller than, and discrete from, the political world of their husbands, but, as Sally Humphreys remarks in her essay in this volume, within that world there was probably a great deal of freedom and a great deal of pleasure.

The Legal View

When viewed solely on legal terms, Classical Athens holds no allure for the modern Western woman.[19] The essence of Athenian law regarding women was to ensure that the child she bore would have the father it was supposed to have in order that property could be handed down to the next generation in confidence and in harmony. To achieve this end, the legal system was so structured that at no moment in a woman's life did she ever have any authority over her own being. Her marriage did not require her consent, and her only possessions were her clothing and her jewelry. At her wedding she passed from the protection of her father, as *kyrios*, to that of her new husband, and should her father die without a male heir, a woman as an *epikleros* could be required to divorce her husband and marry her father's brother, so as to assure a male heir in her father's line. (Marriage to one's uncle was permitted and was not uncommon.) Lacking rights of citizenship, a woman of a respectable Athenian family could not be described as an Athenian, but only as the wife of an Athenian. This circumlocution probably presented few problems, since women were not supposed to be spoken of at all.

As the story of Danae dramatizes, a father lived with an ongoing anxiety that his unmarried daughter would adhere to her true nature and indulge her sexual curiosity and promiscuity (see **Danae**). So serious was the loss of virginity that when Solon, the sixth-century lawgiver, abolished the conditions under which a citizen could be enslaved, he left intact the provision that a father could sell into a slavery a daughter who had become sullied in this way.[20] Solon presumably was referring to virginity lost through promiscuous behavior rather than rape, but we have no evidence that this harsh measure was ever enacted, perhaps because the law was an effective deterrent. We do know that an unmarried maiden who was a victim of rape could claim substantial damages, probably to sustain her as a now unmarriageable woman, or to augment her existing dowry to a magnitude that would be irresistible to a prospective suitor. The provision shows clearly that motivation was not a factor in passing judgment on the predicament. Whether as the result of rape or willing participation in a love affair, an unmarried girl without her virginity was considered to be damaged goods, her worth severely diminished.

Adultery or rape in the case of a married woman was only marginally less serious. Whether the wife was raped or was the willing participant in an affair, the husband was required to divorce her. In the case of an affair, the stipulation was prompted not only because of the possibility of pregnancy, but also because of the belief that once the taboo of infidelity was broken, it could no longer retain any effectiveness. In the case of adultery, we are told that a husband had the right to kick his wife and to strip off her clothes, but he could not maim or kill her.[21] She was also henceforth forbidden to wear jewelry or to participate in public sacrifices, a penalty that emphasized that her offense was considered to be as much against the community as against the husband. Should the adulterer be caught in the act, he could be killed; a lesser penalty, probably a fine, awaited him otherwise. The tradition that an adulterer could be punished by having a radish pushed up his anus does not seem to have a legal basis. Philandering husbands, by contrast, enjoyed a double standard.

Fig. 2. The Agora, the Panathenaic Way, and the Acropolis. Photograph John Dean.

A bride brought to her marriage a dowry of money, and it has been argued that the invisibility of her dowry resulted in less prestige for the Athenian wife than she would have received were she living, for example, in the city of Gortyn in Crete, where dowries consisted of land, which was highly visible, tangible, and prestigious.[22] Even in the form of money, however, the dowry was an important asset that bolstered the wife's moral authority; Plato complains that a high dowry resulted in slavery for the husband.[23] The dowry would eventually function as the dowry of a woman's sons' daughters, at a time when the woman herself was either deceased or a widow living with a married son.[24] That the dowry would not serve as the dowry for a daughter indicates its critical importance to the household's well-being, such that the funds could not be spared while the household was intact. The dowry was apparently not, however, available to the husband to spend, and, should his property be seized, the dowry could not be confiscated. Should the marriage fail, the husband was obligated to return the dowry, at eighteen percent interest, to the wife's father. Although divorce seems to have been rare, the provision regarding the return of the dowry was a reminder to the husband that the wife's relatives had an on-going investment in the marriage and that they would maintain a certain vigilance over her well-being.

The many constraints that Athenian law placed upon women obscure the fact that society took great care to ensure that all marriageable women could marry. The concern was probably less humanitarian than prompted by the anxiety that there be no unmarried, sexually available women to constitute a disruptive force. Exposure of baby girls controlled the annual crop of marriageable maidens, and the further loss of women through childbirth regularly produced widowers who were prospective suitors. Even during the Peloponnesian War when the male losses were extremely heavy, we do not hear of unmarried women. It has been argued that the citizenship law of 451, decreeing that a citizen must have as parents a citizen and a daughter of a citizen, was a means of assuring that men chose their wives from women of good stock rather than from foreign lineage, thereby preventing the creation of spinsters in respectable Athenian families. Sally Humphreys, however, convincingly argues that the law's objective was to prevent Athenian families from contracting powerful alliances through marriages to dynasties outside of Athens.[25]

The sober picture of women's modest stature in the eyes of Athenian law must be tempered by the realization that Athens was a small community and that a woman's family kept a watchful eye on her husband, with mistreatment of the wife interpreted as an insult to her blood family. It is, however, an unavoidable truth that a woman had no opportunity on her own for either legal initiative or legal recourse. In legal terms, an Athenian woman was as helpless as the image that Hephaistos fashioned out of clay and named Pandora. And like Pandora, a woman's influence over men had to be exerted through other than legal channels.

The Biological View

Two aspects of a woman's biology prompted interpretations with far-reaching consequences for Greek thought. First, because in sexual intercourse a woman was the penetrated partner, she was considered to be a passive being, not the master of her own body.[26] Second, because a woman's physiology was such that she appeared to be perpetually receptive to sexual intercourse (in contrast with her male partner), she was viewed as insatiable, unable to control any physical craving at all, be it for food, alcohol, or sex. In a society that highly prized a man's self-control and his ability to establish limits for himself, a woman's perceived anatomical and physiological shortcomings were of devastating significance and underlie the fundamental attitude toward women in Greek culture. An extreme illustration of this mindset is found in the story of the mythical seer Teiresias, who had the distinction of having passed some years of his youth as a woman.[27] When Teiresias was asked whether a man or a woman enjoyed sexual intercourse more, he replied that a woman derived nine times the pleasure from sexual intercourse that a man did. Woman as a voracious force is a pervasive image in Greek myth.

We know from the Hippocratic writings that the ancient Greeks considered the uterus the source of most of women's physical and emotional ills. Our word "hysteria" literally means "wombiness."[28] The prevailing medical view was that being unmarried was severely injurious to the health of a physically mature young woman, because her virginal state blocked the flow of menstrual blood, at the same time as the absence of sexual intercourse resulted in the desiccation of the uterus. A further malady to which both unmarried and married women were susceptible was the wandering of the uterus through the body, causing madness and a shortness of breath that could result in suffocation. Pregnancy was believed to alleviate most of these symptoms, but could not have been a reliable cure, because, especially in the fourth century, women regularly sought aid in the healing sanctuaries of the god Asklepios. Both menstruation and childbirth carried overtones of contamination; after childbirth, a house was considered to be polluted (*miasma*) for three days or more.

The medical association of a wandering uterus with suffocation is consistent with the well-attested correlation of a woman's genitals with her throat. Pegasos and Chrysaor, for example, were born from the Gorgon Medusa's neck cavity after her decapitation (see **Gorgons** and **Women as Containers**). Giulia Sissa has commented upon this association in the instance of the Delphic oracle.[29] The

priestess was a virginal woman who sat over Apollo's tripod while her body absorbed fumes believed to be the god's breath. The priestess would then translate these fumes into riddles. That women were essentially identified with their sexuality and, by extension, their throats is also clear from the way in which mythical heroines die. Some women, such as Phaedra and Erigone, die by hanging; others die in their own bed and bedchamber, the sexual connotations of which are self-evident.

The degree to which a woman was believed to be the parent of her own children is not completely clear. In a famous passage in the *Eumenides* of Aischylos, Athena states that the father is the true parent and that the woman is only the nurse of the seed.[30] Many scholars argue that the goddess' comment was merely a tactic to exonerate Orestes, guilty of matricide, and that contemporary or slightly later medical writings express a firm belief in the equal role of the mother.[31] It used to be argued that a preference for the primacy of the mother was indicated in the prohibition that children from the same mother could not marry each other, whereas half-siblings born of the same father could. A recent counter argument, however, reasonably points out that the intent of this regulation may have been to facilitate the retention of a dowry within the father's family.

The imagery medical writers used to describe the female anatomy is consonant with the metaphors elsewhere encountered in mythology, literature, and art. Hippocrates compared the uterus to a cupping jar (see **Women as Containers**).[32] The word *amnion*, referring to the membrane that surrounded the fetus, was also the term for a vessel intended to contain sacrificial blood (see **Women as Containers** and **Iphigenia**).[33] Aristotle further compares a young woman's menarche with the blood shed by an animal wounded in a hunt (see **Pursuit Scenes** and **Women as Animals**).[34]

The Moral View

A woman's biological and physiological makeup were considered to be such that she was without the capability to control herself or resist outside influences, including emotions, which were believed to be external forces.[35] In Euripides' *Hippolytos* a woman is said to be less capable than a man in withstanding Aphrodite,[36] and in Aischylos' *Libation Bearers* it is said that women are ready to dare anything for love.[37] Comments about women's lust pervade Aristophanes' comedies.[38] By contrast, those goddesses who had embraced celibacy, Artemis and Athena, were considered trustworthy caretakers of children.

Our fullest discussion for the perception of the female nature is in Aristotle, who believed that in a woman "the deliberative faculty in the soul is present, but ineffective," in contrast to a child where the deliberative faculty is "present but undeveloped."[39] Because of a woman's natural moral weakness, Aristotle recommended that a woman should be married young and put into a house.[40] Xenophon echoes this position. Noting that women and men have memory in like degree, and ceding that the female nature is not inferior to that of a man, Xenophon nonetheless argues that the female nature lacks intellectual strength.[41] Several centuries previously, we find in Homer the comment that women were weak, lacking a sense of proportion, and in need of being controlled.[42]

There was considerable apprehension in Greek thought that, should her true nature remain unconstrained or become unleashed, a woman would wreak colossal damage on society. Clytemnestra, the Danaids, and the Lemnian Women kill their husbands, and Medea murders her own children, observing that "when wronged in respect to bed, no heart is more bent on destruction" (see **Medea**).[43] Women's threat to men was not only in terms of physical violence. Among the female mythical beings with bestial forms evocative of woman's feral nature were the Sirens, who posed lethal threats to men solely by means of their words (see **Sirens**). So potent, in fact, was a woman's speech that Mary Lefkowitz has commented that whereas the Christians found a woman's body to be dangerous the Greeks were distrustful of her mind. The sixth-century lawgiver Solon permitted a man to make bequests only if it could be proven that at the time of his decision he had not been under the influence of drugs, illness, or the persuasion of his wife.[44] Other passages in Greek literature confirm the overwhelming forcefulness of a woman's speech; Pandora received from Hermes the gift of "crafty words," and soft whisperings were considered the irresistible tool of a woman's seductiveness (see **Pandora** and **Gesture and Gaze**).

A woman's gaze also carried immense power, as was discovered by unsuccessful adversaries of Medusa (see **Gorgons** and **Gesture and Gaze**). Although the downcast gaze prescribed for a respectable woman was ostensibly an expression of submission and modesty, the goal of this recommended demeanor was also to defuse her weaponry. Exchanged glances between a man and a woman led to, or signified, mutual attraction, and the moment when the bride was unveiled and looked up at her husband was thought to be fraught with eroticism and mutual attraction (see **Gesture and Gaze**).

Society's strategy to combat the dangerous implications of women's nature was multi-pronged. Girls received little formal education and they were married young. As wives, they were insulated in the women's quarters of the houses and directed to conceal their bodies behind voluminous folds and to avert their gazes. Ultimate control was through sexual intercourse, which was also the recommended treatment for women's physical and emotional ailments. In Euripides' *Trojan Women*, Andromache remarks that "one night, they say, undoes the hatred of a woman in her husband's bed."[45] The notion that it was man's capability, even his (not completely onerous) duty, to control women by means of sex gave strength to the metaphor of woman as an untamed animal to be pursued and subdued by men (see **Women as Animals** and **Pursuit Scenes**).

The critical irony in the perception of woman as a feral being was the simultaneous assumption that a woman was also to be the virtuous embodiment of the home and family. Accommodating these contradictions was the conviction that a woman could transcend her basic nature with the aid of men and man-made institutions, such as marriage. Thus an animal with which women were frequently compared was the horse; unmarried girls were called fillies, lacking the harness.[46] The image implied that, like a horse, a woman's beauty and nobility would not be diminished by domestication but would be enabled thereby to flourish and to serve others (see **Women as Animals**).

It has been pointed out that the pervasive anxiety that women would overthrow society is not the result of farfetched reasoning. As Marilyn Arthur points out, women did not have a stake in the political or social system, and it is a classic truth that those who have nothing invested in a system are most likely to undermine it.[47] Arthur points out that the lawgiver Solon, writing in the sixth century, was acutely cognizant of the degree to which women were excluded from the social system and of the need, if not to remedy the situation, at least to rationalize it. One long-lived tradition to explain women's lack of citizenship traced it to the competition for the patronage of Attica between Athena, who produced an olive tree, and Poseidon, who created a spring.[48] When the Athenian women voted in favor of Athena (women were apparently enfranchised at this time), the Athenian men punished their sexual favoritism by taking away the women's right to call themselves Athenians and to give their children their name. While the rationalization behind the story is apparent, its survival not only begs the question of a different social structure in an earlier era, but also intimates at ongoing and unresolved tensions.

Men: The Ideal

> There are three reasons to be grateful to the gods:
> that I am human; that I am Greek; that I am a male.
>
> Thales, quoted by Diogenes Laertius 1.33

The ideal Greek man was handsome, athletic, intelligent, cultured, well-born, skilled in hunting and in warfare, and celebrated in glory for his triumphs over adversaries, be they in battle, in the palaestra, or in the Assembly.[49] He was expected to be aggressive, independent, verbal, competitive, and self-disciplined. All this was to be instilled in a young boy as he grew to adulthood in a highly competitive environment and under the public and intense scrutiny of a unforgetting community, where he would live for the rest of his life.

It has often been remarked that many of the qualities that distinguished the ideal man were exactly the opposite of those considered desirable in the ideal woman.[50] A man was supposed to be an assertive and dominant master of his household, whereas a woman was expected to be submissive and passive. A man was expected to be a highly public and articulate figure in the political life of the polis, winning for himself a glory that assured him fame even after his death. By contrast, a woman was raised to be invisible and silent, completely absent from the public life of the community, and so undistinguished that, as Perikles remarked in his funerary oration, her greatest achievement was not to be spoken of at all. Such a polarization of gender profiles can be partly attributed to the demanding and inflexible standard of manhood that was both defined and made more desirable by the strategic assignment to women of exactly the opposite qualities.

It is noteworthy that the traits that distinguished the ideal man were also antithetical to the qualities believed to be innate to a woman's true nature. A woman was viewed as intrinsically irrational, insatiable, promiscuous, vindictive, and incapable of self-control. The ideal man, on the other hand, was master of his own cravings and emotions and was a fundamentally rational being, with the exception of brief lapses. Like the first, this second antithesis has also been ascribed to what we might call inverse projection, but here there are also suggestions of voyeurism. Greek myth and imagery repeatedly express the almost irresistible attraction to men of women's irrationality and lack of self-control; we are reminded of Pentheus' fatal obsession to spy upon the Bacchantes in their mountain rampages. Foucault shrewdly commented that the outsider represents the part of ourselves that we most fear and from whom we derive vicarious gratification of what cannot be released in ourselves.[51] The Greeks' unyielding yardstick for manliness may have rendered inevitable not only the polarization of the genders but also their responses to this antithesis. Theatrical performances by male actors playing the roles of women in the throes of childbirth or about to murder their children must have been satisfying to the audiences on some level or these kinds of dramas would not have enjoyed the popularity that they did.

A Boy's Rise to Manhood

A baby boy was born to a father who was at least thirty years of age and probably somewhat older. Men came into their full civic rights at the age of thirty, when they became eligible for a magistracy and participation in the Council. Also at this age, their share of their patrimony was settled upon them, had this not occurred earlier. For these reasons, most men postponed marriage until they were thirty, the age that Hesiod, writing in the late eighth century, also recommended.[52] Many scholars believe that the reason why civic maturity and the division of patrimony did not occur at a younger age was to ensure that a boy would reach adulthood either after his father's death or when his father was elderly. In this way the clashes between father and son, inevitable in as highly competitive a society as Classical Athens was, could be minimized, and, indeed, Barry Sutton estimates that half of the youths in Athens had lost their fathers by the time they reached the age of eighteen.[53] The phenomenon of fatherless youths created a need for the presence and exam-ple of older males, and Athenian society filled this void with rituals specifically for young men, with ephebic (military) service and with homosexual relationships.

The son of a citizen was under the supervision of a male pedagogue from the ages of six to about thirteen, during which period he received instruction in reading, writing, music, and athletics. He almost certainly accompanied his father regularly to the public spaces of the city, but, because his father passed so much time in political circles, a boy would also have spent a significant amount of time in his home together with his mother and sisters.

A growing boy also spent a great deal of time in the palaestra, or exercise grounds, where only men were permitted and where everyone exercised in the nude. As he passed into adolescence he would have found himself admired by older youths who were probably in their twenties and who gave their young friends gifts and compliments. So many prominent men in Classical Athens, including Themistokles and Aristeides, participated in homosexual relationships when they were youths that it is difficult to believe that the practice was discouraged, although it is certainly likely that a father disapproved of his son's liaison with any man of less than extraordinary worth.[54] Should the youth accept the blandishments of his admirer, the relationship became a physical one with the adolescent boy either the penetrated partner in anal intercourse or the recipient of intercrural intercourse. Whatever the nature of the relationship, the young boy was expected to adhere to a specific demeanor; he was supposed to be shy and passive, not giving in to his lover too soon and not displaying pleasure in the sexual advances.

The function of homosexual relationships has been much debated over the past century, and assessments can be closely correlated to the mores of the decade in which a scholar was writing. Although in some traditional societies studied by anthropologists, homosexual acts function as the initiation of the boy entering adulthood, many contemporary scholars prefer to attribute the Athenian version to a military culture that placed tremendous emphasis on male aggressiveness. It is usually agreed that homosexual relationships fell out of fashion during the fourth century for several reasons, among them the bleaker economic picture that reduced the leisure time required for the lavish courting of the loved boy, and the greater visibility of women, whose obscurity during the fifth century was surely responsible for the evolution of an elaborate ritual of male courtship. The most convincing explanation for the decline of homosexual relationships is the Greeks' apparent inability to reconcile the act of having once been penetrated in the manner of a woman with the quality of self-mastery that characterized the ideal man. It appears that what could never be overcome was a lingering uncertainty that a youthful homosexual experience might have ultimately diminished one's manhood.

At the age of about sixteen a boy was officially registered in his father's phratry, an important body of men consisting of blood relatives and close associates. At the age of eighteen he was registered in his deme, which was a geographical unit, and he also received the rights of citizenship; at twenty he would be able to take part in the Assembly. Between the ages of about eighteen and twenty, a youth entered military service as an ephebe, an experience that seems to have been a thrilling introduction to adulthood.[55] Posted outside the city in the Piraeus or on the frontiers, ephebes honed their mastery both of military procedure and of hunting. The coincidence of intense ephebic hunting with the raging hormones of adolescence probably explains why myths of courtship were typically envisioned as vigorous armed pursuits of fleeing maidens. Freud was said to have been delighted to discover that he had not been the first to recognize the link between aggression and eroticism.[56]

Ephebes were accorded honored positions in several festivals, among which was the Oscophoria, sacred to Theseus. As part of the ritual, an ephebic race was preceded by a procession of two youths dressed as girls, who were thought to commemorate the young women whose lives Theseus saved by killing the Minotaur. It has often been remarked that transvestism is a common element in rituals that demarcate a life passage for males, and the status of being an ephebe can classified on several grounds as a *rite de passage*, involving stages of separation and re-entry.[57] Dressing as a female graphically emphasized the behavior and the qualities that youths had to leave behind on their road to manhood.

By the age of twenty-two a youth had outgrown his homosexual relationship as a loved one, and might now enter another homosexual relationship, this time as the active lover. He had, by now, surely made the acquaintance of hetairai (prostitutes), and he would continue to do so after his marriage. It is also possible that he continued to enjoy homosexual relationships into his married years as well. At the age of thirty he would marry a fourteen-year-old girl with whom he had only the barest acquaintance, if indeed they had even met, and the difference in their ages was matched only by the discrepancy in their education and sophistication.

The pressurized atmosphere for males in Classical Athens should not be underestimated. As a boy, a youth, and a man, he was supposed to distinguish himself, and therewith his family, in every possible arena. He could lose his rights of citizenship if he wasted his patrimony, abstained from supporting his parents, shrank from military duties, or fled from the field of battle. He lived in a city-state that was operating under a new and untested form of government, whose ever-emerging flaws must have created enormous apprehension and misgivings. After the defeat of the Persians in 480, Athens experienced residual anxiety and intermittent warfare for some decades, coupled by a gnawing self-doubt that the fiber of the citizenry was eroding. The outbreak of the Peloponnesian War in 431 brought economic distress, disease, and, ultimately, disillusionment with public life. Throughout these decades of enormous political and social stress, Athenian males were constantly being measured against an almost unattainable standard. Not all of the aggression and hostility could be channeled into hunting, warfare, and athletics. Attitudes toward women in Classical Athens have to be weighed against this backdrop.

Socialization of Males to Females

> The pillar of the house is the male children.
>
> Euripides, *Iphigenia in Taurus* 57

A young boy growing up in Athens realized almost immediately that his was a privileged status. He would have heard whispered stories of baby girls who had been exposed in deserted areas, and he would have listened to adult comments that a man without sons was not a full fledged member of the community, because, as Thucydides remarks, that man had no children whose lives were at stake.[58] Herodotos commented that a certain Kleomenes died childless, having only a daughter.[59] A boy would also have been aware from a young age that the distinction of being an Athenian citizen was a supreme privilege and honor available only to men. In a city as obsessed with political affairs as Athens was, rights of citizenship were of immeasurable importance; Thucydides remarks that a man who takes no interest in politics was not a man who minded his own business, but a man who had no business in Athens at all.[60]

Notions of male primacy were thus easily internalized. No less clear to a maturing boy would have been the compartmentalization of femaleness. Artemis and Athena were goddesses deserving of the highest respect, even fear, but they were celibate deities without husbands or children. Demeter, revered goddess of the Eleusinian Mysteries, was the quintessential caring mother, but she seemed not even to have a husband, and no one would call her sexy. Aphrodite, on the other hand, was tantalizing, magnetic, but it was difficult to imagine her managing a household or offering wise counsel. By contrast, Hera was very much of a wife, but largely a complaining one, and Hestia, keeper of the hearth, was downright colorless. Such facile categorizing on a divine level had earthly counterparts, because a boy would watch his father or older brothers disappear in the direction of a brothel or speak with enthusiasm of the flute-girls at the last symposium. Demosthenes provides us with a more precise classification: "We have," he remarks, "mistresses for our pleasure, concubines for daily service to our bodies, but wives for the procreation of legitimate children and to be faithful guardians of the household."[61]

Inferior status and compartmentalization were not the only sentiments about women that a growing boy would absorb. Traditional lore offered him scary maxims. Plato remarks that a cowardly man would be born again as a woman,[62] and Demokritos stated that to be ruled by a woman was the final hybris for a man, hybris meaning an infliction of shame and dishonor.[63] Aristotle tells us that in radical democracies, women "dominate the houses and spread gossip about their men."[64] The many visual aids that reinforced these messages in a maturing boy's mind include vase-paintings in which hetairai are being battered (p. 109, fig. 10). Some of the popular wisdom and artistic interpretations are clearly a product of projection. Women, for example, are customarily portrayed in literature as lovesick, but papyri and tablets offer remedies only for male sufferers.[65] An artistic counterpart of such fanciful thought are the vase scenes on kylixes (drinking cups for men) in which women perform oral sex on dildoes.[66]

The isolation of both unmarried and married females from respectable families was so extreme that most of the women with whom maturing youths had any ongoing contact were either hetairai (prostitutes) or the daughters of low-born foreigners living in Athens or the Peiraeus. The latter group does not appear to be represented in art, but in Early Classical vase-painting we frequently encounter scenes in which men present hetairai with gifts while dangling a money purse to indicate that they are negotiating the fee for the service (no. 38). The popularity of this subject on drinking vessels used in all-male symposia is thought-provoking evidence that there existed a yearning for courtship ritual that was elsewhere absent in men's lives, except in homosexual relationships. That the void remained unfilled is indicated by the plethora of vase scenes in which suitors, equipped with the weapons of warriors or hunters, vigorously pursue fleeing maidens (see **Pursuit Scenes**). The repression inherent in the violent depictions of this metaphor for courtship is a reminder that a youth of good family would never have had the opportunity to court a young woman of the class from which his future wife would have to belong. Not every pursuit scene has overtones of brutality, but the large number of highly aggressive examples testify to the freedom with which fantasies were translated into images to inspire or persuade others.

A young boy would have watched his sister marry soon after puberty when she was about fourteen, an age that found him still enjoying athletics in the palaestra, flirting with his first male lover, and looking forward to his period of ephebic service. When he did marry at the age of thirty, he was a man of the world, accomplished and experienced in categories that ranged from warfare to poetry. Perhaps he was pleased that his young bride came to him, as we read in Xenophon, knowing only about spinning and weaving, but otherwise completely innocent.[67] Or perhaps he momentarily pondered the lifestyle of the pre-eminent leader, Perikles, who not only lived openly with the foreign-born courtesan, Aspasia, but also welcomed her presence and her opinions in political and social gatherings. Regardless of an Athenian citizen's view of Perikles, a young husband knew that before him lay the experience succinctly evoked in a conversation between Socrates and Critobulos. Socrates asks his friend, "Is there anyone to whom you entrust a greater number of serious matters than your wife? And is there anyone with whom you have fewer conversations?"[68]

Women and Democracy

It has often been observed that in ancient Athens the status of women declined with the introduction of democracy. In the aristocratic age, which extended as late as the early sixth century, wealthy and well-born women were probably as conspicuous for their

Fig. 3. Marble Herm from Siphnos, Athens, National Archaeological Museum, inv. no. 3728, ca. 490 B.C.

influence as we know they were for their finery. But although Hesiod and Simonides, writing in the late eighth and sixth centuries respectively, railed against materialistic self-indulgence to the point of misogyny, the diminution of women under democracy was not a direct objective, but rather a supporting strategy of the new system.

It used to be argued that, because orderly inheritance of property was critical to the survival of a democracy based on land ownership, a woman's procreation and, in effect, her autonomy had to be closely supervised. Recent studies, however, have discarded this theory to argue that the essence of the democratic system was not to regulate or equalize the assets of each citizen, but rather to create an equality among the male citizenry on the basis of each man's identity as a master, *kyrios*, of his own household of women, children, and slaves. Extrapolating from the fundamental conviction that the definition of a man was to be master of his own self, so must the definition of a citizen be his mastery over a group of individuals submissive to him. In essence women's subordination was an intrinsic part of the democratic system.[69]

Masculinity is, indeed, a subject of great interest in the late sixth and early fifth centuries. It is during these years that we first encounter the herm, a pillar bearing male genitals with an erect penis and surmounted by a man's head. A herm was placed outside the door of each house as a symbol of the household, and several herms were even set up as a public monument to manly valor in battle. In his essay in this volume, Andrew Stewart points out that an intense emphasis on manhood inevitably brings with it enormous pressure on individual men to live up to an unrelenting standard. Probably reflecting such strain are the early fifth-century vase-paintings that depict abused hetairai and Amazons crushed in combat with Greek warriors (no. 120).

An economic factor is probably also a part of this equation. For most of the fifth century, Athenian citizens enjoyed an affluence that was impressive, albeit derived from the assets of their less powerful neighbors. The leisure time afforded by this prosperity enabled citizens to indulge their thirst for political affairs and even to acquire slaves who eased their wives' labors in the home. The wives of citizens undoubtedly carried responsibilities, but these women did not need to contribute to the household income. By contrast Elizabeth Barber has shown that the ancestors of those women were vigorous textile producers, whose contributions were essential to the economy in the Bronze Age, when women appear to have enjoyed a higher status in society.[70] That women of the fifth century contributed little to the Athenian economy beyond procreation could not have strengthened their position.

Women in the Late Fifth Century

The Peloponnesian War had dire economic and social consequences for Classical Athens and for the lives of the citizens' wives. We know that the polis lost much of its population during the plague, and we receive the impression that more men than women succumbed to it. The city also suffered a huge loss of male citizens in battle, as many as one third in the debacle at Syracuse. With the substantial loss of men during these decades, women came to constitute a larger proportion of the population, and surely a louder voice, than ever before. The inevitable disruption of war also had the result that women began to move about the city more freely. We are reminded of their celebration of the Adonia in 415 B.C., on the eve of the departure of the Athenian fleet for Syracuse. The women's incessant wailing was more than annoying, casting a sinister pall over what turned out to be a disastrous venture. Despite the inauspicious overtones of the evening, however, the women carried on with the festival, impervious to criticism (see no. 61).

Still other forces played a role in transforming late fifth-century society. Of critical impact over the course of the Peloponnesian War was the growing disillusionment with public life and public leaders and a renewed appreciation for the home, the family, and the traditions and rituals that had always been entrusted to women's safekeeping. We also know that during the last decades of the fifth century Athens acquired a more international population and that new wealth came into the hands of lesser families. The result was that class lines began to be dissolved and that homosexual relationships, always restricted to an elite core, began to fall out of favor, such that the need for courtship ritual could be redirected to women. All these social shifts, on so many levels and in such intensity, combined to release Athenian women from many of the constraints their mothers and grandmothers had experienced.

The art of the later fifth century reflects these changes and also suggests that women were now the ultimate recipient of a great number of the vases. To please this new market, painters turn away from bawdy symposium scenes, frenzied Maenads, and violent clashes between Greeks and Amazons encountered in Early Classical vase-painting. In their place we find domestic scenes in which women are gathered with their friends or children, and softened pursuit scenes, in which the maiden appears receptive to her suitor (nos. 42-46, and 114-116). Above all, we encounter bridal scenes on vases of specific shapes intended as wedding gifts to the bride. The representations are clearly intended to please the young wife, for in these romanticized renditions, the groom, of whom the young bride would certainly be apprehensive, admiringly turns toward her, while Eros flutters above, symbolic of their mutual attraction (see **The Wedding**).[71] The new mood is also apparent in sculpture. On votive reliefs Demeter and Persephone are now warmly affectionate (nos. 83, 84, and 86), and on a grave stele a mother plays with her young child (no. 6).

The changes extend to style as well. Both transparent fabric and modelled drapery that tellingly accentuate every curve clothe even Athena, who appears to enjoy her new sexual appeal (no. 65). Even mortal women are depicted in this manner on grave reliefs. Domestic vignettes in vase-painting present similarly attired women in possession of a new vocabulary of self-confident gestures and poses. The development almost certainly mirrors changes in contemporary mores.

Moreover, the trend both in art and in the social fabric is irreversible. In fourth-century painting and sculpture, women stand with self-assurance and gesture freely; Aphrodite even dispenses with her clothing. And with the coming of Philip and Alexander, Athens finds herself a much less important city in a much wider world, enveloped by a new social order in which women behave very differently from their Classical, even their Late Classical, predecessors.

ELLEN D. REEDER
Walters Art Gallery

1. Aristotle, *Rhetoric* 1361a. See the superb essay in Fantham et al. (1994a); the following discussion owes much to that synthesis. See also the comments in Lefkowitz (1986).
2. Lonsdale (1993) 232.
3. Pomeroy (1983) 208 n. 2; M. Golden, "Demography and the Exposure of Girls at Athens," *Phoenix* 35 (1981) 316-31.
4. Hesiod, *Works and Days* 702.
5. Aristotle, *Economics* 1.3.1, 1343b. See Foucault (1985) 175-76.
6. Du Boulay (1974) 33, 63, 131-33.
7. More recently, Cohen (1991) 153ff. It should be noted that young girls left their homes to serve Artemis as Little Bears at Brauron and to serve Artemis as Arrephoroi on the Acropolis. No tradition implies that this was the first venture for these girls beyond the confines of their homes.
8. Plutarch, *Perikles* 13.15.
9. Euripides, *Ion* 184ff.
10. Hyperides, frag. 205. Demosthenes 43.62 tells us that only women sixty years and older would participate with female next of kin in a funeral. For older women beyond childbearing, see Bremmer (1987) 198-204, who remarks that women of this age were also priestesses and probably supervised maenadic ritual with its ancient associations with procreation (see **Maenads**).
11. Demosthenes 4.35.
12. For the detailed analysis of the agricultural festivals of the Attic year, see Brumfield (1976).
13. Xenophon, *Oikonomikos* 3.11-13; see Plutarch, *Moralia* 405c 3-11, quoting Xenophon, *Oikonomikos* 7.5.
14. Euripides, *Herakleidai* 777-83.
15. Plutarch, *Theseus* 18.2.
16. Plato, *Laws* 6.771e, recommends that a groom approach the bride on the wedding day as a stranger.
17. Euripides, *Trojan Women* 653-56.
18. Homer, *Odyssey* 6.180-84. See the discussion in Redfield (1982) 196-201.
19. Sealey (1990); Just (1989) 95; Foxhall (1989) 22-45; Patterson (1991) 52-54.
20. Plutarch, *Solon* 23.2. For a provocative discussion of rape and adultery, see Scafuro (1990).
21. Aeschines, *Against Timarchus* 1,183.
22. Leduc (1992) 292.
23. Plato, *Laws* 774c.
24. Leduc (1992) 280.
25. For the citizenship law of 451, see Humphreys (1993) 24.
26. Hesiod, frag. 275 MW; Ovid, *Metamorphoses* 3.316-38. See Halperin (1990) 97, 129, 133.
27. Hesiod, frag. 275 MW; Ovid, *Metamorphoses* 3.316-38.
28. Plato, *Timaeus* 91a-d. See Fantham et al. (1994c) 183-205; King (1983); Hanson (1991) 82-123; DuBois (1988) 171; Veith (1965) 7-22, 38, 42; Ussher (1992) 79-86.
29. Sissa (1990) 51, 53, 166.
30. Aischylos, *Eumenides* 658-61.
31. Halperin (1990) 139; DuBois (1988) 122-4.
32. Hippocrates, *On Medicine* 22 (1.628); Hanson (1991) 88, 120.
33. Empedokles, frag. 70 and see **Women as Containers**.
34. Aristotle, *History of Animals* 58 1b1-2 and *Peri Gynaikeion* 1.6, 72 Littré; King (1988) 120.
35. Just (1989) 179-82.
36. Euripides, *Hippolytos* 966-70.
37. Aischylos, *Libation Bearers* 594-601.
38. Aristophanes, *Thesmophoriazousai* 491-97; *Lysistrata* 551-54; *Ekklesiazousai* 465-8, 616-20.
39. Aristotle, *Politics* 1.1252a24-b14, 1259a37-b10, 1260a3-24, 1260b12-25.
40. Aristotle, *Nicomachean Ethics* 7.7, 1150b 15; *Politics* 7.16, 1335a25.
41. Xenophon, *Oikonomikos* 106 and *Symposium* 29.
42. Homer, *Odyssey* 15.19.
43. Euripides, *Medea* 263-66.
44. Plutarch, *Solon* 21.3; Demosthenes 46.14; Aristotle, *Athenian Constitution* 35.2.
45. Euripides, *Trojan Women* 665-66.
46. For the comparison of women to horses, see Aristophanes, *Lysistrata* 672-80 and 1308. See also **Women as Animals**.
47. Arthur (1984) 24-25.
48. Augustine, *City of God* 18-19; Tyrrell and Brown (1991) 180-81; Vidal-Naquet (1981) 198-99; (1986) 216-17.
49. For a recent discussion of manhood, especially in relation to Mediterranean societies, see Gilmore (1990), who notes that the almost universal function of manhood is to propagate, provide, and protect. He also observes (pp. 11-17, 120-21) that a consistently recurrent concept in most societies is that manhood is an artificial, precarious, and elusive status.
50. Just (1989) 154.
51. Foucault (1967); Ussher (1992) 141. See Foucault (1985) 80, for self-mastery in men versus women, such that (p. 184) a woman's virtue could be viewed as "proof" of her submission to a man.
52. For the age at which a man should marry, see Solon, frags. 27, 9-10, West (about 28-35 years of age). Aristotle, *Politics* 7, 1335a6-35, recommends that a man be 37. Hesiod, *Works and Days* 695-705 also agrees on the age of about thirty.
53. For the relative ages of fathers and sons, see the superb discussion in Strauss (1993) 67-71.
54. For the homosexual experience, see Halperin (1990) 90-98; Sutton (1993) 13-14; Cantarella (1992) 17-64; Dover (1984) 146-50; Dover (1978) 151, 201-203; Dynes (1992) 136, 405, 321.
55. For the ephebic experience, see Versnel (1990) 46-48; Vidal-Naquet (1986) 85-99.
56. S. Freud, *Standard Edition of the Complete Psychological Works*, ed. and trans. J. Strachey in collab. with A. Freud (1ondon 1953-1974) vol. 23, 244-48.
57. For the transvestism of the Oscophoria, see Serwint (1993) 420-21; Vidal-Naquet (1986) 114-17.
58. Thucydides 2.44.3.
59. Herodotos 5.48.
60. Thucydides 2.37.
61. Demosthenes 59.22.
62. Plato, *Timaeus* 90e.
63. Demokritos B 111 DK, quoted by Stobaeus 4.23.39.
64. Aristotle, *Politics* 1313b; see Fantham (1994a) 111.
65 Winkler (1990) 90.
66 Keuls (1985a) 82-83.
67. Xenophon, *Oikonomikos* 7.6.
68. Xenophon, *Oikonomikos* 3.11-13.
69. For a discussion of the emphasis on masculinity in Athenian democracy, see Halperin (1990) 102-104; Fantham et al. (1994a) 75. See also Pomeroy (1975) 78; Leduc (1992) 239.
70. For comment upon women's historic economic participation through textile production, see Barber (1994) 278-83.
71. For a discussion of the romanticization of wedding scenes, see Sutton (1981) 173, 186-88.

THE LAST HOURS OF THE PARTHENOS

Strange as now it may seem, in Greek myth most heroines are young women who have just reached puberty and are on the verge of leaving that status, either to become wives or mothers, and so lose their autonomy, or literally to die.[1] This was the time when girls (parthenoi) were perhaps fourteen years old, and ready for marriage.[2] When the gods wanted to punish Prometheus for bringing fire to mortals, they created a young woman with "the attractive appearance of a parthenos." According to the poet Hesiod, her beauty makes her dangerous to men, along with her "lies and crafty words and a thief's character."[3] In his account her name is Pandora because each of the gods gave her a gift; in the Attic vase-paintings nos. 79 and 80 she is called "Anesidora" and is created by Athena and Hephaistos.[4]

Epimetheus took her in, without realizing what he was doing; no. 81 shows her as an Earth goddess, rising out of the ground. The Eros flying over her head shows that Epimetheus is falling in love with her.[5] As Hesiod tells the story, the parthenos opened her jar (pithos) and let cares and diseases loose in the world. When a parthenos has beauty combined with intelligence and persuasion, its effects can be exciting, and/or devastating, as was the case for Epimetheus. He was deceived by her beautiful appearance and deceitful words and took her into his house; only then when it was too late did he understand that "he had something evil."[6]

The gods realize that it is at this time in her life that the parthenos has the greatest appeal. When Aphrodite set out to seduce the mortal Anchises she assumed the form of an unwed parthenos.[7] Like Pandora, she succeeds because she is both beautiful and deceitful; she tells Anchises just what he wants to hear. It is as parthenoi that mortal women attract the attention of the male gods or mortal heroes, not simply because they are beautiful but because of their courage, intelligence, or physical strength.[8] Cyrene caught the attention of Apollo because she wrestled with lions.[9] Atalanta participated in the hunt for the Kalydonian boar and defeated the hero Peleus in wrestling (he is gazing at her before the match in no. 118); she is shown with athletes in nos. 117 and 119. She ran races against her suitors, but in no. 117 Eros is flying over her head, which suggests that she will lose the race to Hippomenes, who is waiting nearby. In the Hesiodic *Catalogue of Women*, she is won by another hero, Melanion. Since he is slower than she, he must resort to trickery, throwing golden apples that she stops to pick up.[10]

Since parthenoi were thought to be capable of competing with men, it is not surprising that they can perform acts of the greatest heroism, volunteering to die in order to save the state or their families.[11] But it is also a time when the parthenos is particularly prone to error. According to the Hippocratic treatise *About Young Women* (*Peri Parthenon*), parthenoi at the onset of puberty are particularly liable to delusions; some become murderous, others suicidal.[12] So the myths often tell of young women who make serious errors of judgment. Like Kassandra or Daphne they reject the advances of gods, whose passion, however brief, would bring them lasting fame and give them distinguished children. Semele was too ready to believe the lies of an old woman who advised her to test her lover and see that he was really Zeus. The old woman was in fact Zeus' jealous wife Hera in disguise, and when Semele saw Zeus in his immortal form she was destroyed by one of his thunderbolts.[13]

This transitional point in women's lives, when they are ready (and able) to become wives and mothers, is of particular interest, because this was considered the main role of women in ancient society. It is what Odysseus wishes for Nausikaa, when he hopes to persuade her to rescue him: "may the gods give you what your heart longs for, a husband and home."[14] Even Antigone—a parthenos whose independence and courage has brought her into particular prominence in modern times—regrets that she must die before her wedding. She chose instead to defy the edict of her uncle King Kreon forbidding the burial of her brother and was condemned to be sealed up in a cave. She complains that she is going to her death "unwept, friendless, unwedded."[15] Grave inscriptions lament the fate of parthenoi who died before their wedding day.[16] Perhaps, as Emily Kearns has suggested, it is this lost potential that makes the parthenos so desirable a sacrifice to the gods in times of crisis: a young unmarried woman is a more valuable victim than a young man, because "she is giving up what is due to her in life."[17]

But there is another reason why the young women in the myths should no longer be girls, and that is that they must be old enough to understand the full consequences of their actions. Or to put it another way, the Greeks liked the survivors (or victims) of heroic experience to be able to describe what was happening to them. Heroines express themselves as eloquently as heroes and suffer as poignantly.[18] Even though most of the literature that has come down to us was written by men, no ancient Greek writer imagined that heroic experience was wholly enjoyable or ever easy for women, any more than it was so for men. Through both their words and actions, the myths show how women were an integral part of the society that denied them political and legal power.[19]

Homer gives us an idea of what an ideal parthenos should be in his portrait of Nausikaa. At the moment in her life when "her marriage is near,"[20] she is beautiful, outstanding among her female companions, and comparable to Artemis.[21] But she is also courageous and intelligent. She is willing to remain and talk to the stranger Odysseus, while her companions all run away, and she speaks with sympathy, understanding, piety, and common sense. She admires the stranger, and wishes that someone like him might be her husband,[22] but, as daughter of the king, she knows how important it is to protect her reputation and maintains her distance. The notion that the two are well-matched is suggested by the poet with great delicacy; each is capable of making a flattering and persuasive speech, and she asks him (and he promises) not to forget her.[23]

But in other myths, the handsome stranger who appears suddenly in an isolated place turns out to be a god in disguise. No. 113 shows how Poseidon appeared to Amymone, who met him when she was out to find water.[24] He has assumed the form of a handsome man, no taller than she (usually the gods are larger than mortals), and she turns back in mid-flight to look at him, held by the erotic power of his glance.[25] His trident is poised to strike the ground and create a spring, which will be named after her; before that, according to tradition, there had been no springs in Argos.[26] The scene is similar to no. 112, where she stops in mid-flight as he reaches out to her; the god can be identified by the trident he holds casually in his left hand. The Dresden painter makes the scene even more dramatic: in no. 111 the god is holding the trident in his right hand and almost appears to be threatening her with it; but Amymone is holding out her arm to him, and so that he can clasp her hand. In no. 116 they are standing contentedly together, as if they were celebrating their wedding.

Gods are almost always attracted to parthenoi just before the time of their marriage, and never after they have taken a mortal husband. Zeus appears to Alkmene disguised as her husband Amphitryon, just before Amphitryon can return to her after avenging the death of her brothers.[27] Unions with the gods always prove to bring both joy and sorrow to the mortal parthenos. The gods cannot be companions to these women, and so abandon them immediately. Some will marry later, and all will bear famous children, who will look after them, so that at end of their lives they can look back on the moment of their encounter with the god with pride and even with pleasure.[28]

Poets like to tell about the moments when the god finds his parthenos and carries her off, but what makes the woman memorable and heroic is the rest of her story. When Odysseus visits the lower world, he meets Tyro, who fell in love with the river god Enipeus. Poseidon came to her in the disguise of the river god while she was waiting beside his streams.[29] Homer's audience would have known that the rest of the story was not so happy: Tyro's father refused to believe that a god was the father of her twin sons Neleus and Pelias. She was persecuted by her stepmother Sidero. The sufferings of her later life contrast vividly with the glorious setting in which the god made love to her. In a tragedy by Sophokles (now almost completely lost) Tyro describes her misery and loneliness: her hair was cut off, and she compares herself to a young mare:

> whom herdsman have seized in the horses' stables with rough grip, and who has had the yellow mane reaped from her neck; and when she comes to the meadow to drink the water of the river, reflected in the water she sees her image, with her hair shamefully hacked off. Ah, even a pitiless person might pity her, cowering beneath the outrage, as she madly laments and bewails the luxuriant hair she had before.[30]

There in Tyro's story is a deliberate contrast between her glorious but brief *partheneia* and the much longer period of her suffering. Comparing herself to a young horse has a special poignancy. When comparing girls to animals that need to be tamed, the poet usually speaks from the man's point of view: "now you graze in the meadows and leap lightly and play; you do not have a skillful experienced rider."[31] But Tyro (or rather, Sophokles) concentrates on what it is like to be the animal herself.

It is characteristic of the Greek view of life to call attention to the contrast between the glorious, but brief, moments of beauty or happiness and the long period of isolation and misery that seem inevitably to follow them. As the poet Pindar puts it, apropos of a young boy's stunning victory in the Pythian games:

> in a moment delight flowers for men, and in a moment it falls to the ground, shaken by a stern decree. Humans (*anthropoi*) are creatures of a day; what is one of them, what is he not? The dream of a shadow. But when the Zeus-given glory comes, a bright radiance lies on men and life is sweet.[32]

What enables humans to survive the long intervals in their lives between these bright moments is their intelligence, and this is why heroic parthenoi in addition to being beautiful must also be wise.

The experience of one heroic parthenos thus can be held up as an example for another. The chorus of old men in Sophokles' drama *Antigone* tell the story of Danae to Antigone, after she has been condemned by her uncle Kreon to be shut in a cave to die. She complains that she is being led away to die "without marriage, without bridal, having no share in wedlock or in the rearing of children." She asks why she has been deserted by her friends, and the gods.[33] The chorus tell her about the fate of Danae. Her father sealed her up in a bronze chamber because of an oracle that said he would be killed by her son. But Zeus contrived to come to her in the form of a shower of gold, as in no. 74. The chorus do not concentrate on the glory of being a "bride" of Zeus but instead emphasize her afflictions:

Danae too endured the exchange of heaven's light for a brass-fastened dwelling, and immured in the tomblike chamber she was held prisoner. Yet she came of an honoured house, my daughter, and had the keeping of the seed of Zeus that flowed in gold. But the power of fate is strange; neither wealth nor martial valor, nor a wall, nor black ships crashing through the sea can escape it.[34]

The chorus do not comment on what happened to Danae afterward, because there is no hope that Antigone could escape from her imprisonment and the certain death that must follow it. Danae survived, even though her father put her and her infant son Perseus out to sea in a box (her sad departure is depicted in nos. 75-77). But the god saw that Danae and Perseus both landed safely on the island of Seriphos. Significantly, the poet Simonides imagined that during that voyage Danae would behave with courage and understanding. As the wind stirs up the waves, she does not become hysterical, but rather talks to her son and explains what is happening to them:

for if the danger were danger to you, you would turn your small ear towards me. But I say that the baby must sleep, and the sea must sleep, and our troubles must sleep; let a change in our fortune come, father Zeus, from you. If there is a rash or unjust word in my prayer, pardon me.[35]

The final lines show that even though she had been chosen by Zeus, she understands completely the limitations of her mortality, even though she too is very young.

Other stories illustrate by negative example why it is important for parthenoi to realize what was unacceptable for them to do, even if they had been loved by a god. Koronis had intercourse with a mortal while she was pregnant by Apollo:

she spurned the god in the folly of her mind, and accepted another marriage, without her father's knowledge, even though she had been loved by Phoebus and bore the pure seed of the god. She did not wait for the bride's table, or the cry of sounding wedding songs, which her young women (parthenoi) friends would sing in evening songs. But she fell in love with what was far off, as many others have also done. There are foolish people who despise what they have nearby and look beyond, hunting vanities with hopes unfulfilled.[36]

As a result of her poor judgment, Koronis was destroyed by fire. Kreousa, another parthenos who was abducted by Apollo, abandons her baby and feels that the god has deserted her. Years after she was abducted by Apollo, Kreousa remembers how she called out to her mother as the god led her into a cave.[37] She complains bitterly that the god abandoned her and that the child she bore to him "is lost, snatched by birds for their dinner, my son and yours, poor thing; and you play your lyre, singing your paeans."[38] Kreousa does not realize that meanwhile she has already met the son she thought she had lost, and she would have contrived to have him murdered had the god not intervened and revealed his true identity.

These myths illustrate the power of ate, the delusion that affects all mortal understanding. Delusions are explained in physical terms by the writer of the medical treatise on parthenoi: all human beings are subject to fears and destructive visions that "drive them out of their senses, so that they seem to see particular gods who are hostile to themselves, either by night, or day, or both." According to this physician, more women than men are affected by "that kind of vision" (opsis) because a woman's mind is less powerful and smaller than a man's. In his view, parthenoi around the time of their first menstrual period are particularly liable to these delusions, which the physician blames on retention of the menses, and prescribes marriage to cure.

But in myth the visions that affect human judgment are understood to be caused directly by the gods. In the Prometheus Bound, the parthenos Io tells how visions in the night (opseis ennychoi) told her to go out to a meadow where Zeus would make love to her: "O most fortunate girl, why do you remain a parthenos so long, when it is possible for you to have the greatest union?"[39] As she tells the story, she refuses to go, until Zeus makes her father drive her out of the house, after which her body and mind are "turned around"; her head is horned, and she goes to the meadow leaping, stung by a gadfly. Like the distraught parthenoi described by the doctor in his treatise, she wishes to die.[40] But since the other characters in the play are gods, they can more clearly understand what has happened: they know that Hera's jealousy is responsible for the madness,[41] and that eventually Io will be rescued by Zeus himself, the very god she now blames for her troubles, and become the ancestor of a famous race. Vase-painters choose a more dramatic and violent moment in Io's story to emphasize the god's concern for the parthenos he loved: in no. 96 the Eucharides Painter concentrates on the moment when Zeus' son Hermes comes to kill Argos, a giant with a thousand eyes who had been sent by Hera, while Io, in the form of a cow, looks on. Another vase-painting shows Zeus stroking the cow Io's head, while Hermes kills Argos.[42]

According to the writer of the medical treatise About Young Women, when a parthenos is not affected by visions (phantasmata), "a desire sets in which compels her to love death as if it were a form of good." He blames this desire on retention of extra blood around her heart. This physician would have diagnosed Antigone's behavior as characteristic of a parthenos ready for marriage; she is reckless and willing to defy Kreon's edict, which says that anyone who tries to bury the body of her brother Polynikes will be put to death by public stoning:

I knew that I would die, of course I knew, even if you had made no proclamation. But if I die before my time, I account that gain. For does not whoever lives among many troubles, as I do, gain by death? So it is in no way painful for me to meet with this death; if I had endured that the son of my own mother should die and remain unburied, that would have given me pain, but this gives me none. And if you think my actions foolish, that amounts to a charge of folly by a fool![43]

Like the parthenoi in the treatise, she is in love with death as if it were a kind of good, and dies by hanging herself once she is sealed up in her tomb, even though provisions had been left for her.[44] The chorus of Theban elders explain her conduct by her inheritance from Oedipus: "It is clear! The nature (gennema) of the girl is savage, like her father's, and she does not know how to bend before her troubles."[45] The chorus see what has happened as the fulfillment of the family curse, the result of "folly in speech and the Erinys in the mind."[46] They tell her that she was destroyed by her "self-willed passion."[47] Her uncle Kreon describes her behavior as willful disobedience and speaks of taming her, as one controls a spirited horse with a tight bridle.[48] Antigone herself believes that by burying her brother she showed "reverence for reverence."[49] Each of them is right, although each only sees part of the picture. Sophokles also makes it clear that it is not coincidental that Antigone is a parthenos who is about to be married. That is the time in a woman's life when she is most capable of daring action, as he shows in the opening scene of the drama, by contrasting Antigone's reaction to Kreon's edict with that of her younger sister Ismene.

These same characteristics help to account for the important roles played in the myths by parthenoi who volunteer to be human sacrifices.[50] Some of these myths may derive from prehistoric rituals in which a young woman was offered as a bride to a god.

The lost epic *Kypria* told of how Achilles' ghost demanded the sacrifice of Hecuba's daughter Polyxena. Perhaps, as Walter Burkert has suggested, the original purpose of the sacrifice was to make it possible for the hero, even in death, to have his share of the women of Troy—he had seen her when he ambushed and killed her brother Troilos.[51] Certainly the account of her sacrifice in Euripides' *Hecuba* emphasizes her physical appeal:

and when she heard the command from her [Greek] masters, she grasped her tunic from the shoulder, and tore it down to her navel; she revealed her breasts and chest—which was as beautiful as a statue's—and falling on her knees spoke most pathetically: "here is my breast, young man, strike it if you wish, or if you like, here is my throat turned towards you." And he, both willing and unwilling, in pity for the girl, cut the passages of her breath with his sword. And as she died, she nonetheless took much care to fall with modesty. hiding what should be hidden from men's eyes.[52]

It is important to note, however, that whatever the original meaning of the myth, in this account the soldiers resist all temptations to indulge themselves. Her body is treated with respect.[53] Some gather wood to build her pyre. In a vivid departure from normal sacrificial practice, where the bystanders sprinkle the victim with grains of barley, the Greek soldiers cover her with leaves, as if she were a victor in the games.[54] They speak of her courage and nobility of heart.[55] In his description of her decision to allow herself to be a willing sacrifice, Euripides concentrates on her courage and intelligence. Although her mother urges her to plead for mercy, she volunteers to die: she was once a princess and does not wish to be a slave, who would be compelled to do household chores and be the bride of another slave.[56] She will not allow her mother to die in her place, because it would subject her old body to indignities.[57] To reveal one's breasts is not intended to arouse so much as to elicit pity from a male audience; by using the gesture in the courtroom the courtesan Phryne managed to avoid a sentence of death.[58]

Polyxena is willing to be sacrificed in order to avoid what she believes to be an even worse fate, but other parthenoi have patriotic motives as well. In Euripides' *Herakleidai* one of Herakles' daughters, a parthenos, offers herself for sacrifice. In later times this daughter was identified with Makaria, who was celebrated in cult and had a spring named after her.[59] In the drama Herakles' children have fled to Athens to seek protection, and their enemies are besieging the city to capture them and kill them. The oracles have called for a parthenos from a noble family to be sacrificed to Persephone.[60] When no Athenian father is willing to give up his daughter, Herakles' daughter immediately volunteers. Since all the children of Herakles received heroic honors in Attica,[61] it may be significant that Euripides chose to portray the heroism of this parthenos rather than that of one of her brothers; even in a world where men make the decisions and fight the wars, critical contributions can be made by women.[62] The gods also request the sacrifice of males: Ares demands the sacrifice of Kreon's son Menoeceus so that Thebes can be victorious over the Argives.[63] Kodros, the last legendary king of Athens, had a tomb on the Acropolis in honor of his heroic self-sacrifice in the war against the Dorians.[64]

But in Athens the children who were ready to die for the state were parthenoi. In his funeral oration for the Athenian dead in the battle of Chaironeia Demosthenes cites the example of the daughters of Leos, who offered to die in order to save their country from the plague.[65] He also mentions the story of the daughters of Erechtheus,[66] who died so that Athens might be victorious in the war against the Eleusinians. The moral issues inevitably raised by myths of human sacrifice made them an ideal subject for drama.[67] Euripides told the story of this heroic self-sacrifice in his drama *Erechtheus*, which now survives only in fragments. We do not have any of the daughters' speeches, but we know from other sources that, although the oracle asked for only one daughter, her two sisters volunteered to die along with her.[68] These heroic parthenoi were honored as the Hyakinthides in cult and in dances by other parthenoi.[69] If this is the sacrifice that is depicted in the east frieze of the Parthenon, the heroism of these parthenoi was evidently a myth of central importance to all Athenians.[70]

Perhaps we can infer from the speeches Euripides gives to Herakles' daughter in the *Herakleidai* the nature of the lines that would have been spoken in the *Erechtheus* by the king's daughters. Like Polyxena in the *Hecuba*, she has personal motives. Should she refuse, no city would take her and her brothers in, and no one would want to marry her or have children by her. But Herakles' daughter is also motivated by altruistic considerations. She uses the same kind of arguments that a male hero would make when faced with the same dilemma. If the Athenians are willing to give up their lives to save hers, how can she not give hers up to save them? She wants to be worthy of her great father: "isn't it better to die than to experience insults that are unworthy of me; that might be appropriate for someone else, but not for someone as distinguished as myself."[71] She must die in order to save her family and so that Athens can win the war against her enemies.

In prehistoric myth the sacrifices of parthenoi to the goddess Artemis in times of war probably originated as a means of atonement for the blood of the animals killed by human hunters.[72] But in Athenian drama the emphasis is on how the mortal characters react to the harsh requirements of the gods.

In Aischylos' *Agamemnon* Iphigenia is described as a parthenos who "often had sung in her father's hospitable halls," and as a virgin (*ataurotos*) had lovingly sung the paean after her father had poured the third libation to Zeus.[73] The detail about her singing at the men's table suggests that Aischylos in this play imagined her as being too young to be ready for marriage. It also brings out the contrast between her promise and her cruel death: gagged so that she cannot utter a curse and subdued by force.[74] The scene is comparable to the portrayal of the sacrifice of Polyxena on an Attic black-figure amphora of ca. 550 B.C., where Neoptolemos slits the throat of a parthenos wrapped tightly in a cloth.[75] In Euripides' *Iphigenia at Aulis* the heroine is old enough to be married and, as a result, is better able to take a decisive role in the drama.

At first in an eloquent speech,[76] Iphigenia begs her father to spare her. She reminds him of the close relationship they had when she was a child; she asks why she should have to compensate for Helen's behavior. Employing a technique that was used to great effect in Athenian courtrooms,[77] she calls on her younger brother Orestes to weep and ask her father to spare her life. She laments in a long lyric aria the judgment of Paris that caused the war and led to the decision to sacrifice her. Then Achilles arrives and assures Iphigenia (who was to have been his bride) and her mother Clytemnestra that he will not allow Iphigenia to die and will defend her against all the other Greeks. In her earlier speech Iphigenia stated that "anyone who asks to die is insane (*mainetai*)."[78] But now—without warning—she states that she wants to be sacrificed. As we have seen, her behavior is characteristic of the parthenoi described by the Hippocratic writers; she actively seeks death, and she displays sudden changes of mind.[79]

Her speech is remarkably persuasive, first because she gives no one a chance to prepare any counter-arguments against her, and then because she makes her self-sacrifice into an act of the greatest patriotic heroism, equal to that of the daughters of Erechtheus and Herakles. In her earlier speech to Agamemnon, she had spoken of the expedition primarily as a means of resolving a domestic quarrel. Now she describes it as if it were a battle for the freedom of Greece (even though Greece was not under siege by the Trojans). She explains that all Greece now depends on her, and by dying she can save the army:

By dying I shall save all this, and my fame will be enviable, because I have rescued Greece. For also it is not right for me to act like a coward (*philopsychein*); for you bore me for all the Greeks, not for yourself alone.[80]

In addition, by giving up her one life she can save the lives of many thousands of men: "one man's life is worth more than that of thousands of women."[81] She sees her sacrifice as means of defending her homeland. She will give her life for Greece, so that Greeks can rule over barbarians, rather than barbarians rule over Greeks. She ends her speech by claiming that the essential quality of Greek civilization is its freedom: "[barbarian civilization] is a slavish thing; but [Greeks] are free."

The climax of her speech effectively deflects the attention of her listeners from the serious moral issues she had raised in her earlier speech about the injustice of her sacrifice. Her act now exemplifies one of the highest ideals of Greek culture, which was claimed in the Peloponnesian war by both Spartans and Athenians.[82] Confident references to the superiority of Greek civilization were commonplace in contemporary poetry and in public funeral orations.[83] Iphigenia's rhetoric, with its patriotic claims, makes Achilles even more eager to marry her, but she persuades him to let her "save Greece, if we can."[84] Her sacrifice will bring "victorious salvation."[85] Although the original ending of the play has not survived, in the text that has come down to us Iphigenia's conduct won the admiration of the entire army: "everyone was amazed by the courage and nobility of the parthenos."[86] While her father weeps and turns his head aside, she stands near him and says: "I am ready for you. I give my body for my fatherland and for all the land of Greece for you to lead as a willing sacrifice to the altar, since this is what the oracle has decreed."[87]

Here, as in the cases of Herakles' daughter and Polyxena, Euripides (or whoever wrote the final section of the drama) takes pains to emphasize the determination and persuasiveness of the parthenos. The contrast with the scene portrayed on no. 101 is striking. There Iphigenia is being led to her death with the same gesture that is used for brides as they are led by their husbands to their new homes.[88] The implication is that she is to be the bride of death, like Antigone who claims that her tomb is her *nympheion*, her bridal chamber. But in Euripides' play Iphigenia acts as bravely and boldly as Menoeceus does when he volunteers to kill himself on behalf of Thebes: "I shall go and stand on the battlements, and slaughter myself over the dark lair of the dragon, since that is what the seer has indicated, and I shall bring freedom to the land."[89]

I do not think that there is any implication in *Iphigenia at Aulis* that Iphigenia is being sacrificed because as a female her life is less valuable than that of her brother Orestes. Her statement that "one man's life is worth more than that of thousands of women" need not be taken as representative of standard Athenian belief about the relative value of male and female lives.[90] In context it is clear that she is exaggerating for rhetorical effect: she is trying to persuade Achilles (who as a character in the play is as vain as he is courageous) to allow her to sacrifice herself. As she sees it, she is saving all of Greece, women, children, and slaves included. Certainly that is what the daughter of Herakles believes she is doing, and what Erechtheus' wife Praxithea imagines will be achieved if she agrees to allow her daughter to be sacrificed in order to save Athens:

> we have children so that we may protect the altars of the gods and our fatherland. Although the city has a single identity, we who live in it are many. How should I destroy all of them, when it is possible for me to offer one life on behalf of all the others? If I know how to count, and can distinguish greater from less, one household in its affliction does not add up to more than the whole city or have equal weight.[91]

Praxithea points out that she would not have hesitated to send a *son* into battle: "so I shall give my daughter, who is not mine except by nature, to be sacrificed for the land. For if the city is going to be destroyed, what share have I in my children?"[92] Her comments make it clear that she regards her daughter's death as equivalent to that of a son in war.

Perhaps it is because modern scholars have been so eager to discover the original purpose of these human sacrifices, that they have assumed they retained some of their original significance in historical times.[93] Whatever their meaning in the past, in Euripides' play the sacrifice of a maiden is hardly the equivalent of a marriage; rather it has become a heroic service to family and state. As we have seen, there is in the surviving texts no special emphasis on sexuality, but rather a concentration on the full potential of women's heroism. It is significant that the plays containing these examples of self-sacrifice were acted during the long and demanding course of the Peloponnesian War. It is also characteristic of the genius of these writers that they chose to endow these heroic parthenoi with the characteristics of real-life young women: passionate temperament, sudden decisiveness, and courageous determination.

MARY R. LEFKOWITZ
Wellesley College

My thanks to Hugh Lloyd-Jones for permission to use his translations of Aischylos' *Agamemnon* and of Sophokles. All other translations are my own.

1. Lefkowitz (1981) 41-47.
2. Cf. Pomeroy (1994) 268-69.
3. Hesiod, *Works and Days* 63, 78.
4. Cf. Simon, *LIMC* I (1981) 790-91; Loraux (1993) 84.
5. Oxford, Ashmolean Museum, inv. no. G 275 (525); *LIMC* V (1990) 643 (s.v. Hermes). The painters of nos. 79 and 81 combine Hesiod's account with other traditions; see West (1978) 164.
6. Hesiod, *Works and Days* 89.
7. *Homeric Hymn* 5.82.
8. Lefkowitz (1986) 30-42.
9. Pindar, *Pythian* 9.26.
10. Hesiod, *Ehoiai* frag. 76 MW.
11. On the ritual purpose of such sacrifices, see esp. Versnel (1980) 145.
12. Some of these effects are noted in other Hippocratic treatises, e.g., *Prorrh.* 2.30.34 (headaches); *de Mul. Affect.* 127.4, 127.19, *de Nat. Mul.* 3.4, *Superf.* 34.1 (hysteria).
13. This seems to have been the plot of a play by Aischylos, the *Xantriae* or possibly the *Semele*; cf. Lloyd-Jones (1971) 567-68.
14. Homer, *Odyssey* 6.180.
15. Sophokles, *Antigone* 876.
16. E.g., *IG* i² 1014 (*CEG* 24); Aristotle, *Athenian Constitution* 7.486, 489, 490, 649; Lefkowitz (1986) 37-40.
17. Kearns (1989) 57; cf. O'Connor-Visser (1987) 197-99.
18. Cf. Lefkowitz (1987) 503-18.
19. Kearns (1990) 338-44.
20. Homer, *Odyssey* 6.27.
21. Homer, *Odyssey* 6.100-109.
22. Homer, *Odyssey* 6.244.
23. Homer, *Odyssey* 8.460-68.
24. Apollodoros, *Bibliotheke* 2.1.4.
25. Cf. Buxton (1982) 84, 112-13; Sourvinou-Inwood (1991) 69; Lefkowitz (1993) 22.
26. Hesiod, frag. 128 MW.
27. Pseudo-Hesiod, *Shield of Herakles* 35-38.
28. Lefkowitz (1993) 17-37.
29. Homer, *Odyssey* 11.236-54.
30. Sophokles, frag. 659 Radt.
31. Anakreon, frag. 72 (417 *PMG*).
32. Pindar, *Pythian* 8.92-97; Lloyd-Jones (1990) 78-79.
33. Sophokles, *Antigone* 916-20.
34. Sophokles, *Antigone* 944-54.
35. Simonides, 543.18-27 *PMG*.
36. Pindar, *Pythian* 3.12-13.
37. Euripides, *Ion* 881-92.
38. Euripides, *Ion* 902-906.
39. Aischylos, *Prometheus Bound* 647-54.
40. Aischylos, *Prometheus Bound* 583-84.
41. Aischylos, *Prometheus Bound* 592, 704, 900.
42. Würzburg, Wagner Museum, inv. no. ZA 48; *LIMC* V (1990) 665 no. 11 (s.v. Io).
43. Sophokles, *Antigone* 460-70.
44. Sophokles, *Antigone* 775.
45. Sophokles, *Antigone* 471-72:
46. Sophokles, *Antigone* 603.
47. Sophokles, *Antigone* 875.
48. Sophokles, *Antigone* 477-78.
49. Sophokles, *Antigone* 944.
50. Cf. Lefkowitz (1986) 95-103; Wilkins (1990) 177-94.
51. Burkert (1983) 65-67; Gantz (1993) 598-603.
52. Euripides, *Hecuba* 557-67.

53. Gantz (1993) 659.

54. Cf. scholia to Euripides, *Hecuba* 573, I 53-4 Schwartz (=Eratosthenes 241 *FGrHist*F14); Pindar, *Pythian* 4.240, 9.123-24; Burkert (1985) 76. Collard (1991) 161, mistakenly conflates the two practices; cf. Burkert (1983) 5 n. 16.

55. Euripides, *Hecuba* 579-80.

56. Euripides, *Hecuba* 349-68.

57. Euripides, *Hecuba* 404-408.

58. Athenaeus 13.590e (=Hyperides, frag. 178 Kenyon).

59. Kearns (1989) 58-59; Pearson (1907) xix; Wilkins (1993) 104-105.

60. Wilkins (1993) 104-105.

61. Kearns (1989) 166-67.

62. Cf. Wilkins (1993) 112.

63. Euripides, *Phoenician Women* 930-35.

64. Scholia to Plato, *Symposium* 208d (Greene, pp. 63-64).

65. Demosthenes 60.29.

66. Demosthenes 60.27.

67. Foley (1985) 40.

68. According to Demaratos 42 *FGrHist* F4 the demand was made by Persephone; but according to Hyginus, *Fabulae* 46.238, it was Poseidon.

69. Brulé (1987) 31-32; Kearns (1989) 59-63, 201-202; Mikalson (1991) 93-94; on the connection of the Erechtheides with this cult, cf. Parker (1987) 212 n. 66.

70. According to Prof. Joan Connelly's new interpretation, as reported in *The Economist* (19 December 1992) p.83 and *The Wall Street Journal* (1 January 1994) p. A10.

71. Euripides, *Herakleidai* 525-28.

72. Burkert (1983) 63-64; Lloyd-Jones (1990a) 312-13.

73. Aischylos, *Agamemnon* 243-46.

74. Aischylos, *Agamemnon* 233-37.

75. London, British Museum, inv. no. 1897.7-27.2; Maas (1973) 42; cf. Gantz (1993) 658; Harder (1993) 180 n. 16.

76. Euripides, *Iphigenia at Aulis* 1211-52.

77. Plato, *Apology* 34c.

78. Euripides, *Iphigenia at Aulis* 1251-52.

79. *Virg.* and *Superf.* 34.1.

80. Euripides, *Iphigenia at Aulis* 1383-87.

81. Euripides, *Iphigenia at Aulis* 1394.

82. Thucydides 2.8.4, 37.2.

83. Aristotle cites a line from Euripides' *Telephos* (frag. 719 Nauck=Handley and Rea [1957] 45) as what "the poets say" (*Politics* I 1252b8); cf. also Euripides, *Andromache* 665, *Helen* 276, and *Orestes* 115; Hall (1989) 197; Harder (1993) 238 n. 136.

84. Euripides, *Iphigenia at Aulis* 1420.

85. Euripides, *Iphigenia at Aulis* 1473.

86. Euripides, *Iphigenia at Aulis* 1561-62.

87. Euripides, *Iphigenia at Aulis* 1553-56.

88. Jenkins (1983) 141; L. Kahil, *LIMC* V (1990) 710 (s.v. Iphigeneia).

89. Euripides, *Phoenician Women* 1009-1112.

90. Cf. Loraux (1987) 34, 48.

91. Euripides, *Erechtheus* frag. 50. 16-21 Austin.

92. Euripides, *Erechtheus* frag. 50. 38-40 Austin.

93. E.g., Foley (1982) 170: "Ironically, the ideal bride and the ideal sacrificial victim become one, as the education for marriage provides the transition to voluntary death."

THE CULT OF HEROINES: KEKROPS' DAUGHTERS

The subject of hero cults has been one of enormous interest to Greek historians and archaeologists, as well as students of Greek religion, in recent years. In 1944 A.D. Nock, the great scholar of ancient religion, in a seminal paper from which my title is derived, set out succinctly just what the worship of heroes entailed for the Greeks and how it was different from the cults of the gods.[1] In the half-century since, intensive excavation in Greece has provided the archaeological material to make Greek hero cult tangible and better understood. We now know of sites where such Homeric heroes as Agamemnon, Menelaos, and Odysseus received cult worship, in some cases as early as the period of the Homeric poems themselves, the later eighth century.[2] The spectacular discovery of a hero shrine at Lefkandi on the island of Euboea in the 1970s has demonstrated the existence of some form of hero cult in the early Iron Age, at least two centuries before Homer's time.[3]

The nomenclature used to describe heroes and hero cult has to some extent obscured the worship of female heroes. To put the question most simply, is a female hero a heroine? Conventionally, "heroine" refers only to literary contexts, the female protagonist in a Greek tragedy, for example. "Hero" is also used in this sense, but in addition there is a use of the term hero in the religious sphere that carries a technical meaning, formulated by Nock and, before him, L.R. Farnell: a mythological or historical figure who, after his death, received cult worship, usually centered around the location of his

Fig. 1. Detail of a column krater, side A. Baltimore, Walters Art Gallery, inv. no. 48.69.

real or imagined tomb.[4] That there were female figures who fall into this same category is proved by the archaeological evidence, for example for Alexandra/Kassandra alongside Agamemnon at Amyklai and Helen alongside Menelaos at the Laconian Menelaion.[5] I propose in this paper to employ the term heroine in a technical and religious sense analogous to that of hero.[6]

The earliest evidence for cult worship of heroines is at present limited to the Peloponnesos, particularly at the sites just mentioned. In Athens and Attica there is no evidence in the eighth or seventh centuries and almost none for the sixth century. The prevalence of references to heroines in the fifth century and later, however, strongly suggests that in at least some cases the cults should go back to the Archaic period or earlier and have simply not left any recognizable trace. For heroes, by contrast, several cults are well attested in the sixth century in Attica, such as those of Theseus, the Dioskouroi, Ajax, and, probably, Herakles.[7]

In the fifth century, of course, literary heroines are conspicuous on the Athenian stage. Yet almost none of these is associated with Athens or Attica.[8] Antigone is from Thebes, Clytemnestra from Argos (though Spartan by birth), and Medea is not a Greek at all but from the far reaches of the Black Sea. It may be no accident that Athenian (largely male) audiences in the Theater of Dionysos were better able to accept the presentation of strong, often defiant women on stage if they were clearly distanced from fifth-century Athens in both time and place. When women specifically connected with the myth-history of Athens do appear on the tragic stage, it tends to be in subsidiary and safely unambiguous roles. Thus, for example, Aithra, the mother of Theseus, appears in the *Suppliants* of Euripides to help persuade her son to ensure proper burial to the Argive heroes who fell before Thebes. A significant exception is Kreousa, the mother of Ion, in a Euripidean play that is more explicitly political than most.[9]

Yet Kreousa, for all her genealogical importance as mother of the eponymn of the Ionian race, was not a figure of cult. Nor was Aithra, in spite of being the mother of the Athenian national hero, who himself became the city's most prominent cult hero after his bones were brought back to Athens, amid great fanfare, by the statesman Kimon in 475.[10] Which Athenian heroines, then, did have cults, and how did they function within the wider context of Athenian religion? In this essay, I would like to consider the most significant example of the cult of heroines in Athens. The daughters of Kekrops—Aglauros, Herse, and Pandrosos—are intimately

Fig. 2. Pointed amphora (side A). Munich, Antikensammlungen, inv. no. 2345.

as Erichthonios but is the same figure who was later king, and I will maintain here the conventional distinction of Erichthonios for the child and Erechtheus for the man. The story is, of course, more complicated than that. Hardly had the daughters of Kekrops received the baby from Athena into their care than they disobeyed the goddess's command not to look in the basket that held him and were driven mad. Their role as *kourotrophoi* was thus short-lived but still essential for giving the newborn from the Acropolis a place in the Athenian royal house as if by adoption.

The death of the Kekropidai is reported in different versions. In the more "standard," they jump to their deaths, in their madness, from the Acropolis rock.[16] An alternative, that Aglauros willingly sacrificed herself on behalf of the city, is attested first in the fourth century and seldom thereafter.[17] This sounds like a belated attempt to make at least one of these heroines conform to a pattern of voluntary maiden sacrifice, of which Athens already had several examples, most notably the daughters of Erechtheus and the daughters of Leos.[18] It also would help to justify why it was in the sanctuary of Aglauros that Athenian ephebes received their arms and swore an oath of loyalty.[19] At the same time, the "older" Aglauros, who paid the penalty for not following orders, might also have served as an effective warning to the future soldiers.

Fig. 3. Pointed amphora in figure 2, detail of side B.

linked to Athenian genealogy, as offspring of the first king of Athens, and their cults were centered around the heart of the ancient city, the Acropolis.[11]

The history of early Athens is told in many versions, none of them earlier than the fifth century and seldom in agreement with one another.[12] One of the few undisputed points is that Kekrops was the city's first recorded king.[13] He reflects Athens' claim to autochthony in that no parentage is named and he was imagined as human only from the waist up, the rest a long snaky tail (fig. 15). There could be no better image of his origins in the soil of Athens. That he ruled Athens in its infancy is suggested by the story, told first on the west pediment of the Parthenon, that he judged the contest between Poseidon and Athena for the naming and patronage of the city.[14] The kingship did not, however, pass to a son of Kekrops (although, as we shall see, he had one) but instead to a second figure who was also, in a sense, autochthonous: Erechtheus. The three daughters of Kekrops, then, form a crucial link in the royal genealogy of Athens, since they were born from the first king and were, however briefly, nurses of the second.[15] He is known in our sources

If the earlier version is indeed the more authentic, it raises the question of how the disturbing motif of disobedience, madness, and suicide contributed to shaping their role as heroines of cult. An interesting parallel is Ajax, whose madness was, at least in Sophokles' version, also induced by Athena and ended in suicide. Since the cult of Ajax was well established by the fifth century, probably both on Salamis and in Athens, the playwright describes the ritual suicide as a form of self-sacrifice with religious overtones.[20] In this light, the suicide of the daughters of Kekrops and the alternate version of Aglauros' self-sacrifice may not be as far apart as it at first appears. All cult heroes are worshipped only after death, and that death most often takes a violent and spectacular form.[21]

The suicide of the Kekropidai served another purpose in the cult of the goddess they served but disobeyed. It was the brilliant insight of Walter Burkert that the story of the daughters of Kekrops is a kind of mythic paradigm for the initiation ritual of the Arrephoria, in which two or four Athenian girls of distinguished family carried a chest that they were forbidden to look into from the Acropolis down to the Sanctuary of Aphrodite in the Gardens.[22] In this context the motif of disobedience and its consequences would have had a practical purpose, as an admonition, in the annual retelling. The ancient sources do not agree on which or how many of the three Kekropidai obeyed Athena. The most common version seems to be that Pandrosos alone tried to dissuade her curious sisters from looking in the chest, but it is unclear whether she alone was also spared their fate.[23]

Fig. 5. Olive Tree Pediment. Athens, Acropolis Museum.

The nature of the death-leap also serves to fix permanently the important topographical association of the daughters of Kekrops with the Acropolis. For two of the three, a sanctuary can be localized there. That of Aglauros was just below the eastern end of the Acropolis, high on the slope,[24] while Pandrosos' sanctuary was above, on the north side of the Acropolis, near Athena's early temple.[25] No sanctuary of Herse is attested, and she is in other ways a more shadowy figure than her two sisters. She may be a kind of doublet of Pandrosos, since both names are from roots with the same meaning ("dew"). Interestingly, however, it is Herse to whom the best ancient sources give the most prominent role in Attic

Fig. 6. Girl from the Olive Tree Pediment (figure 5). Athens, Acropolis Museum.

genealogies. In one account she became the mother of Kephalos by Hermes, and in another her child by the same god was Keryx, ancestor of the Eleusinian priesthood of the Kerykes.[26] There may be indirect reflections of these traditions on Attic vases that predate any of the late sources by several centuries. A small group of red-figure vases, including one in the Walters Art Gallery (fig. 1), shows Hermes pursuing a young woman who flees to a kingly figure who must be her father.[27] Since, however, other sources name Pandrosos or Aglauros as Hermes' beloved, we cannot be certain she is Herse. The incorporation of Kephalos into the family of Kekrops may be responsible for such visual juxtapositions as we

Fig. 7. Amphora. New York, Metropolitan Museum of Art, inv. no. 53.11.1.

find on the krater in Palermo (no. 72) decorated with the birth of Erichthonios on one side and Eos pursuing Kephalos on the other, or on a cup by Douris, which shows Kekrops present at the abduction of Kephalos.[28]

The existence of distinct and geographically separate sanctuaries of Aglauros and Pandrosos raises the question of whether the three daughters were more often regarded as a corporate entity or as having separate identities.[29] Certainly in comparison to the daughters of Erechtheus or the Leokorai, whose individual names are not even recorded until quite late, they have a greater degree of individuality. The very fact that one obeyed Athena while the other two did not (even if the identification of that one varies in the sources) undermines their collective identity. Yet in some contexts, especially in the visual arts, the threesome is clearly the central element, and they are not always fully differentiated.

As we shall see, the period from soon after the Persian Wars to the end of the fifth century saw the greatest interest in the daughters of Kekrops, at least in the visual arts, and probably in cult as well. The defense of Athens in 490 and again in 480 seems to have reminded the Athenians of some of their indigenous heroes and prompted the introduction of new cults or the revival of old ones. A conspicuous example is Boreas, the North Wind, the Athenians' "son-in-law"[30]—by virtue of his relationship with Oreithyia, daughter of Erechtheus—who came to their aid by wrecking the Persian fleet off Artemision. Soon after 480, Boreas' abduction of Oreithyia becomes one of the favorite subjects of Classical red-figure painters and in at least one instance even includes the daughters of Kekrops (figs. 2 and 3).[31] It is also in these years that the birth of

Erichthonios first appears,[32] while the mature Erechtheus and Kekrops are both depicted as eponymous heroes of two of the ten recently instituted Kleisthenic tribes.[33] How much earlier can we trace the cults of the Kekropidai on the Acropolis?

Though Kekrops himself is not well attested before the fifth century, Erechtheus features in our earliest recorded references to the Acropolis, in Homer. Athena's primitive temple there is known to the poet as "the strong house of Erechtheus," possibly a reminiscence of a Bronze Age tradition that the mythical kings of Athens ruled from the citadel of the city.[34] The association of hero and goddess on the north side of the Acropolis is preserved in the nickname of the Classical successor to the Archaic temple of Athena, the Erechtheion. If the story of Erechtheus' origins on the Acropolis, his "step-mother" Athena, and her entrusting of him to the daughters of Kekrops was also known in the Archaic period, as seems likely, we might expect to find traces of it in the surviving iconography. The evidence is meager but suggestive.

A very early black-figure fragment found on the Acropolis and attributed to Sophilos shows two women side-by-side, one of them labeled Pandrosos (fig. 4).[35] Her companion should be Aglauros, while Herse may not yet have become a necessary part of the threesome at this early stage. The provenance alone is strong evidence for the Kekropidai's early association with the Acropolis, but unfortunately not enough remains to infer the context.

One of the most intriguing visual references to the Archaic sanctuary of the Acropolis is the olive tree incised on the mid sixth-century poros pediment that takes its name from this detail (fig. 5). The nature of the building that this pediment adorned is unknown, but its small dimensions suggest some kind of treasury. The pediment depicts a small roofed shrine of ashlar masonry set against the background of the olive tree, and there were at least three figures

Fig. 8. Marble votive relief. Athens, Acropolis Museum, inv. no. 702.

Figs. 9-10. Cup (sides A and B). Frankfurt, Liebieghaus, inv. no. ST V 7.

as well.[36] A female figure has a round disk on her head of the type used to cushion a hydria (fig. 6). Because of this detail, and the possible resemblance of the structure to a fountain house, recognition of the scene's religious significance was for many years diverted by the suggestion that it represents a mythological narrative, the ambush of Troilos by Achilles.[37] But this story, set at Troy, has no relevance to the Acropolis setting, while the olive tree so meticulously rendered is surely meant to be the sacred olive that Athena caused to grow on the north side of the Acropolis and that was still an important token in much later times. As has been recognized in recent years, the pediment represents a cult scene localized on the Acropolis itself.[38]

But what sort of cult scene? When the Classical Erechtheion was built, the olive tree was just to the west of it, within the precinct identified as the Pandroseion.[39] On this basis we may suppose that the pedimental scene is also set in this area. The architectural structure would represent the temple of Athena, not the huge and complex one erected ca. 560 (the so-called Old Athena Temple or Dörpfeld Temple), but its predecessor in heroic times as imagined by an artist of the sixth century. The female figures, votaries or priestesses of the goddess, could be none other than the daughters of Kekrops.[40] Whatever the one figure carried on her head has not survived, but it need not have been a water jar. A black-figure vase only ten to twenty years later than the pediment may offer an important clue (fig. 7).[41] The context of the vase clearly relates to the Panathenaic festival: the shape is that of the prize amphorae only on a smaller scale (a so-called pseudo-Panathenaic), and the scene

is dominated by a striding figure of the armed goddess similar to that on the prize vases.[42] Here, however, instead of being surrounded by Doric columns, she is flanked by two votaries, a male flute-player and a woman holding out a wreath. As was first suggested by Herbert Cahn, the rectangular object on the woman's head is the folded peplos.[43] It rests on a circular pad similar to the girl's on the Olive Tree Pediment. This is the first and perhaps the only depiction of the peplos of Athena in Archaic art.[44] If the pediment did indeed include the peplos woven in historical times by the Arrephoroi, but set in the mythical past, this would strengthen the link between these historical Athenian girls and their role-models, the daughters of Kekrops.

Several objects found on or around the Archaic Acropolis seem to belong to a cult of three closely associated female divinities or heroines. Best known is a fine marble votive relief of three dancing girls, preceded by a flute-player and accompanied by a young boy (fig. 8).[45] The Kekropidai are, of course, not the only threesome worshipped in this area. We might think first of the Charites, or Graces, who had a sanctuary at the entrance to the Acropolis.[46] The dancing pose may seem more appropriate to Charites than Kekropidai, though the boy is hard to explain. Erysichthon, younger brother of the Kekropidai, is mentioned in some of the ancient sources and occasionally depicted with them on fifth-century vases, as we shall see (figs. 9 and 14).[47] The fruit held by the lead dancer finds a parallel on a black-figure votive plaque from the Nymphe sanctuary on the south slope of the Acropolis.[48] She also carries a wreath in her upraised left hand, while the girl behind her holds both a long sprig and a lotus bud. The third figure, only about half preserved, is probably male. But what we have suggests tokens of female beauty and of vegetation, a connotation implied in the dewy names of two of the three Kekropidai.

A similar triad appears on each side of a ritual vessel, probably a sprinkler, from the same sanctuary.[49] Here a seated, veiled woman is

Fig. 11. Detail of a column krater. San Antonio Museum of Art, inv. no. 86-134G (63).

43

Figs. 12-13. Alabastron, sides A and B. Athens, National Museum, inv. no. 17917.

flanked by two standing women, one of them holding out a flower to her. From under the handle, a small boy approaches with his offering of a cock. The women are surely not the daughters of Kekrops this time. Perhaps the seated figure is Nymphe herself, a bridal goddess (possibly an aspect of Aphrodite)[50] and the other two her worshippers. Nevertheless they suggest again how strong the presence of young, unmarried women was in the sanctuaries on and around the Acropolis.

In Archaic iconography, then, the daughters of Kekrops are elusive at best and never explicitly connected with the story of Erichthonios. It is only after the Persian Wars that this part of the myth is developed, and then in such different ways as to suggest that this charter myth of Athens was still evolving throughout the fifth century and into the fourth.

A cup painted only a few years after the victory over the Persians in 480 encapsulates the theme of Athenian patriotism as expressed in a new genealogical consciousness (figs. 9 and 10).[51] It is also the first certain depiction of the three daughters of Kekrops—in a manner that will not be repeated again.

An enormous snake has suddenly emerged from the dense foliage of a cave-like setting, rearing its head and baring its teeth. Two of the terrified girls flee the monster, still holding the sprigs that help to characterize them. They are met at the threshold of their father's palace by the third sister, who reaches out with both hands in a protective gesture. Kekrops himself sits inside, accompanied by his young son Erysichthon. Both also stretch out their

hands to receive the two disobedient daughters. The scene is drastically telescoped in the Archaic manner, since, even if the palace of the king were on the Acropolis, it would not be in sight of the cave under the slopes of the citadel. By combining the two halves, the painter perhaps wanted to stress the contrast between the one obedient sister and the two who were not, a motif that is present but not so strongly emphasized in the later iconography. This, coupled with the contrast between the quiet domestic setting at the left and the wild and dangerous outdoors at the right, presents the three girls as both positive and negative exempla of a central tenet of Athenian gender ideology. A woman's proper place is in the home, under the watchful eye of her father and brothers. Those who stray outside are asking for trouble. Outdoor places, such as the fountain house where strange men and other threatening creatures might lurk, were thought to be fraught with danger for Athenian women.[52] The snake, which can appear suddenly out of nowhere, is emblematic of the dangers.

Neither Athena nor the baby Erichthonios is included in the scene (and the chest has been displaced, beyond the handle, to the other side of the cup, at the left of fig. 10). The snake itself is punishment enough without the goddess's intervention. Interestingly, no preserved scene actually shows or alludes explicitly to the deaths of the girls, and it is worth asking if this element could be a fifth-century elaboration to help explain the origin of the cult or, alternatively, an early variant that was never fully accepted. When Kreousa relates the story to Ion (our earliest preserved reference to it), he questions its veracity and she has no reply.[53] On the Frankfurt cup, it looks very much as if the two disobedient daughters actually escape to the safety of their father's home, chastened but otherwise unharmed. Likewise, when, in the next generation, the vase-painters first depict the goddess Athena chastising the three girls, there is no indication that they will pay for the indiscretion with their lives.[54]

The finest version of this episode in the Early Classical period is on a column krater in San Antonio attributed to the Orchard Painter (fig. 11).[55] Athena is resplendent in a decorated helmet, long aegis fringed with snakes, and chiton embroidered with dolphins on the hem. Only the slightly comical Gorgoneion, looking like a churlish Mouseketeer, detracts from the solemnity of the scene. A small detail links the scene to the Frankfurt cup: the two disobedient girls each carry a tendril, while the third sister does not. It must, then, be the good Pandrosos who, on the krater, moves off in the opposite direction, looking sympathetically toward her sisters, but from a distance. She keeps both arms tightly enveloped in her mantle, a symbol of modesty and proper breeding that helps underline the contrast with the other two.[56] There are no references at all to the rest of the story: no baby, basket, or snake, yet the meaning is clear. The only aspect that is not clear is the nature and consequences of Athena's wrath. Certainly girls who provoked the wrath of Athena did not usually get off lightly; one thinks of Arachne, for example. But the vase-painters are strangely ambiguous about the outcome.

Figs. 14-18. Five details of a rhyton. London, British Museum. inv. no. E 788.

In an even briefer extract from the larger story, Athena confronts one of the sisters with a mildly reproachful look on an alabastron of about the same date (figs. 12 and 13).[57] Fragments from the Acropolis of the same period seem to have a comparable scene, with Aglauros' name inscribed.[58] A stately Athena calmly stretches out her hand toward the girl. We have moved far from the ferocious snake on the Frankfurt cup.

By the middle of the fifth century, then, both the birth of Erichthonios and the punishment of the Kekropidai are well established in Attic vase iconography. In these same years, a unique object occupies a special place in the imagery of Kekrops and his daughters. A spectacular rhyton modeled by Sotades takes the form of a Sphinx.[59] The actual drinking cup is decorated with a frieze that comprises three pairs of figures (figs. 14-16). Though none is inscribed, the key to an identification is in the unmistakable half-man, half-snake Kekrops carrying the scepter of kingship. In his other hand he extends a phiale to Nike, who will fill it from a jug. The other four figures should then be Kekrops' children: two daughters hurrying in from the right, the third standing before their young brother Erysichthon, who is seated on a rock. Given the family grouping, the occasion for Kekrops' celebratory libation can be none other than the birth of his successor Erichthonios. The scene is a modest precursor to the much more elaborate version on the Kekrops Painter's name-vase (no. 73), where Nike once again pours the wine for libation. The division of the three daughters on

the rhyton corresponds to that on the earlier cup in Frankfurt: the two disobedient girls, Aglauros and Herse, flee the unseen snake in an agitated state, while the dutiful Pandrosos waits with her well-behaved brother. The excited gesture of Aglauros, with both arms outspread, anticipates that on the later Berlin cup (no. 70), where it has been reduced to a generic expression of excitement.[60] Once again the contrast between obedient and disobedient girls is clear, yet their punishment is secondary in importance to the joyous news of the divine child.

The first vase to acknowledge explicitly the connection between Erichthonios' birth and his being entrusted to the daughters of Kekrops is a pelike of the mid-fifth century, sadly too fragmentary to allow us to infer many of the details (figs. 19 and 20).[61] On one side, the birth and the baby's reception by Athena are not unlike the scene on the contemporary hydria in London (no. 67). On the reverse is preserved only part of the overturned basket, along with the hems and feet of several women, Athena and one or two daughters. Also fragmentary is a later cup, which, as ingeniously interpreted by John Oakley, would have similarly shown the girls caught by Athena in the act of opening the chest.[62]

It is only a small step from the Leipzig pelike to the scenes of the birth of Erichthonios in which one or more of the Kekropidai appear as a proleptic reference to their future role as his nurses. This combination, especially popular in the last third of the fifth century, appears earliest and most fully on the Kodros Painter's cup in

Fig. 19. Fragment from a pelike (side A). Leipzig University, inv. no. T 654.

Fig. 20. Fragment from a pelike (side B). Leipzig University, inv. no. T 654.

Berlin (no. 70).[63] All three girls rush to witness the miraculous birth: Herse enters behind the proud father Hephaistos, while her two sisters approach from the other side of the cup. Their father Kekrops is also present at the birth for the first time since a black-figure lekythos of ca. 500 (the earliest representation of the birth of Erichthonios that we have),[64] suggesting a concern for the continuity of Athenian kingship, which is further expressed in the inclusion of even later (and unrelated) kings, Aegeus and his brother Pallas.

In the final decade of the century, the motif of the Kekropidai witnessing the birth of Erichthonios was handled by both painters

and sculptors in a variety of ways. Indeed, so popular must the theme have been in the visual arts that even Euripides acknowledges it, when he has Kreousa tell her son Ion the story of Athena's entrusting the baby to the daughters of Kekrops (here called Aglaurids), and he replies, "as she does in pictures?"[65] Two major sculptural monuments of the last two decades of the fifth century would have been well known to Euripides' audience. The subject of the Erechtheion frieze is one of the great unsolved puzzles of Classical iconography, but the prevalence of young female figures and children among the surviving fragments has suggested to some that the birth of Erichthonios was depicted.[66] The carved frieze on the base of Alkamenes' cult statue for the Hephaisteion certainly showed the birth of Erichthonios, as Pausanias implies.[67] Reflections in Neo-Attic and Roman reliefs led Evelyn Harrison to reconstruct a scene that includes the three daughters in a dance-like pose.[68]

On a Meidian squat lekythos in Cleveland (Cleveland Museum of Art, inv. no. 82.142, Neils [1983]), the three daughters watch from above, appearing only from the waist up in a rocky landscape. Could this be a topographical reference to their sanctuaries in a cave (Aglauros) and on the Acropolis (Pandrosos)? By the very end of the century, the type of composition we find on the krater in Fulda (no. 73) is especially favored, with figures disposed on several levels.[69] The woman observing from the upper left, as Kekrops and Athena pour a libation in honor of the newborn, has been identified by Erika Simon as Aglauros.[70] Her two sisters are behind her, in the handle zone. The Eros (or perhaps Pothos) beside Aglauros would then symbolize the forbidden desire to open the chest that sits in front of the olive tree of Athena.

It is not until the last years of the fifth century that the combination of both scenes, the birth and the punishment, as we have it on the fragmentary Leipzig pelike (cf. figs. 19 and 20), will occur again, this time in a far more complex and subtle narrative. The vase, a pyxis excavated in Athens in the 1970s, still awaits full publication, but the one published illustration indicates that the scene of the punishment ran around the entire body of the vase.[71] A vigorously striding Athena pursues one of the girls, while a second flees in the other direction. The snake rears up in front of Athena's olive tree. Even more remarkably, a complete set of inscribed names reveals that, in addition to Athena and the three daughters, this fullest preserved pictorial version also included some minor Attic heroes and heroines (Pylios, Chryseis, Eunoe), divinities (Hermes, Nike), and allegorical figures (Basileia). On the lid of the same vase was depicted the birth of Erichthonios, amid a group that includes Kekrops and an additional personification, Soteria. Thus the link between the two Erichthonios scenes is strengthened through the association with Kekrops and his family.

Although the Athens pyxis is unique in enlarging both scenes to include a number of new figures, the basic schema is in each case the established one familiar since the second quarter of the fifth century. But these last years of the century, with their heightened interest in the myth, not surprisingly also brought reinterpretations in both art and literature. The battered fragments of what was once a fine squat lekythos in Meidian style, found in the sanctuary of Apollo Maleatas at Epidauros, have long been known but only recently understood correctly, thanks to a painstaking study and reconstruction by Georgia Kokkorou-Alevra.[72] Here we have, in one sense, the "missing link" between Erichthonios' birth and the punishment of the daughters: Athena entrusting the baby to the three girls. Yet there is no chest, and no hint of the terrible outcome. Instead the scene, set in an idyllic landscape (in which the olive tree once again appears), is more reminiscent of that other episode of a divine child—Dionysos, given into the care of the Nymphs.[73] Other, even more modest, vases of this period seem to transport the Kekropidai and the baby in their charge to the kind of "paradise garden" that is characteristic of Athenian escapist art in the last years of the Peloponnesian War.[74] In these modest vignettes we seem to have a return to the original role of the daughters of Kekrops in early Athenian cult, as *kourotrophoi*, or nurturers of the young.[75]

This survey of the iconography of the daughters of Kekrops necessarily ends with the close of the fifth century, as the series of images comes to an end. If the Peloponnesian War called forth a wave of patriotism expressed in the representation of local heroines and heroes, then the war's disastrous conclusion may have made such imagery seem irrelevant and passé. This is not true of the associated cults, of course, since religious practice has its own steady rhythm, and old established cults were usually unaffected by the vicissitudes of war and politics. Indeed, much of our evidence for the cults of Aglauros and Pandrosos comes from inscriptions of the Hellenistic period, when they appear to have been more active than ever.

What sets Kekrops' daughters apart from the host of other female figures in Athenian legend and ensured their primary importance in both art and cult is their intricate web of associations with the city goddess Athena. The myth of Erichthonios is one of the very few in which Athena plays the role of a *kourotrophic* goddess, and the Kekropidai take over that role from her. They are her priestesses, yet by the Classical period they had priestesses of their own, which is not common in hero cults. Aglauros is the patron of the Athenian ephebes, who are otherwise in the service and under the protection of Athena herself. As the Kekropidai are votaries of Athena in the myth, so too in cult are they the heroines who "represent" the goddess and mediate most directly between her and her mortal worshippers.

H.A. SHAPIRO
University of Canterbury

1. Nock (1944).
2. For the sanctuary of Agamemnon near Sparta, see Cook (1953); on the Menelaion: Catling (1976); on the cave of Odysseus on Ithaka: Benton (1938-39). The question of the mutual influence of these cults and the spread of the Homeric epics is much debated; see, for example, Coldstream (1976), Price(1973), and, most recently, Antonaccio (1994).
3. See Popham et al. (1982).
4. See Nock (1944); Farnell (1921); Snodgrass (1988).
5. On Alexandra/Kassandra, see Pausanias 3.19.6; Salapata (1993) 189-90.
6. Even now English usage in regard to gender-specific language is evolving. In American English, for example, the term actress is still widely used, while in British English it has virtually died out, and female performers are regularly referred to as actors. While such "unisex" terms may seem to some less sexist, there is equally the danger that terminology like hero and hero-cult will give the erroneous impression that only males were so worshipped. I therefore retain the term heroine.
7. I have summarized the evidence for these cults in Shapiro (1989) 142-63. Perhaps the earliest well-attested hero in Attica is Akademos, eponymous hero of the Academy, whose Late Geometric sanctuary has been located: see Lauter (1985) 159-63.
8. See Foley (1981) and Lefkowitz (1981) 4-11. On the prevalence of Theban heroes on the Athenian stage, see Zeitlin (1993).
9. See the detailed analysis in Loraux (1981). I shall return to this play below.
10. See my paper, Shapiro (1992).
11. The most thorough recent study of the daughters of Kekrops, their myth, cult, and iconography, is that of Brulé(1987) 28-175.
12. On the royal genealogies, see Brommer (1957).
13. For the sources on Kekrops, see B. Knittlmeyer, *LIMC* VI (1992) 1084-85 (s.v. Kekrops).
14. See Palagia (1992) 40. On the figures in the west pediment usually identified as Kekrops and his daughter (B and C), see now Weidauer and Krauskopf (1992).
15. On the dual name Erichthonios and Erechtheus, see Kron (1976) 37-39.
16. For all the ancient sources on the daughters of Kekrops, see Powell (1906) and U. Kron, *LIMC* I (1981) 283-85 (s.v. Aglauros, Herse, Pandrosos). In another variant, Athena kills them outright.
17. Philochoros (*FGrHist* 328 F 105) reports the self-sacrifice of Aglauros.
18. On this motif see the essay by Mary Lefkowitz in this volume.
19. Demosthenes 19.303. For all the sources and the text of the oath, see Merkelbach (1972). A further association between Aglauros and the ephebes occurs in the festival of the Plynteria, when the statue of Athena Polias was taken to the sea, in a procession accompanied by the ephebes, to be washed (see Simon [1983] 46-48). A late source, Hesychius (s.v. Plynteria), connects Aglauros with this festival.
20. See Burian (1972). Herakles' suicide on Mt. Oita, as portrayed in Sophokles' *Women of Trachis*, is also a kind of sacrificial ritual, this time in preparation for his apotheosis.
21. For the deaths of heroines see Loraux (1987), esp. 31-38, on the death of virgins.
22. Pausanias 1.27.3; Burkert (1966); the thesis further developed by Schmidt (1968). On the Arrephoria see Simon (1983) 39-46; Robertson (1983)
23. Pausanias 1.18.2, specifies that Pandrosos remained obedient. Aglauros is the one sister implicated in all the versions. Harrison (1977b) 270, describes Aglauros as "the most death-directed" of the three sisters.
24. Dontas (1983). The sanctuary was surely in existence by the time of the Persian Wars (Herodotos 8.53) and probably by the mid-sixth century (Polyaenus 1.21.2).
25. Travlos (1971) 213 and 218, fig. 281.
26. As mother of Kephalos, see Apollodoros, *Bibliotheke* 3.14.3; as mother of Keryx, see the sources in *LIMC* I (1981) 285 (s.v. Aglauros, Herse, Pandrosos).
27. Baltimore, Walters Art Gallery, inv. no. 48.69; *ARV²* 510,3; *CVA* Baltimore 1 (U.S.A. 28) pl. 15.3-4; *LIMC* VI (1992) no. 20 (s.v. Kekrops). For other vases with similar scenes cf. *LIMC* I (1981) nos. 33-35 (s.v. Aglauros, Herse, Pandrosos).
28. On this cup see below note 33.
29. On this problem see Kearns (1989) 26.
30. Herodotos 7.189.

31. Munich, Antikensammlungen und Glyptothek, inv. no. 2345; *ARV*² 496.2. For Boreas and Oreithyia in vase-painting, see Kaempf-Dimitriadou (1979) 36-41, 105-109. This is the only instance of the subject in which the names of Kekrops (who is shown fully human) and his daughters are inscribed, though there are many other vases with similar figures.

32. For the literature on this scene see below on nos. 75-85.

33. For Kekrops and Erechtheus as eponymous heroes, see Kron (1976) 84-103, 32-83. A beautiful representation on a recently published vase may be added to her catalogue: cup by Douris, Malibu, J. Paul Getty Museum, inv. no. 84.AE.569; Ober and Hendrick (1993) 61. The scene of Eos pursuing the Athenian hero Kephalos is framed by three kings, Kekrops and Pandion (their names inscribed) and perhaps Erechtheus.

34. Homer, *Odyssey* 7.81. Cf. Homer, *Iliad* 2.547, where reference is made to Erechtheus in the Athenian entry in the Catalogue of Ships. On both passages see the commentary of Kirk (1985) 205.

35. Athens, National Museum, Acropolis Collection, inv. no. 585; *ABV* 40, 17; Bakir (1981) 26-27, pls. 35-36, figs. 64-65; 67-68. For discussion of this fragment see Kron, *LIMC* I (1981) 286, no. 4 (s.v. Aglauros, Herse, Pandrosos) and Shapiro (1989) 104-105.

36. The fundamental publication of the Olive Tree Pediment is Heberdey (1919) 16-28, figs. 7-12. For the fullest recent study see Kiilerich (1989).

37. This interpretation was evidently first fully argued by Buschor (1922). Heberdey, however (supra note 36, p. 21), had already insisted that the subject could not be a non-Attic myth.

38. Hurwit (1985) 245. The full exposition of this theory is that of Kiilerich (1989).

39. Travlos (1971) 218, fig. 281 (the olive tree indicated as Q).

40. Aglauros was considered the first priestess of Athena, according to Philochoros (*FGrHist* 328 F106). On the historical priestess of Athena on the Acropolis, who was drawn from the clan of the Praxiergidai, as the "real life correlative" of Aglauros, see Kearns (1989) 25.

41. New York, Metropolitan Museum of Art, inv. no. 53.11.1; *ABV* 298,5.

42. For the full publication of the vase see Bothmer (1953-54). On pseudo-Panathenaics see most recently Neils (1992) 42-46.

43. H. A. Cahn, in Monnaies et Médailles S. A. 11 (1953) 33, no. 320.

44. See, however, Mansfield (1985) 343-44 n. 109, who rejects the identification of the object as the folded peplos and believes instead that it is a kanoun (sacrificial basket). On the peplos generally see now E.J.W. Barber, in Neils (1992) 103-117.

45. Athens, Acropolis Museum, inv. no. 702; Brouskari (1974) 58-59; *LIMC* I (1981) no. 25 (s.v. Aglauros, Herse, Pandrosos).

46. Pausanias 1.22.8. See E.B. Harrison, *LIMC* III (1986) 192 (s.v. Charis, Charites) on the Charites as gate-protectors. Earlier Harrison (1977b) 269 considered both identifications for the girls on the Acropolis relief, Aglaurids and Charites, and concluded that the Charites are more likely.

47. On Erysichthon see U. Kron, *LIMC* IV (1988) 18-21 (s.v. Erysichthon II). He is to be distinguished from the figure of the same name, known from Kallimachos (*Hymn to Demeter* 22-117) and Ovid (*Metamorphoses* 8.738-878), who ate his family out of house and home.

48. Athens, Acropolis Museum, inv. no. NA 57.AK.2; Brouskari (1974) 92.

49. Athens, Acropolis Museum, inv. no. NA 57.AA.44; Brouskari (1974) 107-108.

50. See LaRocca (1972-73).

51. Frankfurt, Liebieghaus, inv. no. St V 7; *ARV*² 386; *CVA* Frankfurt 2 (Germany 30) pls. 60-62. Cf. also the discussions of the vase by Kron (1976) 68-71, Weidauer (1985) 197-99), and Keuls (1985b) 256-57. The other scenes on the cup show the departure of Triptolemos from Eleusis and, in the tondo, Poseidon pursuing a woman, probably Aithra, the mother of Theseus.

52. On scenes of women at the fountain house see most recently Manakidou (1993); on the dangers see Boardman (1991) 93-95, discussing a puzzling black-figure vase that shows a large snaky monster that has suddenly appeared at a fountain-house.

53. Euripides, *Ion* 274-76.

54. An early Apulian vase is the only version of the punishment of the daughters of Kekrops that may allude to their dire fate: Malibu, J. Paul Getty Museum, inv. no. 77.AE.93; Mayo (1982) no. 18. A fierce Athena lunges at Aglauros and Herse, who truly seem gripped with madness as they flee. Pandrosos sits mournfully beside the closed chest. Other details of the scene unknown in any Attic version, such as the nude Erysichthon trying to spear the snake, suggest the influence of a now-lost play.

55. San Antonio Museum of Art, inv. no. 86-134G (63); Shapiro (1981) 20-21; *LIMC* IV (1988) 933 no. 29 (s.v. Erechtheus).

56. On the motif of women wrapped up in their mantles as a symbol of *aidos* see **Aidos and Sophrosyne** in this volume.

57. Athens, National Museum, inv. no. NM 17917; *ARV*² 735.107; Schmidt (1968) 203-204.

58. Athens, National Museum, Acropolis Collection, inv. nos. 508-509; *ARV*² 973.7-8; Smith (1939) pl. 22, b.d; *LIMC* I (1981) 289, no. 17 (s.v. Aglauros, Herse, Pandrosos).

59. London, British Museum, inv. no. E788; *ARV*² 764.8; most recently discussed and analyzed by Hoffmann (1994).

60. Hoffmann (1994) identifies as Athena the woman carrying a spear or scepter on the Sphinx's base (fig. 18), but she does not have any of Athena's distinctive attributes (helmet, aegis). On the other side of the base is a running satyr wielding a club (fig. 19). It seems thus better to assume that both figures are unrelated to the scene above.

61. Leipzig University, inv. no. T654; *ARV*² 585.35; Kron (1976) 58, 71, pl. 2; *LIMC* I (1981) 287, no. 6 and 288-89, no. 16 (s.v. Aglauros, Herse, Pandrosos).

62. Paris, Musée du Louvre, inv. no. 980.0820; Oakley (1982b). Closely related is the lekythos in Basel (no. 66), fully published by Schmidt (1968), only here the baby is not shown at all.

63. An enigmatic scene on a slightly earlier hydria of ca. 440 may show one of the Daughters alongside Athena as the baby Erichthonios appears at an altar: see Schmidt (1968) 206-207.

64. Lekythos in Palermo: Kron (1976) pl. 1.

65. Euripides, *Ion* 271 (trans. A.P. Burnett). Cf. Zeitlin (1994) 155. Later in the play, Ion decorates his tent with an embroidery of Kekrops and his daughters (1163-64). On this basis Harrison (1977b) 281, no. 59 suggests that a similar scene may have been woven into the peplos of Athena at this time.

66. See Felten (1984) 114-17 for a summary of interpretations of the frieze.

67. Pausanias 1.14.6.

68. Harrison (1977b).

69. Cf. the multi-level composition on a fragmentary bell krater of ca. 400 in Thessaloniki, plausibly identified by Brommer (1972) 452 as the birth of Erichthonios. Among the preserved figures is a woman who should be one of the daughters of Kekrops.

70. Simon and Hirmer (1981) 152.

71. Athens, Archaeological Collection A 8922; preliminary publication in *ArchD* 31, B¹ (1976) 30, pl. 35a. Cf. other brief discussions of the vase by Burn (1989) 67; by M. Zaphiropoulou-Mitropoulou, in *LIMC* IV (1988) 62 (s.v. Eunoe); and by the present writer, in Shapiro (1986) and Shapiro (1993) 37-38.

72. Athens, National Museum, inv. no. NM A21903; *ARV*² 1314.15, 1708.10bis; Kokkorou-Alevra (1988).

73. Perhaps most famously on the kalyx krater by the Phiale Painter, Vatican Museums, inv. no. 16586; *ARV*² 1017.54; Oakley (1990) pl. 38.

74. E.g., two squat lekythoi in the manner of the Meidias painter, illustrated and discussed by Burn (1987) 22 and pls. 12-13. On the notion of the paradise garden see her remarks 19-21.

75. On the daughters of Kekrops as "kourotrophic heroines" see Kearns (1989) 23-27 and Price (1978) 101-117, who records several instances where one or another daughter of Kekrops was worshipped together with a goddess named simply Kourotrophos. A joint cult of Aglauros, Pandrosos, and Gaia Kourotrophos is attested in the Salaminioi inscription of 363/3: see Schmidt (1968) 210. On the priestess in charge of this cult, see Garland (1984) 86-87.

THE ECONOMICS OF HESIOD'S PANDORA

Hesiod tells the myth of Pandora in two versions, the first in the *Theogony*, a cosmogonic poem, and the second in the *Works and Days*, a didactic work of wisdom literature. In each case, she figures as the outcome of a game of wits between Prometheus and Zeus that revolves around a series of deceptions and counterdeceptions in connection with an exchange of gifts. Zeus wins, of course, and in return for the theft of fire, he has Hephaistos, the artisan god, fabricate the first woman as a molded creature, who astounds men by her god-given beauty and ruins them by her thievish nature.

In recent years these narratives have attracted a great deal of attention, which can be ascribed both to the development of more sophisticated techniques for interpreting the discourses of myth and to the current interest in the cultural construction of gender categories. Newer methods address the underlying logic and coherence that govern the structure, language, and content of mythic narrative, and aim to situate a given myth in its literary and sociocultural contexts in order to take account of its wider ideological resonances in the very processes of cultural formation. Despite differences in detail and purpose, the two versions have been taken as complements of one another, two halves of a single extended narrative that mutually illuminate the double-sided question of the origin of woman and woman as origin. Let me first recall the outlines of these two accounts.

The version in the *Theogony* begins with Prometheus' fraudulent division of the portions of the sacrificed ox allotted respectively to gods and men. Zeus chooses the inedible bones concealed beneath a covering of gleaming fat. For men is reserved the meat hidden under the unappetizing casing of the animal's belly. In angry retaliation, Zeus refuses to give (i.e., hides) celestial fire, whereupon Prometheus steals it, hides it in a hollow stalk, and brings it to men without being seen by the gods. When Zeus perceives "the gleam of fire," he counters by creating woman as a "beautiful evil" (*kalon kakon*), an "anti-fire" (*anti pyros*)—an exchange "instead of" or "in recompense" for fire. Hephaistos fashions her of earth in the likeness of a young virgin; Athena robes her as a bride in silvery garments, with a veil, garlands of flowers, and a golden crown. Thus adorned, she is an wonder to behold (*thauma idesthai*) but also a dangerous trap (*dolos*) and, brought to men, she is a continual source of woe to mortals (*pêma mega thnêtoisi*), an unwelcome supplement to those with whom she dwells.[1]

Like a drone she sits within the house and reaps the toil of others into her belly. And a second evil is added to the first, for if a man avoids marriage he looks forward to an old age without any children to care for him, and his estate is divided after his death among his distant kinsmen. But even for a man who relents and takes a good wife, let us say—that is, one whose heart is in agreement with his—Hesiod still maintains that "all through life, in her and by her, misfortune will come to balance out the good."[2]

The version in the *Works and Days* begins with a second unhappy consequence of Prometheus' deception of Zeus in that now the gods also keep hidden from men the source of their livelihood (*bios*, i.e., the grain that must be seeded in the earth). Again in his anger at the theft of fire, Zeus determines to create a great woe (*mega pêma*) to delight men, while encompassing their destruction.[3] This time, the description is recounted in far more detail.

Hephaistos molds the lovely shape of a maiden out of water and earth, with a face resembling the immortal goddesses but endowed with the "voice and strength of humankind." Athena is to teach her weaving, Aphrodite to pour grace (*charis*) over her head and "cruel longing and cares that weary the limbs." Hermes adds a shameless (doglike) mind and a thievish nature. Athena now dresses her like a virginal bride, while Aphrodite's representatives, the Graces (Charites) and Persuasion (Peitho) give her golden necklaces, and the Hours (Horai) crown her with spring flowers. At the end, Hermes names her Pandora because, as the text says, "all (*pantes*) the gods gave her a gift (*doron*), a sorrow (*pêma*) to men who live on bread."[4]

Now follows the familiar story of how Pandora was sent as a bride to Epimetheus who, although previously warned by his brother Prometheus (Foresight) to accept no gifts from the gods, in true fulfillment of his name (Afterthought), he takes her in and regrets it later. For Pandora's first act is to remove the lid of the jar, releasing all the evils and diseases that now silent and invisible wander over the earth and, by Zeus' will, only Hope or Elpis is left behind in the jar,[5] an ambiguous quality to whose meaning we will shortly return.

We owe the most influential analysis of this myth to the French scholar, Jean-Pierre Vernant,[6] (with further elaborations and refinements/correctives by Nicole Loraux and Marylin Arthur [Katz]).[7] Vernant demonstrates a series of homologies, inversions, and correspondences between all the different elements in these narratives: the various animal parts of the sacrifice apportioned by Prometheus (*Theogony*); the fire first hidden, then stolen, then hidden again (*Theogony*, *Works and Days*); the grain now hidden in the earth (*Works and Days*); the jar that conceals all evils (*Works and Days*); and the first woman, lovely to look at but defined as a belly (*Theogony*). Taken together, these now define the new and permanent quality of human life—its ambiguity and deceitfulness—a mixture of evils concealed under beautiful exteriors and virtues under ugly ones.

In one or another of her aspects, Pandora herself corresponds to each term of these several transactions that always operate under the seemingly opposite modes of giving or not giving gifts (hiding/stealing), but that on closer inspection prove to be variations on the single theme of giving through concealment and trickery. Like the sacrificial portion of food offered to the gods, Pandora has a beautiful exterior and a worthless interior. Like the portion offered to men, concealed in the paunch (*gastêr*) of the ox, she is a hungry belly, insatiable of food. Above all, in inverse return for the celestial fire stolen by Prometheus, the woman comes equipped with a thievish nature and is later likened to a fire that consumes man by her appetite for both food and sex.[8] Seed, on the other hand, applies to the germ of technological fire, which, unlike its celestial parent, must now be engendered and stored in a hollow container (the narthex stalk): it applies too both to the seed the farmer must plant within the earth as well as the one which he deposits in his wife's belly to produce children.

Pandora therefore emerges as none other than the symbol of ambiguous human life. In her appearance, her gifts given to her by the gods, she echoes the divine. By her bitch-like mind and the primacy of her bodily requirements she approaches the bestial. By her human voice and status as wife she is human. But, as Vernant concludes, she is also the reverse of man, forming another breed that is fundamentally different from him. Man and woman cannot converse with one another because she conceals the truth in order to deceive. At the same time, the conditions of her creation establish the fundamental triad of activities that are central to Greek views of culture: sacrifice (relations of men and gods), agriculture (men and nature), and marriage (men and women). The last two categories are especially linked in Vernant's discussion by the analogy, so familiar in Greek thought, which likens the woman to the earth and gives men the task of seeding both the womb and the soil.

Viewed from a cross-cultural perspective, however, the story of Pandora can be classified as a variant of a wide-spread myth that both creates woman as a secondary category following the creation or prior existence of men and also associates her creation with the origin of what is conveniently called the "human condition"—that is, with bringing death and evil into the world along with the laborious toil of human existence. While the Greek version subscribes to this general aetiological pattern, it goes much further in its negative evaluation of woman as a separate and alien being, the first exemplar of her race or species, the *genos gynaikôn*.

In the first place, woman is not created as a companion to assuage man's loneliness, as we are told, for example, in the biblical account of Adam and Eve (*Gen.* 2:21),[9] but rather as a punishment (not even merited through human fault). Second, there is no reconciliation after the fact, since male and female retain a drastic asymmetry without any basis for a division of labor that would make them ultimately partners, albeit unequal ones, in the conduct of mortal existence. Thus, while Vernant's reading of the cultural implications of the myth of Pandora remains valid in general terms, it cannot explain the special features of Hesiod's economy—his insistence on the fact that only men work while women remain perpetually idle, compared to useless drones who sit within the house, "filling their bellies up with the products of the toils of others"[10] and providing a source of endless resentment.

Women could contribute to the household, for example, with their typically feminine skills of weaving, already given by Athena to Pandora.[11] Male and female could be active in their respective domains, as Xenophon's *Oikonomikos* prescribes, the man working outside to increase his household's wealth and the woman managing the inside stores. Above all, as wife and mother, woman is herself also a giver of gifts, because she produces children from her belly and gives them nurture (*trophê*).

Hesiod only elliptically acknowledges that woman is needed to provide offspring, viewing this reliance as a second source of evil that follows upon the first complaint that had characterized her as a drone: "Whoever avoids marriage (*gamos*) and the baneful works of women (*mermera erga gynaikôn*), and will not wed, reaches deadly old age without anyone to tend his years (a *gêrokomos*), and though he at least has no lack of livelihood while he lives, yet, when he is dead, his kinsfolk divide his possessions amongst them."[12]

All is inference. Nothing is stated directly—neither sex nor procreation. We typically take this passage to mean that if the creation of woman interrupted the presumed commensality of men and gods, when they shared the same food, it also confronted man with a mortality which she alone can remediate through the compromise of providing progeny to take care of him in his old age, children who will live on after his death and, as his substitute(s), maintain (and increase) the fruits of his labor. But in extracting this reading, we also fail to take the full measure of the evasions and ambiguities that complicate both this text and that of the account in the *Works and Days*, where, in the context of agricultural labor, woman's sexual and reproductive roles remain still more discreetly obscured. Let us take a closer look.

First is the problem of sexuality itself: a natural instinct, fueled by the mysteries of desire and accompanied by pleasure in sexual contact, yet also fraught with ambivalence. In Hesiod, woman's beautiful exterior, enhanced by alluring adornments, elicits only the *thauma* (wonder) of the gaze,[13] while the *pothos* (desire) she arouses in the *Works and Days* through Aphrodite's influence is qualified as "painful" (*argaleon*), linked only to "cares that devour the limbs."[14] We note further that in both texts, far from "cleaving

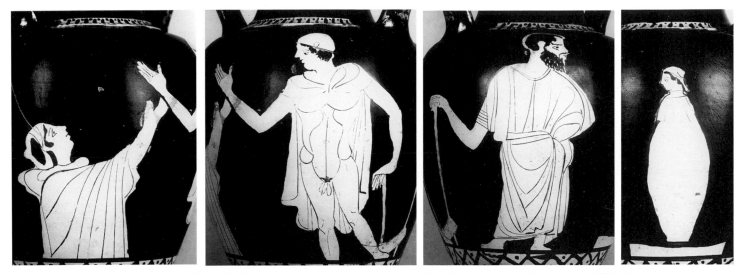

Figs. 1-4. Details of a neck amphora from Basilicata. The figures have been interpreted as Pandora rising from the ground; a youth; Epimetheus; and Elpis (Hope), who remains in the pithos. London, British Museum, inv. no. F 147, late 5th century B.C.

together and becoming one flesh" as the biblical account tells us (*Gen.* 3:24-25), or even "mingling in love (*philotês*)," as the euphemism in Greek texts (and elsewhere in the *Theogony*) would have it, man and woman remain distinct and disjoined entities. Pandora may be arrayed as a bride in a proto-version of marriage and given as a wife to her foolish husband Epimetheus in the *Works and Days*,[15] but nowhere, oddly enough, are we told of any carnal activity between them or again, as the parity of the biblical story suggests, of a mutual awareness of themselves as genitalized beings once they have come into their fallen state (cf. *Gen.* 2:25 and 3:7).

The dangers of sexuality as encroachment on the autonomous male body and the potential imbalance of its humors, the limitations or qualifications set to its unrestricted enjoyment, its separation from a specified love object, and the attribution of unbridled (extravagant) sexual appetites to women are characteristic and recurrent features of Greek attitudes. Later medical and philosophical texts will spell out the dangers to men's health in taking sexual pleasure, as Foucault's astute analysis reminds us,[16] but the framework in its most negative form is already in place in Hesiod, particularly in the context of woman's creation as an *anti pyros*, a "fire" that takes the place of the one that was stolen. Sex is treated as an unequal transaction by which woman steals man's substance, both alimentary and sexual, and by her appetites even "roasts man alive and brings him to a premature old age."[17] Thus in the *Works and Days* men are later warned to beware of making love in the summertime, because this is the time when "women are most wanton, but men are feeblest, since Sirius, the Dog Star, parches the head and the knees and the skin is dry through heat."[18] No wonder that sexuality is viewed as a less than mixed blessing, since men and women do not share the same rhythms or seasons of desire, and woman's desire, in any case, consumes the man and robs him of what is his own.

But the second and corollary point may be more essential. This is the ambivalence about women's reproductive capacities, which may account even better for the notable imbalances we find in Hesiod's economic system. As Loraux points out, in the *Theogony* woman is not even modeled in "the canonical image of the reproductive good wife. If the text implies that with the woman, marriage appears and therefore reproduction, the function of fecundity is hidden. Nothing indicates that the woman is expected to 'imitate the earth' as the standard Greek representations of fertility suggest."[19] On the contrary. Hesiod separates woman from the bountiful earth by inverting the usual etymology of her name from an active to a passive construction, from the one who gives to the one who is given. Not "the giver of all gifts," as a related epithet of Gaia (Earth) indicates, "Pandora" is here glossed as "the one to whom the gods have given all gifts."[20]

Additionally, the suppression of woman's fertility also means ignoring the value of her experience in childbirth, the *ponoi* of her suffering and travail. In other Greek contexts these are sometimes made equivalent to the trials and labors (*ponoi*) of men engaged in battle and other heroic endeavors, exemplified in Medea's famous statement that she would rather stand three times in the van of battle than bear a single child.[21] In Hesiod, by contrast, only men have *ponoi*, the doleful exertions of daily life, attributed in fact to woman herself who has imported them into his present existence.[22]

The significance of these two omissions is again reinforced by comparison with the parallel story in *Genesis* of Adam and Eve: Expelled from the garden of Eden, the male is condemned to bring forth his daily bread by the sweat of his brow (i.e., agriculture) and the female to bring forth children in pain and travail (*Gen.* 3:16-19). Their mutual dependency is further emphasized by God's earlier injunction that they be fruitful and multiply, populating the earth with their numberless progeny (*Gen.* 2:28).

So to put it briefly, the biblical story reflects not only a shared existence and responsibility, once woman has been created, it suggests an economy of abundance, proliferation, and expansiveness, while the Hesiodic tale is rooted in an economy of scarcity, parsimony, and man's anxious surveillance over what he has patiently accumulated by himself and for himself.[23] To cap it all, far from being characterized in the *Theogony* as the "mother of all mankind" as Eve is named (Hava) in the biblical account (*Gen.* 3:20), Pandora is described instead as the origin only of the *genos gynaikôn*, the "race of women," as though to deny, or at least, to elide the drastic notion that men are from women born.

What factors might account for this harsh outlook on life? What are the underlying issues in Hesiod's account that sees woman only as a rapacious and famished belly, "a companion to Plenty but not to Poverty," a creature who takes everything without giving in return? Various socio-economic explanations have been proposed: (a) a change in methods of agriculture, particularly the plough, better suited for men, that devalues women's contribution to subsistence, (b) a disembedded social organization of the Greek polis in this Archaic period (8th century) in which the private *oikos* or household is separated from communal, especially, public life, (c) a growing scarcity of land and resources relevant to this age of colonization, and (d) class distinctions between aristocratic and so-called peasant attitudes.[24]

All these hypotheses may be valid to some degree with respect to the proposed time and place of Hesiodic composition, but they cannot account for the enduring prestige of these texts, particularly, as the canonical account of the creation of the present world order under Zeus' hegemony (over against competing versions). Hesiod's extreme rancor toward woman, while open to compromise and mitigation in other spheres of interest, still remains the touchstone of an underlying attitude concerning this intrusive and ambivalent "other," who is brought into a strange man's household and forever remains under suspicion as introducing a dangerous mixture into the desired purity of male identity and lineage,[25] whether in sexual relations or in the production of children.

A further point is that in both texts, Pandora's creation is an integral part of a larger and more complex narrative. Each time she is a means to other ends, introduced as the outcome of a quarrel between two males over the apportionment of rightful shares. In the *Theogony*, her story is a part of the larger struggle for power among divine forces, the result of the strife between Prometheus and Zeus. In the *Works and Days*, Hesiod's dispute with his brother Perses over the division of their inheritance leads to the use of the Pandora myth as both explanation and admonition, accounting for the current conditions of our existence and warning what men must do to survive in the harsh environment of the Iron Age.[26] Yet in both versions, Pandora's creation marks a conclusive rupture between men and gods, which means that her presence not only defines the categories of male and female in the human sphere but also stands at the intersection of relations between gods and mortals. Given the anthropomorphic nature of Greek divinity, mythic discourse habitually dramatizes the issues of gender, sexuality, and reproduction from a double perspective, and perhaps nowhere more clearly than in the confrontation between divine and human worlds underlying the two Hesiodic accounts. Given the limitations of space, I will confine my analysis to the human world—the status of children and problems of production and reproduction in the household.

Household Economies

There is a persistent strain of ambivalence in Greek thought about the nature and value of children, who, although treasured as bearers of the family line, are also a source of potential disappointment and sorrow. They may turn out well, of course, but, like the woman herself, they may eventually bring trouble to a man's household. A reference to just such an idea may be implied in an ambiguous passage in the *Theogony* that concludes Hesiod's remarks about marriage and its discontents:

> For a man who chooses to marry and gets an agreeable wife...
> evil still continually contends with the good,
> but [for] he who meets up with an *atartêroio genethlês*
> lives always with unceasing grief in his heart,
> and this is an evil that cannot be healed.[27]

The crux of the problem lies in the interpretation of *genethlê*. Does it mean "race" (i.e., of women) or "progeny" (children)? If *genethlê* refers to woman, then the passage contrasts two kinds of wives: a good one (in which case, the negative still vies with the positive) and a baneful type, whose effect is unrelieved misery and woe. On the other hand, if we ask *why*, even in the case of an agreeable wife, evil is still said to contend with the good, then we may prefer to read *genethlê* as "progeny," since, even under the best of circumstances, children may well prove a mischievous bane to their parents. Each reading has its merits, and since the word appears nowhere else in Hesiod, scholarly opinion remains divided.[28] But this uncertainty may well be the essential point,[29] as reflecting the double ambivalence about women *and* the necessity of having children, the latter most fully expressed in the famous choral ode in Euripides' *Medea*:

> ...those who have never had children, who know nothing of
>   them,
> surpass in happiness those who are parents.
> The childless, who never discover
> whether children turn out as a good thing
> Or as something to cause pain, are spared
> many troubles in lacking this knowledge.
> And those who have in their homes
> the sweet growth of children, I see them always
> worn down by worry.

First how to bring them up well and leave them something to
   live on.
And then whether all their toil is for progeny
   who may turn out well or not remains unclear.

Finally [I paraphrase here], even under the best of circumstances, death may still carry them off.[30]

Even more decisive, however, for my argument is the fact that the vexed passage in the *Theogony* containing *genethlê* occupies virtually the same structural position in the narrative as does the mention in the *Works and Days* of the Elpis or Hope that remains in Pandora's jar. Each text marks the conclusion of the episode, each followed by a similar tag line: "So it is not possible to deceive or go beyond the mind of Zeus,"[31] and "So there is no way to escape the mind of Zeus."[32] In context, Elpis functions as yet another ambiguous quality that also shares in this world of mixed good and evil, a sign of the uncertainties of the future to which human life is now consigned, good if it inspires men to work and assure their livelihood, to fill their pithos (jar) with grain, bad if it lulls an idle man into illusory expectations for the future.[33] But taken as an image that embodies an idea, the Elpis that is left in the jar most closely corresponds to the child (or the hope of the child) residing in its mother's womb. In this reading, Pandora's *pithos* can be correlated with the *gastêr* (belly), her defining feature in the *Theogony*, and like the *gastêr* of the sacrificial portion that contained the edible portions of the ox, the pithos too is an independent repository that conceals something within.

References in other texts to the child as the Elpis or Hope of the household provide a telling argument for this identification.[34] But a more precise indication is the fact that later medical and philosophical texts associate and even correlate the womb with a container or jar. Throughout the Hippocratic corpus and the works of later, more sophisticated anatomists, the woman's uterus is likened to an upside-down jar, furnished with two ears or handles. The *stathmos* or *pythmên* (in Latin, the *fundus*) refers to the base or bottom of the jar now located on the top, the *stoma*, *os*, or mouth, lies at the bottom, and the neck (the *aychên*, *trachelos*, or Latin *cervix*) opens in a downward direction. The jar/uterus is modeled on features of human anatomy. It too has a mouth and a neck. This nomenclature is also pertinent to the wide-spread idea of a correlation between women's sexual and oral appetites, emphasized in the Hesiodic text as located below in the rapacious belly (*gastêr*) that fills up on man's substance. Popular and medical notions insist on a symmetry in woman between the mouth and the belly, as reflected, for example, in a number of prescriptions for gynecological therapy. A jar, as in Hesiod, has "lips" (*cheilê*),[35] and so does a womb.[36] The analogy continues in the notion of a seal or stopper that is needed to prevent entry, with the aim of preserving virginity, or, conversely, to retain the seed deposited in it in order to allow a successful pregnancy to occur.[37]

What does it mean then that Pandora comes equipped with her own jar, and that she removes the lid to open it, releasing a swarm of ills that now wander silently and invisible all over the world, leaving only Hope within? This action is what now determines man's condition—that he will suffer "ills, hard toil, and heavy sicknesses which bring the fates of Death upon him,"[38] with only Hope to deceive or console him. *Elpis*, of course, is a general, even abstract concept. Yet we may understand it better in the light of Pandora's actions. If the implicit analogy between Pandora and the jar holds true, then it is difficult to escape the conclusion that to open the pithos is equivalent to the breaching of her virginity, while to close the jar upon the *Elpis* that remains within marks the beginning of pregnancy, not yet brought to term. Under these circumstances, it is equally difficult to resist the idea, even though nowhere directly stated, that what escapes from the jar equally escapes from the vulva in the most negative encoding of female sexuality,[39] and Hope or the child, uncertainly placed between evil and good, is the single best, if still unsatisfactory, result.[40]

Even more to the point in Hesiod's text of the *Works and Days* is the preference, explicitly stated, for a family consisting of a single child: "There should be an only son (*mounogenês pais*) to feed his father's house, for so wealth will increase in the home."[41] The prospect of a second son elicits the ominous remark that in that case, better to die old, or as the text is often read, the only son in turn should have another only son.[42] We find this attitude also expressed elsewhere,[43] but in the Hesiodic economy in which women and offspring are viewed only instrumentally and only in relation to the dynamics of masculine acquisition and retention, the possible proliferation of children is viewed as a significant threat.

Woman is therefore defined as an economic liability. If her continuing reproductive capacity is to be tapped only once, thereafter she is an unnecessary surplus who does not increase the household wealth, but rather with her gluttonous appetite for both food and sex, she diminishes the resources of both house and husband. She thus neither resembles the fields that are worked outside nor the once bountiful earth of the Golden Age. Marriage and agriculture may be understood as two related spheres in which men toil and deposit their seed, but in the case of Pandora, they are also disjoined. If man once took freely from the unstinting produce of earth, woman now takes from the abundant stores accumulated by man, who, since her creation, has had to become the sole author of his own sources of nurturance.

Finally, the emphasis on raising an only child has a more pointed significance if we consider its thematic relevance to Hesiod's personal status as represented in the *Works and Days*. He is certainly *not* an only son: the entire poem is framed as a protreptic exhortation to his good-for-nothing brother Perses. We cannot recover the full details of Hesiod's complaints, but two issues seem to be evident. First, Hesiod has been in some kind of litigation with his brother over the division of their father's estate. Perses has somehow acquired more than his share by stirring up quarrels and has bribed the judges to sanction this unfair division. He has encroached on property that is not his, that rightfully, in fact, belongs to Hesiod. If brothers must share, the portions at least ought to be equal, thereby satisfying the demands of *Dikê*, or Justice. But having one heir and one heir only to the patrimonial estate would do more than forestall the possibility of a fraudulent division leading to destructive Eris (Strife)—it would obviate the need for any division at all.[44]

At one level, as Vernant has observed, the dispute between Hesiod and Perses concerning the fair division of their inheritance parallels the unequitable sharing of the sacrificial meal in the *Theogony* between Zeus and Prometheus. But the characterization of Perses in the *Works and Days* also gives rise to a second analogy, for this Perses is an idler who must be persuaded to accept the divine necessity of labor, so that he does not end up as a burden to others or even as a beggar. "If he had filled himself up with a year's supply of grain in reserve," says Hesiod, "then he could turn to the quarrels and strife in the agora to lay his hands on another's goods."[45] It is after this first address to his brother, in fact, that Hesiod tells the story of Pandora as the founding myth of why men are obliged to work and to accumulate the means of life through agricultural toil.

In the *Theogony*, as we have seen, Pandora is compared to a useless drone, "no companion to Poverty but only to Plenty," who sits within and consumes another's goods. In the *Works and Days*, we learn that the gods gave her a shameless mind and a thievish nature. Perses, we may note, combines both her qualities in his unregenerate state. Like Pandora, he is deceitful and thievish.[46] Like her, he intends to acquire for himself what belongs to another. Like woman, he is an idler who does not work and belongs with Hunger (*limos*) rather than Satiety (*Koros*), and he too is "like the stingless drones who waste the labor of the bees, eating without working."[47] Pandora is the opposite of the "bee wife," who, as the Archaic poet Semonides tells us, is the single and only paradigm of the virtuous wife. Perses, in turn, is a bee with no sting in him, a drone, like the woman within the hive that is the house, assimilated now to her earlier identification as a drone in Hesiod's *Theogony*.

Two inversions therefore come into play. First is the opposition between animal and human worlds, in which the bee community inverts the usual division of roles to assign the active part to the female and the passive one to the male.[48] Although the woman-drone seems to occupy a position reserved for males, the analogy is operative only with regard to the management of the household, which, like a hive, consists of bees and drones. The industrious woman may well be compared to a bee if she fulfills her domestic functions, or if not, she can be called, as here, a lazy drone who fills her belly with the fruit of another's work. For the man, however, whose place is out of doors and in the fields, the image of the drone in the hive can only apply if he loses his masculine dignity by refusing to work (*aergos*) and, like a woman, by living off the toil of oth-

ers. Thus despite the proper alignment of male and drone, the indictment of Perses only attains its full resonance as an allusion to the Pandora of the *Theogony*—Pandora, whose story is told to Perses yet again, now in the context of the god-given necessity that decrees men must now earn their living by tilling the fields. In short, if Perses is a drone, it is because woman, in negation of her positive image as the bee wife, provides a pertinent analogue to Perses himself.

The result is that Pandora occupies a double position in Hesiod's system of the household. She is, first of all, the potential overproducer of progeny, who, in bearing more than one child, poses the risk of a fraternal rivalry that is exemplified in the *eris* between Hesiod and Perses. Yet she also serves as the model for Perses himself: a drone, a supplemental and unwelcome addition who takes what is not hers rather than working or giving in return.

Perses, however, may be persuaded to assume his proper masculine role and to enter into the economy of labor by which he may rightfully prosper as well as participate in the generalized social rules for exchange and reciprocity. ("Give to the one who gives, but do not give to the one who does not give....Give (*dôs*) is a 'good girl', but Seize (*harpax*) is a bad one, the giver of death").[49] Pandora, by contrast, remains ambiguous, excluded from participating in the household economy. Defined as an outsider, unwillingly brought by the man inside his house, she carries within her belly the equally ambiguous Elpis who, even if turning out well for man's future, is still restricted to the grammatical category of the singular (*mounê*), not the plural.

Several important consequences attend this Greek view of woman's origin and functions. We note first by contrast that the myth of Adam and Eve justifies both the social, even organic, dependency of wife upon husband and her subordination to his authority, the first through her birth from Adam's rib after his creation, the second through God's specified punishment for Eve, along with travail in childbirth, that her husband rule over her. Yet in Hesiod, oddly enough, while woman's inferior status is strongly implied, the husband's control over his wife is not established as a "natural" social rule. Woman seems in fact to retain an intrinsic power over man. She can, by her appetites, enfeeble and impoverish him, seduce him and rob him. ("Do not let a flaunting woman coax and cozen and deceive you: she is after your barn").[50] Man has no effective means of retaliation, no sure way of exercising his authority. He can perhaps only minimize her inherent danger by taking a young wife, as he later advises, and hoping thus to socialize her in his ways."[51] But in essence, his only options are to avoid woman by shunning marriage altogether, thereby losing his patriliny and irrevocably fragmenting his substance, or to suffer the miseries she inflicts upon him. On the other hand, by undermining the woman's maternal functions of both nature and nature, the myth separates her from the true underlying sources of her power. The story thereby ratifies woman's secondary and derivative status in man's household, emphasized all the more by the mode of Pandora's own creation, since as an artisanal product, accompanied by another artisanal product (the jar), she is also separated at the outset from the natural processes of generation by which the entire universe came into being.

In sum, the remarkable feature of Hesiod's versions of the origin of woman is precisely the elision of physical contact between the sexes. In its further refusal to utter the name of "child," the text not only cannot name the woman as mother, but also cannot empower the male as the father. The relationship between man and woman is rather an economic one, framed in the disparity between producer (he) and consumer (she), between ownership and appropriation, abundance and lack, between self and intrusive other. As a result, paternity too is commodified, translated elliptically into economic terms as the requirement of the male ego. Man needs the support of someone to tend him in his old age and to conserve and increase the legacy of his material assets. Fatherhood means the continuation of his property in the hands of his heir. The triumph of paternity is projected instead into the world of the immortal gods—in particular, on Zeus who is *both* the first and only instance of a divine child requiring nurture *and* the sovereign ruler who earns the title "father of gods and mortals." Thus it is only the gods who can accomplish what men desire and dream of, exempt from both time and death, but if the price for mortals is high, it is probably woman, in the final analysis, who must pay the greater share.

FROMA I. ZEITLIN
Princeton University

This is a revised section of a longer essay, "Signifying Difference: The Case of Pandora" in *Playing the Other: Gender and Society in Classical Greek Literature* (Chicago 1995).

1. Hesiod, *Theogony* 561-91.
2. Hesiod, *Theogony* 594-609.
3. Hesiod, *Works and Days* 46-58.
4. Hesiod, *Works and Days* 59-82.
5. Hesiod, *Works and Days* 56-104.
6. Vernant (1980b) 168-85 and (1989) 21-86.
7. Loraux (1981) 75-117; Arthur [Katz] (1982) and (1983). See too Pucci (1977).
8. Hesiod, *Works and Days* 704-706.
9. I acknowledge but do not discuss here the problem of the two accounts in *Genesis* of human creation, the first of which suggests that male and female came into being at virtually the same time ("And God created man in his own image, in the image of God created he him; male and female created he them" [1:27]). Both versions, however, insist on the parity of one male and one female, destined to form the first couple.
10. Hesiod, *Theogony* 599.
11. Hesiod, *Works and Days* 63-64.
12. Hesiod, *Theogony* 602-606.
13. Hesiod, *Theogony* 575, 581, 582, 588.
14. Hesiod, *Works and Days* 66.
15. Cf. Hesiod, *Theogony* 511-14.
16. Foucault (1985).
17. Hesiod, *Works and Days* 705.
18. Hesiod, *Works and Days* 586-89.
19. Loraux (1981) 88-89.
20. Hesiod, *Works and Days* 80-82.
21. See Loraux (1989b) and (1989c).
22. Hesiod, *Works and Days* 90-92.
23. The economy of scarcity and parsimony is best summarized in Hesiod, *Works and Days* 354-69. On the biblical worldview, see, for example, Eilberg-Schwartz (1990) chap. 6 and Cohen (1989) chap. 1.
24. See, for example, Sussman (1984).
25. See especially the fine study of Pucci (1977).
26. Vernant (1989) 32-35.
27. Hesiod, *Theogony* 607-12.
28. Many scholars prefer "wife," including West (1966) *ad loc* and Snell, *LfgrE*, s.v. *genethelê* (see also, Loraux [1981] 95 n. 103), but the dilemma remains unresolved.
29. Woman and child can often be conflated, as, for example, in the parable of the lion cub in Aischylos, *Agamemnon* 681-749. The problem of *genethlê* in Hesiod is heightened by yet another ambiguity in that the preceding passage never mentions the word "child" at all. What we hear instead is that "the man who does not marry...reaches baneful old age without anyone to look after him" (605). This caretaker or *gêrokomos* is a word invented for the occasion (and found only here in Archaic and Classical literature). It is sufficiently obscure that West (1966) *ad loc* feels obliged to make clear that the text refers to "the son, not the wife," a claim he deduces (not without reason) from the well-known rule that the son is expected to provide *gêrotrophia* for his parents in return for his own nurture. So too, in the sentence that follows, the son as heir to his father's possessions is not named but merely implied; his identity is inferred in fact from the alternative, that in his absence, it is distant kinsmen (*chêrôstai*) who will later divide the man's estate (605-607).
30. Euripides, *Medea* 1090-1110.
31. Hesiod, *Theogony* 613.
32. Hesiod, *Works and Days* 105.
33. For convenient summary of the many views on Elpis (as good, bad, or both), see especially Verdenius (1985) 66-71; for bibliography, Noica (1984). I concur for the most part with Vernant (1989) 78-86, that *Elpis* is an ambiguous quality (like *Eris*, *Zêlos*, *Aidôs*, and *Nemesis*).

34. Significantly mentioned in funereal epigrams (e.g, *Palatine Anthology* 7.389, 453) and grave inscriptions nos. 661 and 720 in W. Peek, *Griechische Vers-Inscriften*. vol. 1. *Grab-Epigramme* (Berlin 1955).

35. Hesiod, *Works and Days* 97.

36. E.g., Aristotle, *History of Animals* 7.3.583 a16.

37. For the medical texts, see Hanson (1990) and (1992). See also Sissa (1990) 53-70 (on mouth and uterus) and 158-62 (on virginal closure). On the idea of a seal or stopper for the uterus, see Hanson (1990) 324-30, who, dissenting from Sissa, distinguishes between the mouth of the uterus and that of the labia. Sissa (1990) 156, understands the pithos in Hesiod as the belly of the woman ("a faithful and fertile wife") but does not discuss the status of Elpis.

  For the equation of child and Elpis, see Hoffmann (1986) 55-89, (72-76), who notes the correspondence between marriage (Hesiod, *Works and Days* 800) and opening a pithos (Hesiod, *Works and Days* 819) in Hesiod's agricultural calendar, but argues for a different significance.

  Might we take *mega pôma* (stopper) of the jar as a pun on *mega pêma* (bane, e.g., Hesiod, *Theogony* 592), as the first woman is called?

38. Hesiod, *Works and Days* 90-92.

39. This is a hypothesis I cannot prove from ancient evidence but can only surmise.

40. Also instructive is a little-known myth, preserved in several late texts (Parthenius, *Erotika* 28; Nicolas Damascius, frag. 19, scholiast to Apollonios of Rhodes, *Argonautica*. 1.1063; Eustathius, *Iliad* 357, 43f.; and Strabo, 13.621c). Piasos, a ruler of the Pelasgians, conceived a passionate desire for his daughter, Larisa, and raped her. Her vengeance was as follows: observing him leaning over a huge pithos filled with wine, she seized him by the legs and plunged him headfirst into the cask where he drowned. See Rudhardt (1981) 739, who is mystified by the tale, but the correlations are not difficult to find. Her action both parodies his plunge into her "pithos" and fittingly repays him in kind, since the use of wine was typically restricted to men, who had access to the containers (pithoi: cf. Hesiod, *Works and Days* 359-69: "Take your fill when the jar is first opened and then again when it is nearly spent" and cf. 597-603). Sexual and alimentary appetites are neatly joined, with the added fact that wine is the substance that encourages sexual desire. "Drunk" with passion, he drowns in a surfeit of his own lust.

41. Hesiod, *Works and Days* 376; cf. 271.

42. Hesiod, *Works and Days* 378. So (West) 1966 *ad loc* and, among others, Pucci (1977) 111. I prefer the first interpretation, which gives a straight progression: one, two, or many sons, but best to have only one. In the case of a second son, you should die old (presumably after having acquired sufficient wealth to divide it), and if you have many, then you need Zeus' assistance, since he can "easily bestow prosperity." As West remarks, this is "a typical Hesiodic provision for exceptions to the general rules at the discretion of the gods."

43. This attitude is not restricted to Hesiod, whatever the economic conditions of his day might have been. Its continuation in the tradition is already mentioned by the various scholia (vetera) *ad loc*, following Plutarch's commentary. See e.g., Xenocrates frag. 97, Aristotle, *Politics* 1274b19ff., and Plato, *Laws* 740b-d, 923cd, referring to optimum family size and population control in the Greek polis. Also, e.g., Golden (1975). Space does not permit a fuller discussion that, among other issues would have to include exposure of the newborn.

44. The scholiast at 376-78 already notes why Hesiod would prefer a *mounogenês*.

45. Hesiod, *Works and Days* 33.

46. Hesiod, *Works and Days* 322.

47. Hesiod, *Works and Days* 303-304.

48. On the problem of bees and drones and gender inversion, see Loraux (1981) 82 and Vernant (1989) 68-73. Roscalla (1988) argues on the basis of ancient evidence that drones are not viewed as males, per se, but rather constitute an alien *genos*, which, like Pandora, enters another's dwelling. Yet, given that "drone" is a masculine noun and "bee" a feminine one, there is no reason, as Roscalla does, to limit the terms of the analogy.

49. Hesiod, *Works and Days* 354-56.

50. Hesiod, *Works and Days* 374.

51. Hesiod, *Works and Days* 700.

SORCERESSES

In Homer's *Odyssey*, when the time comes for Odysseus to take leave of the sorceress Circe at the end of a long stay at her wondrous island to make his way to the Underworld as she has decreed, she clothes him as an act of solicitude and hospitality for a man with whom she has shared the joys of Aphrodite.[1] She dresses herself in a silvery robe, puts a golden belt round her waist and a veil to her head; but it would seem that she does this because, to her, it is the natural thing to do and not because she wishes to please Odysseus, whose mind is set on departure. Here, and here only, the ambiguous term *nymphe* is applied to Circe, a term which can mean a young girl or a bride, but also one of those semi-divine beings who dwell in trees and rivers. If a young woman is called a Nymph, a note of endearment is often implied, and it should be recalled here that it is Odysseus, only when remembering Circe in his tale of the adventure, who terms her *nymphe*.

In the moment of farewell, the sorceress finds an inimitable manner of parting from Odysseus. Silently she had taken her leave, in order to tether two animals for sacrifice by his ship; he will have need of them at the entrance to Hades. Unseen, she has once again taken care of the hero. "She had slipped past us with ease; and when a god wishes to remain unseen, what eye can observe his coming and going?"[2]

So it is stated that Circe is a goddess. This is the end of the main Circe episode in Book 10 of the *Odyssey*. At the beginning there had also been an invisible Circe, whose charm enthralled Odysseus' companions as they stood before her door, listening as she went ingeniously about her tasks (or this, at least, must be the men's impression). At first there is only her lovely voice, singing as she walks to and fro at her great loom. Between these two non-meetings with Circe—her manifestation as a mere voice and her unseen slipping past—Circe shows herself first to be a powerful and dangerous sorceress before she becomes a generous hostess whom Odysseus "tamed" or even "subjected," in the sense that the Greek word *dmethesia* is used to describe the union of immortal women with mortal men.[3]

Odysseus' adventure with Circe, as later recounted by the hero at the Phaeacian court, reveals the full gamut of potentialities implicit in the scintillating nature of such a great sorceress. Within her sphere, Odysseus experiences extreme situations. Circe is able to lead him to the entrance of the Underworld and back to the world of the living. It is in her power to teach him how to protect himself from deadly dangers on his way.

Circe, probably the best known of ancient sorceresses, is a goddess, not a mortal woman, and certainly not a wicked old witch like those in the Grimm fairy tales. The ugly old sorceress does not figure in Classical Greek literature. Next to Circe, it is Medea who best embodies the nature of a sorceress in the Classical world. That the two great enchantresses are more than kindred spirits is demonstrated in Greek mythology by giving them a common kinship. Both descend from the sun-god Helios—Circe is his daughter, Medea his granddaughter. It is Helios who provides Medea with the snake-drawn winged chariot for her flight from Corinth after she has taken her awful revenge on her faithless husband Jason. A princess, she has grown up in the distant country of Colchis, beyond the Black Sea. It was there that she met Jason, who had come with the Argonauts to obtain the Golden Fleece. She helps him to fulfill his task and returns with him to his Greek homeland. Her first deed there, revealing her as a powerful sorceress, is the revenge on Pelias. The wicked king had usurped the throne that rightfully belonged to Jason and sent his young rival on the perilous mission to bring back the Golden Fleece. Medea cleverly makes use of Pelias' daughters as unsuspecting instruments of her revenge and evades persecution herself. She dismembers an old ram, boils it in a cauldron with her magic herbs, and reanimates the creature in the shape of a young lamb. The Peliades, who want to perform the same miracle on their aged father, are horribly deceived: instead of being rejuvenated, Pelias loses his life.

What are the characteristics of the special arts of the two mythical sorceresses Circe and Medea? What differences exist between these figures, with their supernatural powers, and what, on the other hand, do they have in common with mortal women? Circe can turn humans into animals, an ability Medea seems to lack, or at least does not employ. The magic potion Circe brews for her victims consists of "terrible poisons" (*pharmaka lygra*),[4] which she blends with cheese, barley-meal, yellow honey and wine—a mixture that compared to the witches' concoctions in *Macbeth* might appear palatable and uncomplicated. For the Greeks it was surely of significance that Circe's potion was designated by the same term (*kykeon*) as the famous mixture that played a particular role in the ritual of the Eleusinian Mysteries. Because Hermes had supplied Odysseus with an antidote, a *pharmakon esthlon*, Circe's magic fails to transform him. We are here confronted with the idea of the symmetry of magical machinations: magic can be successfully counteracted with a magical antidote, but it takes a god to thwart Circe. In condition and bewail their loss. The contradiction here (*Odyssey* 10.236) to the preceding lines has often been noted, for there it is written that the potion makes them "lose all memory of their native land."[5] It may well be that various sources have come to bear on this passage; in any event, Circe's magic seems to be imbued with the power of transforming the outward appearance of her victims into animal shape as well as influencing their innermost selves by inflicting loss of memory.

We can equally observe in the mythology regarding Medea that the tale does not always exhaust the full capabilities a mythical sorceress possesses or that she appears consciously to restrict these powers. Medea has the ability to rejuvenate or maybe even render immortal, but, in the case of the unfortunate Pelias, she does not make use of her ability, stops short, as it were, of a (possible) completion. A closer investigation of this essential trait of Greek magic—the whole range of possibilities from good to evil—is called for in connection with the figure of Medea. Circe, who could transform the innermost being of her victims, is content in Homer, whatever the poet's reasons may have been, to restrict herself to outward metamorphoses. To be sure, this is the crueler form because the victims suffer under their changed condition. In many cases, vase-painters have been successful in depicting the horror of the disfiguration. On an amphora in Berlin (fig. 1),[6] the Phiale Painter gives touching expression to the sad situation: the man, already half transformed with an animal's tail and the head of a pig, in an eloquent gesture of despair, covers his face with his hand as he moves away from the ruthless sorceress. But it is significant that, having entered into a loving relationship with Odysseus, Circe does not merely change the enchanted men back into their original shape, but makes them *younger, taller, and handsomer*.[7] The sorceress here exercises her magic in the reverse sense, a positive act which surpasses even the symmetry of transfiguration and restoration.

The pictures of the Archaic and Classical periods on which Circe appears—mostly on vases—characteristically dwell on the dangerous sorceress who turns humans into animals and on her conquest by Odysseus. The tamed Circe of the Homeric *epos*, who ends up as Odysseus' partner and helper, seems no longer to be of great interest. It is Odysseus' behavior that is evidently the decisive factor for these Greek vase-painters and their customers, how he menaces the sorceress with his drawn sword, forcing her to flee and drop the bowl containing the *kykeon*. Such pictures must have had a reassuring effect in that they presented the reinstatement of valid order. The woman who had been experienced as threatening had been put under restraint; she was robbed of her dangerous power. In pregnant form such images appear as an epitome of what, in many interpretations, has been conceived as the essence of the tale of Circe: man's mastery in his involvement with womankind. Ezio Pellizer sees this reflected at two levels in the Circe myth: on the one hand, in the personal experience of the young man in his initiation into adult life and, on the other hand, in a social experience, namely the endeavor to free the relationship between the sexes of

Fig. 1. Amphora by the Phiale Painter. Berlin, Antikenmuseum, Staatliche Museen zu Berlin, Preussischer Kulturbesitz, inv. no. F 2342.

addition to her *pharmaka*, the sorceress' equipment includes a wand, the *rhabdos*, with which she does not merely touch her victims but strikes them. Circe can be seen with this wand on vases from the sixth and fifth century, but more often with the bowl in which she mixes her potion, the *kykeon*.

According to Homer, Circe transforms Odysseus' companions into swine, while her previous victims, still to be seen prowling about her house, had been turned into lions and wolves. But they are only animals in their outward shape; they retain their human senses and are hence able to realize the full extent of their frightful its threatening aspect and establish a balance integral to human relations.[8] It is interesting that a thematic shift can be observed on vases from the sixth to the fifth century. On pictures of the Classical period a defeated, fleeing Circe is substituted for the Archaic image of the sorceress who, in spite of the appearance of an angry Odysseus, is still convinced of her powers. The effort to tame a threatening female element goes along with the ideals prevalent in Classical Athens and corresponds to the behavior expected of women in the Greek polis. It is no mere accident that, on early pictures of the Archaic period, Circe, while still in full possession of her powers of magic and surrounded by Odysseus' companions in various stages of transformation, is not painted as a woman would normally be depicted but in the stance of an Archaic youth, a kouros. The same exceptional stance was also used to representations of hetairai (fig. 2).[9] It is as though the sorceress was felt not to accord with the "norm" of female behavior but, rather threateningly, to incline toward the side of men, leading a life responsible to no one but herself.

It is a noteworthy peculiarity that Odysseus, in Homeric epic, merely simulates a lethal attack on the sorceress; he acts as if he were intent on murder, "...as though I meant to kill her."[10] It was Hermes who had already advised him to pretend "...as though you meant to take her life."[11] It is predestination that Circe's life be spared—apart from the fact that her divine nature makes her immortal anyhow. Odysseus meets her as the annunciated whose coming Hermes had repeatedly foretold. We can assume that the sorceress will henceforth renounce her power of turning men into animals.

One characteristic that Circe, as she appears in the *Odyssey*, has in common with Medea and that does not immediately fit in with our notion of a sorceress is the superhuman knowledge both have at their disposal when assisting the heroes with whose perilous paths they are connected. Circe gives Odysseus not only precise instructions how he should proceed at the entrance of the Underworld, but also helps him afterward to sail in safety past both the Sirens and Scylla and Charybdis. Medea goes even further when, in Pindar's fourth Pythian ode, she is able to prophesy the Argonauts' fate.

Medea employs *pharmaka* in a greater diversity of ways than her kinswoman, although metamorphoses are not her affair. For Medea, too—or rather particularly in her case—the ambivalent use of magic potions becomes clear. She uses her *pharmaka* to a salutary end in Colchis, for Jason at any rate, protecting her lover from the bulls' fiery breath and putting to sleep the serpent, guardian of the Golden Fleece. On the other hand, her magic has a lethal effect in Corinth when she takes revenge on Jason and her rival. It is interesting that Medea's magic, with the exception of the myth relating to the dismemberment of Pelias, seems closer to "reality" than Circe's. Transforming men into pigs, lions, or wolves evidently exceeds the limits within which even mortal women may try their hand at mixing potent drugs. In part at least, Medea's arts are not far from the field of medicine and herbal remedies. This fits

in with the further fact that, unlike Circe who remains on her wondrous island, "beyond this world," Medea enters into painfully close association with the world of human beings and is driven from one spot to another, repeatedly forced to flee. Medea's magic (this applies for the figure as transmitted in Greek literature but perhaps not yet for the earliest stages of the myth) always has an aim in view; it is a reaction to events which she had not initiated, whether in the case of her help in the dangers faced by Jason or in taking her revenge. Admittedly, it would be judging Circe's acts too superficially to see in them a frivolous *l'art pour l'art*, in complete contrast to Medea's different manner of proceeding. Circe also has reasons why she must deprive men of their human shape; however, her "reasons" are not "practical" but have their deeper roots in myth itself.[12]

Although as a foreigner from distant Colchis she seems barely integrated in society, in Corinth Medea is little more than a woman who is particularly apt at mixing poison, as many a Greek woman in a post-mythical age might also have been. At any rate, she is not a figure who makes her appearance conspicuously as a sorceress. It has repeatedly been noted—correctly—that the Medea of Euripides' drama, that is to say the mythical figure as formulated in the Classical period in Athens, has few or no features of a sorceress. Not even the snake-drawn chariot is explicitly mentioned in Euripides' text, which other sources attest for the end of this play, first performed in 431 B.C. In consequence, the relinquishing in Classical tragedy of wondrous and magical elements lets us see Medea as a human being with her own destiny; bizarre displays, which characterize many later versions of the Medea myth, do not detract here from the tragic entanglements of the figure. Furthermore, the view of a sorceress making use of her potential power only to a limited degree and in a most purposeful manner was in accordance with the classical inclination toward the rational, though it cannot be denied that irrational forces were never entirely absent from the Greek way of thinking.

Medea's full personality as a sorceress is revealed, however, in the tale of the revenge on Pelias. It is this myth that best acquaints us with the effective radius, the full scope of a sorceress in antiquity. It is within her power both to tear apart and correspondingly to join together again, to reanimate the dismembered figure as a rejuvenated being. What Medea demonstrates before Pelias' daughters on the dismembered old ram, which jumps from the cauldron in the shape of a young lamb, she no longer completes on their aged father. Pelias is led to his death in accordance with the will of the vengeful Medea. If she wishes, Medea does make use of her particular ability of curing and rejuvenating what had been torn apart, to the advantage of certain individuals: she is said to have rejuvenated Jason's old father Aison, Jason himself, and the nurses of Dionysos. (Here we may remember Circe who gave back to her former victims their human shapes, but in a more handsome form.) It is interesting that mention is made of Medea not only demonstrating *ad oculos* but also effecting hallucinations. According to one source she merely led Pelias' credulous daughters to believe in the ram's

Fig. 2. Cup, with Circe in a "male" stance. Boston, Museum of Fine Arts, inv. no. 99.518.

rejuvenation.[13] Medea made a vision of a young lamb appear in the cauldron. To do this, other special abilities were evidently necessary that perhaps go beyond the sphere of magic in a narrower sense. This special version of the myth of the Peliades' deception touches on the complex problem of the use of hallucinogenic substances in ancient Greece (a highly controversial question, for instance in connection with the mystery cult in Eleusis).

To what extent did magic have any bearing on the life of the Greeks, apart from the domain of myth? In the last centuries of antiquity, after the end of the Classical period, magical practices of all kinds were on the increase. One of these is already attested in Athens for the close of the fifth century, the custom of the so-called *defixiones*,[14] magic maledictions in the form of a curse inscribed on small metal plaques and prescribing the evil which was meant to befall the hated adversary or rival. The intention was to constrain the volition of the cursed person or even cause his or her death. The various types of love-spells were pleasanter; such a love-spell could also be inscribed on one of the metal plaques in an attempt to force the beloved to return one's love. These spells had doubtless been practiced since time immemorial and were not restricted to the form of *defixiones* attested since the Classical era. The magic love-wheel, the *iynx*, seems to have been in use for quite some time. In his fourth Pythian ode, Pindar describes it as Aphrodite's invention and gift to mankind. It is not the sorceress Medea who makes use of the magic wheel; the goddess of love approaches Jason and teaches him with what magic charms he can win Medea's heart—in accordance with the will of the gods, who have further plans for both Jason and Medea.

A closer look into the historical testimonies of magical practices in ancient Greece will make it clear that it is the rule rather than the exception for the man to be the one to apply sorcery. Jason with the love-wheel is thus by no means a surprising figure. The said

curse-tablets, the *defixionum tabellae*, provide interesting information as to how the two sexes made different use of magic. Four of the five different categories[15] of use are evidently restricted primarily to male society: curses intended to eliminate opponents in law-suits, competitors in sport or in economic affairs, or slanderers and thieves. One might be tempted to assume that the *defixiones amatoriae* intended for love-spells might have been of interest—perhaps of more interest—to women. In fact, if we can believe the sources from the Classical period, they were barely used by them. (I am indebted to Fritz Graf for calling my attention to an unpublished plaque from Pella, dated to the fourth century B.C., with the help of which a woman wished to keep her lover from marrying another woman, possibly the only extant erotic *defixio* from pre-Roman Greece for which a woman was responsible.)

The practice of *defixiones* is representative, so to speak, of an unofficial use of magic in everyday life, for which apparently no complicated knowledge was required. "Professional" sorcerers, more feared than respected, worked in a different field. Numerous negative remarks in ancient literary sources inform us of their strange existence. The individual activities of these men are not of import for us here, but it is of interest that, at least in Classical Athens, they had no female counterparts in their "trade."[16]

A similar situation existed in Europe in the Middle Ages. At first magicians alone are versed in the art of magic and through this possess dangerous power. Not until the Late Middle Ages, as the result of a chain of complex motives, are women held responsible for pernicious magic; witch-hunts set in. In his book *Zauberpraktiken*, Christoph Daxelmüller investigates this complex process and remarks, for instance: "The witch's crime was her use of forces to which she was considered to have no right, her exercise of power for which she had no authorization. Written history of the phenomenon of witch-hunts, to which the Enlightenment of the eighteenth century put an end, may be understood also as an attempt to make clear the patterns of disciplinary measures involved in socialization."[17]

It seems that respectable women in ancient Greece during the Classical period were adjusted to the social order to such a degree that they could not risk contact with the marginal sphere of magic even if, from a modern point of view, their most personal interests were at stake. Calling to mind the forms of marriage which, as a general rule, were arranged by fathers, it seems evident that marriage as a social institution provided women with scant scope for active construction of their own future and thus, perhaps, left them little motivation to cast love-spells.

It has become clear that a Medea who came to Greece from a foreign land had to remain an outsider in every respect, a *pharmakos xeina*, a foreigner endowed with magical powers and knowledge of herbs and drugs.[18] Attention can be drawn in this respect to a curious notion contained in a fragment from Melanippides' *Danaids* (fifth century B.C.): The Danaids, who are evidently compared to the Amazons, appear in this text as virile, untamed beings of the great outdoors, who pass their time with hunting and driving chariots, but who also collect aromatic herbs.[19] Here, too, the impression of the foreign is at the forefront, something contrary to the norm, but which may well be endowed with exceptional knowledge and abilities.

Sorceresses, where such beings existed, were therefore outsiders—for Athenians in any event. Whenever their services were called for, one had to look for them elsewhere. An allusion in Aristophanes' *Clouds*[20] is instructive: Strepsiades suggests soliciting one of the Thessalian sorceresses (*pharmakides*) so that she might cast a spell on the moon and conjure it down from the sky, an ability attributed to sorceresses because of their close association with the moon and with the sorceress-goddess Hekate. Some vase-paintings have been interpreted as depicting this incantation of the moon: an Attic squat lekythos in the British Museum, dated to the last quarter of the fifth century B.C.,[21] shows a large full moon with the head of Selene embossed on it, a youth and a maiden to each side of it. The face of the moon-goddess on the rayed disc is turned toward the woman, not the young man. This indicates, presumably, that the woman has a more intimate relationship with the moon. Is the woman here casting a love-spell on the young man? It is most regrettable that a very interesting krater, formerly in the Hamilton Collection and known from Tischbein's engraving, is now lost.[22] It depicted two naked women (which have been compared to Aristophanes' *pharmakides*). One holds a sword, the other a wand—surely a sorceress' *rhabdos*. Between the two, the moon shines down from the sky, with a female head—that of the moon-goddess Selene. With their arms raised, the sorceresses hail and implore the goddess. The remnants of the inscription have been convincingly completed to read *klythi potnia Selana* (Hear us, Lady Selene). On Tischbein's engraving, the only extant testimony of the depiction, it has been thought that a chain is just perceptible as a dotted line

leading from the moon down to earth. This would fit the ability of the Thessalian sorceresses, as attributed to them in Aristophanes: to draw the moon down to earth so that Strepsiades could put it in a box "like they do mirrors" and keep a close watch on it. The incantation of the moon depicted these two vases is evidently very close in content to the later literary evidence. In Theokritos, the *pharmakeutria* Simaetha, who is the only woman who actually lets us look over her shoulder as she casts her nocturnal love-spell, is jealously in love and also implores "Lady Selene." Thessaly, which was traditionally reputed to be the homeland of sorceresses, the *pharmakides* who were knowledgeable about magical herbs and drugs and which still had this reputation after antiquity, is also connected with Medea, the great mythical sorceress. A scholiast referring to the passage in Aristophanes' *Clouds* mentioned above claims pragmatically that Thessalian magic can be traced back to the fact that while fleeing, doubtlessly in the snake-drawn chariot, Medea threw down her magic casket over Thessaly. It is the casket that usually characterizes Medea in depictions of the Classical period.

Perhaps it has become clearer, from the foregoing, why and to what extent the mythical sorceresses Circe and Medea must have been regarded as exceptions in the Greek, and especially in the Athenian, world. Both represent a form of emancipation for which there was no place in the reality of Greek society in the Classical period. Circe remained reassuringly distant on her wondrous island; the images of this sorceress concentrate increasingly on how she is conquered by Odysseus: Circe has to drop the bowl containing the dangerous *kykeon*. Medea is deprived to a great extent of her original nature, which was akin to the gods'. She becomes a human among humans, even though she must remain an outsider. Contrary to many other authors, it is not my opinion that Euripides made Medea more dreadful and frightening. Rather, it seems a miracle that he was still able in his day to depict this heroine as a human being with her own tragic destiny. Admittedly, this humanizing process also amounts to a loss of power. Whereas Circe must stop turning men into animals, Medea loses (almost) everything that once made her more divine than human.

MARGOT SCHMIDT
Antikenmuseum Basel und Sammlung Ludwig

1. I am particularly grateful to Elizabeth Fridrich (Basel) for her careful translation of my article. She would like to dedicate this translation, which appears in a catalogue of the Walters Art Gallery, to the memory of her mother, born Anna Sass in Baltimore on 22 April 1910.

    In view of the profusion of secondary literature on the two renowned mythological figures Circe and Medea, to whom this article is primarily devoted, it is naturally not possible in the limited space available to give more than an extremely scant bibliography. The respective articles in *LIMC* can be recommended as a useful orientation on the evolution of these two myths and on the extant literary and pictorial sources. On Circe: F. Canciani, *LIMC* VI (1992) 48-59. On Medea: M. Schmidt, *LIMC* VI (1992) 386-98. On Jason and Medea: J. Neils, *LIMC* V (1990) 629-38. With regard to Circe in the *Odyssey*, one may consult, e.g., G. Crane, *Calypso: Background and Conventions of the Odyssey* (Frankfurt 1988) esp. 30-85, with bibliography. One of the most recent articles on Circe is J.-M. Moret, "Circe tisseuse sur les vases du Cabirion," *RA* (1991) 227-66.

2. The English translation is quoted from the Penguin edition of the *Odyssey* (E.V. Rieu, 1946).

3. E.g., Hesiod, *Theogony* 1000 and *Ehioai*.

4. Homer, *Odyssey* 10.234ff.

5. Cf. Crane (1988) 32f.

6. *LIMC* VI (1992) 9 (s.v. Kirke).

7. Homer, *Odyssey* 10.395f.

8. Pellizer (1979) esp. 82.

9. N. Himmelmann seems to have been the first to notice this: "Erzählung und Figur in der archaischen Kunst," *Abhandlungen Mainz* (1967) 74, 2. The representation of Circe in this "male" stance can be seen best on the famous cup in Boston (fig. 2), Museum of Fine Arts, inv. no. 99.518; *LIMC* VI (1992) 14 (s.v. Kirke). The non-Attic pictures (ibid. l.c., 4 and 19) may also be compared. Most similar to Circe in this respect is the hetaira and aulos-player depicted on the olpe by the Princeton Painter in Basel, Antikenmuseum und Sammlung Ludwig, inv. no. K 411; *CVA* Basel 1 (Switzerland 4) pl. 26, 3-5.7.

10. Homer, *Odyssey* 10.322.

11. Homer, *Odyssey* 10.295.

12. On Circe, reference may be made to the interesting interpretation attempted by A.H. Ashmead and K.M. Phillips, Jr. (*Studies in Classical Art and Archaeology*. Festschrift P. von Blanckenhagen, G. Kopcke and M.B. Moore, eds. [Locust Valley, N.Y. 1979]

52, pls. 10 and 12) who, on the Brygos Painter's lekythos in Providence, Rhode Island School of Design, inv. no. 25/ 078 (*ARV* 384.84), wish to see Circe enthroned with a hawk or falcon as an eloquent attribute since according to one, disputed, etymology the name Circe is derived from *kirkos*, a kind of hawk or falcon. Cf. Canciani, *LIMC* VI (1992) 50 (s.v. Kirke). In this respect the strange lines in Lykophron's *Alexandra* (1312 ff.) are called to mind, where Medea is termed a crow (*kerais*). Cf. M. Schmidt, rev. of Meyer (1980), in *Gnomon* 56 (1984) 64.

13. Meyer (1980) 41 ff., in particular discusses this version as traceable in the Hypothesis to Euripides' *Peliades* and in Hyginus, *Fabulae* 24, and considers it to be depicted in certain pictorial sources, especially on the well-known relief of Medea and the Peliades, previously in the Lateran, now in the Vatican Museum, Rome. Cf. rev. by M. Schmidt, *Gnomon* 56 (1984) 60.

14. In particular Graf (1994) with general information.

15. Graf (1994) 141ff., with literature.

16. In view of this fact, it is evident that for the pre-Hellenistic period, Graf (1994) had to work almost exclusively with material relating to the magical undertakings of men.

17. Daxelmüller (1993) 178f. The original German text is: Das Verbrechen der Hexe bestand darin, dass sie sich einer Kraft bediente, die man ihr nicht zustand, und dass sie Macht ausübte, die ihr nicht zukam. Die Geschichtsschreibung des neuzeitlichen Hexenwahns, der mit der Aufklärung im 18. Jh. endete, ist zugleich ein Versuch, die Strukturen sozialer Disziplinierungsmassnahmen aufzuzeigen.

18. As in Pindar, *Pythian* 4.234.

19. Melanippides, frag. 757 *PMG*.

20. Aristophanes, *Clouds* 749.

21. *LIMC* II (1984) 43 (s.v. Astra).

22. *LIMC* II (1984) 45 (s.v. Astra).

NUPTIAL NUANCES: WEDDING IMAGES
IN NON-WEDDING SCENES OF MYTH

Thanks to the evidence preserved on Athenian painted pottery we have a much better understanding of the ancient Greek wedding ceremony, for the scenes found on some of these vessels not only provide pictures of events referred to in literary sources, but they sometimes furnish evidence for those not mentioned. Recent studies have helped us to perceive more clearly the parts of the ceremony shown on individual vases and to understand the formal pictorial language developed by vase-painters for wedding depictions.[1] That elements of wedding iconography were used in depictions not only of human weddings but also of mythological ones should not be a surprise, since the Greek gods are anthropomorphic and human in most of their customary behavior. But wedding motifs are also employed in scenes of myth where no wedding proper takes place, lending these images more than one layer of meaning, just as metaphor, simile, and other literary devices do in literature. This has often gone unnoticed, and no overview or analysis of the use of wedding imagery in non-wedding scenes of myth has ever been written. This is the goal of this essay, which will focus on Athenian red-figure vases, where these images occur most frequently. Before turning to our main theme, however, let us first briefly review the development of wedding iconography, since we will be referring to various standard wedding motifs.

Wedding scenes first appear on Attic pottery for certain in the seventh century B.C. and become popular on Attic black-figure vases of the sixth century. More than ninety percent of these show the procession between the bride's father's house and the groom's, the crucial moment of transition for the bride, when she leaves her old home for the new. A chariot is normally the mode of transportation for the couple. In a few cases the figures are labeled, such

Fig. 1. Detail of a hydria in the manner of the Lysippides Painter. Florence, Museo Archeologico Nazionale, inv. no. 3790.

as on a hydria from the last quarter of the sixth century B.C. in Florence in the manner of the Lysippides Painter (fig. 1),[2] where Peleus and Thetis stand in a four-horse chariot, accompanied by gods and deified heroes afoot. They include Thyone (the deified Semele), Dionysos, Apollo, Herakles, Athena, Hermes, Aphrodite, Amphitrite, and probably Ares and Poseidon. In other black-figure wedding scenes there is nothing to suggest that any of the figures are immortal,[3] while on still others there is a mix of mortals and gods.[4]

The mix is clearly meant to raise the status of the bridal couple,[5] in a manner similar to that found in ancient Greek wedding songs, where they are often compared to gods and heroes. Very likely a chariot was not actually used in most weddings, since the literary sources mention only carts in connection with mortal weddings. Probably the chariot is another element employed to raise the cou-

Fig. 2. Drawing after a bell krater. Reading Art Museum, inv. no. 32-772-1.

Fig. 3. Detail of a skyphos by Makron. Boston, Museum of Fine Arts, inv. no. 13.186.

ple's status. Typical iconographical motifs found in other black-figure wedding processions include the wreath the bride may hold and the manner in which she holds the veil or mantle away from her face in the gesture referred to as the *anakalypsis*.

Many red-figure wedding scenes are found on loutrophoroi and lebetes gamikoi, two special ritual shapes connected with the actual ceremony. The loutrophoros was used to carry water for the ritual bath of the wedding and was also placed on tombs of those who died unmarried (nos. 22-27). The exact use of the lebes gamikos (nos. 28 and 55-59) in the ceremony is uncertain, although its inclusion in numerous wedding scenes indicates that it had a role.

Fig. 4. Detail of an amphora by the Berlin Painter. Vienna, Kunsthistorisches Museum, inv. no. 741.

Chariot processions are also found on red-figure vases. On one loutrophoros (no. 27) the groom lifts his bride into a waiting chariot, while other members of the procession stand ready behind them. The foot procession (*chamaipous*), however, is much more popular. Typically the groom reaches for or grabs the bride's wrist or hand in the gesture known as *cheir' epi karpo*, while looking back at her. The bride, beautifully dressed with veil and often a stephane (the bridal crown), looks on demurely. The veil is normally adjusted by her main attendant, the *nympheutria*, who is located behind her. The bride's or groom's mother usually stands with torches before the couple, and Eros often hovers between them. Different points in time during the procession are shown on different vases. There are also varying forms for the stephane. Either the mantle is pulled up over the back of the head, or there is a separate veil. Several loutrophoroi in the exhibit demonstrate these characteristics well (nos. 24, 25, and 102). A wreath hanging in the background is another element typically found in wedding scenes (nos. 24, 27, and 56).

The most common red-figure motif, however, is the preparation and adornment of the bride. Typically she is shown seated among

Fig. 5. Detail of a hydria by the Tyszkiewicz Painter. Munich, Staatliche Antikensammlungen und Glyptothek München, inv. no. 2425.

attendants, who either assist her in getting dressed or carry baskets, caskets, ribbons, or wedding vessels. The bride's actions vary. Two of the more interesting motifs show her binding her hair or holding a musical instrument, as two lebetes gamikoi by the Washing Painter in Athens[6] and New York illustrate (no. 55). Note the loutrophoros held by one of the attendants on each and the assistance of Eros on the first.

Even though the procession and bridal adornment are the two most popular scenes on red-figure vases, a wide range of other moments is also shown. They include the procession for the waters of the bridal bath; the bath itself; the *anakalypteria* (no. 26), that is the ritual unveiling of the bride to the groom; and the *epaulia*, the final day of the ceremony when gifts were brought to the couple

Fig. 6. Detail of a loutrophoros by Polygnotos. Toronto, Royal Ontario Musuem, inv. no. 929.22.3.

and the bride received her friends and relatives in her new home after the wedding night. Red-figure wedding iconography is decisively richer and more varied than its black-figure counterpart, and by the third quarter of the fifth century some painters had begun to specialize in it, the Washing Painter being the best example.

As with black-figure vases, red-figure scenes show the gods and heroes being married in the same format as humans. A good, but not well-known, example is on a bell krater with lug handles once in the possession of Samuel Rogers and now in Reading (fig. 2).[7] Dionysos is shown looking back and grabbing the wrist of his bride Ariadne *cheir' epi karpo*. A woman with torches, possibly Dionysos' mother Semele, leads the procession. Behind the bride is the *nympheutria,* who holds a fillet in a pose similar to that on other wedding vases (nos. 24, 26, and 102). Poseidon stands behind her, and Eros approaches from the right holding a fillet. The same iconographical conventions are used for the foot procession in human weddings. A chariot procession for Peleus and Thetis is found on the exquisite name-piece of the Peleus Painter (no. 110), so both types are also used for heroes and immortals.

Several mythological brides-to-be are at times depicted as brides. In the case of Iphigenia, as on a white-ground lekythos by Douris in Palermo of 490-480 B.C. (no. 101),[8] this fits in with the story, since she was brought to Aulis on the pretense of becoming Achilles' bride. Note her rich dress and the way she holds her veil in

a gesture resembling the *anakalypsis.* Teukros, the brother of the greater Ajax, leads her to Artemis' altar to be sacrificed. He holds a drawn sword in his left hand and looks back at her in the same manner that grooms do in many red-figure scenes of wedding processions, while reaching back with his right hand to grab her *cheir' epi karpo*, an irony that would not have been lost on any Greek viewer.

In other cases the use of bridal attire clearly alludes to the future. So when Paris leads Helen away to Troy on an early fifth-century skyphos by Makron in Boston (fig. 3),[9] he does so *cheir' epi karpo*. Her veil is adjusted in back by Aphrodite who serves as the *nympheutria,* and Eros adjusts Helen's stephane while Peitho looks on from the right holding a flower. Aeneas leads the procession on the left. The actual wedding, we know, took place later in Troy.

A chariot procession is used in place of the foot procession for the abduction on a fourth-century squat lekythos in St. Petersburg.[10] Paris in rich oriental garb mounts the vehicle, in which Helen stands ready, her right arm around his back, her left hand holding out her drapery. Aphrodite, or more likely a statue of her, stands by the horses holding a phiale and incense burner, as Hermes waits before the chariot to serve as *proegetes*, the leader of the wedding procession. One Eros flies in front of Helen holding out two torches; another is behind Paris. The two youths on the left are probably Helen's brothers, the Dioskouroi.

Helen is also frequently depicted as a bride in scenes of her recovery by Menelaos during the sack of Troy. On an amphora in Vienna by the Berlin Painter of 470 B.C. (fig. 4),[11] the pursuit is still in progress, yet she wears bridal veil and stephane, a clear allusion

Fig. 7. Detail of fragmentary kalyx krater. Sarajevo, National Museum, inv. no. 33.

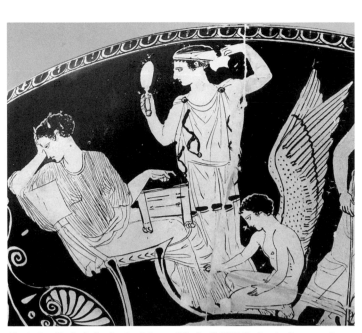

Fig. 8. Detail of a kylix by the Painter of Berlin F 2536. Berlin, Antikensammlung, Staatliche Museen zu Berlin Preussischer Kulturbesitz, inv. no. F 2536.

to the fact that they will once again live together happily married. This is already implied by the sword, which falls from Menelaos' hand.

Several vases show Menelaos taking possession of Helen after having been awarded her hand in marriage. On a hydria in Munich by the Tyszkiewicz Painter of 480-470 B.C. (fig. 5)[12] Menelaos claims her *cheir' epi karpo*, looking back at her in the same manner as the groom in scenes of the foot procession that we saw earlier. In her left hand she holds a fruit, very possibly a *malon* (apple or quince). These we know were eaten by the bride before she entered the bridal chamber on the wedding night in order to sweeten her speech and taste to the groom.[13] The bride on a loutrophoros by Polygnotos of 440 B.C. (fig. 6)[14] holds one in a similar fashion while she is led forth by her groom. The armor and weapons of Menelaos indicate that this is not the wedding proper, but that the wedding iconography is used to indicate the outcome.

Helen was the mythological bride *par excellence*, as evidenced by her famed beauty and her many husbands.[15] It is not surprising, therefore, that many of the mythological scenes connected with her should contain elements of wedding iconography. Let us consider two other examples. On a fragmentary kalyx krater in Sarajevo of ca. 420 B.C. (fig. 7)[16] Paris in oriental dress sits in the wilds of Mt. Ida awaiting Hermes, who leads the three goddesses to him for judgment; little remains of the three lovelies on this fragment. Eros flies toward Paris, indicating already who his choice will be and why, but the painter has also shown him making a wreath, not a normal activity for a shepherd. Wreaths are one of the motifs often found in wedding scenes, as we noted before, since they decorated the houses of the couple's parents and were often carried by brides and worn by the couple, and there are several depictions of brides making

them.[17] The one that Paris makes alludes, as does the presence of Eros, to what is on his mind and to the future.

On the Painter of Berlin F 2536's name-piece, a cup of 430 B.C. (fig. 8),[18] Helen sits on the left, next to a comrade who primps herself in a mirror. Eros bends over, making ready to adjust Helen's sandals, a motif frequently found in scenes of bridal adornment. A squat lekythos in Boston in the manner of the Meidias Painter of 420-410 B.C. is a good example (fig. 9).[19] The bride pulls up her veil, and female attendants stand to each side. The one on the left holds the stephane, and Eros bends over to adjust the bride's sandals. We know from the literary sources that there were special bridal sandals called *nymphides*, so attention to them in scenes of bridal adornment is understandable.

The left-hand side of the scene on the Berlin cup thus recalls one of bridal adornment, the primary difference being the way Helen looks away in a distraught manner with downturned mouth from the approaching Paris who is about to be introduced by the bearded man with scepter in the middle, probably Menelaos. Both Helen's actions and the wedding motifs suggest the future. In this case she appears not to be pleased with what the future holds.

Another category of scenes very often having wedding iconography are those with figures who may be referred to as "pseudo-brides." These include victims of rape, concubines, and willing, pre-marital partners. The first group is the most common. Not infrequently the pursued or abducted woman is dressed as a bride with stephane and/or a veil or mantle pulled over her head, sometimes held away from the face with one hand in the gesture of *anakalypsis*. This is exactly how Oreithyia is shown on a stamnos by Hermonax in the Hermitage of 460 B.C., where she is pursued by Boreas, the north wind.[20] Pursuit scenes were extremely popular on red-figure vases between 490-480 and 430-420 B.C. and in some

Fig. 9. Detail of a squat lekythos in the manner of the Meidias Painter. Boston, Museum of Fine Arts, inv. no. 95.1402.

Fig. 10. Kalyx krater by the Coghill Painter. Lisbon, Calouste Gulbenkian Museum, inv. no. 682.

cases were clearly perceived of as weddings of a sort, paradigms, as evidenced both by the presence of wedding iconography in them and their use on wedding vases.[21] The depictions of Helen being pursued by Menelaos can also be thought of as falling into this category, and many of the vases discussed here can be considered members of more than one group, helping demonstrate how wedding iconography can affectively give a single scene several levels of meaning. I will not attempt in each case to indicate every group to which a vase can belong.

The daughter of Leukippos who is escorted away by one of the Dioskuroi on the main side of the upper frieze of a double register kalyx krater in Lisbon by the Coghill Painter of 440 B.C. (fig. 10),[22] also wears bridal dress, including stephane and veil. This part of the scene is reminiscent in many respects of a chariot wedding procession, such as one on a pyxis by the Marlay Painter in London of 430 B.C. (fig. 11).[23] Both couples are shown in the chariot, and a companion leads them on the Lisbon krater in the same fashion as the *proegetes* does on the Marlay Painter's pyxis. Apollo stands by as if a member of the wedding party, as does the woman with torches on the London pyxis, but the fleeing woman behind the chariot belongs solely to the rape aspect of the scene, as do the remaining figures of the frieze not visible here.

The foot procession is used in place of the rape of Thetis on a stamnos by the Berlin Painter in Palermo.[24] On one side Peleus is shown leading Thetis *cheir' epi karpo* to Cheiron, while on the other side her sister Nereides flee to old man Nereus, their father, on the back, just as companions do on the backs of countless vases where a rape is shown on the front.[25] Thus rape takes place on foot or in wagons, just as wedding processions do.

Still different types of wedding motifs are used in several scenes showing the rape of Europa. On a fourth-century fish plate in the Hermitage, Europa sits on the back of a bull moving across the fish-laden sea in the direction of Zeus, who sits on a diphros holding a scepter. Poseidon sits not far away. Accompanying Europa are a group of Erotes with ribbons, tympana, and caskets, and Nereids atop hippocamps. They are her wedding train, accompanying the bride on the procession to her new home, just as relatives, friends, and Erotes do in depictions of the wedding procession.[26] Remember that ribbons and caskets, among other things, are often carried by these accompanying figures.

Good examples of the last two types of pseudo-brides, that is concubines and willing, pre-marital partners, are Briseis and Ariadne. On a skyphos by Makron in the Louvre of 480 B.C. (fig. 12),[27] Briseis is led away *cheir' epi karpo* by Agamemnon, who turns around to look at her like a groom. She is heavily veiled and performs the gesture of *anakalypsis* with her left hand. The herald Talthybios and the hero Diomedes accompany them. She will not be a legal wife to Agamemnon, but will, he hopes, perform certain

Fig. 11. Pyxis by the Marlay Painter. London, British Museum, inv. no. 1920.12-21.

Fig. 12. Skyphos by Makron, Paris, Musée du Louvre, inv. no. G 146.

and Danae is here preparing herself to be the bride.[29] This vase can also be counted under the previous heading of pseudo-bride.

Having discovered the child's birth, Danae's father Akrisios set the two adrift in a chest across the sea, to avoid being killed by his grandchild, as an oracle had foretold. On the name-piece of the Danae Painter, a hydria (no. 77), we see the pair in the chest as Akrisios, his wife Eurydike, and a nurse look on. Danae is shown as a

Fig. 13. Fragment of a lekanis. Bonn, Akademisches Kunstmuseum, inv. no. 354.

of a wife's functions. Upon returning Briseis to Achilles, Agamemnon swears up and down that he had not touched her. This is apparently not his intent in this scene.

A fragment from the lid of a lekanis from the last quarter of the fifth century in Bonn (fig. 13)[28] shows Ariadne bedecked in veil and stephane as she sleeps deeply on Naxos, while Eros or Hypnos hovers above and Theseus is off to the right, making ready to leave his pseudo-bride for a night. Her bridal attire refers not only to this night, but to her forthcoming marriage to Dionysos, which we saw earlier on a vase.

A third group of women with whom wedding iconography is often associated are motherly figures. Danae, the mother of Perseus, is a good example. On a kalyx krater of 490 B.C. by the Triptolemos Painter (no. 74), Danae sits atop her bed binding her hair, as Zeus in the form of golden rain descends into her lap. Perseus, as we all know, will be the result of this shower. The binding of hair is part of the bridal preparations, as we noted earlier in our discussion of a lebes gamikos by the Washing Painter in Athens,

Fig. 14. Detail of a volute krater by the Painter of the Berlin Hydria. Boston, Museum of Fine Arts, inv. no. 00.347.

Fig. 15. Detail of a hydria by the Semele Painter. Berkeley, Phoebe A. Hearst Museum of Anthropology, The University of California at Berkeley, inv. no. 8.3316.

Fig. 16. Details of the hydria in figure 15 [after *CVA* University of California (U.S.A. 5) pl. 49a-b].

bride with veil and stephane, just as she is on a contemporary fragment by the Phiale Painter (no. 78). We know that she will later attract the attention and advances of King Polydektes when she lands on Seriphos. Her bridal attire, therefore, is not only related to her role as mother, but also to her future when her attractiveness will be crucial to their survival, just as the bride's allure is crucial to the continuation and therefore the survival of the *oikos* (family).

Leto is one of the best examples of the motherly type. She, Artemis, and Apollo form the Delian triad found on many vases. Very often Leto is shown bride-like, with veil and stephane, as on the left of a volute krater in Boston by the Painter of the Berlin Hydria of 460 B.C. (fig. 14),[30] where she makes a wreath. Apollo stands on the right holding out a phiale for libation in his right hand toward Artemis who stands frontally in the center, looking toward him. Apollo holds a bow and laurel staff in his left hand, and Artemis carries an oinochoe and lyre. The bridal motif can only refer to Leto's motherhood, for she is most famous for giving birth to these two gods.

In the tondo of a magnificent cup from near mid-century in Munich by the Penthesilea Painter,[31] Leto serves as the backdrop to Apollo as he seeks revenge against Tityos for his attempted rape of her. The youthful god strides forward, sword raised over his head in the pose of Harmodios from the Tyrannicide Group, as the cowardly perpetrator cowers on knees below. Leto is beautifully adorned with stephane and veil, which she holds out in the gesture of *anakalypsis*. Not only is her role as mother reflected in her attire, but also that of a victim of attempted rape. Once again we see how wedding iconography can add more than one layer of meaning to a vase-painting.

A similar combination of meaning is found on the name-piece of the Semele Painter, a hydria from the turn of the century in Berkeley with the birth of Dionysos (figs. 15-16).[32] Semele lies asleep in the middle beneath a garland bough, as Zeus' thunderbolt descends upon her from directly above. Hermes carries the child to safety on the left, while Iris, sent by Hera on the far right to abduct the child, arrives too late. Zeus and Aphrodite accompanied by an Eros sit above. Of particular interest are the women who stand at the top outer edges of the picture holding caskets and ribbons, the right one of whom is accompanied by Eros. They are a type of figure commonly found in wedding scenes as part of the bride's party.[33] Once again the wedding iconography refers to both the pseudo-bride and Semele's role as mother. This is also a good example of the close ties between weddings and death, for Zeus' thunderbolt will destroy his lover.

Another group of scenes with wedding iconography are chthonic.[34] The namepiece of the Persephone Painter, a bell krater of 440 B.C., is an excellent illustration (no. 82). The goddess' return from the underworld is the subject. She ascends from a slit in the ground and is decked out with a beautiful stephane, while her mantle still clings to the lower part of her head. Hekate leads the way holding out two torches, just as mothers do in scenes of the wedding pro-

Fig. 17. Detail of a bell krater by the Group of Polygnotos. Stockholm, The National Museum, inv. no. 6.

cession. Hermes stands off to the side, and Demeter, her mother, waits on the right. Persephone is often shown in bridal attire, which relates on several other levels, since she is the victim of a rape and the bride and wife of Hades.

A mid fifth-century volute krater once associated with the Group of Polygnotos (no. 81) provides another example. Inscriptions secure the identity of the figures. On the right Pandora ascends from the earth as Epimetheus, her husband to be, stands ready to assist her. Eros flies above with outstretched hands in the direction of Epimetheus. On the left Zeus stands frontally, looking right in the direction of Hermes who moves toward the couple holding a flower, while looking back at Zeus, as if the messenger god had been sent by Zeus to make her even more attractive. Pandora is dressed as a bride with stephane and veil, which along with Eros allude to her future wedding to Epimetheus.

A nearly contemporary bell krater in Stockholm from the Group of Polygnotos (fig. 17)[35] has been variously interpreted. Earlier the

Fig. 18. Detail of a lebes gamikos by the Washing Painter. New York, Metropolitan Museum of Art, inv. no. 16.73.

scene was identified as the *anodos* of Persephone or Pandora, but more recently by Shapiro as being derived from *Aithon*, the satyr play of Achaios of Eretria based on the story of Erysichthon.[36] After cutting down trees in Demeter's sacred grove, Erysichthon was punished with an insatiable appetite that led him eventually to gobble himself up. The figure ascending from the earth in this case would be Demeter. But no matter who she is, the scene is chthonic, and the wedding motif is lent by the ascending figure's short hairstyle, which is a type preserved primarily for brides on several vases by the Washing Painter with scenes connected with her adornment. A lebes gamikos by the Washing Painter in New York (fig. 18)[37] is one example.

Wedding iconography is also used occasionally with mythological figures who do not fall exactly into any of the groups described above. Two examples will have to suffice here. Polyneikes is shown bribing Eriphyle with the necklace of Harmonia on a column krater near the Nausikaa Painter in Palazzolo Acreide of 440 B.C.[38] Eriphyle with outstretched hands sits in the center on a klismos, a veil around her head and stephane, as the bearded Polyneikes lifts the necklace out of its container. A nurse holding one of her sons, most likely Alkmaeon, stands behind her. The bridal attire refers to her marriage and family, as does the presence of her son, helping to remind the viewer just what she is betraying by accepting the bribe that will lead to both her husband Amphiaraos' death and her own by the hand of her son Alkmaeon.

A unique representation of Atalanta pursued by Erotes occurs on a masterful white-ground lekythos by Douris in Cleveland (fig. 19).[39] A richly decorated veil covers her head as she flees right, looking back. The Eros behind her extends a wreath toward her head with his left hand. Originally he held a whip in his right hand, now incorrectly restored as a floral spray, similar to those the two other Erotes framing the pair hold. The essence of the scene is that the virgin huntress is fleeing from marriage. Although this depiction reflects the psyche of the mythological Atalanta, it also parallels the psychology of any uncertain bride, who will have to leave her former life for an entirely new one. The mythological figure and her situation as represented on this vase are applicable to any human bride, and this scene would certainly have found a sympathetic viewer in any Athenian woman.

It is interesting to note that both the fine, early white-ground lekythoi by Douris are close in style and have unique subject matter associated with weddings. Were they both originally made with an eye for use as wedding gifts, as funerary gifts for women who died before they were married, or as special dedications? The Iphigenia lekythos (no. 101) was found in a sanctuary of Demeter and is an appropriate offering for Persephone, Demeter's daughter, who has associations with both weddings and death.

The last figures we will briefly consider are the two female gods most closely tied with the wedding, Hera and Aphrodite. They are often shown in bridal attire, often in scenes where it plays no role other than to remind the viewer of the goddesses' character. So, for

Fig. 19. White-ground lekythos by Douris. Cleveland Museum of Art, inv. no. 66.114.

example, Hera on a cup by Aristophanes and Erginos in Berlin of 410 B.C.[40] is shown wearing a stephane and veil while fighting against the giant Phoitos as part of a Gigantomachy. Her garments reflect not only her role as a deity of marriage, but also her place as Zeus' consort and mother of gods.

In other cases bridal dress can allude to a part of the story. For example, the bridal aspect of Aphrodite is overly stressed on a cup by Makron in Berlin in a scene of the Judgment of Paris, where she is heavily veiled and surrounded by a swarm of fluttering Erotes.[41] That marriage to Helen is what she used to bribe Paris is very clear.

Before concluding it is important to note that the use of wedding imagery is not limited to myth. A skyphos of Corinthian form by the Phiale Painter in Palermo (fig. 20)[42] is a good example of its use in an everyday scene. On one side a veiled and wreathed woman sits on a klismos working wool on her leg, one of a housewife's standard duties. Her heavy veil is not what somebody at work would wear but is clearly a reference to the wedding. Meanwhile the wreathed groom stands before a door on the other side of the vase. By placing her in what will be her new world, the painter has indicated to the viewer one of the things that all normal brides would and should end up doing, for the making of fabrics was one of a wife's most important duties.

Wedding iconography is not limited to Athenian painted pottery. It is used, for example, on South Italian red-figure vases, sometimes with different scenes or figures than their Attic counterparts. A good example is Andromeda, who in Athenian scenes of her exposure is regularly depicted in oriental garb but in South Italian representations is often shown as a bride. A late fifth-century Apulian volute krater from the Sisyphos Group in Malibu demonstrates this well (fig. 21).[43] Dressed in bridal attire Andromeda is being bound to the stakes on the left, while Perseus seals the pact with Kepheus, her father, by a handshake on the right. In return for killing the sea monster, Perseus will be able to marry her. This handshake is part of the *engye*,[44] the formal contract of marriage between the bridegroom and bride's father. It is depicted on the back of a loutrophoros in Boston (no. 24). The gifts below can end up being either funeral or wedding gifts, depending upon the outcome. The close relationship of these two rituals is also demonstrated here.

Returning now to Athenian mythological vases, we have seen that certain types of scenes and figures lent themselves readily to being depicted in connection with wedding motifs. These include brides-to-be, several types of pseudo-brides, mothers, and chthonic figures. And from these groups, certain figures in particular are especially prone to being depicted in this way, including the oft-shown figures Helen, Leto, Hera, and Aphrodite, and such less frequently depicted ones as Danae and Iphigenia.

Not surprisingly, the categories that use bridal motifs are ones that have a relationship to the wedding. Use of the imagery with brides-to-be foreshadows the actual event, a narrative technique used with other types of action in Greek vase-paintings. Pseudo-brides are true brides in one crucial respect, that is the sexual union which took place, though they have not taken part in the ceremony officially recognizing this union. Motherly figures are ones who have properly performed the primary goal of marriage, that is the production of offspring to ensure the continuation of the *oikos*.

Fig. 20. Detail of a skyphos by the Phiale Painter. Palermo, Fondazaion Mormino, inv. no. 788.

Several scenes of bridal adornment show the bride holding a male child, such as on lebes gamikos by the Washing Painter in Munich (no. 56). This may either reflect an actual custom where the bride comes in contact with a male child to encourage fertility, or it may foreshadow her future role in the same fashion as the bride working wool on the Phiale Painter's skyphos.[45] The similarities between the rituals connected with death and marriage have long been noted, so that the chthonic group is yet one more example of this close relationship.

The most important aspect of this wedding iconography, however, is the way it is used as a pictorial language to deepen the meaning of a scene beyond its immediate action. Just as literary devices can be used in various ways, so can wedding iconography. It can produce irony, foreshadow a future event, enrich an image through metaphor or simile, or allude to a figure's psychological state. And just as imagery does in literature, it produces more than one level of meaning, so that in many cases several different aspects of a figure or scene can be implied by its use.

The study of Greek poetry has always been attractive and intriguing because of, among other things, its complex and poly-semantic nature. Often it offers an alternate thread or possible nuance of interpretation that is sometimes clear and more certain than at other times, so that an allusion can be faint, obvious, or somewhere between. This leaves the interpretation open to question, and hence, the poem is in some ways more interesting or intriguing. Similarly, on many of the vases we have looked at in this essay there can be little doubt of the use of wedding iconography, while on other vases its use remains unclear—leaving the tantalizing possibility open but unresolved in the viewer's mind. Thus the same complex interrelationships and patterns of thought are found in the work of both vase-painter and poet, exhibiting a cultural unity in the mind's processes across media.

It is perhaps disheartening to think that much of what we have deciphered in this essay would have been immediately evident to an ancient Athenian looking at one of these vases, for they would know a bride and a reference to a wedding when they saw it. But our knowledge of the wedding has always been hampered by the nature of our sources. No single description of the entire ritual is preserved; rather we have to interpret and collate references to different parts of the ceremony from different parts of the Greek world and from different times. The reason for this must be that weddings were such a common event that there was no need to describe one in full. It is also only recently, with the increased attention given to the ceremony, that the use of wedding imagery in many non-wedding situations has been recognized in various types of Greek verse, particularly Athenian drama.[46]

Athenian literature reflects the greater attention paid to the role of women in the second half of the late fifth century B.C. The vases, with their overwhelming emphasis on the bride, show how the wedding was very much "her day" in antiquity, as it is today. It should not be surprising, therefore, that female mythological figures are primarily the ones with whom wedding iconography is used in non-wedding scenes. In addition the number of wedding vases increases dramatically at this time and, along with this, an increase in the number of vases on which wedding iconography is used in non-wedding scenes. This increased attention to women and their world is exactly what we see in Euripides' plays, as the oft quoted words of Medea to Jason illustrate: "I would much prefer to stand three times by my shield (in battle) than to give birth once."[47]

The vases we have looked at in this essay are in many ways as complicated and intriguing as a work of Greek literature. As our understanding of their pictorial language grows, so, too, our appreciation of the complex and multi-faceted images of ancient Greek women that many of these vessels give us.

Fig. 21. Detail of a volute krater by the Sisyphos Group. Malibu, J. Paul Getty Museum, inv. no. 85.AE.102.

JOHN H. OAKLEY
The College of William and Mary in Virginia

For photographs and permission to publish them, I am very grateful to: F.A. Norick, T. Babineau (Berkeley), H. Getter, U. Kästner (Berlin), W. Geominy (Bonn), C.C. Vermeule III (Boston), A.S. Bour, A.P. Kozloff (Cleveland), F. Nicosia (Florence), M.C. Hipólito (Lisbon), J. Burns, K. Hamma, M. True (Malibu), F.W. Hamdorf (Munich), E.J. Milleker, C.A. Picón (New York), A.-N. Malagardis (Paris), E. Rystedt (Stockholm), J.W. Hayes (Toronto), and A. Bernhard-Walcher (Vienna). Earlier versions of this paper were read in Athens, Greece at the Annual Meeting of the American School of Classical Studies at the University of Missouri at Columbia and at Duke University's Symposium on Greek Vase Painting. I would like to thank my hosts W.D.E. Coulson, W. R. Biers, and K. Stanley at these events, and H.A. Shapiro and R. H. Sinos for their useful thoughts on an earlier draft.

1. Sutton (1981); Oakley and Sinos (1993); and Sabetai (1993).

2. Florence, Museo Archeologico Nazionale, inv. no. 3790: *ABV* 260.30, 264, and 691; *Para* 114; *Add²* 68.

3. E.g., Heidelberg University, inv. no. 72/1; *AA* 92 (1977) 15, figs. 1-2, and 29, fig. 11.

4. E.g., London, British Museum, inv. no. B 174: *ABV* 141.1; *Add²* 38; Oakley and Sinos (1993) 86, fig. 65.

5. Krauskopf (1977); Oakley and Sinos (1993) 28-30.

6. Athens, National Museum, inv. no. 14790; *ARV²* 1126.4; Oakley and Sinos (1993) fig. 23.

7. Reading (Penn.) Art Museum, inv. no. 32-772-1: Jenkins (1989) 11, figs. 10:9(b) and 12:10(b). J. Neils very kindly told me of the vase's current location and supplied other information about it. The winged female figure underneath the left handle and not illustrated here is a type commonly found in wedding scenes and should be connected with this side of the vase.

8. See also Kiel, Kunsthalle, Antikensammlung, inv. no. B 538 (*CVA* Kiel 1 [Germany 55] 81, figs. 35-36, pls. 39-40.1-4), where she is dragged to the altar wearing a stephane.

9. Boston, Museum of Fine Arts, inv. no. 13.186; *ARV²* 458.1, 481, and 1654; *Para* 377; *Add²* 243; Oakley and Sinos (1993) 98, fig. 86.

10. St. Petersburg, State Hermitage Museum, inv. no. 1929; *LIMC* I (1981) pl. 389, Alexandros 65; *LIMC* IV (1988) 531, no. 172 with bibliography and pl. 322, Helene 172.

11. Vienna, Kunsthistorisches Museum, inv. no. 741: *ARV²* 203.101; *Add²* 193; *LIMC* IV (1988) pl. 337, Helene 260. See ibid. pls. 339-42 and 348-49 for some other examples.

12. Munich, Antikensammlungen und Glyptothek, inv. no. 2425: *ARV²* 294.65 and 1642; *CVA* Munich 5 (Germany 20) pls. 227.5-6 and 230.1. I follow the interpretation of Schefold and Jung (1989) 116-17. Others prefer to see the actual wedding here, but his outfit precludes this in my opinion. The scene may conceivably be a softened version of the Recovery of Helen, although he doesn't threaten her as in depictions of this theme.

13. Plutarch, *Moralia* 138d, *Quaestiones Romanae* 279f, and *Solon* 20; Oakley and Sinos (1993) 35.

14. Toronto, Royal Ontario Museum, inv. no. 929.22.3; *ARV²* 1031.51; *Add²* 317.

15. For Helen most recently, see Austin (1994).

16. Sarajevo, National Museum, inv. no. 33; *CVA* Sarajevo 1 (Yugoslavia 4) pls. 46 and 48.

17. Reilly (1989) 419-20 and 424-26; see also Athens, Acropolis Museum, inv. no. NA-57-Aa 1923: Oakley (1990a) pl. 24E. For wreaths in general, see Blech (1982). For wreaths in weddings, see ibid. 76-81 and 336, 355 n. 103a; see ibid. 453 for wreaths in scenes of the Judgment of Paris. On another level the wreath can allude to victory in the contest.

18. Berlin, Staatliche Museen zu Berlin Preussischer Kulturbesitz, inv. no. F 2536; *ARV²* 1287.1 and 1689; *Para* 473; *Add²* 358; *LIMC* I (1981) pl. 384, Alexandros 46.

19. Boston, Museum of Fine Arts, inv. no. 95.1402; *ARV²* 1326.71; *Para* 478; Oakley and Sinos (1993) 67, fig. 30 and 16-18 for the motif and bridal sandals.

20. St. Petersburg, State Hermitage Museum, inv. no. b 2070; *ARV²* 484.10; *Para* 512; *Add²* 248; *LIMC* III (1986) pl. 112, Boreas 30.

21. Most fully demonstrated by Sourvinou-Inwood (1987a).

22. Lisbon, Calouste Gulbenkian Museum, inv. no. 682; *ARV²* 1042.1 and 1679; *Para* 444; *Add²* 320; *LIMC* III (1986) pl. 472, Dioskouroi 197; Prange (1992) pl. 3,1 and *passim* for the iconography of the scene most recently.

23. London, British Museum, inv. no. 1920.12-21.1; *ARV* 1277.23, 1282, and 1689; *Add²* 357; Oakley and Sinos (1993) 92-94, figs. 75-78.

24. Palermo, Museo Archeologico Regionale, inv. no. V 762; *ARV²* 207.139; *Add²* 194; *LIMC* III (1986) pl. 190, Cheiron 40.

25. E.g., on a stamnos by Hermonax, a student of the Berlin Painter: Rome, Vatican Museums, inv. no. 16526: *ARV²* 484.21; *Add²* 248; *LIMC* I (1981) pl. 284, Aigina 23; Kaempf-Dimitriadou (1979) pl. 14,5-6 and see her lists for other examples.

26. St. Petersburg, State Hermitage Museum, inv. no. BB 90; Barringer (1991) 660, fig. 1 and 666, no. 2 with earlier bibliography and passim for other examples.

27. Paris, Musée du Louvre, inv. no. G 146; *ARV²* 458-59.2, 481, and 1654; *Para* 377; *Add²* 243; *LIMC* I (1981) pl. 197, Agamemnon 52; and Shapiro (1994) 15, fig. 7 and 13-16, where he notes the wedding iconography. See also Briseis on the cup in London, British Museum, inv. no. E 76; *ARV²* 406.1 and 1651; *Para* 371; *Add²* 232; *LIMC* III (1986) pls. 133, Briseis 1 and 136, Briseis 14.

28. Bonn, Akademisches Kunstmuseum, inv. no. 354; *CVA* Bonn 1 (Germany 1) pl. 27.7.

29. Sabetai (1993) 40.

30. Boston, Museum of Fine Arts, inv. no. 00.347; *ARV* 616.1; *Add²* 269; *LIMC* II (1984) pl. 236, Apollon 651B. For other examples, see ibid. pls. 246-47.

31. Munich, Staatliche Antikensammlungen und Glyptothek, inv. no. 2689; *ARV* 879-80.2 and 1673; *Para* 428; *Add²* 301; *LIMC* II (1984) pl. 275, Apollon 1071.

32. Berkeley, Lowie Museum, inv. no. 8.3316: *ARV²* 1343.1 1681, and 1691; *Add²* 367; Schefold (1981) 28, fig. 19.

33. Schefold (1981) 28. Marina Sgourou first pointed this out to me. For a good example of this type of figure, see Tübingen University, inv. no. S./I0 1665; *ARV²* 1498.10; *Add²* 383; *CVA* Tübingen 4 (Germany 52) pl. 49.

34. The motherly, chthonic figure Gaia, the Earth, when represented in scenes of the birth of Erichthonios wears a crown several times (nos. 70-72) and in a depiction of the birth of Ploutos a crown (stephane) and veil: Istanbul, Archaeological Museum (*LIMC* IV [1988] pl. 98, Ge 28).

35. Stockholm, The National Museum, inv. no. 6; *ARV²* 1053.40 and 1680; *Add²* 322.

36. Shapiro (1990a).

37. New York, Metropolitan Museum of Art, inv. no. 16.73; *ARV²* 1126.6; *Add²* 332. For the motif, see Sabetai (1993) 43-45.

38. Palazzolo Acreide, Museo Judica; *ARV²* 1110.1; *Add²* 330; *LIMC* III (1986) pl. 607, Eriphyle I 6.

39. Cleveland, Museum of Art, inv. no. 66.114: *Para* 376.266bis; *Add²* 241; *CVA* Cleveland 1 (U.S.A. 15) pls. 32-34 and 35.1.

40. Berlin, Staatliche Museen, inv. no. F 2531; *ARV²* 1318-19.1 and 1690; *Para* 478; *Add²* 363; *CVA* Berlin 3 (Germany 22) pl. 119.2-3.

41. Berlin, Staatliche Museen Preussischer Kulturbesitz, inv. no. F 2291; *ARV²* 459.4, 481, and 1654; *Para* 377; *Add²* 244; *CVA* Berlin 2 (Germany 21) pls. 84-86.

42. Palermo, Fondazione Mormino, inv. no. 788; Oakley (1990a) pls. 131D and 132C-D.

43. Malibu, J. Paul Getty Museum, inv. no. 85.AE.102; *CVA* Malibu 4 (U.S.A. 27) pls. 190-92.

44. Oakley and Sinos (1993) 9-10 with earlier bibliography.

45. Kauffmann-Samaras (1988) and Sabetai (1993) 49-69.

46. E.g., Carson (1982), Seaford (1987), and Rehm (1994).

47. Euripides, *Medea* 250-51.

RAPE?

Rape is an ugly word and an uglier deed, and it is easy to condemn the ancient Athenians' apparent obsession with it. As one influential critic has written:

> In the case of a society dominated by men who sequester their wives and daughters, denigrate the female role in reproduction, erect monuments to the male genitalia, have sex with the sons of their peers, sponsor public whorehouses, create a mythology of rape, and engage in rampant sabre-rattling, it is not inappropriate to refer to a reign of the phallus. Classical Athens was such a civilization.[1]

Fifth-century Athenian vase-paintings often show a god or mortal pursuing a woman, grabbing her, or occasionally carrying her off (nos. 74, 106-108, 111-116, and 121 and figs. 1, 2, and 5-8). The male protagonist is sometimes nude or scantily clad but never has an erection, and with one exception (cf. fig. 8) his victim is always fully dressed. The act may be attended by his triumphant accomplices or her terror-struck companions. Its physical consummation is never shown, perhaps because this would violate even the vase-painters' limited sense of decorum, or because they were more interested in the process than in the outcome, or both. In any case, since these pictures total over 750 (see Appendix) and embellish ten percent of the objects in the present exhibition, on the face of it Keuls' stern assessment seems not ill-judged.

The catalogue of perpetrators is impressive: the gods Apollo (fig. 1), Boreas (fig. 2), Dionysos, Eros, Hades, Hermes, Pan, Poseidon (nos. 111-116), Zephyros, Zeus (no. 74), and one goddess, Eos (figs. 3-4); the heroes Kastor and Polydeukes (figs. 5-6), Peleus (nos. 106-108 and 121), Theseus (no. 121, fig. 7), and Lokrian Ajax (fig. 8); and an assortment of anonymous characters from kings to ephebes. Some attempt the deed only once, others with quite startling frequency. Though Attic painters first treat the theme shortly before 550, and its various subsets overlap, heroic pursuits and abductions are most in vogue around 500-475; divine ones around 475-450; and ephebic pursuits around 450-425.

At first sight this onslaught of facts looks overwhelming, but we do the ancient Athenians no service by drawing a one-dimensional picture of their society and then reviling it. For numerous though these scenes are, they appear on less than four percent of all fifth-century vases; each type was popular for only just over a generation; they are sometimes found on women's vases as well as men's

Fig. 1. Apollo pursues a woman (Kreousa?). Detail of an Attic red-figured hydria from Capua, attributed to the Coghill Painter. Ca. 440. London, British Museum, inv. no. E 170. [*ARV*² 1042.2.]

(nos. 111, 113, and 116); most of the stories are set in the distant past; the Athenians did not invent them; several ended with the victim's acquiescence; they directly conflict with the Athenian code of self-restraint; they show gods chasing women almost as frequently as mortals do, and chasing boys more often; among the immortals, the most frequent offender is a female, Eos; and the most determined mortal perpetrators, the drunken Centaurs and insatiable Satyrs (figs. 9-10), are figures whom one is definitely not supposed to emulate. Finally, though the Greeks are popularly supposed to have had a word for everything, and certainly had words for pursuit (*dioxis*) and abduction (*harpage*), they had no word specifically and exclusively for what we call rape.

All this complicates the issue considerably, and on closer inspection the problems only multiply. Not the least of them is my own limited perspective. An Anglo-American male scholar living in the 1990s, discussing pictures painted by men on vases usually intended for men, but sometimes also for women, and prevented by Athenian androcentism and the accidents of survival from knowing Athenian women's views about them, has a narrow and filtered view at best. Striving to make a virtue out of necessity, I want to consider the status of these images as male fantasies, produced by and mainly for men in the context of the symposium: a locus of homosociality that was essentially a mirror of the polis. Why were pursuits, abductions, even rapes so interesting to Athenian fifth-century males? Why did they choose to represent them as a distinct social discourse at this particular time?

Myth and Reality

As one might expect, it was Homer who mapped the relations between the sexes when the world was young. At one point in the *Iliad*, Zeus rather tactlessly courts Hera by contrasting his present feelings for her with all he has felt for others in the past:

Hera, ... never before has love for any goddess or woman
so melted about the heart inside me, broken it into submission,
as now: not at the time when I loved the wife of Ixion
who bore me Peirithoos, equal of the gods in council,
nor when I loved Akrisios' daughter, sweet-stepping Danae,
who bore Perseus to me, pre-eminent among all men,
nor when I loved the daughter of far-renowned Phoenix, Europa,
who bore Minos to me and Rhadamanthys the godlike;
nor when I loved Semele, or Alkmene in Thebe,
while Semele's son was Dionysos, the pleasure of mortals,
nor when I loved the queen Demeter of the lovely tresses,
nor when it was glorious Leto, nor yourself, so much
as now I love you, and the sweet passion has taken hold of me.[2]

Clearly, Zeus and the typical convicted rapist in late twentieth-century America have little in common. Whereas the latter is usually a socially marginalized young man driven by primitive feelings of neediness, impotence, envy, hatred, and aggression—virtually a

Fig. 2. Boreas abducts Oreithyia. Detail of an Attic red-figure pointed amphora from Vulci, attributed to the Oreithyia Painter (name-piece). Ca. 470. Munich, Antikensammlungen und Glyptothek, inv. no. 2345. [*ARV*[2] 496.2.]

throwback to what the nineteenth century called the "savage"— Zeus is none of these things. The august king of the gods, he claims to be love's victim, and boasts of his offspring. Yet his word for "broken into submission," *damazein*, is cognate with Homer's word for "wife," *damar*, and exactly that which the Greeks normally employed not only for animal-tamers but also for men who "tame," "subdue," or "subject" women against their will.[3] By stating the matter in this way, they transformed what we regard as the crucial issue of the woman's consent into her eventual recognition of and submission to the man's superior power and better judgment. More sinisterly, as Ann Bergren has remarked: "The plot of the *harpage* [or] 'abduction' is appealing to men...because it provides the opportunity for both transgression and rectification of society's social order: both the illicit pleasure of taking another man's woman and the glory or (re)appropriating the woman in legitimate marriage, often through mortal combat."[4]

Being purely male fantasies, these would be of no interest to a modern investigator. If the woman acquiesced, she would want to know whether she was dissembling or not; what kind of pressure was employed; whether her feelings changed afterward; and so on. The contradictions are self-evident, and feminists explain them as a matter of control. "In the patriarchal world, erotic desire and marriage are too dangerous to be joined. The implication is that the only proper marriage will be rape, because it *must* be against the desire of the woman; the only proper bride is the intact virgin; the only proper motherhood is that which comes about as a result of rape. Desire (on the part of the woman) and reproduction are incompatible."[5] Divide and conquer: Greek men, this theory asserts, sought to control women's sexuality by fragmenting it into the oppositional categories of erotic desire and fecundity, or (in fifth-century terms) between erotic "play" and the "work" of conjugal sex for procreation's sake.[6] One might compare Susan Brownmiller's startling assertion that "from prehistorical times to the present ... rape has played a critical function: it is nothing more or less than a conscious process of intimidation by which *all* men keep *all* women in a state of fear."[7] Yet though the issue of control, or rather power, is crucial, this extreme position has come under attack from many sides. Indeed, an apologist for Zeus could argue that not all his conquests fled his advances, that some positively welcomed them, and that his "loving" and progeny-oriented behavior conforms more closely to the widespread practice of polygyny than to serial rape. Classical Athens was a polygynous society, as were Sparta and Macedonia.[8] Furthermore (as will appear), Greek folk wisdom and the medical theory based upon it insisted that a woman's pleasure actually promoted, even enabled her fecundity: the two were by no means so starkly opposed as some assert.

On one famous occasion, the issue was still more highly charged. Warned that the sea-nymph Thetis would bear a son greater than his father, Zeus wisely decided to yoke her to a mortal, thus ensuring that her child could never threaten his own supremacy. Choosing Peleus for the role, he gave him leave to subdue her if necessary (nos. 106-108 and 121):

> Of all the other sea-sisters, Zeus subjected me to a mortal, to Peleus, Aiakos's son, and I had to endure mortal marriage much against my will.[9]

She tried to escape by changing into a lion, snake, and other beasts, but Peleus held on until, exhausted, she at last gave in. All the gods attended the wedding (nos. 109 and 110).

Where Homer led, others soon followed. Hesiod's *Theogony* or "Genesis of the Gods," composed around 700 from both Greek and Near Eastern sources, narrated the history of the cosmos from a primeval chaos (*hybris*, "outrage") to the triumph of Zeus and the patriarchy.[10] After describing the lawless hegemonies, copulations, and unpleasant fates of Ouranos and Kronos, he turns to the loves of Zeus and his generation. Yet since his focus is patriarchal and genealogical, he too barely separates marriage, seduction, and rape. Zeus "married" Metis (886), Themis (901), and Hera (921); but Eurynome "bore him" the Graces (907), and Maia "went up to his holy bed" and conceived Hermes (939). He in turn "came to the bed" of Demeter, who conceived Kore (912); "loved" Mnemosyne, who bore the Muses (915); and "joined in passion" with Leto, Semele, and Alkmene (920, 940, 944), who produced Apollo, Artemis, Dionysos, and Herakles. The amours of Poseidon, Ares, Hephaistos, Dionysos, and Helios follow (930-962; cf. no. 113), then goddesses who mated with mortal men: Demeter with Iasion, Harmonia with Kadmos, Kallirhoe with Chrysaor, Eos with Memnon and Kephalos, Thetis "subject to" Peleus, Kirke and Kalypso with Odysseus, and so on (963-1020; see figs. 3 and 4, nos. 106-110, 121, 131, and 133).

A bridge passage then leads into a second epic, now preserved only in fragments: the so-called *Catalogue of Women*. Taking its cue from the *Iliad* and *Theogony*, it sang of those mortal women who caught the gods' attention and celebrated their heroic offspring: Eurynome and Poseidon (Bellerophon), Europa and Zeus (Minos, Sarpedon, Rhadamanthys), and so on. It included long digressions on Atalanta (nos. 117-119), the Argonauts, and others, then continued by way of a lengthy reprise of Zeus' passion for Alkmene to yet another epic, the *Aspis*. This related the exploits of Alkmene's son Herakles and gave an extended description of his shield, based on Homer's account of Achilles' great shield in Book 18 of the *Iliad*.[11]

The *Catalogue* and *Aspis* were composed around 600-550 by Hesiod's imitators, but along with the *Theogony* they offered a comprehensive panorama of divine and heroic sexual activity that no rivals could match. Meanwhile, others had taken up the theme. The *Homeric Hymn to Apollo* recounted the god's progress from insatiable womanizer (fig. 1) to panhellenic deity; the *Hymn to Aphrodite* constructed a theology of divine-mortal love, and investigated the complexities of a goddess' passion for a man (cf. figs. 3

and 4); Stesichoros sang of Europa and Helen; Sappho of the loves of Aphrodite, Eos (figs. 3 and 4), and Selene; the *Theseis* of those of Theseus, the Amazon queen included;[12] and their rivals and successors of yet others. Finally, around 450, Herodotos represented the origins of the Persian wars as a series of tit-for-tat abductions of Io, Europa, Medea, and Helen. The metaphors of pursuit and flight first appear in Sappho and thereafter swiftly become commonplace, as do those of hunter and quarry.[13]

In face of this awesome palimpsest of primeval promiscuity, and the fact that myth is usually thought to have furnished the Greeks' blueprint for reality,[14] it is a relief to find that in ancient Athens the *crime* of rape is almost invisible. Among the scores of trials known to us from forensic speeches and other texts, there is not one case of it. For evidence about its very existence one has to turn to indirect sources like tragic drama, where the plot often turns upon what Walter Burkert[15] has aptly called this "girl's tragedy," or New Comedy, where Menander based several of his plays on the fate of a child thus conceived, and on one occasion vividly described the victim's terror and dishevelment. Yet tragedy deals only with gods and heroes, and like their modern equivalents, the TV sitcoms, Menander's plots are by no means straightforward reflections of normal everyday life.[16]

Even classical Athenian law on rape is problematic—as one would expect when Greek had no single word for it. For like most premodern societies the Athenians tended to treat adultery, seduction, *and rape* as property offences against the woman's male guardian (*kyrios*), but then went one stage further, implicitly defining them as potentially contaminating the city itself. Once again the central issue was not consent—the forcible violation of a woman's body—but the damage done to a citizen's honor, estate, and bloodline if his unmarried daughter or sister lost her virginity or his wife got pregnant by another man. Not surprisingly, if he caught the offender in the act and killed him, the law held him blameless. Loss of face apart, in the first case he would find it almost impossible to marry the girl off, compelling him either to offer a lavish dowry to attract the undiscriminating or (failing this) to maintain her in home-bound spinsterhood for ever; and in the second the paternity of his existing and future children would be besmirched. If they were male, a charge of bastardy could result in their exclusion from citizenship and all its benefits, including both owning real propery and inheriting it; if female, their marriage prospects would be drastically reduced. Indeed, after Perikles' citizenship law of 451 (see below) no Athenian citizen could legally marry a bastard in any circumstances.

Abduction (*harpage*) of a woman, boy, or slave (cf. figs. 1-8) was not strictly speaking an offense, but illicit sex with them was, and could be prosecuted under three heads: *moicheia*, *biasmos*, and *hybris*. *Moicheia* was adultery, and a public action against the offender could be brought by any concerned citizen, for the crime corrupted the state too, by potentially insinuating bastards into the citizen body.[17] If the woman's husband caught the adulterer in the act he could legally kill him, or if he got him convicted he could beat him up with impunity. He then had to divorce his wife or lose his citizen rights (for any future children would be suspect), and she was banned from public religious ceremonies on pain of physical punishment short of death.[18]

Though rapists could also be killed with impunity if caught in the act, unlike adulterers they could be prosecuted under two different statutes, both of which covered other offences too. A charge of *biasmos* or "assault" treated forcible rape as simple battery; only the woman's *kyrios* could bring the prosecution, and the penalty was monetary; indeed some argue that its whole point was precisely to recover damages in order to cover the victim's increased dowry or her living expenses should the effort to find a husband fail.[19] A charge of *hybris* or "outrage," on the other hand, highlighted the shame and dishonor done to both the victim and her family, though this term covered an even wider variety of transgressions than *biasmos*, from verbal abuse to mugging. Since Greek men were most protective of their women, jealously guarded their modesty, and were easily enraged by insulting behavior to them, *hybris* was a serious offence and could be fatal for the perpetrator.[20] Yet there is no certain case of prosecution of sexual offences under this law, and some have argued that it may never have been employed to this purpose.

On such uncertain evidence it is obviously hazardous to speculate about the incidence of rape of free women in classical Athens. It has always been a notoriously underreported crime, and the tortuous, shame-filled circumlocutions of raped and seduced women in Attic drama suggests that this society was no exception.[21] Indeed, given the potentially catastrophic social consequences of extramarital sex for everyone concerned, one suspects that most citizen families would probably have done virtually anything to hush it up.

Yet in modern "face-to-face" Mediterranean societies, rapes are infrequent, usually committed by outsiders, and often only upon women caught alone outside town—like Apollo caught Kreousa (fig. 1). As in antiquity, close-packed living conditions, the honor code, and the stern tribunal of public opinion both closely circumscribe behavior and mandate instant revenge, making rape both extremely risky and virtually impossible to conceal.[22] In Athens, had it been common, one might expect both more prosecutions and more moralizing about it. Athenians were notoriously litigious, and lawsuits were a time-honored way of damaging a bad neighbor or a political opponent. What better way to achieve this than to allege that he had let another man penetrate his house and his wife, and that his children were probably bastards? As for the moralists, aside from occasional remarks to the effect that women in a city overrun by the enemy might well be raped (cf. fig. 8), and universal condemnation of the practice, the only thinker to address the issue of rape in peacetime was Plato. Yet even he devotes only a few lines to it, less than he does to accidental death by mule kick or lightning bolt—which kill men too.[23]

Fig. 3. Eos pursues Kephalos. Detail of an Attic red-figure calyx-krater attributed to the Achilles Painter. Ca. 440. London, British Museum, inv. no. E 463. [*ARV*² 991.55.]

Finally, since all but the poorest could easily satisfy their sexual appetites with a slave or a prostitute, it would be stupid to try to rape a free woman when these were so readily available. A slave's body was her master's property, so he could have sex with her whenever he chose; whores were cheap; and syphilis and AIDS as yet unknown.[24] As Antisthenes (a pupil of Socrates) once shouted after an escaping adulterer, "You idiot, that comes risk-free for an obol!"[25]

Sociologists tend to explain the phenomenon of "low-rape" societies in two ways: gender relations are stable, and/or female authority and power are high.[26] The first was apparently true of archaic and classical Athens, but not the second. Yet Greek attitudes to *hybris* against free women and the other evidence cited above suggest that rape may also be infrequent when *respect* for women is high, their dignity and integrity are vigorously defended by law and custom, and social cohesion is strong. More bleakly, it may be particularly rare when nonpersons like slaves are readily available to satisfy men's sexual desires. So why were erotic pursuits and abductions so popular in fifth-century Athenian vase-painting (figs. 1-9)?

Theories[27]

The basic problem posed by these images and their cognates (same- and opposite-sex courting scenes, explicit erotica, and so on) was succinctly stated by K. J. Dover in 1974: "What enabled the Greeks of the late Archaic and early Classical periods to achieve a considerable rupture of the inhibitions which are manifested in so many cultures and were operative in the early Archaic period? ...

Fig. 4. Eos apprehends Tithonos. Tondo of an Attic red-figure cup from Vulci, attributed to the Penthesileia Painter. Ca. 460. London, British Museum, inv. no. E 72. [ARV² 885.93.]

[For] the latter half of the Classical period seems to have returned to the spirit of Homeric inhibition and patched up a breach which had been opened in the interval." ²⁸

The most comprehensive study of the genre, by Sophia Kaempf-Dimitriadou, appeared five years later. She confined herself to divine amours but both summarized previous attempts to interpret them and suggested some new ones. Classifying them into three types (gods-women; gods-boys; goddesses-boys: figs. 1-6), she correctly stressed their almost complete congruence in both chronology and composition (they begin around 500 and disappear around 430), then looked for motives and meanings. Do they signal that the gods are close in nature to mortals, even all too human at times? Or (since many were found in graves) do they promise the beholder a kind of apotheosis? Or (as she prefers) do they demonstrate divine power to intervene in human affairs, and more specifically, its deployment on occasion for the good of Athens? Finally, when humans struggle against their abductors does this demonstrate the tragedy of the human condition, and when they do not does this indicate that we too should take heart and trust to luck?²⁹

In 1985 Eva Keuls took a much harder line. She saw all the heterosexual scenes as preludes to rape, "dramatizing the power of the male over the female. This is especially true of the story of Zeus and Semele,… which is virtually a mythological blueprint of the relationship between the sexes in Classical Athens. Translated into societal terms, the male has the power, marries at his choice solely for the purposes of reproduction, deprives the female of credit for genetic motherhood, and destroys her."³⁰ Yet not only may one doubt that all or even most Athenian men married solely for the purposes of reproduction, that most Greek thinkers derided the female contribution to genetics, and that Athenians made a habit of "destroying" their wives, but this explanation could apply to any traditional, patriarchal society, and does not explain why this particular imagery was popular at this particular place and time.³¹

The following year, but too soon to address Keuls' work, Froma Zeitlin also questioned Kaempf-Dimitriadou's conclusions. As she remarks, "all [her] suggestions immediately displace this show of sexual energy to the metaphorical plane as exemplifying the profound cultural energy of this momentous historical period."³² Wondering even so whether they "address some new concern with human sexuality," she concludes that "there is no way to read with certainty these scenes that symbolize both a threat and a promise and hesitate between public and private motives."³³ More positively, she observes that they are commonest around 500-470, just like explicit heterosexual lovemaking scenes (in fact, Table 1 shows that the pursuits peak somewhat *after* 470); at this time too, Maenads in Dionysiac scenes begin to resist the advances of Satyrs. After the mid fifth century, though, a more tranquil mood takes over, the explicitly erotic pictures disappear, and the pursuits become elopements, suggesting that "the combativeness of the erotic style that enjoys a certain limited run may perhaps be seen as a transitional point between a more unfettered sexuality to one that stresses love over lust."³⁴

In 1987 Christiane Sourvinou-Inwood presented a semiotic and structuralist version of Keuls' thesis, focusing on the young man or ehpehe who pursues a girl on numerous vases (no. 121, fig. 7). Agreeing with Sir John Beazley that he is probably Theseus, she also stressed the sexual violence of the theme. An ancient precursor of the *Taming of the Shrew*, it documents the girl's forcible conversion from unmarried parthenos to wedded woman. Specifically, it characterizes her as "a wild thing to be pursued and captured and tamed through marriage; the violence of the wrenching of a girl from her familiar world and transfer to an unfamiliar one and to the jurisdiction of a strange man; the subduing of the female by the male—an important Greek notion which is itself a polysemic signifier articulating other values; and defloration and the sexual relationship as acts of physical domination of the woman. Thus the metaphorical relationship between erotic pursuit and marriage also expresses the notion that the acculturated form of marriage which belongs to civilized society also contains within it the wild marriage to which on the surface it appears to be contrasted."³⁵

More recent work has advanced the debate only marginally. Sourvinou-Inwood has refined her thesis in two further essays and in a collection of essays called *Pornography and Representation in Greece and Rome* (a question-begging title), edited by Amy Richlin, Alan Shapiro offers a nuanced reconsideration of same-sex abductions, based partly on Kaempf-Dimitriadou and Zeitlin.³⁶ Robert Sutton also briefly addresses the late fifth-century tendency to convert these scenes into elopements (figs. 5 and 6), remarking perceptively that since they usually appear on women's vases, they may have been deliberately re-crafted for the female gaze. "Directed, like today's popular romances and romantic films, at a mass feminine audience, [they] may also have been a means by which ancient women were able to grapple with and transcend the cares of their existence."[37]

Finally, Robin Osborne has taken up the theme of female erotic pursuit, represented on these vases by the winged Eos (figs. 3 and 4) in an essay entitled "Desiring Women on Athenian Pottery."[38] In it, he argues that Eos' wings characterize female desire as both evanescent and un-human, and concludes that "in limiting scenes of female pursuit to the case of the winged Eos, pot painters were able both to suggest that women *did* desire men and to suggest that female desire could not be active in the real world. [So]... by playing with the contexts in which they showed Eos' pursuit, painters presented the sexual desire of Eos as socially threatening, like the excess of the Satyr, and as potentially overpowering for men (like Helen). [Although] the development of this imagery may well have no implications for the history of sexual relations, and ... it shows little interest in female sexual desire as such, insisting on female desire could be construed as justifying aggressive male sexuality." The case of Eos, in other words, proves the rule: far from offering a serious challenge to the paradigm, it merely reinforces it.

Work and Play, Gods and Mortals

Before commenting on these proposals, what of the pictures themselves (cf. figs. 1-7)? First, they uniformly contrast the would-be rapist's eagerness with the victim's reluctance. Interestingly, the Greeks often conceptualized the difficult transition to adulthood as a forced abduction (*harpage*). Mythological exemplars like Ganymede and Thetis (nos. 106-108 and 121) apart, testimonia to this range from the complex Cretan rituals of homosexual rape, through Plutarch's explicit statement that the Spartan marriage was a kind of abduction, to the Athenian groom's gesture of grasping the bride by her wrist.[39] In figs. 1 and 7, as the intruder bursts into the girl's closed, presexual world she raises one or both hands in shock and repugnance—a gesture which, ironically, opens her body to the rapist's advance. At the prospect of offspring-producing "work," her proverbial wantonness and lust for erotic "play" has abruptly disappeared.[40] Even though several of the myths ended with her acquiescence, consent is not an issue—unless the backward glance hints that sexual curiosity is beginning to win out. The Greeks were well aware of the erotic power of the glance, and especially of its tendency to inflame the desire of both parties alike.[41]

Yet the male's lack of an erection, his frequent characterization as a hunter, and the omission of Eros suggest that on these occasions his main aim is not sex *per se* but the girl's capture and acculturation—even though he often brandishes a branch, trident, or spear suggestively across his groin (no. 121, figs. 1 and 7). Contrast the bestial, lecherous, and perpetually horny Satyrs, whose sole aim is pleasure, and whose customary fate is frustration (fig. 10). In this way the painter tries to mask the contradiction that underlies the whole genre, namely, that although the man ostensibly wants to acculturate his prey, chasing frightened women for sex is countercultural, an eruption of the bestial in himself. Growing Athenian sensitivity to this issue is evidenced by the fact that just as the fash-

Fig. 5. The Dioskouroi abduct the Leukippidai. Drawing by Karl Reichhold of an Attic red-figure hydria attributed to the Meidias Painter. Ca. 410. London, British Museum, inv. no. E 224. [*ARV²* 1313.5.]

Fig. 6. Kastor abducts Eriphyle. Detail of the hydria in figure 5.

Rape illustrates the gods' power not only to take any woman they want, but unfailingly to produce splendid offspring from the union. As Poseidon said after raping the hapless Tyro in her sleep,

> You can be happy, woman, in our love
> even as this year turns, you will give birth
> to splendid children: matings of the gods
> are never barren. Care for—tend—your sons
> Go home, keep silent, tell no-one; but know
> Your lover was Poseidon, god of tremors.[45]

Of course, gods never chose mortal women randomly, but because of their intelligence, beauty, courage, or breeding—their fitness, in other words, to be mothers. Evolutionary biologists should approve.[46] Furthermore, these unions were confined to a fixed period in world history, and were spectacularly successful: they created the heroic age, and when they ceased, so did the race of heroes. Thereafter, gods and men were permanently separated by the will of Zeus, and the Race of Iron began. The turning-point was Peleus' match with Thetis (nos. 106-108 and 121). Their wedding (nos. 109 and 110) was the last occasion when gods and men feasted together, and the permanent separation of the two races and the decline of that of the heroes—all willed by Zeus—is already a fact in the *Iliad*.[47]

Indeed, Zeus often had still wider goals in mind. For example, he intended Hades' abduction of Persephone and her return to earth every six months (no. 82) to link the infernal and upper worlds: this is one theme of the *Homeric Hymn to Demeter*. For this and other reasons, both she and Demeter accepted it in the end.[48] He also pre-destined many heroes to found cities—a mission of intense interest to late Archaic and early Classical Greeks. Hekataios of Miletos, Hellanikos of Lesbos, and Pherekydes of Athens all discussed these foundations extensively in prose, and Pindar's odes are often structured around the founding hero of the victorious athlete's city and his exploits. Recently, scholars have argued that these rapes drama-tize the violence inherent in colonization, city-founding, and con-stitutional change, and reveal the conflicts generated by the exclusion of women from citizenship and the political process.[49] Athens itself was refounded in mythical times by Ion, the product of Apollo's rape of Kreousa (fig. 1) who eventually became the eponymous hero of the Ionians as his descendants spread across the Aegean.[50] The Athenians also founded many colonies in the late sixth and fifth centuries, not all of them successful, and in 478 chose Apollo's shrine at Delos as the center of their new Aegean alliance, the Delian League.

Not only did such divine lineage bring much honor upon cities, but it could pay unexpected dividends.[51] In Athens one particular abductor, Boreas, the god of the north wind (fig. 2), turned out to be a potent ally before Marathon and again during the Persian inva-sion of 480:

ion for these scenes was taking hold, around 500-475, Maenads turn from welcoming or at least tolerating the Satyrs' advances to active resistance or flight, exactly as in fig. 1.[42]

The gods have no interest in acculturation: all they want is a one-night stand. This suggests that, though the format is the same what-ever the protagonist's status (no. 121, figs. 1 and 7), for the moment at least the two races might profitably be kept apart. The Greeks were well aware that the divine world operated by a different logic from their own, for immortals have few cares about the future and none about death. Though familiar in their humanity, and even ridiculous or pitiable on occasion, the gods nevertheless remain a race apart: separated from mankind by the ritual of sacrifice, often inscrutable and capricious, and "in a certain sense the polar con-trast to man...related [to him] as type and antitype."[43] As Ion com-plains in Euripides' play of that name, referring to Apollo's rape of Kreousa (fig. 1) and using the formal terminology of the *dike biaion*,

> I must rebuke Apollo:
> What's wrong with him? He rapes young girls, and then
> takes off? He fathers children secretly,
> then lets them die? Phoibos, not you! Pursue
> the good, O mighty one! For if a man
> commits a crime, the gods exact their due.
> So is it just that you, who write the laws
> for men, incur the charge of lawlessness?
> Suppose—just let's hypothesize, no more—
> that you pay up for every rape you've done,
> Poseidon, you, and Zeus the Lord of Heaven.
> Your crimes would gut the temple treasuries![44]

It is said that the Athenians had asked Boreas to aid the Greeks because of a new oracle that had reached them, commanding them to "seek help from their son-in-law." For Boreas, according to Greek legend, had abducted and married a woman of Attica, Oreithyia daughter of Erechtheus. So the Athenians, reckoning that this marriage made Boreas their son-in-law, and seeing, while they lay with their ships at Chalkis in Euboia, that the wind was rising, or perhaps even before it freshened, sacrificed to Boreas and Oreithyia, entreating them to come to their aid and to destroy the ships of the barbarians, as they had done once before off Mount Athos. Whether it was owing to this that Boreas fell with violence on the barbarians at their anchorage, I cannot say; but the Athenians declare that they had received aid from Boreas before, and that it was he who had now caused all these events. So when they returned home they built a temple to him on the banks of the Ilissos.[52]

Boreas blew in from Thrace, an area where Athenian colonization was particularly intense, and it was to Thrace that he had abducted Oreithyia. Predictably, this event first appeared on Attic red-figured vases in the 470s, and (though skeptics explained it away as simply a tragic accident in a high wind) it remained popular into the second half of the century (fig. 2). Likewise Eos' abduction of Kephalos (fig. 3): the offspring of Hermes' rape of the Athenian princess Herse and a formidable hunter, he married Oreithyia's sister Prokris, but Eos seduced him even so. (Aphrodite had cursed her with everlasting nymphomania after catching her in Ares' bed.) Though not as politically-charged as the Boreas-Oreithyia story, that of Kephalos was no doubt popular largely because of his Athenian roots. The two are paired on a stamnos of the 460s in Karlsruhe.[53]

As mentioned earlier, it was Zeus who ordained the culminating act of divine-human intercourse, Peleus's union with Thetis (nos. 106-108 and 121). This encounter broke all the rules, for in the past any mortal who had tried to rape a goddess had always come to a sticky end. Ixion, for example, was sentenced to spin on the wheel for eternity for thus assaulting Hera (a classic case of *hybris* or *biasmos*). Yet as already explained, Peleus was heaven's instrument. His wedding (nos. 109 and 110) not only provided the occasion for the last joint feast of gods and men, but also sparked the disastrous argument among Hera, Athena, and Aphrodite as to who was the fairest. This event and its consequences were narrated in a now-lost seventh-century epic by Stasinos of Miletos, the *Kypria*. Zeus had Eris ("Strife") throw down a golden apple inscribed "for the fairest;" Paris was called in to judge the case; Aphrodite bribed him by offering him Helen, the wife of the Spartan king Menelaos and the fairest woman on earth; he seduced and eloped with her (the prototypical case of *moicheia*); and so began the Trojan War. Meanwhile, Thetis had given birth to none other than Achilles, the "best of the Achaeans."[54]

Yet in the final analysis this encounter too was a power-play, dramatizing male dominance and phallic potency at women's expense, all under the guise of "taming" a wild *parthenos* into recognizing male superiority and better judgment, and giving her a child who would become the greatest hero of all. As Christiane Sourvinou-Inwood has justly noted,[55] Thetis' desperate attempts at metamorphosis both articulate the wild animality of the *parthenos* in narrative terms and dramatize her rage at this humiliation. By chronicling her forced passage from nature to culture, from Artemis' wild domain via the marriage-bed of Aphrodite to the domesticity of Hera and Hestia, these pictures become paradigms for mortal marriage, symbolizing the bride's reluctance to abandon her life of "play" for the offspring-producing "work" of conjugal sex. On the Niobid Painter's great Naples krater (no. 121) these issues are doubly underscored by pairing the theme with a picture of a young hunter pursuing a girl, and subordinating them both to a magnificent panorama of the defeat of the Amazons. For Amazon society was the exact converse of the civilized polis, the classic case of female dominance (*gynaikokrateia*) where women ruled, fought, and mated at their own convenience, heedless and disdainful of men and their society.[56]

Perhaps the most compelling treatment of Thetis' rape is on Peithinos' splendid cup in Berlin (no. 106), where the hero doggedly clasps her in an iron grip, trying to lift her bodily into the air. Yet Peithinos was not content to stop there. Not only is his name pro-

Fig. 7. Youth (Theseus?) pursues a woman. Detail of an Attic red-figure hydria from Nola, attributed to the Niobid Painter. Ca. 460. London, British Museum, inv. no. E 198. [*ARV*² 606.79.]

Fig. 8. Lokrian Ajax drags Kassandra from the Palladion. Detail of a red-figure cup signed by Euphronios as maker and attributed to the painter Onesimos. Ca. 490. Malibu, J. Paul Getty Museum, inv. no. 83.AE.362. [*Add* 404.]

grammatic (it means "Mr. Persuasion"), but on the exterior of his cup he assembled two groups of men passionately courting boys in a gymnasium on one side, and more shyly "chatting up" young women on the other. Since he signed at least one other vase, he surely chose these scenes to illustrate his personal credo rather than adopted a nickname to fit them. They have attracted some interest of late, as scholars have attempted to unravel the overall message of the ensemble.

Unhesitatingly identifying the young women as courtesans or *hetairai*, Eva Keuls argues that it "contrasts extra-marital sex, based on negotiation and free will, with marital sex based on compulsion."[57] Robert Sutton, on the other hand, thinks that "the total message is something like 'Woo girls with sweetness, and boys more directly, but force may be needed to subdue an unwilling nobler bride and sire a son like Achilles."[58] This tacitly recognizes that although Peithinos' women are clearly not slaves, they offer no further clues at all as to their status; purses and other signs of mercenary sex are conspicuously absent. Instead, one offers her partner a flower (in the flower of her youth, she is giving it to him to pluck), and all three are heavily draped and bow their heads—the classic sign of female modesty or *aidos*. Since even in the contemporary scenes of explicit lovemaking the status of many of the women is problematic,[59] Peithinos' studied reticence clearly invites us to suspend judgment. If he had thought it important to identify actors or venue, he would no doubt have done so: not social commentary but courtship ritual is his theme, and is appropriately served by the elegant refinement and fastidious delicacy of his style. Quite possibly he is simply contrasting violent, heroic-style abduction with his own culture's reliance on persuasion, not force: Peitho, the goddess of persuasion, was indispensable to Greek weddings, and was often included in courtship pictures.[60] The point would then be: "Force may have been acceptable—even necessary—back then, but isn't now"—a message echoed a generation later in Aischylos' *Danaids* trilogy, where the flower-plucking metaphor occurs several times.[61] And Athenian literature regularly portrays men as primarily lusting after boys, and women as sexually insatiable. Peithinos, however, treats both sexes' desires with the same fastidious delicacy as he does their bodies and clothing.

Peithinos' cup takes us into the mortal realm. Yet contrary to what one might expect from Greek mythology and the remarks of recent critics, on the vases only one hero frequently chases after women: Theseus. From his many amatory exploits[62] the painters selected three: his abductions of Antiope[63] and Helen, and his pursuit of an unnamed girl sometimes identified as Periboia (no. 121, fig. 7—if the man is indeed he). Eight scenes of the Dioskouroi abducting the Leukippidai (figs. 5 and 6), three dozen of Ajax son of Oileus dragging Kassandra from Athena's statue at the sack of Troy (fig. 8), and numerous anonymous pursuits complete the roster (fig. 7). Herakles' endless amatory adventures are ignored in favor of his role as the protector of women and scourge of rapists (fig. 9).

Theseus' abduction of Antiope has been plausibly explained as a forced rectification of the Amazons' antisocial attitudes about marriage; it turned out happily since she came to accept her new situation and even fought on his side against her sisters when they attacked Athens in revenge.[64] Attic artists became interested in it when their Ionian compatriots fell under Persian rule in the late sixth century and especially after their own navy sacked Sardis, the Persian provincial capital of Ionia, in 499; the Amazon counterattack appears shortly after the Persian invasion of 480 and the victories of Salamis and Plataia.

As for his abduction of Helen, which he and Peirithoos carried out together, the texts often pair this with their attempt on Persephone (which is never shown in vase-painting).[65] The two heroes thus tried for the grand prize in both sublunary worlds: earth's most beautiful woman and the queen of Hades. Yet since Helen was prepubescent at the time, and the two got four years' incarceration in Hades for the attempt on Persephone (according to some, Peirithoos was kept there for eternity), this pair of stories perhaps belongs among those cautionary tales whose moral is the Delphic maxim of "nothing to excess."[66]

The Theseus "Periboia" pictures (no. 121, fig. 7) have been exhaustively analyzed by Christiane Sourvinou-Inwood, whose views I summarized above. Unfortunately only three are actually inscribed with Theseus' name, and on one of these his quarry is impossibly named Thetis. Seventy-nine others look sufficiently like them for Sir John Beazley (1968) to have suggested that the protagonist is also Theseus (though he left fifteen more unassigned), and Sourvinou-Inwood emphatically agrees.[67] Yet since the three inscribed versions are relatively late in the series, the unnamed youth may still be a generic ephebe later conflated with the insatiable Athenian. The theme was popular from ca. 475-425, supplanting the abductions of Helen and Antiope in the repertoire. A political motive has been alleged, for the Philaid clan claimed descent from Periboia, and Kimon, who dominated Athenian politics from the mid-470s to his death in 459, was a Philaid.[68]

The abduction of the Leukippidai by the Dioskouroi, on the other hand, was part of a vendetta between the twins and their cousins the Aphareids; a very ancient tale, it also resulted in marriage.[69] At Athens, it too could have carried political weight, since the Dioskouroi were Spartans and the Aphareids Messenians. Under Kimon, Athens helped the Spartans against the Messenian revolt of 462 but Spartan suspicions of Athenian radicalism soon got them sent home. This move backfired, for as relations between the two states worsened, the Athenians and Messenians found themselves increasingly allied, and in 425 jointly defeated the Spartans at Pylos. Around 410, however, the Meidias Painter converted the theme into something more like an idyllic elopement (figs. 5 and 6), surely, as Sutton has argued, to cater to the interests of a female clientele.[70]

Finally, Ajax's assault on Kassandra (the most beautiful of Priam's daughters) during the sack of Troy was roundly condemned as sacrilege—though in the tradition that was current through the Classical period he stopped short of actually raping her in the sanctuary. This was apparently a Hellenistic invention.[71] Agamemnon then claimed her and took her back as his concubine to Mycenae, where they both perished at the hands of the vengeful Clytemnestra. The scene was quite popular around the time of the Ionian Revolt (which ended with the sack of Miletos in 494) and the Persian invasions that followed. Vases like Onesimos' great cup in Malibu (fig. 8) emphasize Ajax's *hybris* and Kassandra's eventual fate by showing her proleptically nude and vulnerable, clinging to Athena's statue; the goddess, in turn, brandishes her spear menacingly at him, but to no avail. Following Homer, Attic tragedy often drew the parallel between penetrating a city and raping or killing a virgin, using Kassandra as one of its prime examples.[72]

Contemporary Horizons

If these scenes spoke to current issues in any way, then their immediate referent was surely located in the realm of human sexual relations, not in the remoter areas of politics, religion, or philosophical speculations about the human condition. Greek art was nothing if not direct, even though the Greeks were perfectly capable of teasing almost infinite subtleties of signification out of its products. So those who interpret this imagery as an articulation of sexual power are surely right: the Niobid Painter's krater (no. 121) virtually proves the case on its own. This does not entail, however, that all they say about the "meaning" of these pictures is acceptable or sufficient.

In particular, the Greek view that unmarried girls or parthenoi were wild animals to be hunted and wrenched from the realm of

Artemis into those of Aphrodite, Hera, and Hestia, and that patrilocal marriage was a kind of abduction, may well help to explain why late sixth- and early fifth-century Athenians liked these particular images.[73] Yet if so, why (for example) were they acceptable if rape was a crime that shamed both parties alike, and brought death or severe injury to the rapist if he were caught? Why is the latter usually characterized as a beardless ehpehe (no. 121, figs. 1 and 7) when Athenian men actually grew beards in their late teens and married around 30? Why were these images popular only at this particular time? And why do same-sex abduction scenes follow exactly the same popularity curve and heterosexual lovemaking scenes describe a fairly similar one?

Once again, it is necessary to stress that these pictures are fantasies, not representations of reality. Athenian men normally married around thirty, but a bearded man pursuing a girl young enough to be his daughter would look ridiculous, even criminal. Yet an ephebe could play the part perfectly, for having yet to reach full maturity he could plausibly be represented as both more susceptible to erotic desire and less able to control it; for during his schooling for citizenship he was the socially marginalized individual and hunter par excellence, a devotee of Artemis and the converse of the mature citizen hoplite.[74] Indeed, as remarked earlier, his lack of an erection, hunting garb, and the omission of Eros all suggest that what he really seeks is not sex *per se* but the girl's capture and acculturation (no. 121, figs. 1 and 7). And given the Greeks' firm belief in eugenics, it was in every girl's interest to select the first in the chase to marry her.

All this makes the displacement easy to understand, but warns us about accepting these pictures either as simple metaphors of male dominance over recalcitrant females, or even more reductively as "ideal representations of normal wedding scenes."[75] Painted by and usually for Athenian men, and dramatizing both the chasm that divides the sexes and the male domination that will eventually unite them, they betray their clientele's anxieties about sexual desire and its outcome. For the pursuer usually has yet to succeed in grabbing his prey or is barely doing so (no. 121, figs. 1 and 7), while she always turns her head back to look him in the eye—suggesting a conflict in the attitudes of both parties alike. As Anne Carson aptly remarks in another context: "The reach of desire is defined in action: beautiful (in its object), foiled (in its attempt), endless (in time)."[76]

Greek women poets like Sappho and Erinna confirm this ambivalence, seeing patrilocal marriage as both a painful dislocation *and* the triumph of a lifetime.[77] Most Athenian girls would probably have agreed, for their fathers usually married them off as soon as possible after puberty; many of them would have had their first child at age fifteen or sixteen. This practice was driven by ideology, not ignorance: the Greeks were keenly aware that teenage pregnancies are not only dangerous for the mother but produce more defective and unhealthy children, but only the Spartans turned knowledge into action, postponing betrothal until after eighteen.[78] No wonder that in no. 121 the girl takes to her heels so fast, and is paired with Thetis and the Amazons!

Yet by their very choice of the imagery of pursuit, abduction, and military victory (no. 121), the Niobid painter and his fellows dismiss feminine reluctance as misguided and irrelevant. Since a girl is too immature to know that male domination is good for her, she will inevitably try to elude it, succumbing only after a struggle whose result is a foregone conclusion. Her backward gaze may anticipate this outcome, perhaps signalling her awakening erotic interest in her pursuer, her realization that the first in the chase should be the best mate. Furthermore, not only must she eventually participate in a formal marriage ceremony (nos. 55-57, 109, and 110), but Greek folk wisdom and the medical theory based upon it asserted that to become pregnant, she must have an orgasm. Only thus would her cervix close and the seed be retained. Indeed, to maximize their chances of a perfect child, both husband and wife were best advised to reach climax together.[79] So for a man to obtain his desired son and heir, not only should he eventually win an immature and frightened girl's consent, but actually bring her to ecstasy too, preferably at exactly the right moment. To illustrate the power of these beliefs, it is worth recalling that they persisted as medical dogma into the eighteenth century and are by no means dead today, as any reader of newspaper advice columns will know.[80]

In these circumstances an Athenian bridegroom's anxiety about his performance must often have been considerable. Even if—like Apollo in Aischylos' *Eumenides*—he thought these notions were only old wives' tales, he still had to consider whether he could afford to take chances.[81] Contemplated from this perspective, this imagery takes on a completely new cast, not only applauding the man's prowess and glorifying his conquest, but simultaneously betraying his fears as well. The Athenian fascination with divine amours is relevant here (nos. 111-115), as are the numerous fifth-century scenes of weddings or less formal reconciliations afterward, regularly attended by Erotes who sometimes crown both bride and groom (nos. 109, 110, and 116). For all reek of masculine wish-fulfilment: gods inevitably sire perfect children, and the Erotes promise equal dividends for mortals too.

Furthermore, since fifth-century Athenians saw the male body as microcosm, metathesis, and manager of the social order of their polis, and were much concerned with the purity and potency of its citizen stock, these fears were of very public interest. When Thucydides and others boasted of Athenian autochthony, or a youth turning eighteen (figs. 3, 4, and 7) swore the ephebes' oath that he would hand his fatherland on to his sons larger and better than he received it, then they were inheriting a strong obligation to safeguard and improve the quality of Athens' human resources. Conversely, any action that a man took that compromised this goal was by definition unpatriotic and in violation of the oath.[82]

Perikles' citizenship law of 451 codified these beliefs. This extraordinary piece of legislation, which has no known precedent in Greek legal practice, stipulated that "no-one should share in the city who was not born of native Athenians on both sides." Perikles thereby defined *any* union between Athenians and foreigners, both Greek and barbarian, as concubinage and its offspring as bastards. By so doing, he proclaimed that Athens' citizen body was now one big, endogamous family. Henceforth, only pure Athenians would share in the benefits of citizenship and thus of empire.[83] Seen in this light, the latest of our vases (e.g., no. 121, figs. 1 and 7) now acquire a solidly political dimension: with external threats growing, they signal the urgency of creating and maintaining a pure-bred imperial elite.

Classical Athens: A "Reign of the Phallus"?

Yet none of this explains why this imagery of pursuit and abduction suddenly became popular in Athens when it did and all but disappeared only three or so generations later. Any explanation must cover both its divine and human dimensions; ideally, it should also cover homoerotic scenes of the same type, which describe the same trajectory.[84] It should also be sensitive to the context for which most of these pictures were painted: the male drinking-party or symposium, with its strong erotic content, propensity to seek release in sexual diversions (both verbal and physical), and central importance in Athenian society as a mirror of the polis itself.[85] The following suggestions come to mind:

1. Sexual: A shift in sexual mores that widened the distance between Athenian men and the objects of their desire.

2. Literary: The appearance of a poem or poems that treated these stories, and gave them wide currency.

3. Socio-political: A change in the status and/or aspirations of Athenian men that was mapped onto the symposiasts' sexual landscape.

Concerning the first, we have no *direct* information about any radical shift in sexual mores in the late sixth century. We do not know, for example, when Athenian men began to believe that strict segregation for women, early marriage for girls, and an ostentatious unresponsiveness by boys to men's public advances were desirable and praiseworthy. Sex-segregation is deep-rooted in traditional Mediterranean societies, but female *seclusion* only appears as families grow wealthier and servants take over jobs like farmwork, shopping, laundry, and drawing water from the well. Even then, the gap between ideal and reality remains wide, for all sorts of occasions from religious festivals to visits to friends and relations play havoc with the rules. Our evidence for ancient Athens suggests that the pattern there was little different.[86] As for early teenage marriage, though the texts cited in the previous section date only from the later Classical period, there is no evidence that Athenian practice during the sixth century was any different from the fifth.[87]

Fig. 9. Herakles, the Centaur Eurytion, and Deidameia. Detail of a red-figure stamnos from Sorrento, signed by Polygnotos as painter. Ca. 440. London, BM 98.7-16.5. [*ARV²* 1027 no. 2.]

What of literature? Though the appearance of the *Theseis* probably ignited the explosion of Theseus scenes in Attic art around this time,[88] the only poetic genres that surveyed the entire sexual landscape were the epics and the new art of Attic tragedy, supposedly invented by Thespis in 534. Yet epic can hardly have arrived in Athens this late, the meager fragments of early tragedy offer little help, and the sympotic genres of elegiac and iambic poetry seem to ignore mythology almost entirely.[89] Aischylos, for example, wrote an *Ixion*, a *Europa*, and an *Oreithyia*, but the first dealt with a story that only appears in art in relation to Ixion's punishment; the second revolved around the death of Europa's son Sarpedon; and the third probably celebrated the founding of Boreas' cult (see Herodotos' account, above), and so probably paralleled rather than inspired the efforts of the vase-painters (fig. 2)—whose pictures are in any case hardly suffused with tragic sensibility. He also wrote a Satyr-play *Amymone*, but since the painted Amymone scenes (nos. 111-116) begin earlier and include no Satyrs, they probably had nothing to do with it.[90] In any case, art is much less often a simple response to literature than an independent manifestation of cultural symbolism: the two are more like cousins than parent and child.

This brings us to current events: the fall of the Peisistratid tyranny in 510 and the momentous social and political upheavals that followed. Between Solon's reforms in 594/3 and the archonship of Kleisthenes in 508/7, Athenians had become impatient with the endless power-struggles among the elite, of which the tyranny was the logical outcome. This impatience must have grown considerably during the latter years of the tyranny (especially as Hippias' rule harshened after Harmodios and Aristogeiton killed his brother Hipparchos in 514) and exploded in fury during the popular revolutions of 510-507. By eliminating regional power-bases and

giving the people of the city (his own district) greater leverage, Kleisthenes' reforms radically shifted the balance of power in the ordinary citizen's favor, and other legislation, culminating in the fully democratic constitution of Ephialtes and Perikles in 462, cemented the change.[91] By then, the newly energized city had beaten off invaders from several quarters, both Greek and Persian; had become Greece's leading power; and had begun to transform its Aegean alliance into an empire. Since most of these pictures occur on vases made for the symposium, an institution that had always been a crucible of Athenian homosociality and was now apparently becoming increasingly "democratized" in its turn,[92] could they be erotic metaphors for these bold, far-reaching, and extraordinarily successful acts of citizen self-assertion?

Louis Gernet and Jean-Pierre Vernant have even argued for a "marriage crisis" in Athens around 500, maintaining that Kleisthenes' reforms of 508 and transfer of power from country to city prompted a shift from aristocratic exogamy to citizen endogamy.[93] This is impossible to prove, but if one considers Athenian gender relations from a Greek perspective, as a kind of zero-sum game where one side's gain is another's loss, it is undeniable that Athenian women now increasingly fitted into the city's signifying space in a most awkward way. If the reforms and the consequent demarcation of public space as an exclusively male preserve consolidated a hard-line segregationist ideology in Athens, it is ironic that the revolutions that brought freedom and equality to men brought the opposite, at least in theory, to women. A woman's domain had always been the home, but in post-Kleisthenic Athens, as her menfolk increasingly expanded their claims, she was soon left with nothing else. Even her house was now guarded by the classic signifier of male dominance and citizen equality: the herm with its unindividualized, bearded face and forbiddingly erect phallus. By Perikles' time Athenian women often seem all but invisible behind this grim façade: even their names, he says, should not be spoken in public.[94]

Strict seclusion of this kind was of course yet another male fantasy, unrealized in practice. Yet Kleisthenes' decisive empowerment of Athenian men and its corollary, an increased male commitment to "keeping women in their place," may well have had the effect of sharpening antagonism between the two sexes. Such antagonism is a favorite theme of Classical writers in Athens; indeed, Aristotle even goes so far as to blame the democracy for letting women dominate the home and gossip outside it about their men.[95] For not only did the reforms compel men to spend much more time in the agora, assembly, and lawcourts, but Athens' increasing involvement in military campaigns that took citizens away from home for long periods cannot but have sharpened suspicions on both sides.[96] There was a tradition that Spartan women stoutly resisted Lykourgos' harsh reforms, and it is tempting to wonder whether these vases hint at a similar gender conflict in Early Classical Athens.[97]

Yet though these events and the conflicts they sparked may have heightened Athenian men's interest in this imagery, they cannot

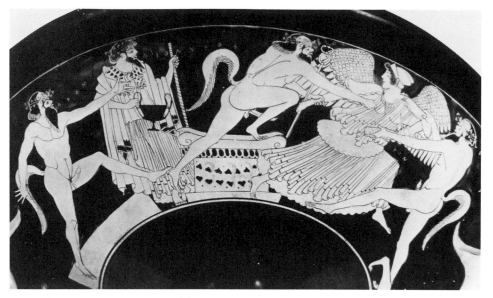

Fig. 10. Three satyrs attempt to rape Iris, while Dionysos looks on. Red-figure cup from Capua, attributed to the Brygos Painter. Ca. 490. London, BM E65. [*ARV²* 370 no. 13.]

themselves have generated it. The relation between art and its context is seldom so straightforward, and this is no exception. For as remarked earlier, these pictures of pursuit and abduction not only begin somewhat earlier than 500 but are embedded in a wider geography of male desire that includes both courtships (of both women and boys) and scenes of explicit sex (with women alone); plotted graphically, they form a series of overlapping bell-curves. Though some examples of each occur both earlier and later, scenes of men courting boys are commonest around 550-500 (no. 106 displays one of the latest); men courting women are most fashionable from ca. 525 to ca. 425 (peaking around 475-450) and effectively bracket the remainder, whose greatest popularity comes at roughly quarter-century intervals. Sex-scenes and heroic pursuits/abductions begin ca. 550 but are most in vogue around 500-475; divine pursuits/abductions peak around 475-450; and ephebic pursuits shortly after 450.

This chronology suggests that the mythological pursuits and abductions represent nothing more nor less than the projection of Athenian male desire first upon the heroic world, and then upon the divine one—or, to put it another way, they mobilize these worlds to promote the cause of Athenian masculine self-assertion. For to adapt a remark by Kaja Silverman, they unabashedly present the circulation of women—whether peaceful or otherwise—as the basic mechanism for defining men as the true embodiments of the social field, and so convey a symbolic privilege upon the male subject.[98] In the present context they enthrone him as an absolutely autonomous yet co-dependent representative of that quintessential "Greek men's club," the Athenian polis.

So by mapping this male bonding upon the sexual landscape, these images perhaps allow us to glimpse the growth of the concept of the self-assertively sovereign Athenian citizen, the *phallos politikos* as Jack Winkler (1990) has aptly termed it. Read in this way, they shamelessly celebrate the ordinary Athenian male's growing confidence in his ability to obtain the object of his desire, whatever it may be. No wonder that many of them precede the momentous events of 510-508, for in some ways these represented the end, not the beginning, of a process: the final, convulsive stage in a chain reaction that had been building for some time.

Since discourse about sex was a prime theme of the symposium, sexual antagonism was a staple of sympotic poetry, and rape is ultimately about male dominance over unwilling females, its metaphorical power in such circumstances is obvious: to this extent, and in the sphere of representation only, these pictures offer some support to Susan Brownmiller's theory of rape as a patriarchal terror tactic.[99] Yet nothing so charged comes without costs: the very fact that these pictures stress female resistance to male control perhaps not only made the hunt seem more exciting to their male audience but implicitly questioned its moral legitimacy in this limiting case.

Eos' abductions of Kephalos and Tithonos (figs. 3 and 4) spotlight the issue by turning it on its head. By showing her pursuing ephebes like those that elsewhere do the chasing, not only do these pictures hint at the evils of *female* dominance (*gynaikokrateia*) and easy capitulation to desire, but nervously evoke their appalling consequence: female control of the phallus. For Homer was explicit that such unions make men "weak and unmanned."[100] Tithonos, for example, wasted away in eternal senescence. The contemporary demand for pictures of the Amazonomachy and their occasional appearance alongside the rapes and abductions (no. 121) may find a place here, for, as explained above, Amazon society was the exact converse of the civilized and male-dominated world of the polis, to be extirpated at all costs.[101]

If the Athenians' rapid construction of a rigorously androcentric—even phallocentric—society indeed stimulated demand for this imagery, then what of its decline after ca. 450? Froma Zeitlin credits a transition to a morality that "stresses love over lust,"[102] but this is to overlook another, related development: the triumph of the classical ethic of self-regulation, summed up in the Greek word *sophrosyne*.

Sophrosyne is the self-knowledge that leads to a measured self-control, a virtue that is conspicuously manifested in such high classical monuments as the Parthenon frieze and the Doryphoros of Polykleitos, both created around 440.[103] In an authoritative monograph published in 1966, Helen North showed how this notion grew from small beginnings in the later sixth century to become the catchword for the age of Perikles and after. Two decades later, Michel Foucault (1985) described the development of classical Greek sexual morality along the same lines, as a matter of self-regulation akin to dietetics. By the fourth century, this species of *sophrosyne* had acquired a name of its own: *enkrateia*, or the establishment of internal control. In the agonistic terminology beloved by the Greeks, the temperate man has fought and won a battle with himself.[104]

In this atmosphere, pursuit, abduction, and rape were acts of self-indulgence akin to gluttony or alcoholism.[105] Indeed, as already explained, the pursuits in no. 121 and fig. 7 had always been a contradiction in terms even within their own semantic field. For whereas they purportedly documented the hard-won conversion of females from nature to culture, the act itself is counter-cultural, a direct expression of the uncivilized and savage in man. Still less should a god succumb to such temptations, as Euripides indignantly reminded his audience in his *Ion* of ca. 410 (quoted above). Furthermore, from the mid-century more and more vases were painted for women, many of whom would hardly want or prize such pictures as figs. 1 and 2 and 5-9. Not surprisingly, then, they were either gradually banished from the "city of images" and confined to the bestial, uncouth, and intemperate Centaurs, as on the south metopes of the Parthenon or the vases of Polygnotos (fig. 9), or sanitized for the female gaze as in figs. 5 and 6. Henceforth, just as Peithinos had forecast (no. 106), in polite society these images were simply no longer acceptable; in effect, they had all but become pornography.

ANDREW STEWART
University of California at Berkeley

Appendix: Heterosexual Pursuits and Abductions in Sixth- and Fifth-Century Attic Vase-painting

Preliminary note: All statistics and identifications are taken from Beazley (1956), (1963), and (1971); his lists include about two-thirds of all known Attic vases. The chronology is rough and ready, for no vases can be exactly dated and the careers of many of his painters overlapped: those who want maximum precision should consult Kaempf-Dimitriadou (1979) 81-109 for Table 1. Beazley's overall picture, however, cannot be far wrong. For black figure, his development is roughly as follows: earliest = ca. 625-575; early = ca. 575-550; mature = 550-525; ripe Archaic = 525-500; latest = ca. 500-475. For red figure, his periods also span roughly a quarter-century each, as follows: early = 525-500; late Archaic = 500-475; early Classical = 475-450; Classical = 450-425; late fifth-century = 425-400.

1. Divine pursuits and abductions:

Date:	625-575	575-550	550-525	525-500	500-475	475-450	450-425	425-400
Total number of vases:	778	752	2343	4478	8819	5115	3754	932
Apollo/woman(1)					4	2	5	2
Boreas/Oreithyia					2	32	6	
Dionysos/Ariadne						1		
Dionysos/woman					1	1		
Dioskouroi/Leukippidai						2	5	1
Eos/Kephalos					5	32	38	1
Eos/Tithonos					4	58	20	
Eos/boy						2		
Eros/woman							6	1
Hades/Persephone						1	1	
Hermes/woman						9	8	
Poseidon/Aithra					4			
Poseidon/Amphitrite						1		
Poseidon/Amymone						3	6	2
Poseidon/woman					3	10	3	
Zephyros/woman						2	1	
Zeus/Aigina						6		
[Zeus]/Europa				2	9	1	7	
Zeus/Io							1	
Zeus/woman					12	21	16	
Totals				2	44	184	123	7

(1) Now often identified as Kreousa: see *LIMC* VI (1992) q.v.

2. Heroic pursuits and abductions:

Date:	625-575	575-550	550-525	525-500	500-475	475-450	450-425	425-400
Total number of vases:	778	752	2343	4478	8819	5115	3754	932
Ajax/Kassandra		1	7	11	5	7	3	
Dioskouroi/Leukippidai						2	5	1
Peleus/Thetis		2	3	30	89	24	3	
Theseus/Antiope				4	4			
Theseus/Helen			2	3	4		1	
Theseus/woman(2)					1	37	45	1
Totals		**3**	**12**	**48**	**103**	**70**	**57**	**2**

(2) But see the text, p. 83, for the argument that most of these scenes are generic.

3. Mortal pursuits: undetermined

Date:	625-575	575-550	550-525	525-500	500-475	475-450	450-425	425-400
Total number of vases:	778	752	2343	4478	8819	5115	3754	932
Kings/women						1		
Warriors/women				2	1	21	10	
Men w. spear(s)/women						2		
Men/women					1	11	1	
Youths w. spear(s)/women						12	3	
Youths/women					1	18	26	
Women/boys					1		1	
Totals				**2**	**4**	**65**	**41**	

1. Keuls (1985a) 1.
2. Homer, *Iliad* 14.315-28 (trans. R. Lattimore).
3. See esp. Calame (1977) I 411-20; Bergren (1989) 4, 15-16, and passim.
4. Bergren (1989) 19.
5. Passman (1993) 58.
6. E.g., Aischylos, *Suppliants* 588; Xenophon, *Memorablia* 2.1.11; etc.: Carson (1990) 149-53.
7. Brownmiller (1975) 15.
8. For critiques of Brownmiller, see e.g., Tomaselli and Porter (1986) xi, 116, 216-19; Paglia (1994) 24-38. For polygyny, see Tomaselli and Porter (1986) 110-111; cf. Lysias 1.30-31; Demosthenes 23.53 and 49.122; Diogenes Laertius 2.26; with Vernant (1988) 57-67; see also Pomeroy (1975) 37, 90-91, 121 (Sparta, Athens, Macedonia); and Cartledge (1981) (Sparta).
9. Homer, *Iliad* 18.432-34.
10. The best critical edition is West (1966); the most easily accessible translation is Evelyn-White's Loeb (1914); on this aspect of the plot see Arthur (1982).
11. For a critical edition see Merkelbach-West (MW) and for a translation of the major fragments and the *Aspis*, Evelyn-White's Loeb (1914). West (1985) is basic; Burkert (1979) 6-7, analyses the structure of many of the tales; Lefkowitz (1986) 30-42, gives a recent survey of them from the woman's point of view; and Stehle (1990) 96-97, discusses the goddess-mortal unions in the *Theogony*.
12. As on the famous amphora by Myson in Paris, Musée du Louvre, inv. no. G 197; *ARV²* 238.1 and 1638; *CVA* Paris, Musée du Louvre 6 (France 9) pls. 34.5, 35.
13. *Homeric Hymn to Apollo* (3) 207-15; *Homeric Hymn to Aphrodite* (5) passim (see esp. Bergren [1989]); Stesichoros frags. 187-93, 195 *PMG*; Sappho frags. 58, 140, 168, 199, and 210 Lobel-Page (see esp. Stehle [1990]); Plutarch, Theseus. 26-28 (*Theseis* frag. 1 *PEG*); Herodotos, 1.1-5. Pursuit etc.: Sappho 1. 21 Lobel-Page; Theognis 1283-94 and 1299-1304, semantically equating boys and women; Aischylos, *Prometheseus Bound* 853-59; Xenophon, *Memorablia*. 1.2.24; Plato, *Protagoras* 309a; Aeschines 1. 170, 195; etc.; others, Dover (1978) 87-9; Carson (1990) 144.
14. Cf. e.g., Keuls (1985a) 51, quoted below.
15. Burkert (1979) 6-7.
16. On rape in Athenian law, see Pomeroy (1975) 86-87, Cole (1984), Scafuro (1990) 133-36, and especially Cohen (1991) 99-106; for cross-cultural comparisons see Brownmiller (1975) and Tomaselli and Porter (1986) 217. For tragedy, see e.g., Euripides, *Hipplytos* 107, *Ion* 437-38 and 880-906, *Auge* frag. 265 Nauck; cf. Burkert (1979) 6-7 and Scafuro (1990). New Comedy: Menander's *Epitrepontes* (esp. 486-90), *Samia*, and *Phasma*; Terence's *Aulularia*, *Adelphoe*, and *Hecyra*; and Plautus' *Truculentus*; with Fantham (1975) 53-55, 66-71; Scafuro (1990) 150.
17. In my view Cohen (1991) 98-132 supersedes all previous discussions.
18. Lysias 1.30-33; Demosthenes 59.66-67 and 86-88; Aristotle, *Athenian Constitution* 57.3; cf. Pausanius 1.21.4 (Ares); Demosthenes, 23.53 (Draco); Plutarch, *Solon* 23 (Solon). As Gale Boetius has remarked to me, by expelling her, the *kyrios* reverses the action of the adulterer, who invades the house and penetrates her: this is how he restores his domestic boundaries, appropriately marked by his ithyphallic herm (see below).
19. Lysias 1.30-33; cf. Pausanius 1.21.4 (Ares); Plutarch, *Solon* 23 (Solon).
20. Aeschines 1.15-16 and 107-108; Lysias 3.6-9; Demosthenes 21.45-50 and 47.53; Dinarchos, *Dem.* 23; Hyperides, *Lykophron* frag. 4b.5-6. Herodotos 5.18-20, relates

how the Macedonians responded to some Persian envoys who molested their women (fondling their breasts) by killing them on the spot.

21. E.g., Aischylos, *Prometheus Bound* 640-57 and *Agamemnon* 1202-1209; Euripides, *Ion* 336-41, 859-62, 874-80, 934, and 1526; Menander, *Epitrepontes* 855-70; Scafuro (1990) 136-51.

22. Euripides, *Ion* 874-80; contrast Lysias 3.23, a unique case; cf. Cohen (1991) 52-53.

23. Herodotos 8.3; Demosthenes 23.56; Hyperides, *Epitaphius* 20; Plutarch, *Alexander* 12 and *Aratus* 31-32; etc. Cf. *Iliad* 3.301; and for further examples see Schaps (1982) 203-204; Cole (1984) 112-14; Cohen (1991) 178. Peacetime: Plato, *Laws* 9 874c; cf. 873e.

24. But apparently not gonorrhea: Grmek (1989) 133-51.

25. Laertius 6.4; cf. Athenaeus 13, 568e. For more evidence see Brandt (1932) 329-39; Keuls (1985a) 153-86, and bibliography p. 427.

26. See P.R. Sanday and Roy Porter, in Tomaselli and Porter (1986) 85 and 223; Paglia (1994) 27, adds the continuing vitality of the nuclear family to the list.

27. In this section I summarize only those scholars who have proposed interpretations for fifth-century heterosexual pursuits and abductions in Attic art, and omit discussions of homoerotic versions (see Shapiro in Richlin [1992] 53-72) and occurrences in non-Attic art. Despite its title, Herbert Hoffmann's *Sexual and Asexual Pursuit: A Structuralist Approach to Greek Vase-Painting* (Royal Anthropological Society of Great Britain and Ireland, Occasional Paper no. 34, 1977) does not address the subject of the present essay: its topic is the (chiefly animal) pursuits found on askoi; Hoffmann's conclusions are challenged and partially refuted by Boardman in *Classical Review* 29 (1979) 118-20.

28. Dover (1974) 207.

29. Kaempf-Dimitriadou (1979) 5 and 43-58.

30. Keuls (1985a) 51.

31. On conjugal love see e.g., Euripides, *Alkestis* passim; Xenophon, *Symposium* 8.3 and 9.7 and Xenophon, *Oikonomikos* 8.4-5; *IG* ii^2 12067; Aristotle, *Nicomachean Ethics* 8.9.4, 1161a23-5; 8.12.7, 1162a16-33; Dover (1974) 211-12; Cohen (1991) 169-70. Female contribution to genetics: e.g., Hippocrates *Peri Gones* 4-9 and 12 Lonie (VII, 474-80, 486 Littré); Censorinus, *De die natali* 5.4; Aetius 5. 5. 1-3; etc., against Aischylos, *Eumenides* 658-66; discussion and further references: D. Halperin, in Halperin, Winkler, and Zeitlin (1990) 278-79; Dean-Jones (1994) 148-70, etc.

32. Zeitlin (1986) 129.

33. Ibid.

34. Zeitlin (1986) 131.

35. Sourvinou-Inwood (1987) 152.

36. Sourvinou-Inwood (1987) and (1991) 29-98; Shapiro in Richlin (1992).

37. Sutton (1992) 31.

38. Osborne (forthcoming).

39. Ganymede: Ibykos frag. 289P; Theognis 1347. Crete: Ephoros, *FGrHist* 70F149 (= Strabo, 10.4.21). Sparta: Plutarch, *Lykourgos* 15.3. Athens: Jenkins (1983). On homosexual abduction and its sequel, anal intercourse, see Bremmer (1980); on heterosexual, Sourvinou-Inwood (1987).

40. On female lewdness, "work," and "play," see Simonides frag. 7 West; Aischylos, *Libation Bearers* 594-601 and *Suppliants* 588; Aristophanes, *Thesmophoriazousai* 491-97; *Lysistrata* 551-54; *Ekklesiazousai* 465-68 and 616-20; Xenophon, *Memorabilia* 2.1.11 and *Oikonomikos* 7.10; Aristotle, *Nicomachean Ethics* 7.7, 1150b15; Aristotle, *Politics* 7.15, 1334b22-28; 7.16, 1335a22-25; pseudo-Aristotle, *History of Animals* 7.1, 581b12-22; see in general Carson (1990) 138-39, 149-53, with other examples—though her references are sometimes faulty. In *Iphigenia at Aulis* 701-703, Euripides represents the union between Peleus and Thetis as resulting from a formal marriage-engagement, or *engye*.

41. See e.g., Homer, *Iliad* 14.294; Sappho frags. 23 and 31 Lobel-Page; Sophokles, *Antigone* 795; Plato, *Phaedrus* 251-55; etc. Cf. Stehle (1990) 107, with references; Frontisi-Ducroux (forthcoming).

42. MacNally (1978); cf. Lissarrague (1990) 62-63. On the hunter metaphor in literature see n. 13, above.

43. Burkert (1985) 188.

44. Euripides, *Ion* 436-47.

45. Homer, *Odyssey* 11.248-52 (trans. R. Fitzgerald). Repeated in Hesiod, *Ehoiai* frag. 31 MW, and later in Euripides, *Alkmaion in Corinth* (frag. 73a. 4 Snell).

46. E.g., Thornhill, Thornhill, and Dizinno, in Tomaselli and Porter (1986) 108 and 117.

47. Homer, *Iliad* 1.261-72, 5.635-37, and 24.62; Hesiod, *Works and Days* 164-78 and *Ehoiai* frags. 1.6-7 and 204.96-103 MW; *Homeric Hymn to Aphrodite* (5) 286-91; cf. Nagy (1979) 213-21.

48. *Homeric Hymn to Demeter* (2) 41-95, with Clay (1989) 210-13; for others, see Passman (1993).

49. E.g., Pindar, *Pythian* 9 (Apollo, Kyrene, and Aristaios); *Pythian* 10 (Zeus, Danae, and Perseus); *Nemean* 5 (Poseidon, Aigina, and the Aiakidai); *Olympian* 7 (Helios, Rhodes, Ialysos, Kameiros, and Lindos); cf. Saxonhouse (1986) 259-61; Joshel (1992). On rape, murder, and colonization, see e.g., Archilochos frags. 17-19, 88, 120 Tarditi; Mimnermos in Strabo 14.1.4; Herodotos 1.146; Thucydides 6.3.2 and 23.2; Dougherty (1993).

50. Euripides, *Ion* passim and esp. 1569-88; cf. Scafuro (1990) 138-51; Loraux (1993) 184-236.

51. Though it could backfire: see Herodotos' acid comment (2.143) upon Hekataios' own claim that Zeus was his ancestor seventeen generations back.

52. Herodotos 7.189.

53. For the rationalizing explanation for the Oreithyia story, see Plato, *Phaedrus* 229c. On Kephalos as a hunter, see Xenophon, *On Hunting* 1.2.5; his abduction is first mentioned in Hesiod, *Theogony* 986; for the whole tale see Ovid. *Metamorphoses* 7.700-830. For the Karlsruhe stamnos see *ARV*² 498.5; *Add.* 251; *LIMC* III (1986) pl. 110 (s.v. Boreas) and pl. 566 (s.v. Eos).

54. For the fragments of the *Kypria* see Allen's Oxford text of Homer, vol. 5 (1914); 36-83 *PEG*; and for a translation, Evelyn-White's Loeb (1914). On the "best of the Achaeans," see Homer, *Iliad* 1.244, 412; 16.271, 274; etc; see Nagy (1979) 26-41 and passim.

55. Sourvinou-Inwood (1987) 152.

56. Sourvinou-Inwood (1987) 138 with references, to which add Keuls (1985a) 54. *Gynaikokrateia*: Herakleides Ponticus, *Politics* 15 ap. Aristotle, frag. 611.43 Rose (Amazons); Aristotle, *Politics* 2.6.6, 1269b25; 5.11, 1313b32-39 defines it as equivalent to tyranny; cf. Dubois (1982); Keuls (1985a) 44-47; Stewart (forthcoming).

57. Keuls (1985a) 218.

58. Sutton (1992) 15.

59. Kilmer (1993) 159-67.

60. See Shapiro (1993) 186-207; Oakley and Sinos (1993).

61. Zeitlin (1987) 137-43.

62. For a list, see Plutarch, *Theseus* and Athenaeus 13, 557a-b.

63. Amphora by Myson, Paris, Louvre G 197, see n.12, above.

64. DuBois (1982) 40; cf. Plutarch, *Theseus* 26-28; cf. Pindar, frag. 175 Snell; Pherekydes, *FGrHist* 3 F 151-53. Some have identified the Amazon behind the naked Greek on no. 121 as her in this role.

65. Diodorus Siculus 4.63; Plutarch, *Theseus* 31. The frescoes of Theseus' shrine in Athens, built by Kimon shortly after he brought the hero's bones back from Skyros in 471, might have done the same: Pausanias 1.17.3-4.

66. Diodorus Siculus 4.63; *Kypria* frag. 10 Allen (13 *PEG*); Alkman frag. 21 *PMG*. Calame (1977) I 281-85, 333-34, argues that Helen's abduction as a child and her seduction by Paris when a woman represent two transitions in a girl's life, for Theseus and Peirithoos took her from a choir of parthenoi when she was sacrificing (i.e., dedicating herself) to Artemis Orthia, while her elopement with Paris took place under the sign of Aphrodite and Peitho. Yet if so, the metaphor is inexact, for she was already married and had produced a daughter, Hermione, when Paris arrived.

67. Sourvinou-Inwood (1987) 133.

68. Barron (1980) 1-4.

69. *Kypria* frag. 7 Allen (11 *PEG*); Lykophron, *Alexandra* 544-49 and scholia; cf. Pindar, *Nemean* 10.60; Calame (1977) I 328-33.

70. Sutton (1992) 30-31.

71. Kassandra: Homer, *Iliad* 13.366, cf. 24.699; Proclus, *Chrestomathia* 239 (p. 108, 2 Allen; p. 89, 15 *PEG*); Euripides, *Trojan Women* 69-72; cf. Pausanius 1.15.2, 5.19.5,

and 10.26.3. Violation in the sanctuary: Kallimachos, *Aitia* ap. scholia to *Iliad*. 13.66. In general see *LIMC* V (1990) s.v. Kassandra; Cohen (1993); Connelly (1993).

72. Hanson (1990) 326, with Homer, *Iliad* 16.100 and 22.468-70; cf. Aischylos, *Agamemnon* 1347-53; Euripies, *Hecuba* 280-81, 303-5, and 536-38; *Trojan Women* 39-47, 69-72, 143-46, 252-70, 307-40.

73. See nn. 13 and 39 above, with e.g. Pomeroy (1975) 19 and 37; Jenkins (1983); Sourvinou-Inwood (1987); Carson (1990) 138-46 and 160-64.

74. See esp. Vidal-Naquet (1986) 106-56; Durand and Schapp (1989); and on beards and the ephebic hunter's dress, Pollux 1.10 and 10.64. Significantly, Aeneas is characterized as a hunter in *Homeric Hymn to Aphrodite* (5) 155-60 just before he strips and "tames" Aphrodite by Zeus' will: see Bergren (1989) 23.

75. Carson (1985) 25.

76. Carson (1985) 29.

77. Sappho frag. 94 Lobel-Page; Erinna, *Distaff* (D.L. Page, *Select Papyri* 3: *Literary Papyri: Poetry* [Cambridge, MA, 1950] no. 120; H. Lloyd-Jones and P. Parsons, eds., *Supplementum Hellenisticum* [Berlin and New York, 1983] no. 401); cf. Oakley and Sinos (1993) 46-47 for possible reflections of this dichotomy in marriage-pictures. But a woman who is self-aware subordinates herself to male guidance: North (1966) 76 and 206; Carson (1990) 142, with references.

78. Age of marriage at Athens: Xenophon, *Oikonomikos* 7.5; Demosthenes 29.43; cf. [Hippocrates] *Peri Parthenoi* 1.16 (VIII, 468 Littré). At Sparta: Plutarch, *Lykourgos* 15.3-4, explicitly making the contrast with "other cities," and citing these reasons. On marriage in the ideal state (Sparta) and the dangers of teenage pregnancies, see also Plato, *Republic* 5, 460e and *Laws* 6, 785b, 7, 833d; Aristotle, *Politics* 7.14.4, 1335a12-30; pseudo-Aristotle, *History of Animals* 7. 1, 582a 17-21, 27-29; cf. Amundsen and Diers (1969); Wells (1975). Angel (1985): Table 4 (repr. Morris [1992a] 76; cf. Grmek [1989] 99-109 for analysis) cites skeletal evidence that the mean age of death for adult women (defined as age 15+ years) in Classical Greece was 36.8 years, as against 44.1 for men; since the average woman bore around 5 children during a period of fertility that has been calculated to last at most 12 years, this gives added poignancy to Medea's famous remark (Euripides, *Medea* 250-51) that she would rather stand three times in the front line of battle than bear one child.

79. This was the *communis opinio* of the Hippocratics: Hippocrates, *Peri Gones* 1.1, 4.1-2 Lonie (VII, 474 and 476 Littré); pseudo-Aristotle, *History of Animals* 10.5, 636b 10-24 and 36-39 (cf. 7. 4, 583b 29-30); etc.; cf. Laqueur (1990) 43-52; D. Halperin, in Halperin, Winkler, and Zeitlin (1990) 278-79, cf. 284 n. 107 (N.B. the view of historians of Greek science that the texts are "the literate representation of Greek folklore"); Hanson (1990) 314-15; Dean-Jones (1994) 156-60. Conversely, if a woman was raped and got pregnant anyway, then it was believed (at least by some in Roman times) that she had tacitly given her consent: Soranus, *Gyn* 1.10 and 37-38; cf. Laqueur (1990) 161-62; Hanson (1990) 315.

80. Summary and evidence: Laqueur (1990) 43-52. On p. 150 he quotes the following from a syndicated question-and-answer column of 10 November, 1987: "I am ashamed to ask my doctor: Do you only get pregnant when you have an orgasm?"

81. Aischylos, *Eumenides* 657-66: a querulous protest against the majority view, and as Hanson notes ([1990] 314 n. 27), contradicted in the *Libation Bearers* by the many hints that Orestes closely resembles his mother; cf. also Aristotle, *Generation of Animals* 2.4, 739a 29-36, cf. 1.20, 727b 34-728a1; discussion, Dean-Jones (1994) 149-51 and 162-66.

82. Thucydides 1.2.5-6; Lykophron, *Against Leokrates* 76, cf. 147-48; etc. On autochthony, denial of the female, and rape, see Saxonhouse (1986); and on the citizen's duty to beget children for the state see Daube (1977), with Plato *Republic* 5, 460a and *Laws* 7, 804d; 11, 923a: Aristotle, *Politics* 2.6.13, 1270b 1-7; 7.14, 1334b 29-30, 1335b 28-30.

83. Aristotle, *Athenian Constitution* 26.4; cf. Plutarch, *Perikles* 33; Aristophanes, *Birds* 1661-66; Athenaeus 577b-c; Patterson (1981) and (1990); see my article, "Imag(in)ing the Other: Amazons and Ethnicity in Fifth-Century Athens," forthcoming in *Poetics Today*.

84. Cf. Kaempf-Dimitriadou (1979) 43; Shapiro (1981) and (1992).

85. Cf. Pantel (1992), with E. Pellizer in Murray, ed. (1990) 177-84, esp. 182: "Without any doubt an important part of the meeting/contest between the symposiasts had as its aim discussion of the effects of love and pleasure."

86. See esp. Cohen (1991) 146-54.

87. Though Hesiod *Works and Days* 697-98 recommends marriage five years after a girl reaches puberty, this says nothing for Archaic/Early Classical Attica; cf. n. 78 above, with Vernant (1988).

88. Cf. Plutarch, *Theseus* 26-28.

89. Cf. n. 13 above.

90. Aischylos, T 78 and frags. 13-15, 88-93, 99-101, 281 Radt; Kaempf-Dimitriadou (1979) 45, argues for the connection, but the *Amymone*, attached to the Danaid trilogy, was produced ca. 463.

91. Cf. Solon frags. 5, 34, and 36 West; Herodotos. 5.66 and 69-78; Aristotle, *Athenian Constitution* 20-21; see in general Sealey (1987) 116-26; Stahl (1987); Manville (1990); Ober (1993).

92. Cf. e.g., Murray, ed. (1990) 66, 111, 144-45, 181; Pantel (1992) 247-52.

93. See Vernant (1988) 67 and passim.

94. Women and the home: comments begin with Homer, *Iliad* 18.495-97; 22.440. Athenian women and the problem of seclusion: Pomeroy (1975) 79-84; Gould (1980) 40, 48-50; Loraux (1993) 116-23; esp. Cohen (1991) 146-59. Herms: Winkler (1990) 35-6, 41; cf. Stewart (1990) 125, fig. 178. Perikles: Thucydides 2.45-46. Cf. Cartledge (1981) and Zweig (1993) for two opposing views on how to interpret the (notorious) freedom of Spartan women: Aristotle, *Politics* 2.9, 1269a29-1271b19; etc.

95. E.g., Euripides, *Hippolytos* 408-10, *Hecuba* 879-87 and *Ion* 398-400; Aristophanes, *Lysistrata* 11-12 and *Thesmophoriazousai* 559-61; etc. Cf. Aristotle, *Politics* 5.11, 1313b 33-38; Cohen (1991) 144-46.

96. See Cohen (1991) 76-83, 151, 159, etc., with e.g. Thucydides 2.40; Xenophon, *Oikonomikos* 7.2-3, 30; and cf. (for the Peloponnesian War) Aristophanes, *Lysistrata* passim.

97. Aristotle, *Politics* 2.6.8, 1270a 7-10; *contra*, Plutarch, *Lykourgos* 14.1.

98. *Male Subjectivity at the Margins* (London and New York 1992) 36.

99. On sexual antagonism in sympotic poetry see most conveniently J.M. Edmonds' *Elegy and Iambus* in the Loeb edition, passim. Terror: Brownmiller (1975) 15; cf. section 1, "Myth and Reality," above.

100. Homer, *Odyssey* 10.341.

101. Kephalos and Tithonos: cf. Hesiod, *Theogony* 984-86; *Homeric Hymn to Aphrodite* (5) 188-90, 218-38; Sappho frag. 58 Lobel-Page; Ibykos frag. 8 *PMG*; Athenaeus 13.566c; etc; cf. Bergren (1989) 33-34; Winkler (1990) 202-204; Stehle (1990). Amazons and *gynaikokrateia*: see n. 56, above.

102. Zeitlin (1986) 131.

103. Stewart (1990) 155-57, 160-62, and figs. 327-46, 378-78.

104. *Enkrateia, sophrosyne*, and sex: Euripides, *Andromache* 595-600; Xenophon, *Agesilaus* 5.1-4; cf. Xenophon, *Memorablia* 1.2.1; 2.1.1, 6.1; 4.5. 9; Xenophon, *Oikonomikos* 12.11-14; Plato, *Republic* 4.430e; Aristotle *Nicomachean Ethics* 3.11-12, 1118b8-1119b19; 7.7, 1150a9-b28; North (1966) 202-203; Foucault (1985) 63-65; Winkler (1990).

105. Cf. Euripides, frag. 282.6 Nauck; Philemon frag. 104 Kock.

WOMEN, BOXES, CONTAINERS: SOME SIGNS AND METAPHORS

"I'm very glad," said Pooh happily, "that I thought of giving you a Useful Pot to put things in."

A.A. Milne, *Winnie-the-Pooh*, chap. 6

"The box of Pandora is proverbial, and that is all the more remarkable as she never had a box at all." It is with these words that Jane Harrison began her article on Pandora.[1] In this way she reminds us of the fact that at no time in ancient tradition is Pandora opening a box, but that the evils of all men were kept shut up in a jar, a *pithos*, buried in the ground. We will not expand on her interpretation of the celebration of the Pithoigia, the opening of the jars on the third day of the Anthesteria, which she connected with the tale of Pandora's opening the jar from which from all evils escaped. The box of Pandora, as shown by Dora and Erwin Panofsky, is a modern invention going back to Erasmus where, for the first time, the idea of Pandora opening not a *pithos* but a *pyxis*, a box, is expressed.[2]

But boxes, chests, and other containers occupy a place that seems important in a woman's world, more specifically in vase-painting, as utilitarian objects but also as sign holders of symbolic values. This is to be the focus of the present discussion. Vase-painters frequently depicted these objects, and their choice shows that the objects had some relevance, not only because they are connected with female activities but also because symbolic values connected with these activities defined, in the eyes of the painters and their clients, the status of women. In a certain way, many of these objects, as iconographical signs, allow a metaphorical expression of views about women. Thus we see women tidying up, putting things in order; using perfumes and jewelry; carrying various objects from one place to another, or spinning wool. And to each of these activities is associated a specific type of chest, box, basket, or container.

To put things in their context it may be appropriate to state a few facts. In a culture that has only limited furniture,[3] chests play an important role,[4] as do all containers of smaller sizes, such as caskets and boxes, whether of metal, wood, terracotta, or wicker.

Greek vocabulary in this area is extremely rich and diversified. Chests are called *kibotos, kiboton, zygastron, soros, antipex, larnax*. Boxes, *theke, kiste, koite, pyxis, kylichnis*. Archaeologists took up the habit of calling *pyxis* what the ancients probably called *kylichnis*, a term connected with *kyklos*, which refers more appropriately to its cylindrical shape.[5] Wicker baskets bear different names according to their function: the *liknon* is a winnowing-basket that may also serve as ritual basket,[6] the *kanoun* is a sacrificial basket with three

points used for carrying grains,[7] and the *kalathos*, with a strong flaring shape, is a wool basket.

To discuss these various aspects in their iconographical context, several mythical tales will be brought to bear in which chests and boxes occupy an essential visual role: the chest in which Danae was kept locked up, the basket where Erichthonios was hidden, and the box where the necklace of Eriphyle was kept. Then we will examine the context of the objects themselves: women's domestic space and their ritual activities, specifically, the wedding.

Mythical Containers

Danae, an Argive princess, was the daughter of King Akrisios, whose story is told by Apollodoros:

> When Akrisios inquired of the oracle how he should get male children, the god said that his daughter would give birth to a son who would kill him. Fearing that, Akrisios built a brazen chamber under ground (*hypo gên thalamon*) and there guarded Danae. However, she was seduced by Zeus, as some say, by Proetus...but some say that Zeus had intercourse with her in the shape of a stream of gold which poured through the roof into Danae's lap. When Akrisios afterward learned that she had got a child Perseus, he would not believe that she had been seduced by Zeus, and putting his daughter with the child in a chest, he cast it into the sea. The chest was washed ashore on Seriphus and Diktys took up the boy and reared him.[8]

As we all know, Perseus grew up and was victorious in various trials, especially against Medusa, the Gorgon he managed to behead and whose head he offered to Athena after freeing Andromeda who had been abandoned to a dragon. Back in Argos, it is by accident that Perseus kills his grandfather with a discus, thus fulfilling the prophecy.

In imagery, painters retained two main episodes about Danae herself: when she received the stream of gold and when she is put in the chest. These two episodes, both connected with forms of confinement, are only rarely associated. This is what makes the kalyx krater attributed to the Triptolemos Painter (no. 74) even more remarkable. On one side Danae is seated on a high bed, her feet resting on a stool. She is raising her head toward the stream of gold falling in her direction and at the same time she is untying the headband holding her hair. The massive bed with its mattress is not a mere dining couch; the objects in the field, mirror and sakkos, show that we are inside a woman's room, the *thalamos*, the bridal chamber. No specific architecture is depicted here, but this indoor space corresponds to that described by Apollodoros: *hypo ten gên thalamon*, an underground chamber. In Sophokles' *Antigone*, at the moment when, on the order of Kreon, Antigone is to be immured alive, the chorus recalls the misfortune of those who met the same fate, specifically, Danae, cloistered in her chamber-grave, *en tumberêi thalamôi*. This underground, enclosed space marks the absolute reclusion in which Danae is held captive, and whose barriers were lowered by Zeus in a stream of gold.

After this first confinement, comes a second when the child is discovered. The obverse of the same krater shows, in the center, the chest in which Danae, carrying Perseus on her arm, is already installed. Akrisios, arm outstretched, scepter at the shoulder, seems to bid farewell, while a carpenter, with a bow-drill, is boring a hole into the thickness of the chest so as to secure its fastening. He is not building the chest, but actually getting ready to shut it definitively by means of dowels. In the oldest depictions of this episode, the carpenter is always present, finishing the job.[9] On a stamnos attributed to the Deepdene Painter (no. 76), the carpenter appears on the reverse of the vase, holding a mallet in one hand and standing next to a maid. The maid can be identified by an inscription as Damolyte; she is standing next to a seated woman, probably the queen Eurydike, and is holding a wicker box of a type seen in wedding scenes (cf. no. 55). This seems to show a play of assimilation on the painter's part between the expulsion of Danae from her father's house and the wedding ceremony. This analogy is repeated, in a different form, on a hydria attributed to the Danae Painter (no. 77): Danae, in the chest, is veiled and wears a diadem in the fashion of young brides. This detail is not an accidental choice; it appears again on a fragmentary krater attributed to the Phiale Painter (no. 78). Painters, thus, first emphasized the closure of the chest, similar to a coffin,[10] then Danae's diadem, giving the scene sometimes funerary, sometimes nuptial connotations.

Some of the depictions of the legend of Erichthonios also play on the idea of confinement, although in a different way. As we know, Erichthonios was born from the Earth impregnated by the desire of Hephaistos for Athena. Here again, Apollodoros recounts:

> Some say that this Erichthonios...was a son of Hephaestus and Athena, as follows: Athena came to Hephaestus, desirous of fashioning arms. But he, being forsaken by Aphrodite, fell in love with Athena and began to pursue her; but she fled. When he got near her with much ado (for he was lame), he attempted to embrace; but she, being a chaste virgin, would not submit to him, and he dropped his seed on the leg of the

Fig. 1. Oinochoe. Paris, Musée du Louvre, inv. no. G 442.

goddess. In disgust she wiped off the seed with wool and threw it on the ground; and as she fled and the seed fell on the ground, Erichthonios was produced. Him Athena brought up unknown (*krypha*) to the others gods, wishing to make him immortal; and having put him in a chest (*eis kisten*), she committed it to Pandrosos, daughter of Kekrops, forbidding her to open the chest. But the sisters opened it out of curiosity and beheld a serpent coiled about the baby; and, as some would say, they were destroyed by the serpent, but according to others they were driven mad by reason of the anger of Athena and threw themselves down from the Acropolis.[11]

The birth of Erichthonios, when the child is entrusted by Gaia, the Earth, to Athena, is subject of an iconography with a clear civic and ideological significance. But painters were also interested in the moment when the ban is broken by the daughters of Kekrops. On a lekythos in Basel (no. 66) it is first the anger of Athena that is emphasized. The armed goddess is running toward a frightened Kekropid, while a snake emerges from the overturned basket. The pelike in London, attributed to the Erichthonios Painter (no. 69), presents a rather more peaceful picture. On the reverse of the vase, two daughters of Kekrops are moving away, while the obverse shows a rock on which the basket lies open. The lid is overturned. The child, protected by a snake, greets Athena who gazes upon it, motionless, holding her helmet in her hand. The role played by the basket in connection with the notion of female curiosity alleged in this legend is twofold; it conceals the child, whose existence must remain unknown, but at the same time, once opened, the basket reveals his heroic presence. Painters, preoccupied by the visual dimension of the episode, successfully brought to the fore the visual effect of the alternately closed and opened basket.[12]

A third legend assigns the box a totally different function, one closer to the daily uses of this type of object. It is an episode connected with the story of the Seven against Thebes. In a fratricidal dispute opposing Eteokles and Polynikes, all means are sanctioned to acquire victory. The intervention of Eriphyle, wife of Amphiaraos and sister of Adrastus, is necessary to allow the departure of the expedition Polynikes wants to lead against his brother to recover power in Thebes. Polynikes bribes Eriphyle by offering her a necklace of great value. Apollodoros summarized the events this way:

> … Amphiaraos, son of Oicles, being a seer and foreseeing that all who joined in the expedition except Adrastus were destined to perish, shrank from it himself and discouraged the rest. However, Polynikes went to Iphis, son of Alector, and begged to know how Amphiaraos could be compelled to go to the war; for the decisions lay with her (Eriphyle), because once, when a difference arose between him and Adrastus, he had made it up with him and sworn to let Eriphyle decide any future dispute he might have with Adrastus. Accordingly, when war was to be made on Thebes, and the measure was advocated by Adrastus and opposed by Amphiaraos, Eriphyle accepted the necklace and persuaded him to march with Adrastus. Thus forced to go to the war, Amphiaraos laid command on his sons that, when they were grown up, they should slay their mother and march against Thebes.[13]

From this story, painters sometimes depicted the moment when Polynikes offers Eriphyle the deadly necklace. He is standing before her, resting on a staff, according to the scheme of conversational scenes. In some cases he is wearing a pilos or a petasos, as if he were a traveler coming from afar.[14] But the most remarkable feature of this series is the very way the necklace is presented to Eriphyle. It is a matter of seducing and tempting her. Each time it is Polynikes who holds the box from which the necklace is pulled out. Now this detail is very unusual in Attic iconography, where grooming tools and jewelry, which are characteristic of a woman's world, are almost always shown in the hands of women, whether they are maids or the household mistresses themselves. It is unusual for a man to hold a casket or a mirror in this way, and the rare instances where a man is seen with a mirror are to be connected with scenes of seduction, as on a pelike from Naples[15] where a male figure holds a purse and

a mirror before a seated woman, or on a skyphos in Oldenburg, where two young men are depicted, one, on the obverse, holding a casket, and the other, on the reverse, a mirror.[16] Painters, by inversing the usual scheme in handing over the box and the necklace to Polynikes, place the seduction on the man's side. But this is not his usual role; it is the woman who must seduce with her jewelry, not be seduced, and even less yield to temptation or betray her husband. On account of this shift, the depiction makes clear that Polynikes' trickery undermines his status as heroic warrior. Visually, Eriphyle's eagerness to get hold of the necklace is emphasized by the outstretched gesture of her hand, as on an oinochoe in the Louvre, where there is, in the center of the composition, a remarkable play of hands around the jewelry box (fig. 1).[17]

Daily Boxes

Boxes and chests are extremely common in iconography, and not everything can be catalogued here. Variants are numerous, whether from the typological or contextual standpoint, but essentially the objects are tied to a woman's space and, as is shown by the three stories already mentioned, to the idea of confinement. It is a matter of putting away, stocking, preserving; sometimes to conceal or to hoard, in short, to exercise a control over an indoor private space, where women are themselves detained. Many compositions where chests are depicted bring this fact to mind. On a now-lost stamnos (fig. 2),[18] two women are folding a piece of cloth; in the field and on a seat placed between them more fabric is shown, as well as a mirror. To the left, a woman is looking on; and to the right is a large chest, probably to hold cloth. Should we see, prosaically, a "scene in a linen room,"[19] or, to the contrary, a ritual scene connected with the peplos of Athena?[20] The matter rests unresolved; but if this scene and that on the reverse, which shows a young man departing while a woman pours a libation, are to be associated, one finds the common opposition between a woman's interior and a man's exterior space. A chest of the same type occupies an essential place on a small skyphos, the iconography of which is quite revealing.[21] On

Fig. 2. Drawing after a now-lost stamnos by the Copenhagen Painter.

Figs. 3 and 4. Sides A and B of skyphos. Malibu, J. Paul Getty Museum, inv. no. 85.AE.265.

one side (fig. 3) a wine amphora is shown resting against a chest; above are a wicker basket and a pitcher. To the right, a ladle, strainer, and a jug, such as those seen in symposium scenes, are hanging from a bronze stand. Other vases and a grille complete this picture, where no human figure is present. The scene is empty. It evokes a domestic interior space, a kitchen or a storeroom. The reverse (fig. 4) holds the key to an interpretation: a woman, followed by a small maid carrying a wine skin on her head, is gluttonously drinking from a skyphos. The scene is meant to be funny and shows, in the manner of Aristophanes, the drunkenness of a woman left to herself, drinking on the sly. This not too flattering picture, the reflection of a man's view on women's world, shows quite well how chests and boxes were used to define women's space. Other scenes have nothing pejorative; the diversity of chests and their contents allows diversified imagery of women. Not only do chests hold fabrics and jewelry, as seen in the case of Eriphyle, but also scrolls on which are inscribed poetic or musical texts. Thus an amphora attributed to the Niobid Painter (no. 44) shows a woman half-opening a casket. Nearby are two female figures holding musical instruments; one is seated and holding a barbiton, the other is standing and is holding a diaulos. The connection between casket and music is even more evident on a hydria attributed to the same artist (no. 45); to the left, a half-open door shows that this is an indoor space, exclusively occupied by women. In the center, a lyre player is seated, tuning her instrument. She is placed on a sort of podium. By her feet, a chest is wide open, and the woman to the left is now holding a scroll she has pulled from the chest and which she is unrolling in front of her companion. To the right, another woman is holding, at the same time, a lyre and a casket; in a way the presence of musical instruments establishes the context, not always explicit, for these boxes.

In Attic imagery, women also appear in connection with other types of containers, more specifically vases and baskets, which help to qualify the general impression of confinement.

In the case of vases, one often sees women carrying hydriae, going to the fountain house where they fetch water. The theme is especially common in black-figure;[22] it allows the depiction of an outdoor space, sometimes with elements of landscape, and exchanges between the house and the world outside of the oikos. Moreover, painters often evoke the risks involved in such outings, and scenes of pursuit or rape at the fountain house are not rare, especially those where Polyxena, with her brother Troilos, is chased by Achilles, or those where Poseidon meets Amymone.[23]

Elsewhere, but always in connection with women, the oinochoe is used for libations, especially in scenes of departure. It is often depicted in the hands of a woman who is pouring, while the man holds the phiale. Not surprisingly potters chose to model some of these oinochoai in the shape of female heads, including several examples signed by Charinos (nos. 47 and 48). In the series of modeled Attic vases, heads of Greek men, citizens, are never represented, but only the heads of non-Greeks and women, in accordance with the anthropological models defined by the philosopher Thales, for example, if the remarks attributed to him by his biographer are to be believed: "He used often to say that he had three reasons to be grateful to the gods: first because by birth I am human and not a beast; second, because I am a man and not a woman; finally, because I am Greek and not a foreigner."[24] This pattern of exclusion, which accords women a less than enviable place, illuminates the choices made by these potters. Through production of vases shaped like heads, one can see a sort of reflection on identity and otherness.[25] By giving the vase the shape of a female head, the performer of the libation and the instrument of libation itself are assimilated.

In the two cases just mentioned, the vases involve forms of exchange and circulation. The same goes for some types of handled baskets which are meant to be carried and which are seen in scenes of harvest, especially in orchards, as on a cup attributed to the Wedding Painter.[26] A large basket of the type used for gathering fruits also appears on a krater attributed to the Orchard Painter,[27] and a similar one appears on a cup by the Painter of Munich 2676 (fig. 5)[28] ("coarse imitation of the late Brygan style," heavily restored). There a standing woman juggles with some sort of balls of irregular shape in front of the wicker basket. Behind her, hanging in the field, is a tall cylindrical basket with three feet and handles; a low chest is resting between the feet of a chair. The gathering of containers of all types clearly defines an indoor space where things are put away and stored. One may be inclined to think that this woman is juggling with fruits, but ball games are often associated with wool working, an activity in which the wicker basket is a frequently depicted tool. It is a basket with a narrow base and with a wide flaring opening, which the Greeks call kalathos. This basket appears on a lekythos by the Pan Painter (no. 62); it is overflowing with large wool balls used by a woman to stuff a cushion. Sometimes a distaff juts out from the kalathos, making more explicit its function in connection with wool working—one of the most frequently depicted activities and which seems quite often, at least in imagery, to keep women busy.[29] The kalathos is thus used to delimit space.

Placed at the feet of women, it is a sign of their economic activity—"economy" being connected etymologically with the *oikos*, the indoor space of the house. The kalathos is sometimes given greater importance by the manner in which it is represented. So it is on the interior of a cup, where two women are depicted standing, a domestic altar and a chair between them; the woman on the right is conspicuously holding a kalathos in one hand and in the other a tendril, whose decorative role in the center of this composition underlines the aesthetic values connected with working wool.[30] These values sometimes take erotic connotations, especially in scenes where Poseidon chases Aithra who is fleeing, frightened, and, in some cases, holding a kalathos in her hand.[31]

This type of wicker basket does not survive archaeologically. There are some rare examples in terracotta, one of which, Attic and of large dimensions, is decorated with an indoor scene depicting women dressing or weaving; one of the women holds a kalathos in her hand.[32] A number of votive terracotta kalathoi from the Geometric period are also known. Of smaller sizes, these kalathoi were offered by women in sanctuaries of female divinities, Demeter at Corinth or Hera at Perachora.[33]

All these objects, chests and kalathoi, sometimes assume a symbolic value beyond their practical function. Terracotta votive reliefs from the sanctuary of Demeter and Persephone at Lokri, in South Italy, are perfect examples. Sometimes of difficult interpretation, they nonetheless allow a glimpse of the play between divine representations and a series of objects defining cultural identities. The kalathos is thus often associated with Persephone, as a characteristic element of Hades' spouse.[34] On a plaque in the Reggio Museum, she appears seated, holding at the same time a kalathos and a casket.[35]

Another type of relief shows a seated goddess in front of a chest on which rests a flat basket she is pulling toward her while lifting the lid; in this flat basket is a liknon, a sort of winnowing-basket, and in it is a child. Sometimes regarded as Aphrodite with the child Dionysos,[36] sometimes as a *kourotrophic* Persephone,[37] the identity of this divine figure remains elusive,[38] but the importance of the various containers—chest, basket, and winnowing-basket—which form a series of barriers protecting the child and from which he is emerging in a sort of epiphany comparable to that of Erichthonios (no. 69) should be kept in mind.

In the same series from Lokri, there are plaques depicting only containers. On one in the British Museum (fig. 6),[39] we see a chest; on it rest a casket, like the chest, a perfume alabastron, a small wicker kalathos, an alabastron, an oinochoe, a third alabastron, and a second casket. These isolated objects, untouched, are self-sufficient. They are not simply descriptive, although they provide archaeologists with interesting information on Greek furniture.[40] These plaques are themselves offerings that depict, in a relatively realistic manner, chests covered with other offerings to the goddess, but also, in a more symbolic way, a feminine space consecrated to a goddess.

Fig. 5. Cup (interior) by the Painter of Munich 2676. Munich, Antikenmuseum und Glyptothek, inv. no. 2676.

Fig. 6. Terracotta plaque, from Lokri. London, British Museum, inv. no. TC 1226.

It is difficult, and it would be unwise, to reduce each of these objects to a single symbolic value and to propose in each case a systematic equivalence between, for instance, the kalathos and Persephone. Interpretations of this type of imagery must preserve some flexibility, taking into account context, especially the relationships between the various elements and the nature of the iconographic support.

Leaving the series of plaques from Lokri, we turn to funerary imagery, relief stelai and white-ground lekythoi. There, the kalathos seems to symbolize, above all, female identity and the virtues of industrious women. Thus, on a fragmentary stele in Basel,[41] a woman is depicted on a seat under which is a kalathos. The same scheme is reproduced on another, older stele in the same museum,[42] as well as on a number of stelai from the Classical period.[43] The so-called stele of Leukothea in Rome,[44] whose style and complex iconography bring to mind the reliefs from Locris, presents the same motif of the kalathos placed under the seat of a female figure, probably a kourotrophic divinity.[45] The kalathos and the seat acquire an explicitly funerary significance on a white-ground lekythos by the Achilles Painter, where they are depicted at the top of a stele to personify the absent deceased,[46] as well as on a lekythos by the Sabouroff Painter, where a casket and a barbiton at the top of a stele apparently refer to the deceased's musical culture.[47] These two objects, casket and kalathos, are not uncommon on funerary stelai and it is no surprise that, by themselves, they can serve as markers for a woman's grave, as is the case on a remarkable funerary monument of the Classical period (fig. 7).[48] The kalathos placed on a casket gives concrete expression to the social identity of the woman.

Apart from the kalathos, other specific types of baskets are equally connected with the world of women, although in a less restrictive manner. They are ritual baskets, the shape, name, and function of which are more closely determined than is the case with chests. First, there is the kanoun, a basket with three points, containing grains and the sacrificial knife;[49] it is seen often but not solely in the hands of women.[50] Thus, on the interior of a cup attributed to Makron (no. 38), a woman is depicted pouring a libation with her right hand while holding a kanoun in her left arm; behind her is a *thymiaterion*, an incense burner. This last ritual instrument appears again on a cup where it is shown open, being filled by a woman who is taking a pinch of perfume from a small box, a *kylichnis* (fig. 8).[51] These ritual gestures clearly show the part of women in

Fig. 7. Grave marker in the form of a chest and kalathos. Athens, National Museum, inv. no. 1052.

sacrificial rites, often as kanephoroi. A small terracotta, found in a female grave (no. 60)[52] shows a young girl carrying a kanoun on her head; with this figurine were found three miniature versions of the kanoun, also in terracotta. The duplication demonstrates clearly the importance of the role of kanephoros and of the kanoun itself for the deceased woman.

Another type of ritual basket is the liknon, the winnowing-basket, whose prime function was to sort out grain but was sometimes used, as we have seen, as a Moses basket, especially for divine children. Thus was the child Hermes[53] placed in a liknon. Some South Italian images, mocking divine epiphanies, place the egg of Leda[54] or a hybrid with the looks of Pan[55] in a flat wicker basket with the same role as the liknon as we saw it in the case of Erichthonios. Last, the liknon reappears in wedding processions, carried among the various gifts of the bridal couple, along with other types of baskets, as well as fabrics from the trousseau.[56]

Boxes on Boxes

In the production of Attic potters, boxes and some vases resembling boxes occupy an important place, especially what archaeologists call a "pyxis," a sort of cylindrical container, of moderate height.[57] Painters deliberately used the correlation between women's space and containers to decorate this type of box by multiplying depictions of baskets and chests. Thus, for example, on a pyxis with high walls (no. 43) depicting five women and a child, the continuous cylindrical frieze is interrupted by a closed door, the only architectural element in the composition, which explicitly shows an indoor space, shut onto itself. In this scene, women are among themselves, playing with pet birds and a little boy; two of these women are carrying chests, while at the center of the composition a kalathos alludes to their textile activities in the *gynaikon*. A similar pyxis, by a follower of Douris (figs. 9-12),[58] reveals many remarkable features. The lid, instead of being topped by a ring, as in the previous example, supports a miniature vase, an *exaleiptron*, a sort of vase for perfume often held by women especially in funerary scenes where it is part of the offerings carried by women to the grave.[59] The cylindrical surface is decorated with three groups of women in connection with three types of containers. The first one is a kalathos placed at the feet of a seated woman, in front of her is a woman holding an alabastron, and in the field, a mirror—all elements connected with female beauty and the manufacture of wool. The indoor space is symbolized by a column near which is another woman holding a basket with handles that is filled with fruits, implying, as already seen, a transfer from outdoor to indoor space. Lastly, in front of a half-open door, a woman is fitting a headband in her hair, while a female companion is approaching her, holding an open chest from which she is pulling a necklace; here again we find the common motif in which a woman is dressing and adorning herself. The painter skillfully brings together the two openings, that of the door and that of the chest, as if to draw attention to the

Fig. 8. Cup (interior) by the Chicago Painter. London, British Museum, inv. no. E 88.

composition's visual play between confinement and opening, between hiding and revealing. Moreover, the artist gave mythological names to almost all his female figures, names corresponding, as Beazley remarked,[60] to Argive heroines: they are, beginning with the seated woman, Helen and Clytemnestra, Kassandra (one of the two women in this group is left unnamed), Iphigenia, and Danae. This series of names does not correspond to any particular episode, but gives a mythical flavor to an ordinary scene that attempts to depict female beauty. We can appreciate the painter's choice; not without irony he gives the name of Danae to the figure carrying the chest.

Not all pyxides are decorated with interior scenes of women's quarters, but painters often retained female themes to decorate vases used by women, such as a group of Maenads on a white-ground pyxis (no. 127). It returns us to an outdoor world where Dionysiac women danced in the grip of divine mania. A type B pyxis in Athens[61] shows a remarkable peculiarity. The box is made of two cylinders fitted together; when the box is closed, the exterior wall covers completely the interior cylinder. The painter cleverly used this double surface: on the outside, on the section of the lid, he depicted women in an open-air scene, using a tree to symbolize this outdoor space, while on the receptacle itself is the indoor scene, visible only when the box is opened. The iconographical opposition, outdoor/indoor, gets concrete expression from the structure of the box, the external part of which is concealing an indoor scene.

This type of interplay is common in Attic pottery. It appears again on a series of small type D boxes, only the lids of which are decorated with a simple scene:[62] a head, part of the body, an animal,

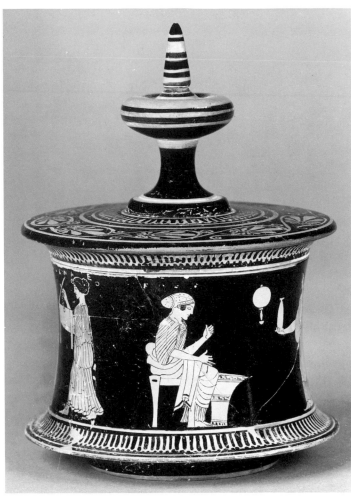

Fig. 9. Pyxis by a follower of Douris. London, British Museum, inv. no. E 773.

Figs. 10 and 11. Continuation of the frieze on the pyxis in figure 9.

but sometimes also with an object such as a vase, a weapon or, in some cases, a casket.[63] The choice of this last motif is certainly not mere coincidence and confirms both the reflexive character of these images and the importance of boxes in the world of women. Other compositions in this series have an explicit sexual nature, especially the phallus-bird[64] associated, on a vase in Athens,[65] with three female sexual organs, as a very crude version of the Judgment of Paris. The English play on words that assimilates the female sexual organs to a box does not exist under this form in Greek, but we find in Aristophanes a joke connecting the word for basket, *kiste*, and the word *kusthos*, a vulgar expression for the female sexual organs.[66]

Women, Wedding, Eros, and Boxes

The interplay just noted between image and support is common on ritual vases used in wedding ceremonies,[67] loutrophoroi and lebetes gamikoi. A fair number of these depictions illustrate, among all the various possible moments, the preparations of the bride and her toilette. Everything that relates to female beauty is evidently appealing to painters who try to provide for it a visual counterpart in their

Fig. 12. Detail of pyxis in figure 9.

Fig. 13. Detail of a pelike. Paris, Musée du Louvre, inv. no. G 551.

compositions. Often the bride is surrounded by female companions, who bring all sorts of baskets and chests, the contents of which remain unknown, but are probably to be connected with the trousseau and wedding gifts. Thus, a lebes attributed to the Washing Painter (no. 55) depicts three women surrounding the bride, who plays a harp; one of them is carrying a loutrophoros, another a chest, and a third one a chest and a checkerboard wicker basket. A loutrophoros in Vienna[68] depicting a procession with the bridegroom holding the bride by the wrist is decorated on the reverse with a woman carrying a kalathos. The same wool basket is also carried by a woman in a scene depicted on the foot of a lebes found in the Kerameikos cemetery.[69] These vases are attributed to the same artist, the Washing Painter, who apparently specialized in the manufacture of ritual vases for wedding ceremonies: Beazley attributed to this painter more than seventy loutrophoroi, unfortunately still unpublished, discovered in the excavations of the sanctuary of the Nymphs, south of the Acropolis.[70] We notice that, on the one hand, even though their iconographical schemes are close, never are two images exactly identical, and that, on the other hand, the existence of baskets, caskets, and boxes is evident in all these scenes. These objects are part of the goods of the bride and are, in a way, a portable part of the oikos she is taking with her. All these objects, whose status and function we have tried to fix in the Attic repertoire, appear again in nuptial scenes, quite obviously because they describe the woman as the one who controls the goods inside the oikos. From this angle, a lebes by the Marlay Painter[71] is exemplary, because all the containers previously described are present: chest, basket, kalathos, *exaleiptron*, sometimes stacked up, a pyxis on casket, a casket on wicker basket—as if to omit nothing of what furnishes an oikos.

In these nuptial scenes, especially in the series of vases attributed to the Washing Painter, winged figures are often depicted, Eros or

Nike, surrounding the bride and her female companions. The presence of such figures should not surprise us; the function of these ritual images does not consist in simply reproducing a ceremony well known to the Athenians, but in illustrating the divine powers behind the rite. Nike is here the sign not of military success, but of accomplishment, the successful outcome promised to the bride. As for Eros, he personifies both desire and beauty.[72] He is frequently repeated, but when he appears only once it is near the bride, whom he often crowns, or between the young couple whom he serenades with his aulos.[73] In scenes of wedding preparations, Eros is also present to underscore the young woman's beauty as she gets ready among her female companions. On a pyxis in New York,[74] he is pouring water for the bath, bringing a casket to a woman who is tying her belt, sitting in the lap of the bride. Thus, Eros in his turn carries a casket as the bride's companions do, a casket which holds the ribbons and clothes used in women's art of seduction and whose contents Eros, in a way, qualifies. The Washing Painter, whose name comes from these scenes of women getting dressed, and for whom they seem to have been a favorite,[75] often depicted Eros alone, in flight, carrying a casket. Sometimes he flies toward an altar,[76] bringing to mind the wedding ritual; at other times, as on a pelike in the Louvre (fig. 13),[77] he is in front of a kalathos, which, as already noted, when associated with a casket could itself define female identity. The same interaction of proximity and association between Eros and the contents of a casket is repeated on a lebes attributed to the same painter:[78] in front of the seated bride who is playing the harp is a standing woman, perhaps Aphrodite, who holds in her left hand a wicker box, while with the right hand she is grasping the leg of a small Eros who is flying away toward the bride. This Eros is no simple divine presence anymore; visible in image,

Fig. 14. Detail of an aryballistic lekythos. Taranto, Museo Nazionale, inv. no. 4530.

he seems real, as if he came out of the box held by the woman. Toward the end of the fifth century, painters often reproduced the figure of Eros, especially in the circle of Meidias;[79] on a lebes attributed to the manner of the Meidias Painter,[80] we see three women, one on the left with a basket and a casket, one on the right with a casket and an alabastron, and the one in the middle with a casket and an Eros seated on her right hand, as if these two elements were complementary. The contents of the caskets depicted in nuptial scenes are rarely visible; there is no reason to describe them. But there is at least one example, Apulian, where a painter has played on the association between Eros and women's caskets. It is a perfume vase, an aryballistic lekythos (fig. 14),[81] depicting Aphrodite seated and nursing an Eros; by her feet is an open casket from which Erotes are escaping. The metaphor between the contents of the casket and its erotic value is here given a concrete expression by the profusion of Erotes spilling from the chest. We find again, in a style that is at once explicit and slightly mannered, the values connected with grace and seduction that remain implicit to Attic imagery.

In trying, as we have, to read Greek culture through a series of specific objects, we were led through a world almost exclusively female, where chests, caskets, and baskets determine the space where they are seen, pointing to their role in managing material goods of the oikos and in domestic production, especially wool working. All these objects are almost exclusively branded as female, and the male is rarely part of this picture. His counterpart can be found in Satyrs who are sometimes humorously depicted in the *gynaikon*. Thus a cup attributed to the Oedipus Painter[82] depicts on the exterior on one side, a scene of armament, and on the other, a woman, seated, spinning wool with two of her companions looking on. The cup compares male and female; in the tondo, and, as if between two worlds, a Satyr holds a casket, as if he were bringing to the women the gifts that characterize them. Beazley rightly noted: "the Satyr should probably be thought of as attending upon women such as those on A."

Another cup, decorated only on the inside (fig. 15),[83] takes up the theme again in a lighthearted fashion: a Satyr, drawn by curiosity, is halfway into an open chest. Unlike Danae, whose torso is

Fig. 15. Detail of a cup (interior) from the European art market.

emerging from the chest, he reveals only his hindquarters and resembles certain Satyrs immerged in a pithos.[84] But the chest here delimits a domestic space, female, where he does not belong. We have seen to what extent the connotations of chests and boxes could vary, and how their polysemantic contents visually characterized, in Attic imagery, the female world. The curiosity of the Satyr infringes, once again, on the boundaries shaping Greek society; he cannot resist and dives, head first, in the women's chest, even if it means losing his head.[85]

FRANÇOIS LISSARRAGUE
Centre National de la Recherche Scientifique

This essay was translated by Eric Brulotte.

1. Harrison (1990) 99.
2. Panofsky (1956) 14-15, quoting Erasmus, *Adagiorum Chiliades Tres* I 233, published for the first time in Basel, 1508. For Pandora's jar, see Hoffmann (1985).
3. Richter (1966).
4. Brümmer (1985).
5. See Milne (1939).
6. Bérard (1979).
7. Deubner (1925); Schelp (1975).
8. Apollodoros, *Bibliotheke* 2.4.1 (trans. J. Frazer).
9. See *LIMC* III (1986) 331, nos. 41, 45, 48 (s.v. Danae).
10. Compare the coffins by the Sappho Painter on the loutrophoros in Athens, National Museum, inv. no. 450 and on the bail amphora now in Brunswick, Bowdoin, both illustrated in Boardman (1974) figs. 264 and 266.
11. Apollodoros, *Bibliotheke* 3.14.6 (trans. J. Frazer).
12. It is curious to note that a fragment showing a boy in a chest was first been interpreted as Perseus, before J. Oakley (1982) demonstrated that it was actually Erichthonios.
13. Apollodoros, *Bibliotheke* 1.6.2 (trans. J. Frazer).
14. *LIMC* III (1986) 844-45, nos. 1, 2, 5, 6, 11, 16 (s.v. Eriphyle I).
15. Naples, Museo Archeologico Nazionale, inv. no. 18426; *ARV²* 1065.7.
16. Oldenburg, inv. no. 12/19634/47; W. Gilly (1978) 60-61, no. 22.
17. Paris, Musée du Louvre, inv. no. G 442; *ARV²* 1065.7, *LIMC* III (1986) 844 no. 4 (s.v. Eriphyle I).
18. Gerhard (1840) pl. 301; *ARV²* 257.17, by the Copenhagen Painter.
19. Picard (1930) pl. 43.1.
20. According to Ch. Lenormant; see Reinach (1899) II, p. 148.
21. Formerly Basel market, Münzen und Medaillen, Auktion 34, no. 169; now Malibu, J. Paul Getty Museum, inv. no. 95.AE.265.
22. Manfrini (1992).
23. Bérard (1983) 20-27; Kaempf-Dimitriadou (1979) 26.
24. Diogenes Laertius 1.33 (frag. 11 A1 DK).
25. Lissarrague forthcoming.
26. Compiègne, inv. no. 1090; *ARV²* 922.1; Bérard (1984) fig. 129.
27. New York, Metropolitan Museum of Art, inv. no. 07.296.74; *ARV²* 523.1.
28. Munich, Antikensammlungen und Glyptothek, inv. no. 2676, name-vase; *ARV²* 393.27.
29. E.g., hydria in London, British Museum, inv. no. E 215; *ARV²* 1082.1, name-vase of the Painter of London 215. On an unpublished lekythos in Paris (Cabinet des Médailles, *ARV²* 624.81 by the Villa Giulia Painter) a spinning woman stands in front of a kalathos and is labeled with the inscription *philergos* (industrious).
30. Rome, Vatican Museums, inv. no. G 72; *ARV²* 955.1 by the Comacchio painter. See also the hydria in Palermo, Adriani (1971) pl. 72: a man on the right and three women, one seated by a chest, one carrying a box and a third holding a kalathos.
31. E.g., hydria in Rome, Vatican Museums, inv. no. 16554; *ARV²* 252.47 by the Syleus Painter. The same kalathos is visible on other cases; see LIMC I (1981) 420-21 nos. 1, 3 and 4 (s.v. Aithra I). Add to these a hydria attributed to the Geras Painter by J.R. Guy in the Dechter collection, Hamma (1989) 45 n. 24. On these erotic values, Keuls (1985a) chap. 9. For a different status in South Italian vase painting, Cassimatis (1990).
32. Williams (1961).
33. See Pemberton (1989) 19-25 and Payne (1962) 303.
34. Prückner (1968) type 14, 51, 52, pls. 4, 10, 11.
35. Zancani-Montuoro (1954) pl. XVIII.
36. Prückner (1968) 31, fig. 3, types 5-12.
37. Sourvinou-Inwood (1978) 114-18.
38. See recently P. Orlandini in Puglisce-Caratelli (1983) fig. 472.
39. London, British Musueum, inv. no. TC 1226; Higgins (1954) 333, pl. 169.
40. See Richter (1957) pl. LVIII, 3 and Richter (1966) 72-78; Brümmer (1985) 50 n. 242, fig. 31b.
41. Berger (1990) 25-70.
42. Basel, Antikenmuseum Basel und Sammlung Ludwig, inv. no. BS 266; Berger (1990) 67, Beilage 7, 2.
43. See Conze (1893) pl. 17, no. 38, 19 no. 40, 23 no. 47; Clairmont (1993) I, 91-92 and VI, 125-126.
44. Rome, Villa Albani; see A. Linfert in Bol (1989) 251-53, no. 81.
45. See Kontoleon (1970) 10 and Rolley (1994) 386.
46. Vienna, Kunsthistorisches Museum, inv. no. 3746; *ARV²* 998.164. See also Amiens, inv. no. 3057.172.33; *ARV²* 1000.200.
47. Berlin, Staatliche Museen, inv. no. 3262; *ARV²* 845.168.
48. Athens, National Museum, inv. no. 1052; Brümmer (1985) fig. 38a.
49. Schelp (1975); Deubner (1925).
50. On the kanephoros see Sourvinou-Inwood (1988) 95-97.
51. London, British Museum, inv. no. E 88; *ARV²* 631.43, by the Chicago Painter.
52. Buschor (1939).
53. Cups by the Brygos Painter, Rome, Vatican and Princeton.
54. Bari 3899; Trendall (1967) 27, no. 18.
55. New York, Fleischman, RVAp I, 4/224a and Trendall in True and Hamma (1994) 129-30, no. 57.
56. E.g., London, British Museum, inv. no. B 174; *ABV* 141.1; Oakley and Sinos (1993) fig. 65. See Krauskopf (1977) 16-28, nos. 3, 4, 9, 14, 15, 27.
57. For the name, see Milne (1939); for the shape Sparkes-Talcott (1970) 173-178 and Roberts (1978).
58. London, British Museum, inv. no. E 773; *ARV²* 805.89.
59. On the shape Scheibler (1964).
60. *ARV²* p. 806.
61. Athens, National Museum, inv. no. 12465; *ARV²* 958.73, by the Comacchio Painter.
62. See Oakley, *CVA* Baltimore, 39-40, pl. 41.
63. Munich, Antikensammlungen und Glyptothek, inv. no. 2726a; *CVA* 2, pl. 99, 2. Edinburgh, inv. no. 1956.477; *CVA* 10-11, pl. 30. Athens, inv. no. 14794; Richter (1966) fig. 398. Athens, Agora; Richter (1966) fig. 397.
64. Boardman (1992).
65. Athens, National Museum, inv. no. 2510; Boardman (1992) 232, no. 9, fig. 5.
66. Aristophanes, *Lysistrata* 1184 and *Peace* 666; see Henderson (1975) 130.
67. See Oakley and Sinos (1993).
68. Vienna, Kunsthistorisches Museum, inv. no. 2027; *ARV²* 1127.11.
69. Athens, Kerameikos Museum; *ARV²* 1127.3 bis. Compare the foot of New York, Metropolitan Museum of Art, inv. no. 07.286.35; *ARV²* 1127.1 (no. 55).
70. *ARV²* 1128.20-92. On this shrine, see Travlos (1971) 361-63.
71. Athens, National Museum, inv. no. 14505; *ARV²* 1277.15.
72. Greifenhagen (1957).
73. Lebes gamikos in Athens, NM 1454, *ARV²* 1178.1, name piece of the Painter of Athens 1454; Loutrophoros in Athens, *ARV²* 1127.14.
74. New York, Metropolitan Museum of Art, inv. no. 1972.118.148; Oakley and Sinos (1993) figs. 20-21.
75. See *ARV²* 1128.106-107, 1129, 108, 1131, 155-160.
76. See *ARV²* 1130.134-139.
77. Paris, Musée du Louvre, inv. no. G 551; *ARV²* 1130.141. See also *ARV²* 1130.140.
78. New York, Metropolitan Museum of Art, inv. no. 16.73; *ARV²* 1126.6.
79. Burn (1987).
80. Ferrara, Museo Archeologico Nazionale, inv. no. 2721 (T 1166); *ARV²* 1322.18; Burn (1987) pl. 48 a-c.
81. Taranto, Museo Nazionale, inv. no. 4530; RVAp I, 15/2, by the Suckling Painter.
82. Toronto, Borowski; *ARV²* 451.3; see J.R. Guy in Leipen (1984) 17.
83. European art market, unpublished.
84. Geneva, inv. no. 16908; Bérard (1984) fig. 173.
85. For their help and advicc, I would like to thank J.R. Guy and O. Murray, for permission to publish photographs, M. Denoyelle, F. Hamdorf, N. Lazaridou, and D.J.R. Williams.

WOMEN'S STORIES

Fig. 1. Sphinx dedicated by the Naxians at Delphi. Delphi, Delphi Museum, inv. no. 365.

The title of this paper was suggested by a TV program on Alzheimer's patients made for the BBC by the poet Tony Harrison, "Black Daisies for a Bride." In an interview shown after the film, Harrison emphasized the close relation between identity and story-telling. In preparation for the film he spent hours walking up and down wards and hospital corridors listening to women who were evidently telling him stories, although he could not identify distinguishable words in their speech. He suggested that it is part of the poet's task to give words to those who have none of their own.

This is also what historians try to do, and what museum visitors do. We must however be aware of the temptation either to parrot or to ventriloquize: to repeat what we have heard from others or to project our own experience uncritically onto the women of other societies.

The aim of this paper is not to provide the viewer with a ready-made story to serve as guide or background to the exhibition but to suggest ways in which the viewer can enter into dialogue with it, can enable it to ask questions as well as asking questions of it—to cast ancient Greek women, perhaps, in the role of the Sphinx (fig. 1), that enigmatic part-female creature who also asked unanswerable questions.

The image of the Sphinx can stand for the three main points that I want to make: about the museum as an institution, about differences between ancient Greece and the modern West, and about the ambiguity of images.

A museum display or exhibit is like a riddle. It juxtaposes objects and images taken out of context, and does so in a way that suggests—given the history of the museum in the modern West as a didactic institution—that there is a "correct" way of reading the connections between them. A specialist in Classical archaeology, Greek literature, or ancient history could supply information to fill in the gaps between objects and between cases and tell a connected story. That suggestion needs to be resisted. In the first place, the stories would vary according to the gender, disciplinary training, and interests of the specialist. Secondly, the objects have arrived in the museum as the result not of one but of a whole series of displacements from context. While the kore from the Acropolis Museum in Athens (no. 1) was made on commission to be set as a dedication in the sanctuary in or near which she was found and where she is now exhibited, this is a rare example of contextual continuity. Loutrophoroi with wedding scenes on them and lebetes gamikoi were, we can be fairly sure, made and painted in the expectation that they would be bought for use in weddings, but many were dedicated on the Acropolis; well-preserved specimens may have been found in tombs. We do not know where and for how long they were kept between wedding and dedication or burial, how they were used, who looked at them. An exhibition is not a shorthand version of a longer story known to experts but an opportunity for provocative juxtaposition, for setting up dialogues in both artistic form and iconographic content between objects that were not originally made with this kind of conversation in mind. The arrangement of objects in this exhibition is not that of a Linnaean taxonomy but more like the arrangement of valued possessions in a private house—personal, provisional, open to question and revision. It may remind us that Greek women could make some decisions of their own about the way they juxtaposed vases, and the images on them, in their homes.

Nevertheless, we need to remember that those homes would probably seem bare by our standards, and that they were sharply divided into male space, open to visitors, and female space, used for women's work—weaving, child rearing, or running the household. Only when kin gathered to celebrate rites of passage would the women of the family be seen in the public part of the house. It is this separation of men's and women's lives that makes it so difficult for us to understand the social experience of ancient Greek women; like the Sphinx, they look at us with women's faces, but the body of practical experience that made up their daily lives was very different from that of the modern suburban housewife.

Leila Ahmed, writing about women in traditional Islamic society, has suggested that one might see Saudi Arabian social arrangements as based on the assumption that men and women belong to separate species from different planets, with scarcely any common tastes or interests, who can only be expected to interact for brief periods and for a limited set of purposes.[1] I suggest we might develop, and modify, this idea by looking at women in male-dominated societies as a species of domesticated animal, and then distinguishing different modes of domestication. There are significant differences in the degree of human intervention in the lives of the "free-ranging" herd animal, the domestic pet, or the victim of factory farming. Women in traditional Islamic society, as early Western female travelers noticed,[2] though living in a highly patriarchal regime, spent almost all their time in female company and were much less subject to ideological pressures to internalize the legitimacy of male domination than women in the Western bourgeois family. They were herd animals rather than domestic pets.

Although the harem favored this cultural independence, and was perceived by Western women travelers in the eighteenth and nineteenth centuries as offering freedoms that they did not enjoy at home,[3] it is not of crucial importance whether women live in extended families or nuclear households. What matters is whether women's social lives are spent in the company of other women or in mixed company. From this point of view the modern Western middle-class marriage—at least before the rise of feminism—represents an extreme in the direction of treating women as household pets that is probably not to be found in any other society—not even in the Western working class.[4]

In societies where men and women lead separate social lives, it is taken for granted that women tell stories and jokes derogatory to men, just as men do to women. There is a female as well as a male locker-room discourse. It is taken for granted that women will deceive men if it serves their ends and they are given the chance.[5] They are clever at making the deceit agreeable; seduction is the role of women (in Greece the domain of Aphrodite), and it is women who are the experts in sexual technique.[6] We find all this in Greek sources, especially in Aristophanes' plays about women (*Lysistrata, Thesmophoriazousai, Ekklesiazousai*) and the comparative evidence suggests that we should believe him. Clearly the two domains were not hermetically sealed off from one another. Small boys heard women's talk as they were growing up, in a society that had no inhibitions about the topics suitable for discussion in the presence of children; hetairai were allowed to join freely in symposium conversations which, when they were present, would afford a favorable reception to gossip and jokes from the female world; there were moments of intimate contact between wives and husbands. When women formed their own groups at religious festivals, or girls appeared to dance in chorus, laughing among themselves, men and boys could see an independent point of view in action; and no

doubt some of the pointed, laughing comments were meant to be, and were, heard. Anyone who has seen groups of girls passing groups of boys during the evening *corso* in a South Italian town can understand the situation.

I do not want to paint too rosy a picture of the possibilities of independent thought—let alone action—for women in ancient Greece; but in trying to understand other societies we may learn more from looking at variations in the degree of women's subordination and helplessness, and less from the general idea of the domination of male discourse, than we do in our own. If women want to change society they have to look beyond details of personal situation. But in historical or anthropological research we have to ask how male domination works and whether women's identity and expectations are shaped consistently and systematically by institutions, vocabulary, texts, and images. How consistently were women presented in the ancient "media" as subordinate and dependent on men? How far did such presentations correspond to their own experience?

We might start at the beginning of Greek literature, by comparing Penelope with Andromache and Briseis. All of them are presented to us as women in societies at war. The poet makes their situations abnormal by lengthening the war, but war in itself was not abnormal. Penelope is managing her husband's property effectively without him; it is the imminent coming-of-age of Telemachus that makes the situation on Ithaca critical for the suitors. (Homer also knows that Agamemnon's wife Clytemnestra took a lover while he was away, though he does not dwell on the point; it

Fig. 2. Interior (tondo) of a kylix. St. Petersburg, The State Hermitage Museum, inv. no. 14611.

Fig. 3. State (Kore) of Phrasicleia. Athens, National Museum, inv. no. 4889.

is in the period of long military campaigns in the fifth century that the story of Clytemnestra's infidelity becomes a major focus of interest.) Andromache has no one in her life but Hector,[7] but this is because her kin are all dead; Briseis, who can be passed from one owner to another, is a prize of war. Authors of fiction often find it convenient to deprive their female characters of kin, as authors of children's stories and TV serials find it convenient to separate children from their parents or orphan them, but in real life a married Greek woman's situation was seriously affected by the presence or absence of male kin who took an interest in her well-being. She could leave her husband easily if they supported her decision to do so; Menander even portrays loyal young brides who insist on staying with their husbands against the pressure of fathers who have decided that the husband's behavior is unpardonable.[8] If she was left in charge of her husband's affairs while he was overseas, it would be an advantage for her to be able to call on the support of her own kin in legal dealings where she needed a male representative; if she was widowed, her kin would arrange a second marriage and/or help her to see that her children were not defrauded by their guardians. The woman who married within her own kindred was in a particularly strong position; if she was in trouble, she could argue her case in person before a family council, as the daughter of Diogeiton does in Lysias 32; her closest male relatives in the kindred might be persuaded to support a plan to allow the sons of a second marriage to inherit or share the estate of her first husband,

as seems to have happened for a time in the case of the estate of Hagnias.[9] On the other hand, sisters who had no surviving male kin in their family of origin, and thus stood to inherit shares in their father's estate as *epikleroi*, had considerable difficulties in pursuing their rights in court; they had to rely on husbands or sons who were not closely tied to each other, would tend to conduct their business when the women were not present, and often failed to maintain a united front, one party or another being bribed or frightened by the opposing litigant into dropping the case.[10]

The invisibility of women in the political arena had advantages for men, yet these same advantages could also put a woman in a position of some power. The process of political argument came increasingly, in the Archaic period, to exclude or minimize appeals to the wishes of the gods and to religious authority, the sole exception being the external authority of oracles whose riddling messages could be the subject of open, purely intellectual debates on interpretation. These changes left religious specialists and male holders of life priesthoods in a problematic position. Religious specialists in Athens, by the Classical period, were expected to confine their interventions strictly to ritual matters and could quickly provoke ridicule if they seemed disposed to claim too much importance for their role and authority. The Hipponikos/Kallias family of Alopeke, which held the office of Torchbearer of the Eleusinian Mysteries in the Classical period, had some political prominence due to its wealth, marriage alliances with other leading families, and service on embassies, for which it was well suited, not simply by wealth but also by membership of one of the Eleusinian priestly families responsible for announcing the truces which cov-

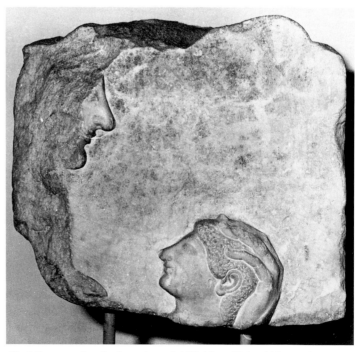

Fig. 4. Fragment of a stele of a mother and child. Athens, National Museum, inv. no. 4472.

Fig. 5. Grave stele of Ampharete. Athens, Kerameikos Museum, inv. no. P695.

ered the period of the Mysteries. This combination of religious and political eminence, however, provoked a notable amount of hostile gossip and attacks in comedy. Most of the male holders of prominent religious offices led politically inconspicuous lives, until Lykourgos, life priest of Poseidon Erechtheus on the Acropolis, took control of a demoralized city after the defeat of Philip of Macedon at Chaironeia.[11]

Priestesses were faced with no such problems. They could enjoy the full dignity of office without facing any contradiction between the extent and norms of religious and of political authority. In choosing the name Lysistrata for the heroine of a play in which the

women in Greece unite to put a stop to the idiocy of a seemingly endless and increasingly destructive war, Aristophanes was obviously associating her with the dignity and authority of the current priestess of Athena Polias on the Acropolis, Lysimache,[12] and with her legitimate transcendence of merely political aims. A prominent priestess both had her own authority in the world of women and, when performing her public role for the city as a whole, was a visible representative of a purer dimension of civic life and authority absent from everyday politics.

Moreover, even in everyday politics—and the closely related contests in the courts—men needed helpers and allies. There was no recognized patron/client system in Athens: the ethos of male political life was fiercely competitive and egalitarian. Often we find men relying on their affines for help, and it seems likely that women played a role here as intermediaries. A woman could act as suppliant on behalf of her husband, with her own father or brothers, or on behalf of her kin with her husband, without the loss of face that a man would have suffered in making a direct request. The very fact that women "don't count" can give them influence.

It is difficult for us to combine, in our picture of ancient Greek women, their evident common-sense recognition that there were circumstances in which they needed effective male protection and representation with a recognition that they also had scope, in other contests, for independent action. Perhaps part of the problem is that we have too ethnocentric a view of what is important and what is problematic in marriage. We should reflect more on the commonplace assertion that marriage took the place in a woman's life that war had in a man's life. This represents marriage as stressful, testing, and dangerous. The primary basis for the comparison was, indeed, the risk that a young married woman would die in childbirth. One was not fully a woman—*gynê*—until one had successfully borne a child, just as a boy was not fully a man until he had been tested in war. But marriage was also testing in other ways. The bride had to manage a stranger, her husband, and a strange household; she had to hold her own among new female neighbors; when she had children, she had to rear them successfully to adulthood. She could not expect her husband to concentrate all his attention on her; he would, for example, certainly go on drinking with friends from his bachelor days, in the company of attractive boys and hetairai, even if he might leave the party before couples paired off for the night.[13] Nor was a woman expected to concentrate all her attention on her husband.

The stories of the Sphinx and of other female monsters, and of the enchantress Circe and Calypso, indicate clearly that seduction is a danger to men, a distraction from the journey of life. At the extreme, to gaze into the eyes of the Gorgon or listen to the song of the Sirens means death. Sexual pleasure should be peripheral in a man's life, not central. Whereas Victorian ideology portrayed the respectable woman as submitting reluctantly to her husband's sexual needs—closing her eyes and thinking of England—the ancient Greeks took the opposite view. It was the respectable man who

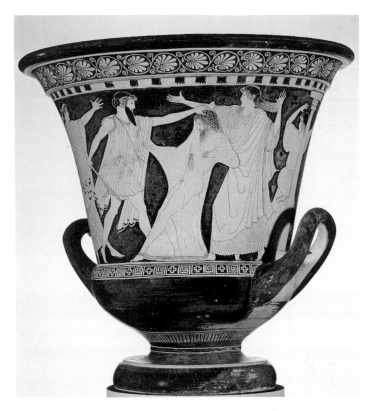

Fig. 6. Kalyx krater by the Dokimasia Painter. Boston, Museum of Fine Arts, inv. no. 63.1246.

should control his physical desires, and women who were incapable of doing so. If unsatisfied, they would resort to masturbation; Herondas' sixth *Mime* represents a conversation between two women about buying dildoes (and they are also shown in vase-paintings (fig. 2). They would also stimulate each other; men do not seem to have found this in any way threatening.

It is no doubt becoming apparent to the reader by now that the stories men told about women were contradictory. There are both psychological and intellectual reasons for this. Women played a large part in a boy's early life; he was treated as a privileged being (as the son of the family), but nevertheless subordinated. For the upper-class boy, his situation as adolescent *kalos* was in some ways analogous, yet much more contradictory. In addition to the demands made on him to measure up to social norms of deference to seniors and successful competition against peers within strictly enforced rules, he was also explicitly targeted as the object of a sexual desire that social norms ordered him not to reciprocate or satisfy. Subsequently, he moved into a position in which he could allow himself openly to express his own desire both for boys—who would meet it with reluctance or rejection—and for women, who were not required to resist. He would only gain social approval, however, by succeeding in other fields: politics and war. Protective, nurturing goddesses (Athena in the *Odyssey*), sexually ambiguous companions in the hunt (the story of Artemis and Aktaeon), and

sexual temptresses would appeal to successive layers in this sedimentation of identity. At the same time, however, on a more intellectual level, maleness was defined against conceptions of the female. Since the female was the unmarked category, its construction did not have to be, and indeed was not likely to be, coherent. Women's sexuality could be stressed in one field of discourse, their modesty in another; they were expected to act out both the extremes of total abandon to grief at funerals and the transcendental dignity of the world of the gods in rituals.

Greek culture, therefore, presented women with contradictory stories about female identity, and this contradictoriness surely left them some room for maneuver. Let us now try to see how it worked out in the visual arts.

We are used to talking about "identifying with" an image or a character in a story; recent feminist work on art history and the media stresses the role of images in shaping women's conceptions of self and of the female body. But the modern world obviously has resources for image-making that were not available in ancient Greece. We have to start by asking *how* women saw images of women, heroines, and goddesses.

In the first place, I suggest, we need to make a distinction, especially for the Archaic period (i.e., until about 500 B.C.), between three-dimensional and two-dimensional presentations of the human body. The free-standing three-dimensional figure occupied the same space as the viewer; it was not surrounded by an invisible frame marking it as "art," as something existing only to be viewed. It was not an image, still less a portrait, but a substitute or proxy. The mourning figure placed in a tomb was put there to make a connection between the dead and the continual process of mourning in the world of the living. The kore in a sanctuary continued the act of worship that had placed her there. The kore standing over a grave (fig. 3) spoke to the passer-by, told her story, and asked for a response of respect and pity:

The sign (*sêma*) of Phrasicleia.
I will always be called kore, having
received this name from the gods
instead of marriage.[14]

The three-dimensional figure normally faced the viewer (herms, which stood by the side of the road, seem to have been an early exception). The story it told—apart from the basic information on age and gender encoded in its figure—was supplied in writing, normally in the form of a first-person address to the spectator.

Two-dimensional representations of the human body, on the other hand, alluded from an early date to narratives through the use of attributes and grouping of the figures. These are depicted in profile, looking at each other, acting out their story in a space cut off from that of the viewer. Frontal faces, in the Archaic period, seem to be mainly confined to Gorgons and Dionysos, both of whom threaten the viewer with the danger that his gaze may lock into

Fig. 7. Terracotta pinax from Lokri. Taranto, Museo Nazionale, inv. no. IG 8332.

imaginative involvement with art. If she looks at a statue of a goddess, the ancient viewer will not identify with it but will interact with it, praying or making an offering—constructing herself in a relationship with a culturally defined other. If, on the other hand, she looks at a statue of woman, she may, particularly if it matches her in age, identify with it in its situation as a figure on view. The adolescent girl who sees a kore in a sanctuary may see in it the model of the image of *aidos* that she herself must present when she is subjected to the gaze of strangers; she may anticipate or re-experience the mixture of tension and pride she will feel as she plays the role of kanephoros (basket-carrier) at a public festival. (It should be remembered that adolescent boys, who were on view in the nude both as statues and in the gymnasium, were much more directly subjected to the voyeur's gaze, in ancient Greece, than women.) The relation to a narrative image is less intimate. The viewer is invited to remember (or imagine, in the case of a funerary monument) a story. If she "identifies with" it, she still has some freedom to choose the character with whom she identifies and the moment of the story she privileges. If reminded of the story of Atalanta, did she dwell more on the ultimate "lesson" of the myth, that even Atalanta was eventually caught by a suitor and married, or on her earlier triumphs in out-running her pursuers? Did she, even, necessarily identify only with female characters, never with male? Always with Medea, never with Jason?[17]

theirs, so that he becomes immobilized by terror or drunkenness and may become possessed by an alien power.[15]

There is, of course, over time, a convergence between the two conceptions of representation. Free-standing three-dimensional figures turn their heads away from the viewer—the bronze god found in the sea near Artemision is a well-known example—and their figures become narrativized: they hurl the discus or tie a sandal. The narrative technique is used for scenes from everyday life as well as mythical stories (as happens also in lyric poetry). Above all, the relief technique is increasingly used in marble for narrativized monuments which take the place of free-standing figures, especially on tombs (figs. 4 and 5).

Nevertheless, I suggest that it is useful to keep the distinction between three-dimensional and two-dimensional figures in mind. Three-dimensional figures have ritual functions. In addition to dedications and tomb monuments, there were cult statues, figurines used in rites to lay ghosts to rest, wax figures used in oath-taking,[16] and figurines pierced with nails and placed in graves to work black magic. I am not saying that Greek sculpture in some way "originated" in magical practices, but that it belongs to a continuum of beliefs and practices in which the focus is on action rather than representation.

This way of thinking about Archaic Greek art suggests that we should expect some corresponding differences in the viewer's

Fig. 8. Detail of a stamnos by the Deepdene Painter (no. 76).

Fig. 9. Interior of a kylix by the Penthesilea Painter, Munich, Museum Antiker Kleinkunst, inv. no. 2688.

Stories were told among women as well as in more public contexts, among men, by poets. Story-tellers adapt tales to their audiences; well-known myths would vary when told by women to each other or children. Possibly the contrast between the high-minded tragic attitude of Phaedra in Euripides' *Hippolytos* and the readiness of her old nurse to engage in romantic intrigue may give us a glimpse of the difference between high-culture versions of stories and the commentary a female story-teller or audience might make in an all-female environment. Such differences in the way stories were told or remembered might also affect the reading of visual images.

Let us consider this in relation to the interpretation of images that, either by association or through metaphor, "stand for" women—textiles and containers. Myths in which textiles play a prominent role seem to represent women in a position of power—fittingly enough, since weaving was the activity through which they autonomously produced wealth for the household. Penelope kept her suitors waiting by weaving and unweaving Laertes' shroud; Deianeira killed Heracles by giving him a poisoned robe, and Medea, perhaps in imitation of the Deianeira story, killed Creon in the same way in Euripides' play; Clytemnestra enticed Agamemnon to walk on a red carpet, entangled him in a net, and murdered him. These stories are not popular on vases, although we have one picture of the death of Agamemnon (fig. 6).

In other myths, where women fare less well or play a less extraordinary role, the metaphors seem to leave openings for alternative

readings. Danae was shut up in an underground chamber made of bronze, visited by Zeus in the form of a shower of gold, and subsequently set adrift with her son Perseus in a chest (*larnax*). One of the primary referents of the images associates them with death: the bronze urn in which bones were buried after cremation is succeeded by coffin (*larnax*) used in inhumation. Like other brides who died young, in the conventional formula of epitaphs, Danae went to the *thalamos* of Hades instead of the bridal-chamber. But there are other readings. A *larnax* was also where a man kept his money;[18] the shower of gold turns into the boy-hero who is stowed away where treasure is stowed, and will surely be reborn and not lost. These were rich themes for women's stories: the tricks by which lovers make their way into the best-guarded houses, often no doubt with the help of a judicious distribution of bribes to slaves, the golden boy, *chryso agoraki* as modern Greeks would say, enclosed in the place where a watchful husband or father kept *his* gold. It seems possible, also, that the *larnax* could suggest the chest (called *chelos* in *Odyssey* 8.438), where women kept their own wealth of woven textiles (figs. 7 and 8). If chests stood in the women's quarters, were they also scary hiding places for small children in their games? Like a Chinese box, the mythical *larnax* contains within it a succession of possible images.[19]

In assuming that women put their own twist on tellings and readings of mythical stories, I merely extend into the women's quarters, with support from Sappho, the freedom of male singers, writers, and artists to select and vary characters and events when they re-presented myths. Greek myth was unstable and speculative, open-ended. Whereas the modern attitude to fiction considers it impossible to go behind or beyond the text—we should not ask how many children Lady Macbeth had—Greek myths, like history, were always open to further questions. The image of the untamed adolescent girl as Amazon could lead to ethnographic theories about the Amazonian mode of reproduction,[20] or to a romanticization of the encounter of the adolescent Achilles and Penthesilea in battle (fig. 9). Amazons also satisfied an interest on the part of sculptors and painters in representing the female form in violent action, in a period when visual representations of monsters appealed less to the imagination and stricter norms of dignity and decorum were being applied to goddesses.

At such relatively obvious surface levels, Greek images of women were shaped by a multiplicity of male interests, among which keeping women in their place hardly played a determining role. The "ideal viewer" of Greek art was not female, except in the case of a limited repertoire of vase shapes made for women's use. A serious study of gender ideology in Greek art would have to move to a more abstract level of analysis, comparing types of action and situation, asking questions, for example, about the gender and status of givers and receivers in scenes where objects are handed over, of rescuers and rescued, heroes and victims, solo performers or participants in relationships. Possibly we might find, at this level, a widespread tendency to allow men an individual identity as actors and to represent women more often relationally and in passive roles. But such research has yet to be carried out, and exceptions to the general trend, if a trend were found, might be revealing in their own right.

It might still be argued that we have some pornographic images from ancient Greece which, even though not painted primarily with a female viewer in mind, represent male domination with a remarkable degree of unambiguous brutality. But even here a reading through the lenses of Greek culture may suggest that there is ambiguity. Multiple-sex scenes (fig. 10) portray either women or Satyrs in the receiving role.[21] There do not seem to be any fully explicit representations of anal penetration of men or of fellatio by men, although one cup shows a man performing cunnilingus.[22] Satyrs were part-human, part-animal male creatures characterized by their inordinate appetite for unregulated drinking and sexual activity; they parody and reverse the norms of well-conducted male social life.[23] Images of Satyrs on drinking cups therefore function, at one level, in the same way as lewd dancers, or the undignified antics of uninvited guests who earned their drink by acting as buffoons, or the helots whom Spartans invited to symposia, after making them drunk, in order to ridicule them.[24] Representations of the outrageous reminded symposium participants, especially the young, of the need to maintain control and not go beyond the permitted limits.[25] Representations of multiple sex with female hetairai presumably carried the same message. Both women and Satyrs were shown passively permitting liberties to be taken with their bodies that would be shameful for the young male *hetairos* (companion) or *eromenos* (love-object).

This example, however, clearly illustrates the ambiguity of imagery as a mode of social control. The young Spartan who joined his elders in tormenting a befuddled helot could scarcely fail to find identification with the victim painful. Pictures of tabooed behavior, even if associated with a sexual code strongly marking the hierarchical distinction between active and passive sexual roles, could not be expected to work so predictably. Their painters acknowledged the normative code, but at the same time suggested pleasure and therefore subversion. As for the female viewer, hetairai, the women most likely to drink from such cups, were in a situation of economic competition against young men for gifts and attention. How would that affect their reactions?

Women's stories are "culturally determined," in the sense that they cannot be understood without a background of historical/ethnographic knowledge. But they are not fully determined. I suggest that the reader should experiment, in looking at the exhibition *Pandora's Box*, with reading, or looking, against the grain both of ancient Greek culture and of our own. Readers I suggest should ask how these images could be read to subvert conventional understandings of ancient Greek society as "male-dominated," not in order to produce a blander and more comforting picture of our Classical ancestors, but in order to take a more critical look both at the stories we tell about them and at the stories we tell about ourselves. Are we too ready to think that lapdogs have a better life than cows?

S.C. HUMPHREYS
University of Michigan

Fig. 10. Detail of a kylix by the Pedieus Painter, Paris, Musée du Louvre, inv. no. G13.

1. Ahmed (1982)527-28; cf. Malti-Douglas (1991).

2. Melman (1992).

3. Ibid.

4. Bott (1957).

5. Handman (1983).

6. Malti-Douglas (1991).

7. Homer, *Iliad* 6.410-30.

8. Menander, *Epitrepontes* act 4; Papyrus Didot 1.

9. Humphreys (1986).

10. Isaeus 5 and 8.40-42.

11. Humphreys (1985).

12. Lewis (1955).

13. Cf. Xenophon, *Symposium* 4.9 and 9.7.

14. *IG* i³ II.1261.

15. Frontisi-Ducroux (1991); Korshak (1987).

16. The figures used in both these two latter examples are called *kolossoi*; Meiggs and Lewis (1969) 5. For figurines to lay ghosts to rest: *SEG* ix.72, 18.

17. Osborne (1994) asks somewhat similar questions about the viewer's relation with kouroi and korai, but comes up with rather different answers. I think he overstresses the differences between representations of adolescent young men and girls, and overlooks the fact that the male viewer of a kouros is presented with an image of the *eromenos*, of the young man at the age when he is a love-object. Osborne's remarks on the influence on sculpture of changes in the relation of aristocratic families to the developing public sphere, and of related changes in practices of dedication and commemoration, are important. On the complexities of the ways in which stories are read by subordinate groups see Steedman (1992), esp. chap. 6.

18. Herodotos 3.123.

19. See Malti-Douglas (1991) 71-75 for Arab parallels.

20. Herodotos 4.110-117.

21. For a fuller discussion of the scene illustrated, see Kilmer (1993).

22. Berlin, Staatliche Museen zu Berlin Preussischer Kulturbesitz, inv. no. 3251; *ARV²* 113.7.

23. Lissarrague (1990) and (1993); Konstan (1990).

24. Lewd dancers: Xenophon, *Symposium*; uninvited guests: Fehr (1990); helots: Plutarch, *Lykourgos* 28.

25. Cf. Herodotos 6.129; Plato *Laws* 637-50.

MALE AND FEMALE, PUBLIC AND PRIVATE, ANCIENT AND MODERN[1]

There are many reasons why the study of the Classical world is a privileged locus for thinking about thinking; not least among them are its many histories, constructed over many centuries in different cultural milieus, each refracting ideological constructions of its present and shaping the constructions of the ancient past by subsequent generations. But not everything is mirage; some things can be determined, and not all constructs have equal value when one is concerned with reconstructing, as much as possible, such determinable aspects of the ancient realities. The fact that we are now aware of the culturally determined nature of our readings of the ancient other makes it possible to generate strategies that will limit its distorting effects to a considerable degree. One of these strategies to limit cultural determination and help illuminate scarce and ambiguous data draws on anthropology. Recent studies[2] have reassessed the alleged seclusion of women in Classical Athens and produced a more complex and convincing picture; the sophisticated approach that produced such results had benefited from the better understanding of the complex modalities of the operation of ideologies and their relationships to lived realities achieved in the anthropological study of living societies, above all in the so-called "Mediterranean societies," a category that includes modern Greece as well as several Islamic societies.

However, I will be arguing that while this understanding has produced beneficial results a different deployment of "Mediterranean societies" for the study of ancient Greek society, and in particular of the position of women, has the potential of itself becoming a new source of distortion; that even when applied with great subtlety and sophistication,[3] the use of contemporary "Mediterranean societies" as a model leads to serious misreading of the ancient realities. I will also be reconsidering a view associated with this approach, which has become widely accepted in recent years, a view most recently formulated as follows: "Like many traditional Mediterranean societies, that of the Greeks was separated into public and private or domestic spheres; the former was the world of men, the latter of women."[4] One version of this approach to the relationship between gender and the public and private spheres articulates an opposition according to which while in the household male and female were complementary opposites; in the public sphere male and female were separate, opposing and unequal. This entails the implication that they were equal in the private sphere.[5] I will be arguing that, on the contrary, while in one particular public sphere, religion, women were complementary and

equal to men, in the private, in the oikos, they were unequal and subordinated to the head of the household, even in religious matters. Another version of this approach[6] acknowledges but underplays the importance of women's role in the public sphere to an extent that makes it possible to compare the position of women in ancient Greece to that of women in modern "Mediterranean societies."

In my view, there are two methodological objections to this approach. First, something which is not of central concern here and which I cannot seriously discuss: the very concept of Mediterranean societies is the result of a particular interpretation of a series of data; it is not uncontroversial fact. As a native of one of the cultures that have gone into the making of this construct, that of modern Greece, I am perhaps better placed than many to recognize the ways in which anthropologists' expectations have shaped their perceptions, let alone their interpretations. These expectations include, for example, the unconscious privileging of distancing from the perceiver's culture and of similarity to societies "instinctively" considered likely to be similar, which leads to the structuring, the making sense, of perceived phenomena through unconscious models based on those societies. In addition, distortion in the very evaluation of observed phenomena results inevitably from the fact that the "societies" under consideration, for example, a Greek mountain village, are *de facto* treated as closed systems, as though they were not part of a wider system, the legal and institutional framework of the Greek state that gives modern women a radically different place from those of classical Athens and that reflects, above all, the social reality and ideology of the urban middle classes, which, incidentally, have always had a more intensive interaction with these "rural societies" than is often acknowledged. This and other problems are further reinforced by an inadequate awareness of the informant's conscious and unconscious strategies of self-presentation, partly in interactive response to the observer's expectations as perceived by the informant; even anthropologists aware of these strategies of manipulation seem all too ready to believe that they have stripped away the final mask and have reached the ultimate level of reality rather than simply a new, more complex mask, corresponding to, and deployed to fulfil, the anthropologist's new and more sophisticated expectations as the informer perceives them. The result of all this is the creation of constructs whose relationship to the lived reality and the normative ideality of the observed society is problematic. These methodological problems are obviously not created by the notion of Mediterranean societies, but, in my view, this concept exacerbates rather than minimizes them. This does not entail that classification into larger categories must necessarily be abandoned. However, the potential danger of blurring distinctions and of structuring perception through alien models that distort each society's reality should be minimized through a rigorous methodology. But this is another story, albeit one not dissimilar to our central one. For the second objection against the deployment of the "Mediterranean society" concept in the study of the ancient world is precisely this potential danger of blurring of distinctions and of structuring perceptions through alien models that distort each society's realities. Even in its most careful version this approach involves the (not always successfully eluded) danger that what was intended as an eye -opening model can slide into, implicitly assume the role of, an explanatory tool, through which scarce and ambiguous data are structured and made sense of. Because of their very scarcity and ambiguity it is possible to structure these data in such a way—and to make such conscious and/or unconscious adjustments to them (such as by overprivileging certain parts of the evidence and underprivileging others, or blurring important distinctions)—as to make the data fit that explanatory model and thus appear to confirm the model's validity, while in fact they reflect the circularity of the investigative process. It is therefore crucial not to allow assumptions about the society under investigation, whether or not they were derived from comparative material deemed to be relevant, to become false structuring centers and create false perceptual filters that will structure the discourse in insidious ways and lead to serious distortions.

It may be argued that when it is used with methodological awareness and centered on explicit similarities such comparative material can be illuminating. However, there are problems with this. First, the identification of similarities is itself ideologically loaded, since classifying different things as similar often depends on stressing some of their aspects and not others. If we study a society for which the evidence is limited and ambiguous with the help of another for which there is much more evidence, the focus on identifying similarities can implicitly underprivilege important differences and end up by, again implicitly, taking the presence of things that look similar in the two societies as an index for the presence of other similarities and thus seriously overestimating the overall similarity of the two systems. Even when the similarities are real, the fact that the elements under consideration would be operating in radically different social and ideological contexts would inevitably have significantly changed their meanings and functions. For every element in a system is also shaped by, and acquires its meanings through, its relation to other elements in the system and with the system as a whole. Thus, when the systems are different, even elements that are superficially very similar have inevitably different meanings. The notion that a woman's adultery dishonors her husband is not limited to ancient Athens and "Mediterranean societies"; it obtains—in combination with another element also taken to characterize "Mediterranean societies," the notion that the public domain is above all a male sphere—in many societies, including until recently at least some sections inhabited by "Western" scholars. However, not only are all the societies that combine these elements not the same in other respects, but there is also wide spectrum of perceptions of both the dominance of the male role in the public domain (from the exclusion of women from everything that is not the world of the home, to a limited participation of all or some women in a few or some public roles, and so on) and of the nature of the adulterous wife's husband's dishonor and the responses it elicits—from Oxford Senior Common Room titters to the expectation that he must wash the dishonor with blood, his wife's, his wife's lover's, or both—depending on a series of associated social assumptions.

I hope to show that there are such serious differences between "Mediterranean societies" and Classical Athens that the use of the former to help us make sense of the latter is inappropriate and leads to a distortion of the ancient realities, and that one of the most fundamental differences pertains to the ways in which women are placed with reference to the public sphere.

The social persona of the large majority of women was defined by their roles within the oikos; most women spent most of their lives in the private sphere; and, we shall see, in a binary symbolic classification men belong with the public and women with the private, the *oikos*. However, it is not the case that in Classical Athens women were excluded from the public sphere; they played an important, active role in public life in religion, as priestesses and other cult personnel as well as as worshippers; that is, they played an active role in a central part of polis activity, in which women were complementary and equal to men. I will return to this. First I will examine the position of women in the private sphere and argue that, far from its being the case that they were complementary and equal with men within the oikos,[7] they were unequal and subordinated to the head of the oikos even in religious matters. When considering these questions it is important not to confuse different categories; what we are talking about here is not respect and love for women within the family, nor the notion that strong women can usurp the power of weak men, but rather a normative structural position, the assumption of a certain amount of power and control that does not have to be "earned" through personal affection. Also, a man who needs his wife's dowry, which went with her, or the husband of a rich *epikleros*,[8] is in a *de facto* weaker position than he ought to be and than husbands normally were, and this was perceived to be undesirable precisely because it reversed the natural and normative order of things.[9]

An interesting articulation of the perception of men's and women's relative position within the oikos, one that speaks of it in hierarchical terms in a normative context is Gorgias fr. 82 B 19 D-K (=Plato, *Meno* 71e), which defines a man's *arete* by his performance in the public sphere and a woman's *arete* as consisting of managing the house well, looking after its contents and being obedient to her husband. A woman's obedience, and thus subordination, to her husband is presented as the normative value. Is this simply male ideality? The problem with *pensée claire* articulations is that the difficulty of disentangling the thinker's creativity from normative ideology makes any reliance on our interpretations potentially vulnerable to circularity. Hence I will not spend much time on Aristotle or Xenophon. I will simply mention that Aristotle's view that the man is the head of the oikos and is in a position of authority toward his wife as well as children and slaves[10] (which is, in my view, not radically different from Xenophon's position,[11] though Xenophon presents a liberal and enlightened version of male headship) converges with the Gorgias fragment and also with the image presented in another genre, one that is much more useful for our purposes because it is by necessity articulated by commonly held assumptions—comedy. In Aristophanes' *Thesmophoriazousai* Mica is claiming that Euripides has made husbands suspicious and as a result women suffer in various ways, one of which is the following: "but the things regarding which before this we could be our own managers, and take away without anyone noticing, barley-meal, oil, wine; not even this is possible any more; for now the men hold the keys themselves, malicious secret Laconian keys with three teeth. And before we could at least open the door secretly by having a three-obol seal-ring made; but now this destroyer of the family,[12] Euripides has taught the men to have little worm-eaten seals and to wear them on their bodies."[13] We can recover the parameters of lived reality that shaped this passage; for this to be capable of functioning as comic discourse, it is necessary that the audience should be taking for granted a state of affairs in which the man is the head of the oikos and his wife manages it for him, under his authority. It is my contention that there is no evidence to suggest that there was any ambiguity or ambivalence in the normative ideology with regard to the notion of the oikos hierarchy and the subordinate position of women.

This subordination of women to men in the oikos mirrors the legal subordination of women. In Attic law a woman never achieved legal majority; she was always under the tutelage and control of a male relative who acted as her guardian, her *kyrios*[14]—the same term as that used for the guardian of male minors. She was entirely dependent on her *kyrios*, and to a much lesser extent on other male relatives,[15] for most things, since she could not act as an independent person in any significant activity except in the cultic sphere. Thus, far from the situation concerning gender in the oikos being different from that in the public sphere, the two are the same, which fits the ways in which oikos and polis interacted in the ancient realities.[16] Indeed, it is at the very least arguable that the legally restricted subordinate position of women is to a considerable extent the result of, reflects, women's subordinate position in the oikos. We know that the legal system concerned itself with the proper functioning of oikos; the oikos was—not wholly and in every respect, but partly—the basic economic unit of the polis. There is some ambiguity as to the extent to which the basic social unit is the oikos or the individual, but in any case the privileged model for "individual" is the head of the oikos. Political power had been rooted in economic and social position and was both in reality and in ideology closely associated with military duties. I suggest that these were the forces that to a very great extent determined women's legal minority status and their exclusion from the political and other non-religious public spheres, that it was the hierarchical articulation of the oikos and the woman's subordinate position in it that determined women's exclusions in the public, in interaction with the importance of military duties, which itself was undoubtedly one of the factors that sustained the perception of man's obvious and natural superiority. I will now try to show that in religion, far from women having a more significant role in the private sphere than in the public, they had a restricted role in the cult of the oikos, while in the public sphere they played complementary and equal roles with men,[17] and that this is correlative with the fact that in polis religion the basic unit is not the oikos, but the individual.[18]

In the most important rite associated with the birth of a child, through which it was incorporated into the oikos, the *Amphidromia*,[19] the father played the central role. This reflected the woman's subordination to her husband in a fundamental aspect of family life, the decision whether to rear a child born to her or expose it. For a child was not admitted to his father's oikos at birth and by right, but only at the *Amphidromia*, a few days after its birth. It was the father who decided whether or not a child would be accepted in the oikos and reared. Even with a legitimate child, it was entirely up to him whether to rear it or expose it.[20] The *Amphidromia* appears to have been in two parts: the first involved a movement around the baby, when the child was examined to decide whether it was worth rearing; in the second the baby was carried around the hearth by a running man, almost certainly the father—a rite of incorporation. The *Amphidromia* articulates, among other things, the subordination of the mother's biological centrality in the production of the new generation to the father's socio-legal and ritual centrality.

The wedding ritual allowed women a more significant role. In legal terms marriage involved a transaction between men, the woman's guardian and the groom.[21] To most intents and purposes, on marriage a woman passed from the guardianship of her father or other male relative to that of her husband. In ritual terms the wedding ceremony dramatizes the transference of the woman from one *oikos* to the other, and her transformation into a woman. The transfer of a woman from one oikos to another is at the very center, legal, ritual, and symbolic, of the Athenian wedding ceremony and of marriage. Correlatively with this ritual centrality of the female, women, the bride, but also the mothers of bride and bridegroom, play an important role in it.

It has often been claimed that the death ritual was the special responsibility of the women of the family. Limitations of space prevent me from setting out here the long and complex argument pertaining to this question. I will only mention that I have briefly argued,[22] and I am arguing in great detail in a forthcoming study,[23] that this notion is based on a conflated perception of the death ritual as an unarticulated whole and also on the elision of a concept that was crucial in Classical Athens. I argue that there was a concept we may call "ritual responsibility," "ritual responsibility" for the conduct of the death ritual, culminating in the burial, and also for the rites of commemoration, the *nomima*, and that this ritual responsibility had to be carried by a male. Also, I argue that women played specific and circumscribed roles in the death ritual, of differential weight in its different parts; they played the dominant role in the first part of the ritual, which involved the embracing of disorder and pollution (correlatively with the fact that in the Greek collective representations and ritual symbolism the male-female opposition functioned as one of the axes of a system of symbolic classification in which women stood for the other pole of the qualities which ideality and collective representations associated with the male, so that the male could be deployed to represent symbolically order, and women disorder). In the second part of the ritual, the *prothesis*, the weight was carried equally by men and women. In the final part, the burial ceremony, the main ritual weight was borne by men. The burial ceremony terminated the period of abnormality; it was the rite through which the dead were finally separated from the living and the new order was restored. Thus, as the plot of the death ritual moved from playing up disorder and pollution and embracing death toward purging pollution, separation from death, and restoration of a new order, the role of the actors on whom the values of pollution disorder and embracing of death had primarily drifted, the women, became less important.[24]

Finally, while in the public sphere women sacrificed both as individuals and as priestesses, on behalf of the polis or of one of its subdivisions,[25] I do not know of any example of a woman sacrificing on behalf of her oikos in the context of an oikos cult, such as that of Zeus Herkeios or Zeus Ktesios. That is because women could not represent the oikos even ritually, even in the private space of the oikos; only the male head of the oikos could do this.

By contrast to this subordinate role in the oikos, in public religion women played a very important role as actors as well as participants, a role that was not subordinated to that of men. Indeed in a fragment of Euripides' *Melanippe Desmotis*[26] the speaker claims that women are superior to men first because it is women who keep the oikoi clean and prosperous; and second, because they play the most important part in religion, a claim she supports by mentioning important cultic offices held by women, such as that of the Pythia. I shall return to this fragment and will consider its connection with practice and normative ideology. Here I want to note that women's value is located in two spheres, the usefulness of their work in the oikos and the fact that men cannot replace them in certain important public religious offices. I should make clear that the exclusion of women from certain cults is not different from the exclusion of men or of other groups from certain other cults.[27] In fact the exclusion of men would seem to be more common than

that of women. Women sacrificed as individuals as well as priestesses and they also very commonly offered dedications in their own right; they could even found shrines.[28]

One of the scholars who deploy the "Mediterranean societies" model, Cohen,[29] acknowledges the fact that women played an important role in Athenian religion, but elides the problems this creates for this interpretation of Classical Athens in terms of the Mediterranean societies model through the device of a reference: "For an investigation of the special role of women in religious life in modern Greek communities see Dubisch (1983)."[30] But this device, and the reference, are misleading, for they implicitly suggest a similarity that can only be sustained through a series of elisions of radical differences. First, the studies that stress the religious role of modern Greek women outside the house are in some ways a challenge to, a refining correction of, perceptions of modern Greek society based on the men-public/women-private dichotomy.[31] Thus, Cohen uses an element that throws doubt on the validity of the conceptual schema at the center of his comparison of Classical Athens and Mediterranean societies and that to a considerable extent differentiates the society that possesses it from another component of the "Mediterranean societies" construct, Islamic societies, as a validating pivot for the comparison. Secondly, and even more crucially, this unexamined comparison between women's involvement in religion in modern and ancient Greece blurs a radical difference. Let us consider very briefly this religious role of women in modern Greece. The study of such roles has shown[32] that "there is no simple correlation of the public/private dichotomy with gender....The expectations of religious practice...can be seen to assign to women distinctly *public* roles in the public arena, defined both in spatial and in social terms."[33] and "Their religious activity .. transcends the localized concerns of neighborhood life as well as well as the exclusive, competitive interests of the family unit."[34] This may not appear on the surface to be radically different from the situation in Classical Athens, but in fact there are radical differences. The most crucial is that in modern Greece women do not hold priesthoods; they do not act as intermediaries between the community and the divinity, on whose proper action the community's prosperity depends. Athenian women were acting as public religious officials; they were not simply operating in the public space and in public, as modern Greek women do, whether as individuals or as chief actors for the family. Priestesses, but also other lesser cult personnel and women performing ritual roles, were acting on behalf of the whole polis or one of its subdivisions. That is, women played an important role in a crucial segment of the public sphere on which, in the Greek mentality, the survival of all the others, the survival of the polis, depended. The polis depended for its survival and prosperity on women doing their job properly, symbolically most strikingly, the priestess of Athena Polias and to a lesser extent the priestesses of other important polis cults, such as that of the Eleusinian cult of Demeter and Persephone and that of Artemis Brauronia. The active role of women was necessary for a proper relationship with the divine; women were not replaceable in their religious roles by men. The very fact that it was a woman, the priestess of Athena Polias, who offered prayers for the polis to the most important poliad deity in the most important polis cult, could not but affect the perception of women's importance in the scheme of things. In contrast, modern Greek women are not even allowed to enter the church's inner sanctum. There is, then, a fundamental distinction between the role of women in ancient Greek religion and in "Mediterranean societies" and indeed until very recently in any Western society. The fact that this radical distinction could be blurred in this way is an example of an unconscious adjustment to make the data fit the explanatory model. Enough blurring from one comparandum to another, enough subsuming of different things into one category, and the resulting constructs end up bearing little relationship to the realities they are meant to illuminate. Such downplaying of important differences illustrates how the explanatory model maximizes distortion by structuring the data to fit even if important distinctions are blurred and important areas marginalized. It is not only in the existence of priestesses that Classical Athens differed from "Mediterranean societies" with regard to the position of women; "the position of women" is not an independent essence, existing apart from the important element that is women's religious role; the position of and perceptions pertaining to women was a system in which—as in every system— each part is given meaning through its relationships with the other parts and with the whole, so the omission of one segment of this system from the assessment of the whole system falsifies the evidence. Thus, the active role of women in religion is an index that the perceptions associated with women are not the same as those in societies in which women do not play this role.[35] Also, perceptions of women cannot be the same in a society that depends on the proper actions of women for its prosperity, on a series of women doing their job properly, performing roles in which they were not replaceable by men. This is one of the things that the *Melanippe Desmotis* fragment articulates. Another difference also illustrates the fact that we cannot have the same element, in essence the same "position of women," in radically different religious and social systems. Not only is the Christian Greek religious system different from that of Classical Athens, with all that entails, but also, and crucially for our purposes, the place and function of religion are radically different. In Classical Athens[36] the polis articulated religion, had ultimate authority in, and control of, all cults, and set in place a particular pantheon and a particular set of cultic observances. The polis was also articulated by religion; cult helped define and gave symbolic identity to polis subdivisions such as tribes, demes, and phratries; all relationships and bonds, including social and political ones, were expressed, and so defined, through cult. One result of this was the centrality of religion; another was the much greater frequency in the performance of festivals and of rituals of various kinds generally and a much greater intensity of interaction within and between different groupings—in most of which women would

have been active not only as participants but also as performers of religious roles. Some of these festivals, incidentally, involved elements such as musical, choral, dramatic, and athletic competitions that gave them a very spectacular nature. In my view, women were present in the theatrical performances.[37] The perception that festivals and rites provided entertainment is, incidentally, explicitly articulated.[38]

There are also differences between women's religious roles in modern Greece and in Classical Athens in the sphere of "family" ritual. For example, in modern Greece women "are the chief agents in all the practices surrounding death beyond the home as well as in it."[39] In Classical Athens, as we saw, the ritual responsibility for the burial and for the *nomima* after death had to be carried by a man.

The differences between the role of women in religion in "Mediterranean societies" and in Classical Athens are even more radical when the comparandum is another component of the construct "Mediterranean societies," Islamic societies. Consequently, the deployment of models based on these societies in the investigation of Classical Athenian society has distorting effects. Even if our perception of Classical Athens is affected by the "Mediterranean societies" model in the vaguest and most implicit way, this still produces an importantly distorted image. Thus, an articulation such as "women were excluded from public life in Classical Athens except for the religious sphere" is already not neutral: it is weighted by culturally determined assumptions and implicitly places this religious role in a position of marginality. In reality, we saw, the religious sphere was central in the ancient polis. A more neutral formulation is that of the interconnected spheres that made up the public domain: "in Classical Athens women had an important place in the religious sphere but were excluded from the political and the military, and they were legal minors."

The constructs based on the deployment of the "Mediterranean societies" model not only distort the position of women in Classical Athens, they also elide the men's dominant role within the oikos. Because men participated fully in all aspects of the public, from most of which women were excluded, because most of most women's lives were spent in, and concerned with, the oikos, and because the public was the privileged part of the public-private opposition, in the symbolic articulation of the Greek collective representations the public-private opposition came to be aligned with the gender opposition, so that the male corresponded to the public and the female to the private. But this alignment should not be taken as the whole story, nor should we take the fact that it corresponds to certain types of male ideality as confirmation of its validity in lived reality.

Let me elaborate a little on the religious roles of women in the public sphere. Space does not allow me even to outline briefly all the many roles women played in cult, as priestesses, holders of various subpriestly offices, players of specific ritual roles such as that of kanephoros, as members of girls' choruses and so on—all these roles performed in honor of the gods on behalf of the community.

But I want to stress that, though some of these roles such as that of kanephoros, for example, involved what may be considered subordinate roles, the higher of these offices, the priesthoods held by women, were not subordinate but were complementary to those of men. Women were not hierarchically subordinated to men in polis cult. Even when a cult had more than one important priesthood the woman priestess was not in a subordinate position. She had her own area of authority on which male priests were not allowed to impinge. Thus, for example, the Athenian demos punished Archias the hierophant for performing a sacrifice on the Haloa while it was not customary to sacrifice on that day, nor was he entitled to perform the sacrifice because it belonged to the priestess.[40] Of course, this is correlative with the fact that different priestly offices had different areas of competence. But the point is that it is this principle that pertains, not one based on gender hierarchy. It is only at the interface of the religious and the political, such as addressing a political assembly, that the priestess' role is different from that of the priest, that priestesses cannot act independently, but need a male relative to act on their behalf.[41]

That women's active role in religion says something about them is one of the notions that is articulated explicitly in the fragment of *Melanippe Desmotis* mentioned above. But would such a notion have been perceived as right, or as an aberrant statement by a bad woman? Because it is a fragment, we cannot be sure about its place in the tragedy, and thus also of its coloring. However, the statement was almost certainly made by Melanippe, and she appears to have been a positively colored character in the play. The fact that the speaker's claim that women are better than men, a claim she justifies by mentioning their indispensability in the oikos and in religion, is in conflict with normative ideology does not necessarily entail that the whole statement would have been rejected, for this claim is explicitly presented as an answer, albeit a polarized answer, to men's censure of women. It thus could have been perceived as an exaggerated version of something recognized as basically true. That all citizen women had a symbolic stake in the religious offices, which in practice only some of them held, is illustrated by the fact that in a forensic context in which the parameters of manipulation were set by what would have sounded convincing to most male citizens, the assumption behind the speaker's argument in [Dem] 59. 110-4 is that all Athenian women would be diminished if a woman who performed the office of *basilinna* though she was not—the speaker claims—an Athenian citizen went unpunished.[42] Therefore the mere eligibility to hold important religious offfice was perceived to be very important to all citizen women. This eligibility was what defined and articulated their identity.

Let us now examine a series of other phenomena that will help us place Athenian women's position somewhat more precisely. If the results of these independent arguments point in directions similar to the conclusions reached so far, this may provide some confirmation for the validity of these conclusions.

Though it would not be correct to say that Athenian society had a true age class system, it is certainly the case that there were important age categories both for boys and girls[43] and that passages into and/or out of these categories were ritually marked. To put it very briefly, in their third year children underwent a rite of "presentation" and blessing in the Choes, the second day of the Anthesteria; between the ages of five and ten Athenian girls were eligible to be bears, undergoing a rite of initiation, the *arkteia*, under the protection and in the service of Artemis;[44] the final stage of an unmarried girl's life, that of marriageable parthenos, was ideologically correlative with the ritual office of kanephoros, though only a minority of girls were actually kanephoroi in polis cults. Marriage marked their passage into womanhood. Boys came of age and were admitted to the phratry, offering the *koureion* sacrifice and cutting their hair[45] at some point probably before age eighteen, when they were inscribed in the demes and served as ephebes[46] before they became fully adult citizens and hoplites. I have argued[47] that these perceptions of female age categories shaped the representation of girls and women, who were depicted through iconographical types corresponding to age bands, types generally based on, but not strictly (and in some cases not much) reflecting, biological age.

Though age class systems have a multifunctional educational, acculturational nature that involves social, ritual, cognitive, military, and political functions,[48] the fact that the military and political functions are part of this system creates a link between age systems class and political control, which is exercised by men,[49] as is the military function. This is why age class systems are predominantly male, both in the sense that they are most frequent for males, and in the sense that even when such systems exist for females they are often assimilated, subordinated, to the male ones.[50] Since this seems to be a general modality (rather than a model applicable to certain types of society), it may be legitimate to suggest tentatively that the fact that insofar as there is something comparable to age class system articulation in Classical Athens it pertains to both males and females and that the latter are not reflections of, or subordinated to, the former but pertain to significant female life categories, may be correlative with the fact that women did have an important public role in ritual.[51]

Let us now consider briefly women's grave monuments. The Greek grave monument existed in the public sphere. It is an anachronistic oversimplification to imagine that the public sphere is to be equated with the public funeral of the war-dead and their collective grave monument invented by the fifth-century Athenian democratic polis. In fact, the emergence and growing popularity of the inscribed grave monument, mostly for men but also for some women, pertains to the preservation of the deceased's memory in the wider community, beyond the family.[52] Cemeteries were public places and the polis regulated by law both what type of private grave monument could be erected at given times and the behavior of the living at these grave monuments. Grave monuments and cemeteries did have a religious significance, but they did not belong exclusively to the religious sphere; they also had an important social dimension, and it is to aspects of the latter facet that legislation limiting the luxury of the grave monuments pertained. Grave monuments made public statements pertaining, above all, to the deceased's social persona. Thus, the fact that in a period in which the inscribed grave monument was the rarest of exceptions, in the Archaic period, a situation that also pertained to some extent also for the fifth century, the fact that women also received such monuments cannot be understood as an extension of usage by unthinking routine, especially since we can see—where this can be ascertained—that the factors determining the choice to erect an inscribed grave monument are the same for men as for women.[53] Consequently, and independently of the factors that led to the choice to erect inscribed grave monuments to some people and not to others, the fact that women received such monuments in the Archaic period and in the fifth century, that registered their lives by articulating their social persona with words and images and naming the monument as the sign of a particular dead woman, entails and is an index of the fact that women were not thought of as ideologically inhabiting only the private sphere. I will not discuss the straightforward case of priestesses' epitaphs. Priestesses held an important public office, and this social persona is articulated in their grave monuments.[54] No one would doubt that they operated in the public sphere, and, besides their grave monuments, there were also statues representing them in the sanctuaries in which they had served.[55]

The type of praise bestowed upon women in the epitaphs of the Classical period also suggests a more complex situation than some present orthodoxies allow.[56] The formulations of praise in women's epitaphs in the Classical period[57] involve terms, and sometimes even formulations, of praise comparable to those used for men. A woman is quite frequently said to be *chreste*, *sophron*, or both, or *agathe* and *sophron* or to have *arete* and *sophrosyne*, or simply *arete*.[58] One woman is said to have loved her husband and *sophrosyne* more than clothes and jewelry.[59] Incidentally, the emotional attachment between man and wife is sometimes described as reciprocal.[60] One woman is said to have pleased her husband and children very much through her behavior and character.[61] Another is said to have been hard-working and thrifty.[62] Once, strikingly, a woman is said to be *eusynetos* (intelligent).[63] Another virtue sometimes ascribed to a woman, as to a man, is that of being *eusebes*, pious.[64] The virtues that are being praised are those fitting for a good wife and mother,[65] except perhaps for the intellectual *eusynetos* to which I will return. It was this social persona of wife and mother, of matron, often represented in images through the 'mistress and maid' schema[66] that defined the large majority of Athenian women; it was one of the two female personae represented in Archaic and Classical grave monuments, the other being that of the unmarried girl of marriageable age, while the representations of men's social persona showed them as athletes, warriors, old men with a stick, or in some cases with the tools of their profession.[67] In the fourth century there was a certain shift toward family-based images, in which the deceased male as well as female was represented as a member of the family group,[68] a trend that began in the later fifth century. Of course, the representation of the persona of wife and mother also carried with it, was also a metonymic sign for, all the connotations associated with that role in Classical Athenian perceptions, including managing the household, participating in certain religious activities, and so on. It is the same as the persona of athlete represented on Archaic grave stelai standing for the whole persona of the young aristocratic male, defining him through activities that straddled the private and the public.[69] To a lesser extent this is true for the persona of the marriageable parthenos or wife and mother; they did not simply pertain to the private sphere. It was her social persona that defined the woman and also made her eligible for certain types of public, religious, office, the marriageable parthenos, for example, to be kanephoros, an office correlative with precisely this persona, this social age group.

Another motif associated with both men's and women's epitaphs is that of people feeling longing for the deceased, which also of course constitutes praise.[70] In the case of women, it is her family or her friends who are said to feel longing for her.[71] In the case of men such longing is often ascribed to a wider group, and the same is true of one woman, Phanostrate,[72] who was a midwife and doctor, and thus came in contact with a large group of people. She is one example of a woman whose social persona is different from that of most others, and who is placed within a circle wider than the private sphere; it could be argued that it was still in private space that she operated, the private space of other people's oikos,[73] but the choice of formulation *pasin potheine* reminds us of the formulations for men. The notion of women's existing on a restricted stage is also challenged somewhat by a series of formulations that do not fit the modern orthodoxy that women are best not spoken of at all, for good or evil.[74] This is based on a passage in Thucydides, 2.45.2, that says so. However, Kallet-Marx has now argued convincingly that this injunction pertains not to all Athenian women, but only to the war widows, toward whom the polis has assumed a relationship comparable to that of *kyrios*, like that it assumed toward the war orphans.[75] If this is right, not only would the injunction not have been relevant to women in general, but also we can locate the context as one being even more conducive to ideological polarization than is already clear by the general framework. In fact, several epitaphs contain formulations expressing the notion that the dead woman had won praise in her lifetime. The formulations may be suggestive of a wider circle, ascribing to this woman a positive social persona.[76] A definite indication of reputation beyond a narrow circle is suggested by praise ascribing *eukleia* (good fame, renown) to a woman, which implies a wide circle and is also used for men.[77]

As to the comparability of the praise for men and for women, though it is true that words of praise do not denote an essence that is unchanged irrespective of the type of person to whom it is ascribed, and indeed the Gorgias fragment cited above illustrates precisely that male and female *arete* are diferent things,[78] and when *sophron* is used for women the self-controlled facet of its meaning would have been dominant,[79] it is nevertheless significant. Moreover, the intellectual virtue denoted by *eusynetos* is especially surprising for a woman since, to my knowledge, this word is otherwise only used once as praise in an epigram of the Archaic or Classical period, as praise for a man lauded for his intellectual qualities.[80] Thus, the epitaphs reflect the most positive end of the spectrum of collective representations about women, the normative ideology about good women (there are, of course, only good women in epitaphs), in which they are not thought of as radically different from men. The other pole, to which have drifted women's potential for wildness and for bringing disorder and catastrophe to men and families, is represented by negatively polarized notions of "bad woman" frequently articulated in tragedy and myths generally.

If it is correct that respectable women were not named in public, such prohibition was not valid in the sphere of religion. Not only were priestesses named, but also, and more significantly, women named themselves in dedications[81] and others named them as dedicators in inventories.[82] Thus, respectable women other than priestesses were named in the public sphere, even in their lifetime. This may suggest that women were named in the facet of the public in which they had a social persona not wholly correlative with that of their position in the oikos and on their relationships to males; they had such a persona in religion, both as priestesses and as individual devotees, and so they were named in the religious sphere.

At least some daughters in at least some phratries were introduced as children to their father's phratry,[83] an important polis subdivision, whose function was not simply, though it was also, religious. This entails that some women had a place in an aspect of the public sphere that was not simply religious. To a lesser degree, all women were taken account of by the phratries because when a man got married he gave the *gamelia*, a sacrifice followed by a meal, to his phrateres, on behalf of his wife.[84] This rite seems to have involved the reception, though not the actual introduction to membership, of the woman to her husband's phratry. The importance of establishing a mother's Athenian citizenship, as a result of Perikles' citizenship law, may have given this rite of reception, which is in fact cited by the orators as a proof of a child's legitimacy, added importance and what one may call a "political" charge.

Let me sum up my main conclusions. First, the deployment of the model of "Mediterranean societies" to help us investigate Classical Athenian society in general and the position of women in particular is methodologically dangerous; it maximizes the intrusion of cultural determination and produces constructs that distort significantly the ancient realities. Second, the role of women in the public sphere of religion had a much more important significance than is allowed by studies in which the investigation of gender roles is structured through the public-private opposition. Third, far from women and men having complementary and equal roles in the private sphere, while the public sphere was hierarchical and the position of the two genders always unequal, in one particular sphere of the public, religion, women were complementary and equal to men, while in the oikos they were hierarchically unequal and subordinated to the head of the oikos even in religious matters. It is only at the interface of the religious and the political that even priestesses have to rely on their male relatives, correlatively with the Athenian women's "legal minority" which, I argued, may be a reflection of their subordination within the oikos. Finally, women also had a (more or less limited) place in aspects of the public sphere that partook of, but cannot be collapsed into, the religious—a limited presence in the phratries and a definite presence in the cemetery and the community's memory through inscribed grave monuments, even when these were extremely rare. The epitaphs reflect the most positive end of the spectrum of collective representations about women, the normative ideology about good women in which they are not thought of as radically different from men.

CHRISTIANE SOURVINOU-INWOOD
University College, Oxford

1. For reasons of space I limited my footnotes to the minimum and mostly refer to recent discussions in which earlier scholarship is noted and bibliography given.

2. Cf. esp. Cohen (1991) 84, 147-67, 218, 236-40 and passim. In my view, Just (1989) 105-25 errs somewhat on the side of underestimating the ideological loading of some of the passages he cites, and thus overestimating women's confinement.

3. As for example most recently, by Winkler (1990) 9-10 and especially by Cohen (1991).

4. Pomeroy (1994) 33.

5. Foxhall (1989) 23.

6. Cf. Cohen (1991).

7. As suggested by Foxhall (1989) 23.

8. A woman whose father died without sons became an *epikleros*, and his estate was passed on through her; in order for this estate to remain in the father's family the right to marry the *epikleros* passed to her nearest male relative in a prescribed order. Even if she was already married such male relatives had the right to dissolve her marriage and claim her in marriage unless she had already had a son. (Cf. Harrison [1968] 10-12; 309-311; cf. 132-38; Leduc [1990] 296-99; Just [1989] 95-98, 102-104).

9. Cf. e.g., Aristotle, *Nicomachean Ethics* 1161a 1-2.

10. Aristotle, *Politics* 1253b, 1254b 13-5, 1259b-1260a.

11. Even Pomeroy (1994) 35 acknowledges that the wife can only have power when her husband delegates it to her.

12. On this word cf. Sommerstein 1994, *ad loc* p.184.

13. Aristophanes, *Thesmophoriazousai* 418-28.

14. Harrison (1968) 108-15; Just (1989) 26-39; Sealey (1990) 36-40. On Athenian women and the law, cf. Just (1989); Sealey (1990) 12-49.

15. For example, she could rely on her original *kyrios* or other close male relative if she was seeking to divorce her husband (cf. Harrison [1968] 43-4).

16. Cf. e.g., the relationship between oikos cults and the polis (Sourvinou-Inwood [1988a] 270-73).

17. Osborne (1993) 392-405 has convincingly demolished the notion that women's exclusion from politics corresponds to a religious incapacity manifested in their exclusion from sacrificing and partaking of sacrificial meat.

18. I have set out the argument on which this is based in Sourvinou-Inwood (1988a) 264-67.

19. On the *Amphidromia* cf. Paradiso (1988) 203-18; Garland (1990) 93-96.

20. Cf. Harrison (1968) 70-71; Garland (1990) 84-93.

21. On the legal aspects of Athenian marriage cf. Harrison (1968) 1-60; Sealey (1990) 25-36; Just (1989) 40-75. On the legal and social aspects of Greek marriage cf. also Leduc (1990) 246-314. On the ritual and its representations, Oakley and Sinos (1993).

22. Sourvinou-Inwood (1987) 24-25.

23. Women and the death ritual, a chapter in a forthcoming book entitled *Women, Religion and Tragedy. Readings in Drama and the Polis Discourse*.

24. Foxhall (1989) 23-24 ascribed the limitation of the role of women at funerals, and the fact that women's participation in funerals was regulated by law, to the fact that funerals also had a public aspect. But, as we saw, it is not a question of the public imposing on the private, it is the structure and ritual logic of the death ritual as a whole that assigns women differemt specific and ultimately subordinate roles. In addition, and most importantly, the notion of ritual responsibility for the death ritual and the *nomima*, which is presented as something important for the head of the oikos and the oikos itself, also shows this, and the ritual subordination of women, clearly.

25. Cf. on this Osborne (1993) 392-405.

26. Euripides, *Melanippe Desmotis* frag. a.1-19 Page (1941).

27. Cf. on such exclusions Sourvinou-Inwood (1988a) 267-70; Osborne (1993) 403.

28. Cf. e.g., *CEG* 2, 744.

29. Cohen (1991) 152.

30. At the end of n. 80 on p.152.

31. Cf. Hirschon (1983) 126-27 and cf. also 113-29 passim; Dubisch (1983) 185-86, 201-2 and cf. also 186-202 passim.

32. With regard to one community (Hirschon [1983]) which is in fact valid for modern Greece in general (cf. also Dubisch [1983] 186-202), insofar as we are talking about sections of Greek society to which these anthropological studies apply at all; for the notion that what is being talked about is "modern Greece" in general is simplisitic. These stories told about "Greek women" by anthropologists certainly do not reflect my own experiences, or my mother's, or indeed even my grandmother's, who was born in the last century.

33. Hirschon (1983) 126.

34. Hirschon (1983) 127.

35. It does not matter what motivates this state of affairs; the fact that it was possible is the significant fact. I will only mention that the number of exceptions to the correspondence in gender between deity and priest (cf. e.g. Holderman [1985] 301-305) shows that this correlation was not felt to be necessary; it was one important factor in a complex nexus of motivating factors.

36. For the discussions on which these remarks are based, cf. Sourvinou-Inwood (1988a) and Sourvinou-Inwood (1990).

37. I cannot discuss this here. Henderson (1991) has made an excellent case for women's presence at theatrical performances. I do not find Goldhill's critique (1994) 347-69 of Henderson convincing. Since the precise ways in which the polis articulated itself in the Dionysia is one of the things that need to be carefully and systematically reconstructed, the structuring of the investigation through assumptions pertaining to this question —and to gender construction—involves methodological dangers. Another route through which the effect of culturally determined assumptions is maximized in this critique is through the implicit deployment of the concept of likelihood; the difference between Goldhill and the discussions he criticizes is in the assumptions that have shaped this (inevitably culturally determined) notion. I discuss the question of women's participation in the Dionysia in Sourvinou-Inwood (1994) 270-71 and n. 9 and in more detail in "Tragedy and Athenian Religion," the Carl Newell Jackson Lectures, delivered at Harvard in April 1994, which will be published in the not too distant future by Harvard University Press. I should add that Goldhill's comment (164 n. 45) that I (in Sourvinou-Inwood [1994]) "may not be cautious enough in using such late evidence to uncover fifth-century ritual" seems to be based on a slight confusion; I did not start with the presupposition that late evidence was relevant to the early period, but produced an argument for a development and change in the spatial articulation of the festival which makes sense of the later attested *eisagoge apo tes escharas*—whether or not ephebes formed the escort from the beginning is not relevant to my case. But, it is worth stressing that, on a more general methodological point, it is not more rigorous to assume that change has taken place in the absence of any evidence for such change than to assume it has not; on the contrary, it is less so, especially when such assumption for change is formulated in the context of an investigation structured by prior assumptions.

38. Cf. e.g., Thucydides 2.38.1; cf. also Hornblower (1991) *ad loc*. and Dover (1993) 57-58 on *paizein*.

39. Hirschon (1983) 127; cf. also Dubisch (1983) 191.

40. [Demosthenes] 59.116-17.

41. Cf. e.g., *LSCG* 35, 16-18 (cf. Pirenne-Delforge [1994] 29-32).

42. [Demosthenes] 59.110-104.

43. I have discussed age categories for girls in detail in Sourvinou-Inwood (1988b) 25-30, 48-58. On girls' ritual offices and initiation rites, cf. also Bremmer (1994) 69-71.

44. As to how many and which girls served as bears, Sourvinou-Inwood (1988b) 114-17; but symbolically they all did.

45. On these complex issues see now Lambert (1993) 163-68.

46. I am assuming there was an *ephebeia* in the fifth century though this is not the place to discuss this question.

47. Sourvinou-Inwood (1988b) 31-67.

48. Bernardi (1985) 144-71, esp. 160-61.

49. Bernardi (1985) 142.

50. Bernardi (1985) 132-42.

51. Of course, this does not alter the fact that the individual rites had specific meanings; for example, the *arkteia* had meanings pertaining to the girls' acculturation and service to the goddess Artemis who presided over girls' transitions.

52. I have set out the discussion and evidence on which the statements pertaining to grave monuments made here are based in Sourvinou-Inwood (1995) 140-297. For a detailed discussion of the mentality associated with the emergence and deployment of the inscribed grave monument cf. ibid. 279-94.

53. For a discussion of this question cf. Sourvinou-Inwood (1995).

54. Cf. e.g., two examples of epitaphs, that for Myrrhine, the first priestess of Athena Nike (*CEG* 1, 93), and that for Chairestrate, priestess of Cybele (*CEG* 2, 566; cf. Daux [1972] 537, fig. 4), which besides her priesthood also referred to her place in, and feelings towards her within, her family. The grave monuments of priestesses and other female cult personnel are discussed in detail by J.B. Connelly in her forthcoming book on priestesses.

55. Cf. the base of the statue of Lysimache, who had been priestess of Athena Polias, found on the Acropolis (cf. the epigram on the base in *CEG* 2, 757).

56. On praise of women in fourth-century epigrams, cf. also Humphreys (1983) 107-108.

57. There is only one archaic expression of praise for women *aidoia*, deserving respect (*CEG* 1, 66; cf. also Stecher [1981] 18); in the Archaic period the theme of praise is not always present in the epitaphs, and some of the few inscribed Attic grave monuments for women were set up for girls who died unmarried, in whose epitaphs other themes were important (cf. e.g. *CEG* 1, 24).

58. *Chreste*: cf. e.g., *CEG* 2, 526, 530; *sophron*: cf. e.g., *CEG* 2, 479, 486; combination of the two: *CEG* 2, 491; *arete*: cf. e.g., *CEG* 2, 493, 510; *agathe kai sophron*: cf. e.g., *CEG* 2, 539; *arete* and *sophrosyne*: *CEG* 2, 611.

59. *CEG* 2, 573.

60. Cf. *CEG* 2, 530 (cf. on this Daux [1972] 545).

61. *CEG* 2, 536.

62. *CEG* 2, 537.

63. Both *sophron* and *eusynetos*: *CEG* 2, 516.

64. Cf. *CEG* 2, 543; 603. Referring (indirectly) to a male as *eusebes*: *CEG* 2, 545.

65. Cf. also Lefkowitz (1981) 26.

66. Cf. Sourvinou-Inwood (1995) 328-37 passim with bibliography.

67. On images of the social persona of the deceased in Archaic and fifth-century grave monuments, cf. Sourvinou-Inwood (1995) 217-78, 328-37.

68. On fourth-century grave epigrams and images stressing the intimate relationships within the family: cf. Humphreys (1983) 107-10.

69. Cf. Sourvinou-Inwood (1995) 222-26, 235-40.

70. On longing for the deceased, cf. Sourvinou-Inwood (1995) 170-72.

71. Cf. e.g., *CEG* 2, 539 (her husband); 543 (her friends), 522 (daughter), 530 (husband); *CEG* 1, 104 (all her friends).

72. *CEG* 2, 569.

73. The *titthe*'s epitaph *(CEG* 2, 571) commemorates a persona that could be said to be in between Phanostrate and most women though nearer the latter, since she performed the services of a surrogate mother within one oikos. On women's work outside the home, cf. Fantham et al. (1994) 106-109; Cohen (1991) 151-52.

74. The easy way out would be to postulate a change between the fifth and fourth centuries; but, as we saw, the change that in fact took place was toward a more family-oriented direction, not a more public one.

75. Kallet-Marx (1993) 133-43.

76. *CEG* 2, 493, 543, 546.

77. Cf. *CEG* 2, 513: she left to her child *megales te aretes euklean agero*, a formulation comparable to that used for a man in *CEG* 2, 570. The significance of this is not altered by the fact that the honour of the dead woman's husband and/ or children was enhanced by the registering of her good reputation; the prestige of the monument's dedicator and members of the deceased's family is often implicated in the erection of a grave monument. What matters is that the claim that she had a good reputation was registered in a public space in the public realm.

78. Aristotle asserts firmly (*Politics* 1260) that virtues like *arete* and *sophrosyne* are not the same for men and women. For a discussion of this question in *pensée claire,* cf. also Plato, *Meno* 71e ff., cf. 73.

79. On the use of *sophron* in Archaic and Classical epitaphs, cf. also Humphreys (1983) 107-108.

80. *CEG* 1, 67.

81. Cf. e.g., *CEG* 1, 259, 273; *CEG* 2, 774.

82. E.g., Inventory III from the Asklepieion, cf. e.g., l.15 (cf. the text in Aleshire [1989] 129-34).

83. Cf. now Lambert (1993) 36-37, 178-88.

84. On the *gamelia,* cf. Lambert (1993) 182-85.

THE CATALOGUE

Representing Women

AIDOS AND SOPHROSYNE

Together with her dress, a woman also sheds her aidos.

Herodotos 1.8.3

A woman should not look any man, even her husband, in the face.

Euripides, *Hecuba* 975

Aidos rests in the eyes.

Aristotle, *Rhetoric* 1384a

The behavior and demeanor expected of a respectable woman could be summed up by the terms *aidos* and *sophrosyne*. *Aidos* can be translated as respectful modesty with strong overtones of sexual shame, an acknowledgment of the popular belief that a woman's sensuality could subvert society unless it were successfully transcended (see **Women as Animals** and **Little Bears**).[1] *Sophrosyne* signified discretion and dignity; Plato defined the term as "doing everything in a quiet and orderly way."[2] A woman exhibiting *aidos* and *sophrosyne* would be modest, submissive, passive, and virtuous. Moreover, she would not speak. Aristotle quotes Sophokles as saying that silence is a woman's glory,[3] and Plato comments that the female mouth was to be closed, speaking only to her husband.[4] A respectable woman would also be practically invisible. In his famous funeral oration, Perikles declared that the greatest glory of a woman was to be least talked about,[5] and orators of the fourth century could observe that some women were too modest to allow themselves to be seen even by male relatives.[6] One of the inevitable—and desired—effects of conforming to this prescribed behavior was a woman's unsophisticated innocence. Xenophon recommended that a bride have "seen and heard nothing when she enters her husband's house,"[7] and an orator could comment that a respectable woman was uncomfortable in the presence of all males, including close relatives.[8] Such shyness was viewed by men as alluring. Athenaeus remarked that *aidos* engendered beauty,[9] and Aristotle observed that *aidos* had an erotic appeal.[10] *Aidos* was one of the first gifts that Hephaistos instilled in his irresistible clay maiden, Pandora (see **Pandora**).[11]

The primary way in which a woman could express *aidos* and *sophrosyne* was by inclining her head and lowering her eyes when in public or in the presence of a man (nos. 18 and19). This comportment was not confined to women. Mature men might adopt the pose in religious contexts where they considered themselves before the gods, and a young man might also present himself in this manner when in the presence of a older man during a solemn moment, for example, the ceremony of betrothal (no. 24).[12] The main difference was that an inclined head and lowered eyes were not expected of a mature man at all times, but were required of a woman who had reached maturity, essentially puberty at the age of about thirteen. It was especially important that the bride behave in this manner as a manifestation of her excellence, or *arete*. Accordingly, in wedding scenes her head is exaggeratedly angled downward, while her eyes, prompted by curiosity, often glance upward as far as is physically possible (no. 18). That an inclined head and lowered eyes signified submissiveness is affirmed by Andromache's comments in Euripides' *Trojan Women*, although her words tell us that the comportment was neither always automatic nor always sincere: "I gave my lord's presence the tribute of hushed lips and eyes quietly downcast. I knew when my will must have its way over his, knew also how to give way to him in turn."[13]

Although the inclined head and downcast eyes were the primary means of expressing *aidos* and *sophrosyne*, a woman was also expected to exhibit a closed silhouette with arms close to her body (see **Gesture and Gaze**). The degree to which her head was covered when she traveled outside the house has been much debated. Most genre scenes in Classical vase-painting are unhelpful, because they show women inside the house in the presence of other women, where, incidentally, they neither incline their heads nor lower their eyes (no. 45). On white-ground lekythoi where women are depicted tending the tomb, we find that in most instances they tend to be draped in their mantles, with their heads either completely uncovered or with the fabric passing over a knot of hair gathered at the back of their heads. In mythological scenes, which parallel genre scenes in terms of female gestures and gazes, we find that goddesses and heroines move freely indoors and outside, with heads uncovered and mantles either omitted or draped with aesthetic considerations foremost. Thus the traditional idea that Greek women traveled outside the home with head and body enveloped may rather reflect the contemporary mores of past generations of scholars. It is more likely that, by the time a girl had reached adulthood, she had successfully absorbed the dictums of her youth as to how a respectable woman should behave. Her reticent body language, carefully draped body, downcast eyes, and absolute silence would, indeed, impart to her the invisibility that Perikles extolled as the female ideal.

1. Ferrari (1990) 185-200; Fisher (1992) 111. For modern times, see du Boulay (1974) 112-117.
2. Plato, *Charmides* 159b.
3. Aristotle, *Politics* 1.13.1260 a 30 after Sophokles, *Ajax* 293.
4. Plato, *Laws* 6.
5. Thucydides 2.45.
6. Lysias 1.22-23; Demosthenes 47.53; Isaeus 3.3-14.
7. Xenophon, *Oikonomikos* 7.5, quoted in *Memorabilia* 405 C 3-11.
8. Lysias 3.67.
9. Athenaeus, *Deipnosophistai* 13.564b; see Ferrari (1990) 188.
10. Aristotle, *Rhetoric* 1384a.
11. Hesiod, *Works and Days* 71.
12. Ferrari (1990) 190.
13. Euripides, *Trojan Women* 653-56 (Lattimore 1959).

GESTURE AND GAZE

The Greeks noticed, appreciated, and viewed with apprehension every means by which they believed that femaleness expressed itself. The shape of the body was only one of many manifestations that included movement, gesture, gaze, hairstyle, clothing, ornament, and voice. Each feature was considered to have its own rich character and distinctive effect upon men. Least captured in Classical art is the voice, but we should remember its special potency. The Sirens are perhaps best remembered for the power of their words, but Pandora was also endowed with an overpowering command of language, and Aphrodite was noted for her *oaros*, the easy, relaxed, intimate speech that "steals the mind" (see **Sirens** and **Pandora**).[1] Conversely, the Gorgons were famous for their terrifying, shrill cry (see **Gorgons**).

Gesture

The evolution of Classical art witnessed, together with an increased skill in rendering the female body realistically, a parallel sophistication in the development both of a vocabulary of gesture and a subtlety in its usage. Little attention has as yet been devoted to differentiating characteristics of gesture among divinities, heroines, and mortals, but, as a general rule, innovations are seen first in the divine realm.

In general terms of body language, a woman practicing *aidos* is characterized by a closed silhouette, with arms close to the torso, whereas a hetaira (prostitute) exhibits an open silhouette (no. 39) that artists deliberately rendered as the diametric opposite (see **Aidos** and **Sophrosyne**). Upraised hands of distress (Thetis in no. 107) or astonishment (compare Pandora in no. 81), when belonging to respectable women, are intended to catch the viewer's attention because they are so uncharacteristic of a well behaved female.

Through much of the fifth century a respectable woman is not shown even touching anyone who is older than a baby, while her prostitute counterpart enjoys easy body contact with male customers (no. 41). Outside of the symposium context, the first expression of affection appears in depictions of deities and in contexts of mother and child. Aphrodite's embrace of her son Eros on the east frieze of the Parthenon is one of the earliest examples (pp. 248-49, fig. 1), and soon afterward she repeated the gesture in the metal relief from which the modern cast no. 17 is derived. At about the same time, Demeter and Persephone begin to express their rapport more overtly, with Persephone consoling her mother by gently placing her hand on Demeter's shoulder (nos. 83 and 86).

Concurrent with the trend toward familiarity is a predisposition for informality. On the east frieze of the Parthenon, Zeus displays his self-confidence and ease by resting his left elbow on the back of his chair (pp. 248-49, figs. 1-2). The gesture enjoys tremendous popularity in the subsequent depiction of women, where it continues to communicate ease, rather than the disinterest that is one of the modern connotations of the gesture. Thus, Aphrodite leans her elbow on a pillar while embracing her son (no. 17); Artemis adopts this gesture while relaxing with her hounds (no. 88); and Athena's left elbow rests on a pillar draped with her aegis (no. 64). Carol Lawton notes that in certain contexts, such as the honorary decree that was probably recorded on this stele, Athena prefers to present an informal aspect of herself by removing her aegis, a tone with which the leaning gesture is very much in keeping.

Classical artists not only expanded their command of gestures; they also refined their existing vocabulary. The gesture of the *anakalypteria*, or the unveiling of the bride, is recognized by the way the fingers of her left hand finger the edge of the mantle or veil in front of the woman's left shoulder (see **The Wedding**). As Maggie Mayo observed, the gesture refers to the moment in the bridal ceremony when, by removing her veil, the bride signals acceptance of her husband and her sexual submission to him (no. 27).[2] In the course of Classical vase-painting the gesture is no longer confined to bridal ceremony. When Amymone adopts this gesture during her pursuit by Poseidon (no. 113), it signals her acquiescence to his advance, a message that is reinforced by the strength of her gaze back at him, to which we will return.

A particularly interesting gesture that undergoes an adaptation of usage during the fifth century is the handshake. It originated as a gesture between men to signify their agreement, such as to a betrothal or to seal an oath (no. 24).[3] In the Archaic period, the handshake was introduced on some grave reliefs to express a bond between the deceased and the survivor. In the later 420's the gesture appears in decree reliefs to signify unity and accord, and Carol Lawton stresses its connotation of equality between participants. At about the same time, if not even earlier, the handshake is introduced into scenes of departure where it replaces the phiale and oinochoe previously held by husband and wife. The substitution is quite significant, because the handshake implies an equality between the couple that was not apparent in scenes where the wife prepares to pour wine into her husband's phiale (no. 18). The first appearances of the handshake in departure scenes are as awkward as they may well have been in actuality. On an amphora from Warsaw (no. 19), the wife continues to incline her head in the traditional expression of *aidos*, but by the end of the century a woman rather aggressively pumps a young man's hand while gazing directly into his eyes (no. 20). By the last decades of the fifth century the handshake is regularly encountered in grave sculpture where a woman may gaze directly into a man's face while confidently shaking his hand (no. 21).

Gaze

> Desire enters the soul through the eye.
> Plato, *Phaedrus* 251b

> Eros drips desire (pothos) onto the eyes like an unguent.
> Euripides, *Hippolytos* 255

A woman's gaze was perceived to be very much intertwined with her sexuality. The lowered eyes of the respectable woman exhibiting *aidos* were only partially intended as an expression of her respect and submission; a woman was also supposed to avert her eyes in order that men might be spared what was thought to be the irresistibly erotic power of her gaze (see **Aidos** and **Sophrosyne**). The phenomenon is well attested in Greek literature; in Homer, the same phrase ("the knees are broken") describes both a warrior receiving a lethal blow in battle and a man overcome by the desire that emanates from a woman's eyes.[4] Similarly, Achilles was said to have been overwhelmed with love for the Amazon queen Penthesilea when she looked up at him as his sword delivered its fatal blow to her (see no. 121). Charms against the evil eye have enjoyed a popularity into modern times, and evidence for the interconnectedness of the eye and the penis can be found in such disparate traditions as the blindness of Oedipus and popular wisdom about the ramifications of masturbation.[5]

The graphic nature of mythic imagery most vividly expresses this phenomenon in the figures of the Gorgons. A man who looked at Medusa while she looked at him was rendered lifeless, recalling Alkman's comment that a woman's gaze is more dissolving, more liquefying than death (see **Gorgons**).[6] On vases in New York (no. 136) and Richmond (no. 135), Perseus is careful to approach Medusa while she is asleep; moreover, the Gorgon's erotic qualities were vividly substantiated by the procreative abilities of her neck cavity, from which Pegasos and Chrysaor were born. The sexual character of her hair and facial features has often been noted (see **Gorgons**).

During the bridal ceremony, the moment in which the bride is unveiled was known variously as the *anakalypteria* and as the *opteria* and *theoretria*, the latter two terms drawn from the verb "to see" (see **The Wedding**). As the veil was removed, the bridegroom caught his first sight of his bride, and she could look at him for the first time with her eyes exposed. In his essay in this volume, Andrew Stewart discusses the Greek belief that conception was possible only if both man and woman experienced orgasm, simultaneously if possible. The mutual arousal necessary to attain this end was believed best capable of being achieved during this moment of looking. Armstrong argued that Aischylos was referring to the compelling impact of the bride's glance when Iphigenia, having just realized that she is to be a sacrificial victim rather than a bride, pulls the veil from her eyes as she approaches the altar in order that the assembled men might witness the full power of her challenge to them (see **Iphigenia**).[7] In a more conventional marriage, the ideal scenario would be that described by Plato who speaks of love flowing in a circuit through the eyes of lover and beloved.[8] Robert Sutton has shown that the presence of Eros hovering over the bride in scenes of the unveiling signifies just this same desire, which was expected to be emitted by her eyes in order to heighten her new husband's response to her.[9] The connotations of the bride's gaze are such that her decision to look into the bridegroom's face was comparable to her gesture of unveiling herself as an expression of her acceptance of her new husband as her sexual partner. One could also say that her decision to meet his glance was a manifestation of her willingness to exert her powers of seduction upon him alone.

The volition underlying linked gazes figures in many pursuit scenes where the fleeing maiden turns to look back into her pursuer's face (no. 113). In these contexts, the deliberateness of the woman's glance indicates that, whereas the man may have initiated the pursuit, the woman has voluntarily chosen to respond.

1. Homer, *Iliad* 14.216; *Homeric Hymn to Aphrodite* 249-51. See Redfield (1982) 196-201.
2. Mayo (1973) 220; Oakley and Sinos (1993) 136, n. 50.
3. Pemberton (1989) 45-50; Davies (1985) 627-40; Lawton (1993) 1-9; Shapiro (1990) 20.
4. Vernant (1991) 101; Homer, *Odyssey* 18. 212 and *Iliad* 5.176, 11.579, 15.332, 21.114, 22.335.
5. Johns (1982) 66.
6. Alkman, PMG 3 (*Pap. Oxy.* 2387) frag. 3, col. 2.
7. Armstrong (1985) 1-12.
8. Plato, *Phaedrus*, 255 c-e; *Timaeus* 91 a-b. See Halperin (1986) 62-3, 66; Halperin (1990) 131.
9. Sutton (1981) 173, 186-8. See Sophokles, *Antigone* 795: "Desire conquers clearly, seen from the eyes of a well-wed bride."

THE WEDDING

Start the wedding song, and through the tents let the pipes cry out,
and the feet start pounding, for this day has come, a blessed one for the maiden.
Euripides, *Iphigenia at Aulis* 433-39

Girls are afraid of marriage, you're supposed to be.
Sophokles, *Women of Trachis* 7-19

Girls are not meant to know about such things.
Euripides, *Iphigenia at Aulis* 891-897

But when we reach puberty we are thrust out...Some go to strange men's homes, others to foreigners',
some to joyless houses, some to hostile, and all this once the first night has yoked us to our husbands,
we are forced to praise and say that all is well.
Sophokles, *Tereus*, frag. 52

Because much of the literature pertaining to the Greek wedding ceremony is found in sources later than the Classical period, we cannot always be certain whether a custom was observed as early as the fifth century B.C. Moreover, information gleaned from a vase-painting often contradicts both the literary tradition and other vase-paintings. Adding more confusion is the painters' tendency to abbreviate and to elide separate moments in the ritual.[1]

The important betrothal, *engye*, often occurred years before the wedding itself and was distinguished by a handshake between the father of the bride and the prospective bridegroom (no. 24). Presumably the bride's dowry was fixed at that time. At some point before the marriage she would no longer be regarded as a *kore* or *parthenos*, but rather as a bride, *nymphe*, a term that also described the semi-divine, unmarried maidens of myth, whose realm was the mountains, woodlands, streams, and springs. The bride and bridegroom may have been distant relatives, but, even so, neither was well acquainted with the other, and on the wedding day they may well have been total strangers. The bride would not be much past puberty, as young as fourteen, although Aristotle urged that she be older.[2] The groom was probably about thirty, in comparison with his new wife, better educated and far more sophisticated.

Before the wedding day the bride dedicated her toys in a sanctuary of Artemis to signify the end of her childhood (see **Persephone and Demeter** and **Athena**).[3] She also dedicated a lock of hair to one of several goddesses, including Artemis. An important preparation immediately preceding the wedding was the bridal bath. Water was brought from the spring, Enneakrounos, located by the Acropolis, in a special water vessel specifically for bridal use, the loutrophoros. The bride would receive others as wedding gifts, and loutrophoroi were also dedicated, presumably by brides, in a sanctuary on the south slope of the Acropolis that was known as the Sanctuary of the Nymph.

The bride was assisted in dressing for the wedding by a *nympheutria*, who was a mature woman other than the bride's mother. Other relatives undoubtedly offered their help. Her wedding garment contained some areas of purple, dyed with a costly substance obtained from the murex, a rare type of snail; for this reason the purple color carried connotations of wealth as well as, certainly, of blood.[4] The bride's belt was tied with a double knot that was known as the bridal, or the Herakles, knot and had such rich connotations that the phrase "loosening the belt" became a euphemism for sexual intercourse. Over the bride's head and shoulders was draped her veil, a piece of fabric that could have a tasselled hem (no. 56). It had been colored to a yellow-orange hue with dye from the saffron plant, which was specifically associated with women, probably because of its traditional use as a medication for menstrual ills (see **Athena**). The bride also wore a great deal of jewelry. In vase-paintings she wears a diadem in the form of a headband from which rise individual elements that resemble leaves. We also find earrings, a necklace, and bracelets. Both bride and groom were outfitted with bridal wreaths made of myrtle, an honor that, as John Oakley observes, was otherwise reserved only for victors in battle and in Panathenaic Games and which conferred a superhuman status upon the bridal pair.[5] Indeed, when completely dressed and veiled, the bride would have seemed as dazzling as Pandora appeared to Epimetheus, or Thetis on her wedding day with Peleus, and wedding guests probably commented upon the comparison (see **Pandora** and **Peleus and Thetis**).

The beginning of the wedding celebration is generally agreed to have taken place in the home of the bride, and here the bride's father officially handed over his daughter to the bridegroom with the pronouncement: "I give her over to you for the ploughing of legitimate children." At the wedding feast guests ate cakes made with sesame seeds and honey, which connoted fertility. During the feast a *pais amphithales*, who was a boy with both parents living, wore a crown of thistle and oak and carried bread in a winnowing basket among the assembled guests, repeating the phrase: "I have left the worse and found the better."[6] It is generally agreed that the wreath, winnowing basket, and phrase refer to the transition from a pre-agricultural to an agricultural society, thereby equating marriage as an equivalent transition from an uncivilized to a civilized way of life. The boy's presence served as a reminder that male children were the desired issue from the couple's union, and boys may have figured elsewhere in the wedding ritual. In vase-painting a boy may carry the loutrophoros for the bridal bath,[7] and scenes on lebetes gamikoi show the bride playing with a baby boy, probably before her wedding in order to bring her good luck (no. 56).

At some point in the festivities the *anakalypteria* or unveiling of the bride took place (see **Gesture and Gaze**). The veil was lifted from the bride's head, probably with her own assistance and certainly that of the *nympheutria*. The action was an actual and symbolic beginning to the disrobing of the bride, and it is generally thought that the action signified the bride's willing acceptance of her husband as a sexual partner (see **Gesture and Gaze**). As Andrew Stewart points out in his essay in this volume, the bride's sexual arousal was considered necessary for conception to take place, and thus the popular belief existed that a newly married man, in the words of Xenophon quoting Sokrates, "desires and is desired in return by his wife."[8] The *anakalypteria* was the first opportunity that the bridegroom had been given to see his bride's face and for her to see his without the intervening veil. Ancient writers accordingly describe the moment as the *opteria* and *theoretria*, words derived from the verb "to see" (see **Gesture and Gaze**).[9] The Greek belief in the erotic power of the gaze and in the importance of the mutual arousal of bride and groom accounts for the figure of Eros who hovers above the bride in scenes of this moment (nos. 24–26).

After the unveiling came the wedding procession to the home of the bridegroom where the bride would hereafter live. The bridegroom led the bride by means of the traditional gesture known as the *cheir' epi karpo*, by which her left wrist was grasped firmly by his right hand (no. 25). In Geometric and Archaic Greek art the gesture was one of abduction. It first enters the wedding context with a late sixth-century vase by Euphronios that depicts the wedding of Peleus and Thetis, and within the wedding ritual the gesture is generally agreed to signify the submission of the bride to her husband, who has now replaced her father as the bride's legal guardian.[10] Indeed, the Greek verb for marriage, *damazo*, carries the additional meaning "subjugate" and "tame," and only the bridegroom was considered to be the one who married. The bride was the one who was married. An archaic term for the bride was *damar*, derived from *damazo*.

In wedding scenes the bridal couple was conveyed to their destination in a chariot, but in actual practice a cart was more probable. We are told that the bride carried with her a barley roasting pan and a sieve, used to process and cook food. The mother of the bride followed the procession holding a lighted torch in each hand, and the mother of the bridegroom greeted the couple at the threshold of her home, also holding two torches (no. 109). As the bride entered the interior of her new home, a basket of dates, nuts, figs, and dried fruit, was upended over the assembled group. This custom, the *katachysmata,* was also observed with the introduction of a newly acquired slave into a household and of a new ambassador to a city-state.[11] The action is generally agreed to have symbolized the prosperity that the new member was hoped to contribute.

The bride carried with her into the wedding chamber a piece of fruit, a *malon.*[12] The custom was undoubtedly a reference to the pomegranate that Persephone ate during her stay in the Underworld with Hades and that obligated her annual separation from her mother (see **Persephone and Demeter**). After the bridal couple entered the wedding chamber, one of the bridegroom's friends stood guard as a *thuroros*, or gatekeeper, to prevent female friends of the bride from rescuing their companion. The custom kept alive the suggestion introduced with the bridegroom's grasp of the bride's wrist that he had forcefully abducted her. As the bride passed the night within the wedding chamber, girls who were her closest friends stood outside the door, singing beautiful *epithalamia* (wedding songs) so that their friend would be comforted by the sounds of their voices.

On the day after the wedding night, the bride welcomed friends and relatives who brought wedding gifts such as the lebes gamikos, which was a unique type of vessel associated exclusively with the wedding. Because it consists of a round basin resting upon a high stand, the lebes was probably originally a food container. Other gifts included baskets, chests, wool baskets, toilette containers (pyxides), oil vessels (alabastra), sashes, and mirrors. The prevalence of containers among the wedding presents may have been a reference to the pithos that Pandora brought with her to her husband Epimetheus and they were undoubtedly regarded as bearing connotations of fertility (see **Containers** and **Pandora**).

The bride's wedding gift to the groom was a *chlanis*, or tunic, that she had woven herself, and it may have been given to him at this moment.[13] The garment was an important demonstration of the most important skill the bride was expected to have acquired before she entered married life, and is another illustration of the degree to which textile production was intimately identified with women, their sexuality, marriage, and procreation (see **Textiles** and **Athena**).

The young wife would remain a *nymphe*, or bride, until the birth of her first child. At that moment she would be considered to have completed her transition from childhood and would henceforth be known as a *gyne*, a married woman.

Although the wedding ritual is endlessly fascinating, only in recent years have scholars turned their attention to it after a long lapse, and much meaning surely still awaits interpretation. There are many elements in the ritual that associate the bride with a wild, uncontrolled, and erotic force that must be overcome: the terms *nymphe* and *damazo*; the verb *meignumi*, which means both to join in sexual union and to join in battle; the bridegroom's grasp of her wrist; and the *thuroros* defending the bridal chamber from the assault of the bride's friends. The bride is also closely aligned with the tilling of the earth in agricultural production. The theme is evident in the *liknon* and the chant of the *pais amphithales*, the barley pan and sieve she carries in the wedding chariot or cart, and the ritual pronouncement of the bride's father that she is being handed over to be ploughed. This last image has many reverberations in Greek literature, from the comment by Antigone that there are other furrows for Kreon's plough,[14] to the mournful cry of Oedipus

that his mother's body was a field of double sowing.[15] Lysistrata comments that a randy husband will remark to his wife: "Now I want to strip off and work the land."[16]

Also interesting are the overtones in the wedding ritual of sacrifice, evident in the dedication of the lock of hair and toys, as well as in the gifts brought to the bride after the wedding night (see **Artemis** and **Iphigenia**). Parallels with Persephone and with funerary ritual have also been noted (see **Persephone and Demeter**). One should also not overlook the bride's associations with wealth. She is ornately festooned with gold jewelry; her garment contains purple; and her arrival in the bridegroom's house is greeted with *katachysmata*. The dowry that she brings with her is only one obvious manifestation of the bounty she connotes, because a fertile young woman who could both bring children into a household and cause it to prosper through wise management was viewed in Greek culture as an immeasurably valuable asset.

Most scenes with wedding ritual appear on vases that were given to the bride as wedding gifts: loutrophoroi and lebetes gamikoi. Because the paintings were deliberately created to please the bride, they offer thoughtful insight into the bride's view of the wedding ritual, an occasion when she would be joined for a lifetime to a man she may hardly ever have met, and with whom she would immediately have her first sexual experience. It may not be surprising that in the vase scenes we detect no note of intimidation, but rather the survival mechanism of romanticization. A favorite subject on the bridal vases is the moment of unveiling, when Eros hovers enticingly above the couple's heads to indicate that they are spontaneously and irresistibly drawn to one another (nos. 24–26).

1. The most complete and recent discussion of the wedding is Oakley and Sinos (1993), where the ancient citations are listed. Valuable analysis is also found in Jenkins (1983); Redfield (1982); Leduc (1992) 235-92.
2. Aristotle, *Politics* 7. 1335 a 6-35. Plato (*Laws* 6.785b) considered sixteen to be the minimum age. The bride of Xenophon (*Oikonomikos* 7.5), however, was fourteen. Soranus commented that fourteen was the age of menarche. See Sealey (1990) 42.
3. *Greek Anthology* 6.280; Burkert (1983) 361.
4. Oakley and Sinos (1993) 16.
5. Ibid. 44.
6. Zenobius 3.98.
7. Simon and Hampe (1959) 40.
8. Xenophon, *Symposium* 8.3.
9. Oakley and Sinos (1993) 25.
10. Homer, *Iliad* 24.267 and *Odyssey* 18.258. For the discussion of the gesture, see Oakley and Sinos (1993) 30-31; Sutton (1981) 181; Jenkins (1983) 140.
11. Scholia to Aristophanes, *Ploutos* 768.
12. Plutarch, *Moralia* 138D; *Quaestiones Romanae* 279f sol. 20.
13. Aristophanes, *Birds* 1693. Pollux 3.39 suggests that the bridegroom was given this at the time when wedding gifts were brought to the bride; Oakley and Sinos (1993) 37, 39.
14. Sophokles, *Antigone* 566-69.
15. Sophokles, *Oedipus the King* 1225-58.
16. Aristophanes, *Lysistrata* 1173.

1

KORE FROM THE ACROPOLIS

520-510
Athens, Acropolis Museum, inv. no. 672

Attic, from the Acropolis
Marble
H (above plinth) 1.03 m., H (plinth) 0.02 m.

Publications: E. Gardner, "Recently Discovered Archaic Sculptures," *JHS* 8 (1887) 167-169, fig. 3; W. Lermann, *Altgriechische Plastik* (Munich 1907) 61-67, fig. 26, pl. 5; G. Dickins, *Catalogue of the Acropolis Museum*, vol. 1 (Cambridge 1912) 209-211; S. Casson, *The Technique of Early Greek Sculpture* (Oxford 1933) 114; E. Langlotz, in H. Schrader, *Die archaischen Marmorbildwerke der Akropolis* (Frankfurt 1939) 90-91 no. 42, pls. 59, 103; H. Payne and G. Young, *Archaic Marble Sculpture from the Acropolis*, 2nd ed. (London 1950) 37, 71, pls. 68, 69.1-2; S. Adam, *The Technique of Greek Sculpture, BSA Suppl.* 3 (London 1966) 48, pl. 21c; G.M.A. Richter, *Korai* (London 1968) 76, no. 118, figs. 373-76; *Marmer in Beeld: Griekse Sculptuur 600-100 v. Chr.* (Amsterdam, Allard Pierson Museum, March 5-June 19, 1994) 21-22, 44 no. 25, pl. II, cover.

Mended from several pieces; missing left forearm and folds beneath it, most of right arm, and front of right foot. Chipping over surface. Carved together with a circular plinth. Upper strap on her right sandal only partially carved, to be finished in paint. Folds beneath her right arm were repaired in antiquity, using Pentelic marble. Red on hair. Painted patterns on her stephane (red and green meander), on the seam of her chiton down her right arm (squares with green borders), on the paryphe (central fold) of chiton (red and green square pattern), on the lower edge of her chiton (red and green meander), and on the border of her himation (red and green meander in front, red and green stripes with red spots behind). Remains of a meniskos.

She stands with her feet close together, her right foot slightly advanced, and she wears sandals. Her left elbow is bent and the left forearm was attached separately. Her right shoulder is lowered, and the missing right hand was just outside her right thigh where it pulled tightly the folds of her chiton across and against her legs. Over a chiton she wears a himation that passes from her left shoulder under her right arm, with the hem edge folded back over the cross-strap to fall in zigzag folds. The rest of the mantle hangs down over her torso and left thigh. She also has a disc earring and a stephane. The hair across her forehead is rendered as two unbroken, scalloped ridges, behind which are vertical locks with horizontal ridges. Over the top of her head her hair is arranged in concentric, smooth ridges; behind her ears the hair forms long wavy locks, four of which fall forward over each shoulder. Her eyebrows are rendered as arching carinations; there is a groove at the base of the upper eyelids; and her eyeballs protrude. The tearducts are indicated.

This maiden belongs to a series of marble statues that were discovered during excavation of the Acropolis at the end of the last century. Inscribed statue bases tell us both that the statues were known as korai (little girls) and that they were dedicated to Athena, who is addressed in the inscriptions as the "kore of Zeus." Through comparison with better surviving examples we know that this kore's left forearm was held horizontally and that the hand held an offering. Her right hand grasped folds of her chiton outside her right thigh. There is no apparent reason why both her gesture and

1

1

draping are the mirror reversal of conventional korai, who wear their mantle fastened on the right shoulder, while the left hand gathers the drapery and the right hand holds the offering.

The sculpture is a superb illustration of the Archaic style. The head has a high dome and the hair is rendered in various unrealistic, but highly decorative, patterns. The eyebrows form high arches, the area between eyebrow and eye forms a concave depression, and the eyeballs bulge, with the upper eyelid passing well down over the eyeball. The Archaic smile is still present, creating a dish-shaped area between cheeks and chin. The torso is largely hidden behind the garments, except for the breasts, which are accentuated by the carefully positioned locks of hair falling over them. The chiton and himation edges form highly stylized patterns and offer a textural contrast to the corrugated locks of hair. The chiton becomes transparent over the legs, clinging closely to all the contours and revealing a not fully credible knee and a pronounced shinbone. The animation of the vivacious smile and protruding eyes combines with the diverse textural contrasts and the tension of the tightly pulled garment to create an impression of vigor, vitality, and joy.

Korai, like their counterparts, the kouroi (statues of nude youths), functioned in the Archaic period as both grave markers and votive dedications. Men as well as women dedicated korai to goddesses, who received as votive gifts both kouroi and korai. Korai differed from kouroi in two important ways. First, a kore's extended hand held a gift, ostensibly for the viewer, whose eyes she engages with her direct gaze. Secondly, a kore is regularly identified by inscription as an *agalma*, an object of delight, whereas kouroi were never, with one exception described by this term.[1] Also identified as *agalamata* were sculptures of horses, and horses with riders. Robin Osborne persuasively argues that the designation of the korai as *agalmata* can be explained by a woman's role within Greek culture, in which she was viewed as a commodity, an object of exchange. Lacking citizenship, but possessing valuable childbearing potential, a woman passed with marriage from the guardianship of her father to that of her husband. The transaction was not necessarily permanent, because should the woman's father die without a male heir, her family could recall her, obliging her to give up her husband in order to marry her father's brother and produce a male heir (see **Women and Men**). In essence, the childbearing potential of a woman was viewed as asset to be managed in a manner analogous to the dedication of a kore as fulfillment of a promised tithe to a deity.[2]

The physically mature bodies of the korai tell us that these maidens were also parthenoi, or physically mature but unmarried adolescent girls. Many of the korai's distinctive characteristics are in accord with the Greek conception of the parthenos, whose vitality was considered to be a manifestation of her fecundity. A girl on the edge of womanhood was viewed as enchanting; she was to be adorned with clothing and jewelry like a doll, in the manner in which Pandora was first fashioned and then ornamented to be a bride for Epimetheus (see **Pandora**). The word for kore in Greek actually means "doll" and also signifies the pupil of the eye, which was thought to reflect back a tiny image of the viewer's form. A maiden's youthful innocence was assumed to be not only a sexual one, because Xenophon tells us that the bride was expected to know little beyond spinning and weaving. Those skills she was expected to have so mastered that the garments of a parthenos, and surely also of a kore, testified to the wearer's skill in textile production, her industriousness, and, surely also in this context, her acknowledgment of Athena's gift of textile manufacture to Athenian women.

In addition to these positive sentiments about parthenoi, Greek culture also harbored considerable apprehension about a young maiden, which this kore can also be seen to embody. A young maiden was thought to possess an active sexual curiosity (see **Danae**, **Erichthonios**, and **Plynteria and Arrephoroi**), an almost uncontrollable spirit (see **Little Bears** and **Women as Animals**), and an irresistibility to men, which could precipitate a man's downfall (see **Atalanta**). Young women who were living at the time when this kore was carved were raised to adopt a demeanor that was almost the direct opposite of the statue's. They concealed their legs and most of their torsos behind their chitons and himations, and they inclined their heads and cast their eyes downward in an expression of *aidos*, which connoted modesty, shame, respectfulness, and submission (see *Aidos* and *Sophrosyne*). By contrast, Kore 672 engages the viewer with her direct gaze and has pulled her garment so closely around her buttocks and legs that very little is not revealed. Even her breasts bulge obtrusively and are further highlighted by the frame created by her long locks of hair. The maiden is not only sexually mature, but also appears to be fully aware of the fact and pleased to be able to delight others with an introduction to it. This tone will soften considerably in the sculptural style of succeeding decades.

Although korai did not function solely as dedicatory gifts to Athena, the number of them offered to Athena calls to mind the prominence of women, and especially parthenoi, in the goddess' cult. Closely associated with Athena were the mythical maidens, the Aglaurides, who, in turn, have been connected with the Arrephoroi, unmarried maidens who took part in a ritual of initiation associated with Athena (see **Athena**, **Erichthonios**, and **Plynteria and Arrephoroi**). Even if the korai were not intended specifically to evoke the Aglaurides or the Arrephoroi, the choice of them as votive gifts is an acknowledgement of Athena's special interest in, and protection of, marriageable maidens as the all-important insurance, even symbol, of the community's survival.

1. Osborne (1994) 90.
2. Ibid. 92.

CARYATID MIRROR

ca. 470
Geneva, George Ortiz Collection

North-East Peloponnese, Sicyon?
Bronze
H 42 cm., Diam (mirror disc) 17.5 cm.

Publications: J. Dörig, ed., *Art Antique. Collections privées de Suisse Romande* (Mayence 1975) no. 227 (illus.); L. Keene Congdon, *Caryatid Mirrors of Ancient Greece* (Mainz 1981) 239-40; Mussche (1982) 192-3, no. 116; C. Rolley, *Les bronzes grecs* (Fribourg 1983) 95-97, no. 75 (color illus.); G. Ortiz, *In Pursuit of the Absolute. Art of the Ancient World from the George Ortiz Collection* (Bern 1994) no. 138 (color illus.).

Repaired at juncture of disc and intermediary element over maiden's head.

The maiden stands with her left leg advanced and with her head turned slightly to her right. In her lowered left hand she holds a lotus bud; in her extended right hand, she holds an apple. She wears a belted chiton with an overfold to the waist. The neckline is rounded, and there are six or seven buttons on each sleeve; below her waist there is a wide fold on each side. Closely set pairs of incised wavy lines originate at the neckline and run vertically over and between the breasts. Beneath the breasts are single, incised lines that radiate to the waist. Over the skirt, the garment is engraved with pairs of undulating lines that pass vertically over each leg to meet between them in a V. The back of the garment is smooth. She also wears slippers. Her hair is rendered as wavy, horizontal locks that pass continuously over the top of her head, creating a slight angle above the midpoint of her forehead. The hair over the back of her head and behind her ears forms delicate wavy lines. The locks are drawn up into a bun at her nape, and she wears a diadem. She gazes ahead and slightly to her right.

The maiden stands on a tripod that terminates in three lion paws, between which are three palmettes. The top of the tripod has the form of an Ionic capital. The intermediary element above the maiden's head takes the form of Ionic volutes, ornamented with two palmettes. The mirror disc has a raised beaded rim enclosing a guilloche rendered as a double row of circles.

The maiden constitutes an exemplary illustration of the way in which the Early Classical style served as a transition between the Archaic and the Classical. Although the manner in which her garment tightly clings to the contours of her shoulders, breasts, and legs calls to mind the Archaic statues of korai, the use of the drapery goes beyond the Archaic style in that it reveals practically the entire curvature of her upper arms. Only a few years later drapery will be employed to model the limbs with curving folds that wrap around the forms to accentuate their plasticity. Also a legacy from the Archaic period is this maiden's vivacity and energy, facilitated and enhanced by the generous tensile strength of bronze, which permits the arms to be held out away from, and in front of, the torso. Another indication of her Archaic ancestry is the even distribution of her weight on both legs. Only a few years later, the weight will be unevenly distributed, and we will see more fully developed the asymmetry noticeable here in the turn of her head to her right and the elevation of her right shoulder. Particularly Early Classical in style is the maiden's face, which no longer exhibits the Archaic smile, but retains the concavity of the mouth area that characterized that smile. The overall impression is a compelling combination of animation and dignity.

It is interesting to keep in mind that this elegant image of a woman was destined for female ownership and use. Because the figurine functioned as the mirror's handle, her tactile forms and surfaces were designed to bring pleasure to a female hand. The figurine's attentive gaze at a mistress attempting to maximize her own appeal reminds us of the degree to which in Classical Greece a woman was cognizant both of the importance of her beauty and of the traditional potency of her gaze (see **Gesture and Gaze**).

The careful and ornate decoration of the figurine's chiton is a reminder of the role that garments played in both a woman's life and her identity. Because nudity in the Classical era was reserved for prostitutes, a respectable woman was inseparable from her clothes, which were viewed as an extension of herself (see **Textiles** and **Pandora**). Fine garments and jewelry both enhanced and symbolized her allure. They also testified to the wealth of her own or her husband's family and to her skills in textile production, the quintessentially female art (see **Textiles** and **Athena**). Skillfully worked garments also demonstrated a woman's industriousness, which, ironically for a society that devalued manual labor in its male citizens, was considered one of the most desirable of female qualities.

2

3

CARYATID MIRROR
WITH APHRODITE

ca. 460
Baltimore, Walters Art Gallery, inv. no. 54.769

Bronze
H (total) 43 cm., H (figure) 15.4 cm., Diam (mirror disc) 15.4 cm.

Publications: Walters Art Gallery, *Handbook of the Collection* (Baltimore 1936) 26 (illus.); F. Poulsen, *Der strenge Stil: Studien zur Geschichte des griechischen Plastik 480-460 B.C.*, *Acta archeologica* 8 (Copenhagen 1937) 19-20, no. 1a; Walters Art Gallery, *Fashions of the Past* (Baltimore 1945) 10 (illus.); D.K. Hill, "9B Column Greece," BWalt 4.7 (1952) 2 (illus.); *An Exhibition of the Treasures of the Walters Art Gallery, Wildenstein* (New York, March 16-April 15, 1967) no. 73; Mitten and Doeringer (1967) 92, no. 88 (illus.); R. Tölle-Kastenbein, *Frühklassische Peplosfiguren Originale* (Mainz 1980) 22-23, no. 2b, 25-26, pls. 7, 10b; L. Keene Congdon, *Caryatid Mirrors of Ancient Greece* (Mainz 1981) 171-2, no. 60, pls. 54-55; *LIMC* I (1981) 20, no. 118 (s.v. Aphrodite).

Largely intact, with some breaks around mirror disc; head of bird in maiden's hand is broken away, and faces of Erotes damaged.

The maiden stands with her right leg advanced. She wears a belted peplos with overfold and slippers. Her left hand clasps folds outside her left thigh; her right elbow is bent, and in the upraised palm and extended fingers of her right hand she supports a long-necked bird. Her wavy hair is center parted and drawn up over the ears; locks are gathered in a bun at her nape. She stands on a convex base supported by three feline feet.

Above her head is the Y-shaped mirror support, with a central palmette flanked by two horizontal half-palmettes whose tips are contoured. Attached at each side is the smooth extended wing of a flying nude Eros, his legs slightly behind him and his arms stretched out to each side. His hairstyle resembles that of the maiden. The mirror disc is lightly convex, and the front bears two concentric circles around the rim; the back has a raised rim and a series of concentric circles. Attached at the top is a frontal Siren with flaring wings supported by S-shaped volutes resting on a flat plate. Flanking the Siren are two birds similar to those held by the caryatid.

Although the circumference of the disc is not that of the cradle, stylistic similarities, particularly of the birds, argue that the parts are original.

The maiden carries her load without difficulty and with a great deal of self-assurance and dignity. Her legs are not indicated beneath her drapery, but the broad, vertical, corrugated folds liken her form to that of a substantial column. Even the folds that fall diagonally from her left hand take on this same tubular form. The artist has skillfully broadened her neck to complement the stem of the mirror support that rises from her head. The result is a graceful silhouette and a convincing proportion of load to weight-bearer. Her head is especially fine, with its elongated eyes and delicately incised strands of hair. Her strong jaw, as well as the rendering of her peplos, indicates an Early Classical date, little more than a decade before the beginning of the Parthenon. Lenore Congdon associates her with the Argo-Corinthian–A group, a center of manufacture identified with the city-states of Argos and Corinth, near Athens.

The presence of the Erotes and the prominence of the birds, which resemble the doves sacred to Aphrodite, suggest that the maiden is the goddess herself, a later counterpart to the caryatid mirror in the Hermitage (no. 15). The presence of Aphrodite is indeed appropriate on a mirror employed by the owner as a means of enhancing her own charms, although the deity's sedate garb and stance contrast strongly with her more provocative appearance only a few decades later (see no. 17).

The Siren at the top of the disc is also a logical member of this gathering, because these bird-women were famous for their magnetic allure through the songs that enticed men to their deaths (see **Sirens**). Probably because of their life-threatening charms, Sirens often perch atop Archaic grave monuments, and the position of the Siren at the top of this mirror disc is surely a reflection of that custom. This Siren would also have served as a reminder to her mistress that a woman's irresistibility to men was considered to reside not only in her appearance, but also in her voice and words.

3

4

FIGURINE OF A MAIDEN

460-450
New York, Collection of Mr. and Mrs. Lawrence A. Fleischman

Argive
Bronze
H 16.1 cm.

Publications: M. True and K. Hamma, eds., *A Passion for Antiquities: Ancient Art from the Collection of Barbara and Lawrence Fleischman* (Malibu, The J. Paul Getty Museum 1994) 67-68, no. 23 (illus.).

Missing the left foot, the front of the right foot, and the element that the figure supported.

The maiden stands frontally with her left leg advanced and relaxed, her face frontal. She wears a girded peplos with an overfold that extends to her waist. Her right hand rests on her right hip, and her left hand is drawn up under the overfold and rests close to the torso above the left breast and beneath the shoulder. Her hair is completely enveloped in a sakkos that is decorated with circles and zigzags and that forms a coil at the back of her head. On top of her head is a hollow tubular element with two ring moldings around the midsection and one at the top.

The form of the attachment on her head suggests that the figure was surmounted by a candelabrum or *thymiaterion* (incense burner), and certainly the heavy columnar folds of drapery and the sturdiness of her wide neck and powerful right arm supply adequate strength for her function as a support and occasional handle. Marion True suggests persuasively that the broad neck, prominent facial features, and the patterns of the sakkos are characteristic of the celebrated metalwork of Argos, with which the caliber of the Fleischman figurine is very much compatible. Particularly noteworthy is the way the contour of her left arm is revealed through her overfold, which is rendered with a fluidity that calls to mind the initial modeling in wax.

The gesture of the left hand beneath the overfold is relatively unusual but may not have been uncommon in daily life, because placing one's hand beneath a section of fabric is a conventional way to judge and exhibit the fineness of the weave (see **Textiles**). The maiden thus appears to be both luxuriating in her peplos and prominently displaying its quality. Although her gesture is found on three other approximately contemporary caryatid bronze mirrors, it probably originated in painting and seems to have characterized the figure of Eriphyle in the slightly earlier *Nekyia*, a wallpainting in Delphi by Polygnotos that depicted the descent into the Underworld.[1] Eriphyle was best remembered for her acceptance of the catastrophic bribe of a necklace and a peplos in order to persuade her husband and son, respectively, to take part in the invasion of Thebes. As an identifying gesture in the wallpainting, Eriphyle's delight in her garment would be highly appropriate. The

4 Detail of rear view

Fleischman figurine, by contrast, need not be Eriphyle herself, nor need the gesture in this context bear negative connotations. The Greeks' selective memory in matters of myth is epitomized by their evaluation of the wedding of Peleus and Thetis as the quintessential mythical wedding, and yet the proceedings were marred by the appearance of the Apple of Discord that precipitated the Trojan War (see **Peleus and Thetis**).

The maiden's sakkos is particularly detailed and is further testimony to the art of weaving, particularly the incorporation of ornamental patterns. This example appears to have long tubular ties that were wound successively around the head to form a decorative coil at the back.

1. Pausanias 10.29.7-8.
2. Gernet (1981) 119-20.

5

FIGURINE OF A MAIDEN FROM A MIRROR

ca. 460
Geneva, George Ortiz Collection

Attic?
Bronze
H 13.33 cm.

Unpublished.

5

135

Smoothed down on top of head where mirror was attached. Right hand missing. Deep gash in brow.

　　　　The woman stands with her weight on her left foot, her right leg relaxed. She wears a girded peplos with overfold; down her right side the folds are closed. She also wears shoes with upturned tips. Her left hand grasps folds of her garment at her side; her right arm was extended in front of her. Her hair is brushed forward to her face and falls in finely engraved locks. Over it she wears a hair covering, which forms two protruding points at the back of the head. Her eyeballs are flat and incised; her jaw is full.

5　Detail

Originally a mirror support, this figurine served as a handle to be grasped by her mistress. The plasticity of the form and its tactile appeal indicate that the artist was sensitive to the maiden's function. The pronounced projection of the right arm was made possible by the greater tensile strength that bronze enjoyed relative to marble; the material was, however, not much less resistant to impact, as the missing hand testifies.

The maiden's dress and the formal gesture of her left hand are consistent with the Early Classical period, when adherence to the Archaic style was still apparent, especially in the absence of torsion and the concealment of the body behind garments of substantial thickness. The projection of the maiden's breasts looks forward to the transparent fabric of subsequent decades, when drapery systems will model the form beneath. The alertness and contained energy of this figurine will soon give way to the effortless composure of the Pheidian style.

6

GRAVE RELIEF WITH MOTHER AND CHILD

420-410
Leiden, Rijksmuseum van Oudheden, inv. no. I 1903/2.1
Six Collection, des Tombe Collection. Acquired in 1902

Attic
Marble
H 67.5 cm., W 46 cm.

Publications: S. Colvin, *JHS* 5 (1884) 205, pl. 39; A. Conze, *Die attischen Grabreliefs* (Berlin 1893-1922) no. 280, pl. 65; G. Rodenwaldt, *Das Relief bei den Griechen* (Berlin 1923) 61-62, fig. 71; H. Süsserott, *Griechische Plastik des 4. Jahrhunderts vor Christus* (Frankfurt 1938) 102 n. 55; A. Kaltenhäuser, *Handwerkliche Gestaltung im attischen Grabrelief des 5. und 4. Jahrhunderts v. Chr.* (Erlangen 1938) 20, 22, 51; Dohrn (1957) 115-19, no. 12, pl. 17a; B. Schlörb, *Untersuchungen zur Bildhauergeneration nach Phidias* (Waldsassen/Bayern 1963) 72; B. Schweitzer, *Zur Kunst der Antike. Ausgewählte Schriften* 2 (Tübingen 1963) 82, pl. 26,1; Leiden. Rijksmuseum van Oudheden, *Artefact. 150 Jaar Rijksmuseum van Oudheden 1816-1968* (Leiden 1968) 46, pl. 85; F.L. Bastet, *Beeld en Reliëf* (The Hague 1979) 26, no. 9 (illus.); R. Stupperich, *Staatsbegräbnis und Privatgrabmal im klassischen Athen* (Münster 1977) 89-91, 93, 108, 123, no. 449; H. Rühfel, *Das Kind in der griechischen Kunst* (Mainz 1984) 148-49, fig. 61; Keuls (1985a) 139, fig. 119; Kauffmann-Samaras (1988) 289-90, fig. 5; Clairmont (1993) vol. 2, 647-50, no. 2.652; Sabetai (1993) vol. 1, 55.

Missing corner above woman's head, corner beneath her feet, her left hand, and child's head.

The stele terminates in a cavetto molding surmounted by a pediment with raised flat borders. Beneath the figures is a thick ledge. The scene is worked in high relief.

A woman is seated in left profile on a klismos, the front legs of which are carved in the round. The woman is also in high relief, with the right breast modeled to the right nipple and the right side of the face indicated to the edge of the right eye. A footstool, set at an angle, supports most of her advanced right foot and the toes of her left foot. She wears a belted chiton, the folds of which cover her left arm and elbow and are visible around her ankles. Her mantle is brought across her waist and legs, and she wears sandals. She has wavy hair, with the locks at her nape pulled up under a fillet that encircles her head. Her left eye is set just beneath the eyebrow, and the upper eyelid overlaps the lower eyelid at the outer corner. Her ear is pierced for an earring, which is absent. Both elbows are bent and the forearms are extended, with the palm of the left hand open and the fingers spread; the tips of the fingers pass behind the garment of the child. The woman gazes ahead of her at the small child that she is about to accept from the hands of the maidservant.

The maidservant turns slightly to her left, her right leg relaxed, her head in right profile. She wears a peplos that reveals part of her right back and side and that is girt at the waist with an overfold. Her hair, which is abraded and was probably left rough for color, is smooth and straight. With both hands she grasps the torso of a small girl; her left hand clasps the child's left side and the right hand grasps the body beneath its right shoulder. She gazes at the child.

The little girl reaches out energetically for her mother, her legs behind her, her left shoulder and arm straining forward. Her torso is almost frontal, her legs in right profile. She is dressed in a long transparent garment that extends to the ankles and covers the left shoulder and upper arm. The billowing folds in front of her indicate that her legs are vigorously kicking out. Her left arm and hand, palm facing out, fingers open, are extended toward the seated woman; the left hand appears to rest on the maidservant's right thumb.

6 (See also colorplate, p. 122)

The carving is a superb example of the way in which Classical drapery of the decades following the Parthenon frieze (442-438) modeled the forms of the body and, even within a single garment, underwent changes in texture and thickness in order to do so. The mother's chiton is rendered as thin, crinkly folds that clearly reveal both nipples and that fall into rounded U-shaped folds where they spill over the girding at her waist. Over her thighs the mantle falls in flat folds with crisp contours; where the fabric lies on the klismos seat outside her left thigh, it forms tubular triangles with open centers. The mantle is pulled tightly over the lower legs, such that most of the contours of the left leg are apparent, and between the legs the fabric forms concentric arcs of tubular folds. The thicker material of the maidservant's peplos is rendered beneath her right shoulder as deep pockets with curvilinear contours. Over her supporting left leg the drapery falls in pairs of cordlike folds, with the folds within each pair linked by a softly concave valley. Over the maidservant's relaxed right leg the fabric is drawn tightly, interrupted by only a few raised, flat, triangular folds.

The child is too old to be a newborn baby, and so the grave relief cannot be honoring a mother who died in childbirth with her baby. Because of the lavishness of the stele in terms of size, height of relief, and composition, it is unlikely to have been commissioned to honor a deceased child, and thus must be commemorating the seated mother. Because a male child was more desired and honored in Greek society than was a baby girl, the fact that this child is female argues that the relief was specially commissioned for this particular family. If so, then the decision to depict the mother with her child, and not with her husband or parents, implies that her maternal affection for her daughter was this woman's most distinctive quality. The high visibility of her breasts is in keeping with contemporary style and may also be an allusion to the woman's maternal aspect; by contrast, the deeply revealing dip of the maidservant's peplos suggests that mistress and servant observed different standards of propriety.

The central group of the baby with arms outstretched to a woman's open embrace must have originated in painting before the middle of the century. The motif appears on so many vases illustrating the presentation of Erichthonios by Gaia to Athena (nos. 67, 68, 70–72) that the prototype of those scenes is also likely to have been the prototype for the motif itself. In later usage the receiving woman is usually the child's mother, a convention that demonstrates how convincingly the vase-paintings with Erichthonios presented Athena as a maternal figure.

A comparison of the Leiden relief with the scene on a lekythos by the Achilles Painter of ca. 450 reveals the sculptor's skill in rendering the servant's grasp of the child and the child's impatience for her mother's arms.[1] And by closely juxtaposing the seated woman and the child, the scene on the relief poignantly conveys a powerful emotional bond between mother and daughter.

The squirming child is the focal point of the composition. Her outstretched left hand occupies the very center of the field and draws our attention both to the open hands of the mother and to the child's impending movement into that space. Uniting the figures even more closely is the concentrated gaze of the woman at the child.

The sculptor has worked the stele in unusually high relief, perhaps in order better to display his masterly ability to render receding planes, especially in the area of the foreshortened footstool and the legs of the woman and maidservant. The high relief lends the figures a freedom of movement that is accentuated by the generous expanse of background to the sides of the figures and over their heads. The high relief and the spaciousness of the scene heighten the energy of the child's squirming form. The sense of immediacy is underscored by the position of the woman's left foot, the toes of which balance tentatively upon the edge of the footstool, as if she is about to move her foot further onto the stool or place it back upon the ground in order better to balance the weight of the child she is about to receive.

1. Berlin, Staatliche Museen Preussischer Kulturbesitz, inv. no. F 2443; see H. Rühfel, *Das Kind in der griechischen Kunst* (Mainz 1984) 109, fig. 43.

7

Vertical crack down center. Stele preserved to waist of figure; missing one akroterion. Faint, incised lines survive from the palmettes that were painted on the akroteria.

Within a naiskos comprising two antae and a pediment stands a woman in three-quarter right profile, her head inclined in right profile. With both hands she holds before her torso the ends of a necklace with beads shaped like pointed amphorae. She wears a peplos or chiton beneath a mantle that is draped over both shoulders and across her waist, with the ends wrapped around the left forearm and elbow. Her wavy hair is center-parted and drawn back to her nape, with the long curly ends flowing freely behind her shoulders. She wears a disc earring. Inscribed on the architrave over her head is the name "Kallistrate": ΚΑΛΛΙΣΤΡΑΤΗ. A second inscription on the horizontal geison reads "Kallisthenes Painaieus": ΚΑΛΛΙΣΘΕΝΗΣ ΠΑΙΑΝΙΕΥΣ.

The carefully executed inscription above the woman's head tells us that her name was Kallistrate. The secondary inscription, less well worked and obviously later, is that of Kallisthenes of Paiania. Paiania was a deme, or district, of Attica, the area in which Athens was located. Clairmont suggests that Kallisthenes may have been a brother of Kallistrate. We know that a single grave relief, often depicting the wife and mother of the family, frequently served as the family grave monument; if such was the case here, surviving relatives may have added Kallisthenes' name to the stele in order to honor him as well.

The relief is beautifully carved, and, in rendering Kallistrate's face, this skilled sculptor has followed the tradition of the Parthenon frieze in positioning the eye directly beneath the brow and in accentuating the upper and lower lids. Indicating a date well after the Parthenon are the softly rounded chin and the softly closed lips, no longer downturned at the corners in the manner of the "Parthenon pout." The drapery points to a date after the beginning of the fourth century, because her garment is no longer transparent, and the drapery falls in clusters of narrow folds that often twist or have angular contours. Also typical of the early fourth century is the way the himation folds cap her right shoulder in a curving sweep, the folds falling into concentric arcs. Familiar, too, from reliefs of the fourth century is the isolation of the figure against the flat expanse of the background, in a manner that recalls the earlier grave stele in Leiden (no. 6).

The stele is a good example of the nostalgic mood in which many of the early fourth-century grave reliefs were executed. Kallistrate's head is almost exaggeratedly inclined in *aidos*, although by the early fourth century this convention may have been less widely observed in actuality (see **Aidos** and **Sophrosyne** and no. 20). Similarly, the delicate, almost affected, gesture of Kallistrate's hands looks back to the Parthenon frieze. Indeed, sentiment permeates the representation, from the long locks of hair designating youthfulness to the innocent gesture of fingering the necklace, suggesting a young maiden's preoccupation with adornment. Such withdrawn absorption so many decades after the Parthenon speaks less of a conservative artist than of the weary, reflective years that followed the eclipse of Athens by Sparta at the

---

7

GRAVE RELIEF OF KALLISTRATE

ca. 400-390
Saint Louis, Saint Louis Art Museum, Museum Purchase, inv. no.
4:1933

Attic
Marble
H 83.4 cm., W 68 cm., Th 10.2 cm.
Inscription: *IG* II² 7061a

Publications: M. Rogers, *Bulletin of the City Art Museum of St. Louis* 18.2 (1933) 14; St. Louis Art Museum, *Handbook of the Collections* (St. Louis 1934) 12; G.E. Mylonas, "The Stele of Kallistrate in the Museum of St. Louis," *Art Bulletin* 18 (1936) 103-105; A. Furtwängler, *Masterpieces of Greek Sculpture*, A. Oikonomides, ed. (Chicago 1964) 421, pl. 78; I. Jucker, *Gestalt und Geschichte. Festschrift Karl Schefold zu seinem sechzigsten Geburtstag am 26. January 1965* (Bern 1967) 139 n. 47, pl. 48,1; B. Schlörb-Vierneisel, "Drei neue Grabreliefs aus der heiligen Strasse," *AM* 83 (1968) 105; *The St. Louis Art Museum Handbook of the Collections* (St. Louis 1975) (illus.); B. Schmaltz, "Verwendung und Funktion attischer Grabmäler," *Marburger Winckelmann-Programm* 1979, 16 pl. 3; Vermeule (1981) 100-101, no. 69, colorpl. 10; B. Schmaltz, *Griechische Grabreliefs* (Darmstadt 1983) 106; K. Herbert, "The Inscription as an Art Form in the Mixed Genre of the Grave Stele: An Example in New York," *Studies Presented to Sterling Dow on his Eightieth Birthday* (Durham, N.C. 1984) 143-48, pl. 9a; *The St. Louis Art Museum Handbook of the Collections* (St. Louis 1991) 16 (illus.); Clairmont (1993) vol. 1, 294-95, no. 1.284.

close of the Peloponnesian War in 404. The period in which this relief was carved saw a disillusionment with public life and renewed appreciation for domestic life and the family, personified on many grave reliefs by the image of the wife and mother. The romanticism and the melancholy of the St. Louis relief may have been prompted as much by the yearning of the age as by sorrow at Kallistrate's death.

8

8

HEAD OF A WOMAN FROM A GRAVE RELIEF

400-390
Cincinnati, Cincinnati Art Museum, The William T. and Louise Taft Semple Collection, inv. no. 1962.389

Attic
Marble
H 22.5 cm., W 14.1 cm.

Publications: W. Siple, "Two Greek Heads on Exhibition in the Museum," *Bulletin of the Cincinnati Art Museum* 2.2 (1931) 41-47; Cincinnati Art Museum, *Sculpture Collection of the Cincinnati Art Museum* (Cincinnati 1970) 38-40.

Head is almost in the round, broken across neck.
    The head is inclined to her left and downward, and she gazes to the side and down. The woman's hair is drawn back from her face under a headcovering (sakkos), which is tied by a cord brought forward from her nape over her ear and behind the roll across her forehead. In front of her right ear are several tufts of hair. Above her right ear, on the side of her head, are the remains of three fingers, evenly separated.

The head is carved almost completely in the round and thus belonged to a monument that was executed in very high relief. Although her right side is completely carved, she is best seen in three-quarter left profile, a position that suggests her torso was also at an angle and thus also almost in the round. Her headcovering and youthful countenance are compatible with a maidservant, and on a grave relief of the early fourth century a similar servant kneels to attend to her mistress's shoes, while the standing woman rests her hand for balance on the side of her servant's head.[1]
    The head is a beautiful example of Classical sculpture. The eyebrow is rendered as a carination in the forehead, and the skin beneath the brow recedes at a sharp angle, with almost no suggestion of fleshiness. The almond-shaped eye, with both lids accentuated, lies closely beneath the brow, and the upper eyelid overlaps the lower eyelid at the outer corners. The lips are bow-shaped, and just beneath the lower lip there is a cleft in the chin. Suggesting a date in

8

139

the early fourth century are the high relief of the carving and the depth and verticality of the bridge of the nose, which causes the inner corner of the eye to be more deeply set than in sculpture of the fifth century. Also supporting a date somewhat after 400 are the slightly upturned corners of the mouth and the narrowing of the jaw, which no longer exhibits the full roundness of counterparts on the Parthenon frieze. The combination of these softened features with the tilted head and sideways gaze conveys a quiet melancholy in keeping with grave stelai of the early fourth century.

1. See the grave stele of Ameinokleia, Athens, National Archaeological Museum, inv. no. 718, in Clairmont (1993) vol. 3, 229-30, no. 370.

9

HEAD OF A WOMAN

ca. 400
Geneva, George Ortiz Collection

"From southwest Asia Minor"
Marble
H 18 cm.

Publication: G. Ortiz, *In Pursuit of the Absolute. Art of the Ancient World from the George Ortiz Collection* (Bern 1994) no. 147 (color illus.).

Broken across the neck. Missing much of nose and chin. Earlobes pierced for earrings. Four holes in the back of the head and two holes above the right ear. The head is almost entirely in the round, only slightly flat in back, and with marks of the claw chisel on the back and right top of the head. Unfinished areas on the right back side indicate that the head was turned slightly to her left.

The maiden's hair is enveloped in a sakkos, the edge of which can be seen along the hairline. A depression delineates the contour of the roll of hair that lies across her forehead under the fabric. The hair at the sides is drawn forward to the face and then brought back over her ears.

The head is so quintessentially Attic that the sculptor must have emigrated to Asia Minor, coerced by the unemployment that followed the completion of the Acropolis building projects and the economic distress of the Peloponnesian War. Typical of the best of Classical sculpture from Athens is the rendering of the eyebrow as a carination in the forehead, meeting at an angle the minimally fleshy area beneath the brow. The eyelids are pronounced, and the upper eyelid overlaps the lower eyelid at the outer corner. The eyeballs are slightly rounded, with the upper part of the eyeball projecting beyond the lower part of the eyeball. The bow-shaped lips are lightly set together and have downturned corners. The maiden gazes down and to her left, radiating reticence and modesty.

The sakkos and the rendering of the head almost in the round are appropriate to a maidservant on an Attic grave monument. It appears that the sculptor brought with him a knowledge not only of his Attic style, but also of Attic forms of sculptural monuments.

10

HEAD OF A WOMAN

390-375
Baltimore, Walters Art Gallery, inv. no. 23.220

Attic
Marble
H 14.6 cm., W 12.6 cm., Th 8.4 cm.

Publications: *Ancient Art in American Private Collections* (Cambridge, Fogg Art Museum, December 28, 1954-February 15, 1955) 27, no. 154, pl. 40; D.K. Hill, "A Beautiful Greek Head," *BWalt* 18.5 (1966) illus.; D.K. Hill, "Greek Head in Baltimore," *Archaeology* 19 (1966) 288; E. Reeder, *Hellenistic Art in the Walters Art Gallery* (Baltimore 1988) 69, 72, no. 3.

Broken away from its background and broken across neck. The back of the hair is roughly worked.

The head is in left profile and in high relief, extending to the right side of the face beyond the outer corner of the right eye. The hair is center-parted with a roll of curls over the hairline; the ends are drawn back from the face over the top of the left ear. At the back of the head the hair is brought up from the nape. The woman gazes in front of her.

10

The traditional composition of these grave scenes was accompanied by an equally conservative mood, attributable to the military and political traumas of the late fifth century, which sparked a disillusionment with public life and a nostalgia for domesticity. On grave reliefs of the fourth century, women were often portrayed with an almost exaggerated dignity and respect as an expression of this reawakened appreciation for family life.

HEAD OF A GODDESS

ca. 440-420
Athens, Agora Museum, inv. no. S 2094

Attic, from the Athenian Agora
Marble
H 28 cm., W 23 cm.

Publications: E. Harrison, "New Sculpture from the Athenian Agora, 1959," *Hesperia* 29 (1960) 369-70, pl. 81a-b; American School of Classical Studies at Athens, *The Athenian Agora: A Guide to the Excavation and Museum*, 2nd ed. (Athens 1962) 126; S. Adam, *The Technique of Greek Sculpture*, *BSA Suppl.* 3 (London 1966) 51; H. Thompson, *The Athenian Agora: A Short Guide* (Princeton 1976) 191; *LIMC* II (1984) 685, no. 859, pl. 510 (s.v. Artemis).

The head has a delicacy and refinement that reveal its date in the first decades of the fourth century, when sculptors were beginning to experiment with a more marked differentiation between male and female faces. Particularly noticeable is the reduction in the emphasis on the lower eyelid, which is now thinner and exhibits a smooth transition to the planes of the face. The profile of the eyeball is also more vertical, contrasting with the fifth-century eye, in which the upper part of the eyeball protrudes beyond the lower. Also noteworthy are the increased depth of the inner corner of the eye and the narrower, rounded cheeks, which contrast with the flatter planes of the cheeks in fifth-century sculpture. The corners of the lips form a horizontal line, contrasting with the downturned corners of the "Parthenon pout," familiar from the Parthenon's east frieze. The chin is also shorter and less protruding than was common in the fifth century. The resulting countenance is youthful, gentle, and innocent.

The head belonged to a relief, of which the most common type for this scale at this time was a grave relief. As this sculpture illustrates, the first decades of the fourth century saw an ever greater depth of relief, and the Walters example would soon be followed by burial monuments in which the head is sculpted almost entirely in the round. Because the woman gazes ahead of her, she may have been seated and looking at a young serving girl standing near her; the head could also have belonged to a figure standing behind a seated figure and gazing across to another standing figure.

Pieces missing from nose and upper lip. Section missing from back of head and nape. Drill hole and two iron pins in neck. Some coarse cutting on the stephane and on the hair behind the ears (probably signs of reuse in antiquity). Two pointed indentations in the forehead hair and one in the chin almost certainly occurred in the process of measuring by Roman copyists.

The head is slightly over lifesize. The wavy hair is center-parted and is drawn back over the ears to the nape. She wears a diadem that ends just above each ear. Above the diadem her hair radiates from the top of the head, forming narrow waves in low relief.

This head is one of the most beautiful of any surviving from the fifth century, and the measuring marks of Roman copyists tell us that the piece was much admired in Roman times as well. The head constitutes a quintessential example of a Classical face from the second half of the fifth century. The eyebrow is rendered as a carination, and the area beneath the brow is minimally fleshy. The eye is set close up under the eyebrow, with a delicate groove delineating the base of the upper eyelid. Both upper and lower eyelid are crisply articulated, and the upper eyelid forms a continuous arc that descends to the tearduct; her left upper eyelid overlaps the lower eyelid at the outer corner. Also characteristic is the flatness of the eyeball, with the upper part of the eyeball protruding over the lower part. The lower eyelid forms a smooth, unbroken curve, with the maximum dip just beyond the midpoint on the outer side. The cheeks have little curvature and even less fleshiness. The lips are full

11

11

and slightly open and are separated by a drilled groove. She has a pronounced cleft under the lower lip and a rounded chin. Along her hairline her hair falls in undulating waves that dip slightly in front of each ear and are then drawn back over the top of the ear, which has a very small lobe. The convenient protrusion of the ear enables the hair to be anchored securely behind it.

The head so immediately calls to mind the head of Artemis from the east frieze of the Parthenon that the Agora sculpture may well have been executed by an artist who had participated in the Acropolis building program. Suggesting only a slightly later date than the frieze (442-438) are such minor adjustments as the greater mass and softness of the hair and the smaller eye, which is set more deeply into its socket. The downturned corners of the mouth, the

so-called "Parthenon pout," have also softened such that the groove dividing the lips is practically horizontal.

The diadem designates the head as that of a goddess, but her identity is unclear. The breakage at the back of the head suggested to Evelyn Harrison that the hair was gathered into a mass at the nape with the locks falling down behind the shoulders. As this hairstyle characterizes the type of the Artemis of Ariccia, there is a possibility that the Agora head belonged to a statue of that goddess. Harrison observed that the piece does not exhibit the weathering typical of a pedimental sculpture and suggested that it belonged to a free-standing statue. The head was probably slightly turned to her right, because the overlapping of only the left upper lid suggests that the face was intended to be seen in three-quarter left profile.

LEKYTHOS
WITH MISTRESS AND MAID

445-440
by the Achilles Painter
Copenhagen, National Museum of Denmark, inv. no. 5624

Attic, from Keratea
Clay
H 35.6 cm., Diam 11.8 cm.

Publications: *ARV²* 997.150; *Para* 438; *CVA* Copenhagen, Musée National 4 (Denmark 4) pls. 170.6a-b and 170a; J.D. Beazley, "The Master of the Achilles Amphora in the Vatican," *JHS* 34 (1914) 221, no. 13; E. Buschor, "Attische Lekythen der Parthenonzeit," *Münchener Jahrbuch der bildenden Kunst* N.F. 2 (1925) 179; J.D. Beazley, *Attic White Lekythoi* (London 1938) 9; N. Breitenstein, *Graeske Vaser* (Copenhagen 1957) pls. 46-47; Reilly (1989) 413, 434, no. 25, pl. 73.

Intact. Red on the peplos of the standing woman, the border of her sakkos, the mantle of the seated woman, the sakkos hanging in the background, and several of the bandelettes.

On the shoulder a tongue border surmounts a pattern of volutes and palmettes rendered in black or brown-black, with several leaves indicated in matte red. Above the scene is a band of meander alternating left and right, enclosing a saltire square.

Seated on a klismos in right profile, legs drawn back, is a woman who holds a plemochoe in her right hand. She wears a chiton, whose sleeve extends beneath her right elbow, and a mantle that is draped over her left shoulder and across her waist and legs to her shins. Her hair is brought up from the nape beneath a fillet, and she gazes ahead of her, over the top of the vase.

Standing before her and facing front, her toes foreshortened, is a woman whose left hand is placed beneath an elongated oval basket, which is decorated with a band of meander beneath the rim. The wreath of leaves beneath the meander may be intended to represent an actual garland. Hanging from the front edge of the basket are three short ribbons decorated with a row of dots and four longer ribbons. The woman's right arm is slightly outstretched, with the palm inward, the fingers extended. She wears a girded peplos with an overfold that extends to mid-thigh; beneath its folds the contours of her legs are seen. Her head is in left profile and her hair is bound up by a covering of fabric (sakkos). She gazes in the direction of the seated woman, but slightly over her head. Both women are barefoot. Hanging in the background are a headcovering (sakkos) and an oinochoe. In the field between the two figures is inscribed "the woman is beautiful," in two lines, *stoichedon*: ΗΥΓΙΑΙΝΟΝ ΚΑΛΟΣ

O ne of the finest of all Classical vase-painters, the Achilles Painter worked in red-figure (no. 112), but is best known for the exquisite draftsmanship on his white-ground lekythoi. In these vases, as this example so well demonstrates, his figures are quintessentially Classical in their stately calm and dignified bearing. Particularly noteworthy are the profiles of his female faces, with their unbroken profile of forehead and nose, the eye rendered as a supine V set close to the eyebrow, and the swelling of the protruding lower lip. The length and fullness of the jaw of the seated woman look

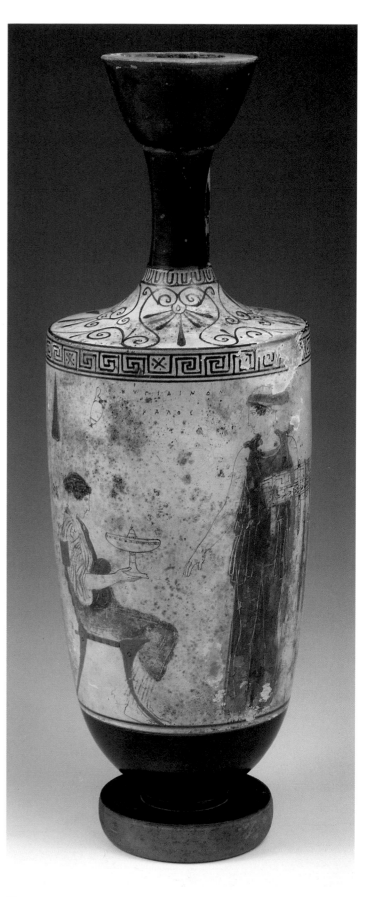

12

12 Detail

12 Detail

back to Early Classical vase-painting and contrast with the standing woman's narrower chin where the cleft beneath the lower lip is, consequently, more pronounced.

It is not only the figures themselves that win our admiration for the Achilles Painter. The skillful way he carefully and generously spaces them enhances the importance of the figures and the scene. Here, the basket carried by the standing woman tells us that she has come to the tomb of the seated woman to offer a burial gift. The deceased holds an elaborate perfume vase of the type that was also given to brides as a wedding gift; to ancient viewers its presence would have called to mind the wedding ceremony, which was the most important celebration in a woman's life.

The separation of the figures, linked only by the quiet gesture of the standing woman, emphasizes the metaphorical space between the deceased and the survivor. The distance is accentuated by the gazes of the women, which do not meet; the seated woman gazes over and beyond the plemochoe, and the standing woman looks over the head of the seated woman. But if the figures are separated by death, the objects in the scene are reminders of how closely

linked the two women are by the lives they lived. The sakkos suspended in the background was a woman's conventional hair covering, and an oinochoe was regularly used by women to pour libations in rituals of departure (see nos. 18 and 20). A further common bond is the basket of funerary ribbons. These baskets were used almost exclusively by women, who bore the primary responsibility for visiting the tomb and maintaining the family burial ground, an expression of the Greek belief that, as bearers of children, women were closer to the thresholds of life and death (see **Women as Containers**).

In contrast with painters of white-ground lekythoi in the early fifth century, the Achilles Painter employs a dilute brown or yellow-brown to delineate his figures. A broader stroke renders the drapery folds of the seated woman's chiton, as well as the contour of her foreshortened right shoulder. Although the flat, regular, folds of the overfold of the standing woman's peplos look back to sculpture of the third quarter of the fifth century, the articulation of the legs beneath the transparent fabric looks forward to the frieze and pediments of the Parthenon.

WHITE-GROUND LEKYTHOS WITH WOMAN AND CHILD

ca. 440
by the Bosanquet Painter
London, British Museum, inv. no. GR 1905.7-10.10

Attic
Clay
H 13.2 cm., W 15.2 cm.

Publications: *ARV²* 1227.10; *Add²* 350; F. Felten, *Thanatos- und Kleophonmaler. Weiss-grundige und rotfigurige Vasenmalerei der Parthenonzeit* (Munich 1971) 21, 23, 61 n. 46, pl. 6.2; Kurtz (1975) 39, 210, pl. 30.3; Keuls (1985a) 139, 141, fig. 122; Robertson (1992) 203, fig. 213. Fragment is broken all around.

A woman is seated in left profile, her left leg crossed over her right leg at the knee. Her left forearm rests on her left thigh, the index finger bent. Her right elbow is placed upon her left forearm near the elbow; her fingers are bent, the index finger most acutely, and her chin rests on the back of the knuckles of her first and second fingers. Her hair is brought up from her nape under a band of fabric that is wrapped twice around her head; the ends of her locks are seen at the back of her head, and a few short curls are brought forward in front of her left ear. She also wears an earring in the form of a double-hoop. Behind her is a vertical line, probably belonging to the grave stele.

The woman's gaze is directed toward a baby boy who is held by a maidservant standing in right profile. The woman's left hand supports the baby under his left shoulder, and her right hand cradles his left hip. The baby turns toward the seated woman, his left arm fully outstretched, his right hand just above the maidservant's right hand. The boy has curly locks below his chin, an amuletic band strung over his right shoulder and around his left hip, and bracelets on his right wrist and left ankle.

White-ground lekythoi conventionally depicted the deceased person appearing together with the survivors. The popularity of this example's scene on later and better preserved lekythoi, as well as on grave reliefs (see no. 6), enables us to identify the seated woman as the deceased mother of the child who is held in the arms of the maidservant. The mother is probably seated on the steps that support the grave stele, the edge of which is rendered by the vertical line behind her back.

In most funerary scenes on lekythoi, the figures stand quietly, such that there is no indication that the survivor can see the figure of the deceased as the artist has depicted him or her for the viewer. The idea is that the sense of the deceased is present at the grave site, and it is to honor and to feel a connection with this presence that

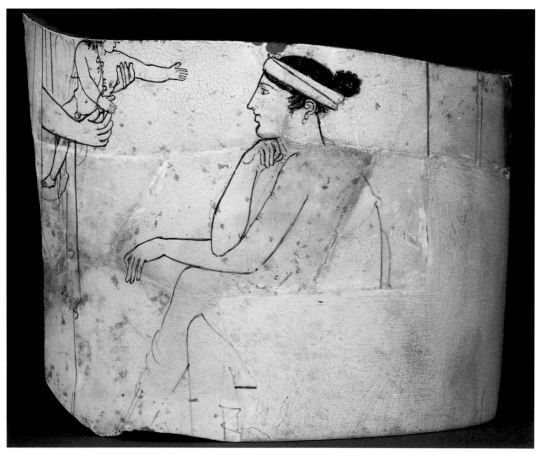

13

145

the survivor regularly visits the tomb. In this scene, by contrast, the child immediately perceives his mother as a tangible entity and eagerly reaches out for her, his energy uncontained by the self-control that distinguishes adult demeanor in Classical art. The boy's unrestrained gesture has, therefore, a double meaning: the exuberance of youth and its special sensitivity to the threshold of birth and death beyond which his mother has now stepped.

Given the obvious affection of the child for his mother, her gesture is initially puzzling. In today's world, the gesture would be understood as one of interested, but relaxed contemplation, detached from intense emotional involvement. That this is not the meaning of the gesture is indicated by the figure of Demeter on the east frieze of the Parthenon (442-438, pp. 248-49, fig. 1). In that scene, each of the Olympian deities is represented with the attributes, or in the pose, most appropriate to his or her divine character. Demeter, as the mother who is almost perpetually grieving for her daughter, Persephone, is seated with her right elbow bent and the back of her right hand brought just under her chin, which is mostly broken away. The gesture obviously signifies mourning, melancholy, and the pensiveness of bereavement, expressed with dignified restraint (see **Persephone and Demeter**). Such, also, is the meaning of the mother's gesture on the lekythos, and her parallel with the figure of Demeter suggests a date for the lekythos contemporary with the Parthenon frieze.

The sure and elegant draftsmanship of this scene shows clearly why the Bosanquet Painter is appreciated as one of the finest of all Classical vase-painters. He handles with ease the mother's complicated pose, successfully rendering the moderate foreshortening of her left forearm. He poignantly juxtaposes the twisting torso and eagerly outstretched arm of her child with the mother's self-contained posture, as she brings her arms close to her torso and responds to her son's overture with only a gaze. Her profile is particularly fine, the length of her chin a legacy of Early Classical drawing. The barely perceptible dip for the bridge of her nose is a subtle detail that softens the otherwise austere profile. Also characteristic of the painter is an avoidance of the added white pigment favored, for example, by the Pan Painter (no. 90).

The motif of the child held securely in the arms of one woman while energetically reaching out for the arms of another probably originated in the prototypical painting from which the vase scenes of Erichthonios are derived (see **Erichthonios**, nos. 67 and 68). In many of these vase-paintings the boy wears a similar amuletic necklace (nos. 70 and 72), and, in Euripides' *Ion* (1428), Kreousa comments that the custom of protecting babies in this way originated with the birth of Erichthonios.

14

LEKYTHOS
WITH WOMAN AT A TOMB

440-435
by the Achilles Painter
Oxford, Ashmolean Museum, University of Oxford, inv. no. 1896.41
(V.545)

Attic
Clay
H 36.3 cm.

Publications: *ARV²* 998.165; *Add²* 313; Kurtz (1975) 38, 40, 46, 51, 214, pl. 36,2; M.J. Vickers, *Greek Vases* (Oxford 1978) nos. 52-53.

Intact. Around the neck are palmettes and volutes; above the scene is a band of three meanders alternating with a saltire square. Red for woman's himation, gray for youth's.

A grave stele is supported by a multi-stepped base; across the top of the stele are three horizontal lines. Facing the stele in right profile is a woman who stands with her left foot advanced and who is barefoot. She wears a chiton beneath a himation that is brought over her left shoulder and draped around her waist and most of her legs, with the ends hanging down her back. In her left hand she holds an alabastron, and in her right hand she clasps the base of a plemochoe (perfume vase). Her hair is brought up from her nape under a wide band; locks in front of her ear curl forward. She gazes downward.

On the other side of the stele a youth stands in left profile, his left arm behind his hip, his right arm extended. His mantle is drawn over his left shoulder, covering his torso and legs to mid-calf; the contours of his legs are revealed beneath. His gaze is ahead but is not focused on her.

The Achilles Painter is much admired for the caliber of his drawing and particularly for his elegant profiles of women. The inner corner of her eye is open; the upper eyelid is accentuated by a second parallel line; and the full jaw reflects influence from the Early Classical period. The woman's toes are minimally foreshortened.

Because the woman approaches the stele with funerary gifts, the deceased individual must be the youth. He is shorter than she is, and perhaps this differentiation indicates that she is his sister or mother. In most funerary scenes on lekythoi, deceased and survivor do not look directly into each other's faces, probably to indicate that the deceased is too removed from the everyday world to focus specifically on a single individual and that the survivor cannot determine the precise location of the deceased even though a spiritual connection with the deceased is being experienced. Here, the woman inclines her head in *aidos* (modesty with overtones of shame), conduct that was expected of her in public and especially if the gathering included men (see ***Aidos* and *Sophrosyne***). Because women at the grave do not always bow their heads, it is

14   14

likely that this woman's action is an expression of her awareness of the deceased youth's presence.

It is interesting to note that the woman chooses as offering gifts objects that are particularly linked with women. Both the alabastron and the plemochoe were vessels that were intended for unguents and perfumes. As expensive and pleasing items, they were conventionally given to the bride as wedding gifts (nos. 28, 56, 58, and 75) and carry connotations of female fertility and adornment. When presented to a deceased woman, we might assume that they are intended to bring delight and comfort; as an offering for a man they probably express the woman's wish to bestow upon him objects with which she herself was intimately linked.

15

CARYATID MIRROR
WITH APHRODITE

ca. 490-480
St. Petersburg, The State Hermitage Museum, inv. no. B 815

Aeginetan?
Bronze
H (total) 28.5 cm., H (figure) 18.6 cm.

Publications: E. Langlotz, *Frühgriechische Bildhauerschulen* (Nuremberg 1927) 99, no. 6 pl. 54a; O. Persianova, *The Hermitage. Room-to-Room Guide* (Leningrad 1972) 72-73; F. Schaller, *Stützfiguren in der griechischen Kunst* (Vienna 1973) 41, no. 100; X. Gorbunova and I. Saverkina, *Greek and Roman Antiquities in the Hermitage* (Leningrad 1975) no. 26; L. Keene Congdon, *Caryatid Mirrors of Ancient Greece* (Mainz 1981) 146-47, no. 27, pl. 24, ill. 27a-c; *LIMC* I (1981) 18, no. 94, pl. 13 (s.v. Aphrodite); *Aus den Schatzkammern Eurasiens. Meisterwerke antiker Kunst* (Zürich, Kunsthaus Zürich, January 29-May 2, 1993) 194-95, no. 100 (illus.).

Mirror disc missing; Erotes have been reattached.

Aphrodite stands frontally, left foot advanced, on a stool whose legs take the form of the lower legs of horses, with hooves. Her right elbow is bent, and two of the fingers of her upraised right hand hold a small fruit. Her left elbow is bent, and two fingers of her left hand clasp folds of drapery at her left hip. She wears a chiton that has a straight neckline edged by a zigzag border, sleeves that cover the upper arms, and a decorative pattern consisting of close-set pairs of wavy, engraved lines. The garment is open down her right side and extends to the arches of her feet. Her himation is fastened on her right shoulder with a decorative knot or brooch and then passes between her breasts; the upper hem is turned over to form a wavy pattern. Over her torso and thighs the mantle falls in stacked pleats. An engraved line is set just inside the edges of the hem, and two horizontal engraved lines over her left thigh beneath her left hand may be additional decoration or intended to suggest folds in the cloth. Behind her right shoulder the fabric falls in stacked pleats. Her shoes have upturned tips.

The hair is center-parted and is arranged in a series of crenelated locks that are drawn to each side of the face, where they pass beneath a loop of similar locks. Similar locks are drawn back from the forehead over the top of the head, pass under a beaded fillet, and then fall to the middle of the shoulders, where they are gathered by a horizontal band, beneath which they fall to the middle of her back. She wears earrings, each of which comprises a disc with pyramidal pendant. The mirror attachment rises from the crown of her head and terminates at each end in a volute with palmette petals; on the back of the attachment is a palmette, the petals of which are incised.

Her head is relatively large for the proportions of her body and is elongated; the face is flat, with little modeling of the cheeks. Her high, arched eyebrows are in low relief, her eyelids are accentuated, and her lips and jaws are full.

Stepping with his right toes upon Aphrodite's left shoulder is a nude, boyish figure of Eros. His left leg is extended slightly behind him, the foot flat; he wears engraved sandals. His arms are stretched out horizontally from his shoulders and are seen against his wings, the tips of which curve upward; on the back of the wings is an engraved pattern. The right hand touches the base of the mirror attachment. A second boyish Eros flies toward Aphrodite's right shoulder, his left knee bent with the foot flat and the right leg extended behind him. The position of his arms and wings echo that of his counterpart. Each boy has long hair that extends to the middle of his back and is surmounted by a fillet; the hair of the Eros on Aphrodite's right shoulder is gathered at the top of the shoulders by a cross-piece similar to his mother's.

Whereas the dress and stiff frontality of the figure are in the Archaic tradition, the curvature of the forms points to an Early Classical date. Around her upper arms the chiton clings so closely that the rounded contours of all but the undermost part of the arms are clearly delineated. In profile view, the artist has skillfully captured the way the weight of her blanket of hair sags forward over her shoulders before being drawn back behind them. The curvature of her shoulders is echoed by the soft swelling of her buttocks. Behind her right shoulder the stacked folds of her himation have plasticity and weight, and the turned over folds of her mantle between her breasts have an appealing lightness and volume. Certain details are less successful, such as the imperfectly positioned and exaggeratedly pointed breasts. The overall impression is one of animation and energy, facilitated by the generous tensile strength of bronze, which permits the ambitiously extended right arm. It has been suggested that the mirror was made on Aegina, an island not far from Athens.

Because the figure functioned as the handle to a mirror, the artist took special care that the form would be a comfortable and gratifying object to hold, and, indeed, its tactile qualities make it a delight to handle, with its varied explorations of curvature and texture. It is interesting to consider that the owner of this prized possession was not male, but a female, who would have derived pleasure not only from handling the forms, but also from contemplating an exquisite female image while preparing her own toilette. Far from a competing presence, the figurine of Aphrodite would have been regarded as encouragement and inspiration, as if to say that an extraordinary mirror such as this one could be owned only by an extraordinary woman.

16

STATUETTE OF APHRODITE

ca. 430
Basel, Antikenmuseum Basel und Sammlung Ludwig, inv. no. BS 272

Marble
H 44.2 cm., W (max.) 20.5 cm.

Unpublished.

Missing both forearms and head, which were added separately; left foot broken off. Area beneath drapery overlying pillar is not carved.

Aphrodite rests her left elbow and lower arm upon a pillar or tree trunk, of which only the horizontal upper edge is visible in frontal view. The rest of her weight is supported by her right leg; her left knee is bent and the foot is slightly advanced. Her right elbow was bent and the forearm was extended. She wears a belted chiton which is buttoned along the length of her right upper arm and which has slid off her left shoulder almost down to the elbow, exposing her left shoulder and the top of her left breast. Her mantle is draped around her back and across her waist and legs. The ends are wrapped around her left elbow and fall in swallow-tail folds over the support, almost completely concealing it.

Although the original statue on which this figurine is based no longer survives, we know from an array of derivative works that the statue represented Aphrodite and was created about 430. Opinion differs as to the precise identity of the original, but a likely candidate is the famous statue of Aphrodite in the Gardens, which was carved by Alkamenes, who was also active in the creation of the Parthenon's sculpture.[1] The location of the sanctuary is thought to have been on the slopes of the Acropolis, but the goddess may have had another sanctuary in the city, and the statue could have been located there.

One of the most distinctive features of the work is the slipping chiton, which has its origins in the reclining figure M (Aphrodite) on the east pediment of the Parthenon. Evocative of Aphrodite's sexuality, the slipping chiton became so closely identified with the goddess that even when borrowed eventually by other mythical figures the mannerism always retained its associations with Aphrodite.

The other distinctive feature of the composition is the leaning elbow, the inspiration for which may ultimately go back to the seated figure of Zeus on the east frieze of the Parthenon (pp. 248-49, figs. 1 and 2). There Zeus casually rests his elbow and arm on the back of his chair, whereas here Aphrodite leans heavily on the support while her right leg bears the rest of her weight. The resulting pose is not only almost impossible to sustain in real life, but also creates a sinuosity that looks forward to the work of the fourth-century Attic sculptor Praxiteles, who was surely mindful of this

16

statue when he created his famous Hermes and the Child Dionysos, as well as the Sauroktonos. The Aphrodite type to which this figurine belongs is important in showing us the degree to which the sculpture of the fourth century was rooted in work of the last third of the fifth century.

On the Parthenon frieze, Zeus' gesture communicates ease and the relaxed posture of self-confidence. In its modified form on the statue of Aphrodite, and in combination with the slipping chiton, the gesture exudes languor and complacency. The suggestion that the goddess would rather be prone than erect is strengthened by the arrangement of her chiton and mantle, which is identical to the drapery scheme of the reclining Aphrodite on the east pediment of the Parthenon. But however strong may be Aphrodite's intimation of barely contained inhibition, she reveals only an exposed left shoulder and a hint of the left breast to fifth century viewers. Not until the fourth century and Hellenistic period will Praxiteles venture to depict the goddess completely in the nude.

Because the Basel statuette displays so many Classical details and no Hellenistic or Roman elements, it appears to have been carved not long after the original statue. Comparison with the many, mostly Roman, copies of the statue underscores how closely the statuette echoes details of the prototype's drapery. Concentric, evenly separated, cordlike folds radiate over the right leg from the top of the left thigh and, where the folds of the chiton spill over the belt, the fabric falls into looping folds. As an almost contemporary copy, this figurine may have been a dedicatory offering in the sanctuary where the life-size original was housed.

1. See *LIMC* II (1984) 29-33, nos. 185-224 (s.v. Aphrodite). For a similar Hellenistic statuette, see J. Marcadé, "Les trouvailles de la maison dite de l'Hermès à Délos," *BCH* 77 (1953) 548-53.

16

MODERN CAST FROM A LOST IMPRESSION WITH APHRODITE AND EROS

original relief, ca. 420
clay impression, ca. 420-400
Berlin, Antikensammlung, Staatliche Museen zu Berlin Preussischer Kulturbesitz

Original relief Attic
Casting clay
H 10.3 cm.

Publications: G. Rodenwaldt, "Ein toreutisches Meisterwerk," *JdI* 41 (1926) 191-204, Beilage 5; D.B. Thompson, "Mater Caelaturae," *Hesperia* 8 (1939) 309, fig. 17; W.-H. Schuchhardt, *Die Kunst der Griechen* (Berlin 1940) 275-76; E. Langlotz, *Phidiasprobleme* (Frankfurt 1947) 85-88, pl. 30; B. Ashmole, *Proceedings of the British Academy* 48 (1962) 232-33; J. Dörig, "Kalamis-Studien," *JdI* 80 (1965) 253-57, 265 fig. 92a; K. Schefold, *Die Griechen und ihre Nachbarn*, Propyläen Kunstgeschichte I (Berlin 1967) 111, 206, pl. 153b; Schefold (1981) 197-98, 370, fig. 268; W.-D. Heilmeyer, "Kopierte Klassik," in *Praestant Interna. Festschrift für Ulrich Hausmann* (Tübingen 1982) 52-62, pl. 6,1-3; C. Rolley, *Les bronzes grecs* (Fribourg 1983) 164, fig. 151; *LIMC* II (1984) 29-30, no. 187 (s.v. Aphrodite); Mark (1984) 300; H. Walter, *Die Gestalt der Frau. Bildwerke von 30,000-20 v. Chr.: Anthropologische Betrachtungen* (Stuttgart 1985) 52-53, fig. 44.

Modern plaster/plasticine impression from an ancient clay impression taken from a metal relief.

The edges of the original relief are visible as a raised band that runs vertically behind Eros and curves down behind Aphrodite. She is seen in three-quarter left profile, leaning with her left elbow upon a pillar that is turned forty-five degrees. Her left leg is advanced with the knee relaxed; her right leg is not shown. She wears a chiton, whose slipping neckline reveals most of her right breast, and a mantle that is draped across her legs, with the ends laid over the pillar beneath her elbow. Either the same fabric or a veil is draped over her head, and the fingers of her upraised left hand draw the fabric away from her left shoulder. Her hair is brought back from her face over her ear. Her head is tilted down toward the face of Eros, and she gazes downward as well. Her right arm lies across the top of his shoulders, and her right hand, the fingers relaxed, hangs over his right shoulder. He is nude and turns his body slightly toward her as he gazes up at her, his face almost in right profile. He has short wavy hair. His right arm is bent at the elbow, and his raised forearm rests along the side of Aphrodite's hand while his right hand clutches her right wrist. His wings open at about forty-five degrees from his body, such that the back of the distant wing is visible.

The scene is one of the most engaging and beloved of surviving Classical compositions. The modern viewer is, however, two steps from the original masterpiece. That work was a metal, probably silver, relief which had been hammered by the repoussé technique. The shape of the frame as well as the curving surface of the cast indicates that the finished relief was attached to a shoulder lappet on a cuirass. Sometime after the metal relief was completed, an impression was made by pressing an unbaked clay slab against its surface. Examination of the several dozen surviving examples indi-

17

cate that clay impressions were made as workshop records, either at the time when a metal relief was completed, or a few years afterward, when the object to which the relief was fastened was returned to the workshop for repair. Because such a small number of Classical metal reliefs survive, the few extant clay impressions offer us valuable insight into the astonishing caliber of late fifth-century Attic metalwork.

The clay impression in which this modern cast was made was discovered in Athens before 1870, when it was known to be in the Rhousopoulos Collection. Sometime afterward, it was sold to an English purchaser and was subsequently lost. Fortunately, before its sale, several modern casts were made by pressing clay into the impression, employing it as a mold. One clay cast was brought to Berlin by Carl Friederichs in 1870, but was subsequently lost. Another modern cast was once in the possession of Ferenc Pulszky of Hungary, and is now in a private collection in Munich. A third cast was known from 1879 and is today in the Akademisches Kunstmuseum in Bonn; it was subsequently fired, which reduced it in size. The example seen here is a cast after the one in Munich, and is, consequently, two more generations removed from the original metal relief.

The scene is unique in Classical art of the fifth century. Aphrodite gazes down at her son, who is depicted as a boy of about four or five years old. He presses his body closely against the legs of his mother and clutches her wrist to bring her arm even more tightly around his shoulders, as he gazes eagerly up at her. The ultimate inspiration was slab 41 of the east frieze of the Parthenon, where Aphrodite was seated beside Eros, who was standing. That slab, unfortunately, is now lost to us, but before its deterioration a plaster cast was made, which in recent years has been modified as more fragments of the original relief have been recovered. The newly restored scene (pp. 248-49, fig. 1) shows that Aphrodite's right arm was interlinked with that of Artemis, who is depicted on the adjacent, surviving slab. Eros, who is here about six or seven years old, looks ahead, in the same direction in which Aphrodite gazes. Instinctively, with perfect confidence and trust, he leans against her knee, needful of, but so reassured by, her supportive presence that he can direct his attention elsewhere.

In contrast to the Parthenon frieze, the metal relief presents a younger Eros, and one far more demanding of his mother's attention. He is clearly the more active figure of the pair, pulling her arm around his shoulders and searching her face as he turns his head upward at an angle that would have been as uncomfortable for him as it was difficult for the metalworker to represent. Aphrodite is much less energetic; her right hand lies limply; her left hand loosely fingers her veil; and she allows the pillar to support most of her weight.

In a modern context, Aphrodite's lolling pose and relaxed clasp of her garment would be interpreted as disinterest and distraction. To some extent, her remarkable restraint is attributable to her immediate prototype, which was surely the type of the Leaning Aphrodite which survives only in Roman copies. The original statue is thought to have been the famed sculpture by Alkamenes for the sanctuary of Aphrodite in the Gardens. For the cuirass relief the metalworker needed only to add Eros and to adjust Aphrodite's glance downward rather than outward. The fact that the Aphrodite of the metal relief represents a modification of a famous motif is surely a partial explanation of the goddess's limited engagement with her son.

We can, however, more fully understand that Aphrodite's leaning elbow does not signify withheld commitment when we examine the figure's ultimate prototype, the figure of Zeus on the east frieze of the Parthenon. In the midst of a gathering of the Olympian gods on the occasion of the Panathenaic festival, he is seated, and rests his left forearm along the back of his chair. The gesture signifies ease, self-confidence, effortless composure, and an absence of tension or anxiety in the anticipation of pleasure. It is this meaning that should be assigned to Aphrodite's leaning elbow, as well as to the leaning elbow of the type of the Leaning Aphrodite.

Similarly, the gesture of Aphrodite's left hand can be compared with that of Hera, who is seated beside Zeus on the Parthenon frieze. As Hera turns around to gaze at her husband Zeus, her left hand draws the folds of her veil away from her head in the traditional gesture of *anakalypsis*, by which the bride unveils herself to her new husband (see **The Wedding**). Why Aphrodite should associate herself with the imagery of a bride is surely explained by the combination of the gesture with her display of maternal affection for Eros. An analogy is again offered on the Parthenon frieze, where Aphrodite entwines her arm with that of Artemis, the goddess who oversees the transition of young girls to marriage. Similarly, the Aphrodite of the metal relief and of the Leaning Aphrodite type is also predisposed to link herself with marriage and motherhood when the occasion is appropriate.

At the same time, the goddess makes no attempt to conceal her sexuality, allowing her chiton to slip down her right breast in the same way the reclining Aphrodite is depicted on the east pediment of the Parthenon. Unrelenting propriety, the goddess' appearance seems to imply, is ultimately unpalatable. Interestingly enough, on the Parthenon's east frieze, Artemis' chiton has also begun to slide off her shoulders, surely to indicate that Artemis' role as the protector of pregnant young wives links her with Aphrodite; after all, Aphrodite's realm is the sexual attraction that facilitates procreation (see **The Plynteria and Arrephoroi**).

Once the leaning elbow and *anakalypsis* gesture are better understood, Aphrodite's demeanor on the relief emerges as regally relaxed, rather than uncaring of her son. Indeed, their emotional bond is confirmed by their exchange of gazes, because, in fifth-century art, figures interacting within a scene do not necessarily look at each other; when they do, as, for example, on the east frieze of the Parthenon, or in departure scenes (nos. 18-20), we are justified in reading into the scene a significant emotional content. Most interlocked gazes seem to be primarily sexual: the bride as she unveils herself for her husband; customer and hetaira embracing at a symposium (nos. 39-41); the fleeing, but perhaps not totally resisting, maiden who gazes back at a pursuing deity (nos. 111-113), and the husband and wife shaking hands as they prepare to take leave of each other for war or in death (no. 19). By contrast, the bodies of Demeter and Persephone are often in very close contact, but their gazes are directed elsewhere in the manner of Eros' on the Parthenon's east frieze; the implication is that a parent and mature child are so indissolubly linked that interlocked gazes are not needed as confirmation of that bond.

The metal relief cannot have been executed very long after the Parthenon frieze. The face of Aphrodite compares very closely with those on the frieze, and the crinkly folds of her chiton find parallels in the figures of Artemis and Aphrodite. Suggesting a slightly later date than the frieze (442-438) are the transparency of the drapery over the breasts and the successful and ambitious foreshortening of the pillar and Eros' wings.

The relief looks forward to the fourth century when Eros will be depicted even younger, and when affection will be even more overtly expressed. The fourth century also witnesses the introduction of the nude Aphrodite, whose sexuality is, therewith, far less contained. No longer will an artist feel compunction for such prudery as did this metalworker, who ensured that voluminous drapery folds separate Aphrodite's right hip from the nude body of her son pressed closely against it.

As an adornment to the left shoulder lappet of a cuirass destined for warfare, the scene with Aphrodite and Eros seems on first thought to be a curious choice. The lappet was, of course, paired with another one, and the subject of the missing mate is an even more tantalizing puzzle. One common denominator that might logically connect the two reliefs and the cuirass is the link between sexuality and aggression. Ares was, after all, the consort of Aphrodite, and the anecdote about Freud's delight upon discovering that long before him the Greeks had recognized the association between Eros and aggression is a familiar one. In this scene, however, Eros is presented as quite capable of another kind of emotional bond, filial affection, and so perhaps the scene on the missing counterpart offered still a different counterpoint. Whatever the subject of the missing relief, the application of this scene with Aphrodite and Eros to a cuirass lappet warns us not to underestimate the introspectiveness of the Classical Greeks. The artist of this relief, or the owner who commissioned the pair, had not only an admirable perspective upon human nature, but also the sense of humor to express it openly.

18 Side A

18

STAMNOS
WITH DEPARTURE SCENE

440-430
by the Kleophon Painter
St. Petersburg, The State Hermitage Museum, inv. no. Б 1148 (St. 1428, B 809)

Attic
Clay
H 42.5 cm., Diam 25 cm.

Publications: *ARV²* 1143.3; *Para* 455; *Add²* 334; Furtwängler and Reichhold (1904-1921) vol. 1, 189; G. Gualandi, "Il Pittore di Kleophon," *Arte Antica e Moderna* 20 (1962) 341-43, 345-46, 360, pl. 107a-b; A. Peredolskaja, *Krasnofigurinye attischeskie vazy* (Leningrad 1967) 183-84, no. 210, pls. 142, 179.3-5; Philippaki (1967) 145, no. 10, 146-147; G. von Lücken, "Zwei Skizzen des Kleophon-Malers," *Wissenschaftliche Zeitschrift Rostock* 19 (1970) 577-78, pls. 15-16, 17.2,4; A. Borbein, "Kanon und Ideal: Kritische Aspekte der Hochklassik," *AM* 100 (1985) 264, pl. 47,2.

Mended from many pieces. On the reverse are three youths. Graffito on foot: ΤΡ.

Above the scene is a tongue pattern; beneath is a band of three meanders alternating with a saltire square. White for beard and hair of man with staff. Inscriptions: Κ[Α]Λ   ΚΑΛΕ   ΚΑ[Λ]Ε.

In the center of the composition a man and woman turn toward each other. The man's torso is turned slightly to his right; his legs and left foot are frontal; and his right foot is shown in three-quarter left profile. He is barefoot. He wears a sleeveless tunic that exposes his right breast and extends to the tops of his knees. Over this is wrapped a fabric or leather strip that covers his lower torso to mid-thigh and is decorated with bands of zigzag between upper and lower borders of angled lines. He also wears the strap of a sword belt over his right shoulder, and part of the sword belt and sword hilt are visible at his left hip. His right elbow is bent, and the uplifted right hand, fingers open, supports a phiale at shoulder height. His left shoulder and arm are concealed by his shield, which bears an eye as a central device; the shaft of his spear can be seen behind his head, extending into the upper border and in front of his left leg. His head is in left profile and he gazes directly at the face of the woman before him. He also wears a crested helmet with the cheekpiece raised; locks of his curly hair are visible beneath the cheekpiece and behind the ear.

The woman stands in right profile, her head bowed, and her eyes directed down toward his waist. She wears a peplos that is open on her right side and has an overfold that extends to the tops of her thighs. The fingers of her right hand clasp the handle of an oinochoe beside her right thigh; the fingers of her left hand draw forward from her left shoulder the fabric of her peplos. Her hair is brought up from her nape beneath a taenia that is wrapped twice around her head; her earring consists of a hoop with three pendants. She is also barefoot.

Behind her stands a man in right profile, his right leg advanced, with the knee relaxed and the foot placed slightly in front of her peplos. He is barefoot. His right elbow is bent, and the right hand rests on the top of a staff. His mantle is wrapped around his left shoulder, torso, and legs. He has a receding forehead, white hair and beard, and he gazes ahead.

Behind the helmeted man stands a woman turned three-quarters to her right. She wears a belted peplos that has a dark stripe down the left side. Her left arm is brought in front of her abdomen, and the fingers are open. Her right arm, bent at the elbow, passes behind the shield of the helmeted man. Her right hand is held vertically, palm facing forward, fingers open. Her hair is wrapped up in a headcovering (sakkos), with one lock visible in front of her left ear. She gazes ahead.

The helmeted young man is departing for war. Although his aging parents are present, the significance of the moment is formally recognized by a ritual of libation in which only the hus-band and wife take part. The wife has just filled her husband's phiale with wine from her oinochoe, which now hangs at her side. He raises the filled phiale and is about to pour the wine onto the ground.

Even though this farewell is potentially a final one, the wife's demeanor toward her husband is remarkably restrained, especially when contrasted with the flustered gestures of the warrior's mother behind him. The wife's head is lowered in the *aidos* appropriate to a proper Athenian woman (see **Aidos** and **Sophrosyne**). *Aidos* carries connotations of respect, modesty, and submission, a note that is further communicated by the gesture of the woman's left hand. In the moment of the unveiling during the wedding ceremony, the *anakalypteria*, the bride uses this gesture to draw the bridal veil away from her face (see **The Wedding**). By this act of undressing herself for her husband, the bride signifies her acceptance of him and her willing giving of herself over to him. In the departure scene the gesture also expresses the wife's allegiance to her husband, but the moment acquires a special poignancy because it is one of perhaps final separation. The allusion to bridal imagery is underscored by the inscriptions also familiar from wedding scenes; the words read *kale*, or "beautiful."

In the moment of the *anakalypteria* the groom looks directly into the bride's face, which is then revealed to him for the first time.

18 Detail of Side A

18 Side B

father's taenia on the St. Petersburg vase has disappeared in the Munich version, where the wife has acquired an ornate earring.

The Kleophon Painter is one of the greatest of all Classical vase-painters. He is particularly admired for the eloquence of his compositions, especially apparent here in the closed contours of the wife and the open, more aggressive profile of the husband. The proximity of her left hand and his phiale sets up an intimacy between them that is frustratingly denied beneath, as the wide expanse of black glaze looms tensely between their torsos and legs. The Kleophon Painter is especially well known for his faces, distinguished by a large eye rendered as a supine V with a second line to accentuate the upper lid and the pupil positioned just under the upper lid. The result suggests respectful dignity and emotional fullness. The fabric of the garments has the texture of a light wool, and the folds fall softly without excessive linear detail. The gently curled fingers of the woman's right hand look forward to the almost affected gestures on the Parthenon's east frieze. Foreshortening is infrequent, but, in the case of the warrior's legs, quite accomplished. The figures overlap only enough to suggest a degree of spatial recession, with the elderly man in the foreground and the arm of the mother passing behind her son's shield.

The elegance of the warrior's accouterments, the accentuation of the departure's significance, and the expression of a genuine bond between husband and wife suggest that the scene may represent a moment in myth. It has been proposed that it depicts the departure of Hector from Andromache at Troy, in which case the flanking parents would be Priam and Hecuba.

The husband in this scene similarly stares directly at his wife's eyes. The artist has tempered this strict adherence to the framework of the ritual by means of several details that reveal the heightened emotionality of the scene. The edge of the man's phiale is teasingly close to the fingers of his wife's left hand, and the horizontal line formed by her raised peplos fold and the phiale's rim underscores the intensity of his gaze. Nor is her gaze directed downward to the ground, but rather as far up toward her husband's face as her bowed head allows. One senses that the couple would prefer a less constricted ritual to signify their separation, and it is not surprising that the libation ritual will soon be replaced in vase-painting, and probably also in real life, with a handshake between husband and wife (see no. 19).

Underlying sketches reveal that the Kleophon Painter made several experimental adaptations before he executed the final version. Even then he must not have been satisfied, because, on another vase, he altered a number of details in order that the wife be more accentuated. The artist painted an almost identical scene on another stamnos, now in Munich, and this latter vase must be the later work. In the St. Petersburg scene the elderly man stands so closely behind the wife that the fingers of his right hand and the tip of his staff touch her back; in the Munich scene, by contrast, the father has been moved much farther away from the woman so that she and her husband form more of a unified pair as the focal point of the composition. Also as a way of accentuating wife and husband, the

19

AMPHORA
WITH DEPARTURE SCENE

ca. 440
by the Painter of the Louvre Centauromachy
Warsaw, The National Museum in Warsaw, inv. no. 147367

Attic
Clay
H 51.7 cm., Diam 26.5 cm.

Publications: *ARV²* 1683, 90bis; *Para* 449; *CVA* Warsaw, Musée National 3 (Poland 6) pls. 14-17; M.L. Bernhard, *Greckie malarstwo wazowe* (Warsaw 1966) 449, fig. 14.

Mended from many pieces. The handles are corded; beneath them is a palmette pattern. Around the neck are two rows of palmettes flanked by leaves upon a base of volutes. On Side B are three men. The scenes have a tongue pattern above; beneath is a band of stopt meander alternating with a cross square.

On side A a woman and a man are shaking hands. She stands in right profile, her left foot advanced. She wears a girded peplos with overfold, a black stripe decorating the edges down her right side. Her hair is gathered up under a broad band that is surmounted by four upright leaves. Her head and gaze are directed downward.

The man stands with his right knee slightly bent, both feet on the ground. He wears a cuirass over a short, pleated tunic. His mantle is draped over his left shoulder and brought over his left forearm, with the ends falling down his left side. His scabbard can be seen behind his left hip. With his left hand he steadies a spear, the end of which rests against his left shoulder. His head is in left profile, and he has short curly hair covering his nape. He gazes directly into the woman's face. Behind him is a bearded, partly bald man, who leans on a walking stick with his right arm. His mantle envelops his body, exposing only his right shoulder He gazes ahead.

19 Side A

The scene is a departure for war, with the warrior positioned in the center of the composition. As the husband bids farewell to his wife, the husband's elderly father looks on, the diagonal line of his walking stick forming a sober counterpoint to the lethal spear of his vigorous son. The focal point of the composition is not, however, the relationship between father and son, but the interaction of husband and wife, where we find that the formality of the scene barely conceals its emotional overtones.

The handshake of husband and wife is isolated against a broad expanse of black glaze, and is accentuated by the diagonal shaft and tip of the spear that both unites the couple and, in its formidable implications, emphasizes their impending separation. Whereas in early fifth-century vase-painting the moment of departure for war was solemnified by the pouring of a libation (see no. 18), this painter has chosen to acknowledge the moment by a handshake that signifies the union, accord, and mutual respect of husband and wife. The substitution is profound; whereas in a libation scene the wife serves her husband with the wine he will pour on the ground, individuals who shake hands are equal participants in the action (see **Gesture and Gaze**).

The painter has not totally abandoned the tradition of the libation scene, because the wife exhibits the traditional female *aidos*, or modesty, inclining her head markedly downward to avoid looking at her husband (see ***Aidos* and *Sophrosyne***). That the tilted head is prompted by strict girlhood training and not a fascination with the handshake is clear from the angle of her gaze, which is not fixed on their hands, but is rather directed as far up toward the husband as the downward inclination of her head permits. Her obviously repressed emotion, in combination with his beardlessness, suggests that they are a young married couple caught in a transition between respect for tradition and more contemporary mores. Indeed, the painter's omission of the husband's helmet and spear lends him a vulnerability that suggests he shares his wife's feelings. Because the pair's lack of eye contact undermines the handshake's quintessential connotation of union, it is not surprising that this awkward accommodation of *aidos* is short-lived. The broad folds and softly inflated texture of the peplos, as well as the pointed chin of the woman, date this vase just after mid-century. In vase-painting and sculpture of the second half of the century, a couple will cement their handshake with an exchange of direct glances.

157

19 Side B

20

BELL KRATER
WITH DEPARTURE SCENE

410-400
by the Dinos Painter
Syracuse, Museo Archeologico Regionale di Siracusa, inv. no. 30747

Attic, "from Camarina, necropolis orientale sporadico"
Clay
H 44.5 cm.

Publications: *ARV²* 1153.17; *Add²* 336; *CVA* Syracuse, Museo Archeologico Nazionale 1 (Italy 17) pls. 20-21; P. Orsi, *Notizie degli scavi di antiquità* 1912, 369-71, fig. 20; J.D. Beazley, "Some Inscriptions on Vases, III," *AJA* 39 (1935) 487-88 figs. 11-12; Brommer (1973) 260 no. B1, 268 no. B1; Kron (1976) 117, 119, 166, 189, 264 no. P8, 274 no. Ak32, 278 no. O1, pl. 13.2; E. Harrison, "The Iconography of the Eponymous Heroes on the Parthenon and in the Agora," *Greek Numismatics and Archaeology. Essays in Honor of Margaret Thompson* (Wetteren 1979) 75-76, pl. 6.3; *LIMC* I (1981) 440, no. 25, pl. 340 (s.v. Akamas et Demophon).

Reassembled from a number of pieces. On Side B a man and two women are engaged in conversation. Above the scenes is a band of laurel over a band of egg pattern; beneath is a frieze of three meanders (right) alternating with a checkerboard square.

On Side A are two departure scenes. In the center of the field a nude man stands with his left leg relaxed and his foreshortened feet facing front. He wears a decorated helmet on the top of his head and a mantle draped behind his back, with the ends brought forward over his left shoulder and right forearm. His left arm passes through the strap of a shield, which is foreshortened, and the left hand holds a spear. A sword belt is brought over his right shoulder, crossing his torso. His right hand holds a phiale, and the arm is extended over an altar toward a woman to his right, at whom he stares directly. Two objects lie on the altar, behind which the front of his right foot passes.

The woman is seen in right profile, the toes of her right foot resting on the ground behind her. She wears a peplos that has an overfold to the waist and two dark vertical stripes down its right side. Her hair is bound into a sakkos, from which two leaves rise vertically, and she wears a dangling earring. The fingers of her right hand barely grasp the handle of an oinochoe she holds at her side; the fingers of her left hand lift folds of her garment in front of her left shoulder. Her eyes gaze directly back into the man's.

Behind her we see a bearded and wreathed man who leans on a staff beneath his left arm; the folds of his mantle are gathered on top of his staff and cover his hips and legs. His right forearm is extended, the palm open, and the fingers outstretched. The fingers of the left hand are similarly open.

Behind the nude warrior is a second couple. The youth, who is taller than the woman, stands in left profile, with the toes of his left foot resting on the ground behind him. His body is enveloped in a chlamys, which extends past his knees, and his petasos hangs behind his back. Two spears, suggesting that he is departing for a hunt, rest in the crook of his left elbow and are steadied by his left hand. He wears a wreath over his long hair, which falls in ringlets past his ears. His right hand grasps the right hand of the woman, and he stares directly at her eyes.

The woman stands in right profile, her left foot advanced, her right foot concealed. She wears a girded chiton with overfold, the sleeves covering her right upper arm. Two dark bands encircle the sleeve hem and decorate the

The transition in departure scenes from libation to handshake and then to direct eye contact is especially interesting when one considers the probable correlation between artistic convention and contemporary custom. Departure scenes on many vases later than this one (no. 20) coincided with the Peloponnesian War and its ravaging effects upon Athenian politics, economics, and morale. In the midst of such turmoil, it would not be surprising if the reticence of traditional ritual yielded to a direct expression of emotion.

20 Side A

right side of her garment from waist to lower hem. Her hair falls to her nape in softly curling ringlets. Her left hand reaches out, palm up, fingers extended, with the finger tips just passing behind the edge of the man's chlamys. Her right arm is bent at the elbow and the forearm raised, her right hand grasping his right hand. She gazes in front of her, in the direction of his neck.

Although the subject matter comprises two departure groups, the focal point is the central male figure, whose frontal stance and appurtenances, as well as his widespread arms, assure him a significant fraction of the field. So closely does this figure recall the style of contemporary sculpture that he is almost certainly based upon a sculptural prototype, and, whether he retains the specific identity of that prototype or not, the allusion is so accentuated that it is likely the Dinos Painter has assigned this figure some mythical identity.

Because he is the focal point of the scene, the libation ritual of the departure has become secondary (see no. 18). The ritual also

seems to have become informalized. The wife's stance suggests movement toward him, whereas he is stationary, and she looks directly at him. This expression of intimacy and emotion are underscored by the father's gesticulating hands, and by the way the edge of the warrior's phiale almost touches her left forearm.

Providing an insightful counterpoint to the libation scene is the couple shaking hands. His spears, broad-brimmed hat, and cloak liken him to an ephebe, a youth on military service who spent much of his time on the hunt, where this young man is probably headed. In this context their handshake of farewell, familiar from High Classical grave stelai and funerary white-ground lekythoi, indicates that it had come to be viewed as an optional substitute for libation (see **Gesture and Gaze**). A handshake differs from a libation in equalizing the participants, so much so that in funerary contexts it can be impossible to identify the deceased (no. 21). That the woman is no longer subordinated is further indicated by the energy with which she raises her right hand to pump vigorously the

159

20 Detail of Side B

youth's limp hand, at the same time as she brings her gesticulating left hand to the edge of the youth's mantle. Moreover, whereas both women now gaze at the men, the necks of both the man and woman in the libation scene are angled so that their heads are slightly inclined downward; by contrast, the neck of the handshaking woman is vertical, lending her a more forthright, aggressive manner. Because of her longer hair and the ephebic garb of the young man, this pair seems to be the more youthful one, and thus the differing manners of the two couples are presented by the painter as a generational rather than individual distinction. At the same time as the painter contrasts the libation ritual and handshake in their formality and structure, he uses the alignment of the rituals not merely to correlate hunting with war as quintessentially male activities, but also to remind the viewer of the life-threatening ramifications of each kind of departure. It is possible that he has used the more traditional libation ritual to underscore the more serious nature of a departure for war.

The style of the Dinos Painter is characterized by his penchant for dilute, broken, and wavy lines in the interiors of the forms; frequently, straight lines terminate in curves. He likes long, extended fingers that hang limply or barely grasp what the hand is holding, and he renders the pupils of the eyes as dots or lines suspended from the upper eyelids. Drapery does not particularly fascinate him, and, on the peplos of the woman paired with the central warrior, the vertical dark strips are not logically located on the fabric's edges but are applied at whim, seemingly as an afterthought. Despite these shortcomings, the Dinos Painter has an a shrewd interest in contemporary behavior, particularly that of women, an interest further manifested on his stamnos with Maenads in Naples (no. 124) and the kalyx krater with Atalanta in Bologna (no. 117).

21

LEKYTHOS-SHAPED GRAVE MARKER

ca. 380
Kansas City, William Rockhill Nelson and Atkins Museum of Fine Arts, Nelson Fund, inv. no. 31-86

Attic
Marble
H 88 cm.

Publication: Clairmont (1993) vol. 4, 29, no. 4.150.

Broken across the neck.

Standing opposite the handle are a man and woman shaking hands. She stands in three-quarter right profile, right leg relaxed, with the toes of the foot resting on the ground behind her. Over her peplos or chiton she wears a mantle which is draped over her shoulders and across her waist and legs. Her left hand fingers the folds in front of her left shoulder. The hand of her extended right arm clasps the right hand of the man in front of her. Her hair is encircled twice by a fillet, and the locks are gathered at the back of her head, where they are wrapped in an ornamental hair covering. She wears a disc earring. She gazes directly at the man, who stands in three-quarter left profile, his left leg relaxed, with the toes of his sandaled foot resting on the ground behind him. His mantle is draped over his entire body, exposing the right breast, shoulder, and arm. The wrist of his left arm, which is enveloped by the folds, rests on the back of his left hip. His right arm is extended, and his hand clasps the hand of the woman. He is beardless and appears to return her gaze.

The couple is flanked by two bearded men whose himatia are draped over their left shoulders and around their waist and legs. Each gazes at the couple.

Grave monuments of the later fifth century occasionally take the form of a lekythos, the vase that was traditionally used to pour a libation of olive oil at the tomb. On this example color would have enhanced the drapery and facial features and was probably used to delineate ornamental patterns around the neck and below the figural scene.

In the later decades of the fifth century, scenes on funerary reliefs and lekythoi often show a male and female clasping hands, and, if the sculpture is uninscribed, there is no way to distinguish the deceased from the survivor. Because each participant in a handshake functions identically, a handshake gives equal emphasis to each figure, who honors the other to the same degree (see **Gesture and Gaze**). Within a funerary context, the gesture signifies the leave-taking that death forces both survivor and deceased to suffer. At the same time, the handshake reaffirms the couple's accord, implying that their union will continue beyond the grave.

Because of the equalizing nature of the handshake, it is not surprising to find in these scenes that the woman usually returns the man's gaze, staring directly into his face, not downward in the age-old modesty of female *aidos* (see **Aidos and Sophrosyne**). In this

scene the symmetry of the couple is striking in that the positions of the legs are identical and the relaxed arms are comparably engaged close to the torsos. The man's head is slightly more inclined than the woman's, but the explanation for this may be that the artist wanted to indicate that the man was taller, and he does, in fact, stoop slightly and dip his head in order to fit within the field.

Because the sculptor has contrasted the handshaking man's beardlessness with the beards of the men flanking him, it is possible that the scene depicts a husband or wife grieving for a youthful spouse in the company of their respective fathers. But despite a reference to, and equal emphasis upon, the families of husband and wife, the focal point of the scene is the handshake. The gesture reminds the viewer that, however short-lived the marriage, the relationship of the couple was of primary importance, not the families from which they came, nor even the fact of death itself.

LOUTROPHOROS-HYDRIA WITH BRIDAL SCENE

ca. 470 BC
by the Pan Painter
Houston, Museum of Fine Arts, Annette Finnigan Collection, inv. no. 37.10

Attic
Clay
H 39.8 cm., Diam 38.7 cm., Diam (lip) 7.9 cm., Diam (base) 7.9 cm.

Publications: *ARV²* 554.79; "The Museum Grows—1931, Annette Finnigan Collections," *Bulletin of the Museum of Fine Arts, Houston* 10.2 (1948); Hoffmann (1970) 398-401, no. 181.

One handle repaired. Under the lip is a band of zigzags over a band of wavy loops. Above the scene on the neck is a band of tongues; beneath is a band of vertical zigzags. Above the scene on the body is a band of tongues; beneath is a band of zigzags. Around the base is a band of rays.

In the center of the scene, the bride moves in right profile, left leg advanced. She presses a loutrophoros against her left side, steadying it with her right hand; it is wrapped with three sashes. Over her chiton she wears a mantle that is drawn over her right shoulder and wrapped around her legs. Her long hair falls down her back and is bound with a rectangular clasp decorated with an X and horizontal lines. Three long strings hand from it. She gazes ahead of her into the eyes of a woman who turns her head back in left profile. This woman carries a wreath in her outstretched left hand, and her hair is wrapped with a taenia. Her body is enveloped in a mantle that is decorated with a black stripe punctuated with dots. Leading the procession is a boy playing the flutes. Hanging in the field above is a wreath.

Behind the bride follows a woman holding a torch in her left hand, her hair bound in a sakkos, and her mantle enveloping her form. She is followed by a female holding a garland in each extended hand. A torch-bearing woman fol-

lows, her hair wrapped in a sakkos, her left hand upraised, palm facing forward. The last woman carries a basket in her left hand; it is decorated with several horizontal rows of chevrons. Over her undergarment she wears a mantle that is draped over her left shoulder and across her body, and her head is turned back in left profile. She gesticulates with her outstretched right hand. Hanging in the field above her right shoulder is a wreath.

Around the neck three women carry a wreath, a torch, and a loutrophoros, which is also wrapped with three red sashes.

The tall vertical handles in combination with the pair of low handles identify the vase as a loutrophoros-hydria. Because the hydria was a water container and thus a vessel intimately identified with women, Viktoria Sabetai has argued that the loutrophoros-hydria was associated with the bride, and that the loutrophoros-amphora was linked with the groom (see no. 23).[1] Indeed, whereas scenes on the loutrophoros-amphora often show the bridegroom grasping the bride's wrist in the symbolic gesture of abduction or domination (no. 23), scenes on the loutrophoros-hydria tend to portray the moments before the bride encounters the groom, as she prepares her toilette for the wedding festivities.[2]

The Houston example depicts the procession for the bridal bath, led by a flute-player and accompanied by companions bearing wreaths and torches. The bride, prominently positioned in the center of the scene, bears her own loutrophoros-hydria. Whereas her full breasts announce her maturity, her long hair indicates her youthfulness, which is further accentuated by the preceding figure's upswept hairstyle, appropriate to a more mature woman. This older woman turns her head back to the bride in encouragement, probably saying a few words to communicate the support and friendship of the bride's companions. The bride meets the woman's glance without an intimation of the bowed head of modesty, or *aidos*, which would be expected of the bride in the presence of the bridegroom and, indeed, whenever she would be seen in public or in the presence of men (see **Aidos** and **Sophrosyne**).

The bride is followed by two women who each bear a single torch; it is interesting to note that in the forthcoming bridal procession, the mothers of the couple will each hold double torches. Also noteworthy is the upraised palm of one of the torch-bearing figures, surely a formal acknowledgment of the solemnity of the occasion. The wicker basket carried by another participant may contain toiletries for the bridal bath; it calls to mind the *kanephoroi*, the virginal basket-carriers who took part in the wedding ritual, as well as in the many religious festivals that punctuated the Athenian calendar (see no. 60). Excavation of loutrophoroi in the Sanctuary of the Nymph on the slopes of the Acropolis suggests that at the conclusion of her bridal bath the bride offered her loutrophoros as a votive dedication, and it is possible that the procession featured in this scene may culminate in that activity.

One of the finest of all Early Classical vase-painters, the Pan Painter is particularly admired for his delicate and steady hand, which excels in long expanses of elegant, unbroken lines. The

Houston example is the only complete surviving loutrophoros by this artist, who is also represented by loutrophoros fragments in Athens, Amsterdam, and Oxford. The painter is better known for his red-figure painting on other shapes (no. 89), as well as for his work in the white-ground technique (nos. 90 and 46). A particular feature of the artist's style is the bride's rectangular hair clasp, which is also worn by Artemis on the lekythos in St. Petersburg and the fragment in Basel.

Most surviving loutrophoroi and lebetes gamikoi date from the later decades of the fifth century, undoubtedly as a result of an increased emphasis upon the wedding ritual within a society plagued by on-going military and economic stresses. The Houston example is thus particularly valuable as an early example of the wedding loutrophoros, whose origins can undoubtedly be traced back to the large Proto-Attic amphorae of the seventh century.

1. Sabetai (1993) 163. See also ibid. 144-46, 159-61.
2. See Langridge-Noti and Oakley (1994) 32; G. Kokula, *Marmorloutrophoren* (Berlin 1984) 116; J. Boardman, "Sex Differentiation in Grave Vases," *AnnArch StorAnt* 10 (1988) 171-79; R.M. Moesch, "Le mariage et la mort sur les loutrophores," *AnnArchStorAnt* 10 (1988) 117-39.

23

LOUTROPHOROS-AMPHORA WITH WEDDING SCENE

ca. 425-420
by the Washing Painter
Houston, Museum of Fine Arts, Annette Finnigan Collection,
inv. no. 37.12

Attic
Clay
H 32.4 cm., Diam. 12.7 cm., Diam. foot 8.4 cm.

Publications: *ARV²* 1127.13; *Add²* 332; Hoffmann (1970) 406-408, no. 183; Sutton (1981) 190, 191, 193, 248, no. W 43; H. Walter, *Die Gestalt der Frau. Bildwerke von 30,000-20 v. Chr.: Anthropologische Betrachtungen* (Stuttgart 1985) 42, fig. 36; Sabetai (1993) vol. 1, 148, 162-68; vol. 2, 17 no. LA4, pl. 6.

Mended. On each side of the neck a woman stands enveloped in her mantle and wearing a sakkos. Beneath (Side A) are two and a half encircled seven-leaved palmettes separated by dots; on Side B are three running meanders (left). On the shoulder there is a band of tongues, beneath which, on Side A, is a band of eggs. Beneath the scene on both sides is an egg pattern, with a ray pattern around the foot.

The bride is turned in three-quarter right profile. Her mantle passes over the top of her head, envelops both arms and hands, and covers most of her body, with the ends drawn over her left arm; a black stripe edges the mantle's

163

23 Side A

hem. The folds of her undergarment cover most of her feet. Her head is inclined. Her left elbow is bent and the forearm is extended. In front of it is seen the right forearm and hand, fingers open, of the bridegroom, who stands almost frontally, his head turned back in left profile, his eyes gazing into the bride's face. He wears a mantle that passes from the right side of his waist over his left shoulder, exposing his right breast; there is a black stripe along its hem. Hanging in the field between the couple is a wreath. Behind the bridegroom a woman stands almost frontally, her head in left profile. She wears a peplos that has an overfold edged by a black stripe; a stripe with zigzag upper border edges the lower hem. She holds a torch in each outstretched hand and her hair is gathered into a bun at the back of her head; she also wears a pendant earring. Behind the bride stands a woman whose right hand is about to touch the back of the bride's head. She is followed by a winged woman who flies toward her in right profile, a sash in her outstretched right hand, her lowered left hand muffled in her himation, which is extends to just above her ankles. She also wears a pleated undergarment, visible at her ankles, and a sakkos, as well as an earring.

The pair of elongated handles elegantly flanking the neck identify this vase as a loutrophoros-amphora. By contrast, a loutrophoros-hydria is recognized by a pair of short handles on the shoulder in combination with a single tall handle inspired by the hydria, a water vessel identified with women (no. 22). Viktoria Sabetai has argued that the loutrophoros-amphora was particularly identified with men and that the most frequently encountered scene on these vases depicts the moment in the ritual when the groom grasps the bride's wrist as he prepares to lead her in the bridal procession to her new home.[1] The choice of subject matter is especially appropriate to a vessel identified with the groom, because this symbolic gesture of domination signified the establishment of a new household in which the bridegroom assumed the identity of his new bride's *kyrios*, or master (see **The Wedding**).

It is interesting to note which elements of the wedding ritual the Washing Painter considered essential for inclusion within the limited space of this modestly sized vessel. Clearly emphasized is the extension of the bridegroom's right hand to the bride's left wrist, although here he seems merely to lay it on top of her muffled hand. Also clearly indicated is his gaze into her face as he turns around to her before moving forward in the procession. The bride's downcast head and gaze of *aidos* are explicitly captured (see **Aidos and Sophrosyne**). The wreath, probably of myrtle, celebrates their marriage. The two flanking figures represent a vital part of the bridal procession; the woman with two torches is the mother or mother-in-law of the bride, and the woman who adjusts the bride's veil is the *nympheutria*, a bridal attendant other than her mother. The winged female bearing a sash is frequently seen on loutrophoroi and has been identified as Nike, affirming the bride's victorious beauty and fertility. Because such winged females also appear in funerary scenes, it is possible that they carry connotations of Underworld deities. John Oakley notes that, in the *Eumenides*, Athena promises the Furies, or Erinyes, that the Athenians will offer to them first fruits during the marriage ritual, with the hopes that children will be born to the new couple.[2]

The custom of giving a loutrophoros-amphora to a bridegroom reminds us that he also received a bridal bath, and there were certainly other ritual activities that attended his preparation for the wedding, although we know little about these details. It is interesting to note that, whereas a grave monument in the form of a loutrophoros honored a maiden who had died unwed, unmarried men as well as unmarried women were honored with loutrophoroi as funerary offerings. The custom is a thought-provoking testimony that for a man as well as for a woman the failure to experience marriage signified in the Greek mind a life that was incomplete.

The Washing Painter was a prolific painter of wedding scenes. He delights in bridal finery, and can be recognized by his signature black stripe edging animated drapery folds. He is also quite charmed by the marriage ritual. He is sympathetic to the bride's simultaneous reticence and curiosity; he has enormous respect for tradition; and he is very much in awe of the special superhuman stature that the bridal couple occupy during the wedding ritual.

1. Sabetai (1993) 163.
2. Aischylos *Eumenides* 834-6. See Oakley and Sinos (1993) 20. For females as Nikai, see Langridge-Noti and Oakley (1994) 51; H. Kenner, "Flügelfrau and Flügel damon," *ÖJh* 31 (1939) 82.

24

LOUTROPHOROS
WITH WEDDING PROCESSION

ca. 425
Boston, Museum of Fine Arts, Francis Bartlett Collection,
inv. no. 03.802

Attic
Clay
H 75.3 cm., Diam (lip) 25.3 cm., Diam. (body) 18 cm.

Publications: Boston, Museum of Fine Arts, *Annual Report* 1 (1903) 62, 71; E. Zevi, *MemLinc* 6 (1937) 353 fig. 5; U. Wintermeyer, "Die Polychrome Reliefkeramik aus Centuripe," *JdI* 90 (1975) 170 n. 134, 171 n. 141; R. Stupperich, *Staatsbegräbnis und Privatgrabmal im klassischen Athen* (Münster 1977) 156 n. 3, no. 11a; Sutton (1981) 189, 250 no. W.52, pls. 13-14; G. Kokula, *Marmorlutrophoren, AM-Beiheft* 19 (1984) 16 n. 16, 117 n. 108, 118, n. 111; Keuls (1985a) 118-19, fig. 102; *LIMC* III (1986) 905 no. 639e (s.v. Eros); R. Hague, "Marriage Athenian Style," *Archaeology* 41.3 (1988) 32; Sutton (1989b) 334-51, pls. 29-33, fig. 1; Sutton (1992) 26-27, fig. 1.10; Oakley and Sinos (1993) 9, 36, 51 (fig. 1), 109-111 (figs. 105-107); Fantham et al. (1994b) 102, fig. 3.16.

Reassembled from several pieces. Around the neck is a woman wearing a wreath and carrying a loutrophoros-hydria; a second woman carries a torch in her right hand and steadies a flat wicker basket on her head. On the shoulder is a band of tongues. Above the figural scene is a band of eggs; beneath is a frieze of three meanders (left) alternating with a checker square. Around the base is a band of rays.

23 Side B

165

24 Detail of Side A

side of her head two Erotes flutter; the one in front of her bears a wreath and the other one carries a necklace. Behind the bride stands a woman who also adjusts the bride's dress, extending her hands to the bride's shoulder and back. This woman's head and body are in right profile. She wears a peplos with overfold, a diadem or taenia into which three leaves have been slipped, and an earring; her hair is bound into a knot at the back of her head. Behind her a wreath hangs in the field.

On the other side of the bridegroom a woman stands turned three-quarters to her right. She wears a chiton and a diadem with three vertical elements; her hair is gathered into a bun at the back of her head; she carries a torch in each hand. Her body slightly overlaps a doorway whose double doors are slightly open, revealing the turned leg and mattress of a bed within; above it is the end of a scabbard. The doorjambs are decorated with broken lines; rows of dots edge the upper and lower edges of the doors, and adorn the door panels at regular intervals. The doors appear to be elevated by one or two steps in front of them. Leaping in mid-air toward the ground from the threshold is an Eros, his legs extended out before him as if he were seated, his right arm behind his right thigh, his left hand at his waist.

Behind the doors a woman stands almost frontally, her hands uplifted in surprise as she gazes downward at Eros. She wears a belted peplos with a kolpos and an overfold that extends to her waist; her hair is gathered into a bun at the back of her head and she wears a pendant earring. Behind her, and with his garment slightly overlapping hers, is a bearded man standing in right profile, wearing a chiton and a mantle draped over his left shoulder and around his waist and legs. He has curly hair, and his head, in right profile, is slightly bowed. His left hand steadies a scepter that is decorated with black bands; his right hand grasps the right hand of a beardless youth who is turned in three-quarter left profile, his head in left profile and also slightly bowed. He wears a tunic beneath a patterned tunic that is decorated across the hips with a band of zigzag with dots across and across the hem with a band of zigzag interspersed with dots; the rest of the fabric bears a ray design interspersed with dots. The youth wears boots and a petasos behind his shoulders, and he steadies two spears in his left hand. Hanging in the field between the two men is a wreath. Behind the youth a woman turns in three-quarter right profile; she wears a chiton and a mantle draped over her left shoulder and around her hips and legs; her hair is bound into a knot at the back of her head. In her left hand she holds a fan, and in her upraised right hand she holds a plemochoe. At her feet is a goose. In front of her a woman stands almost frontally, her head turned in left profile. In her upraised left hand she holds a phiale; her right hand holds the cords of a chest. Hanging in the field are two wreaths. Lettering in the field reads ΚΑΛΕ, probably referring to the bride.

The bridegroom moves to his left, his feet widespread, with the toes of his right foot resting on the ground behind him. He wears a dotted mantle that is draped over his left shoulder and wrapped around his waist and legs. His head is turned back to the bride in left profile, and he wears a wreath of pointed leaves over his short curly hair. His left hand grasps his mantle folds at his side; his right hand grasps the edge of the bride's hand. Above his head are the letters ΚΑΛΟΣ. The bride stands in three-quarter right profile, her head slightly bowed. She wears a chiton that has a rounded dotted neckline and a mantle that is draped over her left shoulder and across her waist and legs. She also wears a wreath or diadem with vertical leaves. Over the top of her head is draped a veil that is decorated with stars and X's and that falls over her shoulders. Her right elbow is bent and the forearm is held horizontally; the palm is vertical and the fingers are outstretched and slightly bent. Her left hand is extended, with the palm down, the fingers outstretched, and the thumb held to the side, such that the bridegroom's hand grasps the side of her hand. On either

Successive moments of the wedding ritual have been successfully telescoped. In the center of the scene, we see that the bridal procession is beginning, as the bridegroom leads the bride forth. The painter shows the groom clasping the side of the bride's hand, but we know that the prescribed gesture called for the groom to grasp her wrist. That gesture was the traditional one of domination, and it implied that the bridal procession was actually a mock abduction (see **The Wedding**).

Although the bridegroom hastens forward in a vigorous stride, he turns around to gaze back into the bride's face. The abrupt turn of his head in the midst of his eager movement forward suggests that the bride has only just been unveiled and her face revealed to the bridegroom for the first time. That the painter has elided the preceding phase of the unveiling (*anakalypteria*) with the bridal procession is also suggested by the gesture of the bride's attendant (the *nympheutria*), who appears to adjust the bride's garments. Meanwhile, the bride's head is bowed, but her eyes are not completely downcast, such that she tentatively begins to meet the bridegroom's glance, a feature seen in other depictions of the *anakalypteria*. Also appropriate to the *anakalypteria* are the two Erotes, who hover around the bride's head, bringing a wreath and a necklace to enhance her desirability. The Greeks regarded emotions as external forces which had an almost tangible presence; thus they believed that the bride emanated a desire that drew the groom to her and her, in turn, to him. John Oakley reminds us that the

24 Detail of Side A–B

24 Side B

24 Detail of Side B–A

167

wreaths of the bridal couple signify the superhuman stature with which they were regarded, because wreaths are otherwise bestowed only upon victors in war and athletic competitions.

Standing in front of the bridal chamber belonging to the home of the bridegroom's family is the mother of the groom. She carries two torches to welcome the bride and to dispel any unbenevolent forces. The doors symbolize both the new status into which the bride will now pass and the intimacy of the bridal bed, which is partially revealed. Above it hangs part of a scabbard to underscore the masculinity of the bridal chamber. Scampering out of the doorway, as if springing down from the bed, is the figure of Eros in the form of a baby boy. His presence surprises the woman standing beside him, and she raises her hands in alarm, the note of levity alleviating the solemnity of the occasion. The larger size of this Eros, in contrast with pair of Erotes adorning the bride, alludes to the baby boys whom the bride will hopefully bear.[1] This Eros would also have reminded the viewer of the custom by which the bride slept with a baby boy before her wedding. Representations on other vases of the bride playing with a baby boy (no. 56) suggest the existence of a further practice, an ancient counterpart to the tradition still observed on Crete, in which a baby boy is placed on the wedding bed or on the knees of the bride.

The two women behind the *nympheutria* probably refer to the ceremony of the *epaulia*, which took place on the day after the wedding night. Gifts carried to the bride include a bowl, a plemochoe for perfumed oils, and a chest for jewelry and toilette articles, all intended to enable the bride to sustain the allure that so successfully seduced the bridegroom during the wedding ritual. The goose, which was special to Aphrodite, underlines all these connotations.

A fourth stage in the wedding ritual is represented by the handshake of the two men. This moment is that of the *engye*, the betrothal of the bride to the bridegroom, which was sealed by a handshake between the bride's father and her future husband.[2] The *engye* was a solemn agreement that was not lightly broken; hence a bridal wreath is suspended between the two men, and they bow their heads in respect for the importance of the moment. The *engye* might well take place years before the wedding, when the bride was still a young girl and the groom much younger than thirty, the age at which he usually married; thus the bridegroom's depiction as an unbearded ephebe is appropriate. The bearded man's royal scepter, as well as the undergarment beneath his himation, befits a mythical personage; these details may point to a specific mythical character or, perhaps, merely allude to the elevated stature of all those participating in the bridal ritual.

1. Sutton (1989b) 346.
2. Ibid. 349; see Herodotos 6.130.

FRAGMENTARY LOUTROPHOROS WITH WEDDING SCENE

ca. 420
Oxford, Ashmolean Museum, University of Oxford, inv. no. 1966.888

Attic
Clay
H 13.5 cm., Diam 15 cm.

Publications: R. Hamilton, *Select Exhibition of Sir John and Lady Beazley's Gifts to the Ashmolean Museum 1912-1966* (London 1967) 90, no. 326, pl. 47; Brümmer (1985) 150 n. 718, fig. 36 a-b; *LIMC* III (1986) 905, no. 639c, pl. 646 (s.v. Eros).

Surviving are base of the neck, stump of one handle, shoulder, and part of the wall.

The bride is led forward by the bridegroom. She wears a chiton that sits low over her full breasts, a necklace, and an himation that is draped over her left shoulder and arm and across her waist. The fabric is ornamented with circles and has a dark stripe along the edge. Over the back of the bride's head is a veil, which hangs down behind her back and over her right shoulder. In contrast to the mantle's pattern, the veil is decorated with a series of horizontal and vertical lines, perhaps to indicate gauzy material. Her hair is curled loosely about her face and is brought up from the nape; two tendrils escape, one before and one behind the ear. She also wears a diadem that tapers slightly at the ends and has a narrow reserved border on each edge. Her head is inclined, and she gazes up from under her lids in the direction of the groom's forearm. Her left hand, palm down and fingers extended, is grasped around the wrist by the thumb and fingertips of the groom, who stands frontal, slightly turned to his right. His upper torso is nude, but himation folds are visible over his left shoulder and upper arm and at his right hip. He has wavy hair, curly locks of which fall down his jawline in front of each ear; another tendril winds down behind his ear. He wears a laurel wreath. His head is in left profile and he stares directly into the bride's face.

Between the couple is the nude, winged figure of Eros; his torso is turned toward the groom. His dangling feet almost rest on the bride's left forearm, and his head is turned back in left profile to the bride's face. In his left hand he clutches a loutrophoros-amphora on which the figure of a woman is depicted; in his right arm he clasps a loutrophoros-hydria. Over his short curly hair he wears a laurel wreath.

Behind the bride and flying toward her is the figure of a Nike who holds a basket and a box. Behind the groom and flying toward him is a Nike who holds a perfume vase in her right hand, a torch in her left. A woman behind her holds a basket.

The loutrophoros was the traditional type of vase used for the bridal bath, and hence vases of this shape were conventionally given as wedding gifts and bear wedding subjects. Even in its fragmentary state, the Oxford loutrophoros depicts most of the vital elements of the wedding ritual: the wedding veil; the bride's inclined head and modest, but curious, glance; the groom's traditional grasp of the bride's wrist; the bride's jewelry and the groom's wreath; the wedding gifts of chests, loutrophoroi, and perfume container; and the torch to light the bride's journey. Particularly

25

characteristic of wedding scenes on vases from the second half of the century is the figure of Eros. Robert Sutton has convincingly shown that the deity's presence signifies mutual sexual attraction between husband and bride (see **The Wedding**). That Eros is moving from the bride to the groom and looks back meaningfully, encouragingly, at her emphasizes the degree to which these vase scenes were directed toward the bride, who was probably the recipient of the Oxford loutrophoros as a wedding present. The romanticization of marriage is one of the most distinctive features of later fifth-century wedding scenes; even if the bride was to be married to a man she barely knew, the vase scenes imply that both husband and wife were spontaneously attracted to each other.

The vase can be dated by the narrow, close-set lines that form passages of concentric arcs over the bride's chiton and cling closely to the contours of her breasts. The agitated curls of the tendrils, and the exaggerated downturned corners of the bride's mouth similarly date the vase well after the Parthenon frieze but before the extreme affectation that we find at the century's end.

26

FRAGMENTARY LOUTROPHOROS-HYDRIA WITH BRIDAL SCENE

430-425
by the Phiale Painter
Boston, Museum of Fine Arts, The James Fund and
Special Contribution, inv. no. 10.223

Attic
Clay
H 17 cm., Diam 14.2 cm.

Publications: *ARV²* 1017.44; *Add²* 315; D. Kyriakou-Zapheiropoulou, "Erithromorphe Lekythos Arith. B.E. 1404 tou Mouseiou Brauronos," *ArchDelt* 34 (1979) A1, 136, pl. 51b; Sutton (1981) 197-201, 253 no. W.63, pl. 15; Oakley (1982a) 113-18, figs. 1-3; G. Schwarz, "Hochzeitsbilder der Parthenonzeit—die Bostoner Loutrophoros und zwei Lekythen des Phialemalers," in *Pro Arte Antiqua. Festschrift für Hedwig Kenner* II (Vienna 1985) 319-25, pl. 53.6-7; *LIMC* III (1986) 905, no. 639a, pl. 645 (s.v. Eros); Reilly (1989) 418, pl. 78a; Reinsberg (1989) 58, fig. 12 a-b; Sutton (1989b) 351-59, pl. 34; Oakley (1990) 42, 73, no. 44, pls. 24c, 25; Oakley and Sinos (1993) 25-26, 83, figs. 60-61.

Reassembled from many fragments. On the neck is a band of tongues. Above the figural scene is a Lesbian cymation.

Only the top of the bride's head survives, in right profile. Her head is tilted downward, and she looks downward; she wears a diadem with a zigzag contour and is seated on a cushioned stool. Standing behind the bride is a woman in right profile, wearing a peplos, a necklace, a triangular shaped earring with three pendants, and a similar but smaller diadem on her hair, which is gathered

26

into a knot at the back of her head. Her head is inclined and she looks down at the bride's head as both of her hands carefully hold the veil just above the bride's diadem. Hanging in the field in front of the woman's head are a lekythos and a hair covering (sakkos) with zigzag ornament. Behind this woman stands a woman in three-quarter right profile, wearing a knee-length tunic over a chiton; the lower border of the tunic has a black stripe and a line of dots along the hem. She carries a ribbon and perhaps a basket, from which a ribbon hangs; another ribbon hangs in the field in front of her. Only part of the following figure survives; this person wears a peplos, and both hands steady a chest, the lid of which is open. A last woman wearing a chiton and mantle stands frontally, her head in right profile. The oval object in front of her may be a mirror that she was carrying.

Flying down toward the bride is Eros, a ribbon in his outstretched hands. Beneath Eros is a beardless youth who turns to his right, his mantle over his left shoulder and a wreath in his short hair. He looks down at the bride. Behind the youth is another beardless youth whose head is at the level of the bride; he wears a similar wreath and a mantle draped over his shoulders, and he also looks across to the bride. Over his head is a large oval basket held in the hands of a draped figure who is largely missing; a black stripe edges that figure's garment. The left hand of the figure grasps the base of the basket; the fingers of the right hand rest on the rim of the opposite side. The side of the basket has been wrapped with a leafy vine; within the basket are a number of small fruits, some of which are bent over at the tips. A ribbon hangs in the field behind the basket.

The artist appears to have elided into one scene several of the most prominent features of the wedding ritual. All eyes are upon the bride, as the *nympheutria*, or special attendant of the bride, raises the veil off her head in the moment known as the *anakalypteria*, or unveiling. She modestly gazes down, but the bridegroom, seated opposite her, looks directly over at her; so central to the unveiling was the bridegroom's first view of his bride's face that the moment was also known as the *opteria* or *theoretria*, words derived from verbs for seeing (see **The Wedding**). Meanwhile Eros flies down to the bride, his presence signifying the erotic impulse that draw bride and groom together at this instant.

The young boy standing between the couple is probably the *pais amphithales*, the boy with both parents living, literally "blooming on both sides" (see **The Wedding**). This youth offered to the guests bread, which he carried in a *liknon*, or winnowing basket, while reciting the words: "They have fled the worse, they have found a better way." The practice expresses the concept of marriage as a progression to a higher state of civilization. Similarly the bride might carry with her to her new home a roasting pan for barley and a sieve, symbolic of the refined foods she would prepare during her marriage. The alignment of marriage with agricultural cultivation is also emphasized in the marriage ritual as the bride's father, addressing the groom, declares that he gives this woman for the "ploughing" of legitimate children. Moreover, the bride often wore a crown of thistle and oak to symbolize the wild state she was leaving as she entered married life. The youthfulness of the *pais amphithales* expressed the hope that the marriage would produce children, and especially boys.

The basket held by the woman behind the bridegroom is probably wrapped with myrtle and holds figs, in reference to the ceremony of the *katachysmata* that occurs a little bit later in the ritual. When the bride enters the home of the bridegroom, she will be showered with dates, nuts, dried fruits, and figs, which those present will scramble to retrieve. The custom was also observed with the introduction of a new slave into a household and at the time when a city inaugurated its sacred and secular ambassadors. The rite signified the incorporation of an outsider, whose addition was expected to bring prosperity and fertility.

27

LOUTROPHOROS
WITH BRIDAL PROCESSION

ca. 430
Berlin, Antikensammlung, Staatliche Museen zu Berlin Preussischer Kulturbesitz, inv. no. F 2372
Sabouroff Collection; Russian inventory number, AK 942. Returned to Berlin in late 1950s

Attic
Clay
H 69.5 cm., Diam 15 cm.

Publications: C. Daremberg and E. Saglio, *Dictionnaire des antiquités grecques et romaines* (Paris 1877-1919) vol. 1, pt. 2, 1528, fig. 1992 (s.v. Corona); vol. 3, pt. 2, 1651-52, fig. 4866 (s.v. Matrimonium); A. Furtwängler, *La Collection Sabouroff* (Berlin 1883-1907) pls. 58-59; Furtwängler, *Beschreibung der Vasensammlung im Antiquarium* II (Berlin 1885) 645-47 no. 2372; G. von Lucken, *Griechische Vasenbilder* (Berlin 1921) 20; Sourvinou-Inwood (1973) 12-21; Sutton (1981) 172, 175-177, 240, no. W14 pl. 10; Jenkins (1983) 137, fig. 1; H. Rühfel, *Kinderleben im klassischen Athen: Bilder auf klassischen Vasen, Kulturgeschichte der antiken Welt* 19 (Mainz 1984) 112-14, fig. 64; Reinsberg (1989) 61-62, fig. 16; Lissarrague (1992) 152-54, fig. 7; Oakley and Sinos (1993) 30-31, 90, figs. 72-73.

Mended from many pieces.

A bridegroom lifts his bride onto a bridal chariot driven by a charioteer. The groom steps forward in right profile. He is barefoot, and his left leg is advanced, with the left foot lifted off the ground. He is draped in a mantle that passes over his left shoulder, covering his body to his lower legs. He also wears a laurel wreath over his shoulder-length hair. His right arm is brought forward, fingers curled, and is pressed against the bride's right hip. She is suspended in air in right profile, her bare feet dangling. She wears a chiton, the crinkled pleats of which are visible over her ankle and blow behind her to indicate her movement. Her himation covers her legs. Over a diadem from which two ele-

27 Side A

ments rise vertically she wears a veil that is draped over her head and falls to her waist, covering her right arm. The fingers of her left hand clasp the veil's folds in front of her left shoulder. Her right elbow is bent and the hand is held, palm up, fingers open, in front of her torso and just above the groom's right hand. The bride gazes ahead. Flying toward the bride is a winged Eros who holds a myrtle wreath in his outstretched left hand. Hanging above the groom's head is another myrtle wreath.

The charioteer stands behind the chariot rail, his head turned back in left profile toward the couple. In each hand he holds reins, and his right hand also clasps a whip. The chariot frame is decorated with a dotted pattern; the wheel has seven spokes. The charioteer's garment is draped over his left shoulder and tied around his waist, with the folds falling over his feet. He also wears a laurel wreath.

Interrupting the reins and the chariot axle is a Doric column, on the other

27   Drawing after A. Furtwängler, *Die Sammlung Sabouroff*, vol. 1(Berlin 1883) pl. 58.

side of which stands a facing woman who holds a torch in each hand as she gazes back in left profile. Over her chiton she wears a mantle that is draped over her left shoulder and covers her left arm and most of her body. To her left stands a bearded man, his right leg advanced and the knee relaxed. He wears a sleeved garment, with his mantle draped over his left shoulder, covering most of his body. He also wears a laurel wreath, and his right hand steadies a staff that has a floral tip.

Behind the groom stands a small child wrapped in a mantle and wearing a wreath. Behind him stands a woman holding two torches.

The vase-painter has telescoped sequential events in the bridal procession. The bride's left hand fingers her veil in the distinctive gesture of the *anakalypsis* that signifies her sexual availability and receptiveness to her new husband (see **The Wedding**). Although she is depicted at the moment when she is being lifted into the chariot just before the beginning of the bridal procession, we realize as we turn the vase that the chariot has already arrived at the home of the bridegroom and his parents. The chariot's horses have been omitted, as if they have moved behind the architectural structure represented by the column, which alone designates the house. That the column does not divide two consecutive moments is indicated by the mother-in-law's torch, which passes behind the column so that the flaring tip is angled toward the charioteer's head. The bearded man's scepter suggests that he is royal and thus that the figures have mythological identities.

The representation of the bride calls to mind Hesiod's description of Pandora, who was fashioned as a bride for Epimetheus (see **Pandora**). Not only is the bride in this scene richly adorned with diadem and veil like Pandora, but she is lifted onto the chariot as if she were a doll, and her objectification recalls the fabrication of Pandora out of clay and water. In this scene the bride is further depersonalized by her passive acceptance of the groom's action and by her lack of acknowledgment of him by either gesture or gaze. Like Pandora, the Greek bride was adorned and then taken to her new home; she was the one who was married, never the one who married.

The small boy behind the groom is probably one of the *propempontes*, who escorted the bridal procession.[1] The winged Eros who flies toward the bride is about to crown her with a wreath, which contrasts with the less emphasized wreath that hangs above the bridegroom's head and is undoubtedly for him. The scene's focus upon the bride is not surprising, because the loutrophoros was intended as a wedding gift for the bride. What is provocative are the connotations of Eros' action. It is generally agreed that his presence in Classical wedding scenes signifies the sexual attraction that both bride and husband experience for each other, as well as the desirability that each person emanates. Robert Sutton has shown that in many scenes Eros is focused almost exclusively upon the bride, for the purpose of accentuating both her irresistibility to the groom and her awakened response to him (see **The Wedding**). Because brides often entered arranged marriages with grooms whom they had hardly met or barely knew, the romanticization of the wedding ritual is an understandable fantasy, and the vase-painter's responsiveness to the bride's point of view is evidence of both a certain empathy and definite marketing skills.

1. Oakley and Sinos (1993) 30.

28

LEBES GAMIKOS
WITH BRIDAL SCENE

420-410
in the manner of the Meidias Painter
Athens, National Archaeological Museum, inv. no. 1659

Attic, "from Eretria"
Clay
H 20 cm.

Publications: *ARV²* 1322.11; *Add²* 363; M. Collignon and L. Couve, *Catalogue des vases peints du Musée national d'Athènes* (Paris 1904) 21, no. 1575, pl. 48; A. Brückner, "Athenische Hochzeitsgeschenke," *AM* 32 (1907) 107, pl. 7; L. Deubner, "Attischer Frühlingszauber," *Festschrift zum 60. Geburtstag von Paul Clemen* (Düsseldorf 1926) 120; G.M.A. Richter and M. Milne, *Shapes and Names of Athenian Vases* (New York 1935) 11, fig. 74; Roberts (1978) 183, pl. 101.1 (drawing).

28 Side A

Mended from several pieces, with parts of the scene missing. Tip of finial broken off.

Above the scene is a band of tongues over a band of eggs. Beneath the scene is a band of eggs.

A woman leans forward in left profile, her advanced right knee bent, with the foot raised off the ground. With both hands she reaches down toward her (missing) foot. She wears a sleeveless, belted, and closely pleated garment, and the contours of her legs are clearly visible through the fabric. She also wears a bracelet, rendered in added white, on her left hand. Her hair is gathered into a knot at the back of her head. She gazes ahead of her, toward Eros, who flies toward her in right profile, an alabastron in his outstretched right hand, and a wreath, in added white, on his hair.

Standing behind her and turning slightly to her right is a woman who wears a peplos that is girded over its overfold, a black stripe edging the upper and lower hems. Her left hand hangs at her side; her right hand steadies a chest. Hanging beneath the chest is a sash with a fringed end. Her hair is gathered at the back of her head and is wrapped with a hair covering, from which several leaves rise vertically. Several ringlets trail down her neck. On each wrist she wears a bracelet, indicated in white.

Behind her and flying toward her in left profile is a winged woman holding a lighted torch in each hand. Her peplos is belted over its overfold, and a black stripe edges the hem of the overfold and skirt. Her hair is gathered at the back of her head in a knot, around which a hair covering is wrapped. A sash, fringed at each end, hangs in the field in front of her.

Approaching the bride from the other side is a woman turned slightly to her left. Over her peplos she wears a mantle that is draped over her left shoulder and brought across her waist and legs, with the ends falling over her left forearm; the hem is edged with a black stripe. Her left hand gesticulates, fingers extended, palm out. Her right hand is largely missing. Her hair is arranged in a manner identical to that of the woman bearing the chest. Flying toward her is a winged woman in right profile, a lighted torch in each hand. Her hair is bound with a hair covering and gathered into a knot at the back of her head.

In the center of Side B a woman turns to her right. Over her chiton she wears a mantle that passes over her left shoulder and over her waist and legs. Her hair is dressed in a fashion identical to that of her companions, and her right hand hangs at her side.

28 Side B

The bride prepares herself for the wedding ritual. As she leans down to adjust her shoe, Eros proffers an alabastron, undoubtedly filled with perfume. An attendant brings a chest with finery to enhance the bride's allure, and sashes celebrating the special occasion hang in the background.

Because feet were thought to have unusual sexual appeal, the bride's shoes were an important part of her wedding regalia. As part of the wedding tradition, shoes were thrown at the bridal couple, undoubtedly to enhance their fertility. The stance of the bride as she reaches for her foot calls to mind the celebrated and approximately contemporary relief of the Sandal Binder from the Nike Temple parapet, and also looks forward to sculptural translations of this pose in the fourth century and Hellenistic period.

The prominence of the alabastron calls to mind its analogous emphasis on the lekythos by the Providence Painter with the story of Danae (no. 75). Because perfumes and ointments were used to anoint both the deceased and the bride, the vessel carried both funerary and nuptial connotations. In the bridal sphere the alabastron had particular erotic associations, because it was customary to anoint with myrrh the genitals of both bride and bridegroom; moreover, myrrh was also used in connection with abortion.[1] For this reason, the juxtaposition of the alabastron with the bridal shoes underscores the erotic undercurrents of the bride's toilette.

As in bridal scenes of several decades before, Eros is depicted as a baby boy (nos. 25-27), but in contrast with his earlier invisibility, he functions here as an actual participant in the narrative. It is clear that the bride sees him, because she has interrupted her dressing to respond to his overture, and she gazes directly into his face. Meanwhile, the bride's companions stand some distance away, as if to emphasize the special, semi-divine space that the bride occupies during the nuptial ritual. The close-set lines of the bride's drapery, especially where they encircle her left leg, are consistent with the style of the late fifth-century vase-painting, as is the relative lack of involvement of the flanking women. The winged females, either Nikai or chthonic divinities, are commonly seen on nuptial lebetes and accentuate the super-human status of the bride during the wedding ritual (see nos. 23 and 57).

1. Sutton (1981) 332-37; myrrh used as a contraceptive and abortifacient, J.M. Riddle, *Contraception and Abortion from the Ancient World to the Renaissance* (Cambridge, Mass. and London 1992) passim; Riddle et al. (1994) 31-32.

GOLD NECKLACE WITH PENDANTS

4th century
Jerusalem, Collection of Batya and Elie Borowski

Gold
L 35 cm.

Unpublished.

The necklace consists of a variety of spherical beads, some with pendants, strung together on a (modern) cord. Eleven large spherical beads, each with three chains ending in pomegranate-bud pendants, are arranged around a loop, with smaller plain gold beads, granulated gold beads, and stone (glass?) beads between them. Sixteen of these smaller beads have small, seed-shaped pendants: six are of a red stone, four are blue stone, and six are gold beech-nut pendants. The spherical beads are formed of two equal hemispheres and are decorated with a repoussé leaf-pattern with granules attached at the tip of each leaf, and coils of twisted wire circling each opening. Hanging from a cylindrical collar at the base of each large bead are three loop-in-loop chains, each anchored in a terminal bead shaped like a pomegranate, of similar design to the bead with leaves and granules on the sides, ending in outspread flanges imitating the case of the flower-bud, represented by inset stones.

This exquisite and unusual necklace is particularly evocative of the finery of the bridal array, since the imagery of the pomegranate has powerful associations with the fertility of the bride and with Persephone, the bride of Hades, Lord of the Underworld, whose marriage endowed mankind with continuing cycles of earthly vegetation (see **The Wedding** and **Persephone and**

29 Detail

29

Demeter). In the story of Persephone's abduction, she was persuaded by Hades to taste part of a pomegranate, and, once she had eaten its seeds, she was obligated to live for part of each year in the depths of the earth. In its elaborate use of gold and colored stones, the necklace is a magnificent example of the beaded necklaces popular in the fifth century, and would have been worn together with a profusion of other golden finery, including earrings, bracelets, hair- and dress-ornaments, and an elaborate bridal crown (stephane). In her gold-drenched appearance, the bride would have glowed as a precious jewel herself, decked in gold like Pandora (see **Pandora**), in accord with her position as a highly valued commodity being brought into her new household, since she represents through her children the continuation of the family line.

The repoussé leaf-pattern with attached granules on the spherical beads and pomegranate terminals is found on many examples from south Russia, and from coastal sites around the northern and eastern Aegean, including several elaborate pieces from the rich tomb known as the Great Bliznitza, now in the Hermitage.[1]

Carol Benson

1. Williams and Ogden (1994) 184-90, nos. 120-22; J. Boardman, "A Greek Cylinder Seal and Necklace in London," *AntK* 13 (1970) 49.

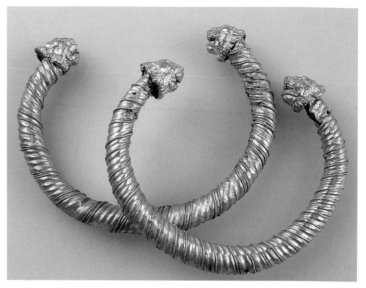

30

30

PAIR OF GOLD BRACELETS

late 4th century
Jerusalem, Collection of Batya and Elie Borowski
Formerly Joseph Ternbach Collection

Gold
Diam. 6.8 cm. and 6.3 cm.

Publications: E. Porada, *Man in the Ancient World* (Paul Klapper Library, Queen's College, New York 1958) no. 180; R. Merhav et al., *A Glimpse into the Past, The Joseph Ternbach Collection* (Israel Museum, Jerusalem 1981); Sotheby's New York, *Antiquities and Islamic Art* (November 24-25, 1987) no. 196 (illus.).

Each bracelet consists of a curved hoop with lion-head terminals. Each lion's head is formed from thin gold sheet in two symmetrical halves, joined down the center of the face. The gold sheet is pierced at the eyes and mouths, and slightly bent under at the edges of the mane. Collar elements, which once masked the join of the heads to the hoop, are lacking; differences in wear and pierced holes below the point of attachment attest to their original placement. The hoop of each bracelet consists of gold sheet laid over a bronze core which is spirally striated to imitate tubes or strips twisted together. The striations in the overlying sheet are lined with gold wire wrapped around the hoop, anchoring the gold sheet in place.

This type of animal-headed bracelet, worn in pairs, is eastern in origin, and became tremendously popular among the Greeks after the Persian wars, when tales of sumptuous Persian riches spread among the Greek cities. Gold and silver vessels, jewelry, and fabrics taken as booty, including the spoils seized from the tent of Xerxes at Plataea, were displayed before the awed and envious Greek populace, inspiring Greek goldsmiths to imitate the eastern forms and motifs.[1]

Many Greek examples are like this pair, with sheet gold covering an alloy core, such as a simple pair from Kourion on Cyprus in the Metropolitan Museum of Art, dated to the second half of the fifth century.[2] Others have hoops of silver with gold terminals, as seen in the magnificent pair from Pantikapaion, now in the Hermitage, dated to the early fourth century.[3] An extremely delicate pair of bracelets with antelope-head terminals, formed of gold sheet twisted into spiral pleats for stiffness, is in the Walters Art Gallery and is dated to the fourth century B.C.[4]

Carol Benson

1. Herodotos 9.80-85; E.D. Francis, "Greeks and Persians: The Art of Hazard and Triumph," in *The Art of Persia: The Art of an Empire*, D. Schmandt-Besserat, ed. (Malibu 1980) 81-82.
2. Williams and Ogden (1994) 250, no. 189.
3. Ibid. 156-157, no. 96.
4. A. Garside, ed., *Jewelry: Ancient to Modern* (Baltimore 1979) 89, no. 267.

31

PAIR OF GOLD SPIRAL EARRINGS OR HAIR-COILS

4th century
Jerusalem, Collection of Batya and Elie Borowski

Gold
L 2.7 cm., W 1.8 cm.

Unpublished.

Gold tubular casings enclosing an alloy core are twisted into a spiral, crowned with elaborate terminals. Each terminal consists of a long, tapered tube crowned by a pyramidal structure, formed by one large globule atop three globules, surmounted by a small piriform bead, with the added decoration of granulation running down the three edges of the pyramidal structure and surrounding each globule. The granulation continues down each tube in six lines, each flanked by plain wires, meeting the peaks and bases of three triangles of grains around the base, above a collar of thick beaded wire flanked by plain wires.

This type of spiral ornament is often described as a hair ornament, but is now identified as an earring, based on a depiction on a Lycian coin, showing a large hole in the earlobe and a spiral ornament worn in the ear.[1] In an excavated tomb, a pair of this type of spirals was also identified as earrings from their placement *in situ* at the level of the ears.[2]

Spiral earrings are common in Eastern Greece from the seventh century down through the Classical period; a pair with elaborate granulation from Kyme, now in the British Museum, is dated to the fifth century, and notable examples have also been found in Bosporus region, including a pair from Pantikapaion, now in the Hermitage, dated to ca. 400 B.C.[3]

CAROL BENSON

1. Williams and Ogden (1994) 34, 95, fig. 30, nos. 5, 47, 93, 145, 165, 172-174. The depiction on the coin was noted by K. Hadaczek (*Der Ohrschmuck des Griechen und Etrusker* [Vienna 1903] 13-16), but the identification as an earring has been doubted by some authors (see, for example, Vickers, *Scythian Treasures in Oxford* [Oxford 1979] 42, pl. XIc). Narrower, tighter spirals such as several pairs from Cyprus must have been worn as hair ornaments: A. Pierides, *Jewellery in the Cyprus Museum* (Nicosia 1971) 29-30, pl. XIX.4-7; pair of spiral ornaments from Marion-Arsinoe, Cyprus, now in the Benaki Museum, inv. no. 1533: A. Bromberg, *Gold of Greece: Jewelry and Ornaments from the Benaki Museum* (Dallas 1990) 42, 107, pl. 19.
2. Y. Kulashnik, in Williams and Ogden (1994) 152, no. 93.
3. Eastern Greek spiral earrings, Higgins (1980) 126-27; Rhodian example, Williams and Ogden (1994) 52, no. 5. Pair from Kyme, ibid. 95, no. 47. Earrings from Pantikapaion, ibid. 152, no. 93.

32

GOLD RING WITH ATHENA

ca. 400-375
Jerusalem, Collection of Batya and Elie Borowski
Greek, said to have been found with no. 33

Gold
H (bezel) 1.7 cm., W (bezel) 1.0 cm., Th (bezel) 0.6 cm.

Unpublished.

On the pointed oval bezel is engraved the figure of the goddess Athena standing in left profile on a cross-hatched groundline, behind an upright shield. Her left leg is bent and slightly trailing, with a lifted heel. She wears a belted peplos with loose overfold; the garment clings to the body, revealing the form beneath. Her hair is worn loose and hangs to her shoulder. In her left hand she holds a helmet with a feathered crest, and in her extended right hand is a small winged figure of Nike. Nike alights on the goddess' hand, her dress billowing back, and one wing visible lifted behind her head; she holds a taenia in both hands. Behind her is a spear or staff. The tapered ends of the hoop are soldered to the bezel.

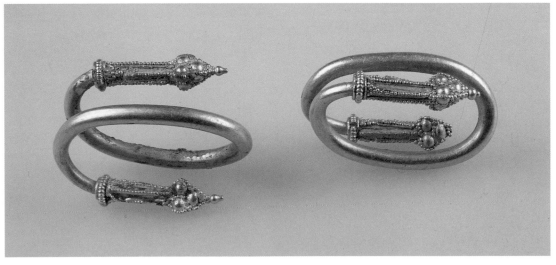

31

32

A thena appears with some of the attributes of the cult statue of
Athena Parthenos, including the large upright shield at her feet
and the winged figure of Nike in her outstretched right hand, but in
its depiction of the goddess as bare-headed, with her crested helmet in her hand, this image is unparalleled. Strikingly, Athena is
shown here as a youthful and simply dressed maiden, like the sim-
plest of the korai dedications on the Acropolis (no. 1). She wears
only a simple belted peplos and is without her customary aegis, in
contrast to her war-like and majestic appearance in her fifth-century cult images and on an intaglio from the British Museum with a
more traditional view of Athena, dated to the third quarter of the
fifth century.[1] Other Classical images of the gentler side of this goddess include the Walters' bronze statuette of Athena (no. 63) and
vases with depictions of a motherly Athena at the birth of Erichthonios (see **Erichthonios** and nos. 66-73). The shape of the ring is
seen in examples ranging in date from the third quarter of the fifth
century into the fourth century;[2] the style of the carving strongly
reveals the influence of "Rich Style" monuments, in the proportions
of the body, the nimble, dance-like pose, and the clinging, revealing
treatment of the drapery.

CAROL BENSON

1. J. Boardman, *Greek Gems and Finger Rings* (London 1970) 198, 288, fig. 486.
2. Ibid. 216 (The Waterton Group).

GOLD RING WITH APHRODITE

4th century
Jerusalem, Collection of Batya and Elie Borowski
Greek, said to have been found with no. 32

Gold
H (bezel) 1.95 cm., W (bezel) 1.15 cm.

Unpublished.

The ring has a pointed oval bezel. On a simple cross-hatched groundline,
Aphrodite stands in three-quarter right view, wearing a thin pleated chiton
covered by a large, clinging mantle which circles her right shoulder, forms a roll
beneath her breasts, and passes under her left arm. The mantle is decorated
with a fine stippled pattern. Her left leg is bent and slightly advanced; her bent
right arm, covered by the mantle, is pushed behind her, while her left arm
extends downward to touch the bird. Her hair is elaborately dressed into a roll
crowning the forehead and is gathered into a bun at the nape; she wears a beaded necklace and earrings. In front of the goddess is an altar on which sits a bird,
perhaps a dove. The hoop is soldered to the ends of the bezel.

33

A phrodite and her attributes are a common theme for women's
finery in the Classical period, evoking a mood of romantic love
and sensual pleasures. The goddess is shown here in a moment of
repose, dressed in elaborate finery, including a fine chiton, which
clings to her breasts, and a sheer, decoratively patterned himation.
She reaches down with a gentle gesture to touch her attribute, the

dove, which perches on a round altar, marking the setting as the goddess's sanctuary.

John Boardman dated the earliest finger-rings of this form to the third quarter of the fifth century B.C., including one example with a figure of Artemis before an altar in the British Museum.[1] Also in the British Museum is a ring with a woman before an altar, on which a large upright eagle stands; the altar is more elaborate and is seen in three-quarter view. The shape of the bezel is more rounded, and the ring has been dated to the mid-fourth century.[2] The simple refinement of the Borowski example, and the goddess' graceful, languid pose, as well as her hairstyle and the fleshy treatment of her jowl, all testify to the ring's fourth-century date.

CAROL BENSON

1. J. Boardman, *Greek Gems and Finger Rings* (London 1970) 216 (The Waterton Group); Williams and Ogden (1994) 52, no. 4 (illus.), with bibliography.
2. Williams and Ogden (1994) 105, no. 58 (illus.), with bibliography.

34

34

PAIR OF GOLD EARRINGS WITH BOVINE HEADS

5th century
Baltimore, Walters Art Gallery, inv. no. 57.589-590

Gold
H (earring) 3.8 cm., L (pendant) 1.6 cm.

Publication: A. Garside, ed., *Jewelry: Ancient to Modern* (Baltimore 1979) 77, no. 238 (illus).

Each earring consists of a hoop from which a pendant with a bovine head is suspended. Each pendant has the form of a biconical bead, one side of which has a repoussé bull or cow head attached as if to a collar. On the front of the bead, a double row of granules covers the join of the repoussé animal-head to the bead. Each head projects forward strongly, and is delicately and carefully modeled, with the ears and horns formed separately and attached. Details of the eyes, nostrils, mouth, skin, and the forelock on the animal's high crown are chased and engraved. Around the equator of the bead is a row of granules, flanked on either side by triangles of granulation arranged in alternating peaks up and down. Decorating the center of the back side of the bead is a large globule surrounded by triangles of small granules. A loop for suspension is attached to the top of the pendant at the collar. The hoop (probably modern) is formed of a hollow gold tube which terminates at one end in a loop with a globule attached at the back; the other end is coiled around the loop. The upper half of the loop is spirally wrapped with plain wire.

Although the bull's head is common in Greek jewelry from the Archaic period, these delicately modeled heads have softer, cow-like features, including a very slender muzzle and a fleshy neck, reminiscent of the fifth-century imagery of Io, the priestess of Hera who was loved by Zeus and turned into a cow by the god in an attempt to shield her from Hera's wrath.[1] As a domesticated animal trained to carry the yoke, the cow was an attribute of Hera and a symbol of marriage. This unusual combination of a cow's head with finery worthy of a bride, with its very elaborate treatment incorporating it into a biconical bead with a decorated back, makes this a rare and outstanding example of the miniature art of the Classical goldsmith, a rival to larger-scale sculpture in both monumentality and naturalism.

The sculptural plasticity of the Walters bovine-head earrings argues strongly for a Classical date, as does the very fine modeling around the animals' eyes, nostrils, and muzzles. The attachment of an animal protome to a circular collar derives from a earlier earring type shaped like a shield, with a projecting central lion-head boss and triangles of granulation around the rim, examples of which were found at Olbia and dated to the second half of the sixth century.[2]

Necklace pendants with bull's heads are fairly common in Greek jewelry, but the use of this type of pendant for an earring is very rare. A crude pendant with a calf's head, identified by its vestigial horns, was found at Kourion on Cyprus and is dated to the second half of the fifth century; like most animal-head pendants, it has a back-plate of sheet metal closing the neck aperture.[3] A bull-head pendant in Boston has a back-plate that protrudes around the edges to form a collar of flat petals around the neck; it has been dated to ca. 400.[4] A bull-head pendant from the Hermitage was found *in situ*, at the neck of a burial in Pantikapaion dating to the second quarter of the fourth century.[5] Several examples of similar, but cruder, necklace pendants are in Berlin and have been dated to the fourth and third centuries B.C.[6] An earring, which is similar in form to the Walters pair, but later in stylistic features, is also in Berlin; it has been dated to the Roman period, but there is no compelling reason to date it so late.[7]

CAROL BENSON

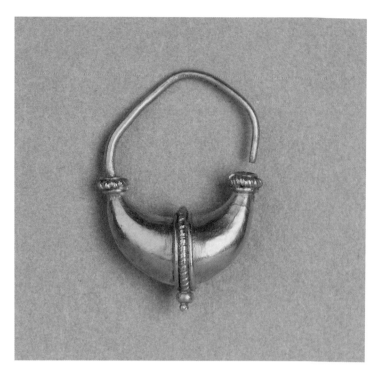

35

1. See Gantz (1993) 198-204. For examples of Io's imagery in cow form, se*LIM-CV*(1990) 665, nos. 4, 7, 11, 13, pls. 442-43 (s.v. Io I).
2. B. Pharmakowsky, "Archäologische Funde im Jahre 1913, Russland," *AA* 1914, 242, fig. 61.
3. Williams and Ogden (1994) 249, no. 188.
4. H. Hoffmann and P. Davidson, *Greek Gold: Jewelry from the Age of Alexander* (Mainz 1965) 237, no. 97, figs. 97a-b
5. Williams and Ogden (1994) 160, no. 100.
6. A. Greifenhagen, *Schmuckarbeiten in Edelmetall*, vol. 1 (Berlin 1970) 42, pls. 19, 6-7; vol. 2 (Berlin 1975) 23, pls. 15.1, 16.5, and 23-24, pls. 15.2, 16.3.
7. A. Greifenhagen, *Schmuckarbeiten in Edelmetall*, vol. 1 (Berlin 1970) 46, no. 7.12, pl. 23.

GOLD BOAT EARRING

5th century
Baltimore, Walters Art Gallery, inv. no. 57.1626

Gold
H 1.8 cm.

Publication: A. Garside, ed., *Jewelry: Ancient to Modern* (Baltimore 1979) 75, no. 236 (illus.).

The earring is of "boat" form and is hollow, formed of sheet gold in two halves. The decoration consists of twisted wire flanked by plain wires encircling the boat at its midpoint; attached below is a globule surmounting a granule. The terminals are similarly decorated with twisted wire flanked by plain wires. The hoop is of plain tapered wire.

This tiny yet elegant earring movingly evokes the youthfulness of the girl who once wore it. A young girl from a proper Greek family prepared for marriage at thirteen or fourteen years of age, and her first gold jewelry may have been the bridal ensemble, in which she appeared bedecked like Pandora with necklaces, earrings, bracelets, rings, and a bridal crown (stephane) of gold (see **Pandora**).

The boat earring is one of the most common Greek earring types, originating from very early contacts with the East through Syria and lasting in popularity in Greece down through the fourth century, when the decorations became increasingly elaborate. The simplicity, delicate proportions, and elegant decoration of this example suggest a date in the fifth century, although such simple examples remained popular throughout the period. Surviving examples of boat earrings represent a range of dates. These include a seventh-century example from Ephesos in the British Museum;[1] a pair and singleton from the fifth or fourth centuries, also in the British Museum;[2] and more elaborately decorated pairs from the fourth century, often with filigree decoration, from Tarentum.[3] A pair with filigree palmettes decorating the undersides was found in a fourth-century tomb from Pantikapaion and is now in the Hermitage.[4] Strikingly similar in form to the Walters example, although larger, is an earring from a Tarentine tomb, now in the Museo Archeologico in Taranto; it has been dated to the second quarter of the fourth century B.C. based on ceramic evidence in the tomb.[5]

CAROL BENSON

1. Marshall (1911) 72, no. 946, pl. IX; Higgins (1980) 119, pl. 21E.
2. Marshall (1911) 179, nos. 1659, 1660-61, pl. XXX; Higgins (1980) 125, pl. 25c; Williams and Ogden (1994) 60, no. 13, 87, no. 38.
3. Earrings from Tarentum: E. De Juliis, *Gli Ori di Taranto in Età Ellenistica* (Milan 1984) nos. 56-68. Another example from Tarentum has filigree running-spiral patterns flanking the decorative bands around the mid-point, dated to the second half of the fourth century. Basel, Münzen und Medaillen AG, B. Deppert-Lippitz, *Griechische Goldschmuck* (Mainz 1985) 179-80, fig. 127.
4. Hermitage, inv. no. P.1845.6; Williams and Ogden (1994) 160, no. 99.
5. E. De Juliis, *Gli Ori di Taranto in Età Ellenistica* (Milan 1984) 150, no. 56.

OINOCHOE WITH HETAIRA AND CUSTOMER

490-480
by the Berlin Painter
San Antonio, San Antonio Museum of Art,
Gift of Gilbert M. Denman, Jr., inv. no. 86.134.59

Attic
Clay
H 28.9 cm., Diam 12.9 cm.

Publications: *Para* 345.184ter; *Add²* 196; Shapiro (1981) 160-61 no. 63; M. Meyer, "Männer mit Geld: Zu einer rotfiguren Vase mit 'Alltagsszene'," *JdI* 103 (1988) 103, 108, 124 no. H1.

Reassembled from many pieces. Missing is left hand of woman and part of her drapery. Oinochoe type 1 with three edged-handle and rotelles. Added red for wreath and taenia, flower carried by man, bud in woman's hand, woman's jewelry.

Beneath the handle is a pointed palmette. Egg pattern above the scene and meander (right) beneath.

A young man, with short hair and the beginnings of a beard, leans forward toward a seated woman, his stick beneath his left shoulder, his weight on his right foot, with the left foot resting on the toes behind him. His upper torso is nude, and his mantle is draped around his waist and legs. In his extended right hand he holds a flower, in his left hand a small bag. His head is in right profile and he gazes downward toward the flower he holds.

Seated before him on a klismos with dotted cushion is a woman with prominent breasts. Her advanced right foot rests on the ground; the heel of her left foot is raised. Over her chiton she wears a mantle that is brought over her left shoulder and across her waist and legs, with the ends passing over her left forearm. The pleats of her chiton cover her lower shins and ankles. She wears a pendant necklace and, on her left wrist, a spiral bracelet. Her head is in left profile, and the long ends of her hair are drawn up at the back of her head under a fillet. She gazes downward in the direction of the flower offered by the man, while the fingers of her extended right arm hold a flower bud just in front of his groin. A mirror hangs on the wall over her head.

A young man has come to bargain for the affections of a hetaira, or prostitute. That he is the visitor is established by the mirror hanging on the wall, which denotes the quarters of a female. To emphasize the point, the Berlin Painter has shown the woman seated and the youth leaning on his walking stick.

Much has been written about the youth's bag, which in other representations is clearly a coin purse.[1] Although it has been suggested that its presence signifies the role of husband as breadwinner, scenes such as that on the San Antonio oinochoe clarify its pivotal role in the negotiating process with a prostitute. The youth may first proffer the red flower, but the money bag is prominently displayed as added encouragement. The woman indicates her willingness to discuss terms by holding out a flower bud toward the man's thighs, surely to tickle him.

36

The Berlin Painter contrasts the uncertain demeanor of the young man with the forthright manner of the woman. His nascent beard establishes his age as an adolescent, in keeping with which are the tentative gestures of his barely extended arms, and the rather clumsy subtlety of the simultaneous offering of both a flower and money. Nor does the youth look at the hetaira, but rather shyly down at the flower. The hetaira, by contrast, fully extends her right arm and displays no reticence in her explicit gesture. Moreover, in complete confidence, she stretches her lower legs out from the chair edge. The painter has so skillfully placed the bag of money behind the flower in her line of vision that it is not clear at which she gazes, the blandishment or the hard currency.

This oinochoe, a wine-jug, was destined to be used at a male drinking party, or symposium, and the scene was intended for a male audience. The popularity of scenes like this one on other vases intended for the symposium shows clearly the degree to which the negotiating phase of a visit to a hetaira was considered to have titillating qualities. By mid-century, however, these scenes disappear from vase-painting although prostitution continued to flourish.

In Greek culture the erotic undercurrents of flowers were age-old. Persephone was gathering flowers at the time when she was abducted by Hades, as if she were herself a flower ripe to be plucked (see **Persephone and Demeter**). Floral imagery was especially prevalent in late Archaic love poetry, not long before this vase was painted.

One of the most admired of all Greek vase-painters, the Berlin Painter displays here the qualities for which he is best known: skilled draftsmanship, especially of faces and jawlines; a simple composition with eloquent gestures; and a masterful balance of the scene to the vase surface.

1. See Sutton (1992) 17, fig. 1.5, inv. no. 4224 by the Penthesilea Painter in St. Petersburg, *ARV²* 889.166, ca. 460. See also Sutton (1981) 291-95.

NOLAN AMPHORA
WITH HETAIRA AND CUSTOMER

485-475
by the Providence Painter
Cambridge, Harvard University Art Museums, Arthur M. Sackler
Museum, Bequest of Frederick M. Watkins, inv. no. 1972.45

Attic
Clay
H 31.8 cm., W (at handles) 17.9 cm.

Publications: *ARV²* 638.43; *Add²* 273; Beazley (1918) 76; *The Frederick M. Watkins Collection* (Cambridge, Fogg Art Museum, January 31-March 14, 1973) 64-65, no. 25; Sutton (1981) 404, no. G75.

Intact, with some overpainting on the wool basket. A band of double palmettes and curving tendrils encircles the vase beneath both figural scenes. Beneath each handle is a palmette with tendrils. On Side B is a bearded man in left profile, draped in a mantle and holding a staff. Added red on Side A for letters, wreath held by woman and wreath worn by man.

On Side A a woman is seated in right profile on a klismos. She is barefoot, and her legs are drawn back, with the toes of her right foot resting on the ground beneath her seat. She wears a chiton beneath a himation that is fastened on her left shoulder and draped over her torso and legs. Her hair is drawn up in a headcovering that is decorated with dots; locks of hair escape in front of her right ear. She also wears a disc earring. Both arms are outstretched, and her hands hold a garland or a ribbon, toward which she gazes. In front of her is a wool basket (kalathos) filled with balls of wool.

On the other side of the basket a bearded man stands in left profile. His left hand holds the grip of a long walking staff over which his upper torso is bent. The toes of his right foot rest on the ground behind him. His mantle is brought over his left shoulder and around his waist and over his legs, with the ends falling over the outside of his left elbow and forearm. His right arm is outstretched before him, with the elbow bent and the forearm raised; his wrist is cocked, the palm faces him, and his fingers are curled, with the index finger touching the thumb. He wears a wreath, and he gazes downward at the woman's hands. Between the heads of the figures is the inscription ΚΑΛΟΣ ("beautiful one"). Another inscription beneath the man's right arm may read ΚΑΛΕ ("handsome one").

Because unmarried girls were almost invisible and the wife of an Athenian citizen had little contact with men outside the home, scenes from daily life in Greek vase-painting rarely portray the interaction of men and women. Even domestic vignettes with husband and wife are rare. By contrast, scenes with men and hetairai (prostitutes) are not unusual, and during the first quarter of the fifth century a popular subject in vase-painting was the financial negotiation between a prospective client and a hetaira (no. 38). In many of those scenes the customer extends a moneybag toward the woman, but the purse need not be present, and sometimes the gift of a flower or ribbon seems to be sufficient, either by itself or as an

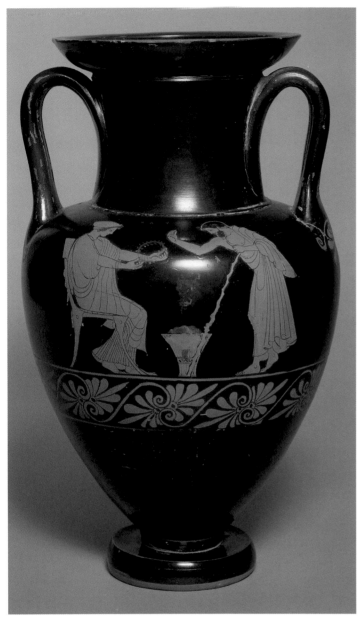

representations and the bargaining process itself. Because respectable Athenian girls were so secluded that courtship of them was impossible, Athenian men had to content themselves with these semi-flirtatious moments of negotiation (see **Women and Men**).

In a number of these scenes a wool basket is present, and the only logical explanation is that an allusion to her domestic nature enhanced a hetaira's appeal to a prospective customer. Indeed, since the ideal woman in Greek society was supposed to be beautiful, intelligent, submissive, and industrious, the inclusion of the wool basket specifically addressed this last criterion. It is also true, however, that the ideal woman was supposed to shy, virtuous, and modest, and it was the insistence upon those qualities in a Athenian wife that was partially responsible for the health of the city's flourishing brothels.

The Providence Painter also executed the lekythos with Danae (no. 75), and in both vases the artist reveals his penchant for simple, elegant compositions that capture a moment of significance and emotional content, with dramatic gestures that focus the action silhouetted against the background. His draftsmanship is fluid, and his composition is always sensitively adjusted to both the curving field and the overall contours of the vase.

38

KYLIX WITH HETAIRAI AND CUSTOMERS

ca. 490-480
by Makron
Toledo, Toledo Museum of Art, purchased with Funds from the Libbey Endowment, gift of Edward Drummond Libbey, inv. no. 1972.55

Attic
Clay
H 11 cm., W (at handles) 36 cm., Diam (rim) 29 cm.

Publications: *CVA* Toledo, Museum of Art 1 (U.S.A. 17) 34, pls. 53-54 (C. Boulter and K. Luckner); Sutton (1981) 291-92, 296, 398, no. G46; Keuls (1983a) 225-26, fig. 14.34a-b; Keuls (1985a) 167-68, 223-24, figs. 141-42, 204; M. Meyer, "Männer mit Geld: Zu einer rotfiguren Vase mit 'Alltagsszene'," *JdI* 103 (1988) 89 n. 13, 105-106, 124.

Repaired, with part of one handle missing and restored. Around the tondo is a band of continuous meander (left). Added red in the tondo for the flames and the bloodstains on the side of the altar, the wine, the tassels on the woman's belt, and the fumes from the incense burner. Narrow reserved band on inner and outer edge of rim; reserved band beneath scenes on underside. Added red

37

advisable prelude to discussion of the precise terms of the transaction. Such is the strategy of the bearded gentleman in this scene. He has apparently just bestowed a garland or ribbon upon the object of his attention, and, while she gazes at it with admiration, he presses his case, gesticulating energetically as he proposes a specific number of coins. There is a slight tension; neither looks at the other, as he tries to assess the exact degree of her pleasure in his gift. His walking stick testifies to his maturity and thus to his previous experience with these kinds of matters; he surely learned long ago that a hetaira's delight at the gift of an inexpensive trifle could translate into a reduced price and a lower overall financial outlay. The popularity of negotiating scenes on vases destined for use by men at their symposia testifies to the titillating currents underlying both these on Side A for flowers and wreath, on Side B for fillets, flowers, and wreaths. Graffito on the underside of the foot.

In the tondo a woman stands turned three-quarters to her right, her breasts, legs, feet, and head in left profile. She wears a chiton with kolpos and overfold beneath a himation that is draped behind her back, with the ends falling forward over each shoulder. The hem is decorated with two parallel lines set slightly in from the edge. Her hair is drawn up from the nape beneath a fillet, with a single long corkscrew lock falling from behind the ear down the left side of her neck. She also wears a disc earring. Her left elbow is bent and the arm cradles the base of a ritual basket (kanoun). With her extended right hand she pours wine from an oinochoe over a flaming altar, which is set upon a two-stepped platform. Behind her, fumes rise from a *thymiaterion* that stands on a raised block.

On the underside is a gathering of men and hetairai (prostitutes). Side A: under one handle is a stool, before which stands a beardless youth, turned three-quarters to his left with his wreathed head in left profile. He leans on a walking stick, which is placed under his left arm, and the toes of his left foot rest on the ground behind him. He wears a himation that is draped over his left shoulder and around his legs, with the folds gathered on top of his stick. His elbow is bent and his upraised left arm holds a small purse; his lowered right hand, brought behind his hip, holds a flower. In front of him, seated in left profile on a cushioned klismos, is a woman who turns her head back in right profile. Over her chiton she wears a himation that is draped around her hips and

legs with the ends brought forward over her lap. Her hair is drawn up in a sakkos, whose ends protrude at the back of her head. Her left hand is upraised, with the index finger and thumb holding a flower. Her right arm is extended in front of her, palm down, and in her extended fingers and thumb she also holds a flower. Hanging in the field behind her are a strigil (scraper), a sponge, and a small net bag with marbles.

The other couple on this side comprises a bearded man in the same pose and dress as his youthful counterpart behind him. His right elbow is bent and his wrist is cocked. The index finger and thumb are in contact, with the rest of the fingers curled. His left hand extends a bag toward a woman who stands before him in three-quarter left profile. Over her chiton she wears a mantle that is brought over her left shoulder, around her back, and across her waist and legs, with the ends draped over her left forearm. Her long hair is brought up from the nape under a taenia; two curly ringlets behind her ear fall down her neck. The index finger and thumb of her left hand are in contact, with the rest of the fingers curled. Her right elbow is bent, with the forearm upraised and a flower in the fingers. Behind her a flute-case hangs in the field, and under the handle is a palmette.

On Side B, a standing woman turns back to man behind her. Her legs and breasts are in left profile, her head in right profile. Over her chiton she wears an himation that is draped over her left shoulder and across her waist and legs; the long locks at her nape are brought up under a taenia; she also wears an earring. Her right hand holds away from her side a pair of double flutes; her left elbow

38 Side A

38   Side B

is bent, forearm uplifted, and the fingers hold a flower. Turned toward her is a bearded man leaning on his walking stick. He is seen in three-quarter left profile, with his left foot frontal and right foot in left profile. His himation is draped over his left shoulder and across his waist and legs, with the ends brought over his left forearm. His left hand grasps the top of a walking stick, which his right hand steadies in the middle of the shaft. Hanging in the field behind him is a mirror.

The last couple comprises a woman seated in right profile on a cushioned klismos. The sleeves of her chiton have been pushed up onto her shoulder, and her himation folds are brought around her waist and legs, with the ends falling over her left thigh. Her hair is wrapped in a headcovering from which locks at the back of her head are pulled through, and from which locks escape to frame her face; she also wears an earring. With both hands she holds a fillet. Her left arm is extended, with the thumb and index finger touching, the other fingers curled; her right elbow is bent and the forearm upraised, with the fingers forming a gesture identical to that of her left hand. Hanging in the field before her is a strigil and a sponge. Facing the seated woman is a bearded man who stands in three-quarter left profile, his mantle draped over his left shoulder. with the folds brought across his legs and the ends draped over his left forearm. His left hand clasps the handle of his walking stick; his right elbow is bent and the forearm is raised; the palm is facing out, with the extended fingers of the hand held vertically.

The tondo depicts a ritual scene of libation, complete with flaming altar and incense burner. As the woman pours wine on the altar, she clasps the *kanoun*, or ritual basket, which by the fifth century had acquired a distinctive form, with its walls divided into three flaring members (see no. 60). The *kanoun* contained the tools of sacrifice, including the knife with which the sacrificial animal would be killed, and barley that would be scattered over its head. In religious processions the *kanoun* was carried only by girls of marriageable age, with whom these baskets were closely identified. The privilege of being named a *kanephoros* (basket-carrier) was much coveted by Athenian maidens, and we can infer from the literary texts that the honor was regularly bestowed only upon the daughters of the foremost citizens. At the culmination of the procession, following the libation shown here, the maidens would give over the *kanoun* to the priests who would then proceed with the blood-letting, from which all women were prohibited.

If the tondo depicts an unmarried Athenian maiden of good birth, her counterparts on the underside provide a sharp social contrast, although the painter has intentionally adorned them in a similar fashion. Two hetairai share the hairstyle of the *kanephoros*,

38 Detail of interior (tondo)

and all of the hetairai are dressed comparably to her, even to the gathered neckline of their chitons. Absent, however, on the underside is the stylish striping of the tondo figure's mantle, as well as its elegant and probably ritualistic draping over both shoulders.

While the *kanephoros* is engaged in pouring a libation, the hetairai participate in a unique form of courtship, as clients and prostitutes negotiate payment by means of the flattery of flowers and the stronger language of moneybags. The lone beardless youth is apparently the least experienced of the men, and his blandishments of flowers have failed even to attract the attention of the hetaira he addresses. Perhaps it is not coincidence that the moneybags are

missing from Side B, where we find both the oldest customer, leaning with both hands upon his walking stick, as well as the most affluent, whose gift of a taenia seems to have pleased the hetaira seated before him. Indeed, the energy of her response is unmistakable as she sits up vertically in the chair, her sleeves pushed upon her shoulders, her mantle folds gathered loosely around her waist. Although it has been suggested that a flower was held in the man's right hand, his fingers could well be uplifted and extended in a gesture of negotiation, as Keuls suggests.

The setting of these negotiations is not unambiguously clear. On the one hand, we would seem to be in spaces belonging to the hetairai, because they are seated and a mirror hangs in the background near a flute case, from which a woman adjacent to it has just drawn her flute. The cushions on the klismoi and the stool also bespeak a domestic environment. On the other hand, hanging in the background on each side are the accouterments of the palaestra: the sponge and strigil. Perhaps they signify both that the men have just come from the palaestra and they fully intend their stay with the hetairai to be of some length.

So prized was the virginity of a *kanephoros* that we can be assured that the maiden on the tondo had been allowed little contact with men, and, indeed, she seems insulated to the point of enshrinement within the tondo's field. When in public or in the presence of men, a young woman of respectable upbringing was expected to adopt a self-contained body language, and to incline her head and direct her gaze downward in a display of *aidos* (see **Aidos** and **Sophrosyne**). By contrast, her counterparts on the underside of the kylix enjoy an unconstrained relationship with men, gesticulating and maintaining direct eye contact as they bargain over finances. Makron's juxtaposition of the scenes was clearly intended as an ironic social comment.

The scene tells us something else about the interrelationship of men and women in Classical Athens. An unmarried man enjoyed little contact with a respectable young *kanephoros*, whom he would never have been allowed to court and with whom his marriage would ultimately be arranged (see **Women and Men**). Outside of his household, his interaction with women was almost exclusively with hetairai. The situation was not so very different for an older married man, who probably had little interaction with respectable women outside of his family and for whom hetairai also comprised the majority of his female acquaintances. Scenes such as this one were popular on male drinking cups for symposium use, because the flirting that attended the negotiations with hetairai filled a void created by a constricting social structure that proscribed heterosexual courtship on any level.

Typical of the first decades of the fifth century is Makron's difficulty with three-quarter views, which he renders with profile legs and profile breasts. His only significant attempt at foreshortening is seen, probably intentionally, on Side B in the left foot of the man whose bent position indicates that he is the oldest figure present. In the spirit of Late Archaic vase-painters, Makron delights in linear patterns, which are especially successful in the rendering of *kanephoros*. His superb draftsmanship is also apparent on his kylix in Berlin (no. 123).

39

KYLIX WITH SYMPOSIUM SCENE

ca. 470-460
by the Tarquinia Painter
Basel, Antikenmuseum Basel und Sammlung Ludwig, inv. no. Kä 415

Attic
Clay
H 13.9 cm., Diam 34.3 cm.

Publications: *ARV²* 868.45; *Para* 426; *CVA* Basel, Antikenmuseum und Sammlung Ludwig 2 (Switzerland 6) 47-48, pl. 26.3, 28-29, 37.3,7, 39.12, Beilage 6.2; J.D. Beazley, "Some Inscriptions on Greek Vases," *AJA* 58 (1954) 190; K. Schefold, *Meisterwerke griechischer Kunst* (Basel, Kunsthalle Basel, June 18-September 13, 1960) 204, 206, no. 220; E. Berger, H.A. Cahn, and M. Schmidt, *Kunstwerke der Antike aus der Sammlung Käppeli* (Lucerne 1963) cat. no. D 12 (illus); K. Schefold, *Führer durch das Antikenmuseum Basel* (Basel 1968) 94 no. 123,2; Keuls (1985a) 168-69, figs. 143-44; Peschel (1987) 211-15, 450, no. 152 (illus.); Reinsberg (1989) 92, fig. 34.

Reassembled from many pieces. Signs of ancient repair.

Encircling the tondo is a band of five to eight meanders (left) alternating with a cross square. Within the tondo a nude youth, right foot raised behind him, turns to a beardless youth in a himation who holds a forked rod in his extended right hand. A sponge, aryballos, and strigil hang in the background.

Beneath the figural scenes on the underside is a band of six meanders (left) alternating with a cross square. On Side A, a nude woman reclines with her elbow pressed against an elaborately decorated cushion. Her left leg is extended out in front of her, her right leg is drawn back under her right thigh, and her right palm clasps her right knee. Her head is turned back in right profile, and she wears a sakkos. Hanging in the field above her right knee is a rhyton, and hanging in the field above her right shoulder is a woven basket in the shape of a pyxis. She gazes at a beardless youth who leans his left elbow on a folded, decorated pillow and extends his right arm forward, with the fingers directed to his companion. A mantle covers his legs, which straddle the woman's cushion. The hair around his face is brushed down over a broad taenia, indicated in red. Hanging above his right arm is a basket.

All of the rest of the men are bearded and all the other woman have short hair brushed down over their ears; all these figures wear a taenia decorated with evenly spaced zigzags. In the second pair the man leans against the legs of the woman behind him. His right hand rests on the back of his head, and he gazes upward in left profile. His mantle covers his genitals and legs. Hanging in the field in front of him is half of a shield in its case. The woman reclines on her left thigh, with her lower legs drawn back. Her left elbow rests on a folded cushion, and her left hand holds a skyphos. Her right hand waves a ivy branch over the head of her companion.

On Side B, a nude woman reclines on her left leg, which is bent back under her thigh. Her right leg is similarly bent, the knee raised. Her head is in right profile as she turns back to gaze at the man behind her. Her left arm is stretched out toward him, and the hand holds the foot of a kylix. Her right elbow is bent and the hand, fingers extended, is above her head. Hanging in the field above her left arm is a basket. The bearded man behind her leans his left elbow on a folded cushion and with his left hand, raises a kylix to his mouth. Both knees are bent, with his mantle draped over his legs, exposing his left foot. His right forearm rests on his knee, the fingers lightly curled. His head is in left profile and he gazes back at the woman. Hanging in the field above his right arm is a taenia.

In the last couple, a nude woman leans against the right leg of the man behind her; his knee is raised and the right lower leg is drawn back. Her right leg is in the identical position. Her left arm is drawn across her waist, with the

39 Side B above, Side A below

188

39 Detail of interior (tondo)

fingers extended; her right arm is outstretched in front of her, and her index finger passes through the handle of a kylix, which she prepares to flip in a game of kottabos. She gazes back in right profile at the man's face. A basket hangs in the field beside her head. He leans his left elbow on a folded cushion and waves an ivy branch in his uplifted right hand. His mantle is wrapped around his legs, with the ends brought under his left elbow and down his left side.

The scene on the underside presents a very clear picture of how hetairai (prostitutes) conducted themselves. In almost every detail, the behavior contrasts markedly with that of a respectable woman belonging to the family of an Athenian citizen. The hetairai are nude, their pubic hair is clearly visible, and the legs of several of them are widespread. Their arms are fully extended out from the body, and they gesticulate freely. They also participate with enthusiasm in the game of kottabos, whereby the player flicked the wine lees from the bowl of the kylix toward a disc suspended some dis-

tance away. Also in contrast to wives and daughters of citizens, almost all of these women wear their hair short, curls rakishly framing their face. Even more remarkably, the hetairai gaze directly into the faces of the male customers; not a single woman displays the downcast head and lowered eyes of *aidos* (see **Aidos and Sophrosyne**).

It is interesting to note that in couples where the man is bearded, he is less aggressive than the animated hetaira he is with. The women's outstretched arms and full nudity contrast with the partially draped figures of the men and the greater composure and restraint of the men's gestures. It is obvious that a hetaira's lack of inhibition was a large part of her appeal to her customer, whose attraction to unconstrained spirits calls to mind the popularity of Atalanta (see **Atalanta**) and the metaphor of a woman as an untamed animal yet to be domesticated (see **Women as Animals** and **The Wedding**).

A notable contrast to the conduct of the bearded men is offered by the beardless youth. He is far more aggressive than the hetaira beside him, whose sagging breasts indicate that she is older than her colleagues. Her hair is gathered into a dignified sakkos, and she leans gracefully upon a pillow, as her right hand rests calmly on her knee. The young man, on the other hand, separates his legs to cradle the woman's pillow, and he reaches out eagerly for her. The painter seems to suggest that a mature man exhibits in the company of hetairai a specific kind of demeanor that a young man must learn. Whereas an inexperienced youth approaches a hetaira with the aggressiveness that he identifies with the ideal of courtship represented by mythical scenes of pursuit, he grows to realize that the purchase of a woman's favors enables him to assume a more passive role.

Energy is rather to be expended in the preceding phase of the relationship, wherein the negotiating of the financial terms of the service takes place. In those vase scenes (nos. 36-38), and presumably also in the actual events, the men's aggressive gestures and gifts of love tokens communicate the tension inherent in the unresolved status of this unusual kind of courtship. In these bargaining scenes the uncertainty of the denouement creates an atmosphere that is as much or more erotic than the ambience of a symposium, where the scenario is already determined. On the Basel kylix, the separation of the bodies and the absence of embraces further diminishes the erotic undercurrents. We can be assured, however, that to the ancient owner the scene had sufficient sexual energy, because he took care to repair the vase after it was damaged, perhaps in a game of kottabos.

40

KYLIX WITH SYMPOSIUM SCENE

ca. 510-500
in the manner of the Gales Painter
New Haven, Yale University Art Gallery,
Gift of Rebecca Darlington Stoddard, inv. no. 1913.163

Attic
Clay
H 9.2 cm., Diam 22.3 cm.

Publications: J. Hambidge, *Dynamic Symmetry: The Greek Vase* (New Haven 1920) 122, fig. 12; P. Baur, *Catalogue of the Rebecca Darlington Stoddard Collection of Greek and Italian Vases in Yale University* (New Haven 1922) 108, no. 163, fig. 36, pl. 15; H. Licht, *Sittengeschichte Griechenlands* II (Dresden and Zürich 1925-1928) 47; Caskey and Beazley (1931) 11; Burke and Pollitt (1975) 46-47, no. 42; Peschel (1987) 89 90, 444, no. 48 (illus.); S. Matheson, *Greek Vases: A Guide to the Yale Collection* (New Haven 1988) 16-17; Reinsberg (1989) 94, 96, fig. 38; Yale University Art Gallery, *Handbook of the Collections* (New Haven 1992) 262 (illus.); J.M. Riddle, J. Estes, and J. Russell, "Ever Since Eve ... Birth Control in the Ancient World," *Archaeology* 47.2 (1994) cover.

Piece of rim and one handle restored; part of youth's right knee missing. Type B kylix; foot in two degrees. Two reserved circles surround scene. Extensive preliminary sketch. Red for wreaths, basket, basket strings, and inscription.

A young man and young woman recline on a bed, about to kiss as they gaze into each other's eyes. The edge of the bed is rendered as a narrow band. The youth is completely nude, and part of his pubic hair and genitals are visible. He leans on his left hip, his back and left shoulder resting against a large pillow, which is decorated with four horizontal bands, each consisting of one of two reserved lines enclosed by black bands with scalloped edging. The youth's left knee is bent, and his lower leg is drawn up upon the couch; only the outer edge of his left thigh is visible, and his left foot is suggested by a curious extension beneath his shin that presumably passes beneath the buttocks of the female. The youth's right knee is also bent, and his lower leg is brought forward over the thighs of the woman. The fingers of his left hand are extended toward the woman's left breast, and his right elbow is hooked around the back of her head, with the extended fingers framing her chin. His head is in left profile, and he has short hair and a wreath. A clump of fuzz on his left cheek indicates his youthfulness. Above his head is inscribed: ΗΟ ΓΑΙΣ ΚΑΛΟΣ ("the youth is fair.")

The woman is completely nude except for a mantle which is brought around her right hip and falls forward over her genitals and the tops of her thighs; the other ends pass beneath both figures and hang from the edge of the bed. The woman also wears a wide necklace in the shape of an arc, the lower contour of which is accentuated by a double line, and the interior of which bears three rectangular groups of dots. She reclines on her left hip and thigh, leaning her upper body against that of the youth. Her knees are bent, and her lower legs are not visible. Her right elbow is bent and the lower arm is upraised, with the fingers grasping a pair of double flutes. The position of her left arm mirrors that of her right arm, and the fingers caress the back of the youth's head. Her face is turned back to his in right profile, and she wears a wreath; the ends of her wavy hair pass under the youth's right forearm. In the background above the woman's right thigh is suspended a basket that is decorated with three groups of horizontal lines and a number of diagonal lines extending from base to rim.

W e are at a symposium with a youth and hetaira (prostitute), who also doubles as a flute-girl. The rim of the tondo functions as a window for the viewer, cutting off the head and foot of the bed, the outer edge of the basket, and the lower ends of the drapery. The pillow conveniently rests against the tondo's curving frame. Oblivious not only to our presence but to that of any other guests, the nude couple abandons all inhibitions. The hetaira's almost total nudity, her outstretched arms, forthright gesture of affection, and her direct gaze into the youth's eyes are a diametrical contrast to the decorum of a respectable Athenian woman. A modicum of modesty is apparent in the way her mantle falls over her genitals, but the similar concealment of the youth's genitals suggests that the modesty may rather be on the part of the painter. The hetaira's wide necklace, which was not a conventional form of Classical Greek jewelry but has antecedents in the Near East, indicates either that she is from the eastern Mediterranean or subscribes to those styles. In either case her ornament, as well as her demeanor, clearly demonstrate her otherness.

The painter, like his contemporaries at the end of the sixth century, was fascinated by the challenge of rendering figures turning in

40 Detail of interior (tondo)

space. An extensive preliminary sketch testifies to both his commitment and the ambitiousness of his enterprise; in the finished painting he even moved the youth's right leg farther up the woman's hip to increase the foreshortening. The painter's difficulties are, however, as apparent as his successes; the legs of the youth are not readily identifiable, and the painter seems to be as confused as we are as to how the thighs are attached to the groin.

Certain features distinctive of late sixth-century red-figure vase-painting are the rendering of the eye as a narrow, undulating oval whose inner corners are closed and the representation of the pupil and iris by a black dot. The chins are deep and jutting, and the ears form a pattern of concentric arcs. Other late sixth-century features are the long fingers with upturned tips and the radiating patterns formed by the extended fingers. One should also note the stacked pleats of the mantle and the linear pattern of the hem edges. Like many of his contemporaries, this painter prefers to work exclusively in undiluted glaze.

The artist has taken pains to emphasize the youthfulness of the customer, who must be in his late adolescence. It is generally agreed that in Classical Athens homosexual relationships involved a boy between the ages of about thirteen and twenty-one and a man in his mid-twenties and older. We do not know how old a youth was when he began visiting hetairai, but homosexual and heterosexual relationships were inevitably concurrent rather than sequential. Indeed, the inscription added here, "the boy is beautiful," is as often seen in scenes where no women are present and where the attractiveness of the youth suggests his desirability to other men. Because the conventions of homosexual courtship stipulated that the younger male was expected to express no affection or pleasure, the enthusiastically demonstrative tenor of symposium scenes like this one offered these youths an emotional release. We should also keep in mind that young men had almost no contact with young women of respectable families. A maturing girl of the class into which the youth in this scene would eventually marry was all but invisible; if she did go out in public, she was enveloped in garments, self-contained in gesture, and warned to avoid eye contact with men (see *Aidos* and *Sophrosyne* and **Women and Men**).

FRAGMENT OF A KYLIX WITH HETAIRA AND CUSTOMER

510-500
by the Kiss Painter
New York, Metropolitan Museum of Art,
Rogers Fund, 1907, inv. no. 07.286.50

Attic
Clay
H 15.3 cm., W 12.2 cm.

Publications: ARV² 177.2; Richter and Hall (1936) 24, no. 9, pl. 8.

Broken all around. Red for the youth's wreath.

A youth turns to his left, his head in right profile. His right hand is at his hip; his left arm is outstretched, with the fingers extended. His mantle frames his back, with the ends brought forward over both upper arms; his genitals are barely visible. He has short wavy hair and wears a wreath. He gazes downward at a woman whose head is tilted up to his in left profile, her arms passing around his neck. Over a pleated undergarment she wears a mantle that is draped around her back, with the ends falling forward over her left shoulder; she also wears a sakkos.

The youth's wreath indicates that we are at a symposium and thus that the woman is a hetaira (prostitute). Indeed, no woman other than a prostitute would be depicted in an embrace and in direct eye contact with a man. This woman is, in fact, minimally attentive to modesty; although her body is concealed by her garments, she eagerly encloses the man's neck in her arms and presses his head down to her as she reaches up to kiss him. There is no question as to who is the more active participant in the encounter, because the youth's left arm is extended outward in surprise whereas his right arm is bent, with the arm drawn back behind his torso, and the fingers barely skimming his right hip. Her eagerness coupled with his passivity is an amusing contrast to the prescribed behavior ordained for each gender; the male was supposed to be ever-aggressive and the female compliant. Suggesting that these conventional strictures could become wearisome is the frequent reversal of these roles in symposium scenes on drinking cups destined for male symposiasts.

The Kiss Painter receives his name from this vase. It is unfortunate that few vases survive by his hand, because he excels in draftsmanship, particularly in faces, drapery folds, and fingers that are delicately fanned. His sense of movement and humor are delightful.

41

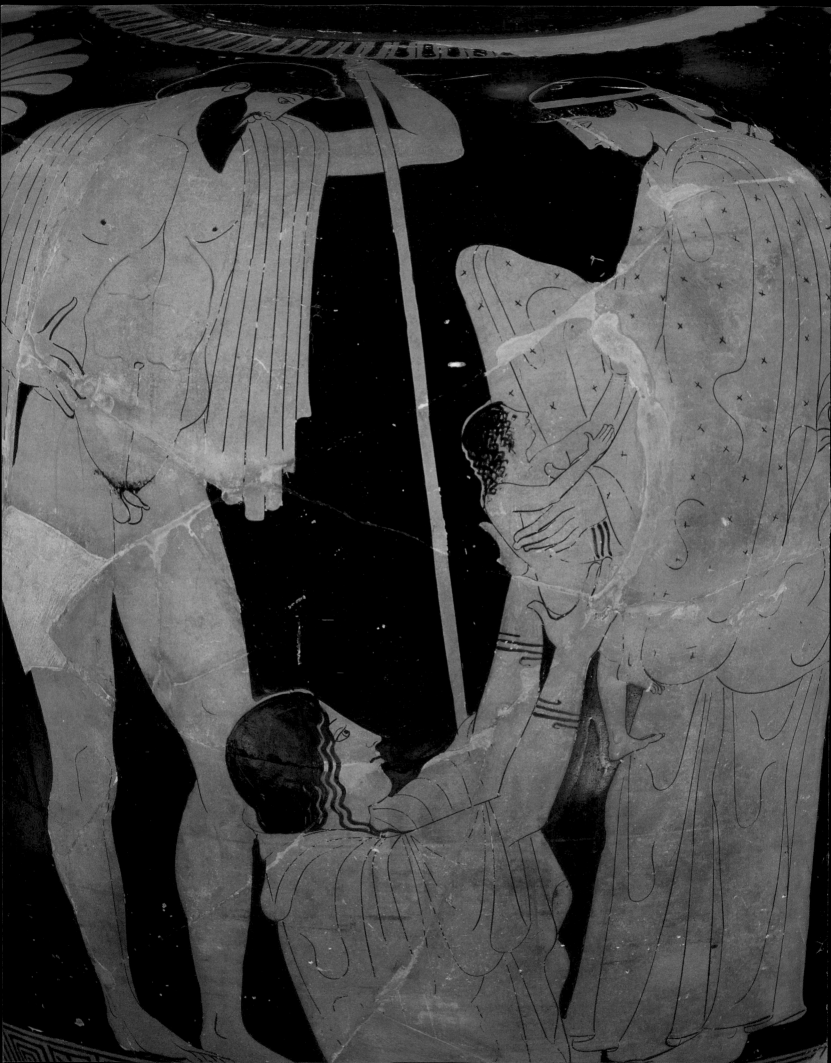

Containers and Textiles as Metaphors for Women

WOMEN AS CONTAINERS

The things of a woman are the things that are within.

Xenophon, *Oikonomikos* 7.3

The wife is the guardian of the things inside.

Demosthenes, 57.122

Keep yourselves nice and clean, so that we women can entertain you with the contents of our kistae [baskets].

Aristophanes, *Lysistrata* 1183-84

Female: having a hollow part.

Webster's New World Dictionary, Third College Edition, 1994

From earliest times we find that the Greeks were fascinated by the image of a pregnant woman containing an unseen baby inside of her. Equally intriguing was the image of a woman possessing the potential to swell up with pregnancy. The logical comparison of a woman's body to a container is well documented in Greek thought (pp. 196-97, figs. 1-2).[1] Hippocrates likened the womb to a cupping jar,[2] and the same word, *amnion*, is used both for the membrane that surrounds the fetus and a vessel for collecting the blood of a sacrificial animal.[3] More specific forms of containment are often mentioned. Aristotle speaks of the womb as an oven,[4] and elsewhere we find the female body correlated with a treasure chamber. The term *muchos* refers both to the interior of a woman's body and to the innermost chambers of a house.[5] A woman's body is also aligned with the earth, which was considered the quintessential womb. In the Greek wedding ceremony the father of the bride addresses his daughter's new husband by declaring that "I give her over to you for the ploughing of legitimate children" (see **The Wedding**). The analogy of a woman's uterus to a furrow was so commonly accepted that Antigone spurned Kleon's advances with the contemptuous remark that "there are other furrows for his plough."[6]

The analogy of a woman to a container permeates everyday customs, rituals, and myths, where we encounter a wide variety of forms of containment. These images can vary from clay vessels to wicker baskets and wooden chests, and also include enclosed rooms in a home and underground storage chambers. Through the metaphor of containment, women and their fertility are ascribed three important connotations: concealment with overtones of withholding, treasure, and mystery, all tinged with sexuality and undercurrents of anxiety. Conversely, containers in myth, ritual, and everyday life are often connected not merely with femaleness and female fertility, but also with the human life cycle. Sheila Murnaghan has eloquently shown how a woman's gift of life was always simultaneously viewed as a gift of mortality, because birth marked the beginning of a life cycle that would inevitably end in death.[7] In Greek myth, it is the role of the mother to tell her child that he will die; so does Hecuba remind Hector of his mortality,[8] and so does Thetis inform Achilles.[9] Moreover, by Greek tradition, it was women who ushered the deceased out of the world through a funerary ritual marked by anguished cries analogous to those that accompanied childbirth.

In many myths babies are put into vessels from which they emerge as if from a second birth, entering a new identity or new situation. Erichthonios, Perseus (son of Danae), and Ion (son of Kreousa) come readily to mind (see **Erichthonios** and **Danae**). Sometimes adults are incarcerated against their will, as in the case

Fig. 1. Minoan larnax from Vasilika Anogeia, Heraklion, Archaeological Museum, inv. no. 1612, ca. 1550 B.C. Courtesy museum.

of Auge who was put in a chest by her father after her affair with Herakles.[10] She ultimately survived, as did Kypselos, who hid in a chest when the Bacchiads tried to kill him.[11] An adult may also be shut up in a chest voluntarily, as occurs in the story of Hypsipyle, one of the Lemnian Women who killed all the men on the island of Lemnos. Hypsipyle decided to spare her father by enclosing him in a chest that she set adrift at sea.[12] The experience of being enclosed in a vessel or chest is not always life-sustaining. At his birth, Adonis was sealed in a chest by Aphrodite, who gave the receptacle over for safekeeping to Persephone.[13] Because Adonis was the child of incest and grew into an unsuccessful hunter who met death in a boar hunt, he was a powerful symbol of effeminacy and depleted masculinity, images which are reinforced by the suffocating surveillance of his female caretakers (see no. 61). Similarly, when Althaea is angered at her son Meleager and decides that his life must end, she removes a firebrand from the chest where she had stored it since her son's birth.[14] Because Meleager immediately dies when the firebrand is thrown on the fire, we know that Althea's protection of the firebrand within the chest had safeguarded her son's well-being.

That an image of a human being in a container carried overtones both of life and of death was in keeping with traditional Greek custom. The placing of bones in a vase or chest (*larnax*, see fig. 1) goes back to the Minoan period, and we are told by Homer that Thetis provided the golden jars in which the bones of Achilles and Patroklos were deposited.[15] Sarah Morris has pointed out that a form of secondary cremation in double vessels is attested for Arkades, with a close parallel observed in seventh-century burials on Crete.[16] As

late as the Classical period the bones of young children and newborn babies were placed in clay vases that have been recovered from the Kerameikos.[17] So closely, in fact, were deceased babies associated with vessels that the slang expression for the exposure of unwanted babies was "to put [it] in a pot."[18] It is not surprising, then, that in one version of the story of Erichthonios we are told that Athena put the baby Erichthonios inside the basket with the intention of rendering him immortal (see **Erichthonios**). There must have been many grieving mothers who cherished the notion that the child whose remains had been placed within a burial vessel would remain there in perpetuity.

Perhaps the most compelling mythical example of the vessel as a metaphor for a woman's body is the pithos (storage jar) that Pandora brings with her to Epimetheus (see **Pandora**). As Froma Zeitlin demonstrates in her essay in this volume, the pithos is an image for Pandora's own body. When she opens the pithos, a host of sicknesses and plagues escapes, in keeping with the Greek point-of-view that children represented a mixed blessing. The fact that Hope does not depart, but remains inside the pithos is also consistent with what Georgia Nugent has described as the optimism with which every new birth is anticipated.[19]

In addition to its reference to the life cycle, the metaphor of woman as vessel carried connotations of treasure. From Mycenaean times onward, a household's most valuable assets, which included wine, grain, and oil, were stored in pithoi.[20] Similarly, a young woman's virginity and her life-giving potential were not only her own most valuable assets, but were also of supreme value to her new husband and to her own family, whose concern it was to safeguard her chastity until marriage. Accordingly, the *Palatine Anthology* could remark that virginity was a treasure to be guarded.[21] It is extremely interesting to note that by Classical times the value of woman as a container was not viewed solely in terms of her own femaleness, but rather included, even gave priority to, the male contribution. Aischylos refers to the female as the treasurer of the man's seed,[22] and, in commenting upon household management, Xenophon includes an obvious sexual reference when he remarks that, in the case of a wife who was a poor manager, the husband's role as provider could be described as pouring water into bottomless jars.[23]

The metaphor of woman as a vessel carried still another meaning, one of concealment and withholding.[24] When Demeter is angered at her daughter's disappearance, she refuses to give forth the annual renewal of vegetation (see **Persephone and Demeter**). The idea that a woman's contained space and its contents were not always available or accessible to men is alluded to the *Lysistrata's* veiled sexual reference to storming the gates of the Acropolis with crowbars.[25] Hesiod carries the idea of refusal to relinquish a step further when he compares women to consuming fires.[26] The distrust of this unseen and hidden territory is palpable.

The vessels that are particularly associated with women further enrich the expression of the metaphor of containment. Because obtaining water was traditionally a woman's task, the water vessel, or hydria, was viewed by many Greek artists as a specifically female vessel. Not surprisingly, scenes painted on hydriae often refer to women's activities, and the distinctive swelling shape was surely compared with a woman's body. When the unmarried Amymone took her hydria as she set out to search for water, she was waylaid by Poseidon who pursued her vigorously until he won her over as his lover (see **Amymone**). The depictions of their rapprochement so strongly resemble wedding scenes that the hydria appears to function as a vessel for the wedding bath, and the suggestion is conveyed that Amymone's own body is a receptacle for Poseidon's semen and eventually for his child. The identification of Amymone's body with her hydria supports Evelyn Harrison's suggestion that the hydria seen beside the Aphrodite of Knidos likewise refers to the goddess's body. Among other vessels associated with women we should note the alabastron, which held perfume, ointments, and especially myrrh. Robert Sutton has noticed that the alabastron, almost alone among vases closely linked with women, is given by a woman to a man.[27] The custom suggests that the alabastron was charged with meaning, perhaps because it is believed to have been used to contain ointments with which the genitals were anointed before sexual intercourse (see no. 122).

Another compelling image of containment inextricably associated with women is the enclosed chamber, especially one within the heart of the house. Not only did the word *muchos* identify both a woman's body and the interior of house, but the same word, *eschara*, referred to both the central hearth of a house and a woman's sexual organs.[28] Deianira secretes within a chest hidden deep in the inner recesses of the house the poison that will destroy Herakles,[29] and Thetis attempts to save Achilles from death on the battlefield of Troy by concealing him within the women's chambers. It is behind the closed doors of the marriage chamber, the *thalamos*, that mythical women such as Iocasta and Deianira choose to die, a tradition that emphasizes the degree to which in death as well as life women were inextricably identified with their sexuality (see **Textiles**).[30]

The comparison of women with sealed or greatly protected chambers finds a parallel in actual custom. The house was generally considered to be under the wife's direction, whose responsibility it was to preserve the goods that the husband procured.[31] These were stored in the aforementioned pithoi, as well as in large chests, where valued textiles were placed.[32] A woman spent the majority of her time within the house, while the man passed his days in the open air public spaces of the city. So pervasive, in fact, was the image of a woman as being contained within the house that ancient writers could speak of women being "locked in" the women's quarters, or *gynaikonitis*,[33] and Aristotle could remark that women were accustomed to living a submerged and shadowy existence.[34] In *Lysistrata* the complaint is voiced that, as a result of the ceaseless war, young girls were growing old in their chambers.[35] It is interesting to consider that same pattern of thinking has continued into

Fig. 2. Breasted ewer from Thera, Athens, National Archaeological Museum, inv. no. 877, ca. 1550 B.C. Courtesy museum.

modern times in traditional Greek villages, where it is said that a woman literally "is" the house, which blooms "like a garden" only when the woman is present.[36]

Women were also identified with underground treasure chambers, of which the most memorable mythical example was the enclosure outfitted as a bedroom (see no. 74) in which Danae was unsuccessfully incarcerated to prevent her inevitable impregnation. From the Bronze Age onward, pithoi could be stored underground, and in the centuries following the collapse of the Bronze Age civilization, we know that the underground Mycenaean tholos tombs, once so richly outfitted with gold, were regarded with awe as treasure chambers. The connotations of underground storage as a hidden place where valuables are concealed offered a logical parallel for Danae's virginity, and, when Zeus takes the form of a rain of gold, he simultaneously penetrates both the chamber and Danae.

In ritual, women were consistently associated with containers. Baskets are featured on vases depicting the cult of the Little Bears, in which young girls served Artemis in her sanctuary in Brauron in preparation for marriage (nos. 98-99). Young girls appointed Arrephoroi carried containers with mysterious contents to and from a sanctuary of Aphrodite (see **The Plynteria and Arrephoroi**). The unknown identity of the baskets' contents and the fact that the girls were solemnly presented with these containers make it clear that the girls were supposed to regard their burdens as an honor and a responsibility intimately linked with the community's own well-being. A similar tone surrounds the kanephoros, the virginal maiden who headed religious processions, carrying on her head a *kanoun*, the basket that contained barley and the sacrificial knife that would be used to kill the animal victim (nos. 60 and 38). Her prominence in religious processions, her role in the wedding ritual, and the fact that she was charged with both an emblem of agricultural sustenance and the religious implement of sacrifice underscore the degree to which a marriageable maiden was thought to be inextricably entwined with the prosperity of the city-state.[37]

Containers pervade the wedding ritual (see **The Wedding**). The bride took her bridal bath using water stored in a vase, the loutrophoros, that was exclusively for wedding use (nos. 22-27, 102). Another distinctive wedding vessel was the lebes gamikos, which surely has its origins in a vessel for food (nos. 28, 55-59). It was customary to place sprigs of myrtle in the mouth of a lebes, obviously to reinforce the couple's fertility. Also figuring in the ritual was a winnowing basket, which referred to the refinement of grain that, together with marriage, was equated with civilized life. When the bride entered her new home, a basket carrying the *katachysmata*, a mixture of figs and possibly coins, was emptied over her head as an expression of the fertility and prosperity that her addition to her husband's household was hoped to bring.

Brides were the recipients of a profusion of vessels, chests, and boxes, which are presented to them by women, never by men.[38] A popular present was the kalathos, a wicker basket that was used in wool working and that consequently signified the bride's industriousness and skill in the arts of textile production (see **Textiles**). Other vessels, such as the pyxis, which was used to store toilette articles and jewelry, accentuated the bride's sexuality. We are reminded of the chest containing Beauty that Psyche obtained from Persephone and could not resist opening, in order to indulge herself.[39] These gifts offer a thoughtful reminder of the degree to which a woman's hiddenness, her secret spaces, and her sexual mysteries were viewed as positive titillating and alluring qualities when their potency was on a controllable scale; one senses that Medea's box of magic would not have been regarded in the same benign way.[40]

Women had the responsibility for maintaining their relatives' graves, and they typically brought to the tomb elongated flat bas-

kets. These contained ribbons to tie around the grave stelai, vessels with which to pour libations on the grave, and branches, which were surely an expression of vitality. The three handles depicted on the basket seen on the Worcester lekythos (no. 53) call to mind the triple elements of the *kanoun* and raise the question whether both kinds of baskets might not share a similar ancestry.

Containers figured in other rituals closely associated with women. The Eleusinian Mysteries are so intimately identified with kistae (baskets or chests) that on the east pediment of the Parthenon Demeter and Persephone are seated upon them.[41] At the Adonia, women mourned the death of Adonis, who was the antithesis of ideal manhood, by means of a ritual that was similarly inverted. Women planted seedlings in broken amphorae, then allowed the young plants to die in the hot summer sun (no. 61).

The Thesmophoria was an exclusively female ritual that was considered to be of such importance to the well-being of the community that its annual expenses were paid from the city's treasury.[42] The festival closely linked women's own fertility with the annual renewal of the earth's vegetation. In its most distinctive feature, women retrieved from underground chambers, or *megara*, the remains of piglets that had been thrown in there some months before. Pigs were intimately linked with fertility, and in Greek slang a women's genitals were referred to by terms relating to pigs.[43] We are told by ancient commentators that the women threw back into the pit images made from dough that represented male genitals. After intermingling the piglet remains with seeds saved from the preceding year's harvest, the women scattered the mixture over the earth, symbolically fertilizing it, with a brief nod to male participation. Especially interesting are the obscenities that the women were said to have uttered freely. The Greek term for obscene language is *aporreta*, literally "unspoken things," and Allaire Brumfield has traced the close correlation between unspeakable sexual language and the hiddenness of women's sexual organs and biological processes.[44] Uttering the unspeakable, Brumfield argues, was a means of driving away infertility and malevolent forces.

Froma Zeitlin has pointed out that underlying the ritual of the Thesmophoria is the theme of opening and closing, and Giulia Sissa has investigated in depth the relationship of these concepts to the metaphor of women as containers.[45] A pregnant woman was envisioned as being filled up; according to a Hippocratic aphorism, the mouth of the uterus closes when the semen is absorbed.[46] Similarly, a virgin was thought to be self-contained, and Hesiod probably refers to this notion when he says that when the wind blows it does not touch the young girl.[47] Offering a sharp contrast to these two states were the mythical Danaids, who murdered their husbands on their wedding nights and in punishment were required eternally to fill their leaking hydriae in Hades. Because the water leaked out as soon as the vessels were filled, the maidens were in effect sentenced to perpetual labor. The correlation of the hydria with a woman's body is sufficiently established that Sissa is surely right when she interprets the torment as a custom-made punishment for a physically mature woman who rejected pregnancy.[48] The Danaids were to be plagued ever after with leaking containers that symbolize their own bodies, which they had refused to allow to be filled up. The fact that Amymone was also a Danaid, although not a participant in the slaughter of the husbands, reinforces Sissa's interpretation of the myth. Just as Amymone is rewarded with a filled hydria, so must her sisters, presumably, regret their choice.

The emphasis upon the vagina as an aperture finds further expression in the close correlation of the vagina with a woman's throat, most graphically expressed in the mythical image of the Gorgon, whose decapitation results in the birth from her neck cavity of Chrysaor and Pegasos (see **Gorgons**, **Gesture and Gaze**, and **Persephone and Demeter**).[49] Another vivid manifestation was the Pythia, the elderly virgin priestess who sat over the steaming crevice at Delphi and conveyed Apollo's responses in the form of riddles. As Giulia Sissa has shown, the Greeks believed that Apollo's breath entered the Pythia's vagina to pass out of her mouth in the form of words.[50] The analogy with sexual union is obvious, and also noteworthy is the image of the Pythia's body as permeable to an outside force. That this idea was popularly applied to women is suggested in Euripides' *Hippolytos*, where it is remarked that women's boundaries are more fluid than men's.[51] The suggestion that women were physically more susceptible than men to outside influences echoes the popular belief that a woman lacked a man's physical, mental, and emotional self-control (see **Women and Men**). Paradoxically, however, it was men's irrepressible curiosity about women's mysterious vessels that triggered their own downfall. In the *Thesmophoriazousai* Aristophanes explores voyeuristic exploits with levity, but in Euripides' *Bacchai* the ramifications are more chilling when Pentheus spies upon the women's world and, in retribution, is dismembered.

1. DuBois (1993) 89-91; DuBois (1988) 132, 147; Loraux (1984) 231, commenting on Bachofen. For Late Cycladic breasted ewers, see C. Doumas, *Thera: Pompeii of the Ancient Aegean. Excavations at Akrotiri, 1967-79* (London 1983) 110, fig. 14a, pls. 62-63.

2. Hippocrates, *On Medicine* 22 (1.628). See Hanson (1991) 88, 120.

3. Burkert (1983) 469, quoting Empedocles, frag. 70. See King (1987); Keuls (1985a) 131.

4. Aristotle, *Generation of Animals* 764a, 12-20. A man accused of necrophilia was said to be putting his loaves in a cold oven; see DuBois (1993) 91. In modern Greece a young woman is said to have a burning oven; see Dubisch (1986) 156. See also Hanson (1991) 119.

5. See Jenkins (1985) 112; Padel (1983) 3-19; Loraux (1987) 74 n. 42. See also Sophokles, *Antigone* 1293, 1295, 1299 and *Women of Trachis* 686.

6. Sophokles, *Antigone* 566-69. Oedipus refers to his mother Iocasta as "this field for double sowing" (Sophokles, *Oedipus the King* 1255-58). Lysistrata (Aristophanes,

Lysistrata, 1173) comments that men will say that "they want to strip off and work the land." Solon remarked (Plutarch, *Solon* 15.5) that "I took away the mortgage stone stuck in her breast."

7. Murnaghan (1993) 48, 72-3; Burkert (1985) 159ff, discusses the concept of death as inherent, coexistent with life; Burkert (1987) 100ff.

8. Homer, *Iliad* 23.82-5.

9. Murnaghan (1993) 55, 62; Homer, *Iliad* 18.54-62.

10. Pausanius 8.47.9, quoting Hecataeus.

11. Herodotos 5.92.

12. Apollonios of Rhodes, *Argonautika* 1.609-26.

13. Apollodoros, *Bibliotheke* 3.14.4.

14. See Morris (1992b) 42; Murnaghan (1993) 45-46.

15. Homer, *Odyssey* 24.36-92.

16. Morris (1992b) 161.

17. Hamilton (1992) 70; U. Knigge, *Der Sudhugel* (Berlin 1976) 13. See Barber (1991) 204 for silks in a bronze funerary urn of the late fifth century from the Kerameikos.

18. Cantarella (1987) 44; Aristophanes, *Frogs* 1190; Plato, *Minos* 315d. The verb *chutrizein* has the meaning "to put in a pot (chutros)."

19. See Nugent (1992).

20. Homer, *Odyssey* 2.337. See Zeus' two pithoi: Homer, *Iliad* 24.524.

21. *Palatine Anthology* 6.444.

22. Aischylos, *Eumenides* 658-61, 665.

23. Xenophon, *Oikonomikos* 7, 18-40.

24. See DuBois (1987) 40, 49.

25. Aristophanes, *Lysistrata* 411.

26. Hesiod, *Works and Days* 704.

27. Sutton (1981) 332-33.

28. Leduc (1992) 240.

29. Sophokles, *Women of Trachis* 686.

30. Sophokles, *Oedipus the King* 1261-62; Euripides, *Hippolytos* 782, 793, 808, 825.

31. Xenophon, *Oikonomikos* 7.12-13.

32. Jenkins (1985) 112; Homer, *Odyssey* 8.95ff, 15.104-110, 21.51-2 and *Iliad* 9.200.

33. Aristophanes, *Thesmophoriazousai* 414-22; Xenophon, *Oikonomikos* 9.5.

34. Plato, *Laws* 781c. See Fantham et al. (1994a) 103.

35. Aristophanes, *Lysistrata* 589-93.

36. Du Boulay (1974) 33, 63, 131-133.

37. See Schelp (1975) 23, 25.

38. Sutton (1981) 332-33.

39. Apuleius, *The Golden Ass*, 139-40; see Tatar (1992) 148-52.

40. See the essay by Margot Schmidt in this volume.

41. Pausanius 10.28.3 describes a painting by Polygnotos of Thasos, in which a woman who introduced the rites of Demeter to Thasos is seated with a kiste on her knees. For the Eleusinian Mysteries, see Burkert (1985) 286.

42. See Fantham et. al. (1994a) 87 for discussion; Burkert (1985) 242ff; Burkert (1983) 349-52; Parke (1987) 123-27.

43. Henderson (1991) 131-32.

44. Brumfield (forthcoming) 73-113.

45. Sissa (1990) passim; Zeitlin (1982) 143-49.

46. See Sissa (1990) 159.

47. Hesiod, *Works and Days* 519-25.

48. Sissa (1990) 153, 162, 171.

49. Loraux (1987) 4, 50-61; Sissa (1990) 51, 53, 166.

50. Sissa (1990) 22-27, 51-53, 166.

51. Euripides, *Hippolytos* 730-31; Sissa (1990) 49.

TEXTILES

By how much men are expert of propelling a swift ship on the sea,
by this much are women skilled at the loom.

Homer, *Odyssey* 7.108-111

We are from this land and worthy of the peplos.

Aristophanes, *Knights* 566

Just as the words "distaff" and "spinster" have survived into modern times as references to women, so in ancient Greece was textile production intimately associated with females. Spinning and weaving were the only skills that Xenophon believed a young bride needed to bring with her to her new home,[1] and during her married life textile production would occupy the lion's share of her time and energy. A woman would manufacture the clothing worn by every member of her family, as well as coverings for beds, cushions, and chests. It is not surprising, then, that the textiles needed to outfit a household were thought to be synonymous with the domesticity of civilized life. Moreover, the extended concentrated effort required from women to produce textiles came to represent the role to which society expected women to conform.[2] The image of Penelope at her loom is probably the best known exemplar of the female ideal, but we also hear of the Nymph Melissa, who turned men from savage ways, introduced *aidos*, or modesty, and invented the wedding veil (see **Aidos** and **Sophrosyne**).[3] Lysistrata comments that women could bring men to peace by the arts of wool work,[4] and, when the Theban women followed Dionysos to the mountains where they engaged in a Maenadic frenzy, Euripides underscores the magnitude of the outrage by telling us that the women had been lured from their looms and shuttles.[5]

As patron goddess of Athens, Athena was credited above all with her gift of *techne*, or craftsmanship, and among its several manifestations, including shipbuilding and horse harnessing, textiles were the most highly valued. Every year Athena was honored with the presentation of a woven cloth, a peplos, which had been prepared by carefully selected women, who wove into the fabric the story of the gods' defeat of the Giants (see **Athena**). The roots of the ritual certainly lie in the Bronze Age, when textile production was the mainstay of the economy on Crete. Elizabeth Barber has commented on representations of elaborate garments on faience plaques found at Knossos,[6] and both she and Erika Simon argue that the processions of women depicted in Mycenaean painting are forerunners of the ritual celebrated in Classical Athens.[7] Writing in the eighth century, Homer tells us in the *Iliad* that as an offering gift Hecuba placed a peplos on the lap of a statue of Athena.[8]

The dedication of votive textiles in Bronze Age ritual is closely related to the critical importance of the society's textile industry, which appears to have been so prominent that cloth was exported as far as Cyprus and Egypt. As documented in the Linear B tablets, women performed the vast majority of the work in producing the textiles, but the administration of the industry was in the hands of men. By contrast, it is quite possible that in the earlier Minoan civilization on Crete women played a more prominent role in the industry, as they certainly did in eastern Mediterranean societies of the late third millennium, where textile manufacture was also a driving economic force. Elizabeth Barber has shown that there is a high correlation between women's pivotal roles in the ancient Near Eastern textile industry and their status in those same societies.[9] It is interesting to note that women's status in those contexts appears to have been not only higher than it was on Mycenaean Crete, but also in Classical Greece, when women manufactured textiles only for their immediate households and when textile production was no longer a serious component of the Athenian economy.

The narrative representations woven into the peplos dedicated to Athena in Classical times also assuredly had predecessors of great antiquity. Indeed, the tradition of storycloths was age-old. The mythical Arachne, transformed into a spider when she spied upon the gods, divulged her observations in an elaborate storycloth that graphically set forth the gods' transgressions.[10] When Philomela's brother-in-law cut out her tongue so that she would not tell anyone that he had raped her, she revealed the outrage by means of a vivid storycloth. Both myths regard the woven narratives as a substitution for a woman's voice, from which we can conclude that Perikles' emphasis upon a woman's silence was probably not a new idea in Classical times.[11] Although the ephemeral nature of textiles would seem to reinforce women's verbal silence in Greek culture, we should keep in mind the widely acknowledged influence of textiles on Geometric pottery. Moreover, given the survival into the Classical period of sophisticated weaving skills manifested in the creation of Athena's peplos, it is more than likely that storycloths, and especially the depictions of the famed Gigantomachy, continued to exert some influence on contemporary artists.

As a laborious, intimate creation of women, textiles were naturally closely identified with them. Kreousa recognized that the youth Ion was her own son when he showed her the swaddling cloth she wove for him as an infant.[12] Mythical women turn to garments as allies, even instruments of their will. Both Medea and Deianira prepared garments dyed with a poison that Elizabeth Barber identifies as the lethal realgar, a sulfide of arsenic that colored garments a dark purplish red.[13] Herodotos tells of the tradition that the Athenian women, angry at a messenger who announced the catastrophic defeat of the Athenian fleet at Aegina, used the dress pins from their peploi to stab him to death, therewith precipitating a decision on the part of the men that women should henceforth wear the chiton, which did not require the long pins.[14] Mythical women also turned to textiles when they decided to commit suicide. Phaedra hanged herself with a cloth, as did Antigone, who deliberately used a knotted veil of the type she would have worn as a bride.[15] It has been shown that a woman's throat was so closely aligned with her vagina that hanging carried overtones of a woman's sexuality and for that reason was almost exclusively a female form of death (see **Women as Containers** and **Gorgons**). The sexual undertones of hanging were reinforced by the role of textiles in the process.

A woman's garments were not merely testimony to her skill and industriousness. They also came to be viewed as an extension of her being, inextricably merged with her. When a bear wandered inadvertently into a sanctuary of Artemis and was killed there, the angered Artemis spread a pestilence over the community (see **Little Bears**). The priest Embaros offered to sacrifice his daughter in atonement, but secretly substituted a goat that had been dressed in his daughter's clothes. The goat was apparently indistinguishable from the young woman, and Artemis accepted the sacrificial animal as a substitution.

The story of Pandora demonstrates the degree to which the inseparability of a woman from her clothing accentuated undercurrents of wealth and sexuality (see **Pandora**). Pandora was created by Hephaistos from earth and water, and over this core the gods adorned her with a profusion of garments and gold ornament. Athena herself bestowed exquisitely woven clothing, including a veil. When Pandora was finally completed, she was a vision of textiles and gold, and her clay core was concealed behind a dazzling curtain, much as a Greek bride would be almost completely hidden to her bridegroom behind a curtain of finery. Pandora is as much her raiment as she is her clay construction, which not only carried no intrinsic worth, but was tantamount to an empty vessel to be filled in pregnancy (see **Women as Containers**). At the same time, however, Pandora's clothing and jewelry, like those of a bride, connoted a value that was immeasurable in monetary terms. The finery signified that the young woman was herself a valuable asset as the potential bearer of children, and, through her weaving skills and hard work, a source of prosperity to her new husband's household.

Fig. 1. Woman spinning, after M. Kliapha, γυναικέσ τησ γησ (Athens 1994) 119.

Textiles were so intensely viewed as an extension of a woman's self that it was thought that the natural state of a female was to be clothed whereas that of a man was to be nude. Male nudity, whether in exercise in the palaestra or in artists' depictions, at all times carried overtones of masculinity and sexuality, but the separation of a woman from her clothing had specific and explicit sexual overtones. The unveiling of the bride was a symbolic and actual first step in her disrobing for sexual intercourse, and the "loosening" of the bride's belt was used as a term for the sexual act itself. Accordingly, women's clothing carried overtones of sexual suggestiveness and allure, connotations which they retain into modern times.

If a woman's clothing signified her skill, industriousness, value, and sexuality, textiles also lent connotations related to the techniques of textile production. Spinning, or the preparation of wool thread, was the most time-consuming aspect of textile manufacture, because preparation of the thread required seven to ten times the length of time needed to weave the thread into a cloth.[16] Moreover, in contrast with weaving, which required a cumbersome loom, spinning could be carried out almost anywhere, and, consequently, ancient Greek women must have appeared to be perpetually occupied with their distaffs and spindles (fig. 1). The incessant action of spinning, the seemingly endless thread, and the skill required to master the craft linked spinning and spun thread with knowledge and intelligence, in the sense of planning and forethought. The Moirai, or Fates, were thought to spin the threads that shape our lives, and Ariadne saved Theseus by providing him with a thread by which he could retrace his steps out of the Labyrinth. Marcel Detienne has shown that the name of Metis, the mother of Athena and the goddess of intelligence, was closely identified with verbs meaning tying and binding.[17] Skillful maneuvering through one's life was thought to involve the identification of a thread that both defined one's way and tied a person to a prosperous course. In myth it is women who are inseparably associated with this ability.

Weaving is a technique by which sets of threads are interlocked into a web. A fabric's essence as a sort of "collaboration" between warp and weft was reinforced by the weaving process, because both the setting up of the warp threads on a loom and the weaving itself were vastly simplified if performed by two or more people working in tandem. These characteristics of weaving find their way into Greek thought as early as Homer, who speaks of Athena and Odysseus weaving a plan together, and weaving a trick.[18] Odysseus' cleverness was one of his most admired and celebrated traits, and hence his collusion with Athena carries only positive overtones for each of them. By contrast, to the Classical Greek poets weaving has taken on connotations of concealment, deceit, and guile specifically associated with women. The imagery pervades the *Oresteia* where Aischylos speaks of Clytemnestra's woven cloth as a snare or hunting net, which he implicitly correlates with the hunting weapons of men.[19] To Euripides, weaving also carries overtones of female guile; the cloth Elektra prepared is described as a deceitful snare.[20]

Textiles figure in all major passages of women's lives to a much greater degree than they do in men's. A young girl serving as an Arrephoros was dressed in a white garment that she might later dedicate to Athena (see **The Plynteria and Arrephoroi**). When she served Artemis as a Little Bear, a saffron colored garment, a *krokotos*, figured in the ritual (see nos. 98-99). As a virginal basket-carrier, or *kanephoros*, a young woman's basket, or *kanoun*, was covered with a special fabric (see no. 60).[21] Garments were particularly connected with wedding ritual. In Book 6 of the *Odyssey*, Nausikaa has a dream that she is to prepare for her wedding and, upon awakening, immediately takes a load of woven goods down to the river to be washed. The bride's garment, veil, and belt were key elements of the bridal ceremony, and after their wedding the young couple was visited by the priestess of Athena who brought with her the sacred aegis, which was draped with a net-like covering.[22] As a wedding gift, the bride presented the bridegroom with a tunic, or *chlanis*, that she had undoubtedly woven herself (see **The Wedding**).[23] A young mother who survived childbirth offered her clothes to Artemis as an expression of gratitude; should she have died in childbirth, her relatives dedicated her garments to Iphigenia (see **Artemis** and **Iphigenia**). A woman prepared a swaddling cloth for her newborn child, and, in the manner of Penelope, wove a shroud for deceased members of her family.

Athena was honored with similar attention to her garments. We are told that, in commemoration of the death of the maiden Aglauros, the clothing of the olivewood statue of Athena on the Acropolis was not washed for a full year. During the annual festival of the Plynteria, the garments were laundered and the statue was enveloped in a shroud, a garment Homer knew as a peplos (see **The Plynteria and Arrephoroi**).[24] The statue was then redressed, but only a month later received a new, richly embellished peplos to celebrate the goddess' birthday at the Panathenaia. During this festival a newly outfitted statue of Athena was honored for the deity's munificence to the Athenian people, among which textile production was viewed as her greatest gift. The goddess celebrated her birthday with her statue elaborately arrayed in the finest garment the Athenian women could produce, and, with this presentation, the Athenian calendar was considered to have come full circle, and the new year could begin.

1. Xenophon, *Oikonomikos* 7.6.
2. To Homer, weaving was women's work, as war was men's work. See Homer, *Iliad* 6.490-3 and *Odyssey* 1.356-9.
3. Detienne (1974) 62-63.
4. Aristophanes, *Lysistrata* 567-86.
5. Euripides, *Bacchai* 105-119, 1236-37.
6. Barber (1992) 116.
7. Simon (1982) 132; Barber (1991) 376.
8. Homer, *Iliad* 6.269-311.
9. Barber (1994) 283.
10. Barber (1994) 153, 240; Barber (1992) 112.
11. Thucydides 2.5.
12. Euripides, *Ion* 1428. In Euripides' *Elektra* (540-42), Elektra is asked if a stranger could prove he was her brother by showing a garment she had once woven for him when he was a child.
13. Barber (1994) 234.
14. Herodotos 5.89.
15. Loraux (1987) 8-19.
16. Barber (1994) 87.
17. Detienne (1978a) 133-74. See also the essay on Peleus and Thetis in this volume.
18. Homer, *Odyssey* 13.386, 5.386, 4.739.
19. Aischylos, *Agamemnon* 1383 and *Libation Bearers* 980. See also *Agamemnon* 1493-94: "lying in a spider's web."
20. Euripides, *Orestes* 25 and *Elektra* 155.
21. Mansfield (1985) 189, 195-96.
22. Mansfield (1985) 189, 191.
23. See Oakley and Sinos (1993) 37, 39; Pollux 3.39; Aristophanes, *Birds* 1693.
24. Homer, *Iliad* 24.796.

42 Side A

42 Side B

42

SKYPHOS WITH SEATED WOMAN

late 5th century
connected with the Penelope Painter
Oxford, Ashmolean Museum, University of Oxford, inv. no. 1934.339

Attic, "from Tithorea"
Clay

Publications: *ARV²* 1302.4, 1689; *Add²* 360; K. Schauenberg, "Frauen im Fenster," *RM* 79 (1972) 5, pl. 6.2.

On Side A a woman sits in right profile on a rocky seat or bench, marked by three black circles with dotted centers, other scattered dots, and straight and wavy lines. She leans forward, chin resting on her upraised right hand. She stares ahead of her and slightly downward. She is barefoot and wears a chiton, the pleated folds of which fall around her ankles. The rest of her body is enveloped by a mantle, the ends of which are wrapped around her neck and shoulders and fall behind her back. Large tufts of wavy hair rise above her hairline and frame her face. Behind her is a closed rectangular door, decorated with bands of dots, circles enclosing dots, and an X. Above the door is an entablature which is extended to one side, forming a porch supported by a pillar. A thin line near the base of the entablature may indicate its underside. Flanking the scene and extending beneath the handles are palmettes and tendrils. Beneath the scene is a reserved line, then a band of rays between glazed bands.

On Side B a maiden runs to her left, her head in left profile. In her outstretched left hand she holds a chest. Her right arm is behind her.

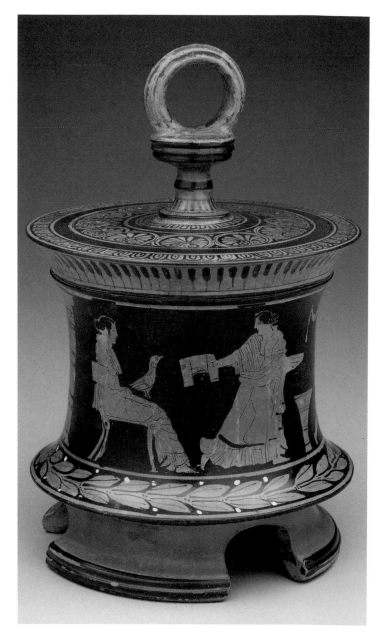

The skyphos exhibits a number of features that date it to the very end of the fifth century. The drawing of the woman is rather sketchy, the wavy, broken lines varying in thickness. The looseness of the style extends even to the hair, which is treated as an amorphous mass, with the fuzzy locks in front of the ear rendered in dilute glaze. Similarly, the eye, mouth, and nostrils are worked in the same relaxed, linear manner. Also looking forward to the fourth century is the emphasis upon the plasticity and voluminous mass of the woman's draped form. This interest will be more fully developed in the generously proportioned clothed women on vases of the Kertch style.

Also representative of the late fifth century is the painter's interest in the setting and in inanimate objects. The ambience of the scene is dependent upon its sense of place, defined by the abbreviated porch and door of the woman's house and by the embellished perch on which she huddles. The vignette has the quality of an observation drawn from real life, and many modern viewers can certainly recall visits to traditional Greek villages where women, enveloped in garments which are usually black, sit quietly in front of the doors of their houses as they watch what seems often to be an absence of activity around them. With a few simple strokes this painter has captured much of the essence of the Greek woman's environment: her home; the door, which calls to mind the doors to the women's quarters of the house; and the garments that conceal, define, and here almost drown the female form (see **Women as Containers**). The seat recalls the episode in the *Homeric Hymn to Demeter*, in which the goddess, overwhelmed by her despair at the loss of her daughter, sits apart from mankind as she broods and withdraws into her misery. The gaze of the woman in this scene, both forward and down, gives the impression that she is partly self-absorbed, partly focused on the world around her. Her demeanor, the arrangement of her garments, and the intimacy of the private setting speak to the Greek perception that a woman's position in a community was at a physical and spiritual distance from the public spaces of the polis.

PYXIS WITH WOMEN

ca. 450
by or near the Aberdeen Painter
Dallas, Dallas Museum of Art, Gift of the Junior League of Dallas, inv. no. 1968.28.A-B

Attic
Clay
H 23.9 cm., W 13.8 cm.

Publications: Hoffmann (1970) 420-26, no. 191, fig. 191a-f; H. Rühfel, *Kinderleben im klassischen Athen: Bilder auf klassischen Vasen, Kulturgeschichte der Antiken Welt* 19 (Mainz am Rhein 1984) 31-32, fig. 16; Keuls (1985a) 109-110, figs. 94, 97.

Broken and mended. Concave sides, with tripodic stand and horizontally fluted base. Lid has fluted ring handle. On the lid is a band of enclosed palmettes between bands of tongue pattern. Above the figural scene on the body is a frieze of stemmed tongues; beneath is a laurel band.

Two closed doors are decorated with four pairs of horizontally dotted bands to suggest studs or rivets. Beside them, seated in right profile, is a woman who wears a chiton beneath a himation that envelops her body. Her hair is drawn up into a bun at the back of her head. A large bird sits on her lap. Moving quickly away from her is a woman who turns her head back in left profile, her hair in a bun at her nape. The toes of her right foot rest on the ground behind her, and the pleated hem of her chiton flares up behind her ankle. Her mantle is wrapped around her waist and legs, with the ends brought forward over her left shoulder. She holds a chest in her extended right hand and steadies a bowl or basket in her left hand. In front of her is a kalathos (wicker wool basket), over which a sash hangs in the background. A nude boy runs in right profile with arms outstretched toward a woman, who stands almost frontally and gazes down at him. Over her chiton she wears a himation that is brought over her left shoulder, covering her arm and most of her body; her right arm encircles the rim of a basket that is pressed against her right thigh. A taenia encircles her head and secures a bunch of hair at the back of her head. The next figure is a woman standing in right profile, a bird perched on the hand of her outstretched right arm. Over her chiton she wears a himation that is brought over her left shoulder and wrapped around her waist and legs; her long hair falls down her shoulders. Running away from this woman is another, whose head is turned back in left profile, her hair blowing out behind her. Her legs are widespread, and the toes of her right foot rest on the ground behind her; the pleated hem of her chiton blows up behind her ankle. Over her chiton she wears a himation that passes over her left shoulder and around her waist and legs. Her left hand holds a chest by her left side, and her right hand grasps folds of drapery beside her right knee.

The pyxis was a vessel associated almost exclusively with women and was used to contain jewelry, cosmetics, and toiletries. The tripod base of this example does not appear on all examples and would seem to be a legacy from a form and perhaps different use inherited from the Archaic period. Also unusual is the fluted ring handle in place of the standard knob.

The double doors identify the scene as taking place in the women's quarters of the house, where women carried out their tasks (represented by the wool basket), spent time with their children (reflected in the presence of the boy), groomed and adorned themselves (to which the hanging sash and chests refer), and enjoyed their leisure hours (to which the bird is an allusion). The two darting women enliven the composition and accentuate the circularity of the figural band; they are probably also intended to suggest that a woman's world had animated as well as idle moments.

The artist's perception, reinforced by the vessel itself, is that the female realm is an environment of enclosures, be they the doors to the women's space or the pyxides, baskets, chests, and kalathoi that harbored women's treasures and their secrets (see **Women as Containers**). We are also in a world where women spend happy and

43 Details of the frieze

intimate moments in the company of other women. So fine an example as this pyxis may well have been a wedding present, in which case the representation would have been created to please a bride. Indeed, a young woman would surely have been delighted both by the scene's assurance of the future camaraderie in her life and by the assumption conveyed by the pyxis itself that she, too, would now have prized possessions to keep safe and private within such an elegant container. As a gift, this pyxis would also function as a subtle advocate for the privacy a woman should value and the discretion she should consistently practice.

205

44

AMPHORA
WITH DOMESTIC SCENE

ca. 460-450
by the Niobid Painter
Baltimore, Walters Art Gallery, inv. no. 48.2712
Formerly, Collection of Raymond Duncan

Attic
Clay
H 45.3 cm., W (at handles) 32 cm.

Publication: E.D. Reeder, "The Niobid Painter in Baltimore," *JWalt* (forthcoming).

Some restoration of neck and lip. Two ledges inside the mouth were probably designed to support a strainer. Above the scene on Side A is a vertical palmette and lotus frieze; above the scene on Side B is a band of slanting addorsed palmettes. Below each scene is a band of two meanders (left) alternating with a cross square. Framing the sides of each scene is a band of net pattern, and there is a tongue pattern at the base of each handle. Graffito under the foot.

In the center of Side A, a woman is seated in right profile on a klismos. She wears a chiton beneath a mantle that is draped around her waist and over most of her legs, with the ends falling over the outside of her right thigh; she has bare feet. The fingers of her left hand are pressed against the strings of a barbiton; her right hand, holding a plectrum, rests against her right thigh. Her head is in right profile and her hair is gathered into a bun at the back of her head beneath a head covering (sakkos) ornamented with bands of dots. Wavy curls frame her face, and she also wears a pendant earring. She gazes up at the woman opposite her. A lyre hangs in the field above her head. In front of the seated woman is a woman who stands almost frontally, her bare feet foreshortened. She wears a peplos with an overfold extending to her waist, and the fingers of each lowered hand grasp a flute. Her hair is gathered at the base of her neck by means of a rectangular clasp, and she wears a diadem, from which three elements rise vertically; she also has a pendant earring. Her head is in left profile, and she gazes over the head of her seated companion to the standing figure at the other side of the scene. This woman stands in right profile and is also barefoot. Over her chiton she wears a mantle that passes over her right shoulder, around her back, and across her waist and legs, with the ends falling over her left elbow. The palm of her left hand, raised to chest-level, steadies a box, the lid of which is being raised by her right hand; the side of the box is decorated with a black rectangle enclosing a reserved rectangle. The woman's hair is gathered into a bun at her nape, and wavy curls frame her face. She wears a diadem, from which four leaves rise vertically, and a round pendant earring. She gazes into the chest.

In the center of Side B, a woman stands turned slightly to her right. She wears a chiton and himation that is brought across her waist and legs, with the ends falling forward over her left shoulder; she is barefoot. Her head is in left profile and her hair is gathered into a bun at the back of her head. She wears a diadem, from which three leaves rise vertically; she also has a pendant earring and a pendant necklace. Her left hand steadies the shaft of a thyrsos, the butt of which rests on the ground; her right hand holds a lighted torch. She gazes at a woman who stands in right profile. This woman wears a peplos, which is belted over an overfold that extends to mid-thigh and which has a black stripe across both the lower hem and that of the overfold. She is also barefoot. Her left hand holds the shaft of a thyrsos, which is almost horizontal; her right arm is bent at the elbow and the hand steadies a phiale in front of her chest. Her head in right profile and her hair is brought up from the nape under a fillet. She gazes toward the other two figures. The last woman stands turned in three-quarter left profile. She wears a chiton and a himation that passes over her left shoulder and arm and is brought across her torso and legs, passing under her right breast; she is also barefoot. In her lowered left hand she holds an ivy branch; her right hand is elevated with the palm facing out, the fingers open. She wears a diadem, from which five rectangular units rise vertically, and her hair is gathered into a bun at the nape. She gazes across to the other women.

This vase is an especially fine illustration of the mastery of harmony and proportion for which the Niobid Painter is particularly admired. Both the height of the figural scenes and the simple compositions consisting of only three figures happily complement the shape and size of the amphora. Similarly, the elegant decorative borders accentuate the contours of the vessel at the same time as they effectively frame the scenes. Characteristic of the Niobid Painter's style are the absence of overlap in the figures and the dignified calm of the poses, which, particularly on Side A, lends the scene an aura of importance. Here the figures have been especially carefully spaced to achieve the optimally harmonious balance of light and dark, and even the lyre hanging in the background is skillfully scaled to the black expanse.

The heavily rounded chins and the voluminous folds of the peplos worn by the flute-bearer indicate a date for the vase just after mid-century. Confirmation is provided by the moderately successful foreshortening of the torsos. The broken wavy lines in the himation of the seated woman on Side A are an attempt to render the flat, raised folds that will be further developed on the Parthenon frieze (442-438 B.C.).

The gathering on Side A must be taking place in the women's quarters of the house. Here, one woman relaxes upon a klismos in the company of her friends and in the proximity of a lyre that hangs ready in the background. Neither the woman with the barbiton nor the woman with the flutes is playing at this moment, but they exchange glances and prepare to collaborate. Their interaction contrasts with the preoccupation of the third woman intent on a lidded box of a type that often appears in wedding scenes as a gift for the bride. Chests such as this one conventionally held jewelry, toilet articles, and book rolls (no. 45), as well as specially prized possessions. The careful way with which the woman disregards her comrades to lift the chest and peer inside the partially raised lid accentuates the privacy of the chest's domain and, by extension, the aura of secrecy that envelops both it and its mistress (see **Women as Containers**). The vertical decorative borders defining the picture reinforce the connotations of enclosure and seclusion inherent to both the chest and the women's quarters of the house.

44 Side A (**See also colorplate, p. 12**)

44 Side B

In Classical vase-painting, the reverse side of a vase is not necessarily related to the subject of the obverse. On this example, however, both the exceptionally careful handling of the scene and the pertinence of the subject argue that Side B was intended as a pendant to the domestic scene on the obverse. The thyrsoi, the torch, the branch, and the phiale tell us that the women are engaged in Maenadic ritual related to the god Dionysos, but their quietly composed manner contrasts markedly with the unbridled behavior familiar in depictions of mythical maenads (see **Maenads**). Historical records inform us that in a number of city-states there existed Maenadic associations of Greek women, who were often wives of the foremost citizens. These women met regularly to carry out specific ceremonies that incorporated elements familiar from descriptions of Dionysiac ritual in myth, including processions to the mountains by torchlight and dancing. Most scholars believe that the activities of these Maenadic associations were highly tamed versions of mythical Maenadic ritual; indeed, we know that by Hellenistic times the associations had the overtones of a kind of women's club that offered members an opportunity to escape temporarily their regulated existences for the pleasure of social interaction with other women. In Athens a group of women were known to carry out Maenadic ritual in association with the Lenaia, a festival to Dionysos, and scenes in Attic vase-painting with this subject have traditionally been linked with that festival. Whether or not the Niobid Painter is here alluding to the Lenaia, it is apparent that he is contrasting this type of female gathering with the one depicted on Side A. The juxtaposition is an eloquent reminder to us that outside the home women did not participate in the public life of the polis, nor venture into the public spaces of the city, where men's gatherings were of a political character. On the contrary, women's space was either in the interior of the home or in a ritual space apart from the heart of the polis, either literally beyond the city limits in the untamed wild or in a sanctuary evocative of the world of nature (see **Women as Animals**).

HYDRIA WITH DOMESTIC SCENE

ca. 460
by the Niobid Painter
New York, The Solow Art and Architecture Foundation

Attic
Clay
H 28.8 cm., W (at handles) 28.6 cm.

Publications: C. Bérard, "The Order of Women," in Bérard et al. (1989) 90-91, fig. 124; E.D. Reeder, "The Niobid Painter in Baltimore," *JWalt* (forthcoming).

Intact. Tongue pattern around the mouth and the bases of the handles. Above the scene is frieze of circumscribed palmettes with lotus between; beneath is a frieze of two meanders (right) alternating with a cross-square.

In the center of the scene, a woman is seated frontally on a klismos that rests upon a two-stepped platform, across the top of which is a dotted band. The fingers of her left hand finger the strings of a barbiton, which rests against her left hip; her right arm is brought over her upper torso, and the first two fingers of her right hand support the instrument's bridge. Her face is in left profile, and she gazes over to a woman standing to her right. Wavy curls frame her face, and the long ends are gathered into a bun at the nape; a taenia is wrapped three times around her head. Over her chiton she wears a mantle drawn across her waist and legs; the ends are brought over the bun at the back of her head and fall down over her left shoulder. Resting on the platform to her right is a chest, the short end of which is decorated with the outline of a rectangle which encloses two dots and a smaller rectangle. The hinged side of the chest is next to the seated woman, and the lid is raised.

Standing next to the chest is a woman who is seen almost frontally, her head in right profile. She wears a peplos belted over the overfold and a sakkos, which is ornamented with a band of beading. Both hands hold the rolled ends of a book roll, and she gazes at the seated woman. Behind her are an abbreviated threshold, entablature, and door jamb, as well as a partly opened door that is ornamented above, below, and across its midpoint with a black band enclosing two reserved semicircles with dark circular interiors.

On the other side of the seated woman, another woman stands almost frontally, her head in left profile. She wears a peplos that has an unbelted overfold and is open down the right side. A black stripe decorates all the fabric's edges, and the pins securing the garment are clearly visible on each shoulder. Her left hand steadies a chest against her shoulder; its side is decorated with a rectangle enclosing a smaller, solid black rectangle. Her right hand clasps the edge of a lyre at her side. She wears a fillet from which an ornament rises vertically above her brow. The hair at her brow is wrapped over the fillet, and her long locks fall down onto her shoulders. She gazes at her two companions. The feet of all the figures are frontal and unshod. Hanging in the field above the head of the seated woman is another lyre, and hanging in the field outside the door is a phormiskos in a bag.

45

The doorjamb and door signify that we are in the women's quarters of a house. The affluence of the household is announced by the profusion of musical instruments and the presence of the book roll. The platform beneath the woman's chair enables the painter to fill the picture field without adding a fourth figure; perhaps he borrowed the motif from theatrical representations.[1]

The scene tells us a certain amount about women's domestic life. The figures attending the seated woman must be her friends, because the diadem worn by the woman holding the chest would not belong to a servant. Nor is it likely that the painter would depict a serving girl, even holding a book roll, as the focus of the attention of the mistress and her companion. In keeping with the sophistication implicit in the book roll is the open door, which suggests that these women are secluded in the women's quarters only by choice. An easy coming and going is further suggested by the woman with the chest and lyre, who appears to be bringing the objects over to her friends. In this atmosphere of intimate camaraderie, the seated woman's mantle has slipped to the back of her head. Although the use of the veil is not yet well understood, it appears that outside the house a respectable woman might drape either her mantle or a separate veil more completely over her head in an expression of modesty (see **Women and Men** and *Aidos* and *Sophrosyne*).

The assemblage of musical instruments implies that the friends have gathered to make music together, and the unwinding of the book roll is clearly connected with this activity. Depictions of a woman with a book roll are not uncommon in Classical vase-painting and are most often encountered in scenes where several women are gathered together.[2] A chest is usually also present, obviously indicating where the book roll is normally stored for safekeeping. In many scenes a book roll is paired with a lyre, and the combination suggests that the texts contain poetry, although some book rolls probably also included musical notation. The frequency with which women and book rolls are depicted in Classical vase-painting tells us that many wives of Athenian citizens could read; however, the consistent and exclusive association of the book roll with portrayals of an affluent lifestyle suggests that literacy was not widespread in the general population.

45 Detail

The scene is testimony to the degree to which the Niobid Painter associated women with chests and doors, imagery whose connotations of enclosure, intimacy, and treasure are particularly evoked in this composition (see **Women as Containers**). It is also interesting to consider that the Niobid Painter assumed that women also accepted and were pleased by these associations, because, as a water vessel, the hydria was particularly linked with women, and superb examples such as this one are often assumed to have been wedding gifts. Certainly, a bride would have been delighted to have been identified with musical skills, literacy, prized possessions, and the leisure of a prosperous household.

A date for the vase shortly before mid-century is indicated by the softening of the seated woman's jaw, which looks forward to vase-painting contemporary with the Parthenon. Supporting that date are the broad, even heavy, folds of the unbelted peplos worn by the woman holding the chest. The fabric's columnar stateliness is also in keeping with the Early Classical style. Foreshortening is both problematic and tantalizing; the open door and the frontal feet are adequately rendered, but the seated woman's left arm is not shown,

and the rendering of her knees and of the front of her legs under her mantle is somewhat awkward.

The similarity of this scene to that on the amphora in Baltimore (no. 44) clearly reveals the Niobid Painter's penchant for simple compositions with a few quiet figures and a balance between light and dark achieved through a skillful distribution of figures and objects. That the Niobid Painter could also respond superbly to the challenge of active and complicated subject matter is demonstrated by the volute krater in Naples (no. 121), but there, too, we encounter the same skilled draftsmanship, majestic profiles, and the linkage of figures by means of a meaningful exchange of glances.

1. In her forthcoming publication of this vase, A. Kauffmann-Samaras relates the platform to scenes of competition and compares the composition to representations of Apollo and the two Muses. I thank her for these comments.
2. H.R. Immerwahr, "Book Rolls on Attic Vases", *Classical, Mediaeval, and Renaissance Studies in Honor of Berthold Louis Ullman*, Charles Henderson, Jr., ed. (Rome 1964) 17-48; H.R. Immerwahr, "More Book Rolls on Attic Vases," *AntK* 16 (1973) 143-47.

LEKYTHOS WITH WOMAN, CLOTH, AND WOOL BASKET

ca. 470
by the Pan Painter
Cambridge, Harvard University Art Museums, Arthur M. Sackler
Museum, Gift of Schimmel Foundation, inv. no. 1991.28

Attic
Clay
H 37.1 cm., Diam (at shoulder) 13.04 cm., Diam (at mouth) 6.9 cm.

Publications: *Ancient Art. The Norbert Schimmel Collection* (Mainz 1974) no. 62 (D. von Bothmer).

The ornament on the shoulder and neck are in red-figure: a band of dotted egg above three red-figure palmettes, the central one pointed down, with tendrils and lotus. Above the figural scene is a band of two meanders (broken), stopt, alternating with a saltire square. Red for woman's mantle.

A woman stands upon a narrow black groundline. Her left foot is in left profile; her right toes are frontal; her breasts and head are in left profile. Over her chiton she wears a red mantle that is brought around her waist and over most of her legs, with the ends draped over her left shoulder, upper arm, and elbow. Her left hand holds the end of an empty rectangular pillow cover; at one of its lower corners, the threads are gathered in a tassel. Hanging from the pillow are the ends of the two strings that are threaded through the sides of the short end and will be pulled tightly to seal the pillow. Each end of the pillow bears a broad stripe flanked on each side by a narrow line. Beneath the pillow is a footstool, the cushion on which is decorated with crosses. In the woman's right hand she holds wool, which she is about to stuff into the pillow. Her head is in left profile, and her wavy hair is brought up from the nape of her neck, with the ends passing under a taenia that is wrapped around her head. Her gaze is directed down, toward a wicker wool basket (kalathos), filled with more circular skeins of yarn, that is just behind her right leg. The inscription in the field reads: ΗΕ ΠΑΙΣ [Κ]ΑΛΕ.

The inscription tells us that the woman is a hetaira (prostitute), and her ample breasts, and the clarity with which they are delineated, support the identification. We know from a number of vase-paintings that spinning and weaving were skills which hetairai were expected to master and in which they were instructed as part of their professional training (no. 50), although it is unclear whether the objective of such instruction was so that the women could pass idle time constructively, earn outside income, or enhance their appeal to potential clients by appearing industrious and domestic. It is clear that this particular hetaira does not have the patience for such time-consuming work, because she does not spin the wool but rather stuffs it as filler for a pillow of a type used at a symposium, to which the festive ribbon wrapping her hair is also appropriate. The painter has created this scene with a light spirit, for he implies that, whereas a respectable woman would

46

211

undertake ambitious weaving projects in order to clothe her family, this hetaira is content with simple pillows and the prospect of the festivities that lie ahead.

Women are a favorite subject of the Pan Painter, who has also given us the tender rendering of Artemis in nos. 89 and 90. His skilled draftsmanship and mastery of fluid line lend his figures a rhythm that echoes the movement and elegance of his decorative borders. As with his lekythos with Artemis in St. Petersburg (no. 90), the Pan Painter offers a bemused, thoughtful commentary on what seems initially to be a quiet moment. The subtlety of the lekythos shape is especially compatible with his manner.

OINOCHOE IN THE FORM OF A WOMAN'S HEAD

ca. 500-490
signed by Charinos
St. Petersburg, The State Hermitage Museum, inv. no. Б 2103

Attic, "from Vulci"
Clay
H 27.7 cm.

Publications: *ARV*² 1531.4; E. Reisch, "Vasen in Corneto," *RM* 5 (1890) 314; E. Buschor, "Das Krokodil des Sotades," *Münchener Jahrbuch der bildenden Kunst* 11 (1919) 12; J.C. Hoppin, *A Handbook of Greek Black-Figured Vases* (Paris 1924) 70-71; J.D. Beazley, "Charinos: Attic Vases in the Form of Human Heads," *JHS* 49 (1929) 44-45, no. 4; O. Persianova, *The Hermitage. Room-to-Room Guide* (Leningrad 1972) 71 (illus.); X. Gorbunova and I. Saverkina, *Greek and Roman Antiquities in the Hermitage* (Leningrad 1975) no. 27; J.R. Guy, "A Ram's Head Rhyton Signed by Charinos," *Arts in Virginia* 21.2 (1981) 2; *LIMC* II (1984) 109, no. 1080 (s.v. Aphrodite).

Inscription incised on handle in two lines : ΧΑΡΙΝΟΣ ΕΠΟΙΕΣΕ.

47 (See also colorplate, p. 6)

48

OINOCHOE IN THE FORM OF A WOMAN'S HEAD

ca. 500-490
signed by Charinos
Berlin, Antikensammlung, Staatliche Museen zu Berlin Preussischer Kulturbesitz, inv. no. F 2190

Attic, from Vulci
Clay
H 27 cm.

Publications: *ARV²* 1531.3; *Para* 502; *Add²* 385; A. Furtwängler, *Königliche Museen zu Berlin. Beschreibung der Vasensammlung im Antiquarium* II (Berlin 1885) 511-12; E. Reisch, "Vasen in Corneto," *RM* 5 (1890) 316-17; E. Buschor, "Das Krokodil des Sotades," *Münchener Jahrbuch der bildenden Kunst* 11 (1919) 12; J.C. Hoppin, *A Handbook of Greek Black-Figured Vases* (Paris 1924) 64-65; J.D. Beazley, "Charinos: Attic Vases in the Form of Human Heads," *JHS* 49 (1929) 43-45, no. 3, fig. 2; G.M.A. Richter, *Archaic Greek Art (New York 1949)* 137, fig. 218; A. Greifenhagen, *Antike Kunstwerke*, 2nd ed. (Berlin 1965) 22, 48-49, pls. 52-53; K. Schefold, *Die Griechen und ihre Nachbarn, Propyläen Kunstgeschichte* 1 (Berlin 1967) 93, 173, pl. IIa-b; Staatliche Museen Preussischer Kulturbesitz Berlin, *Führer durch die Antikenabteilung* (Berlin 1968) 123; J.R. Guy, "A Ram's Head Rhyton Signed by Charinos," *Arts in Virginia* 21.2 (1981) 2; Mussche (1982) 182, no. 107; *LIMC* II (1984) 109 no. 1080, pl. 109 (s.v. Aphrodite); W.-H. Schuchhardt, et al., *Neue Belser Stilgeschichte 2: Griechische und römische Antike* (Stuttgart and Zurich 1987) 22, fig. 15; Staatliche Museen Preussischer Kulturbesitz, *Antikenmuseum Berlin: Die ausgestellten Werke* (Berlin 1988) 112-13, no. 5.

Inscription incised on handle in a single line that extends over the top of the handle and halfway to the handle root: ΧΑΡΙΝΟΣΕΠΟΙΣΕΝ.

Both vases have been reassembled. Each vase has the handle, mouth, neck, and shoulder of an oinochoe resting atop the head and neck of a woman. The shoulder of the St. Petersburg example bears a band of horizontal palmette (running right) that are enclosed by tendrils, with a vertical petal separating every second palmette. On the Berlin vase, the palmettes move in the opposite direction, but, as in the St. Petersburg example, the vertical petal over the maiden's forehead is placed off-center.

Each of the faces is framed by four or five rows of tiny shell curls that were painted red; those on the topmost layer are the terminations of long, thin locks rendered as ribbing, which was certainly worked by hand after the piece emerged from the mold. Behind the hair on the Berlin head there is a band of meander; on the St. Petersburg example, the meander is replaced by a band of meander with saltire square. Across the back of the head between the ears the decorative scheme is reversed.

On both vases most of the back of the head is covered with a hair covering that takes the form of a series of diamonds or lozenges formed by the intersections of diagonal black stripes; a smaller reserved diamond is placed in each intersection. Within each diamond or lozenge are four alternately reserved and glazed smaller diamonds. On the St. Petersburg vase, the ends of the locks across the nape are wrapped in a netting, rendered as parallel lines intersecting diagonally. On the Berlin vase, this band of netting does not envelop the hair ends but passes over the lozenge head covering farther up onto the back of the head. The final decorative detail on both heads is a pair of knobs that sit beneath the base of the handle atop the bands of meander with saltire square. Each knob is decorated with narrow radiating lines; on the Berlin example, the two knobs are connected by three looping black lines resembling chains.

48

The faces are distinguished by high arching eyebrows, rendered as glazed lines, the curvature of which continues down the sides of the nose. The almond-shaped eyes, which are protruding and slanted, are outlined in black glaze. On the St. Petersburg vase, the iris is rendered by a black line enclosing a sphere in dilute glaze, with the pupil a glazed dot. On the Berlin vase, a narrow reserved band separates the raised, glazed pupil from the iris, whose interior retains traces of red. In each case, the eyes gaze downward. Also on each vase, the lips are slightly smiling and were accented in red. The base of the neck is encircled by a black band.

Both vases were discovered in the same tomb in Vulci and are here reunited for the first time. They are remarkably similar, and Charinos gave equal attention to each. In addition to the variations in decorative patterns, the St. Petersburg example is slightly larger, and on the Berlin example the pupils are in relief, the knobs on the back of the head are linked by chains, and the inscription rather elegantly and adventurously extends down the handle.

The ornate head coverings on each example suggest a combination of embroidered fabric, netting, and hair ornaments; the discs, which are linked by chains on the Berlin vase, have a counterpart in the bridal brooches that characterized traditional Greek jewelry used into modern times. On both vases the faces are animated and charming. The Archaic smile, almost completely relaxed, and the elevated outside corners of the eyes create an expression of innocent enthusiasm, tempered by the downcast gaze expressive of *aidos*, the sense of modesty and shame becoming in a young maiden (see **Aidos** and **Sophrosyne**). The heads are rendered with such a masterly sense of sculpture that they compare well with the series of korai from the Acropolis. Stylistic comparison, especially of the incipient self-awareness in the expressions, points to a date in the beginning of the fifth century.

Throughout the Archaic and Classical periods, Attic potters created head vases that were almost exclusively in the forms of women, Satyrs, and Africans. Beazley noted that Charinos himself potted two examples with the head of a woman on one side and the head of an African on the other. The pairing suggests that Charinos was implying an equation between women and Africans, both in terms of social status, because each group did not have the legal rights of Athenian male citizens, and in terms of morality, because both women and Africans were viewed as lacking the self-control and self-mastery that characterized the Athenian citizen. Schuchhardt suggests that the women depicted in the head vases are prostitutes, both because of the finery of their head covering and because the vases were almost certainly destined for symposium use where prostitutes were present. However, the *aidos* of the downcast gazes, appropriate to a respectable young woman rather than a prostitute, suggests that we should rather adopt a more generic identification. Because of the proliferation of female head vases among the figurine vases of the late fifth and fourth centuries,[1] Delivorrias suggested that the woman Charinos depicts is Aphrodite, but this identification is also unlikely in light both of the outsider status of head vase subjects and Charinos' predisposition for correlating females with Africans.

The oinochoe is a vessel shape particularly well suited to a head vase, because the oinochoe's shoulder can sit atop the human head in the manner of a hat. Moreover, the curving contours of the oinochoe's body are so similar to the shape of a human head that the outlines of the vessel do not entirely vanish in the transformation to the form of a human head. One should note that in these examples the human head takes precedence over the oinochoe shape, which must adapt to it, and in this feature the Charinos vases contrast markedly with the earlier Archaic head vases in the form of kantharoi. The latter type required that the human head undergo drastic distortion in order to conform to the contours of the kantharos, which itself suffered little alteration. By the end of the Archaic period such distortion was no longer acceptable, nor, apparently, was the practice of drinking out of a human head, in the manner of animal-headed rhytons and mastoi (drinking cups made in the shape of a woman's breast). The shape of the oinochoe, which was a jug for wine, was an ideal solution, and the popularity of the oinochoe form for head vases led to the figurine vases of the late fifth century where, indeed, the entire series adopts the form of an oinochoe. The oinochoe shape was particularly appropriate to a female head vase, because, in leave-taking ritual, women traditionally poured wine from an oinochoe into the phiale of the departing warrior (nos. 18, 20).

Although these two head vases were found in a tomb, their original destination was certainly for the (all-male) symposium. One can well imagine how much these vases would have been admired as a welcome decorative variant to the customary array of kraters, amphorae, and kylikes among which they would have been displayed. In considering the significance of the context and use of these head vases, one should remember that, at the time when Charinos created these two, head vases in Athens were not being made of Greek men, but only of women, Satyrs, and Africans, all marginal members of society. Indeed, these two elegant examples by Charinos constitute concrete embodiments of the traditional metaphor that likened women to hollow containers created by men from clay (see **Pandora** and **Women as Containers**). The vases thus offer not only evidence for the objectification of elaborately draped and adorned women, but also insight into the degradation that accompanies comparison to an inanimate object without a power of its own (see **Textiles**). In the easy camaraderie of a drinking party one can well imagine how enthusiastically these vases might have passed from hand to hand, amid ribald remarks that they were to be used, upended, and filled.

1. M. Trumpf-Lyritzaki, *Griechische Figurenvasen* (Bonn 1969) 60-65, pls. 23-25.

49

BRONZE SPINDLE

5th century?
Copenhagen, National Museum of Denmark, inv. no. 4955

South Italian, "from Cumae?"
Bronze
H 26.8 cm., Diam 4.5 cm.

Unpublished.

A slender dowel thickens a quarter of its length from a perforated tip above a flat disc. At the opposite end of the dowel there are two more discs: a smaller one set slightly in from the tip and a much larger one a fourth the distance down the shaft.

The spindle was a tool essential to the spinning of wool. The unspun wool fiber was bound to a long stick or board, known as a distaff, which was held in the raised left hand (if the spinner was right-handed). The spinner's right hand fed the fiber into a twist that was created as the spindle, to which the end of the new fiber was attached, rotated like a top. As the spun yarn lengthened, the spindle eventually reached the ground, at which point the spinner had to stop and wind the new yarn onto the spindle. An experienced spinner did not need to interrupt the spinning process but could manipulate the spindle like a yo-yo to take up the finished yarn around the spindle. The disc, or spindle whorl, near the lower tip of the spindle functioned to reduce any wobbling and to prolong the spin.

Spinning yarn was far more time-consuming than weaving it; it is estimated that seven-tenths of the time required to make a garment would have been spent in spinning the wool (see **Textiles**). Because spinning could be carried out almost anywhere and was easily interrupted, it was particularly well suited to women tending young children, and hence became the quintessentially female task from earliest times. Not surprisingly, its omnipresence as a chore gave rise to such mythical motifs as the threads spun by the (female) Fates. A Greek girl would learn to spin at an early age and would spend much of her adult years spinning and weaving. Elizabeth Barber suggests that most ancient spindles were wood, with the spindle whorls of clay.[1] Gold, silver, and bronze examples have, however, been recovered from contexts as early as the Early Bronze Age, and in the *Odyssey* the spindle Helen uses is made of gold.[2] If the Copenhagen example were not for actual use, it would have been intended as a votive offering.

1. Barber (1994) 37.
2. Homer, *Odyssey* 4.125-26, 130-32; see Barber (1994) 209.

50

HYDRIA
WITH WOMEN AND SPINDLE

440-430
by the Washing Painter
Copenhagen, National Museum of Denmark, inv. no. CHR.VIII.520

Attic, "from Nola"
Clay
H 18.7 cm., W (at handles) 18.2 cm., Diam 14.7 cm.

Publications: *ARV*² 1131.161 and 1684; *Add*² 333; *CVA* Copenhagen, Musée National 4 (Denmark 4) pl. 154.2, 155.1; B. Schröder, "Die Polygnotische Malerei und die Parthenongiebel," *JdI* (1915) 116, pl. 3; E. Suhr, *Venus de Milo: The Spinner* (New York 1958) 47 (illus.); C. Isler-Kerenyi, "Chronologie und 'Synchronologie' attischer Vasenmaler der Parthenon-Zeit," *Zur griechischen Kunst: Hansjörg Bloesch zum sechzigsten Geburtstag am 5. Juli 1972, AntK Beiheft* 9 (Bern 1973) 29; Sutton (1981) 356; Williams (1983) 96, fig. 7.4; Boardman (1989) 97, fig. 209; Reinsberg (1989) 123-24, fig. 67; Beard (1991) 30; Sabetai (1993) vol. 1, 195; vol. 2, 34, no. H13, pl. 8.

Reassembled from a number of pieces. Tongue pattern around the lip. Above the scene is a band of Lesbian cymation; beneath the scene is a frieze of three meanders (left) alternating with a checker square. Red for the thread.

A woman is seated in three-quarter left profile on a klismos, the cushion of which is cross-hatched. Her left forearm rests along the back of the klismos, with the fingers of the hand relaxed. Her right forearm is upraised and the fingers are curled, with the palm facing her. She wears a belted chiton and a himation that is draped over her legs; a black stripe borders the hem. Her feet are bare and her left foot is stretched forward, the heel resting on the ground. Her head is in left profile and her hair is drawn back from her face and secured by a hair covering that passes around her head. She gazes ahead of her in the direction of her right hand and of a nude woman who stands in right profile, her left leg relaxed with the toes resting on the ground behind her. She is spinning thread and her raised left hand grasps a stick around which wool is bunched, while the fingers of her right hand draw the yarn that hangs vertically and winds around a spindle that is suspended just above the ground. The woman wears a band, with amulet, around her thigh, and a taenia is wrapped twice around her hair. Behind her is a klismos, upon the seat of which a garment is lying. Hanging in the field above the seated woman is a sash.

Spinning and weaving were the two most important household tasks that a Greek woman performed, and her skill and industriousness in these areas were barometers of her worth as a wife (see **Textiles**). The sash hanging in the background, the klismos, and the casual relaxation of the seated woman are appropriate to the women's quarters of a house, where such activity would take place. The nudity of the spinner, however, suggests that we are not in a conventional home.

In Classical vase-painting a respectable woman is always clothed, even when shown in the company of other women in the women's quarters of the house (nos. 42-46). Hetairai, by contrast, are usually nude only when in the company, and embraces, of male customers in symposium scenes (nos. 39, 40). While not entertaining their clients, hetairai are fully dressed, for example when negotiating the financial aspects of their services (nos. 36-38) and even when receiving gifts from customers who have just entered a brothel.

Spinning is, however, an activity that takes place within a brothel, and both Dyfri Williams and C. Reinsberg have commented upon vase scenes in which either the madam or an unoccupied hetaira busies herself with spindle and wool. It would appear that a prostitute's attraction to customers was considered to be enhanced by her mastery of the skills desirable in a wife. Accordingly, the scene on the Copenhagen hydria must show us the training in spinning that would be given a prospective hetaira, whose familiarity with domestic skills does not yet equal her comfort with nudity. The seated woman, who must be the madam of the brothel, is obvi-

ously unperturbed by her comrade's appearance. Indeed, she seems to have stipulated the nudity, because the garment resting on the seat of the klismos implies that the young woman was wearing clothes until the beginning of her lesson. The relaxed self-confidence of the madam is communicated through both her extended leg and the position of her forearm along the back of the klismos. This gesture of assured ease first appeared with the figure of Zeus on the east frieze of the Parthenon (p. 249, fig. 2) and was rapidly adopted by Classical vase-painters for representations of women at leisure (see **Gesture and Gaze**). The curled fingers of the madam's right hand suggest that she is beckoning or instructing her young associate, who is clearly responding to her employer's direction.

The young hetaira wears the thigh ornament known as the *periamma*. While popular with hetairai, *periammata* were worn by respectable Athenian women as well. Robert Sutton notes that a bride can be depicted with a thigh ornament,[1] and in his *Thesmophoriazousai* Aristophanes mentions *periammata* in a context that refers to Athenian women in general.[2] Only the woman's nudity, therefore, changes this scene from one that could as easily be a domestic vignette within the women's quarters of a house. Indeed, the hydria was a vessel shape particularly associated with women, and we cannot assume that this example was targeted only for purchase by a hetaira or a customer in search of an appropriate gift for a prostitute. A respectable Athenian woman might reason that if a male Athenian citizen found a prostitute's attraction heightened by her industriousness as a spinner, then these domestic skills must have an underlying sexual appeal. A scene such as this one could actually be interpreted as confirmation that a wife's mastery of spinning intensified her sexual desirability to her husband.

The Washing Painter is especially fond of depicting women, and he is best known for his loutrophoroi and lebetes gamikoi, those distinctively female vases that were presented to the bride as wedding gifts (nos. 55-59). Nudity does not figure in those wedding scenes, unsurprisingly, and the Washing Painter's lack of experience in depicting a nude female is quite apparent here. As is typical of the representations of nude female torsos in Classical vase-painting, the body resembles that of a man, complete with the curving musculature of shoulders and back, the delineation of the muscled abdominal area, and developed thighs. The softening and slenderizing of the female body will not be accomplished until well into the Hellenistic period.

1. Sutton (1981) 101.
2. Aristophanes, *Thesmophoriazousai* 256.

HYDRIA WITH MOTHER, CHILD, AND NURSEMAID

ca. 440-430
attributed to the circle of Polygnotos
Cambridge, Harvard University Art Museums, Arthur M. Sackler
Museum, Bequest of David M. Robinson, inv. no. 1960.342

Attic, "from Vari"
Clay
H 34.6 cm., Diam 24.6 cm.

Publications: *CVA* Baltimore, Robinson Collection 2 (U.S.A. 6) 31-32, pl. 43.1; Dohrn (1957) 93, 116, pl. 16b; F. Frost, *Greek Society* (Lexington, Mass. 1971) 82; Sutton (1981) 221, 259, no. F5, pl. 18; Williams (1983) 93-94, fig. 7.2; Keuls (1985a) 73-74, fig. 58.

Around the rim is a band of egg pattern. The figural scene has a border of laurel leaf and berry above; below is a frieze of three meanders (left) alternating with a dotted saltire square.

A woman is seated on a klismos in left profile, her bare feet on a raised plinth, which is probably a footstool. Over her chiton she wears a mantle that is wrapped around her waist and most of her legs. With both hands she steadies the buttocks and legs of a nude baby boy who is seen in left profile, a cord with a bulla (amulet) passing under his left arm. He kneels on the woman's right thigh as he stretches both arms forward toward a standing woman in front of him. The seated woman's head is in left profile and her hair is wrapped in a head covering with zigzag ornament from which curly locks escape in front of her ear. She gazes into the eyes of the standing woman, who leans forward with both arms extended. Her left hand clasps the torso of the boy under his right arm; the fingers of her right hand are extended. Over a finely pleated garment, she wears a belted long-sleeved tunic, whose neckline, sleeve edges, and lower hem are edged by a black band supporting a series of short perpendicular bands; she is barefoot. Her long hair is drawn back over her ears, and the wavy locks are gathered at the nape. Behind her is a loom with newly woven cloth, each side of which has a woven border similar to that on the maidser-

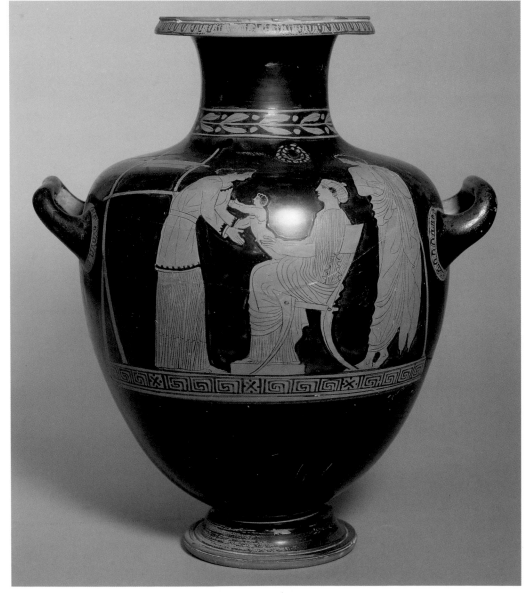

51

vant's dress. Behind the seated woman is a man who wears a mantle draped over his left shoulder and around his waist and legs. His left hand rests upon a staff, and the fingers of his right hand are slipped inside his mantle at his waist. His upper torso is frontal, but his legs are in profile, the toes of the right foot on the ground behind him. He has short curly hair and the beginnings of a beard, and he looks over toward the maidservant and child. Hanging in the field is a wreath.

The loom tells us that the scene takes place in the interior of the house, probably in the women's quarters. The mistress, identified as such by her seated posture, hands her son over to the nursemaid, whose tunic bears a border so close to that on the woven cloth wound on the loom as to suggest that the maidservant spends much of her time weaving under her mistress's supervision. The serving girl's leaning pose contrasts with the relaxed and self-assured posture of the boy's mother, who is now finished playing with her son, or possibly nursing him. The boy's eagerness for the arms of his nurse is quite natural, because she probably gave him most of his daily care, and the motif is surely ultimately inspired by depictions of the child Erichthonios being handed from the arms of his mother Gaia to the goddess Athena (see **Erichthonios**). Given the prototype of the image, it is interesting to note that in Classical sculpture (no. 6) and vase-painting (no. 13) it was conventional for the child to reach out its arms to its mother from the embrace of its nurse, probably because this affirmation of filial love was certainly more pleasing to the affluent parent who purchased the vase or sculpture. The scene's emphasis upon the nursemaid's importance to the child is further accentuated by the mother's and maid's exchange of glances, which ignores the complicated maneuver of the handing over of the boy to underscore the mutual bond between the two women in their affection for the child. The placement of the scene on a hydria, a water vessel distinctively associated with women, is further argument that the scene was painted with the intent of pleasing the vase's female owner, possibly as a wedding gift.

The female environment and the walking stick tell us that the man is the guest, or intruder, in this setting. His almost complete beardlessness implies that he is the youthful bridegroom and new father; thus the wreath hanging in the background may allude to the couple's recent wedding. Although husbands were about thirty years old at the time of marriage, wedding scenes consistently present the bridegroom as beardless, probably to stress the man's newness to marriage and to minimize the difference in age between the bridegroom and his fourteen-year-old bride. The pose and gesture of the husband are somewhat awkward. Whether through limited competence or indecision, the painter has suggested by the man's raised right heel that he is approaching the women; by contrast, his frontal torso and relaxed right hand indicate that he stands patiently as a contented onlooker. Although the man is obviously not totally comfortable in this setting, where he is clearly subordinate to the main action, his presence is a pointed reminder to the viewer

that a husband was envisioned as an essential component to the female domestic harmony evoked by male child, loom, and industrious, loving servant.

HYDRIA WITH FUNERARY SCENE

460-450
attributed to a pupil of the Niobid Painter
Cambridge, Harvard University Art Museums, Arthur M. Sackler Museum, Bequest of David M. Robinson, inv. no. 1960.341

Attic, "from Vari"
Clay
H 39.5 cm., Diam 30.6 cm.

Publications: *ARV²* 617.13; *CVA* Baltimore, Robinson Collection 2 (U.S.A. 6) pl. 35; D. Robinson, "Illustrations of Aeschylus' *Choephoroi* and of a Satyr-Play on Hydrias by the Niobid Painter," *AJA* 36 (1932) 401-405, pls. 14-15; *The David Moore Robinson Bequest of Classical Art and Antiquities* (Cambridge, Fogg Art Museum, May 1-September 20, 1961) 17, no. 100.

Restored is the chiton around the lower legs of the woman at the far proper left. Around the lip and below the scene is a band of egg pattern. Above the figural scene is a band of lotus and palmette. The handle attachments are surrounded by a tongue pattern. Added white for the branches.

In the center of the scene, a woman stands in right profile. With both hands she holds a large wicker basket, the side of which is rendered as three horizontal bands of zigzag. Rising over the rim are the tops of eight lekythoi, as well as several branches. Sashes hang over the side. Over her chiton she wears a mantle that is draped over her left shoulder and upper arm, enveloping her waist and most of her legs. Her hair is drawn back from her face to her nape. In front of her, a hydria rests on the ground. On the other side of it, a woman stands frontally, her head in left profile and her short hair brushed down toward her face and over her ear. She raises her right arm, fingers extended, in a gesticulation to her companion; her left hand is raised to her hair below her ear. She wears a chiton and a mantle that is draped over both shoulders. The third woman in the scene stands frontally, her head in right profile as she gazes over at her companions. She wears a chiton and a mantle that passes over her left shoulder and falls over her torso and much of her left leg. Her left hand, fingers extended and separated, is brought to her chest; her right hand is raised to the back of her hair, which is brushed down to fringe her forehead and cover her ear.

Three women gather to honor the dead, the remains of whom are apparently contained in the large hydria that is the focus of their attention. The use of a vessel as a burial container is well attested for the Classical period, and remains of children placed in clay vessels have been found in the Kerameikos (see **Women as Con-**

52

tainers). That a hydria was also used for this purpose is confirmed by Lucian, who tells us that the remains of Demosthenes were placed inside a hydria.[1] The association of the hydria with the dead and particularly with women goes back to the Mycenaean period when a hydria, together with a drinking cup, was placed in the grave, obviously with the intention that the deceased should not be thirsty.[2] E. Diehl assumes that these hydriae were filled with water before they were buried, and also notes that the hydriae were particularly, possibly exclusively, placed in women's graves. By Classical times the hydria was also used to hold the water with which women washed the dead. Because it was a woman's responsibility to obtain the water needed for her household, the hydria was associated with her in everyday use as well, and hydriae were surely also presented to the bride as a wedding gift (see **The Wedding** and no. 116). The Cambridge example was found in a tomb as a funerary offering,

and, given the age-old associations of women with hydriae, it is likely that the grave belonged to a woman.

The scene on this vase is an informative glimpse onto the world of women's role in funerary ritual. The woman in the center holds the funerary basket, which in vase-paintings is carried almost exclusively by women. The branches inside the basket are surely myrtle and will be placed around the tomb.[3] Also intended as an offering are the lekythoi, which hold olive oil that will first be poured on the ground in libation. The sashes were conventionally wrapped around the funerary stele and were probably also tied around the neck of burial vessels. The short straight locks of hair on the two flanking women were a tradition of female mourning, as were their gestures of rending their hair in lament.

Preparing the body for burial and tending the tomb were two of the most important responsibilities that women carried. Their liminal status in Greek society had various manifestations, but none more graphic than their close associations with the entry into and departure from life. Just as women brought new life to birth or, as midwives, assisted with that passage, so did women also ease the transition from life to death and maintain ties with departed family members. Women figured strongly in the funeral itself, washing the body and mourning the deceased, probably in a kind of structured lament not unrelated to the sophisticated antiphony that has been observed in Greek village funerary ritual of modern times.[4] It is interesting to reflect that the funerary ritual encouraged through institutionalization an emotionality in women that was generally considered to be one of their fundamental weaknesses. In the Archaic period, female mourners gradually became so desirable and prolific that the lawgiver Solon sought to control the excessive costs of private funerals by restricting the number of female mourners that a wealthy family could enlist or employ.[5] Once the funeral was over, it was the duty of women to visit the tomb regularly, and this task was probably an enjoyable activity shared with other family members and female friends.

The large, distinctive basket for grave offerings was made of wicker and appears to have been oval in shape. Although by the Classical period, basket weaving seems to have become a commercial, and surely male, occupation,[6] in early times basketry was probably a female activity, because the techniques are closely related to weaving, which was always a female preserve (see **Textiles**). The basket's near exclusivity to women in funerary ritual suggests an ancient origin for the association, and perhaps also a relationship with the *kanoun*, another woven basket exclusively identified with virgins in religious processions (see no. 60 and **Women as Containers**).

1. Lucian, *Demosth. Enkom.* 29. See E. Diehl, *Die Hydria. Formengeschichte und Verwendung im Kult* (Mainz 1964) 147.

2. Diehl (1964).

3. Euripides, *Elektra* 324, 512.

4. Seremetakis (1993d) 119-49.

5. Plutarch, *Solon* 12.5, 21.4-5.

6. D.A. Amyx, "The Attic Stelai, Part III. Vases and Other Containers," *Hesperia* 27 (1958) 268.

WHITE-GROUND LEKYTHOS WITH WOMEN AT A TOMB

450-445
by the Achilles Painter
Worcester, Worcester Art Museum, Gift of Miss Mary Felton Sargent in memory of her cousin, Miss Mary S. Felton, daughter of President Cornelius Felton, Harvard University, inv. no. 1900.65

Attic
Clay
H 33.4 cm., Diam 11.6 cm.

Publications: *ARV²* 997.151; *Add²* 312; A. Fairbanks, *Athenian White Lekythoi*, vol. 1 (New York 1907) 217, no. 35, pl. 9,1; Beazley (1918) 164, no. 24; S.B. Luce, "The Diphilos-Dromippos Lekythoi," *AJA* 23 (1919) 30-31, fig.7; Worcester Art Museum, *Art through Fifty Centuries* (Worcester 1948) 15, fig. 14; D. Buitron, *Attic Vase Painting in New England Collections* (Cambridge, Fogg Art Museum, March 1-April 5, 1972) 134-35, no. 74.

Reassembled with some restoration. Around the neck is a band of egg pattern. Around the shoulder are palmettes and volutes. Above the scene is a band of alternating left and right triple meanders separated by a saltire square. A line serves as the groundline.

A woman stands in right profile, her right knee relaxed. With both hands she holds a large flat-bottomed basket, which has three curved handles and which is wider at the brim than at the base. The side is decorated, from below, with a band of laurel, a narrow band of pairs of vertical lines, and a band of meander. Hanging down the side of the basket are four sashes, decorated with a row of dots; the string ties dangle below. The woman wears a peplos that is belted over the overfold, and her hair is gathered up at the back of her head and bound by a taenia. She is barefoot. Hanging behind her in the field is an oinochoe. The woman gazes over to her companion, who returns her gaze. This woman stands frontally, her bare feet foreshortened. The palm of her upraised left hand steadies the base of a plemochoe; her right hand hangs at her side. She wears a chiton with a kolpos that extends to mid-thigh, and her hair is gathered at the back of her head, with small curls framing her face. The inscription reads "Hygiainon is beautiful."

Two women bring offerings to a grave. The wicker basket was used almost exclusively by women to carry grave gifts, in this case the sashes that would be wrapped around the grave stele. The plemochoe carried by the other woman was a perfume vessel, a conventional grave, as well as wedding, gift. It is not clear whether one of the figures is the maidservant of the other or whether the woman with the plemochoe is the deceased (see no. 12). Noteworthy is their exchange of glances, which expresses a shared solemnity of feeling.

The three handles of the grave basket recall the three handles that distinguish the *kanoun*, another flat-bottomed wicker basket exclusively associated with women (see no. 60 and **Women as Containers**). The *kanoun*, carried in ritual processions only by an unmarried virgin, alluded to the maiden's potential to give life. The

53

53

funerary basket has a related connotation, because it was the responsibility of women to bring nourishment to the dead, both by honoring them with libations and by sustaining their memory through regular visits.

Although the Achilles Painter also worked successfully in red-figure (see no. 112), he is particularly admired for his white-ground lekythoi with funerary subjects (see nos. 12, 14). The compositions typically feature a very few dignified figures captured, as here, in a quiet moment. The elegant profiles of his women show clearly why the artist is usually heralded as the epitome of the Classical style. The painter's skill in draftsmanship is also evident throughout this scene, and especially in his delineation of arms and hands. Equally distinctive is his technique, because here, as on most of his white-ground vases, the Achilles Painter drew in dilute glaze, and his colors, even the second white, were applied before firing.

54

WHITE-GROUND LEKYTHOS WITH WOMAN AND MAIDSERVANT

ca. 450
by the Thanatos Painter
London, Collection of Claude Hankes-Drielsma.
Formerly, Collection of William G. Helis, Jr.

Attic
Clay
H 25.7 cm., Diam 8.3 cm.

Publications: *ARV²* 1230.44; *Add²* 351; Shapiro (1981) 112-13, no. 44; Sale Catalog, Sotheby's, New York, *Antiquities and Islamic Art*, December 14, 1993, no. 28.

On the shoulder is a band of egg pattern above palmettes linked by tendrils. Above the scene is a meander band. Red on woman's chiton and himation.

A grave stele wrapped with sashes rises above a four-stepped base. On top of the stele is a young boy, who crouches on his left leg, with the knee bent; his right knee is bent and raised. He gazes to his left toward a young woman who approaches in left profile, stooping beneath the weight of the basket on her head. Her upraised right hand steadies the front edge of the basket, and several long sashes spill over its sides. In her outstretched left hand, she cradles the base of an alabastron. She has short, straight hair and a snub nose.

Standing on the other side of the stele in right profile is a woman who wears a chiton beneath a mantle that is draped over the back of her head and wrapped completely around her arms, torso, and most of her legs. She gazes ahead of her. Hanging in the field behind her is a length of fabric.

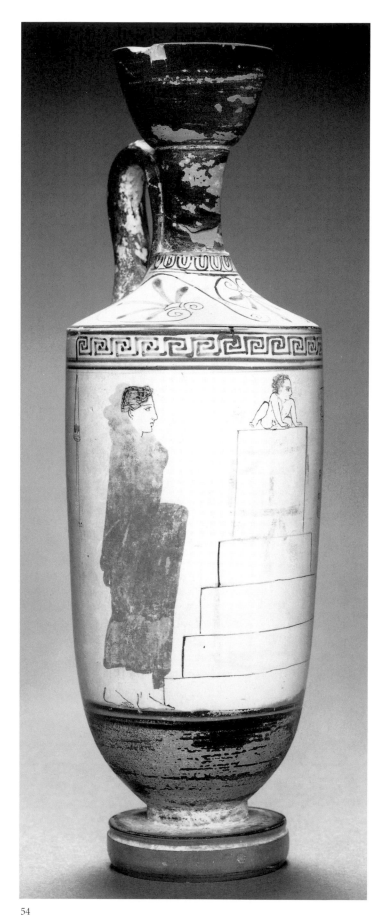

54

223

54 Detail

The stele commemorates the death of the baby boy who is seated on top of it, as his mother and her servant approach with burial gifts. The scene provides telling insight into a Greek household, because the rendering of the maidservant's nose suggests that she is African. Her servitude is emphasized by her stooped pose, even though the weight of the sashes could not have made the basket an onerous burden.[1] The mistress of the house, by contrast, holds nothing, and the envelopment of her arms in her mantle accentuates her unavailability to assist with carrying the offerings. There is no suggestion in her demeanor of the inclined head of *aidos*, modesty and submission; she is rather shown here as the figure in control, the individual being served (see **Aidos and Sophrosyne**).

Given the fact that his mother is present, it is interesting that the boy gazes away from her in the direction of his nurse. The boy's pose is of a type familiar from contemporary terracotta figurines, wherein the head is turned to the side of the lowered leg, but the painter could certainly have reversed the placement of

mistress and maid. The direction of the boy's gaze thus implies either that his foremost affection is for his nurse as his primary caretaker, or that his primary interest is in the funerary presents he is about to receive.

The female head covering (sakkos) hanging in the background accentuates the female ambience of the grave site. As givers of life, women were thought to be closer than were men to the thresholds of life and death, and thus women prepared the body for burial and carried to the tomb baskets with sashes they had woven to wrap around the grave stele. A common grave gift was the alabastron, a distinctively female perfume vase that was given to the bride as a wedding present to underline her allure and fecundity.

The Thanatos Painter worked exclusively in white-ground lekythoi with funerary scenes, and he was strongly influenced by the Achilles Painter (nos. 12, 14).

1. Compare the lekythos by the Bosanquet Painter in Berlin where the servant girl stands upright and balances a stool on top of her head (Boardman [1989] fig. 270).
2. M. Trumpf-Lyritzaki, *Griechische Figurenvasen* (Bonn 1969) 80-81, pl. 29.

55

LEBES GAMIKOS WITH WEDDING SCENE

ca. 430-420
attributed to the Washing Painter
New York, Metropolitan Museum of Art, Rogers Fund, 1907,
inv. no. 07.286.35

Attic
Clay
H 51 cm.

Publications: *ARV²* 1126.1; *Para* 453; *Add²* 332; Richter and Hall (1936) 182-83, no. 145, pls. 146, 174; Ginouvès (1962) 273, n. 5-7; Wegner (1963) 102-103, fig. 65; A. Krug, *Binden in der griechischen Kunst* (Hösel 1968) 63, 65; S. Roberts, "Evidence for a Pattern in Attic Pottery Production Ca. 430-350 B.C.," *AJA* 77 (1973) 436 n. 19; G. Comotti, "Una antica arpa, la 'magidis', in un frammento di Teleste (fr. 808 P)," *Quaderni Urbinati di Cultura Classica* N.S. 3 (1983) 57-71; D. Paquette, *L'Instrument de musique dans la céramique de la grèce antique* (Paris 1984) 194-95, no. H2; A. Bélis, "L'organologie des instruments de musique de l'antiquité: chronique bibliographique," *RA* 1989.1, 132; M. Maas and J. McIntosh-Snyder, *Stringed Instruments of Ancient Greece* (New Haven 1989) 153; Reilly (1989) 421 n. 60; *LIMC* VI (1992) 361 (s.v. Nike); Robertson (1992) 225-26, fig. 233; Sutton (1992) 30, fig. 1.11; Oakley and Sinos (1993) 20, 69, fig. 36; Sabetai (1993) vol. 1, 22, 34, 42, 70; vol. 2, 3, no. LG1, pl. 1.

Reassembled from many pieces. Around the neck is a band of tongues; above the scene is a frieze of egg pattern; beneath the scene is a band of tongues. Ray pattern around the base. Above the scene on the stand is a band of three meanders (left) alternating with a checker square; beneath are two reserved lines above a band of rays. The scene on the base shows two pairs of women separated by kalathoi; two of the women hold kalathoi and a third woman holds a sash. The women wear chitons and himatia and two of them wear sakkoi. Red for the fillets on the loutrophoros-hydria on Side A.

On Side A the bride is seated in right profile on a diphros, her bare feet resting on a footstool, which is rendered as a low platform. Both hands finger the strings of a harp. She wears a chiton beneath a mantle that is draped over her legs. Her head is inclined and she gazes downward, her hair drawn up from her nape beneath a broad fillet. Behind her a woman stands in three-quarter right profile, her hands clasping a loutrophoros-hydria that is tied with two sashes. She wears a peplos that has an overfold to the waist and that is decorated with a broad stripe at the hem. Her hair is also drawn up beneath a fillet, and she wears a crescent earring and a bracelet. Her head is inclined and she gazes downward. Behind her is a diphros, whose cushion has a pattern of two bands flanking a line of zigzag. Behind her a winged woman flies forward in right profile, a tendril in each outstretched hand. She wears a chiton with a kolpos, and her hair is bound in a sakkos.

In front of the bride, a woman stands in three-quarter left profile, wearing a chiton beneath a mantle that is draped over her left shoulder and across her waist and legs. Her left hand fingers her mantle folds at her waist, and her right hand steadies the base of a chest that she holds in front of her. Her head is in left profile, her hair gathered into a knot at her nape, and she gazes ahead of her. Behind her a shorter female stands almost frontally, her head in left profile. She wears a peplos that is girded over an overfold. A chest studded with dots rests on her left forearm and hand, and a basket is balanced on her head and steadied by her right hand. It is decorated with a horizontal band of dots between panels that alternate dark and reserved with lines and zigzag. Behind her and flying toward her is a winged woman dressed identically to her counterpart under the other handle; she carries a sash in her lowered left hand and a basket in her upraised right hand. The basket is decorated with several horizontal bands, one of zigzag.

On Side B a woman stands almost frontally, her arms at her sides; she wears a peplos that has an overfold to her hips. She gazes in left profile to a woman who turns toward her, holding a basket in her left hand. On the other side of the central woman is a third woman who stands in front of a klismos with a patterned cushion. She turns in three-quarter left profile and, over her undergarment, wears a mantle that envelops her left arm. She steadies a basket in her upraised right hand. Hanging in the field on each side of the scene is a sash.

The lebes gamikos was a distinctive form of marriage vessel, and most examples were surely presented to the bride as wedding gifts. The type probably originated as a food container. Because we can assume that the representation on this vase was intended specifically to delight the bride, the scene tells us much about those aspects of the ritual that were thought to be especially pleasing to her. Here she concentrates on her harp while women approach, bearing gifts for her. Because the bride does not wear either veil or wreath, nor is in the process of dressing herself or being dressed, the occasion must be the *epaulia*, the day after the wedding feast and bridal procession (see **The Wedding**). Now the bride receives presents from her friends and family, especially chests and woven wicker baskets, in which the new wife will store her jewelry, toilette objects, and precious clothing. The profusion of containers in this scene suggests a wealth of personal possessions. The loutrophoros-hydria wrapped with ribbons is the vessel of the wedding bath that preceded the ceremony (nos. 22, 26); perhaps the bride will dedicate this gift at the foot of the Acropolis in the Sanctuary of the Nymph, where a number of loutrophoroi have been found.

55 Side A

225

55 Side B-A   55 Side B   55 Side A-B

The harp is a reminder of the music that accompanied all phases of the wedding ritual: the procession to the bridal bath, the wedding feast, the bridal procession to the home of the groom, and the epithalamium that was sung by the bride's companions as they passed the night outside the bridal chamber. Its presence carries other connotations as well. The bride's withdrawal into her music-making as her companions enter her presence suggests her absorption into her new identity as a married woman. To a young bride, the depiction of a new wife enjoying her harp would also have brought reassurance of leisure time in her future married life. Another promising note is introduced with the shorter girl carrying the basket on her head. Her carefully delineated breasts announce her maturity and consequent usefulness, and she is probably a serving maid, whose presence testifies to the affluence of the bride's family's circle.

The winged females beneath the handles may be Nikai, whose presence would allude both to triumphant female beauty and to the fertility which Nikai protected and bestowed.[1] John Oakley notes the appearance on funerary vases of winged females who are deities of the Underworld and suggests that their counterparts on lebetes have the same identity. As forces of fertility, chthonic deities were honored along with the Olympian gods in wedding ritual. Indeed, in Aischylos' *Eumenides* Athena promises the Eumenides (Furies)

that the Athenians will bring them offerings in connection with marriage ritual.[2]

The base of the lebes injects a more serious note that offsets the illusion of idle ease celebrated in the main scene. Here we find as many as four wool baskets (kalathoi), which allude to the spinning and weaving that would constitute one of the primary, and time-consuming, responsibilities of a married woman. Indeed, as much as a bride was appreciated for her seductive charms, she was also valued for her industriousness and her mastery of the skills of textile production (see **Textiles**).

Women are the Washing Painter's favorite subjects, whether as brides of respectable families or prostitutes in a brothel (no. 50). The painter is fond of female finery, especially garments with wide stripes along the edges, which he likes to drape in decorative patterns. Affluence appeals to him too: vessels, containers, musical instruments, and furniture of a comfortable life which his subjects enjoy in a mood of quiet leisure.

1. E.M. Langridge-Noti and J. Oakley, eds., *Athenian Potters and Painters*, December 1, 1994-March 5, 1995, Gennadius Library, American School of Classical Studies (Athens 1994) 51; H. Kenner "Flügelfrau und Flügeldamon," *ÖJh* 31 (1939) 82; I.S. Mark, *Nike and the Cult of Athena Nike on the Athenian Akropolis* (Diss., New York University 1979) 45-52 and 292-93.

2. Aischylos, *Eumenides* 834-36.

LEBES GAMIKOS WITH WEDDING SCENE

440-430
by the Washing Painter
Munich, Staatliche Antikensammlungen München, inv. no. 7578

Attic, from Athens
Clay
H 63 cm., Diam 27.5 cm.

Publications: *ARV²* 1126.3; *Add²* 332; J. Sieveking, "Berichte. Museum antiker Kleinkunst 1925-1927," *Münchener Jahrbuch der bildenden Kunst* N.F. 6 (1929) 91, fig. 28; E. Buschor, "Ringende Flügelknaben," *AM* 71 (1956) 206, Beilage 118; S. Roberts, "Evidence for a Pattern in Attic Pottery Production Ca. 430-350 B.C.," *AJA* 77 (1973) 436; T. Hadzisteliou Price, *Kourotrophos: Cults and Representations of the Greek Nursing Deities* (Leiden 1978) 45; H. Walter, *Die Gestalt der Frau. Bildwerke von 30,000-20 v. Chr.: Anthropologische Betrachtungen* (Stuttgart 1985) 42, 44, fig. 36; Kauffmann-Samaras (1988) 287-88, fig. 3; Reilly (1989) 426-27, pl. 81; Oakley and Sinos (1993) 18, 20, 72, fig. 40; Sabetai (1993) vol. 1, 22, 25, 43, 45, 55, 90-91, 98, 101; vol. 2, 5, no. LG3, pl. 2.

Mended from many pieces. Above the scene is a band of tongues over an egg pattern. Beneath the scene are an egg pattern and a band of rays. Above the scene on the base is a meander, beneath a band of egg over a ray pattern.

A woman is seated in right profile on a stool, whose back far leg and underside are indicated. She wears a chiton with a short overfold and a mantle that has a black stripe across the hem and that is draped over her waist and legs. Her hair is gathered into a knot at the back of her head, and she also wears a taenia and an earring. With both hands she supports the nude body of a baby boy whom she is about to hand over to a caretaker; her left hand clasps his left thigh, her right hand his right arm. She gazes at him. Standing in left profile in front of her is a woman wearing a chiton and a mantle that frames her back and is wrapped around her waist and legs. Her left forearm is extended in front of her and the hand clasps folds of a receiving cloth, which is wrapped around her right hand. The extended left arm of the baby boy passes behind the cloth, and he looks over in right profile to the standing woman, who returns his gaze. Hanging in the field just above the seated woman's head is a wreath; hanging beside it is a sash.

Behind the seated bride stands a woman who faces front, her head in right profile, her gaze directed across to the baby boy. She wears a peplos that is belted over its overfold; both overfold and lower hem are edged with a black stripe. Her hair is gathered up at the back of her head, with a long ringlet falling forward over each shoulder. With both hands she holds behind her back the end of a cloth that extends to her hips; its fringed lower edge is clearly visible. Following behind her is a young girl who is almost frontal, her head turned in right profile. She wears a sleeveless pleated garment that is girded once at the waist and again just above the knees. Her hair is gathered to the back of her head. With her left hand she steadies on her head a large chest, the side of which is rendered as two rows of black squares alternating with vertical zigzag panels beneath a horizontal band of meander. On top of this chest is another smaller box, the side of which is vertically striped at irregular intervals. Her lowered right hand holds a long stick, which broadens just above hand and then tapers at its tip; it is probably a distaff, because a wool basket (kalathos)

56 Side A

rests on the ground behind her. Behind her is a flying winged woman, who wears a chiton and a sakkos. She holds a sash in her extended right hand.

Behind the woman with the receiving cloth stands a woman in left profile who holds a large loutrophoros-hydria with both hands. Over her chiton she wears a mantle edged with a dark stripe; it passes over her hips and legs, with the ends thrown over her left shoulder. Her hair is gathered at the back of her head, and she wears an earring. Behind her and flying toward the bride is a winged female holding a sash in her lowered left hand and an alabastron in her raised right hand. She wears a chiton and a sakkos. All the figures are barefoot.

On the base a woman stands in left profile, her right hand resting on the back of a klismos. She wears a chiton and a mantle that exposes only her right shoulder and upper arm; her hair is gathered in a knot at the back of her head. Approaching her is a woman who holds a kalathos in her left hand. Behind her stand two females turned toward each other. One holds a kalathos in her extended right hand; the other woman holds a sash in her lowered right hand.

56 Details of figures on Side A

The wreath suspended over the head of the seated woman tells us that we are witnessing the preparation of the bride for the wedding ceremonial. One companion comes forward with the loutrophoros-hydria, a form of loutrophoros that was particularly associated with women and that was used for the bridal bath.[1] Another attendant holds behind her back the bridal veil, which is decorated with stars and bears a fringed border. Meanwhile, the bride has just been playing with a young boy, who is now being handed over to an attendant. The activity must represent a custom still observed in modern Crete, wherein the bride bounces a baby boy on her knees or lets him play on her bed, with the hope that male children will be born to her.[2] Ancient commentators tell us that it was customary in some parts of Greece for a bride to sleep with a baby boy either before or after her wedding.[3] The Greek preference for male over female children is succinctly summarized by the comment of Herodotos that a certain Kleomenes died childless, having only female children.[4] To avoid that predicament, boys figured prominently in the ancient wedding ritual. A *pais amphithales* (a boy with both parents living) circulated among the wedding guests carrying a winnowing basket, and another youth, a *propempontes*, took part in the wedding procession (see **The Wedding**). It is also likely that a boy was included in the procession that accompanied the bride to her bridal bath.

The depiction of both the boy and the receiving cloth that the attendant holds was surely ultimately inspired by a lost painting that served as the prototype for a series of vase-paintings in which the boy Erichthonios is being handed over by the mother goddess Gaia to Athena, the boy's nurse (see **Erichthonios**). The motif of a child reaching out from the arms of a woman to the embrace of another woman enjoyed considerable popularity in sculpture and vase-paintings of the second half of the fifth century, with the child exhibiting varying degrees of animation or passivity (nos. 13, 6).

It is interesting to note that in several depictions of Erichthonios the receiving blanket Athena holds is given special prominence in the scene (nos. 67, 68, 72). In Euripides' *Ion* the receiving blanket is described as a *peplos*, the same word for the garment with which Athena was honored every year at the Panathenaia (see **Textiles** and **Athena**). The prominence of the peplos in the story of Erichthonios, who was Athena's nursling, suggests that the receiving, or swaddling, cloth was viewed in Athens as an important symbol of motherhood, family life, and the textile arts bestowed by Athena and intimately linked with married women (see **Textiles**). The theme is underscored in this scene by the proximity to the swaddling cloth of the wedding veil, which is also depicted prominently.

The young girl bearing the chests is probably a servant girl, bringing jewelry or cosmetics with which the bride will soon be adorned. As is typical of representations of young girls, the double girding of the garment indicates that the girl has been outfitted with an oversized garment into which she will eventually grow. The dowel that she holds in her right hand is probably a distaff, around which will be tied the unspun wool soon to be taken from the wool basket beside her. The winged women flanking the other figures are frequent participants in scenes of bridal ritual and are thought to represent either Nikai or Underworld deities (nos. 23, 28). Here they bring sashes to honor the occasion, and one also holds an alabastron, or perfume vessel, underscoring the scene's emphasis upon the bride's sexual allure and fertility.

The kalathoi, or wool baskets, on the base of the lebes develop the theme of textile production introduced in the main scene. The baskets remind the viewer that spinning and weaving were the quintessential skills that a bride was expected to bring with her into her marriage and were activities in which she would pass innumerable hours, many of them inevitably tedious.

In the Classical era the lebes gamikos was exclusively associated with the wedding and apparently served no other function than to hold sprigs of myrtle evocative of fertility and joy. By contrast, the forerunner of the lebes was undoubtedly a form of krater that was used for cooking food. The prominence of a food vessel in wedding ritual is particularly apt because, as Marcel Detienne has pointed out, marriage was viewed as a transition from an uncivilized way of life to a civilized state characterized by cooked food.[5] Indeed, the bride carried a roasting pan with her in the marriage procession. The swelling forms of both the sizable lebes gamikos seen here and the smaller versions that typically date from the end of the century (nos. 28, 58) were also evocative of another kind of sustenance for which the new wife would be responsible: the birth of children, who would ensure the continuation of the family line and, ultimately, the survival of the community (see **Women as Containers**).

1. Sabetai (1993) 163; see also no. 22.
2. Kauffmann Samaras (1988) 286-99.
3. Pollux 3.40; Kallimachos, *Aetia* iii, frag. 75.
4. Herodotos 5.48.
5. Detienne (1989) passim; see also Tyrrell (1991) 77-82.

LEBES GAMIKOS WITH WEDDING SCENE

ca. 440
University, Mississippi, University Museums,
The David M. Robinson Collection, University of Mississippi

Attic, "from a cemetery near Vari in Attica"
Clay
H 56.8 cm., H (with lid) 64.2 cm., Diam (max.) 23.9 cm.

Publications: *CVA* Baltimore, Robinson Collection 2 (U.S.A. 6) 36-38, pl. 50-51; D.M. Robinson, "A New Lebes Gamikos with a Possible Representation of Apollo and Daphne," *AJA* 40 (1936) 507-19, figs. 1-4; Krieger (1973) 45-47, 49-50, 61-64, 77, 106-108, 121, 159, no. 40.

Mended and restored. Egg pattern around the lip and the base of the handles. Above the scene is a tongue pattern; beneath is a band of two and three meanders (right) alternating with a checker square. Around the base is a band of rays.

On Side A a woman is seated in right profile on a klismos. She wears a chiton and a mantle that is wrapped around her waist and legs. Her hair is wrapped with a taenia that passes over a bun of hair at the back of her head, and she gazes into a mirror that she holds in her right hand. A woman faces her, standing in left profile, her right leg relaxed, and her right hand fingering folds of drapery in front of her right shoulder. Over her chiton she wears a mantle that is draped over her left shoulder and around her most of her body; her hair is also gathered into a bun. Flying towards her is a winged female wearing a chiton belted over its overfold; her arms are extended out from her body, and her head is in left profile, her hair gathered into a knot. Behind the seated woman stands a woman who is almost frontal, her forearms raised, with the fingers extended. Her head is in right profile and she gazes at the seated woman. She wears a peplos that is belted over its overfold, and her hair is gathered into a knot at the nape.

On Side B a woman is seated in left profile on a klismos. Her left hand is enveloped in folds of her mantle, which is draped over her chiton. Her right hand steadies a chest that she extends toward a woman who stands in right profile, her left hand on the side of the chest. The standing woman wears a peplos with an overfold, and her right forearm is raised, with the fingers extended. Behind the seated woman stands a woman who is almost frontal, her head turned in left profile, her right forearm raised with the fingers extended. Behind her is an altar, toward which a winged female flies in left profile; over her undergarment she wears a mantle that completely envelops her arms. The hair of all of the women is gathered into a bun at the nape; the seated woman also wears a diadem. A sash hangs in the field over her head.

The base has a band of meanders (right) alternating with a checker square above a band of laurel. Beneath is a band of ray. Peleus, wearing a mantle, boots, and a laurel wreath, with a petasos behind his shoulders and two spears in his lowered right hand, is seen in three-quarter right profile as he runs after Thetis, his left arm extended, with the palm up, fingers open. She flees, with her head turned back in left profile to gaze back at him. Her right elbow is bent, with the forearm brought in front of her torso; her left hand holds folds of her skirt. Facing her is her father, Nereus, holding his staff. Behind him is a dolphin followed by a woman who runs away from Peleus, gazing back at him. She holds a stalk in her right hand.

As the bride admires her reflection while preparing her wedding toilette, she is attended by two solicitous companions (see **The Wedding**). On the other side of the lebes, the bride is shown again, now accepting a chest that contained jewelry or toiletries. The winged females under the handles are a familiar presence in bridal scenes on loutrophoroi and lebetes gamikoi and are probably to be identified as Nikai or Underworld divinities (see nos. 23, 56). The altar may refer to rituals that preceded the wedding festivities, perhaps the offerings (*proteleia*), including locks of hair, that the bride would dedicate in a sanctuary of one of several goddesses, including Artemis.

The most remarkable feature of the vase is the presence on the base of a scene of pursuit (see **Pursuit Scenes**). The dolphin in the field before the running maiden with the tendril identifies the participants as the mortal Peleus and the goddess Thetis, who would assume the forms of many animals, including a dolphin, in her efforts to avoid accepting Peleus as her husband (see **Peleus and Thetis**). The conventional depiction of the couple's encounter is a wrestling match, but here the painter has adopted a well-known form of pursuit that Christiane Sourvinou-Inwood characterizes as a youth with the petasos, cloak, and spears of an ephebe hastening after a fleeing maiden.[1] Sourvinou-Inwood argues that the youth's grasp of the spears in an non-threatening manner emphasizes the metaphorical nature of the pursuit as analogous to courtship, and her interpretation is confirmed by the gaze of Thetis, who turns her head back to look directly into Peleus' eyes (see **Gesture and Gaze**). So thoroughly did the Greeks believe in the seductive power of a woman's gaze that Thetis' willingness to return Peleus' glance expresses her willing responsiveness to his advance. The remaining figures in the scene are the elderly Nereus, who was Thetis' father, and a Nereid, one of Thetis' sisters.

The placement of this scene on a vase created as a wedding gift to please a bride tells us a great deal about Classical modes of thought. It is clear that the pursuit scene as a metaphor for courtship was sufficiently pleasing to the Greek female that its representation was acceptable on a wedding vase. Significantly, however, the scene almost totally lacks the violence that characterizes other pursuit scenes, especially those depicting Poseidon and Amymone (see **Amymone**). Indeed, Peleus' left hand is gracefully extended, with the fingers slightly cupped and the palm turned upward, such that his gesture is more expressive than aggressive. Clearly, the metaphor of pursuit as courtship was most acceptable to the Greek bride when it was presented in a softened form.

The inclusion of the myth on this lebes is a vivid example of a selective approach to myth that is characteristically Greek. After all, Thetis initially did everything in her power to try to avoid becoming Peleus' bride. That, however, was surely not the aspect of the story that appealed to the bride, who undoubtedly preferred to regard the pursuit as the preliminary episode in a drama that culminated in the most glorious wedding in Greek mythology (nos.

57 Side A-B   57 Side B   57 Side B-A

109, 110). The winged figures on the lebes remind us that during the wedding ritual the bridal couple was considered to be elevated to a superhuman stature (see no. 23), and it was probably not unusual for a particularly beautiful and richly adorned bride to receive comments from wedding guests that at this moment, on this day, she was Thetis herself.

1. Sourvinou-Inwood (1987) 131-53.

LEBES WITH BRIDAL SCENE

ca. 410
by the Painter of Louvre MN 558
Athens, National Archaeological Museum, inv. no. 1658

Attic
Clay
H 16.5 cm., H (with lid) 23.8 cm., Diam (max.) 17.4 cm.

Publication: *ARV*² 1320.1.

upper and lower moldings bears a band of dots, and there is a scroll on each foot. Over her chiton she wears a mantle that is brought over her right shoulder and is belted at the waist, forming an overfold at the hips, with the open ends hanging down over her right leg. A black stripe edges the hems. She wears a beaded necklace and a bracelet on her left arm, both in added clay. Her hair is gathered high on the back of her head, and she wears an ornamental headpiece rendered in added clay.

Following her is a woman in left profile, her left knee relaxed. In her uplifted right hand she holds a necklace. Her left hand steadies a chest that has beading along the horizontal upper edge. Her belted peplos with overfold has a black stripe edging upper and lower hems; she also wears a necklace and a bracelet on each wrist. Her hair is wrapped with a piece of fabric, and curly locks protrude at the back of her head.

Flying toward her back is a winged female in left profile wearing a belted peplos that has a black stripe edging its overfold. Her lowered right hand holds a sash decorated with dots, its borders paralleled by a series of horizontal lines; the ends are fringed, indicated in white. Her hair is knotted at her nape.

Behind the bride is a klismos facing the opposite direction; on the seat is a large pillow covered with close-set straight and wavy lines. In front of the klismos and approaching the bride in three-quarter right profile is a woman who stands with her right knee relaxed. Her left hand steadies a chest decorated with egg pattern and spirals; on top of it is a plemochoe with stripes to indicate fluting. In her right hand she holds a sash and another chest. The side of this chest is decorated with two rows of black squares alternating with striated ones. The sash is decorated with dots between pairs of horizontal lines and has fringed ends. Behind this woman and flying toward her is a winged woman in right profile bearing an alabastron and a sash in her right hand. Another sash is in her lowered left hand; both sashes are decorated like the other ones in the scene.

The last figure in the center of Side B is a woman hastening to her left, left leg advanced with the knee bent and her head turned back in left profile. In her right hand she carries a necklace in added clay; her left hand holds a sash and a chest decorated with a row of black dots across its mid-section. The edge of the lid bears a band of dots, and a decorative ornament in added white surmounts each end of the lid. The woman's hair is bound into a knot at the nape.

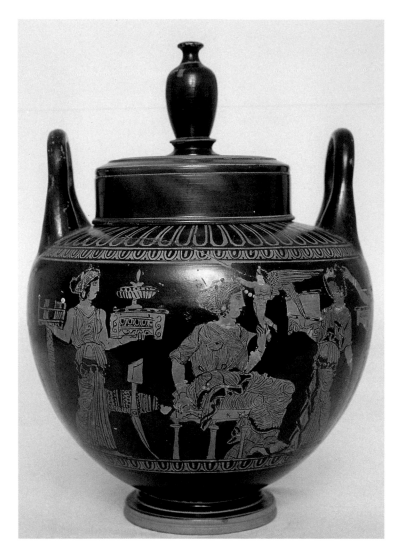

58   Side A

Minor repairs. Lid has tall alabastron handle.

Above the scene are bands of tongue and egg pattern. Beneath the scene is a band of egg.

In the center of the scene, a woman is seated turned in three-quarter right profile, her ankles crossed. She is barefoot, as are all the other figures. Her head is in right profile, and she stares straight ahead. Her right hand rests on the side of her stool, which is decorated with a star and a cross along the side piece. Over her belted chiton she wears a mantle that is draped over her thighs and legs; it is bordered with a black stripe edged with dots. Her wavy hair is gathered into a knot at the back of her head; she wears a sphendone crowned by a diadem with a meander pattern. She also wears a ball earring, a beaded necklace, and a spiral bracelet on each arm, all in added clay. A glazed bracelet is also on each arm. Her left elbow is bent, and the upraised fingers draw a triangular passage of fabric in front of her left shoulder. Just behind her first two fingers are seen the left lower leg of Eros, who flies toward her in three-quarter left profile, a beaded necklace rendered in added clay held between his outstretched arms.

Facing the bride is a woman who turns slightly to her right, her left leg relaxed. In her lowered left hand she carries a sash ornamented with horizontal lines and dots. Her right hand steadies a chest, whose lid is raised. The

It is the bride's moment, and the attention of all the figures is focused upon her. She is as richly bedecked as she was during the wedding ceremony itself, wearing earrings and bracelets. Her hair is elegantly wrapped in an elaborate hair covering, but the wedding veil is no longer in evidence. Alone of all the figures she is seated, probably in the home of her husband and parents-in-law, where she will now live. The procession of female figures bringing gifts to her tell us that this scene depicts the *epaulia*, which was believed to follow the wedding night.

With the fingers of her left hand the bride draws folds of fabric in front of her left shoulder in the gesture familiar from the wedding ritual and known as the *anakalypsis*, or the unveiling, when the bride signifies her acceptance of, and submission to, her new husband by beginning her own disrobing (see **The Wedding** and **Gesture and Gaze**). For this reason the gesture became associated with married women, among whom the bride can now number herself.

The figure of Eros is familiar from wedding scenes where the groom stands beside his new wife as Eros focuses his attention primarily upon the bride. Here, the presence of Eros in the absence of the bridegroom accentuates the deity's close affiliation with the bride, to whom he was believed to bring the desirability that would make her sexually alluring to her husband (see **The Wedding**). Because the Greeks believed that emotions were external forces, the bride becomes literally endowed with desire, such that Sophokles could remark that "desire conquers, bright, from the eyes of a happily wed bride"[1] (see **The Wedding**). It is also interesting to note that Eros does not bring the bridal wreath customary in scenes of the wedding ceremony itself, but rather a necklace. The gift emphasizes the god's interest in sustaining the bride's erotic appeal, at the same time as it equates Eros with the wedding guests, who also bring necklaces.

The inclusion in the scene of five chests suggests that the quintessential wedding gift was a chest, and the examples seen here are carefully decorated with a wide range of ornament. One of the women appears to have taken a sash from her chest, and another offers a necklace that must have been stored in the one she carries. The other chests would be destined for similar precious possessions, such as the toiletries that would enhance the bride's allure. The plemochoe and the alabastron would similarly have contained perfumes to sustain her sexual appeal. In the ancient mind the chests and vessels would have carried connotations also shared by the lebes on which the scene is painted: allusions to fertility and the

life cycle, of which the bride herself was the prime exemplar (see **Women as Containers** and **Pandora**). The plethora of sashes in this scene were surely woven by the women who bring them and speak to the joy and honor of the occasion. Together with the elaborately adorned cushion on the klismos, the fabrics are a forcible reminder of the degree to which textile production was a uniquely female art and one synonymous both with a married woman and domestic life (see **Textiles**).

The winged females, which are often seen on lebetes, have been variously identified as Nikai and as chthonic (Underworld) deities, for whom it was customary to offer libations as part of wedding ritual (see no. 23). Their presence here, together with that of Eros, reminds us that every bride was envisioned as inhabiting a suprahuman sphere, coming to occupy through the wedding ritual a status approximating that of the divine brides Pandora and Thetis (see **Pandora** and **Peleus and Thetis**). As a wedding present to a bride, this lebes would certainly have been treasured all her life as testimony to an unsurpassed moment when she was the honored center of attention, richly adorned (here with as many as three necklaces), endowed with sexual allure, inundated with a profusion of gifts, and elevated to a super-human stature with divine attendants. And the lebes itself, the protector of the woman's special personal possessions, would have been an ever-present reminder of the degree to which in Greek thought women were identified with fertility, mystery, and treasure (see **Women as Containers**).

It is ironic that such honor was enjoyed by every woman simply by virtue of her biological maturation, whereas formal acknowledgment of successful or fatal childbirth was almost non-existent. By contrast, a young man would receive comparable attention only at a older age and only if he could claim an exceptional achievement, perhaps an athletic victory or extraordinary conduct in battle.

The late fifth-century style of this vase-painting is manifested in the generous use of added clay and the close-set drapery lines that wrap tightly around the limbs, even radiating from the bride's nipples. The exaggerated relaxation of the bride's hands results in gestures that are almost affected. Whereas Eros is still depicted as a baby boy, he is now a more active participant in the scene, proffering a necklace and practically touching the bride's hands; however, faithful to the convention of earlier bridal scenes, the bride continues to be unaware of his presence. Also noteworthy is the relative profusion of objects and accouterments relative to the number of figures in the scene.

58 Side B

1. Sophokles, *Antigone* 795-801.

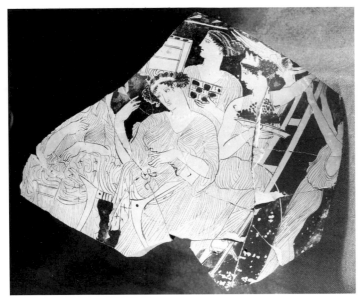

59

FRAGMENT OF
A LEBES GAMIKOS
WITH WEDDING SCENE

ca. 380
attributed to the painter of Athens 1454
Paris, Réunion des Musées Nationaux, Musée du Louvre,
Départment des Antiquités grecques, étrusques, et romaines
inv. no. CA 1679

Attic
Clay
H 15.5 cm., W 19 cm.

Publications: *ARV*² 1179.3; *Para* 460; *Add*² 340; G. Nicole, *Meidias et le style fleuri dans la céramique attique* (Geneva 1908) 144-47, pls. 8.2, 9; A. Neppi Modona, "Adonia e Adonidos Kepoi nelle raffigurazioni vascolari attiche," *Rendiconti, Atti della Pontifica Accedmia Romana di Archeologia* 27 (1953) 179, no. 3; M. Milne, *AJA* 60 (1956) 201; D.B. Thompson and R.E. Griswold, *Garden Lore of Ancient Athens, Excavations of the Athenian Agora. Picture Book* 8 (Princeton 1963) fig. 50; N. Weill, "Adoniazousai," *BCH* 90 (1966) 668-70, fig. 4; Atallah (1966) 180-82, fig. 40; A. Delivorrias, "Das Original der sitzenden 'Aphrodite-Olympias'," *AM* 93 (1978) 11-12, 21, pl. 13.1; *LIMC* I (1981) 227, no. 46, pl. 169 (s.v. Adonis); Burn (1987) 27, 42; C. Bérard, "The Order of Women," in Bérard et al. (1989) 96-97, fig. 132; Boardman (1989) fig. 299.

Assembled from several pieces. Part of a laurel band survives above the figures' heads.

A woman is seated on a klismos in left profile, her upper torso almost frontal. Her left forearm rests on the back of the klismos, and her right forearm is raised with the wrist cocked and the fingers extended toward her face. She wears a chiton with an overfold that extends just below the breasts; her belt is tied with a bow. A mantle decorated with a cross-pattern is wrapped around her waist and most of her legs. Her center-parted hair falls into short tousled curls which spill over her taenia or diadem at her ears. Her head is inclined

downward and she gazes down and to her right.

Behind her is a ladder, which is being mounted by a barefoot woman who turns back, with her head in left profile, to gaze at the seated woman. Her right hand steadies a plate with a pyramidal mound of small spheres. She also wears a chiton with an overfold that extends beneath the breasts, and over her short wavy hair she wears a diadem from which three leaves rise vertically. Her left arm is extended in the direction of a higher rung of the ladder. Also supporting the ladder with uplifted arms is a female who stands in left profile, wearing a girded chiton. On the other side of the ladder a nude winged Eros extends his arms toward the (missing) left hand of the climbing woman. In the background a fourth woman stands with torso frontal, head in left profile, with a taenia wrapped several times around her hair, which is drawn up to the back of her head. With each hand she steadies a chest; the smaller one in her left hand bears a checkerboard pattern; the side of the other's lid is decorated with a line of short bands. The last figure in the scene is seated, apparently on a stool, such that she rests her left forearm on the knees of the other seated woman. She is dressed similarly to her companion, and the fingers of her right hand are brought to her chest. Above her left shoulder are the feet of what must be another flying Eros.

This scene has traditionally been interpreted as a representation of the Adonia, but it is more likely to be a depiction of bridal ritual. A woman ascending a ladder in the presence of Eros also appears on the squat lekythos with the Adonia in Karlsruhe (no. 61). On this fragment, however, the woman does not carry a broken vessel with seedlings, but rather a plate that may hold food or possibly balls of myrrh. Moreover, the most prominent figure in the scene is the woman seated in the foreground, wearing a head ornament that is probably a diadem. The maiden on the ladder looks around to this seated figure, behind whom hovers a woman carrying two chests, which are the quintessential wedding gift. Of great significance is the fact that the fragment belongs to a lebes gamikos, a type of vase exclusively associated with the wedding and usually bearing a bridal scene. Indeed, a ladder is seen in the background of a bridal scene on a lebes in Athens, and it is likely that in both contexts the ladder refers to the bridal chamber and hence to the wedding night.[1] In keeping with this allusion would be the pensiveness of the bride, which finds parallels in scenes depicting presentations of gifts to the bride on the day following her wedding night (no. 55). The bride's solemnity and withdrawal are probably intended to suggest the new soberness of mature womanhood.

The relaxed gesture of the bride's left forearm is ultimately derived from the figure of Zeus on the east frieze of the Parthenon (p. 249, fig. 2), and a date for this fragment in the 420s is also suggested by the close-set figures, the affected gestures of the cocked wrists and fingers, the sentimental nod of the seated woman's head, and the close-set lines of drapery folds that radiate from her nipples. It interesting to note the rendering of the climbing woman's right leg; the painter has carefully delineated the rear contour of thigh and lower leg, even though we are to understand the leg as concealed by the drapery folds.

1. Athens, National Archaeological Museum, inv. no. 1452; Edwards (1984) 64, pl. 19.

TERRACOTTA FIGURINE OF A KANEPHOROS (BASKET CARRIER)

Come, prepare the baskets for the sacrificial rite.

Euripides, *Iphigenia at Aulis* 433-39

...pure as an Athenian kanephoros.

Aristophanes, *Lysistrata* 1314-15

500-450
Munich, Staatliche Antikensammlungen München, inv. no. Schoen 154

Terracotta
H 20.7 cm.

Unpublished.

White slip over surface.

A female stands frontally on a square base. With both hands she steadies on her head a basket with a cylindrical base and three fan-shaped vertical elements. Over a pleated undergarment she wears a mantle that is draped over both shoulders, with the folds falling over her legs below her knees. Her hair is center-parted and is drawn back over her ears, and she looks straight ahead.

60

The figurine is simply made, with the back smooth and unmolded. The cylindrical arms were probably shaped by hand, together with the flat elements of the basket. The worn details of the face and drapery indicate that the mold had seen intensive use. That this use took place over a period of time is indicated by the discrepancy between, on the one hand, the Archaic stylistic features as the rolled hairstyle, bulging eyes, and symmetrical swallow-tails of drapery and, on the other hand, the mid fifth- century context in which the figurine was found. Use of a mold well into a later stylistic period is a frequent phenomenon in terracotta manufacture.

The maiden is a *kanephoros*, an unmarried virgin who functioned as a ritual basket carrier in one of the many religious festivals that dotted the Attic calendar.[1] *Kanephoroi* were featured in the Panathenaia and also took part in many lesser festivals dedicated to both male and female deities. *Kanephoroi* were also closely identified with the wedding ritual; thus Iphigenia, anticipating a wedding that is in actuality her sacrificial death, calls for the baskets to be brought forth.[2] Being chosen as a *kanephoros* was a special honor testifying to a young woman's virtue and exceptional qualities, so much so that in *Lysistrata* we encounter the phrase, "pure as an Athenian kanephoros."[3] The famous slaying of the tyrants Hippias

and Hipparchos by Harmodios and Aristogeiton was said to have been prompted by Hippias' charge that Harmodios' sister, a *kanephoros*, was not a virgin.[4] Serving as a *kanephoros* was one of the few occasions in which unmarried, but marriageable, young women were in full public view, and the richness of their adornment is attested by temple inventories which record the dedication of their clothes and jewelry.[5]

The *kanephoros* carried on her head a *kanoun*, which was a flat basket with three handles. Schelp has shown that its origins can be traced back to about 1000 B.C. and suggests that it evolved from a basket that was used in Bronze Age ritual, related to the one depicted in the procession of women on the Hagia Triadha sarcophagus.[6] He further proposed that both the *kanoun* and the *kistae* carried by the ritual maidens known as Arrephoroi shared a common Bronze Age origin (see **The Plynteria and Arrephoroi**). Originally, the *kanoun* was probably a food basket,[7] but by Classical times the *kanoun* held barley, a knife, and a taenia. In Athenian festivals, the procession reached its culmination when the *kanephoros* handed the *kanoun* over to a male priest, who would sprinkle the barley over the head of the sacrificial animal and then use the knife to slaughter it. Parts of the meat would be burned upon the altar as a gift to the gods; the internal organs would be roasted and eaten immediately, and the rest of the meat would be prepared as part of the feast of the festival. Because in Greek thought cooking was equated with a higher form of civilization, the uncooked barley represented a primitive state in human culture, believed to have been superseded with the introduction of sacrifice.[8]

The association of a fertile young woman with a ritual to ensure fertility and human well-being was explicitly expressed in the basket as a metaphor of a virgin's life-giving potential (see **Women as Containers**). Indeed, on a fragmentary terracotta *kanoun* from Lindos, on Rhodes, a figure is represented inside the *kanoun*.[9] The solemnity with which *kanephoroi* carried their burden communicated the sentiment that a young woman's ability to give life was a responsibility and honor she should regard with awe and respect, and a similar tone surrounded the ritual of the baskets that were presented to the Arrephoroi. One is reminded of mythical young women, such as Aglauros and Pandora, who disobediently open containers from which children emerge (see **Erichthonios** and **Pandora**). Even Danae and Persephone exhibit a curiosity that contrasts with the disinterested formality that is displayed by *kanephoroi* and Arrephoroi as role models for maturing young girls (see **Danae** and **Persephone and Demeter**).

During the ritual procession the *kanoun* was apparently veiled with a covering (*skepasma*), which appears to have been occasionally adorned with an aegis and was described by ancient commentators as a net-like cloth, made by plaiting pieces of yarn (see **Textiles**). Recovering the contents of the *kanoun* therefore involved an act of unveiling as well as an act of opening. The action is reminiscent of the bridal ritual and also calls to mind the image of the container on the kalyx krater from Fulda (no. 73). Here the chest, presumably with the baby Erichthonios inside, is completely covered by an elaborate fabric.

Finally, one should consider how closely the *kanephoros* was associated with the sacrificial animal, even bearing the weapon by which it dies. The proximity calls to mind the tradition of maiden sacrifice and suggests a further link with the strong Greek prohibition that women must not be allowed to draw blood, a proscription that in effect excluded women from engaging in animal sacrifice (see **Iphigenia**).

This figurine was found in Athens in the grave of a young girl. Buried with her were small clay offering baskets, another *kanephoros*, a jointed doll, a loutrophoros, and several lekythoi. The gifts are poignant testimony to her contemporaries' view that the ultimate pleasure and fulfillment that awaited a young woman— and which this girl would miss—were the dual experiences of being a *kanephoros* and a bride.

1. Burkert (1983) 344-46.
2. See *Suda* (s.v. epaulia); Oakley and Sinos (1993) 38; Schelp (1975) 25; Deubner (1925) 212, quoting scholia to Theokritos 2.66.
3. Aristophanes, *Lysistrata* 1314-15.
4. Thucydides 6.56.57
5. Loraux (1993) 169; Parke (1977) 143.
6. Schelp (1975) 18-28.
7. Deubner (1925) 213.
8. Tyrrell (1991) 77-82.
9. Schelp (1975) 54, pl. 3.1.

61

SQUAT LEKYTHOS WITH ADONIA SCENE

ca. 390
circle of the Meidias Painter
Karlsruhe, Badisches Landesmuseum, inv. no. B 39 (278)

Attic
Clay
H 14 cm.

Publications: *CVA* Karlsruhe, Badisches Landesmuseum 1 (Germany 7) pl. 27.1-4; G. Nicole, *Meidias et le style fleuri dans la céramique attique* (Geneva 1908) 149-50, pl. 8.3; K. Schefold, *Untersuchungen zu den kertscher Vasen* (Berlin and Leipzig 1932) 140, no. 4; Metzger (1951) 92, no. 41, pl. 7,2; *LIMC* I (1982) 227, no. 47, pl. 169 (s.v. Adonis); Edwards (1984) 62; Badisches Landesmuseum, *Wege zur Klassik* (Karlsruhe 1985) 151, pl. XVII; C. Bérard, "The Order of Women," in Bérard et al. (1989) 96-97, fig. 131; Lissarrague (1992) 187-88, fig. 30.

Above the figural scene is a laurel band with gilded berries; beneath is a band of eggs. Beneath the handle is a thirteen-petal palmette above a pair of volutes that terminate in two tendrils enclosing a fourteen-petal palmette beneath. Winding from the pair of volutes toward the figural scene are more tendrils, volutes, leaves, and reserved circles with dots. Added clay and gilding for the wings and jewelry. Added white for the woman on the ladder, the vegetation, and the inscription that reads: ΚΑΛΟΣ ΚΑΛΕ.

A woman stands on the lowest rung of a ladder that extends into the ornamental band above the scene. She leans over in right profile, and her hands clasp the base of a fragmentary amphora which has been broken off around its midsection and in which seedlings are growing. Her hair is gathered into a knot at the back of her head, and she wears a taenia, to which two round elements are attached, and a disc earring. Her mantle is wrapped around her hips and left arm, with the ends falling down in front of her left thigh. Also holding the base of the amphora is a nude Eros who stands in three-quarter left profile. His head is in left profile, and he has short curly hair. Between the figures is the upturned upper half of the amphora, in which seedlings are also growing. Behind Eros and resting on a low plinth is a vessel that has a round basin with horizontal handles and a tall, flaring base; small balls emerge from the rim. Standing next to the vessel is a woman in left profile, the toes of her left foot resting on the ground behind her. She wears a peplos that is belted over its overfold and has a stripe down her left side. She also wears a bracelet and her hair is gathered at the back of her head into a knot. Her hands are upraised at her waist. Her counterpart at the opposite side of the scene is a woman who turns in three-quarter right profile, her right leg relaxed. She is similarly dressed and her hair is tied back; she also wears a diadem from which elements rise vertically and a disc earring. Her hands are also upraised at her waist.

The scene depicts the festival of Adonis, an annual rite that was celebrated exclusively by women to commemorate what was perhaps the most unsuccessful of all Greek heroes. Born on Cyprus from an incestuous union of his mother (Myrrha) with her father, Adonis was said at birth to have been placed by Aphrodite upon a lettuce leaf inside a chest entrusted to Persephone for safekeeping. Adonis grew into a handsome youth, but died in the course of a boar hunt, when he was gored in the thigh.[1] Aphrodite's protection of Adonis and his reemergence as a youth recalls the Mesopotamian cult of Dumuzi-Tammuz.[2] Indeed, Adonis' cult is thought to have entered Greece through Cyprus, the direction from which Aphrodite also ultimately originated. Our first references to the Adonia in Athens date only from the middle of the fifth century, when the celebration was gaining a popularity that continued well into the fourth century. An influx of eastern people into Athens in these years can only partly account for the broad acceptance of a festival that obviously claimed a particular meaningfulness. Most scholars have found that significance in the fact that Adonis perfectly embodied the antithesis of Greek manhood, claiming only impure lineage and inadequate physical skills, and lacking the distinction of having fathered a son. His failure as a hunter was compounded by the sexual overtones of the wound in his thigh. Intercrural intercourse was a common practice in homosexual relationships, and the boar tusk's penetration of Adonis carried connotations of castration.

Not surprisingly, Adonis has been the object of much scholarly attention. As an ephebe manqué, incapable of making the transition to the responsibilities of adulthood, Adonis has been compared with Melanion, Melanthus, Hippolytos, other mythical youths who rejected women and integration into community life in order to live as isolated hunters in the wild. Iphigenia, Atalanta, and Persephone share with Adonis certain elements characterizing incomplete transitions, but are not exact counterparts because of the vastly different roles expected of adult women in contrast to adult men, who were supposed to be dominant and self-sufficient masters of their own selves (see **Iphigenia**, **Atalanta**, and **Persephone and Demeter**). By this standard, Adonis falls so far short that in Jungian analysis he is categorized as a puer, indissolubly attached to his mother and the epitome of a male's innate fear of regression.[3] Stehle, noting the tradition that lettuce was a source of sterility in men, but of fertility to women, correlates Adonis with other mortal men of myth reduced to sexual incapacity by a goddess's love.[4] To Stehle, Adonis responds to fundamental fantasies nourished by both genders: a woman seeking sexual possession of a son, and a man surrendering to a helpless state under maternal care. Given all of Adonis' shortcomings, it is often argued that Athenian society commemorated his death in order to clarify officially what was considered completely undesirable in a male, and probably also in the harvest cycle.[5] The Adonia may have been exclusively observed by women not only because male participation was an uncomfortable idea, but also because the female context underscored Adonis' image of effemi-

61

nacy and effeteness. The ritual probably also carried the underlying reminder that it is a woman's responsibility to give birth to a son who will become a man.

Because the festival does not seem to have ancient roots in Athens, its structure merits particular attention as a conscious selection of actions and imagery deliberately chosen to express most accurately the meaning of the cult. At the height of mid-summer's heat, women planted fast-growing seeds of fennel and lettuce, possibly also wheat and barley, in broken clay vases.[6] The containers were placed on the rooftops of houses, where water was deliberately withheld from them so that the young shoots quickly wilted and died in the blazing sun. We also hear of the use of frankincense and of loaves of myrrh in the ritual. As the sprouts died, the women wailed for the dying vegetation and the dead Adonis, assembling in groups for all-night gatherings known as *pannychides*.

The women's planting of the seedlings in containers is an obvious metaphor for women's ability to give birth and nurture new life, and the seedlings clearly symbolize the brief lifespan of Adonis and

61 Details of figures flanking the main scene

the rooftops settled over the polis like an ominous cloud.[10] So sinister, in fact, did the wailing appear to be that the ritual would surely have been curtailed or suppressed had it not enjoyed a broad popularity among the female population of the city. The incident thus provides interesting evidence that women were allowed a considerable freedom in the rituals they chose to support. Eva Keuls suggests that the opportunity was not lost upon the participants and that the women's incessant wailing during those critical moments in 415 was a deliberate protest against the war.[11]

The scene on the squat lekythos in Karlsruhe contains the essential elements of the Adonis festival: the seedlings growing in broken vessels, and the women who carried them to the rooftops where they would die. The unbroken basin behind Eros was thought by Hafner to be an incense burner, and this would be in keeping with the myrrh and frankincense that we know figured in the ritual and that were customarily burned in the shape of small spheres. The presence of Eros embodies the erotic atmosphere of the festival, and it is possible that the figure on the ladder is Aphrodite herself. The rich ornamentation of the women underscores the connotations of sumptuous luxury that was traditionally associated with Adonis' homeland in the eastern Mediterranean, and the elaborate vegetal pattern beneath the handle and elegant notes of added gilding further the effect of precious sensuality. The function of the vase is exquisitely suited to its decoration, because squat lekythoi were conventionally used to hold prized oils and perfumes.

Characteristic of late fifth- and early fourth-century vase-painting in the Meidian style are the close-set and wavy lines for the drapery, the almost affected gestures, and the use of added white. Also typical is the emphasis on subjects that focus on women, be they mythical, domestic, or ritual scenes. With this vase one senses the pride in personal possessions that would energetically stimulate the development of the decorative arts, and particularly jewelry, during the course of the fourth century.

his inadequate masculinity (see **Women as Containers**). What is distinctive about the ritual is that by planting the seeds in broken vessels and then deliberately allowing them to die the women were behaving in a manner that was the diametric opposite of the role expected of them in society, just as Adonis was the direct antithesis of Greek manhood. For this reason, Burkert has described the Adonia as an example of a ritual of inversion or a ritual of rebellion, the objective of which was to act out what was most feared and most discouraged as a means of overcoming anxiety and of accentuating desirable behavior.[7] The extremity of the ritual can be better appreciated when one considers that in Greek culture a female murderer was an even more abhorrent figure than a male murderer; indeed, women were not even allowed to draw blood in animal sacrifices.

The erotic undercurrents of the festival are powerful and were probably a large part of its popularity with female participants. Weill persuasively suggests that the festival must have been fraught with sexual jokes about impotence and the need to nurture wilting penises.[8] Detienne argues that the festival was predominantly celebrated by hetairai (prostitutes), whose preoccupation with promiscuity rather than procreation would be in keeping with Adonis' failure to father a son.[9] He further believes that incense figured prominently within the ritual as an evocation both of the debauchery associated with the eastern Mediterranean and the incestuous sexual union that produced Adonis. The Adonia also had subversive overtones. We learn from Aristophanes and Thucydides that in 415, at the time of the preparation for departure of what became the disastrous Sicilian expedition, the wailing of the women from

1. Hesiod, frag. 139 MW; Thucydides 3.46-8; Panyasis frag. 27 *PEG*; Aristophanes, *Peace* 420; Aristophanes, *Lysistrata* 87-98; Apollodoros, *Bibliotheke* 3.14.4; Ovid, *Metamorphoses* 10.298-514. See Gantz (1993) 102, 729.
2. Burkert (1985) 176ff; Burkert (1987) 79 rejects the idea of a dying and rising god.
3. Segal (1991) 74.
4. Stehle (1990) 88-125. For lettuce, see Humphries (1993) 44-45.
5. Burkert (1979) 106ff.
6. For a discussion of the date of the festival, see Plato, *Phaedrus* 276b; Thucydides 6.30; Weill (1966) passim.
7. Burkert (1979) 122.
8. Weill (1966) passim. After eating a lettuce leaf, Hera was said to have given birth to Hebe.
9. Detienne (1977a) 66-67.
10. Aristophanes, *Lysistrata* 387-96. For the Sicilian departure, see also Plutarch, *Nikias* 13.2.7 and *Alkibiades* 18.3-4. For other expressions of male aversion to the festival, see Aristophanes, *Peace* 420. See also Fantham (1994a) 78.
11. Keuls (1985a) 395. She also ascribes to Athenian women the castration of the Herms.

ATHENA

Athena...teaches tender maidens in the house and puts knowledge of goodly arts in each one's mind.

Homeric Hymn to Aphrodite 10-11

And did Athena take him forth from the Earth?
Yes, in her maiden (parthenos) arms.

Euripides, *Ion* 269-70

Certainly the first myth about Athena to be learned by a young child in Classical Athens concerned the story of her birth from the head of Zeus, motherless and fully armed. The tradition explained the special favor in which the Athenians believed they were held by Zeus, and also accounted for the goddess' warlike character and her aversion to marriage and motherhood.[1]

In actuality, the Athenians did not honor Athena so much for her martial connotations as for her gift to them of *techne*, or craftsmanship. Whereas shipbuilding and the chariot were viewed as important examples of *techne*, the goddess' pre-eminent gift was considered to be the art of textile production: spinning and weaving (see **Textiles**). This craft was the quintessential realm of women, and it is with women that almost every one of Athena's rituals is associated. The goddess was honored each year with a peplos which was traditionally woven by selected women of the city, and which was surely a thank offering for her role in the defeat of the Giants.[2] Participating in the preparation of the fabric were several young girls, the Arrephoroi, who subsequently took part in a ritual that is generally agreed to have resembled an initiation rite of puberty, involving the transport of concealed contents in a container (see **The Plynteria and Arrephoroi**). The Arrephoroi of cult have, in turn, been identified with the mythical Aglaurides, three daughters of King Kekrops of Athens, and, in his essay in this volume, Alan Shapiro emphasizes the prominence of their sanctuaries on the slopes of the Acropolis (see also **Erichthonios**). Aglauros was especially honored on two occasions each year: in the annual oath-taking by the new ephebes, and during the Plynteria, the festival that celebrated the bathing of the statue of Athena (see **The Plynteria and Arrephoroi**).

The ritual evidence attesting to Athena's special tie with women is buttressed by the mythical tradition. It was said that, in the contest between Athena and Poseidon for the patronage of Attica, the women of Attica voted for Athena, and for this they were punished by being excluded from Athenian citizenship.[3] The story sounds much like a late rationalization of an existing practice, but the fact that a special rapport between women and Athena was cited as the basis for the rationalization argues for its long-standing tradition.

Although the epithet Parthenos (a physically mature, but unmarried maiden) cannot be attested for Athena before the Classical period, the surviving literary references imply a long popular vision of the goddess as a parthenos, and her close ties with the Arrephoroi and the Aglaurides additionally support this identification.[4] We should also remember that the Late Archaic statues of pubescent girls known as korai (no. 1) were essentially parthenoi. It is noteworthy, too, that during the festival of the Plynteria the ancient statue of Athena was bathed in preparation for her reception of a new peplos. The ritual recalls that in which the bride is bathed and clothed in preparation for her wedding (See **The Wedding**). We should also remember that the ancient olivewood statue of Athena was heavily ornamented with a diadem, earrings, necklace, a golden aegis, and a golden owl and thus very much resembled a bride, Pandora herself, and a *kanephoros*, or virginal basket-carrier (see **Pandora** and no. 60).[5] It is not insignificant that the Plynteria was considered sacred to Aglauros, another parthenos who would never marry.

Athena's name appears in Linear B; this and the fact that in the *Iliad* she is the recipient of a peplos dedicated by Hecuba argue that the goddess was similarly honored in Bronze Age cult, where storycloths were almost certainly dedicated as votive offerings (see **Textiles**).[6] It is also likely that in Bronze Age cult Athena was honored by processions of women similar to those depicted on both a wallpainting from Tiryns and the Hagia Triadha sarcophagus; the latter scene includes an offering basket that is thought to be the predecessor of the *kanoun* carried in Classical ritual (no. 60).[7] On a fresco from Thera, a scene of women gathering saffron is featured so prominently that the activity must have been regarded as a ritual (p. 240, figs. 1-2).[8] Indeed, in Classical times saffron, the stamen of a kind of crocus, was viewed as a cure for menstrual ailments and was so closely identified with women that the bride's veil was dyed with saffron and the girls serving Artemis as Little Bears wore saffron colored garments (see **The Wedding, Iphigenia**, and **Little**

Fig. 1. Detail from Fresco of the Saffron Gatherers, Thera, 1800-1500 B.C. Courtesy Idryma Theras, Petros M. Nomikos.

Bears). A passage in Euripides' *Hecuba* suggests that the peplos woven for Athena was also saffron-colored.[9]

Several decades ago, Herington observed that the Classical Athenians seemed to recognize two facets of Athena: a peaceful mother deity who survived in the Athena Polias and a martial parthenos honored in the Parthenon.[10] He argued that the distinction had ancient antecedents, but Elizabeth Barber, noting that the loom used in Bronze Age Greece originated in Old Europe, argues

Fig. 2. Drawing of the Fresco of the Saffron Gatherers, Thera, 1800-1500 B.C. After Marinatos (1984) 62.

on an analogy with Old European precedents that these seemingly diverse characteristics can be accommodated within a single tradition.[11] Barber points out that the Vilis of age-old Slavic tradition are thought to be young women who died before giving birth, either unmarried or the victims of childbirth. Like Athena, the Vilis are honored with the dedication of ritual fabric and are thought to be part-bird; in the *Iliad*, Athena actually assumes the form of an owl.[12] Although childless, Vilis are viewed as potent forces of fertility on the grounds that the generative potential that had not found expression during their lifetimes could be harnessed to enhance the fertility both of humans and of the agricultural cycle.

The close association in the Vili tradition of childlessness with maternal nurturance finds a provocative echo in the ancient traditions that surround Athena. Robert Parker has noted the very early origin of the story of Erichthonios, who was born from Earth to become the nursling of Athena (see **Erichthonios**).[13] In several Classical vase-paintings depicting the goddess' warm reception of the boy (nos. 67, 68, and 72), the artists have spotlighted the swaddling cloth that Athena holds. In the *Ion* Kreousa describes the swaddling cloth as a "peplos," an unsurprising usage of the word because the peplos was, in fact, simply a rectangular length of fabric that could be used in a multitude of ways.[14] Athena thus bestows on Erichthonios what the Athenian people present to her, and it is likely that the ritual dedication honored the goddess's generative capacity in her identity both as a parthenos and a mother deity. As Herington himself noted, it was not until the political strategizing of the late sixth and early fifth centuries that the martial and parthenogenic aspects of the goddess were given precedence.[15]

1. Hesiod, *Theogony* 678-86, 693-705. See Burkert (1985) 139ff; Loraux (1984) 11, 77, 134, 139, 177, 211, 212; Barber (1991) 362, 380, estimates that the peplos was five to seven feet long and four to five feet wide; Ridgway (1992) 127.
2. See Barber (1992) 113.
3. Augustine, *City of God* 18.9. See Tyrrell and Brown (1991) 180-81; Vidal-Naquet (1981) passim.
4. Herington (1955) 9-15.
5. Herington (1955) 23.
6. Homer, *Iliad* 6.209-311, 14.178-9. See Barber (1992) 112; Barber (1994) 153, 240.
7. Schelp (1975) 20.
8. Marinatos (1984) 62-68; Doumas (1992) 127-75.
9. Euripides, *Hecuba* 466-74. See Barber (1991) 232, 362; Barber (1992) 103.
10. Herington (1955) 11, argued for distinguishing the mother goddess aspect of Athena from a martial parthenos aspect on the grounds that the Greeks viewed virgins as "pugnacious."
11. Forthcoming in a volume in memory of Marija Gimbutas.
12. Homer, *Iliad* 1.319-23.
13. Parker (1986) 190-202.
14. Euripides, *Ion* 1428.
15. Herington (1963) 65-70.

62

PROTOME (BUST) OF ATHENA

460-450
Munich, Staatliche Antikensammlungen München, inv. no. NI 6711

Terracotta
H 20.8 cm.

Unpublished.

Mended, with a diagonal join visible across aegis.

The protome comprises the head to waist, including the upper arms down to the elbows. Athena is frontal and wears a peplos beneath an aegis adorned with six winding snakes and a Gorgon face. Her center-parted hair is brought back over each ear, and the locks on top of the head are slightly wavy, with the lock closest to the face especially undulating. Flanking the face are long locks to the shoulders, scored horizontally. Her headdress comprises a narrow band beneath a higher one, of equal height throughout.

The protome was a traditional type of votive dedication and was usually molded from terracotta. Reflecting the venerable history of the protome are several conservative features in this example. The neck is rendered as a flat expanse, and the ears are missing. Moreover, the shoulders are rotated to the front, although the fastenings of the peplos would normally occupy the top center of the upper arms. Also retained from Archaic depictions are the horizontally scored masses of hair flanking the face and the high headdress that does not taper as its curves round the head.

Combined with these traditional features is a superb Early Classical handling of the face. The eye is set closely beneath the eyebrow, which is rendered as a carination of the forehead. The upper and lower eyelids are especially wide, thereby accentuating the eye. As will be distinctive of sculpture from just after mid-century, the upper part of the eyeball projects over the lower part. Distinctively Early Classical are the fullness of the jaw and the cleft in the chin beneath the mouth. The slightly downturned corners of the mouth look forward to the "Parthenon pout."

The protome's combination of traditional and contemporary features reminds us that Archaic depictions of Athena present her as a mature woman. It was the Classical period that envisioned her in her identity as a parthenos, a physically mature, but unmarried young woman. The Munich protome captures that period of transition when, beneath her heavy locks and ponderous headdress, the countenance of a youthful, maidenly goddess begins to emerge.

FIGURINE OF ATHENA

ca. 450
Baltimore, Walters Art Gallery, inv. no. 54.766
Purchased from Brummer in 1929

Bronze
H 14.4 cm., W 7.9 cm.

Publications: Walters Art Gallery, *Fashions of the Past* (Baltimore 1945) 12 (illus.); D.K. Hill, *Catalogue of Classical Bronze Sculpture in the Walters Art Gallery* (Baltimore 1949) 86, no. 185, pl. 38; F. Eichler, *Gnomon* 23 (1951) 61; H.G. Niemeyer, *Promachos: Untersuchungen zur Darstellung der bewaffneten Athena in archaischer Zeit* (Waldsassen/Bayern 1960) 91, no. A2; E. Bielefeld, *IstMitt* 12 (1962) 32 n. 40; H. Hoffmann, "Master Bronzes from the Classical World," *Apollo* 86 (November 1967) 340, fig. 18; Mitten and Doeringer (1967) 96, no. 92 (illus.); W. Fuchs, *Die Skulptur der Griechen* (Munich 1969) 185, fig. 194-95; G.K. Sams, *Small Sculptures in Bronze from the Classical World* (Chapel Hill, W.H. Ackland Memorial Art Center, March 7-April 18, 1976) no. 23; A. Leibundgut, *Die Römische Bronzen der Schweiz III: W. Schweiz, Bern und Wallis* (Mainz 1980) 50; R. Tölle-Kastenbein, *Frühklassische Peplosfiguren Originale* (Mainz 1980) 48-49, no. 8b, 51-52, pl. 35; Keuls (1985a) 39-40, fig. 18; Neils (1992b) 12, 149, no. 8; R. Thomas, *Griechische Bronzestatuetten* (Darmstadt 1992) 94-95, fig. 86.

Missing spear in left hand.

Athena stands with her left knee slightly relaxed. Her left elbow is bent and the hands of her upraised left hand steadied a spear, now missing. Her right forearm and hand are outstretched, with the fingers extended; on the upraised palm and thumb an owl is perched. She wears a girded peplos with overfold that is open on her right side. Her head is inclined to her right and downward, and she gazes down in the direction of the owl. Over her long hair, which tapers to the middle of her back, she wears a helmet with raised cheekpieces. The base of the helmet crest is indicated by two parallel ridges, and there is a winged, long-tailed Sphinx on the crown.

63

With admirable subtlety the artist has rejected the strict frontality of his Archaic predecessors. As Athena raises her left arm to support her spear, her left shoulder is correspondingly elevated. The effect of the effort is reflected in both the diagonal fold of drapery that originates at her left nipple and the more emphatic fold in the middle of her back. The asymmetry continues at her waist where, over her right, supporting leg, her right hip is minimally elevated. These departures from verticality are accentuated by the inclination of Athena's head, which leads our eye first to her owl and then across to her left knee. The folds of her overfold have plasticity, and the tubular folds over her supporting right leg are rendered with volume and an interesting variation in width.

Athena's gaze is directed toward a point on the ground that is somewhere in front of her right foot. The inclination of her head is more extreme than the gaze requires and also more extreme than would suffice should she be gazing down at imaginary worshippers. Her head is rather bowed in *aidos*, or modesty, which was becoming in all women, including goddesses, and prescribed as well for youths and even grown men before the gods (see **Aidos and Sophrosyne**). Here the connotations of *aidos*, shame, shyness, and respect, are underlined by the gentle and affectionate gesture of her hand beneath the owl and the absence of her aegis and Gorgoneion. Even her helmet is pushed back upon her head, with the Sphinx functioning more as a decorative headdress than apotropaic device. Lacking her trademark emblems of power, Athena is presented as non-combative and unthreatening. The figurine epitomizes the transition that Athena's image underwent during the first part of the fifth century, because this demure, even shy, maiden has moved well beyond her militant image in earlier times and looks forward to her even more literal portrayal as a parthenos in the second half of the century (see **Athena** and nos. 65 and 70).

It has often been suggested that the Walters figurine was inspired by a famous statue that has not survived. Leibundgut points out similarities with the type of the Martigny Athena, and Tölle-Kastenbein suggests that a statue on which she was based served as the prototype for the Elgin Athena. The Sphinx on the figurine's helmet was a well known feature of the approximately contemporary Pheidian statue of Athena Parthenos, and Jennifer Neils points out that on coins of the Roman period, which are certainly based on a lost prototype, an owl also perches on Athena's right hand.

63

DECREE RELIEF WITH ATHENA

ca. 410-400
Baltimore, Walters Art Gallery, inv. no. 23.177

Attic
Marble
H 50.8 cm., W 20 cm., Th 16.6 cm.

Publications: Walters Art Gallery, *Fashions of the Past* (Baltimore 1945) 9 (illus.); E. Reeder, *Hellenistic Art in the Walters Art Gallery* (Baltimore 1988) 70, no. 1; C. Lawton, "An Attic Document Relief in the Walters Art Gallery," *JWalt* 51 (1993) 1-9; M. Mangold, *Athenatypen auf attischen Weihreliefs des 5. und 4. Jhs. v. Chr., Hefte des Archäologischen Seminars der Universität Bern. Beiheft* 2 (1993) 48, 73, no. 57, pl. 10.2.

Broken down both sides with top and bottom edge preserved; chipped over front. The moldings above and below the scene consist of a fillet above an ovolo. The inscription above the scene reads:]ΝΟΣ[. The inscription beneath the scene reads:]ΝΕΡΙ[.

Athena stands almost frontally, turned slightly to her right with her left leg relaxed. She wears a girded peplos with kolpos and an overfold, as well as sandals. Her left elbow rests upon the top of a pillar over which her aegis is draped; the pillar is shown from the corner and includes the receding side. Her right arm was at her side. Her head, in left profile and extending to the base of the upper molding, is inclined, and her gaze is also directed downward. To her right are the remains of a scepter.

64

The inscriptions identify the sculpture as belonging to a decree or record relief. This kind of monument typically takes the form of a narrow upright rectangle, on which a scene featuring a deity rises above an often lengthy inscription of a public document, such as an honorary decree or a formal alliance. The lettering dates this relief to the late fifth century, and Lawton suggests that the inscription named the person with whom the document was concerned.

Supporting a date for the relief at the end of the fifth century are the corded folds of Athena's peplos and its transparency over her relaxed leg, whose contours are clearly revealed. The foreshortening of the pillar is also compatible with this date.

Athena is here portrayed as composed and relaxed, heir to the tradition of timeless effortlessness introduced on the Parthenon frieze. It is, however, a solemn event that she witnesses, for the carved inscription formalizes an official decree, and so we must be careful not to mistake the self-assured gesture of the goddess's leaning elbow for casual disinterest (see **Gesture and Gaze**). Though first seen in the figure of Zeus on the Parthenon's east frieze (p. 249, fig. 2), Athena's leaning gesture was more directly inspired by a lost statuary prototype, the so-called Leaning Athena. The date of that work is unknown, but it obviously predated an echo of the type that appears on the decree relief of Apollophanes of Kolophon of 427/6. The substitution in this scene of a pillar for the Leaning Athena's shield is surely due to influence from the type of the

Aphrodite in the Gardens (ca. 435, see no. 17), where the angle of the goddess' body is more extreme. The verticality of Athena's stance on this relief compares well with the figure of Amymone on a contemporary hydria in New York (no. 116).

Consistent with her depiction in vase-painting and sculpture of the last decades of the fifth century, Athena is here presented as an unassuming maiden (see **Athena**). The shield of the statuary prototype has been replaced by a pillar, and she has even removed from her torso her aegis, which is of diminutive size. The Gorgoneion is larger than we would normally find it on the aegis, but it is so appropriately scaled to the pillar that its primary function appears to be decorative. Also compatible with the softened presentation of the goddess is her unbelted overfold, which does not follow the type of the Leaning Athena, but is rather inspired by the dress of Demeter, Hera, and Hygeia, goddesses of comforting, maternal character. This benign impression is further reinforced by the downward tilt of Athena's head in *aidos*, or modesty (see **Aidos and Sophrosyne**). Athena's portrayal is particularly in keeping with her later fifth-century image as a young mother (see no. 70) and an adolescent maiden (see no. 65).

Athena's quiet and informal demeanor suggests to Carol Lawton that the scene accompanied an honorary decree. In Lawton's reconstructed composition, a deity with a scepter stood between Athena and the honored individual, who would have been depicted in smaller scale.

65

STATUE OF ATHENA

late 5th century
Athens, Agora Museum, inv. no. S 1232

Attic, from the Athenian Agora
Marble
H 66 cm., W 28 cm., Th 24 cm.

Publications: H. Thompson, "The Excavation of the Athenian Agora. Twelfth Season: 1947," *Hesperia* 17 (1948) 175-76, pl. 51, 1-3; P. Amandry, "Chronique des Fouilles en 1947," *BCH* 71-72 (1947-48) 429, fig. 5; Thompson, "The Pedimental Sculpture of the Hephaisteion," *Hesperia* 18 (1949) 234, 239-40, pls. 51, 52.1; S. Adam, *The Technique of Greek Sculpture*, BSA Suppl. 3 (London 1966) 51; H. Thompson and R. Wycherley, *The Athenian Agora* XIV: *The Agora of Athens. The History Shape and Uses of an Ancient City Center* (Princeton 1972) 148 n. 152; A. Delivorrias, *Attische Giebelskulptur und Akrotere des fünften Jahrhunderts* (Tübingen 1974) 22-24.

Pentelic marble. Missing head, which was made separately and set in a shallow socket. Broken across right arm and across thighs. There is a hole in the left upper arm for the attachment of the lower arm. There are six holes in the points of the scalloped edge of her aegis; two more holes are on each shoulder; and there are two close-set holes in the center of her belt. The piece is carefully finished in back. Two *deltas* (Δ) are scratched into the surface, one on the left shoulder, the other on the left breast.

Athena, shown half lifesize, stands with her left leg advanced, the knee relaxed. She wears a belted peplos with an overfold that extends to the top of her thighs. On top of this is an aegis, where a Gorgoneion is centered between her breasts and appears to be suspended from two cords that pass around Athena's neck. The scalloped contour of the aegis has a raised, rounded molding, in which holes were pierced for the addition of metal snakes; metal ornaments were also fitted into the holes in her belt. In back, her long hair falls down her shoulders to the bottom of her aegis.

The figure is an excellent example of late fifth-century sculpture. The female body is remarkably well understood. The contours of Athena's upper back and shoulders are accurately rendered, and her breasts are correctly positioned. Although the fabric is not transparent, it is very thin, and it clings closely to the contours of the breasts, without, however, revealing the nipples. Over her torso the fabric falls into narrow and close-set folds, and on each side of her waist the fabric spills over her belt with a graceful liquidity. On her right side, several folds bifurcate before they pass under the belt; on her left side, the folds form angular loops with fairly deep pockets. Beneath the belt over her left hip each tubular fold admits a concave furrow that runs part way down its length. Consistent with a date at the end of the fifth century is the Gorgoneion's benign countenance, which testifies to the process of beautification that the image underwent during the last half of the fifth century (see **Gorgons**). Here the Gorgoneion is suspended from a cord in the manner of a pendant necklace.

The statue was probably dedicated as a votive offering but has also been tentatively linked with the east pediment of the Hephaisteion. No specific prototype can be identified, and it is possible that the statue has been only loosely inspired by statuarial predecessors.

Statues such as this one remind us that female nudity in fourth century and Hellenistic Greek sculpture has its roots in late fifth century sculpture. The left armhole is cut so deeply that much of the side of the torso is revealed. On Athena's right side, the fabric invitingly reveals the base of her breast and then teasingly skirts the rest of its contours, while exposing much of the side of her torso down to her waist. The suggestive glimpses of exposed skin combined with the clinging fabric over the breasts create an impression of sultry sexuality that indicates the direction sculptors of succeeding decades will explore.

This statue is of particular importance and interest because the possessor of such overt and youthful sexuality is Athena, patron goddess of the polis of Athens. The goddess was traditionally regarded as a parthenos, a term that signified an unmarried, but sexually mature, maiden (see **Athena**). Even so, the conventional Archaic and Early Classical depictions of Athena primarily accented her martial character, even though Archaic sculptors and dedicators were clearly convinced that Athena would find pleasure in the statues of adolescent girls, the korai. In the fifth century, by contrast, concurrently with the increasing juvenescence of all the goddesses, artists began to experiment with the literal portrayal of Athena as a parthenos. On the east frieze of the Parthenon, she is coupled with her sometime mate Hephaistos, and her aegis lies in her lap (pp. 248-49, fig. 1). In a late fifth-century decree relief (no. 64), the sculptor has rendered her with a graceful and demure demeanor, even though her role is that of official witness to the formalization of a decree. The same emphasis upon the ripe sexuality of adolescence is apparent in contemporary vase-painting. In scenes that represent Athena receiving the child Erichthonios from the earth goddess, Gaia, Athena is portrayed as a desirable maiden

65

65

who is also warmly maternal (see **Erichthonios**). On this statue from the Agora, the sculptor has tempered the youthful innocence connoted by the adolescent form by tilting the upper torso slightly backward, and giving the abdomen a slight forward thrust. The

resulting impression of stability and supreme self-assurance endows the figure with the dignity and regal bearing befitting a goddess, even a youthful one.

THE PLYNTERIA AND ARREPHOROI,
WITH THE PANATHENAIA AND THE PARTHENON

Having placed on their heads what the priestess of Athena gives them to carry—
neither she who gives nor they who carry have any knowledge of what it is—
the maidens descend by the natural underground passage.

Pausanias 1.27.3-4

Athenian religious festivals are often viewed in isolation from one another, but the Plynteria, the ritual activities of the Arrephoroi, and the Panathenaia were so directly linked that they should be considered together.

On the day of 30 Pyanopsion, during the festival of the Chalkeia, which was sacred to Hephaistos and perhaps to Athena Ergane (Athena of weaving), four Athenian girls were selected to be known as Arrephoroi and to live in seclusion on the Acropolis.[1] Also at this time a loom was set up on which a new peplos for Athena would be woven, and the process for selecting the weavers and approving the design for the Gigantomachy pattern was initiated. For the next nine months the weaving continued, with the participation of two of the Arrephoroi.

The seventh month following the Chalkeia saw the observance of the Plynteria, on 25 Thargelion.[2] In this ceremony the ancient olivewood statue of Athena Polias was undressed, bathed, and wrapped in a shroud in commemoration of Aglauros, who jumped to her death from the Acropolis (see **Erichthonios**). In keeping with this time of mourning, the sanctuaries were closed and no sacrifices were held. The olivewood statue was then redressed. At some point in the ritual baskets of sweetmeats made with figs were carried through the city.

One month after the Plynteria, in the month of Skirophorion, the ritual of the Arrephoria took place. The four girls placed on their heads baskets (kistae), the contents of which, Pausanias tells us, were unknown to their bearers. The girls carried their burdens down to the Sanctuary of Aphrodite in the Gardens, where the contents of the kistae were exchanged for other unknown contents. The girls again carried their kistae back up the Acropolis, at which point they were discharged as Arrephoroi and returned to their homes.

A month after the Arrephoria, and nine months after the beginning of the weaving process, the Panathenaia was observed on Athena's birthday, 28 Hekatombaion.[3] At this time, the olivewood statue of Athena was presented with the newly woven peplos.

It is generally agreed that the Plynteria and the Arrephoria were of ancient origin, and it also widely agreed that the Panathenaia had earlier antecedents as well, even though the festival was reorganized during the sixth century (see **Athena**). The antiquity of the rituals makes them promising sources of insight into the character of Athena's worship, and what immediately emerges from a comparative analysis is the common theme of renewal. Athena is presented with a new peplos on her birthday, which ushers in the new Athenian year. The presentation of the peplos was preceded not only by bathing the statue, but also by shrouding it in the manner used to prepare a body for burial. The fact that Aglauros was honored in the Plynteria is entirely appropriate, because Aglauros was a parthenos whose death prevented her from marrying and giving birth. The removal of the shroud and the subsequent redressing of the statue during the Plynteria calls to mind the new beginnings celebrated with the dressing of a bride. Moreover, the baskets of sweetmeats made with figs also have parallels in wedding ritual (see **The Wedding**).

In the activities of the Arrephoroi, the creative aspect of textile manufacture is directly linked with puberty, sexuality, and procreation. The girls' actions so immediately call to mind the story of the Aglaurides that most scholars agree with Walter Burkert that the myth of the Aglaurides was fabricated to explain the more ancient ritual of the Arrephoroi.[4] The Aglaurides were the three unmarried daughters of Kekrops to whom Athena entrusted a kiste in which, unbeknownst to them, the baby Erichthonios was concealed. When one or more of the girls could not repress their curiosity and opened the kiste, the baby boy was revealed together with a protective snake or snakes. The unexpected sight so terrorized the girls that one or more of them jumped off the Acropolis to their deaths (see **Erichthonios**).

247

Fig. 1. The central section of the east frieze of the Parthenon, 442-438 B.C. The figures have been identified as Hermes, Dionysos, Demeter, Ares, Nike (or Iris), Hera, and Zeus; the five figures of the peplos scene; and to the right, Athena, Hephaistos, Poseidon, Apollo, Artemis, and Aphrodite, with Eros standing at her knee. Photo montage, courtesy British Museum and D. Widmer.

Through its links with the later myth of the Aglaurides, we can surmise that the ritual of the Arrephoroi was closely related to sexuality. Like the Aglaurides, the Arrephoroi are entrusted with containers whose contents are unknown to them, but which were obviously evocative of sexuality and birth, because the destination of the girls' journey is a sanctuary of Aphrodite. In the myth, the baby Erichthonios was born when Athena threw upon the earth a bundle of wool with which she had wiped away Hephaistos' semen; Burkert suggested convincingly that the initial contents of the Arrephoroi's kistae included wool related to the weaving of the peplos. The second set of contents obtained in the sanctuary of Aphrodite must have been symbolic of the baby Erichthonios; ancient lexicographers mentioned biscuits in the form of snakes and phalluses.

Many elements in the ritual have analogies with girls' puberty rituals in other cultures.[5] The Arrephoroi are secluded on the Acropolis for the duration of their period of service, and the ritualistic recognition of their sexual maturity is aligned with both the skills expected of a mature woman (textile production) and the industriousness that the activity required. The Arrephoroi's unresisting acceptance of their mysterious burden formally demonstrated both their submission to society's mores and their acceptance of responsibility in matters of sexuality, childbearing, and probably also childrearing. Moreover, the maidens' journey could be said to affirm and renew the two greater truths of the earth's fertility in creating Erichthonios and Athena's own nuturance of the child as her nursling.

In the ritual of the Arrephoroi society's expectations of a young girl are made clearly manifest. The presentation of a container to an unmarried girl has parallels not only with the Aglaurides, but also with Pandora; with puberty the maturing girl receives as a gift the potential to nourish life, and she is simultaneously given instruction in how to use that gift, which she may or may not follow (see **Women as Containers** and **Pandora**). It is noteworthy that the Arrephoroi are never told of the nature of both sets of contents that they carried. They nevertheless submit obediently to their mysteri-

ous directives, in contrast with the eagerness of the Aglaurides who open the forbidden kiste. It is clear that both myth and ritual advocate self-control in the matter of a young girl's sexual curiosity, with the myth providing a graphic illustration of the ramifications of disobedience.

A second social value transmitted in the ritual pertains to textile production. Two of the Arrephoroi join with the accomplished older women in weaving the peplos, and only when the cloth is near completion do the Arrephoroi carry out their specified journey. The ritual's implication that the acquisition of the textile arts was a prerequisite to marriage finds a mythical parallel in the tradition that Pandrosos, the only daughter of Kekrops not to look inside the kiste, was rewarded by Athena with the gift of weaving. The message in both the myth and the ritual is that the girl who complies with what is asked of her is rewarded with the knowledge of textile manufacture, which was synonymous in Greek thought with a worthy wife, domestic life, and even civilization (see **Textiles**). The ritual of the Arrephoroi thus illuminates for us the Greek view of a young girl's preparation for marriage; she serves Athena to learn the textile arts, as in her service to Artemis she learns to repress her nature as an untamed animal (see **Little Bears**).

The sequence of rituals discussed here offers a dramatic illustration of the role of clothing in defining status and changes in identity. During the period when the new peplos was being woven for Athena, we are told that the Arrephoroi wore distinctive white garments. Also concurrently with the weaving, the old statue of Athena was undressed, shrouded, and then redressed during the Plynteria. We assume that, upon the presentation of the new peplos during the Panathenaia, the statue was again undressed and redressed in the freshly woven garment that had been elaborately worked with the story of Athena's part in the defeat of the Giants.

The emphasis in these festivals on renewal, expressed ritualistically through a nine-month period of textile production, bathing, dressing, and journeying, helps us understand the motivation behind the depiction of the creation of Pandora on the base of the statue of the Athena Parthenos within the Parthenon. Here the

motherless goddess Athena was paired with the motherless mother of all women (literally the "race" of women), from whom all the generations of humankind would descend. Although details of the base's representation are unclear, we know that Pandora, who would be the first mother, was depicted as a bride, richly bedecked in finely woven garments that were the special gift and creation of Athena (see **Pandora**).

The Parthenon

Given the fact that both the cult of Athena and base of the statue of Athena Parthenos emphasized the theme of renewal and revitalization in tandem with the sexuality and procreative abilities of young women, it is difficult to refute Ira Mark's interpretation of the much debated east frieze of the Parthenon (fig. 1).[6] Mark argues that its subject is marriage, sexuality, and motherhood as the quintessential combination of elements that secured the continuation of the Athenian community. Mark points out the pairing of Athena and Hephaistos, and the wreath symbolic of bridal finery worn by Zeus' long-suffering wife Hera. Of particular interest is the linking of arms by Artemis and Aphrodite, beside whom stands her son Eros. The goddesses shared one very important common concern, because Artemis was the protector of young girls through marriage to motherhood and the sexuality of Aphrodite's realm represented the vital element that ensured conception, as Andrew Stewart discusses in his essay in this volume. Given this it is not surprising that Aphrodite wears the veil associated with married women, and Artemis lets the edge of her chiton slip suggestively from her shoulder in a manner that will soon become the hallmark of Aphrodite.[7]

Other elements in the scene reinforce Mark's interpretation. It is noteworthy that the two maidens who are usually identified as Arrephoroi carry small chests. The stool balanced on the maidens' heads has been convincingly connected with chthonic worship and is most likely in this context a reference to the cult of Pandrosos, who was honored with a sanctuary on the Acropolis.[8] The young

child holding part of the peplos is probably a boy assisting with the ritual, who thus finds a parallel with the *pais amphithales*, the boy with two parents living who participated in the wedding ritual as a reminder of its specific objective, the birth of a son (see **The Wedding**). All the elements in the scene can be thus comfortably explained as an expression of the essence of Athena's cult: an emphasis upon the unmarried maiden's transition to sexuality and motherhood as a means of securing the community's future.

1. For the Arrephoroi, who were thought to be ages seven through eleven, see Aristophanes, *Lysistrata* 641-47. See also Burkert (1966) 1-25; Burkert (1983) 150; Mansfield (1985) 271-77; Parke (1987) 218-21.
2. For the Plynteria, see Herington (1955) 30; Mansfield (1985) 139, 143, 370-73, 391, 439.
3. For the Panathenaia, see Mansfield (1985) 2-8, 18, 139-43.
4. Burkert (1966) 1-25; Burkert (1985) 225ff.
5. Lincoln (1991) 91-109.
6. Ira Mark (1984) 289-342. See also Jenkins (1985); Loraux (1984) 212.
7. Serwint (1993) 415 suggests that the exposure of Artemis' left breast refers to her aspect of mothering and care for the young.
8. Schäfer (1987) 197-98; Simon (1982) 141-42.
9. Mansfield (1985) 293, 354 n. 129.

Fig. 2. Detail of Zeus and Hera from the east frieze of the Parthenon, 442-438 B.C. Courtesy British Museum.

ERICHTHONIOS

Great-spirited Erechtheus, whom once Athena, daughter of Zeus reared,
but the grain-giving soil bore him, and Athena set him down in Athens, in her rich temple.

Homer, *Iliad* 2.547-49

Earth, Mother of all and oldest of all, who nourishes all things living on land,
all creatures that walk upon the land and all that move in the deep or fly in the air.

Homeric Hymn to Earth, Mother of All, 1-4

Great mother of the Olympian gods, dark Earth.

Solon, frag. 363-67

The myth of Erichthonios is an exemplar of myth's organic character. Of ancient origin, the story was clearly enriched over time and was subject to considerably different artistic interpretations, even within the art of the fifth century.[1]

It is usually agreed that Erichthonios and Erechtheus shared the same mythical tradition and that Erichthonios was the infant form of Erechtheus. In the version known to the Classical period, the smith-god Hephaistos one day became enamored of Athena and pursued her vigorously. Taking advantage of the god's lameness, the goddess escaped, but his semen fell upon her thigh. Athena used a piece of wool to wipe away the semen and then threw the wool upon the earth. Where it landed, the baby boy Erichthonios was born from Earth, or Gaia, who subsequently handed the child over to Athena, who became his nurse.

Athena put the boy in a kiste, a basket or small chest, and handed the container over for safekeeping to the three unmarried daughters of king Kekrops of Athens. The girls, Aglauros, Herse, and Pandrosos, were instructed not to look inside the basket, but Aglauros, and possibly Herse, could not restrain their curiosity. When they lifted off the lid and saw the baby Erichthonios guarded by one or more snakes, they were so terrified by the sight that they jumped off the Acropolis to their death. The obedient daughter, Pandrosos, was rewarded by Athena with the gift of weaving, and she became the first mortal woman to weave garments for mankind.

Some elements in the story are certainly older than others. The myth as we have it in the Classical period has three parts: the attempted rape by Hephaistos; the birth of Erichthonios from Gaia and his transfer to the care of Athena; and the incident with the daughters of Kekrops. The oldest of these is the segment about the birth of Erichthonios from Gaia and the nursing of the child by Athena. It appears in the *Iliad*'s Catalogue of Ships, which, even should the lines be a later interpolation, are at least of sixth- century date. Robert Parker argues that the vignette of Hephaistos' pursuit is a later addition, and the episode certainly seems to have been inspired by the conventional pursuit of a young maiden by an athletic and invariably successful suitor (see **Amymone** and **Pursuit Scenes**).[2] It is important to note that the addition of Hephaistos modifies Gaia's contribution, because no longer does she bear the child spontaneously, but rather accepts the semen of Hephaistos who thus becomes the child's father.

In his essay in this volume, Alan Shapiro notes that the daughters of Kekrops are not linked with Erichthonios until after the Persian Wars, although they have extremely early roots. Similarly, Robert Parker follows Walter Burkert in arguing that the participation of the Aglaurides was fabricated in order to explain the much older ritual of the Arrephoroi, who carried baskets with mysterious contents to a sanctuary of Aphrodite below the Acropolis (see **The Plynteria and Arrephoroi**). Indeed, aspects of the Aglaurides episode conveniently integrate certain features of the Acropolis, including its sacred snake, the nearby sanctuary to Pandrosos, and that of Aglauros on the lower slopes. One should also note that the strongly didactic ring of episode's underlying theme of disobedient young women echoes the more artfully concealed message in the ritual of the Arrephoroi, expressing the same apprehension that physically mature young women will explore their sexuality before marriage (see **The Plynteria and Arrephoroi**).

Especially interesting is the image of the child Erichthonios inside a container, a motif that has overtones both of a nurturing womb and a burial enclosure (see **Women as Containers**).[3] Here, the raising of the lid leads to the boy's emergence from the kiste in a virtual rebirth, as Erichthonios repeats his first epiphany from the arms of Earth, or Gaia. The process, even to its functioning as a second birth, has close parallels in the story of Danae (see **Danae**). Apollodoros' interpretation of Athena's action shows us the degree to which the connotations of the container had become recognized by his time and suggests the ease with which the motif could be employed in conscious myth-making. Writing in the second century B.C., Apollodoros explains that Athena put the boy in the chest to render him immortal, but that Aglauros' premature opening of the container obviated the process, a transparent parallel to the damaging curiosity of Demophoon's mother in the story of Demeter as told in the *Homeric Hymn to Demeter*, which was composed between about 650 and 550 B.C. Because a mother's birth of a child is also a gift ultimately of death, Aglauros' opening of the kiste functions as a mythical parallel to the birth process itself, as she interrupts the child's potential immortality to bestow mortality upon him.

Even though the incident with the Aglaurides was a subsequent addition to the story of Erichthonios, the tradition is in keeping with the associations of fertility and procreation with which the daughters of Kekrops were identified from their earliest appearance. It has been shown that the names Herse and Pandrosos are derived from words for "dew," whose analogy to semen was acknowledged even in ancient times. Moreover, we know that the same priestess on the Acropolis attended to the cults of Aglauros, Pandrosos, and Gaia Kourotrophos.[4] The apparently age-old prominence of the Aglaurides in the cult of Athena testifies to the goddess' primal association with generation and, by extension, with young women (see **Athena**).

The nurturing, if not fully maternal, action of Athena in her caretaking of Erichthonios is certainly compatible with the life-sustaining character of a goddess who was believed to protect the well-being of the Athenians and to renew the prosperity of the community each year. Elizabeth Barber has shown how closely the role of Athena as a source of fertility is intertwined with her identity as a parthenos, a fecund, but unmarried maiden (see **Athena**). The role of Gaia as Erichthonios' actual mother was always a prominent part of the story, but became accentuated for political reasons during the sixth and early fifth centuries in order to emphasize that the Athenians were literally "natives" of the soil of Attica, in contrast with their fellow Greeks in other city-states who were regarded as interlopers.[5] On the Parthenon's west pediment, where the contest between Athena and Poseidon was depicted, the presence among the attending figures of members of Erichthonios' dynasty stresses the autochthonous nature of the Athenian (male) citizens and complemented the depiction of the creation of Pandora, the ancestress of all women, on the base of the statue of Athena Parthenos within.[6] Because Hephaistos was both the father of Erichthonios and the creator of Pandora, the representations combine to offer exceptional honor to the lame god of the smith.

The Artistic Tradition

The myth was extremely popular in Classical vase-painting, but experiences a shift in emphasis over the course of the century in response to changing political and social currents. In the middle of the century the maternal aspect of Athena is paramount; by century's end the theme of autochthony is foremost.

Because so many of the vase representations of this myth closely share a number of common elements, we can be certain that there existed a common artistic prototype, one that was both prestigious and sufficiently appealing to artists that certain features were consistently retained even in otherwise individualistic reworkings. This prototype was surely a painting that was much earlier than the probable appearance of the story on the base of the cult statue in the Hephaisteion.[7] Common to almost all the vase renderings, and therefore stemming from this prototype, is the depiction of Gaia rising up from the earth with only her upper torso visible. She consistently has long locks of hair, as if to suggest that those who live below the earth have no interest, time, or daylight for fashionable hairstyles. The baby Erichthonios also consistently reaches eagerly for Athena, at whom he gazes, a motif that will enjoy a broad popularity on later grave reliefs, where the squirming child reaches alternately for its mother or its nurse (no. 6).[8]

There are also repeated consistencies in the representations of Athena. Her Gorgoneion is either absent or pushed behind her back, surely, as has been suggested, in order not to frighten the child.[9] Erichthonios often wears an amuletic necklace strung over his right shoulder, and in Euripides' *Ion* Kreousa remarks that the custom of protecting babies in this way stems from the tradition surrounding Erichthonios' birth.[10] Most significant is the swaddling fabric that Athena holds and into which she is about to receive the child. It is always ornately decorated, like the other garments in the scenes, obviously to stress the importance of the gift of weaving that Athena bestowed upon the people of Athens. But the fabric has considerable significance in its own right. In the *Ion*, Kreousa speaks of the "peplos" that she wove as a swaddling cloth for the baby Ion. The word "peplos" is so often associated with a woman's garment we forget that the term merely signifies a square expanse of fabric. The garment Athena holds in the vase scenes is therefore also a peplos, and thus Athena presents to the future ancestral king of the Athenian people the same gift with which she herself is honored at the Panathenaia (see **Athena**).

A final common element shared by most of the vase scenes is an expression of surprise on the part of one of the onlookers, for example, the figure of Kekrops on the kalyx krater in Palermo (no. 72). The figure of a woman rising upward is a familiar motif in Greek art (compare Danae, Pandora, and Persephone), and the gesture of surprise is a frequent accompaniment of the woman's emergence or reemergence. Because the motif of a female rising up is so clearly correlated with the annual renewal of vegetation, it is likely that celebrations of this renewal incorporated in them a ritualized expression of surprise in order to emphasize that the revival of life was not automatically anticipated but was received with gratitude and wonder.

The pairing of the story of Erichthonios with the story of Eos and Kephalos is too frequent to be coincidental, appearing on the vases in Palermo (no. 72), Berlin (no. 70), and Richmond (no. 71). Kephalos was the son of Herse and Hermes, and it is possible that a celebrated dramatic performance, perhaps a dithyramb, linked these two traditions and served as inspiration to the vase-painters (see **Eos and Kephalos**).

1. Homer, *Iliad* 2.547-48; Euripides, *Ion* 9-26, 260-82, 273-74, 496; Euphorion frag. 7 PW; Apollodoros, *Bibliotheke* 3.14.6; Hyginus, *Fabulae* 166 and *De Astronomica* 2.13; Ovid, *Metamorphoses* 2.552-61; Pausanius 1.18.2, 1.27.2. See Gantz (1993) 233-38; Loraux (1984) 126-35; Burkert (1985) 226ff; Parker (1986) 190-202.

2. See discussion in Parker (1986) 193.

3. Schelp (1975) 28 suggested that the *kanoun* of the *kanephoros* was descended from this basket. See no. 60.

4. Schäfer (1987) 197; Schmidt (1968) 208.

5. Strauss (1993) 44.

6. Castriota (1992) 150.

7. Harrison (1977a and 1977b) passim.

8. In the description of Ion's birth, which is generally agreed to adhere closely to the story of Erichthonios' birth, Kreousa comments that the baby stretched out his arms to her. Euripides, *Ion* 961.

9. See Arafat (1990) 52, who comments on the Athena Velletri. See also Harrison (1977a) 153-54.

10. Euripides, *Ion* 1428.

LEKYTHOS WITH ATHENA AND AGLAUROS

435-430
by the Phiale Painter
Basel, Antikenmuseum Basel und Sammlung Ludwig, inv. no. BS 404

Attic
Clay
H 47 cm., Diam 12.7 cm.

Publications: *CVA* Basel, Antikenmuseum und Sammlung Ludwig 3 (Switzerland 7) 54-55, fig. 21, pls. 29.7-8, 32.2-3, 34.4; E. Berger, *AntK* 7 (1964) 99; E. Berger, "Die Hauptwerke des Basler Antikenmuseums zwischen 460 und 430 v. Chr.," *AntK* 11 (1968) 63 n. 21; K. Schefold, *Führer durch das Antikenmuseum Basel* (Basel 1968) 101-102, no. 131,3; Schmidt (1968) 200-212, pls. 73-74; Brommer (1973) 258, no. B4; C. Isler-Kerényi, *Chronologie und Synchronologie attische Vasenmaler der Parthenonzeit, AntK-Beiheft* 9 (1973) 25; Kron (1976) 71-72, 253 no. E29; Loeb (1979) 181; *LIMC* I (1981) 289, no. 19, 295, pl. 212 (s.v. Aglauros); Schefold (1981) 51-52, 363-64, fig. 61; Oakley (1982b) 222, pl. 9c; Neils (1983) 288 n. 18; Brümmer (1985) 20 n. 127; Oakley (1990) 35, 83, no. 106bis, pl. 84, fig. 13b; Gantz (1993) 237.

Reassembled. The forehead, upper lip, and index finger of Aglauros, as well as the lower lip of Athena, are somewhat worn, and the contour of Aglauros' forehead is restored. Lines for the preliminary sketch are visible throughout. Graffito on underside. Around the neck is a band of tongues above a black-figure band of three palmettes with tendrils and dots. Above the figural scene is a frieze of three meanders alternating left and right separated by a saltire square. Beneath the scene is a band of running key pattern to the right.

Athena moves forward vigorously in left profile, her right leg advanced well in front of her left. She wears a chiton, her aegis, and a mantle that is draped around her waist, with the ends brought forward over her left shoulder. Over her long hair she wears a crested helmet that extends into the upper border. She also wears a necklace, and she clasps her spear in her left hand. Her right arm is extended, and her right hand grabs the left forearm of a maiden who is fleeing, her right leg advanced, the toes of her left foot resting on the ground behind her just in front of Athena's right foot. Both of her arms are raised, palms forward, fingers extended and separated. Her head is in right profile, and she gazes back into Athena's eyes. She wears an ungirded peplos with an overfold, a bracelet, a necklace, an earring, and three leaves in her hair, which is bound into a knot at the back of her head. Between the two figures can be seen a tilted basket decorated with two rows of a glazed square alternating with a reserved square enclosing a vertical zigzag. Emerging from the basket is a coiled snake, whose head thrusts upward toward the fleeing maiden.

The overturned basket (kiste) tells us that Aglauros has just disobeyed her instructions and has opened the basket to reveal the baby Erichthonios protected by snakes (see **Erichthonios** and **The Plynteria and Arrephoroi**). The boy is not shown, but one snake coils upward, its eyes on Aglauros. Athena also looks at the girl, the goddess' glaring expression accentuated by the abraded surface around her pouting lower lip. Athena is very angry, and she lunges forward to grab Aglauros' left forearm, the angle of her spear and her helmet's contour intensifying her aggressiveness. The literary tradition tells us that Aglauros jumped off the Acropolis to her death in fright from the sight of the baby and snakes in the basket, but the Phiale Painter implies that Aglauros' fear was mostly inspired by the rage of Athena. In his essay in this volume Alan Shapiro points out that the story of the Aglaurides did not become attached to the myth of Erichthonios until the beginning of the fifth century, and the lateness of the tradition could account for the different explanations for Aglauros' fatal leap.

The composition is based upon the well-known pursuit scene, in which a male god pursues a mortal maiden, whose fear is often expressed by her upraised arms (see **Pursuit Scenes** and no. 113, also by the Phiale Painter). In the context of this myth, the composition also recalls Hephaistos' unsuccessful pursuit of Athena, which resulted in the birth of Erichthonios. In pursuit scenes the maiden often looks back into the eyes of her male pursuer as an expression of her responsiveness to his advances (see **Gesture and Gaze**). Here, the exchanged glances between Aglauros, the parthenos (unmarried maiden), and Athena, the quintessential parthenos, have a similar sexual undercurrent and remind the viewer of Athena's narrow escape from Hephaistos' assault and Aglauros' newly acquired sophistication in sexual affairs (see **Athena**).

The Phiale Painter has provided a simple, but effective composition, in which the basket and the curvilinear contour of the snake are framed by the stark angles of Athena's and Aglauros' legs and by the interlinking of their arms. The mass of Aglauros' peplos coupled with the unbroken, flowing lines of its folds reflects influence from the Parthenon's metopes and compare well with the rendering of Amymone on a contemporary lekythos by the same painter (no. 113). Also by the Phiale Painter are the fragment with Danae in Oxford (no. 78) and the stamnos in Warsaw depicting women in Maenadic ritual (no. 125).

A dramatically different image of Athena is presented in contemporary renderings of an earlier moment in this same story (see nos. 68, 70).

HYDRIA WITH GAIA, ATHENA, AND ERICHTHONIOS

470-450
by the Oinanthe Painter
London, British Museum, inv. no. GR 1837.6-9.54 (E 182)

Attic, "from Chiusi"
Clay
H 37.4 cm.

Publications: *ARV²* 580.2 and 1615; *Para* 392; *Add²* 263; *CVA* London, British Museum 6 (Great Britain 8) pl. 85.1; Smith (1896) 159-60; B. Sauer, *Das sogenannte Theseion und sein plastischer Schmuck* (Berlin-Leipzig 1899) 60; A.B. Cook, *Zeus: A Study in Ancient Religion*, vol. 3 (Cambridge 1940) 182-84, pl. 22; Metzger, "Dionysos Chthonien," *BCH* 68/69 (1944-45) 330-32, fig. 12; Metzger (1951) 105-106; S. Papaspyridi-Karusu, "Alkamenes und das Hephaisteion," *AM* 69/70 (1954-55) 82; E. Simon, *Die Geburt der Aphrodite* (Berlin 1959) 51; *EAA* V (1963) 626, fig. 781 (s.v. Oinanthe); R.J. Hopper, *The Acropolis* (London 1971) 52; Brommer (1973) 262, no. B2; Bérard (1974) 36-37, 119-20, 148, pl. 2, fig. 6; Boardman (1975) 180, fig. 329; Kron (1976) 56-58, 249, no. E2; Metzger (1976) 295-98, fig. 1; Loeb (1979) 169-70, 339-40, no. Er4; Neils (1983) 275, fig. 2; *LIMC* II (1984) 999-1000, no. 477, pl. 754 (s.v. Athena); Mark (1984) 313 n. 119; *LIMC* IV (1988) 173, no. 14 (s.v. Ge); ibid., 929, no. 3 (s.v. Erechtheus); Arafat (1990) 52-54, 188, no. 2.19, pl. 12a; Gantz (1993) 236; Loraux (1993) viii, 135-36, pl. 3.

Around the mouth is a band of tongues. Above the scene is a frieze of ivy; beneath is a band of five meanders alternating left and right separated by a saltire square. Added purple for ends of taenia, fillet of Oinanthe, and inscription.

The earth goddess Gaia is seen in right profile to her waist, a mantle draped over her undergarment and around her shoulders, over the ends of her long hair. A sash is wrapped around her head, looped up at the back, with three leaves inserted above her forehead. She gazes up at Athena. Her right hand holds the left knee of Erichthonios; her left hand supports his left side as he twists around toward Athena, his arms outstretched to her, his head in right profile, and his eyes directed to her. She returns the gaze, standing in left profile, her right leg advanced, her upper torso bent over toward him. With both

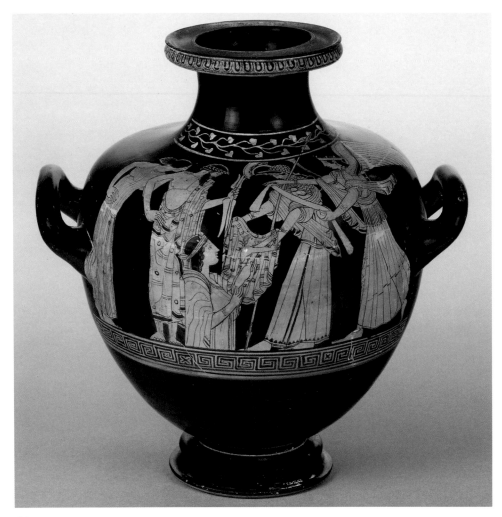

67

outstretched hands she holds behind him a piece of fabric that is decorated with bands of three horizontal lines separated by circles. She wears a garment that has an overfold to the waist and a scalloped lower hem; she also wears her aegis (which has been turned around to her back) and a mantle that is draped around her back, with the ends brought forward over each elbow. Her long hair is gathered at her nape and tied in a knot, and on top of this she wears a crested helmet that is cut off by the upper border; she also wears bracelets. Her spear leans against her left shoulder and overlaps the upper border.

Rushing forward in left profile, with her arms in front of Athena, is a winged female. Over her long undergarment is a diplois (double cloak) with fringe around the midsection; over this she wears a mantle that is draped behind her back, with the ends brought forward over each elbow. Over her long hair she wears a diadem from which three leaves rise vertically; she also wears bracelets and an earring.

Behind Gaia stands Zeus, who is almost frontal, his head in right profile as he stares down at Erichthonios. He holds his thunderbolt in his left hand; his right hand rests on his hip. His mantle is draped over his left shoulder, around his waist and legs, and over his long hair, which is plaited into a braid that encircles his head; he wears a wreath. Behind him, with her left hand resting on his right shoulder, is a woman who leans forward, her head in right profile as she gazes over at Erichthonios. She wears a sleeveless chitoniskos with a kolpos, and her hair is gathered into a knot at the back of her head. Above her head is inscribed ΟΙΝΑΝΘΕ ΚΑΛΕ ("Oinanthe is beautiful").

Gaia, the true mother of Erichthonios, hands the boy over to Athena who will henceforth care for him (see **Erichthonios**). In contrast to the maternal accent on Athena seen in other contemporary renderings of this subject, the emphasis in this scene is on the divine lineage of the child and his future identity as a monarch. As a Nike rushes forward to bestow a sash upon the boy in honor of his special stature, Athena stands formally apart from the boy without touching him, her hands concealed in the folds of the receiving blanket. Also lacking in maternal softness is her appearance, because her crested helmet is firmly in place on her head; its presence would have reminded the ancient viewer of the fear with which the baby Astyanax reacted to the sight of his helmeted father Hector in Book 6 of the *Iliad*.[1] Athena is also equipped with a spear, the tip of which is uncomfortably close to the baby's body. We receive the impression that Athena accepts the boy in his official identity as a future king of Athens, not as a beloved quasi-son.

Meanwhile, looming over the baby's head is the sizable thunderbolt of Zeus, who takes the place of the figure of Hephaistos seen on a stamnos in Munich (no. 68). The presence of Zeus alludes to the popular belief that, as the daughter of Zeus, Athena had special access to the god and his supreme powers; for this reason, it was believed that the citizenry of Athens under Athena's patronage enjoyed special favor with Zeus (see **Athena**). The god's presence in this scene implies his approval of Erichthonios and his continued commitment to Athens under Erichthonios' leadership. The political character of the scene is further accentuated by the prominence of the blanket, against which Erichthonios is framed. The blanket is an example of the textile arts that Athena will teach the Athenians, and, as a "peplos," it is also a reminder of the peplos that the Athenians would weave for Athena as an annual gift in gratitude for such generosity (see **Textiles**).

The maiden labeled Oinanthe leans upon Zeus' shoulder in a pose that is more common in vase-painting of the later fifth century. Its appearance on a vase of this early date argues that the prototype lay in painting, although a celebrated later sculptural translation is quite possible. Oinanthe was said to be one of the nurses of Dionysos,[2] and on the basis of her nurturing character she may have been included here. Appropriate to her Dionysiac associations are her prominent breasts and the lack of inhibition apparent in her familiar gesture.

1. Homer, *Iliad* 6.466-70.
2. Nonnus, *Dionysiaca* 14.225.

67 Detail

68

STAMNOS WITH GAIA, ATHENA, AND ERICHTHONIOS

470-455
by the Painter of Munich 2413
Munich, Staatliche Antikensammlungen München, inv. no. 2413
WAF

Attic, "from Vulci"
Clay
H 39.3 cm., W (at handles) 38 cm., Diam 31.4 cm., Diam (of lip) 19.3 cm.

Publications: *ARV²* 495.1 and 1656; *Para* 380; *Add²* 250; *CVA* Munich, Museum Antiker Kleinkunst 5 (Germany 20) pls. 252-55.1-2; Jacobsthal (1927) 137, 139-40, 172, 176, 183, 199, 205-206, pl. 100; Furtwängler and Reichhold (1904-1921) vol. 3, 95-98, pl. 137; Buschor (1940) 180-82, fig. 202; A.B. Cook, *Zeus: A Study in Ancient Religion*, vol. 3 (Cambridge 1940) 184-85, pl. 23; A. Greifenhagen, *Griechischen Eroten* (Berlin 1957) 26, 28-31, 72, figs. 21-24; Philippaki (1967) 103; Brommer (1973) 262, no. B1; Bérard (1974) 36, 148, pl. 2, fig. 5; Boardman (1975) 193, fig. 350.1-2; Robertson (1975) 218, 253, pl. 86a; Kron (1976) 57-58, 65, 249, no. E4; Metzger (1976) 295; Simon and Hirmer (1976) 127, pl. 175-177; Brommer (1978) 22-23, 208, no. B5; Loeb (1979) 168-69, 339, no. Er3; Robertson (1981) 79-80, fig. 118; Schefold (1981) 52-53, 364, figs. 63-64; Kardara (1982) 22-23, fig. 8; Shefton, "The Krater from Baksy," in Kurtz and Sparkes (1982) 176; Neils (1983) 275, figs. 3-4; *LIMC* II (1984) 999, no. 476 (s.v. Athena); Mark (1984) 313 n. 119; Keuls (1985a) 42-43, fig. 21; E. Simon, "Early Classical Vase-Painting," in *Greek Art: Archaic into Classical*, ed. C.G. Boulter, *Cincinnati Classical Studies*, New Series 5 (Leiden 1985) 71, pl. 63b; Simon (1985) 194-95, fig. 178; H. Walter, *Die Gestalt der Frau. Bildwerke von 30,000-20 v. Chr.: Anthropologische Betrachtungen* (Stuttgart 1985) 44, fig. 39; *LIMC* III (1986) 864, no. 98 (s.v. Eros); *LIMC* IV (1988) 173, no. 16, pl. 98 (s.v. Ge); ibid., 648, no. 217, pl. 403 (s.v. Hephaistos); ibid., 929, no. 6 (s.v. Erechtheus); Arafat (1990) 53-54, 188, no. 2.21, 198, no. 4.59, pl. 13; Robertson (1992) 176-77, figs. 186-87; Gantz (1993) 236; Loraux (1993) viii, 125, pl. 4.

Reassembled. Restored are the neck and mouth, part of the ornament, and small parts of figures. Above the figural scene is a band of tongues; beneath is a band of two meanders (left) alternating with a saltire square. Around the handles is an elaborate palmette-volute ornament. On Side B are a seated Zeus with phiale, a standing Nike, and two Erotes.

Gaia rises up out of the ground, her torso visible in right profile to just above the waist as she extends both arms upward, her hands supporting the baby Erichthonios by his buttocks and left side. She wears a sleeved garment or a mantle that passes over her long hair, of which two long curly ringlets fall forward over her right shoulder. She also wears two snake bracelets. Her head is in right profile, and she gazes upward toward the child. Standing opposite her in left profile, right leg relaxed, is Athena, who wears a voluminous mantle studded with stars over her longer undergarment and beneath her aegis, which is turned to her back. Her head is in left profile, a ribbon bound around her long hair and tied at her nape, where her long hair is gathered. Her right arm is enveloped in a piece of fabric that is decorated with similar stars, and her left hand, fingers extended, touches the right side of Erichthonios, who turns toward her in three-quarter right profile, curly hair to his shoulders. He gazes up at her, meeting her eyes. His arms are extended upward, with his left foot pressed against Athena's right thigh, and his right knee bent such that the toes touch the folds overlying her right thigh.

Behind Gaia stands Hephaistos, his left knee relaxed, his upraised left hand resting on his staff, his right hand on his hip, the index finger extended upward toward his breast. His mantle is draped behind his back, with the ends brought forward over both shoulders, and he gazes downward at Erichthonios. Flank-

68 Side B

68 Side A (**See also colorplate, p. 194**)

ing the figures is a pair of Erotes standing on tendrils. The one behind Athena holds a tendril in his right hand and a lyre in his left hand; the other Eros rests his left hand on his hip, while his right hand grasps an end of the spiral tendril on which he stands.

In contrast with other treatments of this subject in Classical vase-painting, the Painter of Munich 2413 has chosen to portray Athena and Hephaistos as proud and slightly anxious parents of a newborn child. Zeus has been relegated to the opposite side of the vase and only Gaia's upper torso is visible, with the result that the couple dominates the scene. Gaia's self-assured gesture, with arms fully extended, contrasts her role as an experienced nurse with the hesitation of Athena as a new mother. Almost every martial note has been silenced from Athena's portrayal. Her helmet is absent, as is her spear, and only the serpent coils on her back indicate that she is wearing her aegis. Her hair is simply dressed with a ribbon, and the forms of her body are lost behind the voluminous folds of her garment, which blend with the identically decorated receiving blanket that she holds in her right hand. Her tentativeness is also evident in the gesture of her right hand, because she has not yet grasped the boy, whose full weight is still being supported by Gaia.

Hephaistos is a similarly benign presence, his body at rest and the infirmity of his lame foot only subtly suggested by the manner in which he leans his weight upon his staff. The angle of the staff accentuates the parallel direction of Hephaistos' gaze down at his son, whose exchange of glances with Athena unites the three figures in a triangular composition. The impression of unity is reinforced

by the youthful Erotes, whose presence alludes to the erotic impulses that led to this moment. Now, however, Hephaistos' previous attraction to Athena is nowhere in evidence, and his attention is completely absorbed by the first glimpses of his son.

The execution of the scene is as masterful as its composition. Particularly noteworthy are the faces of Hephaistos and Gaia, where the line denoting the upper eyelid extends well beyond the pupil to indicate eyelashes and to create an expression of benevolent goodwill. An elegant S-curve renders the nostrils, and the jaws are full, in keeping with the Early Classical date. Also exquisitely drawn are the Erotes and the palmettes and tendrils beside them. The overall effect is one of quiet lyricism, an extolling of parent and child with no hint of the complicated events that preceded this moment or would soon follow hereafter.

69

PELIKE WITH ATHENA AND ERICHTHONIOS

440-430
by the Erichthonios Painter
London, British Museum, inv. no. GR 1864.10-7.125 (E 372)

Attic, "from Kamiros"
Clay
H 26.5 cm.

Publications: *ARV²* 1218.1; *Add²* 349; Smith (1896) 243; A.B. Cook, *Zeus: A Study in Ancient Religion*, vol. 3 (Cambridge 1940) 238-39, 248, pl. 29.a-b, fig. 154; *EAA* III (1960) 420, fig. 512 (s.v. Erittonio); R.J. Hopper, "Athena and the Early Acropolis," *Parthenos and Parthenon, Greece and Rome* suppl. to vol. 10 (1963) 3, pl. 1c; R.J. Hopper, *The Acropolis* (London 1971) 53; Brommer (1973) 263, no. B7; Kron (1976) 71, 252, no. E28, pl. 7.3; *LIMC* I (1981) 289, no. 18 (s.v. Aglauros, Herse, Pandrosos); Kardara (1982) 22-23, fig. 9; *LIMC* II (1984) 1000, no. 480, pl. 754 (s.v. Athena); Keuls (1985a) 123, 125, fig. 107; *LIMC* IV (1988) 933-34 no. 36 (s.v. Erechtheus); Boardman (1989) 98, fig. 250; Gantz (1993) 236-37.

On Side B two females stride forward to their left, legs widespread. The leader has short hair and bare shoulders; she holds before her chest bunched folds of her mantle, which covers her body to the ankles. The other female has spiral curls around her face and turns her head back in left profile. Her mantle passes over her head and completely over her body, concealing her arms and hands.

Above the scenes is a band of laurel; beneath the scene is a band of three meanders alternating left and right separated by a cross square. Added purple on side A for wreath and rays of diadem.

Athena stands turned in three-quarter right profile, her spear in her right hand, her left hand in front of her, fingers clasping her helmet. She wears an ungirt peplos with overfold and a taenia, and her hair is gathered into a knot at the back of her head with soft curls framing her face. Her head is in right profile and she gazes at baby Erichthonios, who rises up out of an oval basket, his torso visible to the tops of his thighs, which are bent forward as if he is seated. He wears a mantle that is draped around his waist, with the ends brought forward over his left shoulder. His right arm is lifted, the fingers extended. He has wavy curls to his nape, and his head is in left profile. Flanking the basket are two spotted snakes, one of which is bearded. The basket rests on a pile of boulders, at the base of which is the upended lid, encircled by a wreath; the lid's wicker interior is rendered by cross-hatching.

This is the end of the sequence of episodes that marked Erichthonios' eventful birth (see **Erichthonios**). The offspring of a near rape of Athena by Hephaistos, Erichthonios was born to Gaia and subsequently handed over to Athena, who enclosed him in a wicker basket that the goddess then entrusted to Kekrops' daughters. In this scene the container has just been opened by the incurably curious maiden Aglauros. The lid lies on the rocks of the Acropolis where she has tossed it in her terror and from which we presume she has just jumped to her death. Rising up from the container, Erichthonios makes his second arrival on earth, again in the presence of Athena. Now, however, he is a toddler for whom nudity is inappropriate, and he no longer reaches out like a baby for its mother's arms. He rather acknowledges Athena's presence with a single upraised hand.

Whereas Athena was a solicitous figure during Gaia's presentation of the infant (see nos. 68, 70), she is now a more sober and distant presence, and she stands formally in a pose probably inspired by sculpture. Although her aegis is absent and she has doffed her helmet, she holds the helmet prominently in front of her so that both its formidable presence and the menacing snake separate her from the boy. The moment is less a reunion of mother and child than a solemn and official second introduction to the goddess of a future king of Athens. And although the dignity of the moment is somewhat personalized by the boy's gesture and Athena's informal attire, the viewer is primarily mindful of Erichthonios' future role as a monarch and of the goddess' benevolent patronage of the Athenian people.

The two rushing figures on Side B must be two of the Aglaurides. Their speed and the backward glance at the cause of their terror and evidence of their wrongdoing suggest that the artist is following the version of the story in which both Aglauros and Herse jumped off the Acropolis to their deaths. What is noteworthy, and perplexing, are the bare arms and bunched folds of the leading, and smaller, daughter, who seems to have been undressed, or not fully dressed, when the lid of the kiste was lifted and the tumult began. It is interesting to note the connection between the mythical Aglau-

69 Detail of Side A

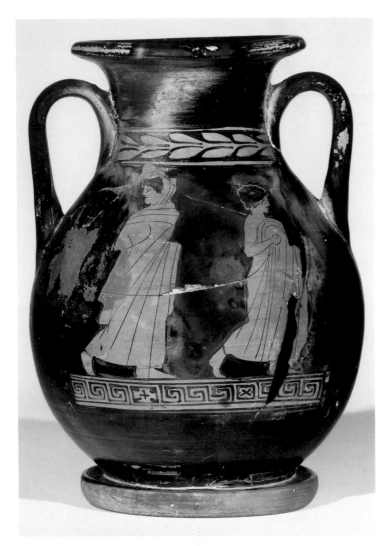

69 Side B

rides and the Arrephoroi of ritual who were closely associated with woven fabric (see **The Plynteria and Arrephoroi**). By pairing Athena and Erichthonios with the daughters destined for death, the artist pointedly connects the birth of a future monarch with what in this context could be described as the sacrifice of the maidens (see **Iphigenia**).

Although not a superior draftsman, the Erichthonios Painter delights in a lively narrative and figures of youthful charm. He is also willing to take liberties with the story in order to achieve the elegantly symmetrical snakes, who were said to have emerged from inside the container not from underneath it.

KYLIX WITH GAIA, ATHENA, AND ERICHTHONIOS

440-430
by the Kodros Painter
Berlin, Antikensammlung, Staatliche Museen zu Berlin Preussischer Kulturbesitz, inv. no. F 2537

Attic, "from Corneto"
Clay
H 12 cm., Diam 31.2 cm.

Publications: *ARV²* 1268.2 and 1689; *Add²* 356; *CVA* Berlin, Antiquarium 3 (Germany 22) 13-14, pls. 113, 116.2, 117.1, 132.4,8; *Monumenti inediti pubblicati dall'Instituto di corrispondenza archeologica* 10 (1877) pl. 39; A. Furtwängler, *Beschreibung der Vasensammlung im Antiquarium* II (Berlin 1885) 718-19; B. Sauer, *Das sogenannte Theseion und sein plastischer Schmuck* (Berlin-Leipzig 1899) 61-63; Jacobsthal (1927) 127, 161, 163, 205-206, pl. 85b; H. Thompson, "Buildings on the West Side of the Agora," *Hesperia* 6 (1937) 67, fig. 40; Buschor (1940) 214, fig. 232; A.B. Cook, *Zeus: A Study in Ancient Religion*, vol. 3 (Cambridge 1940) 185-87, fig. 95; S. Papaspyridi-Karusu, "Alkamenes und das Hephaisteion," *AM* 69/70 (1954-55) 81, fig. 36,1; Brommer (1957) 152-64, pl. 21.1-2; Brommer (1973) 262 no. B1, 263, no. B8; W. Real, *Studien zur Entwicklung der Vasenmalerei im ausgehenden 5 Jh. v. Chr.*, Orbis Antiquus 28 (Münster Westfalen 1973) 24-25; Bérard (1974) 37, 148, pl. 2, fig. 4; Kron (1976) 59-60, 63, 65-66, 79-80, 139, 250, no. E5, pl. 4.2, 5.2; Metzger (1976) 295-96, fig. 2; Brommer (1978) 21-23, 208, no. B1, pl. 16,1; Kaempf-Dimitriadou (1979) 17, 20-21, 92, no. 201, pl. 11.6; Loeb (1979) 171-72, 340-41, no. Er6; *LIMC* I (1981) 287, no. 7, pl. 210 (s.v. Aglauros, Herse, Pandrosos); ibid., 363, no. 39, pl. 280 (s.v. Aigeus); Schefold (1981) 54-55, 316-17, 364, figs. 65-66, 457; Neils (1983) 275-77, figs. 5-6; *LIMC* II (1984) 1000, no. 478 (s.v. Athena); *LIMC* III (1986) 774, no. 274, pl. 578 (s.v. Eos); Staatliche Museen Preussischer Kulturbesitz, *Antikenmuseum Berlin: Die ausgestellten Werke* (Berlin 1988) 126-27, no. 4; *LIMC* IV (1988) 173, no. 17 (s.v. Ge); ibid., 648, no. 218 (s.v. Hephaistos); ibid., 929, no. 7 (s.v. Erechtheus); Boardman (1989) 98, fig. 238; Arafat (1990) 52-53, 55, 188, no. 2.22, pl. 14; Gantz (1993) 236; Loraux (1993) ix, 41, 61-63, pl. 5a-b.

70 Detail of interior

258

70 Detail of Side A

Reassembled with small section (face of Pandrosos) missing from Side B. Tondo encircled by a band of six meanders alternating left and right and separated by a cross square; within, Eos moves to her left, her head turned back in left profile. She carries Kephalos, who is depicted as a young boy with a laurel crown over long ringlets. In the field are inscribed ΗΕΩΣ and ΚΕΦΑΛΟΣ Beneath the scenes on the exterior is a band of six meanders (right) alternating with a cross square. Elaborate palmettes and tendrils beneath each handle.

On Side A all the names are inscribed. Gaia rises up out of the earth, her body visible to her knees. She is turned in three-quarter right profile, her right knee relaxed. She is completely wrapped in her mantle, with only her hands visible. Her left hand supports Erichthonios' left side, and her right hand is visible beside his right thigh. Her scepter rests against her left shoulder. Her head is in right profile, and she gazes up at Athena; a long ringlet falls forward over each shoulder, and she wears a diadem decorated with a tongue pattern, from which four leaves rise vertically. She also wears an earring. Erichthonios is seen in right profile, a string with an amulet (periamma) passing around his right shoulder, His legs dangle, and his arms are stretched up toward Athena. She stands in left profile, her right leg advanced, with both knees bent and her upper torso leaning forward. She wears a chiton with a kolpos to mid-thigh and her aegis, which has been turned to her back. Her hair is gathered onto a bun at the back of her head and over this she wears a diadem. She also wears bracelets, and an earring, and her spear rests against her left shoulder. She gazes intently into Erichthonios' eyes.

Behind Gaia stands Kekrops, whose form below his thighs is that of a coiled serpent. He wears a tunic that is girded over the overfold and a mantle that passes behind his back, with one end brought forward over his right upper arm, the other end grasped by his lowered left hand. He steadies a staff in his upraised left hand. He gazes over at the child, a wreath on his curly hair. Behind Athena stands Hephaistos, his right, misshapen foot advanced, his right hand grasping the handle of his walking stick. His left hand rests on his left hip. His mantle is draped over his left shoulder and around his left forearm. His wreathed head is in left profile and he gazes over at the central group. Behind him Herse hastens forward, her right leg advanced. She wears a peplos with an overfold. Her right hand fingers her garment at her right shoulder; her left elbow is bent and the hand is outstretched, palm upward, fingers extended. The folds of her peplos blow out behind her left ankle. Her hair is gathered into a knot at her nape.

On Side B the names are inscribed. Hastening forward with right leg advanced, head turned back in right profile, is Aglauros, her right hand upraised, her knotted hair surmounted by a diadem. She also wears bracelets and an earring. Behind her rushes wreathed Erechtheus, his staff in his right hand, his left arm behind his waist, the folds of his pleated undergarment blowing up behind his left ankle. His mantle envelops most of his body. In the center, standing almost frontally, is Pandrosos, who wears a pleated garment with kolpos and overfold. Her hands are upraised on either side of her, palms facing outward, fingers extended. Approaching her in left profile is wreathed Aigeus, his staff in his left hand, his right hand upraised in gesticulation. The last figure is Pallas, who stands almost frontally, his left hand on his hip, his right hand resting on his walking stick. His head is in left profile, and he wears a mantle over his left shoulder and arm and around his waist and legs.

In this much admired work, still a different slant is given the moment that is also portrayed on nos. 68-69, 71-72. Here the central group of Gaia, Erichthonios, and Athena is without a male presence. The composition is a tightly self-contained unit with the baby framed within the crossed staff and spear. Erichthonios' arms parallel those of Athena, and Gaia's head is placed just behind the boy's, so that their gazes form a single line to Athena's eyes.

Athena is here an affectionate young mother. Her helmet is set aside, and the blanket is omitted so that her hands can reach out for Erichthonios. Her hidden right hand is presumably already in contact with the boy because it has passed behind his left side. The figure of Gaia is more prominent than in other versions of the scene because here she rises up out of the ground to her knees. She is also a far more presentable presence, no longer ponderous or unkempt as on other vases. Her staff is also unusual and signifies her divine stature. Gaia and Athena are here united as nurse and mother in their shared concern for the baby in a composition that has counterparts on later grave reliefs (nos. 6, 13), where a child reaches out from his nurse's embrace for the arms of his mother. The painter is thus presenting both goddesses as comparable maternal forces in the boy's life.

Similarly, Hephaistos and Kekrops form a balanced pair flanking the central group. Hephaistos is the natural father of the boy, but Kekrops will be a strong earthly paternal presence. Each wears a wreath, and Kekrops carries a staff as counterpart to the walking stick that supports Hephaistos' lame leg.

In this scene's emphasis upon the extensive and divine lineage that Erichthonios can claim, the presence of Kekrops' daughter Herse is logical. She will marry Hermes, and their son Kephalos will catch the eye of the goddess of dawn, Eos, whose abduction of the boy is the subject of the kylix's tondo (see **Eos and Kephalos**). Here, Herse fingers her garment in the bridal gesture of unveiling, probably both to signify that she is of marriageable age and to allude to the future divine elements in her own lineage (see **The Wedding**).

The theme of family and ancestry is continued on Side B, where the two other daughters of Kekrops are joined by legendary kings of Athens: Erechtheus (with whom Erichthonios will be confused), Aigeus, and Pallas. Standing before them and encouraging them onward is Aglauros, the impulsive daughter who will open the forbidden basket to reveal Erichthonios. Meanwhile, the obedient daughter Pandrosos stands with arms spread in a gesture of agitation befitting her hesitation to join her sister's escapade.

The Kodros Painter's draftsmanship is superb, his fabrics endowed with soft textures and rhythmic lines that reflect the contemporary style of the Parthenon frieze. The delineation of the central group with Gaia is outstanding, and the gracefulness of Athena's form and the boy's outstretched arms is especially admirable. It is interesting to note the artist's difficulty in providing Gaia with a foreshortened right hand that is still elegant. Gaia's hand seems barely to touch the boy's right thigh, although her gentle gesture is in keeping with the mood of the group.

70 Detail of Side B

KALYX KRATER WITH ATHENA, GAIA, AND ERICHTHONIOS

ca. 410
by the Nikias Painter
Richmond, Virginia Museum of Fine Arts,
The Arthur and Margaret Glasgow Fund, inv. no. 81.70

Attic
Clay
H 37.9 cm., Diam 41 cm.

Publications: Neils (1983) 277, fig. 7; M.E. Mayo, "Tradition and Imagination: Five Centuries of Greek Ceramic Art," *Apollo* 122 (1985) 430, 432-33, figs. 8-10; *LIMC* III (1986) 764, no. 124 (s.v. Eos); J. Oakley, "A Calyx-Krater in Virginia by the Nikias Painter with the Birth of Erichthonios," *AntK* 30 (1987) 123-30, pls. 18-19; *LIMC* IV (1988) 648, no. 221, pl. 403 (s.v. Hephaistos); ibid., 930, no. 11, pl. 632 (s.v. Erechtheus); Boardman (1989) 167, fig. 322; Arafat (1990) 52-53, 56-57, 188, no. 2.25, pl. 15; Carpenter (1991) 74, fig. 111.

Reassembled, with minor restorations. Above the scene is a frieze of slanting addorsed palmettes; beneath is a frieze of three meanders (left) alternating with a checker square, above a band of egg pattern. Extensive added white, especially for Erichthonios. On Side B Eos pursues Kephalos; both are labeled. Eos is winged and wears a peplos, diadem, and earring. Kephalos holds two spears in his right hand and wears a chlamys, petasos, headband, and sandals. Behind Eos a youth wearing a mantle prepares to hurl a stone. The uneven groundline and the vegetation above Kephalos' head refer to Mt. Hymettos, where the seduction took place.

On Side A all the figures are labeled except Gaia, Erichthonios, and the owl. Athena leans forward in left profile, her right foot on a rock. She wears a chiton beneath a peplos, as well as an aegis and a helmet rendered in checkerboard pattern; the helmet is crested. Gaia is seen in three-quarter right profile, rising out of the earth to her knees. She wears a belted peplos with overfold and a stephane over her long hair. Her right hand clasps Erichthonios' right thigh and the fingers of her left hand support his left side; he wears an amulet over his right shoulder and turns with both arms extended to Athena, whose hands are stretched out to him, her right hand touching the left side of his face.

Behind Athena a winged Nike strides forward, wearing a belted peplos with straps crossing her chest; over her left arm is a shield, and in her right hand is a spear. In front of her an owl is suspended frontally, a wreath in its claws. Beneath the Nike is Aphrodite, seated to her right and gazing at the central group. She holds a scepter in her left hand, and wears a belted peplos, a mantle over her lap, a sphendone, a diadem, sakkos, earring, necklace, and bracelets. Behind her stands Zeus, with mantle and wreath, a thunderbolt in his left arm, a scepter in his right. A youth is seated in three-quarter right profile behind Zeus, his head turned back to the central group, a staff in his left hand; the poorly preserved inscription may be read "Epimetheus" or "Prometheus."

Above Gaia's head, in a curve of landscape, is the upper torso of Hermes, who wears a petasos and mantle and carries a caduceus in his right hand. Behind Gaia stands Hephaistos, who leans on a walking stick under his left arm. His right hand is on his hip; his left hand gesticulates, and he wears a decorated tunic and mantle, sandals, and a wreath. Behind him is Apollo, seated in three-quarter left profile, his head turned back in right profile. He wears a mantle draped over his waist and legs and a wreath over his long locks; his left hand steadies a laurel staff. Beside his right knee is a tripod on a column.

71 Side A

In contrast with Athena's demeanor in other depictions of this moment, it is an eager goddess whom we see here, bending over markedly, with her weight pressed on a boulder, which must represent the Acropolis. Her hand even gently caresses the side of Erichthonios' face. His figure is rendered in a white that is superimposed on Athena's hands, and the technique lends the boy a divine aura, as well as a weightlessness within Gaia's grasp. The vehemence of his reach for Athena equals the intensity of her gesture toward him and results in one of the most emotional of the surviving portrayals of this moment. Also noteworthy is the special dignity accorded Gaia, who is visible to her knees and who wears a prodigious crown over her curly locks, which have the same texture and length as Athena's. Nike is also a prominent figure in this scene, standing just behind Athena with the goddess' shield and spear, to remind us that Athena's formal presence and official identity are only briefly relaxed during this maternal interlude.

Subsidiary to the main scene at which they are respectful spectators are the boy's father Hephaistos and Aphrodite, the catalyst of the unsuccessful rape. Zeus as Athena's father is another appropriate presence here, and Hermes is also a fitting guest because he was the god both of travelers and of children. Hermes will also become the father of Kephalos, the youth pursued by Eos on the other side

of the vase. Kephalos' mother will be Herse, one of the daughters of Kekrops to whom the chest containing the baby Erichthonios will soon be entrusted.

John Oakley suggests that the seated figure behind Aphrodite is more likely to be Epimetheus than Prometheus, because Epimetheus will be the recipient of Pandora, who will open her forbidden container (see **Pandora** and **Women as Containers**). The allusion is apt in this scene, because the daughters of Kekrops will disobediently open the chest in which the baby Erichthonios will soon be placed. And just as Pandora will be considered the founder of the race of women, so will Erichthonios be honored as the ancestral king of the Athenian (male) citizens. The story of Pandora will decorate the base of the statue of the Athena Parthenos, and it is widely agreed that the story of Erichthonios adorned the base of the cult statue in the temple of Hephaistos. John Oakley further suggests that the inclusion in the scene of Apollo, a tripod, and the owl with wreath behind Athena indicates that the vase honors a victorious dithyrambic performance, perhaps presented during the Thargelia, a festival closely linked with Apollo. A dithyramb was an ode sung by a chorus of fifty men or boys, and such choregic competitions were a regular part of many Attic festivals, with the winning poet awarded a wreath and a bull, and the sponsoring tribe the

71 Detail of Side B

71 Details of figures over the handles

recipient of a tripod. A victorious dithyramb on the subject of Erichthonios might well have included references to pertinent mythical figures, such as Epimetheus and even Eos and Kephalos, a subject found on several vases depicting the birth of Erichthonios (see nos. 70 and 72).

The Nikias Painter exemplifies the style of late fifth-century vase-painting in his use of multiple groundlines, isolated figures often in three-quarter poses, affected gestures, and pronounced inclinations of heads. He delights in ornamental patterns, such as stripes on drapery hems, which enliven his figures, and he excels in such varied drapery effects as billowing and clinging folds. The energy of his winged figures, such as Eos, the Nike, and the owl, complements the emotional intensity that infuses Athena's reception of her young charge.

KALYX KRATER WITH THE BIRTH OF ERICHTHONIOS

late 5th century
in the manner of the Talos Painter
Palermo, Museo Archeologico Regionale di Palermo, inv. no. 2365

Attic, "from Chiusi"
Clay
H 42.8 cm., W 42.8 cm.

Publications: *ARV²* 1339.3; *Add²* 367; A.B. Cook, *Zeus: A Study in Ancient Religion*, vol. 3 (Cambridge 1940) 187-88, pl. 24; S. Papaspyridi-Karusu, "Alkamenes und das Hephaisteion," *AM* 69/70 (1954-55) 82, fig. 36.3; Brommer (1957) 153, 155, 157, pl. 21.3; Brommer (1973) 208, no. B2, 263, no. B10; Kron (1976) 56, 60, 63, 65-66, 91-92, 100, 250, no. E7, 260, no. K6, pl. 4.1; Metzger (1976) 295-98, fig. 3; A. Greifenhagen, "Zeichnungen nach attisch rotfigurigen Vasen im Deutschen Archäologischen Institut, Rom," *AA* 1977, 215-16, no. 20, fig. 22; Brommer (1978) 21-23, 208, no. B2; Kaempf-Dimitriadou (1979) 17, 86, no. 125; A. Greifenhagen, "Addenda II zu Zeichnungen nach Vasen," *AA* 1981, 305, no. 2.215; Neils (1983) 277; *LIMC* II (1984) 1000, no. 479 (s.v. Athena); *LIMC* III (1986) 763, no. 120 (s.v. Eos); *LIMC* IV (1988) 173, no. 18, pl. 98 (s.v. Ge); ibid., 648, no. 219 (s.v. Hephaistos); ibid., 930-31, no. 12 (s.v. Erechtheus); Arafat (1990) 53, 55-56, 188, no. 2.24, pl. 12b.

Mended from many pieces. The upper border has a frieze of slanting addorsed palmettes; beneath the scene is a band of ivy between bands of egg pattern. On Side B winged Eos pursues a man (Kephalos or Tithonos) who holds a staff and looks behind him, his hands upraised. Behind her is a man who carries a staff and runs off in the opposite direction.

On Side A the torso of Gaia is visible to mid-thigh as she rises up from uneven, rocky terrain, where three plants emerge. She wears a chiton ornamented with dots, and with borders of spiral pattern at the neck, waist, and sleeves. Her belt is tied in a bow. Her mantle is draped over both shoulders and has a broad, black stripe along its edges. Long curly ringlets tumble down over her shoulders, and she wears a stephane, from the top of which rise a row of six upright leaves.

With both hands Gaia holds the baby Erichthonios, but her hands do not directly touch the baby and she does not look at him but, rather, upward at Athena. The baby's hips and legs are enveloped in a mantle, the black border of which suggests that it is part of Gaia's own mantle. With her left hand she supports the baby at the left side of his waist, her hand passing under the fabric. Her right hand steadies his right thigh and knee, which is bent, and the boy's right foot is pressed against her chest. Erichthonios wears an amuletic band over his left shoulder and across his chest, and on his short curly hair there is reserved diadem. His torso is turned in three quarter left profile toward Athena, and he leans and stretches forward, both arms extended to her. His head is in right profile, and he looks up at Athena.

Athena is rendered in a smaller scale than Gaia and stands with her left leg relaxed, her spear resting in the crook of her left arm. Her upper torso is covered by her aegis, which is decorated with a diamond pattern and bears no Gorgoneion; snakes wind from all of its edges. Beneath her aegis can be seen her peplos, which extends to the ground and is belted, with an overfold that reaches her hips. She is barefoot. Athena's hands are in front of her torso and hold a piece of fabric, also decorated with dots. Her right hand is enveloped in its folds; her left hand no longer survives. Her long hair falls down behind her shoulders, and on top of her head she wears a crested helmet, cheekpieces raised. The helmet has the same scale pattern as Gaia's crown. Athena gazes in front of her, toward Hephaistos, who is behind Gaia.

72 Side A

Flying above Erichthonios' head in left profile is a Nike, her garments flying out about her legs. Her wings are spread and her hair is drawn up into a top-knot at the crown of her head. With both hands she holds a large wreath directly above Erichthonios' head.

Behind Athena we see Kekrops in left profile, rendered in the same scale as Gaia. Below the waist his body takes the form of a serpent whose coils echo those of the snakes on Athena's aegis. His tunic covers his body to his hips and is decorated with interlinked palmettes; a band of egg pattern decorates the neckline, and a series of arcs decorate the hem. His left hand steadies a spear; his right hand is upraised, the palm facing out, fingers open in surprise. He has a long beard, ringlets to his shoulder, and a wreath. He stares upward at Athena.

Beside Gaia there is an olive tree, and behind this is Hephaistos, his left knee bent and the left foot resting on a rock, which is barely indicated. His orna-mented tunic bears a field of crosses enclosed by bands of rays. Narrow bor-ders of running spiral decorate the edges of his neckline, belt, and hem. He wears sandals, the thongs of which are tied around his ankles. He has a short beard, and upon his hair, which extends to his nape, he wears a wreath. His right elbow is bent and he holds tongs in his upraised right hand. He stares ahead, over Gaia's head, at Athena. Behind him and flying toward him is a Nike holding a wreath in both extended hands. Her wings are outspread, and the folds of her sleeveless, belted peplos billow out behind her.

In this scene the presentation of Erichthonios by Gaia to Athena has been given the aspect a formal ritual with solemn political overtones for the Athenian polis (see **Erichthonios**). The rocky ter-rain and the olive tree specify the hallowed ground of the Acropo-lis, sacred to Athena, and the omnipresent and elaborate textiles further emphasize the goddess' magnanimity to the Athenians through her gift of weaving (see **Textiles** and **Athena**). The pair of women is flanked by the boy's two fathers, Hephaistos as the bio-logical father and Kekrops as the dynastic patriarch. As in the other examples of this scene, the child squirms in his nurse's arms as his adoptive mother approaches, and so heartily struggles to be free of Gaia that he kicks his leg against her chest. She, in turn, accepts her subordinate stature and refrains even from touching the skin of the child as she gazes upward respectfully at Athena.

Unlike other representations of the scene, Athena does not lean over or reach eagerly for the child, but stands erect with dignity. She

72 Detail of Side B

263

does not even look at the boy but exchanges glances with Hephaistos, whose tongs are a reminder of the god's gift of metalsmithing to the Athenians. Athena holds the ornately patterned fabric before the child almost as an official vestment, and the voluminous folds fall as a curtain separating her from the boy and thereby further accentuating the formality of the occasion. The hovering Nike descends to present the boy with a wreath to signify the sacredness and triumphal character of the moment. The other Nike honors Hephaistos with a second wreath.

Although the surprised gesture of Kekrops expresses his wonder at the event, the painter has taken pains to show that Kekrops very much belongs in this gathering. He is rendered on the same scale as Gaia, and he further shares her unruly long ringlets. The prominence of his serpent coil bears witness to his special affiliation with the Underworld. Moreover, the angle of his spear echoes that of Athena, creating a comfortable rhythm pairing those two figures. Indeed, Kekrops is presented as a most appropriate surrogate earthly father to Erichthonios.

It has been suggested that this vase scene is directly drawn from a sculptural prototype on the Acropolis, and the subject would certainly be most appropriate to that context. The birth of Pandora was represented on the base of the statue of Athena Parthenos, and, like Erichthonios, Pandora also owed her existence to Hephaistos (see **Pandora**). The important difference was that, whereas Hephaistos artfully fashioned the female progenitor of all women, he was regarded as the biological father of the Athenian male citizenry.

KALYX KRATER WITH ATHENA AND KEKROPS

410-400
by the Kekrops Painter
Fulda, Museum Schloss Fasanerie, Hessische Hausstiftung,
inv. no. AV 77

Attic
Clay
H 57.5 cm., Diam 53 cm.

Publications: *ARV²* 1346.1; *Para* 482; *Add²* 368; *CVA* Adolphseck, Schloss Fasanerie 1 (Germany 11) pl. 46-48, reviewed by J.D. Beazley, *AJA* 61 (1957) 111; F. Brommer, *Antike Kleinkunst in Schloss Fasanerie (Adolphseck)* I (Marburg 1955) 9-10, pl. 20; Brommer (1957) 153, 157, pl. 22.1; E. Buschor, *Medusa Rondanini* (Stuttgart 1958) 33, pl. 47.2; *EAA* II (1959) 450-51, pl. 631 (s.v. Cecrope); Brommer (1973) 208 no. B3, 262 no. B4, 263 no. B11, pl. 17; Bérard (1974) 37; Kron (1976) 61-63, 65-66, 91-92, 100, 250 no. E11, pl. 5.1; Simon and Hirmer (1976) 152-153, pls. 226-27; J. Floren, *Studien zur Typologie des Gorgoneion* (Westfalen 1977) 129, no. 88, fig. A; E. Harrison, 'Alkamenes'

Sculptures for the Hephaisteion: Part II, The Base," *AJA* 81 (1977) 273; Brommer (1978) 21-23, 208, no. B3, pl. 17; *LIMC* I (1981) 287, no. 8, pl. 211 (s.v. Aglauros, Herse, Pandrosos); B. Shefton, "The Krater from Baksy," in Kurtz and Sparkes (1982) 176; Neils (1983) 281, figs. 11-12; Simon (1983) 52-53, pl. 14.2; Simon (1985) 194-95, 197, fig. 180; *LIMC* III (1986) 21, no. 6, pl. 15 (s.v. Attike); *LIMC* IV (1988) 302, no. 177, pl. 175 (s.v. Gorgo, Gorgones); ibid., 648, no. 220, pl. 403 (s.v. Hephaistos); ibid., 930, no. 10, pl. 632 (s.v. Erechtheus); Arafat (1990) 57, 188, no. 2.28.

A few pieces reattached, with a section missing from the rim on Side B. Above the figural scenes is a band of ivy; beneath is an elaborate band of lotus, palmette, and volute pattern. Above the scene on Side A are many inscriptions, reading ΚΑΛΟΣ and ΚΑΛΕ. On Side B Herakles brandishes his club as he approaches the Cretan Bull in a landscape of trees and vegetation. A Nike flies towards Herakles with a laurel wreath. Seated above the bull is Athena, and behind her a Nike leans on a shield. Above and behind Herakles, Apollo is seated, wearing a laurel wreath and clasping the trunk of a laurel tree; beneath him a woman stands in right profile, wrapped almost entirely in her cloak, from which only her right hand protrudes.

On Side A Athena stands almost in the center, on an invisible groundline that is even with the tops of the handles. Her left leg is relaxed and her head is in left profile. Her left hand steadies the shaft of her spear and she holds a phiale in her extended right hand. Her chiton is decorated with stars and crosses and has a band of palmettes around the hem. The Gorgoneion of her aegis is partly hidden by her mantle, which is brought across her waist, with the ends falling forward over her left shoulder; the mantle's hem has a large band of rays. Over her long hair she wears a diadem, from which four leaves rise vertically; she also wears bracelets and a necklace. Opposite her is Kekrops, his body beneath the waist winding into snaky coils, his hair and beard white. He wears an elaborately ornamented tunic on which a Nereid rides a seahorse over a field of rays flanked by decorative borders at upper and lower hems. His mantle passes behind his back, with the ends brought forward over each elbow. In his right hand he holds a phiale; in his left hand are a reclining lamb and branches. His staff rests against his left shoulder. Between the figures is a laurel tree, and on the ground is a wicker chest, whose herringbone pattern is visible at its base. A fabric decorated with stars and a band of ray pattern has been thrown over the chest. Four stalks grow in front of the chest, one behind. Flying above the tree toward Athena is a winged Nike in a long garment, an oinochoe in her right hand, branches in her left. Her hair is bound at the back of her head and she wears a diadem, from which three leaves rise vertically.

Above and behind Kekrops are three females. One is seated to her right, with her head in right profile and her eyes directed at Athena, who returns her glance. A small Eros leans toward her, his left hand extended to her right shoulder. Her right hand, resting on her right knee, is grasped by the left hand of a female, who turns her head back to a third maiden, whose left elbow rests on her companion's right shoulder and whose right hand is extended to the other's side. All three females wear ornamented garments, the central figure wears a sleeved tunic that extends to mid-thigh.

Beneath Kekrops is seated a bearded male, his right hand resting on the shaft of his scepter. Standing in front of him, with head turned toward him, is a woman who rests her left hand on the handle of a volute krater; behind her is an incense burner. On the other side of the krater, a woman wearing an ornamented tunic over her chiton leans her left elbow on a bed, an oinochoe in her right hand, her head turned to her right and upward. Lying on the bed is Poseidon, his left hand steadying his trident, a coverlet draped over his waist and legs. He wears a wreath and gazes upward at Athena and Kekrops. A low table is before him, and an Eros stands on the mattress, holding a tray with grapes in his left hand, while gesticulating with his right hand. In the field behind Poseidon is a tripod.

Above Poseidon and behind Athena sits a woman, turned in three-quarter left profile, her left forearm resting on a shield with a Gorgoneion, her right

73 Side A

hand steadying a helmet. She wears a chiton, a mantle, crossed bands between her breasts, a necklace, and a leafy wreath over her long locks. Behind her Hermes leans forward on his bent left knee. He holds a caduceus and wears boots, a winged cap on his head, and a mantle draped behind his back. He faces a bed on which Hephaistos reclines. The god is seen from the back, his tongs in his left arm (which is not shown), a phiale in his right hand. Above the phiale flies the figure of Eros, an oinochoe in his right hand, a wreath in his left hand.

For this impressive and elaborate vase, the Kekrops Painter chose to depict a moment in the story that his contemporary colleagues ignored (see **Erichthonios**). The baby Erichthonios, newly received by Athena from Gaia, has just been enclosed in a wicker container and is about to be handed over to mortal caretakers for safekeeping. In the literary tradition, the kiste (basket or chest) is entrusted to the three daughters of Kekrops, king of Athens, but here Kekrops himself accepts the chest on behalf of his daughters, who are assembled behind and above him. The primary focus of the scene is the official and solemn implications of the ceremony and therefore on the special ancestry claimed by the Athenian citizenry. Maternal warmth and the adolescent antics of undependable young maidens are of secondary importance.

In contrast with the affectionate Athena who lovingly accepts the child from Gaia in the immediately preceding moment of the myth (see nos. 68, 70), Athena is here regally posed, with her hand on her spear and her aegis securely in place; her rendering is almost certainly inspired from statuary. Athena holds a phiale, which a winged female hastens to fill from an oinochoe, and is joined in this ceremony by Kekrops, who also holds a phiale, as well as the offerings of a sacrificial lamb and sacred branches.[1]

The focus of the ceremony is entirely on the chest, whose wicker side is almost hidden beneath a richly ornamented fabric of the same pattern as seen in Athena's chiton and in the mantles worn by both figures. The elaborate cloth is obviously the receiving cloth that Athena will extend toward Erichthonios in other vase scenes, and its presence here alludes to the arts of weaving that Athena invented and that she would present to the Athenian people (see **Textiles** and **Athena**). One version of the story tells us that Athena taught weaving to Pandrosos as a reward for refraining from looking inside the chest.

The fabric may have an additional significance. In Euripides' *Ion*, which is usually believed to be an allusion to the myth of Erichthonios, Kreousa speaks of the swaddling cloth, or "peplos," that she

73 Detail of Side A

73 Detail of Side B

wove for her baby Ion (see **Textiles**). The concentrated focus in this vase-painting on a woven garment that is also a peplos emphasizes the degree to which the receiving cloth was an important element in the story of Athena's reception of Erichthonios. It is possible that the Athenian ritual in which Athena was presented a newly woven peplos may have been seen as an allusion to the story of Erichthonios. A parallel alignment between ritual and myth exists between the ritual of the Arrephoroi and the story of the Aglaurides (see **Athena** and **The Plynteria and Arrephoroi**).

Of the three daughters grouped behind Kekrops, the seated woman nearest to her father is probably Aglauros. Unabashedly curious, as is her character, she looks across to Athena, who returns her glance, in a manner that calls to mind the earlier linked gazes of Athena and Aglauros on the lekythos by the Phiale Painter (no. 66). The exchange of glances surely refers to the future outcome of the baby-sitting assignment, when Aglauros will disobey Athena's

explicit instructions and will lift the lid off the chest to discover the baby Erichthonios inside. At the moment we see depicted here, the maiden is still unaware of the chest's contents, but the figure of Eros or Desire hovering at her shoulder is a reminder of the sexual undercurrents that will ignite her curiosity.

It is interesting to note that Aglauros clasps the hand of her sister, either Pandrosos or Herse. The gesture appears, perhaps for the first time, on the east frieze of the Parthenon, where Artemis and Aphrodite link arms in an expression of their shared realms, those of young maidens and sexuality, and it is possible that a deliberate allusion to that relief is intended here (pp. 248-49, fig. 1). This second maiden wears the *kandys*, a sleeved Persian tunic also worn by the female standing at the foot of Poseidon's bed below the chest. Evelyn Harrison believes that the Arrephoroi also wore the *kandys*, in which case this detail would underline their association with the daughters of Kekrops (see **The Plynteria and Arrephoroi**).[2] The last of the daughters is also noteworthy for the intimacy of her gesture as she rests her left elbow on her sister's shoulder. The representation illustrates the considerable degree of familiarity that characterized gestures among women in late fifth-century vase-painting. Only gradually would such informality be introduced into sculpture.

The presence of a tripod and wreath on the kalyx krater in Richmond (no. 71) suggested to John Oakley that the Richmond krater refers to a victory in a dithyrambic competition, where choruses of youths and men competed in song. On the kalyx krater from Fulda, we can probably read a similar meaning into the tripod over Poseidon's head and the wreath that the winged boy brings to the already wreathed reclining Hephaistos. Indeed, on Side B, a Nike carries a prominent wreath toward Herakles as he prepares to overwhelm the Cretan Bull. Bulls were awarded as the prize to the victorious poet, and it is quite possible that this krater was also painted to commemorate a victorious dithyramb on the subject of Erichthonios, perhaps with a reference also to the defeat of the Cretan Bull.

The Fulda kalyx krater is a superb example of late fifth-century vase-painting. The painter exults in richly adorned figures who are scattered over the vase surface on multiple groundlines. There is little overlap among the figures, who are presented largely as self-contained motifs and interact minimally interact with each other. The painter exhibits a notable interest in inanimate objects, whether furniture, attributes, or landscape details. Although the style is characterized by a high degree of technical skill in three-quarter views and foreshortening, one senses the artist's frustration with the constraints of the vase surface, which he no longer attempts to accentuate or complement.

1. Erika Simon suggested that the ritual celebrates the birth of a divine child; if so, we would have to assume that Kekrops is cognizant of the contents of the chest, while his daughter behind him as yet remains ignorant. Simon (1985) 194-95.

2. Harrison (1977b) 273.

DANAE

Some say that Zeus had intercourse with her
in the shape of a stream of gold
that passed through the roof into Danae's lap.

Apollodoros, *Bibliotheke* 2.4.1

So love takes hold of earth to join in marriage,
and showers, fallen from heaven brought to bed, make the earth pregnant,
and she in turn gives birth...

Euripides, frag. 44n (trans. Grene)

Danae was the unmarried daughter of Akrisios, King of Argos. When Akrisios was informed by an oracle that his daughter was destined to bear a son who would kill him, he attempted to circumvent the prediction by locking Danae in an underground chamber reinforced with bronze. But Zeus became aware of Danae and visited her in the form of a shower of golden rain, which was able to penetrate the earth and pass through the roof of her cell. A boy was born to Danae, who, with the help of a nurse, kept secret from Akrisios the existence of his grandson Perseus. When at last Akrisios discovered that part of the oracle had already come true, he locked Danae and her son in a chest, which he then set adrift upon the sea, expecting that it would sink. But the chest floated safely and landed on the island of Seriphos. Here it was discovered by a fisherman, Diktys, who called it to the attention of his brother, King Polydektes, who forced Danae to marry him. After Perseus grew to be a youth, Polydektes sought to eliminate him by sending him to obtain the head of the Gorgon, Medusa. When Perseus returned triumphant from the journey, the hero used the Gorgon's head to lithify Polydektes. Thereupon, Perseus and his mother returned to Argos where, intentionally or by mistake, Perseus killed his grandfather, thereby fulfilling the oracle's prediction.[1]

Danae is locked up twice by her father, once in an underground chamber to isolate her virginity, then in a chest which is intended to be her tomb. The dual connotations of enclosures signifying both life and death are pervasive in Greek thought. Danae's underground chamber particularly calls to mind such Mycenaean tholos tombs as the Treasury of Atreus, which was partly built underground and covered over with earth, and which had a doorway ornamented with bronze. Both in tholos tombs and in the earlier and simpler underground burial chambers, the body was placed inside together with funerary gifts of gold. With similar care is Danae incarcerated, and she is likewise the recipient of a golden offering from Zeus. Moreover, Danae could herself have been considered a form of wealth, because in Greek society an unmarried young woman was prized both for her ability to create new life and for her virginity; the irony in this story is that it is Danae's very assets that are the source of Akrisios' anxiety.

The imprisonment of Danae in an underground chamber has further associations. The image of women in, and of, the earth is as old as Gaia herself, and Persephone passes much of each year underground as the bride of Hades (see **Erichthonios** and **Persephone and Demeter**). Pandora is actually made of earth, and on a volute krater in Oxford (no. 81) she rises up out of the earth upon being presented to Epimetheus (see **Pandora**). And as earth is fertilized by rain, so is Danae impregnated by means of a golden shower, a transparent image for semen.

The story of Danae enjoyed particular popularity in antiquity, undoubtedly because it dealt with basic apprehensions in Greek society. The oracle's prediction that Akrisios would meet death at the hands of his grandson was not beyond credibility. By Greek custom, the son of a married daughter belonged to the household of his father, and, should relations between the families grow hostile, son and grandfather could well find themselves in opposing camps. Akrisios' dilemma speaks to a common anxiety of the inability to control one's offspring, and, by extension, one's own fate (see the essay by Froma Zeitlin in this volume).

A Greek male's anxiety about the behavior of his daughter extended well beyond the future threat of a grandson. Akrisios was only one of the earliest of a long line of helpless fathers who have thought of locking up their beautiful and uncontrollable adolescent daughters. Akrisios' strategy is, in fact, only an exaggeration of normal Greek custom, which was guided by the reasoning that to keep an available woman invisible was to keep her safe from other males. Nor was Danae totally cooperative, because ancient sources leave little doubt that Danae was responsive to Zeus' overture. The Classical historian Pherekydes tells us that Danae literally "welcomed" Zeus' gold, and the Triptolemos Painter (no. 74) depicts her gazing unabashedly up at the shower of gold that she eagerly gathers into her lap. This intimation of Danae's sexual receptivity is echoed in another, possibly post-Classical, version of the story where we learn that she was locked up in the chamber because Akrisios discovered that she was having an affair with her uncle, Akrisios' brother.[2] The theme of the unmarried, but sexually curious, maiden recalls the stories of Aglauros and Persephone, and finds parallels in the rituals of the Arrephoroi and the Little Bears (see **Erichthonios, Persephone and Demeter, The Plynteria and Arrephoroi,** and **Little Bears**).

When Akrisios discovered that his unmarried daughter had given birth to a son, he found himself in a position that Athenian law regarded with the utmost gravity, because an unmarried girl who was no longer a virgin brought extraordinary shame upon her father. Although by the sixth century Athenian citizens could no longer be sold into slavery, Solon decreed that this prohibition did not apply to an unmarried daughter who was no longer a virgin, the reasoning being that a parthenos without her virginity had ceased to exist as a free woman.[3] Akrisios chose a solution of no less duress; while he shrinks from killing his daughter, his punishment carried the high probability that both the disobedient daughter and feared grandson will sink into the sea (see **Iphigenia**). His willingness to countenance his daughter's death calls to mind the Greek euphemism for the exposure of an unwanted baby girl upon a deserted hillside; the phrase was "to put [her] in a pot."

The chest afloat upon the sea is an evocative image, because it carries for its occupants both the threat of death and the prospect of life. As an analogy to a woman's body, the motif of the container bears paradoxical connotations, because the Greeks viewed a mother's gift of life as also one, ultimately, of death (see **Women as Containers**). Moreover, whereas containers usually functioned to shelter valuables, children were buried in clay vessels as late as the Classical period. In the story of Meleager, his mother Althaea keeps within a chest a firebrand that she withdraws when she decides that the time has come for her son to die.

The emergence of Danae and Perseus from the chest is also a motif with recurrent echoes. Perseus comes out of the chest to begin life anew in a new land, and thus the experience for him is analogous to the emergence of Erichthonios, first from the arms of Gaia, and later also from a woven basket (see **Erichthonios**). Danae's emergence from the chest also signals a rebirth from death because she becomes a bride, the implication being that she has continued to remain a virgin. The motif of a woman rising up from an enclosed space has analogies with other mythical figures: Gaia who hands the child Erichthonios over to Athena, and, of course, Persephone on her annual return to her mother (see **Persephone and Demeter**). Even Pandora bore such connotations (see no. 81).

For every male listener who identified with Akrisios, there were surely as many women who would have sympathized with Danae, her future predicted almost as soon as she was born and her fate seemingly in the hands of her father. To many unmarried girls the myth must have spoken graphically of sexual excitement, and there were surely some female listeners who were gratified by the theme of revenge upon a father for the sacrifice of his daughter (see **Iphigenia**). Even the image of Danae on Seriphos would have spoken to a female audience, because wives have often been compared with exiles in a foreign country (see **Circe** and **Medea**). Parted from their families at marriage, brides never truly became integrated into the households of their husbands, and this liminal status is reflected in the Homeric custom by which the stranger to a house asks the wife to intercede with her husband.

As a dramatic story, the myth of Danae could be said, in modern parlance, to have it all: the seduction of a beautiful woman, family disintegration, a perilous sea journey, triumph over a monster, and a loving son's fatal vengeance upon his mother's husband and his own grandfather. Not surprisingly, all three major tragedians took up the myth, as did a number of other prominent poets. Pindar summarizes the myth in *Pythian* 12, written in 490, and, at approximately this same time, Simonides of Keos wrote a majestic lament of Danae to her young son, spoken while both were adrift on the sea. It has been suggested that both Pindar and Simonides were inspired by the tetralogy of Aischylos that is probably also to be dated about 490. The names of three of these four plays survive for us: the *Phorkides* (which must have dealt with Perseus' triumph over Medusa), the *Polydektes* (surely Perseus' subsequent defeat of Polydektes), and the satyr play, the *Diktyoulkoi*. Fragments of the latter play deal with the arrival of the chest on Seriphos and indicate that Polydektes was not present; thus we can be certain that Aischylos followed the version in which Polydektes marries Danae sometime well after her arrival. It has been suggested that the fourth drama by Aischylos dealt with the seduction of Danae and the building of the chest, in which event that work may well have influenced the approximately contemporary vase by Triptolemos Painter (no. 74). The grandeur of the Providence Painter's depiction (no. 75) would also seem to echo the majestic tenor of Aischylean tragedy.

In 467, the poet Aristeas triumphed with his play *Perseus*, of which we have only the title, but a stamnos by the Deepdene Painter (no. 76), dating ca. 470-460, could be related. Not long afterward, Sophokles took up the subject with his *Andromeda*. Three more names of Sophoklean plays dealing with the Danae story have survived, but it is unclear if these titles all refer to the same work or to separate plays: *Larisaioi, Akrisios,* and the *Danae*. The Sophoklean dramas may have exerted some influence on the Phiale Painter when he took up the subject in about 440 (no. 78).

The basic themes and motifs in the myth of Danae find echoes in many other familiar traditions. The enclosure of Perseus in the chest recalls the story of Moses; the disgorgement of mother and son from the sea calls to mind the story of Jonah; and the experience of an unwed virgin who is impregnated by a god and becomes the mother of an exceptional son is the foundation story of Christianity.

1. For the story of Danae, see Pherekydes *FGrHist* 3 F 10; Sophokles, *Antigone* 944-50; Pindar, *Pythian* 12.17-18; Apollodoros, *Bibliotheke* 2.4.1-2; Simonides 543 *PMG*; Hyginus, *Fabulae* 63. A full description of the chest may have been in Hesiod's *Catalogue of Women* or the *Ehoiai*, frag. 135 MW. See also Gantz (1993) 300-304; Scafuro (1990) 129.

2. Still another tradition said that Danae was raped by her uncle: Apollodoros, *Bibliotheke* 2.41; Gantz (1993) 300.

3. Plutarch, *Solon* 23.

74 Side A

KALYX KRATER WITH DANAE

490-480
by the Triptolemos Painter
St. Petersburg, The State Hermitage Museum, inv. no. Б 1602
(St. 1723, B 637)

Attic, "from Cerveteri"
Clay
H 41 cm., Diam 45.7 cm.

Publications: *ARV²* 360.1 and 1648; *Para* 364,1 and 512; *Add²* 222; E. Gerhard, "Danae, ein griechisches Vasenbild," *Winckelmannsprogramm der Archäologischen Gesellschaft zu Berlin* 14 (1854) 1-10; G.M.A. Richter, *Ancient Furniture: A History of Greek, Etruscan and Roman Furniture* (Oxford 1926) 63, fig. 162; Caskey and Beazley (1954) 11-13; K. Schauenberg, *Perseus in der Kunst des Altertums* (Bonn 1960) 3, pl. 1,2; G.M.A. Richter, *The Furniture of the Greeks, Etruscans and Romans* (London 1966) 60, fig. 318; A. Peredolskaja, *Krasnofigurinye attischeskie vazy* (Leningrad 1967) 45-46, no. 42, pl. 30, 169.8, 170.1; Boardman (1975) 139, fig. 306; Simon and Hirmer (1976) pls. 164-65; *LIMC* I (1981) 450, no. 3, pl. 343 (s.v. Akrisios); Schefold (1981) 240, 372, fig. 336; J. Oakley, "Danae and Perseus on Seriphos," *AJA* 86 (1982) 113 n. 7; Mark (1984) 307 n. 89; Brümmer (1985) 48-49, fig. 12a; *LIMC* III (1986) 327, no. 1, 331, no. 48, pls. 243, 247 (s.v. Danae); J.-J. Maffre, "Une nouvelle représentation de Danaé recevant la pluie d'or," *Studien zur Mythologie und Vasenmalerei. Konrad Schauenberg zum 65. Geburtstag am 16. April 1986* (Mainz 1986) 71, 74; Gantz (1993) 302.

Reassembled. Beneath the scene is a frieze of dots. Red for the stream of gold on Side A. White for the beard and hair of Akrisios on Side B; red for his taenia.

On Side A Danae is lounging in three-quarter right profile at the foot of a bed, her feet in right profile on a footstool before it. Over a chiton with an overfold to her waist, she wears a himation that is wrapped around her waist and knees; she is barefoot and she wears a disc earring. With both hands she binds a long sash around her head, passing the ends over long locks of hair that have been brought up from her nape. Her head is in right profile and she gazes upward, in the direction of two streams of large drops that fall vertically onto her lap. Each vertical support of the bed is decorated with palmettes and a star; the support beneath the head of the bed terminates in a palmette. The sagging mattress is elaborately decorated with a pattern of lines and dots arranged in a diamond pattern. A large pillow at the head of the bed bears identical bands of

stripes down its seam. Hanging in the background is a mirror and a hair covering (sakkos). In front of Danae's face is inscribed: ΔΑΝΑΕ.

On Side B in the center is a large chest, the hinged side on the viewer's right, the lid raised halfway. Decorating the front of the chest are ten starbursts and three circles enclosing dots, which are possibly air holes for the occupants. Standing inside or behind the chest is Danae, her left hand cradling the buttocks of her nude son. He is in left profile; his left arm rests on top of his mother's left arm; his right hand holds a ball; and his left foot rests on the rim of the chest. His short locks curl around a fillet, one end of which hangs from his nape. Danae's right arm is bent at the elbow and the forearm is upraised, the hand bent back, with the fingers extended and the palm facing up. Danae wears a chiton, with a kolpos at the waist, and a mantle that is brought forward over each shoulder, the dark band along the hem forming a zigzag pattern. Her hair is gathered up from the nape to the back of her head, and she wears a diadem, from which a number of elements rise vertically. Her head is in right profile and slightly inclined, as she gazes down at Perseus.

On the other side of the chest's lid, Akrisios stands in three-quarter left profile, his feet together, with his toes almost under the lion-paw of the chest. Akrisios' scepter rests in the fingers of his left hand and against his left shoulder, and his right arm is stretched forward, the fingers extended. He wears a pleated, sleeved garment beneath his mantle, which is brought forward over his left shoulder and upper arm, and passes across his waist and legs. His head is in left profile and over his white hair he wears a fillet. To Danae's right is a bearded and bandy-legged carpenter in right profile, his exaggeratedly hunched shoulders obviously misshapen. The toes of his left foot rest on the ground behind him. A piece of cloth, edged with a stripe, is tied around his waist. His short hair is brushed forward to his face and down to his nape, curling at the ends. His right hand grasps the bow of a bow-drill, which his left hand is manipulating. At the man's feet is an upturned hammer.

269

74 Detail of Side B

On Side A we are within Danae's underground chamber, where her father Akrisios has enclosed her in hopes of escaping the ominous prophecy (see **Danae**). She has made of it a female space, hanging her mirror and a hair covering on the wall, with luxurious fabrics decorating her pillow and bed. The mattress sinks invitingly, cradling her form, which comfortably melds with it. The careful delineation of her breasts announces her maturity. The golden rain has begun to fall from the roof of her chamber, the ceiling of which coincides with the fascia that separates the krater's lip from the vessel wall, such that Danae's chamber appears to be the kalyx krater itself (see **Women as Containers**). In two vertical streams the rain falls precisely onto the drapery lying on Danae's lap, and the image would have reminded ancient viewers that the word *kolpos* referred both to folds of drapery and a woman's vagina.[1]

Far from being terrified or resistant to this inexplicable shower, Danae gazes directly upward at the source, intent and curious, and it is clear that the Triptolemos Painter has chosen the version of the myth in which Danae "welcomed" Zeus' golden stream (see **Danae**). Indeed, one senses from the fact that Danae was adorning her hair that she was hoping her attractiveness would elicit some kind of response. Indeed, her manner of binding her hair calls to mind the similar practice of symposiasts, and she even sits at the end of the bed, where an hetaira would recline during a symposium. With exaggerated insistence, however, the painter tells us that Danae is never to be confused with an hetaira, because her feet rest primly on a footstool beside the bed.

An uninhibited Danae is certainly in keeping with the vase she adorns, which was used to hold wine at a symposium. The kalyx krater took its name from the shape of a flower about to blossom, and the familiar association of ripe young women and flowers is best known from the story of Persephone, who was reaching for an appealing narcissus when she was abducted (see **Persephone and Demeter**). One can imagine the kinds of bawdy comments that this scene must have inspired at symposia. Certainly, the vertical stream of wine poured into the krater would invite comparison with the rain falling onto Danae's lap, and one can also imagine that guests might propose comparisons between Danae and the assembled hetairai. With this portrayal, the Triptolemos Painter becomes the first in long series of artists over many centuries who were captivated by the eroticism of Danae's seduction.

With Side B, the comforting curves of Side A give way to a harsh angularity consonant with the ugly moment at hand. The welcoming couch is replaced by the obdurate chest, and the underground chamber into which liquid penetrated gives way to another sealed container that will float upon the sea. The painter has not made completely clear just where Danae is standing. She would seem to be within the chest, because her feet are not visible beneath it; on the other hand, Perseus' left foot rests horizontally on the chest's edge as if he were outside it. Despite the ambiguity of her position, Danae's gestures and gaze express decisively both her distress and her resolution. She clutches Perseus and looks down at him, her nose practically touching the bangs on his forehead; meanwhile, her right hand is thrust out in distress. The angled lid of the chest accentuates the physical and emotional separation of father and daughter (and, should Danae be inside the chest, her line of sight as well). Akrisios' stiff vertical stance and rigid gesture communicate his position clearly. Meanwhile, the carpenter carries on, attentive only to the task assigned him, as oblivious to the drama enacted in his midst as Danae, Perseus, and Akrisios are ignorant of the denouement that will soon unfold.

The painter shows the same subtle skill in this scene as he did in its pendant. The lid of the chest is unable to open all the way because of the protruding fascia, which designated the chamber's ceiling on Side A. The continued assertion of the fascia reinforces the associations of the chamber, chest, and krater itself as forms of enclosure Danae cannot escape (see **Women as Containers**). Also interesting is Danae's appearance; her hair is now fully dressed and she wears a diadem as well, with the folds of her himation skirting the nape of her neck as though they have just slid off her head. The diadem, as well as well as the hint of a veil, reminds the viewer that Danae's forthcoming voyage also functions as an unorthodox bridal journey that will bring her to her future husband Polydektes.

Of special interest is the rendering of Perseus. In contrast with most other depictions of the story, he is nude, clasped to his mother's side, and four or five years of age, rather than a baby. Interest in the embraces of mother and child will not develop until the second half of the fifth century, and even then mothers are shown embracing babies, not the maturing boy that we see in this scene (no. 6). The protectiveness with which Danae envelops Perseus, contrasted with the innocence with which he clutches his ball, captures the mother's fierce allegiance to her son and offers a thoughtful counterpart to the intense relationship between Demeter and Persephone (see **Persephone and Demeter**).

The Triptolemos Painter is as skilled a draftsman as he is a master of composition and the nuance of imagery. Especially noteworthy is Danae's face on Side A, with her elegant almond eye. The stacked pleats, rendered with such fluidity of line, are in keeping with the date of the vase, in the last years of the Archaic style.

1. Henderson (1991) 140.

LEKYTHOS WITH
DANAE AND THE CHEST

480-470
by the Providence Painter
Toledo, Toledo Museum of Art, Purchased with Funds from the
Libbey Endowment, Gift of Edward Drummond Libbey, inv. no.
69.369

Attic
Clay
H 40.5 cm., Diam (at shoulder) 13.5 cm.

Publications: *CVA* Toledo, Museum of Art 1 (U.S.A. 17) 29, pl. 44; *Auktion 40 Basel*
(1969) 58-59, no. 98; K. Luckner, *Toledo Museum News* 1 (1972) 83; Brommer (1973)
273, no. B16; Kurtz (1975) 47, 214-15, pl. 37.2; *LIMC* I (1981) 451, no. 5, pl. 343 (s.v.
Akrisios); *LIMC* III (1986) 331, no. 43 (s.v. Danae); Carpenter (1991) 103, fig. 146;
Gantz (1993) 302.

75

Reassembled. On the shoulder is a band of tongues above a chain of five palmettes, the central palmette inverted and flanked on each side by a lotus.
Above the figural scene is a band of three stopt meanders (right) alternating
with a checker square. Added red for bracelet and for thong around alabastron.

In the center of the scene is a large chest with lion-paw feet and raised lid.
The upper border is decorated with a frieze of two lions flanking a boar; there
are also several stars, narrow bands of dots, and two circles enclosing dots.
Inside the chest can be seen the head and shoulders of Perseus, whose head is
in left profile as he gazes up at his mother's face and stretches his arm to her,
fingers extended and touching. She stands in right profile, right foot slightly
behind her, and she leans over the chest as her right hand clasps its edge. Her
left hand is held above the center of the chest and steadies an alabastron, the
neck of which is tied with a cord or thong, the end of which hangs down the
side. Over her chiton Danae wears a himation that is brought over her left
shoulder and upper arm, passing around her waist and most of her legs. Small
curls frame her face, with longer locks hanging down behind; her taenia is tied
at the back of her head in a bow. She also wears a disc earring and a spiral
bracelet.

Akrisios stands on the opposite side of the chest, turned in three-quarter
left profile, his bearded head in left profile. His scepter has a floral upper tip
and a lower end in the form of a spearhead; the shaft rests in his left hand and
against his left shoulder. His right arm is outstretched horizontally toward
Danae, with the fingers extended and slightly separated; he also looks over at
her. Over a long pleated undergarment, he wears a mantle wrapped around his
waist and legs, with the ends passing over his left shoulder and arm. He also
wears a fillet over his hair, which forms curly locks around his hairline and
tumbles over his left shoulder in several curly ringlets.

We are at the moment in the drama when the chest has been
finished, the carpenter has left, and Perseus has already been
placed within (see **Danae**). Dwarfed by its size, he turns to his
mother for comfort, his gesture and gaze echoing other scenes in
which young children appeal to their nurse or mother for solace
(nos. 6, 13, and see **Erichthonios**). Danae tries to console Perseus,

leaning over the chest and resting her right hand on its edge in a gesture that parallels the line of her son's arm. She looks down at him, oblivious to her father's presence. Meanwhile, Akrisios concentrates his attention exclusively upon her, and the stiff horizontality of his arm and the open fingers communicate his anger and distress. Appropriate to the duality of his emotional state is the peculiar combination of a floral finial to a scepter that terminates in a menacing spearhead just beneath the figure of Perseus.

The focal point of the composition is the alabastron that Danae holds over the midpoint of the chest and over her son's head. The vessel is carefully framed by the chest lid below it and by the animated arm of Akrisios that passes just behind it. The precision of the vase's placement lends it and Danae's gesture the formal overtones of ritual. Indeed, whereas an alabastron was a perfume vessel enjoyed by women in everyday use, it is most often seen in the hand of a woman who brings it as either a wedding gift (nos. 56, 58) or an offering for the grave (no. 54). In both uses, the vessel is balanced, as here, in the slightly cupped palm of the hand, a gesture whose formality underscores the ritualistic import of the gift-giving.

Perseus' fate does indeed relate closely to both funerary and bridal ritual. Soon to be interred in a chest that Akrisios hopes will sink into the sea, Perseus will foil death, emerging to a new life, first on Seriphos, then in a triumphant return to Argos (see **Women as Containers**). Danae herself will also experience a rebirth, becoming in the process the bride of Polydektes, and it is as a bride that she is depicted by the Phiale Painter (no. 78). Nothing is as it appears to be at this moment, and the rather large silhouetted lions and boar on the chest's side remind the viewer that the hunt is not yet over. The scene's participants, however, are completely unaware of the denouement, and at this moment Danae is convinced that the chest will become her son's tomb. In grave scenes on lekythoi, the survivor does not appear to see the deceased, but here Danae and Perseus intently exchange glances, as Danae prepares to join her son on his deadly journey.

Both the majesty of this scene and the complexity of its imagery suggest inspiration from drama. The elegance, however, is the vase-painter's own. As on the Nolan amphora in Cambridge (no. 37), the Providence Painter excels in balanced and harmonious compositions that accentuate the meaningful gestures linking the participants. On both vases the scenes and the vase contours are gloriously complemented by rhythmic and graceful patterns of palmettes rendered on a generous scale.

76

STAMNOS WITH DANAE AND AKRISIOS

470–460
by the Deepdene Painter
New York, Metropolitan Museum of Art, Rogers Fund, 1917,
inv. no. 17.230.37

Attic, from Rome
Clay
H 38.1 cm., W (at handles) 39 cm., Diam 31.4 cm.

Publications: *ARV²* 498.1; *Para* 381; *Add²* 251; G.M.A. Richter, "Red-Figured Athenian Vases Recently Acquired by the Metropolitan Museum of Art," *AJA* 27 (1923) 279-81, figs. 16-18; G.M.A. Richter, *Ancient Furniture: A History of Greek, Etruscan and Roman Furniture* (Oxford 1926) 92; Jacobsthal (1927) 86, 138, 173, 200, pl. 97a; Richter and Hall (1936) 112-14, no. 82, pls. 85-86, 173; Caskey and Beazley (1954) 12; T. Howe, "Illustrations to Aeschylos' Tetralogy on the Perseus Theme," *AJA* 57 (1953) 273, pl. 76.4; Neumann (1965) 74-75, fig. 36; G.M.A. Richter, *Furniture of the Greeks, Etruscans and Romans* (London 1966) 74; Philippaki (1967) 80-85, no. 1, pl. 41.3; Brommer (1973) 273, no. B5; *LIMC* I (1981) 451, no. 6, pl. 343 (s.v. Akrisios); J. Oakley, "Danae and Perseus on Seriphos," *AJA* 86 (1982) 113 n. 7; Brümmer (1985) 54 n. 255, fig. 14c-d; *LIMC* III (1986) 331, no. 49 (s.v. Danae).

Reassembled from many pieces. Upper part of Akrisios restored. On the mouth there is a pattern of egg and dots between two reserved bands; there is a tongue pattern on the shoulder. Around the handles are palmette, bud, and scroll designs, with egg pattern at the attachment of the handles. Below the scenes, two addorsed meanders alternate with dotted cross squares.

On Side A a large chest with lion-paw feet is seen from the side, its raised lid skirting the back of Danae's head. She stands inside, turned in three-quarter right profile, with her head in right profile; she appears to look out and down. Her left hand, fingers curled, is brought to her chin; the extended fingers of her right hand rest on the head of Perseus, which is in right profile. Over her chiton Danae wears a mantle draped over both shoulders. Curly waves frame her face, with longer locks falling down behind her shoulders. She wears a fillet, a pendant earring consisting of a disc from which three chains are suspended, and a necklace. Perseus has curly locks that cover his nape, and he wears a himation, from which his right hand emerges, fingers extended. He gazes over at Akrisios who stands close to the chest, his slightly advanced left foot passing behind the lion-paw foot. Over a pleated sleeved undergarment, he wears a mantle that is draped over his left shoulder and around his waist and legs. He has a long beard, and he wears a wreath over his hair; the ties of the wreath hang behind. In his extended right hand he holds upright a scepter with a floral tip. Inscriptions read: ΓΕΡΕΥ[Σ], Perseus; and ΑΚΡΙΣΙΟΣ, Akrisios.

On Side B a woman is seated in right profile on a stool. She wears a chiton and a mantle that is draped around her body to her knees, exposing only her hands. Her left hand grasps the shaft of a scepter; her right hand is brought to her mouth. She also wears a sakkos and a disc earring with pendants. Standing almost frontally beside her, with her head in left profile, is a woman who wears a pleated garment with a kolpos and overfold. In her left hand she steadies a round or oval basket; with two fingers of her right hand she pinches her nose. She has short curly hair and an inscription in the field identifies her as Damolyte. To her left stands a man who turns slightly to his left, his head in right profile. His mantle is draped about the mid-part of his body; his left arm is bent with the forearm and hand upraised, the fingers open; and his right hand holds a hammer by his side.

76 Side B

76 Side A (**See also detail, p. 107**)

The construction of the chest is completed and Akrisios is about to set his daughter and grandson adrift on the sea (see **Danae**). Danae and Perseus are already in the chest, but in no way reconciled to their fate. Danae does not yet crouch down, but stands upright, partly resisting, partly frozen in horror, as she brings her hand to her mouth. Meanwhile, the baby boy Perseus extends a hand of pleading to his grandfather, and Danae, ever mindful of her son whose lot she will soon share, rests a comforting hand on his head. Akrisios' vertical scepter divides the scene and the adversaries. Although Akrisios' feet are confidently in contact with the menacing lion-paw foot of the chest, his upper torso is as removed from his scepter as are Danae and Perseus; the physical and emotional gulf between father and daughter seems impassable.

Side B is probably to be thought of as part of the same scene. Holding the royal scepter and depicted in the seated position that designates her as the mistress, Danae's mother sits with dignity, bringing her hand to her mouth in an expression of concern that is far more restrained than that of her daughter. Less inhibited is the nurse, who is recognized by her short hair, as well as by her unrefined gesture; she pinches her nose to keep away the ugly stench of Akrisios' punishment. Meanwhile the carpenter holds on to his hammer while lifting his hand in agitation, in contrast to the mechanical demeanor of his counterpart in the kalyx krater by the Triptolemos Painter (no. 74). On this vase no one accepts Akrisios'

order without some degree of remonstrance, neither child nor adult, family member nor servant.

The basket carried by the servant has the linear patterning of wickerwork and thus resembles the large oval or round baskets that women carried when they visited the graves of family members. The baskets conventionally held sashes, branches, and lekythoi (no. 52). The basket's presence in this scene renders more explicit the funereal overtones of the punishment and the analogy of the chest to a grave (see **Women as Containers**). The combination of the basket with the expressive reactions of those assembled vividly captures the rawness and enormity of the family schism.

The Deepdene Painter worked on a number of stamnoi, many of which, like this one, are characterized by their high shoulder, which tapers to a narrow, high base. Recognizable features of the painter's style are the small iris and the gesture of the upraised hand, both of which are used to express surprise and agitation.

77

77

HYDRIA WITH DANAE

ca. 450–440
by the Danae Painter
Boston, Museum of Fine Arts, Francis Bartlett Collection,
inv. no. 03.792

Attic
Clay
H 40 cm.

Publications: *ARV²* 1076.13; *Para* 449; *Add²* 326; P. Hartwig, "Danaé dans le coffre: Hydrie appartenant au Musée de Boston," *MonPiot* 10 (1903) 55-59, pl. 8; G.M.A. Richter, *Ancient Furniture: A History of Greek, Etruscan and Roman Furniture* (Oxford 1926) 91, fig. 223; Caskey and Beazley (1954) 12; Richter, *Furniture of the Greeks, Etruscans and Romans* (London 1966) 74, fig. 384; S. Karusu, "Die Schutzflehende Barberini," *AntK* 13 (1970) 42, fig. 5; Brommer (1973) 273, no. B12; *LIMC* I (1981) 451, no. 7, pl. 344 (s.v. Akrisios); J. Oakley, "Danae and Perseus on Seriphos," *AJA* 86 (1982) 113 n. 7; Brümmer (1985) 71, fig. 23b; *LIMC* III (1986) 331 no. 50 (s.v. Danae); Gantz (1993) 302.

Around the rim is a band of tongues. Above the scene is a band of lotus and palmette; beneath, three meanders (left) alternate with a saltire square.

The chest is seen from the corner, its raised lid invading the upper border. The chest has large paw feet and a palmette in the center of the front; the lid is edged with a border of black and reserved squares; the black band just above Danae's head is thought to represent joinery. Her head and shoulders are in left profile as she gazes downward at Perseus, of whom only the wreathed head is visible. Danae wears a diadem, from which six elements rise vertically, and her veil or mantle passes over the back of her head.

Standing slightly behind the corner of the chest and turned in three-quarter right profile is a young maiden, whose long hair is gathered in the center of her back by a rectangular clasp, from which several cords dangle. She wears a peplos with an overfold to the waist, and her right hand, fingers extended and palm vertical, is held just beneath her face. Her left hand clasps the edge of the chest, and she gazes down at Perseus. Behind her a taller woman stands frontally, her left foot in profile. She wears a peplos that has an overfold to the tops of the thighs and a black stripe edging upper and lower hems. Her right hand clasps her left upper arm, and her left elbow is bent, with the forearm passing over her right wrist to her right shoulder. Her head is in right profile and her hair falls in short straight locks that edge her jaw; she looks over at Danae and Perseus. Behind her a bearded man stands almost frontally, his left foot in profile. He leans slightly upon a walking stick grasped by his left hand; his right hand is raised in front of his chest, fingers extended, palm facing Danae. His mantle is wrapped around his body, exposing his nude torso; he also wears a wreath upon his wavy hair that covers his nape.

Unlike the scenes on the St. Petersburg, Toledo, and New York vases (nos. 74, 75, and 76), Danae is here thoroughly ensconced in the chest, and the intertwinement of her fate with that of her son is indicated by both their linked gazes and the folds of her mantle or veil, which seem to pass behind Perseus' head. Also unlike the other vases, Danae is oblivious to the family she will soon be leaving. She is completely unresponsive to her father's expostulations, here suggested only by his raised hand, which contrasts with his more vehement gesticulations in the other scenes. It is interesting to note that the eyes of all the bystanders are directed primarily at Perseus, a reminder that the boy's potential to precipitate his grandfather's death has not only instigated the sea voyage, but still remains undiminished.

The short straight hairstyle of the woman beside Akrisios suggests that she is the child's nurse or conceivably Danae's mother; in either case, the crossed arms communicate agitation, as well as frustration at her inability to alter the course of events. Meanwhile the younger female raises her hand to bid an emotional farewell to Danae and Perseus. Her long hair, with the hair ornament familiar from depictions of Artemis (nos. 89, 90), identifies her as a parthenos, who is, therefore, close in age to Danae and probably her sister. The maiden's heartfelt grief accentuates the obduracy of Akrisios, who stands as far away from his daughter as he can. The simple composition eloquently contrasts the women's rapport with the divisiveness of grandfather and son, who are, at the same time, intimately linked by the gruesome prophecy. The painter has effectively rendered the emotional havoc of a disintegrating family.

Both the diadem and the fabric passing over the back of Danae's head are appropriate to a bride (see **The Wedding**). Danae is depicted in the same way in scenes representing the chest's arrival on Seriphos in the presence of the Polydektes, Danae's future husband (no. 78).[1] The consistent rendering in Classical vase-painting of Danae as a bride probably derives from a common prototype and, in alluding to her future life as the wife of Polydektes, underscores the chest's connotations as both a tomb and a receptacle, from which Danae and Perseus will emerge to a new life (see **Women as Containers**).

1. Oakley, *AJA* 86 (1982) 111-15.

FRAGMENT OF A BELL KRATER WITH DANAE AND PERSEUS

440-435
by the Phiale Painter
Oxford, Ashmolean Museum, University of Oxford, inv. no. 1917.62

Attic
Clay
H 10.5 cm., W 16.5 cm.

Publications: *ARV²* 1018.75 and 1678; *Add²* 315; *CVA* Oxford, Ashmolean Museum 1 (Great Britain 3) 22, pl. 25.4; R. Engelmann, "Danae und Verwandtes," *ÖJh* 12 (1909) 168; E. Tillyard, *The Hope Vases* (Cambridge 1923) 81, pl. 22.137; H. Luschey, "Danae auf Seriphos," *BABesch* 24-26 (1949-1951) 27; C. Clairmont, "Studies in Greek Mythology and Vase-Painting," *AJA* 57 (1953) 94; Brommer (1973) 273, no. B10; *LIMC* I (1981) 451, no. 8, pl. 344 (s.v. Akrisios); J. Oakley, "Danae and Perseus on Seriphos," *AJA* 86 (1982) 112; *LIMC* III (1986) 331-32, no. 51 (s.v. Danae); Boardman (1989) 61, fig. 127; Oakley (1990) 25, 78, no. 75, pl. 57d.

Broken all around.

Rising up from the chest is the upper torso of Danae, seen in right profile. She leans forward slightly, and brings her right hand toward her head, which is tilted downward; she also gazes down. Over wavy hair, which frames her face in front of her ear, she wears a diadem decorated with a series of three dots arranged in a triangular cluster. Rising from the top of the diadem are two leaves. She wears a chiton and a mantle that is brought forward over her right shoulder; a veil with a scalloped edge lies over her diadem and extends halfway down her right upper arm.

Beside Danae is the boy Perseus, his shoulders and head seen in right profile. He wears a mantle, which envelops his right arm, held before his chest. He wears a taenia over long curly locks of hair that tumble onto his shoulders. His gaze is directed upward toward a man who stands in front of the chest, his right knee relaxed, the hand of his extended right arm steadying a vertical scepter around which a dark band is wound. The man wears a sleeved pleated garment beneath a mantle that covers most of his torso.

The scepter identifies the man as a king, either Akrisios (in which case the scene is one of departure) or Polydektes (in which case the chest would be arriving on Seriphos). That the latter moment is more probable is indicated by several features on the Oxford fragment. The monarch with the scepter compares well with the figure of Polydektes on a fragment from the Athenian Agora, on which the arrival of the chest on Seriphos is depicted.[1] It is also noteworthy that the depiction of the Seriphos episode was a popular theme with contemporary vase-painters. Finally, Danae's dress and demeanor on the Oxford fragment have pointed bridal overtones, which must be an allusion to her forthcoming marriage. She wears the bridal veil, which is recognized by the scalloped edges that indicate its fine texture. Moreover, her notably downcast head and gaze are especially in keeping with the *aidos* expected of a bride; the Phiale Painter renders a bride in just this

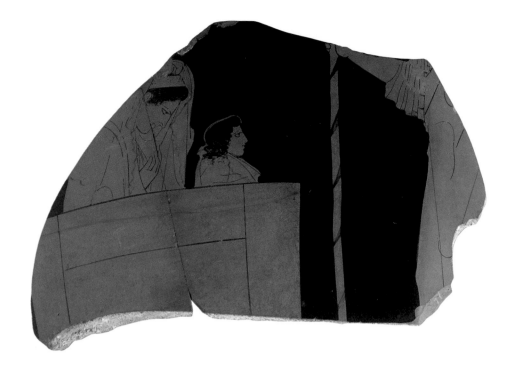

78

manner on lekythos that was once in Basel (see **The Wedding** and ***Aidos* and *Sophrosyne***).[2] Perseus' self-possessed gesture and steady upward gaze toward Polydektes are also appropriate as a harbinger for the next phase of the drama, which will belong almost exclusively to him.

Noting the popularity of the Seriphos episode of Danae's travails in vases contemporary with the Oxford fragment, John Oakley has suggested a common literary origin. This work could not be Aischylos' *Diktyoulkoi* (ca. 490), because we are fairly confident Polydektes did not appear in that play. Another, and more contemporary, inspiration could have been the *Perseus* by Aristeas (467), possibly a play by Sophokles, or another unidentified work.

The Phiale Painter is represented here by the lekythos in New York with Amymone (no. 118), the stamnos in Warsaw with women in a Dionysiac ritual (no. 136), and the lekythos in Basel with Athena and Aglauros (no. 78).

1. Oakley, *AJA* 86 (1982) 112.
2. Oakley (1990a) 86, no. 123 quater, pl. 100a-b.

PANDORA

The myth of Pandora has enjoyed remarkable longevity. The term "Pandora's box" is very much a part of everyday usage, and the custom of keeping a hope chest is still a familiar tradition.

Our principal source is the poet Hesiod, who relates the story both in his *Theogony* and his *Works and Days*, which are dated to about 700 B.C.[1] In each poem the myth is presented in a slightly different way so as to reinforce the theme of Hesiod's specific context, and such obvious manipulation on the part of the poet suggests that the nature of the story he inherited could have had a somewhat different emphasis.

Hesiod tells us that before Pandora existed, only men lived on the earth, without women and without sickness or hardship. One day the god Prometheus ("forethought") deceived Zeus by offering him a choice between two piles of offerings: in one mound the desirable meat was concealed under an ox hide; in the second pile the bare bones were buried beneath a covering of gleaming fat. Zeus chose the latter offering and was enraged when he realized the trick. The themes of deceit and concealment find echoes in the creation of Pandora.

In anger at Prometheus, Zeus hid fire from men. In turn, Prometheus stole fire from the gods by hiding it in a fennel stalk which he then gave to men. With these actions the themes of concealing and giving enter the story.

Prometheus knew that Zeus would not fail to respond to his newest escapade, but he did not know how or in what form retribution would come. Suspecting that Zeus would take advantage of Prometheus' less intelligent brother Epimetheus ("afterthought"), Prometheus instructed Epimetheus not to accept any gift from the gods. But, Hesiod tells us, the overpowering sight of Pandora would make Epimetheus forget his brother's command.

Zeus asked Hephaistos to fashion from earth and water a beautiful maiden. Hephaistos endowed her with *aidos*, modesty, and provided her with an intricately worked golden diadem that depicted all types of creatures of the earth and sea (see **Aidos and Sophrosyne**). Athena dressed Pandora in beautiful garments the goddess had woven herself and even taught the maiden the skills of weaving. Aphrodite gave her grace and *pothos*, a word that means sensuous longing,[2] and necklaces and crowns were added by the Graces, the Hours, and Persuasion. Negative qualities were added,

interestingly enough by a male god, Hermes, who endowed the clay maiden with crafty words and a deceitful nature. When Pandora was completed she was presented to all the gods, who heartily approved of their handiwork. Hesiod tells us that they called her Pandora, because everyone on Mt. Olympos had given her a gift. She was, Hesiod tells us, a *kalon kakon*, a beautiful evil. Zeus sent Hermes to accompany Pandora to Epimetheus, as a present, and Epimetheus did not hesitate for a moment to accept this ravishing gift.

Pandora appears either to have arrived with a big clay vessel, a pithos (p. 278, fig. 1), or to have had immediate access to one, and Hesiod tells us that she lifted the lid off the pithos and that plagues and diseases escaped. Only *elpis*, a word various translated as "hope" and "wishful thinking," remained inside the pithos, and Hesiod implies that this *elpis* was henceforth available to all mankind to offset the effects of the destructive forces that had escaped. Hesiod tells us that after Pandora opened the pithos men were no longer free of plagues and diseases and that Pandora became the progenitor of the "race" of women. The poet also tells us that Pandora was only one of two evils Zeus gave to man; the second evil was the prospect that an unmarried and childless man would have no children to look after him in his old age.

In her essay in this volume Froma Zeitlin argues convincingly that Pandora's pithos represents Pandora's clay body, and that the act of opening the pithos signifies the opening up of Pandora's body through sexual intercourse and childbearing.[3] The motif of the container traditionally carried connotations of a woman's body, and mythical children are constantly associated with containers, as indeed in real life even into Classical times deceased children were buried in vessels (see **Women as Containers**). The apparent contradiction of an image connoting both birth and death is inherent to the life process itself, because, as Sheila Murnaghan has shown, intrinsic to the birth of a child is recognition of that child's mortality, as a life cycle begins that will inevitably end in death.[4]

Hesiod's description of the pithos' contents is also compatible with Zeitlin's interpretation. Greek mythology provides ample evidence that in Greek thought children were not considered to be an unmixed blessing, but rather a potential source of destructive intergenerational and interdynastic conflict. At the same time, the Greeks also appreciated that apprehension was offset by *elpis*,

Fig. 1. Clay pithos from Knossos, London, British Museum, inv. no. A 739, ca. 1450 B.C. Courtesy museum.

whether that be optimism with which a newborn child is welcomed or, as Georgia Nugent proposes, the wishful thinking that enables humans to endure distress by means of fantasy or denial.[5] The *elpis* inside Pandora's pithos also resonates with the story's overarching themes of withholding, because anxiety that children might not be born at all from a woman mirrors the gods' earlier refusal to bestow fire upon men.

It is interesting to note that Hesiod does not tell us that Pandora was forbidden to open her pithos, and yet the tradition of Pandora's disobedience has endured to the present day. The explanation is probably that the theme of sexually curious girls was well known in Greek myth (see **Erichthonios**), and, indeed, rituals such as that of the Arrephoroi reveal a strong apprehension that unmarried girls would explore their sexuality before marriage (see **The Plynteria and Arrephoroi, Persephone and Demeter, Danae,** and **Erichthonios**).

As Hesiod tells the story in the *Theogony*, Pandora was a brilliant counter in the game with Zeus that Prometheus had heretofore been winning. Like the bones wrapped in glistening fat, like the fire hidden in the fennel stalk, Pandora was literally and figuratively the epitome of irresistible packaging. Beneath her sparkling exterior of gold jewelry and fine garments, there were only earth and water, as well as a thieving temperament and the overpowering weapon of language. Like the bones in Prometheus' arrangement of the sacrificial offering, there was nothing of value behind her golden exterior. The point is reinforced in the *Works and Days* when Hesiod follows his discussion of Pandora with a description of the first generation of men on earth, who had been made by the gods, Hesiod tells us, entirely of gold.

Both the skill with which the story of Pandora is fitted into the poems and the poet's well known misogyny tempt the reader to identify as Hesiod's contribution most of the unflattering aspects of Pandora's story. On the contrary, however, many of these elements appear to have been intrinsic to it. Pandora is unquestionably inferior to a man. Whereas in Greek thought men were apparently created by the gods, Pandora was manufactured by a craftsman, who labors in his workshop as if he were producing one of the clay vases or clay statuettes with which Hesiod was familiar. Moreover, Pandora's role is utterly passive, first as the object of a Hephaistos' craft, then as the focus of the gods' attention as they ready her for presentation, and finally as a gift conveyed by Hermes to Epimetheus. Finally, she is so laden with adornment that she disappears behind her finery, and her identity appears to lie almost entirely in her embellishment.

The fact that many of these features find parallels in Greek custom indicates that they are not the product of Hesiod's imagination. The inseparability of a woman from her clothes and ornament is a pervasive current in Greek thought (see **Textiles**). Moreover, Pandora's experience mirrors that of the traditional Greek bride, who was carefully adorned, even hidden behind, a profusion of finery and presented to a husband as unfamiliar to her as she was to him. She was also expected to be passive to the point of objectification, as we see in vase-paintings where the bridegroom lifts his new wife on a chariot to take her to her new home (no. 27). Sarah Morris has observed that Hesiod's account of the dressing of Pandora (and by extension we might include the actual practice of the dressing of the bride) can be compared with Homeric arming scenes of men.[6] The analogy reflects the Greek sentiment first noted by Vernant that marriage was to a woman what war was to a man.[7] Both institutions were considered to embody the culminating experiences for their respective genders, and each offered the prospect of death, whether in battle or in childbirth.

Pandora's inferiority constitutes a vivid contrast to the powerful female divine presences to whom the story indirectly refers. Pandora's clay essence associates her with Gaia, the goddess of Earth, who is described by Aristotle as the ultimate mother (see **Erichthonios**).[8] We know that the ancient Greeks were conscious of the correlation of Pandora with Gaia, because in depictions of Pandora's creation she rises up out of the soil in the manner in which Gaia is consistently represented (no. 81). Similarly, the diadem Hephaistos creates for Pandora bears representations of all kinds of untamed animals that live free in the wild. This is the realm of the Mistress of Wild Beasts, who was thought to have originated in the hunting and gathering phase of human existence and who later became identified with Artemis (see **Artemis**). Pandora's ties to Gaia and the Mistress of Wild Beasts, the two most powerful ancient goddesses, are so antithetical to the subordinate status of the clay maiden that the story of Pandora must have originated at a time when female divine forces were no longer pre-eminent, perhaps after or toward the end of the Bronze Age.

Hesiod, writing ca. 700 B.C., enthusiastically adapted the Pandora narrative to his own purposes. He passionately denigrates Pandora's clay interior, contrasting its worthlessness, nothingness, with the wealth of her exterior in order to reinforce the larger themes of concealment and guile that characterize the context in which he has chosen to integrate Pandora's story. Another manifestation of Hesiod's heavy hand in the Pandora tradition is the discrepancy between his bitter comments on the after-effects of Pandora's creation and the more modest negative expectations aroused by his earlier description of her fabrication, where her only undesirable qualities were the ones Hermes bestowed on her. Further evidence that Hesiod invented rather than originated the Pandora story is the ease with which he glosses over the existence of the pithos, as if he expects his audience to know this fact.

In Classical vase-painting a bride was the recipient of wedding gifts that include a profusion of containers, and it is interesting to reflect whether the pithos of Pandora is either an antecedent or early evidence for the custom (see **The Wedding**). If either were the case, we would have reason to believe that the vessels presented to the Greek bride would have been consciously viewed as emblems of fertility. In any event, the obviously positive connotations of these wedding gifts reinforce the acute possibility that Hesiod's accentuation of the dour nuances of Pandora's pithos was his own contribution.

There is a contradiction in the story of Pandora in that Hesiod tells us that Pandora was the progenitor of the "race" of women, and yet at the same time implies that the birth of all children followed her arrival. A similar attempt to distinguish female from male ancestry is seen in Athenian thought, where the lineage of Athenian men was traced back to Erichthonios, whereas the progenitor of all women was identified as Pandora. Yet Erichthonios was the son of Gaia, and by Classical times it was believed that Gaia had been impregnated with the semen of Hephaistos (see **Erichthonios**). In the minds of the Athenians, therefore, both Athenian men and all women could trace their ancestry back to both the Earth and Hephaistos, with the textile-producing skills of Athena intimately linked with procreation and marriage (see **Athena**). It is not surprising, therefore, that the descendants of Erichthonios appeared on the west pediment of the Parthenon, and that the story of Pandora's creation was depicted within the temple on the base of the statue of Athena Parthenos (see **Athena**).[9]

1. Hesiod, *Works and Days* 60-89 and *Theogony* 570-606. See also Gantz (1993) 154-64; Lévêque (1988) 49-62; Loraux (1984) 73, 126, 128; Loraux (1978) 49-53; Vernant (1974) 176-84.
2. See Vernant (1991) 107, where *pothos* is described as desire in the sense of grieving for what cannot be attained over an unbridgeable distance.
3. See also DuBois (1988) 47, 57, 59; Sissa (1990) 156.
4. Murnaghan (1993) 48, 72-73.
5. Nugent (1992); see also Gantz (1993) 157.
6. Morris (1992) 32; Homer, *Iliad* 14.166-8.
7. Vernant (1974) 23.
8. Aristotle, *Generation of Animals* 716a 14-17.
9. Pausanius 1.24.7.

79

WHITE-GROUND KYLIX WITH PANDORA

ca. 470-460
attributed to the Tarquinia Painter
London, British Museum, inv. no. GR 1885.1-28.1 (D 4)

Attic, "from Nola"
Clay
Diam. 31.9 cm.

Publications: *ARV²* 869.55; *Para* 426; *Add²* 299; A.H. Smith, "The Making of Pandora," *JHS* 11 (1890) 279 n. 1; Smith (1896) 389-91; A. Murray and A. Smith, *White Athenian Vases in the British Museum* (London 1896) 29, pl. 19; H. Philippart, *Les coupes attiques à fond blanc* (Paris 1936) 41-46, no. 28, pls. 19b-20; A.B. Cook, *Zeus: A Study in Ancient Religion*, vol. 3 (Cambridge 1940) 201-202, pl. 27; S. Karusu, "Alkamenes und das Hephaisteion," *AM* 69-70 (1954-1955) 72-73, fig. 37; J.D. Beazley, "Hydria-Fragments in Corinth," *Hesperia* 24 (1955) 317 n. 43; D. and E. Panofsky, *Pandora's Box* (New York 1956) ii, 96, frontispiece; Lendle (1957) 66, 68-70, pl. 2; *EAA* V (1963) 931, fig. 1142 (s.v. Pandora); Bérard (1974) 162; Mertens (1977) 174, no. 61, 181, pl. 32.3; Brommer (1978) 24, 208, no. B1; Loeb (1979) 149-52, 336, no. Pa3; *LIMC* I (1981) 790, no. 1, pl. 642 (s.v. Anesidora); Schefold (1981) 73, 365, fig. 89; Simon (1982b) 146, pl. 39a; Wehgartner (1983) 67-68, no. 68, 90, pls. 22.1-2, 23.1; Simon (1985) 225, fig. 213; *LIMC* IV (1988) 648, no. 223 (s.v. Hephaistos); Boardman (1989) 38, fig. 73.1-2; Arafat (1990) 61; Gantz (1993) 158; Shapiro (1994) 66-67, fig. 41; *LIMC* VII (1994) 164, no. 1 (s.v. Pandora).

Assembled from many pieces. In the tondo the hair is rendered as black strokes on a wash of brown. The peplos of Anesidora is brown with purple borders and white asterisks; the mantle of Hephaistos is brown with purple borders. The girdle of Athena is purple and her aegis is purple, with white detail; white also for the Gorgon and in the border. The diadems of Anesidora and Hephaistos are in added, gilt clay. Exterior: beneath the figures is a band of meander (left) alternating with a cross square; beneath each handle is a double palmette. Purple for the fillets and wine; white for the beard of the old man.

The scene in the tondo is set within a narrow brown circle, and the figures stand on a thin black groundline. In the center a female stands frontally, feet together with bare toes foreshortened, hands at her side fingering the overfold of her peplos, head turned in left profile. She wears a diadem above long, wavy locks of hair that fall down behind her back. The overfold of her peplos extends to the top of her thighs. A purple stripe edges her neckline, the lower hem of her overfold, and the selvedges beneath her right shoulder; white asterisks are scattered over the surface of the fabric. Over her head is inscribed:]ΝΕΣΙΔΟΡΑ.

To the right of Anesidora is Athena, identified by the inscription over her head. She stands in right profile, with her head in right profile, and she leans forward slightly. She wears a finely pleated chiton that has a deep kolpos; the ends of her belt are visible at the top of her thighs. Her aegis is draped over both shoulders in the manner of a shawl; it has a border of chevrons and is edged with a number of coiling snakes. Athena's right arm is bent at the elbow, and the sleeve covers the elbow. From its wide opening, Athena's bare forearm emerges, angled upward; the hand probably adjusted the shoulder fastening of Anesidora's garment.

To the left of Anesidora stands a beardless male, whose name is inscribed in the field behind him: Hephaistos. He stands almost in left profile, his feet bare with the toes of the advanced right foot extending under the hem of the central figure; the heel of the left foot is slightly raised. The edge of his mantle is

79 Interior

folded over, and the garment is brought across his waist, covering his body to his knees; the ends are brought forward over the left shoulder and upper arm. The mantle's purple border is visible at the lower edge, over his left shoulder, and across his waist. His curly hair frames his face; at the back of his head the hair is gathered up to pass under a diadem. His left hand holds a hammer at his side; his right hand adjusts Anesidora's diadem.

Exterior: Side A. Behind a haltered horse, which stands in left profile, is a youth who stands almost frontally, draped in a mantle. He exchanges glances with a second youth who leads the horse forward; he is draped in a mantle, carries two spears in his right hand, and wears a petasos behind his shoulders. Next to him a woman stands in right profile, a flower in her upraised right hand. Behind the horse a woman stands in right profile, a phiale in her uplifted left hand, a slightly tilted oinochoe in her right hand; wine spills onto the ground. She wears a chiton, a mantle, and a sakkos. She gazes toward a bearded man in a mantle, who stands in left profile, a walking stick in his lowered right hand. All the men wear fillets.

Side B. Behind a horse in right profile is a woman standing in left profile, her hair wrapped in a sakkos, a mantle draped over her chiton and enveloping her body, and a flower in her upraised right hand. She gazes at a man who is turned slightly to his right, his left leg crossing over his right leg, with the toes of his right foot resting on the ground. His mantle is draped over his left shoulder and upper arm and brought across his body; the folds are bunched at his left hip upon a walking stick on which he leans. His right hand is on his right hip, and his uplifted left hand holds a money purse. He is bearded and gazes back at the woman before him. Standing at the horse's head is a youth with mantle, spear, and petasos. Behind him approaches a youth wrapped in his mantle and carrying a stick in his lowered right hand. All the men wear fillets.

The inscription identifies the central figure as Anesidora, a synonym for Pandora that carries the same ambiguous meaning, "giver" or "recipient of" all gifts (see **Pandora**). The scene captures the moment when the process of creating Pandora is not yet complete, and she stands stiffly and frontally, like a doll or statue, as Athena and Hephaistos add the finishing touches to this marvel that Hephaistos has just fashioned out of clay. True to his skill as a

280

79 Side A

79 Side B

metalworker, Hephaistos places a metal diadem on her head, and Athena, the inventor of weaving, is almost surely adjusting the peplos she has just bestowed on Pandora.

Pandora is not only distinguished from the flanking deities by her passivity. Athena and Hephaistos are much larger and they adopt a proprietorial manner. Hephaistos' right hand sits just above the full breadth of Pandora's head as he reaches forward to the edge of the diadem that sits just above her forehead. At the same time, the toes of his right foot slide just beneath the hem of her peplos and almost touch her toes; such forwardness on his part accentuates the extent to which she is yet inanimate, a created object. We sense her appeal to Hephaistos in the fact that the painter has depicted him as a virile young man who has no apparent need for the walking stick to cope with his lameness, here only subtly intimated by his raised left heel. The artist seems to imply that a god of such youth and beauty could only create a like image which would appeal to his vibrant masculinity.

Athena is also rendered as a figure of grace and female charm, who delights in adornment, be it of herself or another. Her slenderness is accentuated by the elegant crinkled folds of her garment, which is tied below her hips in a manner more stylish than functional. Even her aegis is drawn around her shoulders like an elaborately ornamented shawl, the snakes a form of exuberant passementerie. Her primacy in this scene is indicated by the fact that Pandora's head is turned toward her in left profile, although we might rather expect Pandora to be turned toward her maker Hephaistos in order to facilitate his adjustment of the diadem. The scene's emphasis upon Athena, and, by extension, upon the clothing for which Athena is responsible, suggests that the kylix might have been made as a dedicatory offering to the goddess (see **Athena** and **Textiles**). Indeed, the scale of the vase and especially of the tondo scene so much surpass those of conventional kylikes that the vase was surely intended for display rather than use. Moreover, the depiction of the birth of Pandora on the base of the statue of Athena Parthenos indicates the extent to which Athena was thought to be pleased by a reminder of her association with Pandora's creation. The petasos and spears of the youth on Side A tell us that we are concerned with an ephebe, a young man who passed the years between eighteen and twenty in military service. The horse was also appropriate to an ephebe's well-to-do status and physical training, and the beardless companion must be an attendant, who was entrusted with the horse's care. The libation scene of departure (see nos. 18-20), coupled with the ephebe's act of leading the horse, suggests that the youth is embarking on military service, while his father, and probably his mother, participate in the ritual of leave-taking. Side B, by contrast, features another well-known vignette, the negotiating for services between a hetaira and a potential customer (see nos. 36-38). The tassel of her head covering dangles saucily as she clasps the stem of a flower which the man must have just given her as a love token. Meanwhile, in the self-assured manner typical of bargaining clients, he leans casually upon his walking stick and cocks his left elbow, his manner belying the intensity of his determination, which is evident in the forthright manner with which he stretches forward his left hand with the money bag. His bearded face contrasts with the youthfulness of the ephebe on Side A, perhaps to indicate the pleasures of mature manhood which the ephebe could anticipate, either during leave or after military service was completed. In the context of the scene with Pandora in the tondo, the underside of the kylix appears to offer a male view of the dual aspects of a man's interaction with women: the respectable, supportive environment of home life, and the more titillating atmosphere of the brothel.

Although the scene in the tondo is fragmentary, the quality of the draftsmanship is clearly apparent here, as well as on the underside. Joan Mertens notes that the Tarquinia Painter, who also executed no. 39, belonged to the group around the Pistoxenus Painter.

80 Side A

80 Side B

80

KALYX KRATER WITH PANDORA

ca. 460
by the Niobid Painter
London, British Museum, inv. no. GR 1856.12-13.1 (E 467)

Attic, "from Altamura"
Clay
H 49.2 cm., Diam 49.5 cm.

Publications: *ARV²* 601.23; *Para* 395; *Add²* 266; A.H. Smith, "The Making of Pandora," *JHS* 11 (1890) 279-80, pl. 11-12; Smith (1896) 285-86; A.B. Cook, *Zeus: A Study in Ancient Religion*, vol. 1 (Cambridge 1914) pl. 38; Jacobsthal (1927) 127 n. 234; T.B.L. Webster, *Der Niobidenmaler, Bilder griechischer Vasen* 8 (Leipzig 1935) 18, 20, no. 12, pl. 14-15; J.D. Beazley, "Hydria-Fragments in Corinth," *Hesperia* 24 (1955) 316-318, pl. 88a; Lendle (1957) pl. 6; E. Simon, *EAA* V (1963) 931, fig. 1143 (s.v. Pandora); D. Aebli, *Klassischer Zeus* (Munich 1971) 124-26, 233, no. 52; Loeb (1979) 152-55, 336, no. Pa4; *LIMC* I (1981) 790-91, no. 2, pl. 643 (s.v. Anesidora); *LIMC* II (1984) 125, no. 1303 (s.v. Aphrodite); ibid., 485, no. 87, pl. 367 (s.v. Ares); J.H. Oakley, "Double-Register Calyx Kraters: A Study in Workshop Tradition," *Ancient Greek and Related Pottery. Proceedings of the International Vase Symposium in Amsterdam 12-15 April 1984*, H.A.G. Brijder, ed. (Amsterdam 1984) 125, no. 1; *LIMC* IV (1988) 700, no. 345, pl. 425 (s.v. Hera); *LIMC* V (1990) 348, no. 742 (s.v. Hermes); ibid., 750, no. 99 (s.v. Iris I); Boardman (1989) 13-14, fig. 5; Arafat (1990) 60-62, 189, no. 2.37, pl. 17b; Gantz (1993) 158; Shapiro (1994) 67-70, figs. 42-44; *LIMC* VII (1994) 164, no. 2 (s.v. Pandora).

Beneath the rim is a band of dart and lotus pattern. Beneath each of the figural scenes is a band of two or three meanders (left) alternating with a cross square, and beneath each handle is a double palmette. Purple for the thunderbolt of Zeus and the fillets. Brown wash for the animal skin of the Maenad on Side B.

On Side A Pandora stands almost in the center, facing front, her toes foreshortened. She wears a peplos that has an overfold to her hips and a pin fastening the garment on each shoulder. Long locks of hair are brought forward over each shoulder and she wears a fillet, the ends of which fall down the back of her head. Her arms hang at her side, and in each hand she holds a wreath (Smith) or a leafy branch (Simon). To her right Athena stands in right profile, wearing a peplos that is belted over its overfold; both hems are decorated with a stripe beside a row of dots. Her hair is gathered at the back of her head, and she wears a diadem that has a row of dots across its midsection. Her spear leans against her left shoulder. Both arms are extended forward and the hands hold a wreath. On the other side of Pandora is Ares, who approaches in left profile, his head turned back in left profile. He wears a tunic, a cuirass, and a mantle draped behind his back and over his right forearm; he also has greaves, a crested helmet with cheekpieces lowered and with dolphin on the bowl, a spear in his right hand, and a shield over his left arm; the device is a four-spoked chariot wheel. Behind this figure is Hermes, who moves away to his left, his head turned back in left profile. He has a short tunic, a mantle, winged boots and a petasos, and he carries his caduceus in his right hand. Behind him a woman stands frontally, her head in left profile. She wears a chiton, himation, a modius (headdress) with two rows of dots, and earrings, and she carries a scepter in her right hand.

Behind Athena stands bearded Poseidon, his upright trident steadied in his left hand, his right hand on his hip. His body is draped in a mantle which passes over his left shoulder, and he wears a wreath. His head is in left profile and he looks around to Zeus, who is seated in right profile on a klismos, his scepter in his left hand and a thunderbolt in his right hand. He wears a mantle and a wreath. Behind Zeus follows a winged female, who stands with her weight on her right leg, the toes of her left foot resting on the ground behind her. She wears a short, belted chiton and winged boots, and she carries a caduceus in her right hand; her left hand rests on her right shoulder.

Beneath this scene is a second row of figures. A flute-player in right profile blows on his double pipes, his cheeks inflated. His mantle is wrapped around his body, exposing only his right shoulder, and he wears a wreath. On each side of him is a pair of ithyphallic Satyrs with beards, snub noses, pointed ears, curved double horns rising backward from the midpoint of the hairline, and bushy tails. They wear abbreviated, tight-fitting garments that cover their buttocks but expose their genitals. The figures are moving rapidly, legs bent and arms extended in various animated gestures.

On Side B the upper frieze of figures depicts six girls dancing to the music of a flute-player, who stands in right profile, his cheeks inflated in the manner of his counterpart on Side A. He wears a long-sleeved garment that extends to his ankles and is decorated with dots; he also wears a wreath. The girl behind the flute-player wears a pleated undergarment beneath a short belted tunic that is decorated at the neckline and hem with a broad stripe and a row of dots. The other maidens wear peploi with overfolds that may or may not be belted and their hair is wrapped in head coverings (sakkoi) from which only a few curls escape. Standing between the last two dancers behind the flute-player is a bearded man in left profile, wearing a mantle and a wreath, and holding a staff in his right hand.

In the center of the lower frieze a woman stands frontally, a thyrsos in her left hand. She wears a pleated garment beneath a spotted animal skin; she also wears a wreath over her long hair. She gazes across to four nude Satyrs who form two piggy-back pairs. The elevated ones wave their arms toward the other figures in the scene, who include, behind the woman, a boy Satyr, holding a hoop in his left hand, and a bearded Satyr who leans on a walking stick and holds a ball in his right hand.

In the upper frieze on Side A, Pandora, newly completed, is being presented to the Olympian gods (see **Pandora**). As in no. 79, she stands stiffly frontal. Here, even her face is facing the viewer, a device that vase-painters employed in rendering the inanimate, such as a deceased person or a mask (no. 82); indeed, seemingly unconscious of her environs, Pandora stares ahead of her. Her main creator, Hephaistos is noticeably absent, probably out of patriotic loyalty to the city's patron goddess, who hastens to claim credit for the achievement. Athena ostentatiously extends a wreath in the manner in which we might imagine a proud mother putting the finishing touches on a bride (see **The Wedding**). Indeed, Pandora is created to be a bride, and the branches or wreaths that she carries call to mind the wreaths worn by bride and bridegroom, as well as the myrtle branches that were placed in the wedding vessels, the lebetes gamikoi (see **The Wedding**).

Poseidon, meanwhile, turns to Zeus as if to share a private comment about this wondrous creation. The winged figure behind Zeus may be Iris whose messenger status makes her a logical counterpart to Hermes near the other end of the scene. The armed warrior beside Pandora must be Ares. The agitation of his martial character is expressed by his energetic advance, although his attention is curiously focused behind him. Ares is probably present because he is the consort of Aphrodite, whose generosity to Pandora made this new creation both irresistible and problematic to men. That forthcoming duality is suggested by the antithesis of Ares' movement and gaze. The mixed blessing of Pandora's creation is further accentuated by the way Ares' spear mirrors Athena's spear, which carries more constructive overtones. The spears create a frame for Pandora that sets her apart from the other gods and accentuates her rigidity.

80 Detail of Side A, with Athena, Pandora, and Ares.

Behind Ares we see Hermes, the messenger god who brought Pandora to the gods and now, in his characteristically volatile way, is speeding away again. The last figure has been variously identified as Hera (Shapiro) or Aphrodite (Simon). Either would be appropriate, because Aphrodite was one of the most powerful of Pandora's benefactors, and Hera is the quintessence of the wife that Pandora will become.

The dancing Satyrs on Side A are usually thought to allude to a Satyr play, which was presented following a tragedian's trilogy. Satyr plays were intended to provide a light resolution to the day's dramatic performances, and they usually parodied a myth. The most logical inspiration for this scene is the Satyr play of 470-460 by Sophokles. The drama was entitled *Pandora* or *The Hammerers*, but because little survives beyond the title we cannot reconstruct it with any confidence.

The dancing girls on Side B are surely performing in one of the many rituals in the Athenian calendar that afforded marriageable young girls their only formal opportunity to be in full public view. These girls constitute the closest real-life counterpart to the Pandora of myth; at the peak of adolescence and soon to be brides themselves, they embody the grace that, Hesiod tells us, made Pandora a "beautiful evil."

With the lower frieze that encircles the vase, we are in the realm of Satyrs. On Side B a family plays under the watchful eye of a maenad who is presumably the mother and who probably alludes to the lack of docility in Pandora's character, as well as the maternal role Pandora will eventually assume.

With his elegant drawing and simple compositions, the Niobid Painter is often regarded as one of the quintessential Classical vase-painters. He is also represented here by an amphora in Baltimore (no. 44), a hydria in New York (no. 45), and a volute krater in Naples (no. 121).

VOLUTE KRATER WITH PANDORA

ca. 450
related to the Group of Polygnotos
Oxford, Ashmolean Museum, University of Oxford,
inv. no. G.275 (V.575)

Attic
Clay
H 48.2 cm., Diam 35.2 cm.

Publications: ARV² 1562.4; *Para* 506; *Add²* 388; *CVA* Oxford, Ashmolean Museum 1 (Great Britain 3) 18-19, pls. 21.1-2 and 32.6; P. Gardner, "A New Pandora Vase," *JHS* 21 (1901) 1-2, 6, pl. 1; C. Robert, *Archäologische Hermeneutik. Anleitung zur Deutung klassischer Bildwerke* (Berlin 1919) 266-67; J. Harrison, *Prolegomena to the Study of Greek Religion*, 3rd ed. (Cambridge, England 1922) 276-83; M. Bieber, *Griechische Kleidung* (Berlin and Leipzig 1928) 14, 16, fig. 18; E. Buschor, "Feldmäuse," *Sitzungsberichte, Bayerische Akademie der Wissenschaften (München)* 1937, 23-27, fig. 9; Lendle (1957) 66-68, pl. 1; *EAA* V (1963) 931, fig. 1141 (s.v. Pandora); A.D. Trendall and T.B.L. Webster, *Illustrations of Greek Drama* (London 1971) 33-36, 39; Bérard (1974) 161-64, fig. 71, pl. 19; M.J. Vickers, *Greek Vases* (Oxford 1978) no. 48; M.L. West, *Hesiod: Works and Days* (Oxford 1978) 164-65; Loeb (1979) 157-61, 337-338, no. Pa6; *LIMC* I (1981) 791 (s.v. Anesidora); Schefold (1981) 73-75, 365, fig. 90; Simon (1982b) 145, pl. 39b; Boardman (1989) 63, fig. 170; E. Simon, "Hermeneutisches zur Anodos von Göttinnen," in *Festschrift für Nikolaus Himmelmann: Beiträge zur Ikonographie und Hermeneutik, BJb-Beiheft* 47 (Mainz 1989) 197, pl. 35.3; Arafat (1990) 60-62, 189, no. 2.36, pl. 17a; LIMC V (1990) 340 no. 643 (s.v. Hermes); Carpenter (1991) 76, fig. 119; Gantz (1993) 68, 158; Loraux (1993) viii, 89, 115, pl. 2; *LIMC* VII (1994) 164, no. 4 (s.v. Pandora); Shapiro (1994) 69, fig. 45.

Under the lip, bands of tongue, laurel, eggs, lotus, and palmette. On the handles is an ivy pattern; beneath them are palmettes. Above the figural scene is a band of tongue; beneath is a frieze of two meanders (left) alternating with a cross square.

At the viewer's right, Pandora rises up from the ground, her body visible only to mid-thigh. She is turned slightly to her right, and her head is in left profile. Her arms are outstretched upward, fingers extended. Curly locks frame her hairline, and a long lock of hair behind her left ear falls to her shoulder. She wears a high diadem that has five leaves rising from the upper edge. She also wears a chiton beneath a veil that is draped over both shoulders, passing over the diadem. Over her head is the inscription: ΠΑΝΔΟΡΑ. Her gaze is directed upward toward a bearded man who looks down at her, an inscription over his head identifying him as ΕΠΙΜΕΘΕΥΣ. He moves toward her, his left leg advanced with the knee bent, his right toes resting on the ground behind him, where they overlap the left foot of the figure behind him. Epimetheus' lowered right hand holds the handle of a three-sided hammer; the hand of his lowered left hand, palm outward and fingers extended, is brought forward to the edge of her sleeve. He wears a belted tunic that extends to mid-thigh and is decorated across the neckline and shoulders, as well as across the lower hem, with a broad stripe beside a row of dots. He also wears a fillet. In the field before him and flying toward him is a nude Eros, whose wreathed head is slightly inclined and who holds a taenia in his outstretched arms.

Behind Epimetheus and moving toward him is Hermes, his left leg advanced, the right leg extended behind him, but the foot not shown. His left hand holds a flower at his waist; his right hand holds a caduceus. He wears a tunic, over which his chlamys is fastened on his right shoulder; a stripe edges the lower hem. He also wears winged boots and a winged cap; curly locks are visible in front of his left ear; others are gathered into a bunch at the back of his head. His head is in left profile and he gazes back at the face of bearded Zeus, who stands frontally, his body enveloped in a mantle that exposes only his right shoulder. Zeus' left arm is beneath his cloak; his raised right hand supports his scepter. The inscription above his head reads ΖΕΥΣ. He also wears a wreath and he returns the gaze of Hermes.

On Side B a beardless youth moves to his left, his left arm advanced, fingers extended, his right hand clasping two spears at his right hip. He wears a sunhat (petasos) behind his shoulders and a mantle. The woman in front of him moves away, legs widespread, arms wrapped in a mantle that lies over her chiton. Her head is turned back in left profile. Behind the youth a woman flees away in the opposite direction. Her right hand is uplifted and her head is turned back in right profile. A tendril is in the field behind the youth and above the spear shafts.

81 Side A

The scene on Side A gives us a later moment in the myth than those seen on the previous examples, because on the London kylix (no. 79) Pandora is being created and on the London kalyx krater (no. 80) Pandora is being reviewed by the Olympian Gods (see **Pandora**). The scene on the Oxford volute krater focuses on the succeeding episode when Zeus sends Hermes to present Pandora, now fully animate, to Epimetheus. Hermes moves away from Zeus who sends him forth on his mission. The two gods exchange conspiratorial glances as a reminder to the viewer of their delight in being privy to a game of deception in which Epimetheus is totally innocent. Indeed, every negative quality Pandora possesses is a gift from Hermes. The flower that Hermes carries usually has connotations of a love token, because it is frequently held by a woman who has just received it from the man in her presence (no. 36, 38, and see **Persephone and Demeter**). In the hands of Hermes the flower probably alludes to Pandora's status as a gift and to Hermes' own

81 Detail of Side B

gifts to Pandora, foremost among which is deceitfulness, one of Hermes' own more prominent traits. The figures in front of Hermes represent the next phase in the scheme, as Pandora is presented to Epimetheus. Oblivious to the chain of trickery in which he is a hapless pawn, Epimetheus steps forward with eagerness. His left hand is brought forward toward Pandora in an expression of wonder and desire; his fingers stop just short of touching her directly, hovering suggestively at the edge of her arm and sleeve. Pandora is, indeed, a wonder to behold, fully alert, imbued with vitality, and unquestionably responsive to Epimetheus' interest. Her adornment closely follows the descriptions in Hesiod. She wears a garment that Hesiod knew as silvery, a marvelous veil, and an elaborate crown.

This moment of physical animation is equaled by the emotional agitation of the encounter. Epimetheus and Pandora have locked their gazes, so much so that it is clear that Epimetheus has completely forgotten Prometheus' warning never to accept a gift from Zeus. As confirmation of the sexual charge between the pair, Eros hovers above Pandora, flying toward Epimetheus as if embodying

285

81 Detail of Side A

the power of her glance. The presence of Eros, the position of the bridal veil on the back of Pandora's head, and the wreath Epimetheus wears liken the scene to representations of the unveiling of the bride, the *anakalypteria* (nos. 25, 26, 102). At this point in the ritual, bride and groom behold each other for the first time, and in vase representations of this moment Eros flies toward the bride to signify the desirability she exudes and the response she awakens in her new husband (see **The Wedding** and **Gesture and Gaze**). The bride consistently maintains the controlled gestures and modest comportment that are in keeping with the *aidos* and *sophrosyne* that characterized a young woman of respectable family (see **Aidos and Sophrosyne**). Pandora provides an amusing contrast to the traditional bride as she spreads her arms above her head and tilts her head back so that she can look Epimetheus fully in the eyes.

What has puzzled scholars is the hammer that Epimetheus carries, a feature not described in Hesiod, where the only tools are those of Hephaistos. A Satyr play by Sophokles, written between about 470 and 460, was entitled *Pandora* or *The Hammerers*, and it is generally thought that the scene on the Oxford vase must reflect elements of this work. Satyr plays were known to parody well-known myths, and the few surviving fragments of the Sophoklean work indicate that the creation of Pandora was parodied by a chorus of hammer-wielding Satyrs who participated in beating the clay that formed Pandora's image.

To what extent the Sophoklean play presented Pandora rising up out of the ground is unclear, but the painter of the Oxford vase need not have turned to drama for this motif.[1] The image of a woman rising up out of the earth was a familiar one, both in Classical vase-painting and in Greek thought. The Earth goddess Gaia is consistently depicted in this way in the series of vase-paintings that depict the story of Erichthonios (nos. 67, 68, 70-72). Pandora and Gaia do, indeed, have much in common, because Gaia is the womb that originates and nourishes all life (see **Erichthonios**). On her part, Pandora is made from earth and water, and the clay pithos that she opens initiates the cycle of life and death among mankind; Hesiod also tells us that Pandora's headdress bears representations of sea and land animals (see **Women as Containers**). Another divine female who rises up out of the earth is Persephone (no. 82). Danae is also an analogous figure, because she is first confined to an underground chamber and then enclosed in a chest, from which she emerges as a bride when she and her son begin a new life on the island of Seriphos (see **Danae**, and no. 78).

1. E. Simon (1982b) 145 suggests that Sophokles presented Pandora rising up out of the ocean, in reference to the tradition that Hephaistos' workshop was beneath the sea.

PERSEPHONE AND DEMETER

He snatched her—she unwilling and lamenting—
in his golden chariot.

Homeric Hymn to Demeter 19-20

...when she [Persephone] saw her mother's sweet eyes,
she left the chariot and horses and leaped down to run to her,
and falling upon her neck, embraced her.

Homeric Hymn to Demeter 385-58

Two things come first in the lives of people.
First, there is Demeter.

Euripides, *Bacchai* 275

The story of Persephone and Demeter is believed to be one of the oldest of Greek myths, and both it and its associated ritual, the Eleusinian Mysteries, continue to intrigue and puzzle scholars. The principal source of the myth is the compelling *Homeric Hymn to Demeter*, which is thought to have been composed between 650 and 550 B.C.[1]

Persephone was a parthenos, a mature but unmarried daughter of Demeter. Persephone's father was Zeus, who in the incestuous Olympian pantheon also happened to be Demeter's brother. One day, as Persephone and her friends gathered flowers in a meadow, the earth goddess Gaia sent up a magnificent narcissus to capture Persephone's attention. As the girl reached out to pluck it, the ground yawned open and Hades, god of the Underworld, emerged with his chariot to abduct the frightened and resisting maiden. Hades was a brother of Zeus, and we are told in the *Homeric Hymn to Demeter* that Zeus had given permission for Hades' action.

Demeter's discovery of her daughter's loss elicited anger, frantic distress, and what a Jungian psychologist has described as clinical depression. The goddess deliberately withheld prosperity from the earth, such that no vegetation or crops would grow, and she rejected pleas from Zeus to restore the earth's vitality. Finally, Zeus sent the messenger god Hermes down to the Underworld to bring Persephone back to her mother. Demeter greeted her daughter's return by restoring life to earth once again. But Persephone was not able to remain permanently with her mother because, just before she had left the Underworld, Hades had persuaded Persephone to eat part of a pomegranate. Because she had consumed its seeds, Persephone was obligated to return for a third of each year to the Underworld as the bride of Hades.

The story is rich in vivid imagery. Like the irresistible narcissus, Persephone is herself a ripe bloom that will be snatched. The anal-ogy lives on into modern times with both the term "to deflower" and the tradition whereby young Greek women gather flowers before their wedding day (see **Sirens**).[2] The pomegranate Persephone consumes, with its reddish color and profusion of seeds, has often been considered an allusion to Persephone's defloration, and the association of the mouth and the vagina is well attested in Greek thought (see **Women as Containers**).[3] Because Persephone has eaten the seeds, she cannot undo her marriage or regain her virginity, but must serve part of each year as Hades' wife. The symbol survived in the Greek wedding ceremony, where the bride carried with her into the bridal chamber a *malon*, which was a category of fruit with seeds that includes the apple and quince (see **The Wedding**). Other examples of the *malon* were the celebrated golden apples that enticed Atalanta to lose her footrace and acquire a husband (see **Atalanta**). Finally, one should remember that Persephone's annual return above ground was traditionally correlated with the earth's regaining of vitality in springtime.

The story of Demeter and Persephone is often interpreted as the story of a mother's loss of her daughter through marriage. By Greek custom, a father had the authority to select his daughter's husband and the time of her marriage, and, as in the case of Persephone, we know that young women were not uncommonly married to an uncle on their father's side in order to prevent family property from becoming divided. After her wedding a young bride moved from her family's home to the house of her new mother-in-law where she found herself surrounded by new faces, including a husband with whom she may have been barely, if at all, acquainted, and another family's household in which she would never be considered to be thoroughly integrated. Because a Greek bride was hardly past puberty, marriage brought an abrupt end to childhood, and this transition was ritually acknowledged just before her wedding when the bride dedicated her toys to Artemis. It is often said that the parallels between bridal and funerary ritual, as well as the analogy with maiden sacrifice, can be explained by the truth that in symbolic terms a rite of passage formally acknowledges the death of a previous identity (see **Iphigenia**). In the case of a girl's marriage, however, the actual circumstances of the transition incorporate the potential of death. Not only did the young bride leave behind childhood, virginity, and her family home, but she faced the ominous possibility that she could die in childbirth within the year or with successive pregnancies. Despite the intimidating nature of the experience, in the eyes of Greek society a young woman's transition to wife and motherhood was viewed as inevitable because of its critical importance to the survival of the community. That no other identity was possible for a maturing girl is manifested in the burial customs that attended a young girl who died before marrying. On her grave stele she would be addressed as the bride of Hades, and the monument over her grave could take the form of a loutrophoros, the distinctive vessel used to hold water for the bride's wedding bath.

Despite the myth's vivid portrayal of Persephone's experience, the accent in the *Homeric Hymn* is very much upon Demeter. Indeed, it has been noted that in a Greek marriage the mother's loss could be said to be the greater one, because her daughter was not only lost from her own protection but also passed into the hands of a mother-in-law who would now be the foremost woman in her daughter's life.[3] The artistic tradition does, in fact, recognize that Demeter's loss is the greater one, because it is Persephone who consistently consoles her grieving mother (nos. 83, 86). The myth offers powerfully moving imagery for an emotional state that probably every mother has at one time experienced—an intense longing literally to stop the world in order to save her child. In the myth, Demeter does not obtain a complete victory, because she loses her daughter for part of each year, but her triumph is beyond what a mortal mother could expect. Nonetheless, the impact on Persephone of Demeter's apparently successful negotiation is far from positive. In perpetuity, Persephone is required to journey between her husband and her mother, and, even more significantly, will never become a mother herself. Because she is prevented from completing the transition from girlhood and never attains the status of wife and mother that in Greek thought defined a woman's ultimate fulfillment, Persephone remains a shadowy figure without a distinct presence, ever acted upon, ever passive.

Froma Zeitlin argues that Demeter does not only mourn her daughter's physical loss, but that the goddess' intense emotional response to the abduction is partially sparked by anger at Persephone's initiation into sexuality.[4] Persephone is, indeed, not quite the innocent she appears to be. The fact that she voluntarily reaches out for the flower that symbolizes her loss of virginity suggests that she shared the same curiosity about sexuality that Pandora and Aglauros, even Danae, displayed (see **Pandora**, **The Plynteria and Arrephoroi**, **Danae**). Moreover, in the *Hymn*, Persephone is suspi-

ciously overly insistent when she tells her mother that she was simultaneously deceived into eating, and forced to eat, the pomegranate.[6] Her contradictory prevarication implies that she knows the motivation of her mother's question and that her acceptance of the pomegranate was not totally ingenuous. It would seem that Persephone had been ready to make the transition from girlhood and was well aware of the nature as well as the force of her mother's resistance.

The myth also offers a provocative picture of Demeter as a goddess who is the sole source of all vegetation on earth and, until her daughter's misfortune, was apparently a generous donor. An apt comparison is with the image of Gaia, the Earth goddess, opening her arms to give over the child Erichthonios willingly to Athena (see **Erichthonios**). We are also reminded that the root of Demeter's name is the verb "to give." The beneficent picture is totally changed, however, when Demeter is angered. Now she becomes awesomely vengeful, and completely pitiless as she keeps all vegetation from growing until her will prevails. It has been suggested that this omnipotent image of Demeter reflects a very ancient point-of-view from an era before the introduction of agriculture when people subsisted by depending entirely upon the earth's giving or withholding of bounty.[7] The specific mention of crops in the *Hymn* is evidence that this image of Demeter survived into the era of agriculture, but elsewhere in Greek thought the tilling of the soil is viewed as having changed the equation dramatically, with male toil now triggering the earth's fertility. So obvious a symbol for male impregnation was the plow's blade that in the wedding ritual the bride's father handed over his daughter to her new husband with the words: "I give her to you for the ploughing of legitimate children" (see **The Wedding**).

The intense closeness of Demeter and Persephone has occasionally been explained as an indication that the figures are actually different aspects of a single divinity, and certainly in other religions a single earth or mother deity is more the norm.[8] Persephone's epiphany from beneath the ground, especially when correlated with the revival of life upon earth, calls to mind images of other rising female figures as forces of fertility; in addition to Gaia can also be cited images of Pandora, and even Danae (see **Pandora**, **Danae**). One should not forget, however, that in the story as recounted in the *Homeric Hymn*, two other mother divinities figure strongly. It is Gaia who sends up the alluring flower that precipitates Persephone's abduction, and it is Demeter's mother Rhea who reconciles her own daughter with the Olympian Gods. The masterfulness of the *Hymn* is that it successfully and poignantly presents these powerful mother forces as alike and yet distinct.

It has been remarked that the story of Demeter and Persephone resembles the description of a ritual, and Henri Jeanmaire pointed out that the traditional name for Persephone, Kore, signifies a young girl of the age of initiation.[9] Indeed, it would not be surprising if some part of the story of Persephone's abduction and Demeter's mourning were acted out, perhaps as a part of the Eleusinian

Mysteries, the elaborate ritual in which Demeter was honored. Elements in the story conform to the fundamental framework of ritual first observed by van Gennep: the removal of Persephone; her existence apart in an enclosure; and her return with a new identity.[10] It is unlikely, however, that the myth of Demeter and Persephone was shaped to explain a pre-existing ritual in the manner in which the story of the disobedient Aglaurides is thought to have been fabricated as an explanation for the ritual of the Arrephoroi (see **The Plynteria and Arrephoroi**). The important difference is that the story of Demeter and Persephone is widely agreed to be of great antiquity, even going back to Neolithic times.

Finally, one should consider the interpretation of the myth from the point-of-view of Jungian psychology. Jean Bolen argues that Demeter's loss should not be viewed only as a female experience, but more broadly as an expression of any deep human loss to which rage and depression are a normal response.[11] The myth tell us, Bolen suggests, that it is out of this abyss that renewal comes.

1. *Homeric Hymn to Demeter*; Homer, *Odyssey* 11.217; Hesiod, *Theogony* 912-14. For commentary on the *Hymn*, see Foley (1994). See also Burkert (1985) 159ff.

2. Lincoln (1991) 74.

3. Henderson (1991) 134, notes that a pomegranate seed was slang for a woman's genitals; see Winkler (1990) 183.

4. This sentiment survived into Greek village life in modern times, see du Boulay (1974) 127.

5. Zeitlin (1982) 149.

6. *Homeric Hymn to Demeter*, 371-72, 413-15.

7. DuBois (1988) 49, 57, 59, 68, 147.

8. Burkert (1979) 132ff.

9. See discussion of Jeanmaire in Lincoln (1991) 74.

10. Lincoln (1991) 99.

11. Jean Bolen, *Demeter and Persephone. The Abduction into the Underworld*. Sounds True Recordings (Boulder 1992).

82

BELL KRATER WITH THE RETURN OF PERSEPHONE

ca. 440
by the Persephone Painter
New York, Metropolitan Museum of Art,
Fletcher Fund, 1928, inv. no. 28.57.23

Attic
Clay
H 41 cm., W (at handles) 50.2 cm., Diam 45.4 cm.

Publications: *ARV²* 1012.1; *Para* 440; *Add²* 314; L.R. Farnell, *The Cults of the Greek States*, vol. 3 (Oxford 1907) 223, pl. 6a; Pfuhl (1923) 566, pl. 218, fig. 556; Richter and Hall (1936) 156-58, no. 124, pl. 123-24, 171; Richter, *Attic Red-Figured Vases: A Survey*, rev. ed. (New Haven 1958) 123-124, fig. 92; T. Kraus, *Hekate: Studien zu Wesen und Bild der Göttin in Kleinasien und Griechenland, Heidelberger Kunstgeschichtliche Abhandlungen* N.F. 5 (Heidelberg 1960) 93; S. Papaspyridi-Karusu, "Hermes Psychopompos," *AM* 76 (1961) 91-106, fig. 58.2; Metzger (1965) 11-12, no. 7; A. Peschlow-Bindokat, "Demeter und Persephone in der attischen Kunst," *JdI* 87 (1972) 94, 148, no. V96, fig. 31; *Antike Welt* 3 (1972) 4, 41, fig. 6; Bérard (1974) 76-77, 99-102, 129-39, pl. 15, fig. 50; Robertson (1975) 326-27, 408, pl. 106a; Loeb (1979) 135-36, 332-33, no. Ko18; Robertson (1981) 106, fig. 146; Schefold (1981) 71, 365, fig. 87; Simon (1985) 101-102, fig. 94; H. Walter, *Die Gestalt der Frau. Bildwerke von 30,000-20 v. Chr.: Anthropologische Betrachtungen* (Stuttgart 1985) 39, 41, fig. 33; C. Bérard, "Festivals and Mysteries," in Bérard et al. (1989) 115-17, fig. 159; Boardman (1989) 61, fig. 121; Carpenter (1991) 36, fig. 44; *LIMC* VI (1992) 990-91, no. 13 (s.v. Hekate); Gantz (1993) 27, 67.

Mended from several pieces; remains of ancient repairs. Beneath the rim is a laurel wreath between bands of tongue. Below the scenes is a band of double meander in groups of three on Side A, groups of five on Side B, alternating with a saltire square. Added red for the fillet of the woman with torches on Side A and those of the men on Side B; also for the flames and inscriptions. On Side B a woman wearing chiton, himation, and sakkos stands frontally, holding a trefoil-mouthed oinochoe. She gazes to her right, at a man who holds a phiale in his right hand and wears a himation and fillet. To her left, a man leans on his staff; he is also dressed in an himation and fillet.

On Side A Persephone returns from the Underworld, attended by Hermes. She rises out of rocky terrain, turned almost in right profile. Her left, advanced knee is bent. She wears a chiton beneath a himation that is wrapped around her right shoulder and arm, passes behind her back and nape, and is brought forward over her left shoulder, enveloping her lower torso and right leg. Her right elbow is bent, with the forearm raised and the fingers extended, palm facing out; her left hand, concealed by her drapery at her left hip, lifts the himation folds to facilitate her ascent. Short curls edge her hairline, and longer straight locks fall down behind her shoulders. Her diadem is decorated with a band of lotus and palmette, and she also wears a pendant necklace. She gazes ahead of her.

Standing beside and just behind her is Hermes, whose face and body are frontal. Over his tunic he wears a chlamys that is fastened on his right shoulder; the folds are wrapped completely around his right arm. His left hand holds his caduceus by his side. He also wears sandals, and over his curly hair he wears a petasos.

In the center of the scene Hekate moves to her left, her legs in profile, her torso frontal, her head turned in left profile, Her left leg is advanced with the knee relaxed, and her frontal right foot is foreshortened. She wears a peplos that has an overfold and that is open down her right side; the selvedges are bor-

85 Side A

dered with a stripe. She also wears a necklace with a pendant. In each hand she holds a flaming torch. Her hair is bunched up at the nape, and her fillet is wrapped three times around her head.

On the other side of her, Demeter stands frontally, both feet frontal and foreshortened. She wears a chiton beneath a himation that passes over her left shoulder and around her waist and legs, concealing her left arm. In her right hand she steadies a scepter that is diagonally striped and terminates in an elaborate floral finial. Her head is in left profile, and she looks across to Persephone. Her hair falls in scallop waves across the hairline and is gathered up in a bun at the nape.

Inscriptions identify the figures as Persephone, Hermes, Hekate, and Demeter.

With regal dignity, Persephone draws aside her mantle in order to facilitate her imminent first step upon the earth (see **Persephone and Demeter**). She gazes across to her mother and formally acknowledges her with an upraised hand. Meanwhile, stationary and composed, Demeter stands waiting, betraying no intimation of the frenzied grief and black despair that preceded, and precipitated, this moment. The stiff verticality of her scepter fur-

ther accentuates the vastness of the separation mother and daughter have endured and are still experiencing. Between Persephone and Demeter stand Persephone's guides, Hermes and Hekate. The frontality of Hermes' body and face, a treatment that Classical vase-painters reserved for such liminal images as masks and the dying, emphasizes the no man's land that he, Persephone, and Hekate still inhabit. The strong diagonals of Hekate's torches and the complementary angle of her body also underscore the distance between the living and the dead. At the same time, her rhythmically flowing garments lend immediacy to the scene by testifying to the progress of the journey and to the impending reunion of mother and daughter.

The solemn tone created by the composition, the poses, and the gestures bespeak a ceremonial context, and, indeed, Persephone's elegant stephane and Hekate's double torches recall the wedding ceremony (see **The Wedding**). Here, however, the bridal journey is inverted. In the traditional marriage ritual the bride's mother follows the wedding procession as it makes its way to the home of the groom, where the groom's mother stands waiting (nos. 102 and

109). Here, by contrast, Persephone, though dressed as a bride, journeys back to her mother. The scene poignantly reminds us that it is Persephone's fate to travel as a perpetual bride between her mother and her husband Hades. Persephone will never complete the young woman's transition to marriage and motherhood, because, although sustained by her mother's love, she is also impeded by it.

The rocky terrain from which Persephone emerges alludes to her new identity as queen of the Underworld, an association that links her with other mythical females closely associated with the earth. As the embodiment of Earth, Gaia dwells under the surface of the ground and, in Classical vase-painting, she allows only the part of her body that is above her genitals to rise above it, as she hands over to Athena the baby for whom she has functioned as a womb (see **Erichthonios**). The step that Persephone is about to take in this scene distinguishes her from Gaia, who shows no interest in rising farther. Another manifestation of the link between women and the earth is Pandora, who was literally fashioned from clay (see **Pandora**). She is usually portrayed as a statue or a doll, but her age-old link with earth divinities is manifested in her portrayal on a volute krater in Oxford (no. 81) where she rises up out of the ground. A further comparable image is the figure of Danae rising up out of the chest (see **Danae**). Danae, too, often wears the stephane of a bride, which she will soon become. With these mythical figures we are repeatedly reminded how compelling to the Greeks was the image of a woman rising up, usually out of the ground, and always bearing connotations of fertility.

This is the only vase attributed to the Persephone Painter, whose extraordinary skill in composition and draftsmanship has occasionally inspired scholars to identify him with other red-figure and white-ground artists.

82 Detail of Side B

VOTIVE RELIEF WITH DEMETER AND PERSEPHONE

420-410
Munich, Staatliche Antikensammlungen München, inv. no. GL.198

Attic, "from Rhamnous"
Marble
H 50.5 cm., W 33 cm., Th 11 cm.

Publications: B. Sauer, *ArchEph* 1893, 36-39; M. Ruhland, *Die eleusinien Göttinnen* (Strassburg 1901) 25; L.R. Farnell, *The Cults of the Greek States*, vol. 3 (Oxford 1907) 264-65, pl. 26b; C. Anti, *ASAtene* 4/5 (1921-22) 74; G. Oikonomos, *ArchEph* (1923) 91; C. Karusos, "Ein attisches Weihrelief," *AM* 54 (1929) 4, no. 5; H. Speier, "Zweifigurigen Gruppen im fünften und vierten Jahrhunderts vor Christus," *RM* 47 (1932) 37, pl. 7.1; H. Süsserott, *Griechische Plastik des 4. Jahrhunderts vor Christus* (Frankfurt 1938) 95-96; G. Lippold, *Handbuch der Archäologie* 3.1, *Die griechische Plastik* (Munich 1950) 197 n. 9; Dohrn (1957) 28; T. Hadzisteliou Price, "Double and Multiple Representations in Greek Art and Religious Thought," *JHS* 91 (1971) 56, no. 5b; G. Despinis, *Symbole ste melete tou ergou Agorakritou* (Athens 1971) 179; R. Kabus-Jahn, "Die Grimanische Figurengruppe in Venedig," *Antike Plastik* XI (1972) 32, fig. 3; Peschlow-Bindokat, "Demeter und Persephone in der attischen Kunst," *JdI* 87 (1972) 113-14, 151, no. R 14, fig. 37; E. Mitropoulou, *Corpus I, Attic Votive Reliefs of the 6th and 5th Centuries B.C.* (Athens 1977) 48, no. 77, fig. 115; G. Neumann, *Probleme des griechischen Weihreliefs, Tübinger Studien* 3 (Tübingen 1979) 57, 59, 65-66, pl. 32b; *LIMC* III (1986) 865, no. 232 (s.v. Demeter); B. Vierneisel-Schlörb, *Glyptothek München* III, *Klassische Grabdenkmäler und Votivreliefs* (Munich 1988) 1-8, pl. 1.

The side to the left of the figures is intact; the side to the right of the figures is broken. The underside and top are smooth. There is rough pointwork on the back.

There are flat moldings beneath the figures. Above the figures' heads is a flat molding, the underside of which recedes at a 45-degree angle back to the plane of the background.

Two women stand side by side, each turned three quarters to her right, with the left leg relaxed and wearing sandals. Each holds between the index finger and thumb of the left hand a scepter, which rests on the outside of the left thigh; each shaft also leans against the left shoulder. The figure to the viewer's right, Persephone, wears a chiton, which has a low, rounded neckline. A mantle is draped across her waist and legs, with the ends brought forward over her left shoulder to hang down the outside of her left thigh. The fabric is very thin, clinging to the right side of her torso, and revealing her right breast and nipple. Folds of her chiton spill over her himation at the waist. Her head is in left profile, and over her short, wavy hair she wears a taenia. She gazes across to the face of the other woman. Her right elbow is bent; her right forearm is not shown; and her right hand clasps the left shoulder of the other woman.

The second woman, Demeter, wears a girded peplos with overfold. In the center of the neckline, the folds dip in a V, and at each side of the waist the drapery spills over the girding to the thigh. The fabric falls closely over the breasts, almost revealing the right nipple. Demeter also wears a mantle that is fastened on each shoulder with the ends falling down behind the legs to the knees. Her head is turned in three-quarter right profile and is tilted to her

83

women share. The figures are well separated, otherwise linked only by Persephone's gaze and by the chiton folds that spill over her right arm. Because the chiton designates Persephone's marriageability, the folds underscore not only the physical bond between the two women, but also the generational distance that is ultimately the reason why they cannot perpetually remain together. Demeter seems, if not oblivious, then at least unresponsive to her daughter's overture. Her withdrawal, communicated by her averted head and gaze, expresses her grief for their forthcoming, and ever recurring, separation, and her lack of receptivity to sympathy calls to mind the similar, self-absorbed depression the goddess experiences in the *Homeric Hymn to Demeter*. Persephone, by contrast, does not focus on her own predicament, but rather on that of her mother, to whom she offers solace. As in the *Homeric Hymn*, the greater sufferer in the story is the mother.

The handling of the drapery dates the relief to the last decades of the fifth century. Noteworthy is the extreme transparency of Persephone's chiton over her breasts, as well as its finely crinkled folds over her right arm and ankles. Demeter's peplos is rendered with cordlike folds over the upper torso and supporting leg. Over the relaxed left leg the fabric is drawn tightly, and at the top of the left thigh are several flat, vertical folds with slightly concave valleys. No folds cut into the plane of the figures. Especially remarkable is the liquidity of the peplos as it spills over its girding, and the similar fluidity of Persephone's mantle where it is drawn across her waist. Typically Classical is the flattened upper surfaces of the arms.

The relief was made for dedication in a sanctuary, and the figures may have been inspired by statuary prototypes that have not survived.

84

right, with her gaze directed downward to her right. Her short, wavy hair is drawn back from her face.

The gesture of affection linking the two women indicates that they are Demeter and Persephone. Because the less revealing peplos was the sedate garment of an older woman and the more alluring chiton was preferred by marriageable maidens, we can identify Persephone as the figure who rests her hand on her mother's shoulder. The gesture is ultimately inspired from vase-painting and finds an antecedent in a scene with Erichthonios of shortly before mid-century (no. 67).

Although Classical depictions of affection between Demeter and Persephone are consistently understated, the subtlety of this scene is remarkable. The figures are completely separated except for the position of Persephone's hand directly on the bare skin of her mother's shoulder, a detail that accentuates the intimacy the

VOTIVE RELIEF WITH DEMETER AND PERSEPHONE

410-400
Athens, Acropolis Museum, inv. no. 1348

Attic, from the Athenian Acropolis
Marble
H 73 cm., W 32 cm., Th 11 cm.

Publications: B. Sauer, *ArchEph* 1893, 36-39, pl. 8; M. Ruhland, *Die eleusinien Göttinnen* (Strassburg 1901) 24-25; L.R. Farnell, *The Cults of the Greek States*, vol. 3 (Oxford 1907) 264, pl. 26a; C. Anti, *ASAtene* 4/5 (1921-22) 74; S. Casson, *Catalogue of the Acropolis Museum* II (Cambridge 1921) 253-255 (illus.); H. Speier, "Zweifiguren-Gruppen im fünften und vierten Jahrhunderts vor Christus," *RM* 47 (1932) 39-40, pl. 11.1; H. Süsserott, *Griechische Plastik des 4. Jahrhunderts vor Christus* (Frankfurt am Main 1938) 94-95, pl. 13.1; G. Lippold, *Handbuch der Archäologie 3.1, Die griechische Plastik* (Munich 1950) 197 n. 8; Dohrn (1957) 28-29; A. Peschlow-Bindokat, "Demeter und Persephone in der attischen Kunst," *JdI* 87 (1972) 115-16, 150, no. R 3, fig. 38; Brouskari

(1974) 170, fig. 363; E. Mitropoulou, *Corpus I, Attic Votive Reliefs of the 6th and 5th Centuries B.C.* (Athens 1977) 49, no. 79, fig. 117; *LIMC* III (1986) 875, no. 376, pl. 588 (s.v. Demeter).

The vertical edge to the figures' left is intact; the edge to the figures' right is broken across the woman's right upper arm. The top of the relief is smoothed, with a cutting for a square clamp. The upper molding and base are badly broken away. Effaced are the faces of the figures and Persephone's right hand and both feet. In front of Demeter's head is the remains of the inscription: ΔΗΜΗΤ]ΗΡ.

Two women are turned slightly to their right. The figure in the foreground stands with her left leg relaxed, her left arm hanging at her side, with the hand, fingers relaxed, by her left hip. Her right arm also hangs by her side, but the hand is drawn away from the right hip and the fingers rest on the left thigh of the woman beside her. Over her chiton, she wears a himation that is brought across her hips to cover her legs, with an overfold extending to mid-thigh. The ends are brought forward over her left shoulder, covering her left arm to her wrist, with the folds falling to the ground. Her head is in left profile and is markedly bowed, and her hair is drawn up from the nape beneath a fillet.

Beside and behind her stands a woman whose left leg is relaxed, the weight resting on the toes; the foot of her right, supporting leg is in profile and wears a sandal. Her right arm is extended out from her shoulder, and her left arm is outstretched behind her companion, with the hand upraised to steady the shaft of a scepter. She wears a peplos, the girding of which is visible at the center of her waist; over her right hip folds are drawn up over the girding and spill down her right thigh. Her head is in left profile, and her wavy hair covers her ear. Outside her right leg, and overlapping part of it, is a raised element with curving contour belonging to a figure or object to her right.

84

The intimate juxtaposition of the figures, as well as the remains of the inscription, identify the women as Demeter and Persephone. Demeter wears the matronly peplos and holds a scepter as she gazes directly in front of her; Persephone, clad in the maidenly chiton, inclines her head in the *aidos*, or shy modesty appropriate to a bride (see **Aidos** and **Sophrosyne**, **The Wedding**). Demeter is the confident protector of her daughter, extending her arm behind Persephone's back, and so assured of her daughter's presence and security that she can focus her gaze in the opposite direction. Persephone, by contrast, stands so close to her mother that her forehead is in contact with Demeter's hair, and her right shoulder is pressed into the hollow beneath Demeter's left shoulder. Moreover, the fingers of Persephone's right hand touch Demeter's left thigh, and the lower folds of her peplos touch her mother's left foot. The utter familiarity and ease with which the bodies are intimately linked recall the group of another mother and child, Aphrodite and Eros (no. 17) where each figure is also so comfortable with the close proximity of the other's body that the eyes can look elsewhere (see **Gesture and Gaze**). The combination in these parent-child groups of linked bodies and averted gazes contrasts with scenes of heterosexual and homosexual lovers, whose bodies may or may not be entwined, but whose gazes are fixedly locked upon one another (nos. 40, 41).

The sculptor of this relief chose not to present Demeter as a mother grieving for a daughter lost each year to Hades. Instead, we see here the commanding mother goddess who was able to suspend all earthly vegetation until her daughter was returned to her

293

care. Proud and triumphant, Demeter dominates Persephone, who is rendered here as the modest young maiden of *aidos* who will never complete the traditional pattern of a young woman's life, by which an adolescent girl left her mother and childhood home for marriage and motherhood (see **Aidos** and **Sophrosyne**). The relief expresses clearly how the interrupted transition freezes Persephone's character such that she perpetually remains the young maiden and shy bride, ever under her mother's care.

The carving is a superb illustration of late fifth-century style. Persephone's chiton is all but transparent, the fabric lying closely over her breasts and the navel barely visible. The fabric of Demeter's peplos is only slightly more substantial, revealing clearly the contours of her right breast. The folds of Demeter's right armhole are carved in very low relief, but nowhere do the drapery's valleys cut into the plane of the figures. Whereas the fabric over Demeter's right leg falls into tubular folds that conceal the leg, the contours of her left leg are accentuated by means of both a tubular vertical fold that originates at her left knee and another that emerges beneath her left knee and curves around her left shin and ankle. The liquidity of the drapery perfectly complements the rhythmic pairing of mother and daughter.

VOTIVE RELIEF
WITH PERSEPHONE

ca. 420
Würzburg, Martin-von-Wagner-Museum der Universität Würzburg, inv. no. HA 1754

Attic
Marble
H 42 cm., W 21 cm., Th 35 cm.

Publication: E. Mitropoulou, *Corpus I, Attic Votive Reliefs of the 6th and 5th Centuries B.C.* (Athens 1977) 50, no. 80, figs. 118-19.

Marble, broken around all edges, abraded over surface, with some dark discoloration.

The relief is carved on both sides. On Side B is a standing man in three-quarter left profile, his left knee relaxed. His mantle is draped around his waist and legs, with the folds bunched under his left arm. His left hand is at his side.

On Side A Persephone stands on her left leg, with her right leg relaxed. Her right elbow is slightly bent, and at her thigh her right hand holds the end of a torch, the tip of which is seen just in front of her left breast. Her left elbow is bent. She wears a chiton, the buttons of which are visible on her right arm. A cord passes over each shoulder and around the outside of each breast. Her himation is wrapped around the waist, with the upper hem turned back and the point of the garment falling down the left thigh; the ends of the himation are wrapped around the left elbow. Beneath her left elbow can be seen the right forearm and hand of another figure.

85 Side A

The key to the identity of the figure is the close proximity of the arm and hand of the missing figure, who touches the maiden's left arm and thigh and whose upper right arm must have been overlapped by the maiden's upraised left forearm. Although the torch can be an attribute of several goddesses, including Demeter, Hekate, and Artemis, in the Classical period only Persephone consistently wears a chiton and is depicted in such immediate contact with another figure, her mother Demeter (see **Persephone and Demeter**). Here, Persephone is typically seen as a parthenos, a mature young maiden of marriageable age, still young enough to be gathering flowers with her friends when she was abducted by Hades. The torch refers not only to the darkness of the Underworld, but also to the wedding torch and, by extension, to the marriage of Persephone and Hades.

Whereas vase-painters had traditionally shown hetairai and their customers entwined in embraces (nos. 40, 41), gestures of intimacy in other contexts were rare before the Parthenon frieze (442-438), where Aphrodite links arms with Artemis, while her son Eros casually presses his body against his mother's leg (pp. 248-49, fig. 1) (see **Gesture and Gaze**). In succeeding years artists experimented with more overt gestures of affection, which are first introduced in representations of Demeter and Persephone. Such easy intimacy is not widespread in mythical contexts before the late fifth century, and in real life it is almost unprecedented in Classical art, with the exception of portrayals of mothers with children (no. 6).

The Würzburg relief is superbly carved, possibly by a sculptor who had contributed to the Parthenon. Suggesting a date one or two decades after the Parthenon frieze is the way the drapery lies closely upon the torso, interrupted by flat folds that occasionally meet in a V. The himation is rendered by cordlike folds which, over

Fig. 1. Side A of a fragment from the same monument as no. 85

Fig. 2. Side B of a fragment from the same monument as no. 85

85 Side B

the left supporting leg, become narrower at they rise and are separated by wide, flat valleys. On the right thigh, as well as on the left thigh of the man on Side B, the fabric forms a wide, flat fold, the midpoint of which is concave. Looking forward to the last years of the fifth century are such details as the undulating neckline of the chiton and the folds that originate at the right nipple. In general, the drapery follows the spirit of the Parthenon frieze in revealing and modeling the forms of the body. Only at the end of the fifth century will the drapery folds penetrate the plane of the flesh and will the fabric falling free of the body take on a life of its own.

Angelos Delivorrias has identified a fragment in a private collection in Athens as part of this relief (p. 295, figs. 1 and 2). He suggests that the relief was a dedication in one of the sanctuaries on the south slope of the Acropolis.[1]

1. I thank A. Delivorrias for permission to publish these photographs.

86

VOTIVE RELIEF WITH DEMETER AND PERSEPHONE

420-415
Athens, National Archaeological Museum, inv. no. 3572

Attic
Marble
H 1.15 m., W 52 cm., Th 15 cm.

Publications: C. Karusos, "Ein attisches Weihrelief," *AM* 54 (1929) 1-5, pl. 1; F. Brommer, *Die Skulpturen der Parthenon-Giebel* (Mainz 1963) 151 n. 30; S. Karouzou, *National Archaeological Museum. Collection of Sculpture: A Catalogue* (Athens 1968) 60; A. Peschlow-Bindokat, "Demeter und Persephone in der attischen Kunst," *JdI* 87 (1972) 115 n. 215; E. Mitropoulou, *Corpus I, Attic Votive Reliefs of the 6th and 5th Centuries B.C.* (Athens 1977) 54, no. 92, fig. 140; *LIMC* III (1986) 867-68, no. 273 (s.v. Demeter).

Only part of the top and the vertical side to viewer's right is intact. Effaced over surface. Inscription on the anta reads ΔΗΜJΗΤΗΡ.

Within a frame formed by an anta and architrave, Demeter stands behind and to the right of Persephone, who is seated. Demeter's torso is turned only slightly to her right, and her head was in left profile. She wears a belted peplos with an overfold that stops short of her belt. Her mantle passes over her head, and is wrapped around her left upper arm; the folds were brought around behind her back and are drawn across her abdomen to her left hip. Her left forearm rests on Persephone's left shoulder at the base of the neck, with the fingers resting on Persephone's torso just above the left breast. Persephone is turned in three-quarter left profile, and her head is in left profile. She gazes ahead of her, and her upper arms are at her side. She wears a belted peplos, and possibly a mantle over her left shoulder. The left arms of both figures overlap the anta beside them.

86

Demeter stands so close to Persephone that her daughter's head is cradled between her mother's torso and left arm. With remarkable intimacy Demeter's left forearm nestles against the side of Persephone's neck, and the fingers rest almost directly on her daughter's breast. The composition brings to mind the representation of Aphrodite and Eros (no. 17), where mother and child share a comparable rapport, bodies intertwined while their attention is directed elsewhere. In the scene of Aphrodite and Eros, it is the young boy who needs the reassurance of his mother's presence; here, by contrast, Demeter is the clinging figure in keeping with the ancient view that Persephone's abduction was a greater loss to Demeter than to her daughter (see **Persephone and Demeter**). The mantle over Demeter's head surely refers to the veil that she wore when mourning the loss of her daughter; its folds, wrapped around Demeter's left forearm, press against her daughter's head and remind the viewer of the intensity of the grief that preceded Persephone's return.

The almost gossamer thinness of the mantle as it frames Demeter's neck and passes across her abdomen indicates a date for the relief within the last two decades of the fifth century. Consistent with that date are the undulating neckline of her peplos and the manner in which the mantle folds are tightly wrapped around her left arm.

Although both homosexual intimacy (no. 106) and heterosexual intimacy involving hetairai (nos. 40, 41) were depicted throughout the fifth century, demonstrative gestures of affection in other relationships were first explored only in the last two decades of the fifth century and only in representations of Demeter and Persephone. In the following centuries, gestures of affection become both more common and much less restrained.

Because the relief was certainly a votive offering, the scene probably included mortal worshippers, whose gaze the goddesses would be returning. The particularly deep-set inner corner of Persephone's left eye accentuates the intensity of her concentration, and, therewith, her complete sense of security within her mother's arm.

Women and the Metaphor of Wild Animals

WOMEN AS WILD ANIMALS

Ruthless as a mountain lioness roaming through the green glades,
she wrought the deed she had set her hands to do.

Euripides, *Elektra* 1163-64

On the whole, the womb is like an animal within an animal.

Aretaeus, *On the Causes and Symptoms of Acute Diseases* 2.11

The close association of women with animals is of extreme antiquity. A goddess depicted in about 6000 B.C. at Çatal Hüyük in southeastern Anatolia was flanked by animals, and an animal skull lay between her legs, as if she had just given birth (p. 304, figs. 2 and 3, see **Artemis**). The same symmetrical representation characterizes Archaic images of the Mistress of Wild Beasts, whom Homer identified with Artemis (see **Artemis**). The Mistress of Wild Beasts, and surely her ancient ancestor, was viewed as the mother of all animals, both the predators that would destroy men and the game that would sustain them.

The age-old linkage of animals and women goes beyond rapport. Homer's Athena actually takes the form of an owl, and there are many other mythical instances where women assume animal form (see **Athena**). Kallisto is changed by Artemis into a bear when she breaks the rules of the forest, and Kephalos has sexual intercourse with a bear, which then turns into a woman (see **Bears** and no. 100). After her famed foot race and turbulent life as a married woman, Atalanta returns to the wild as a lion (see **Atalanta**). Mythical maidens are also regularly demanded in sacrifice to atone for the killing of a sacred animal that has been wrongfully hunted down. The maidens escape their fate when an animal is substituted in their place. Iphigenia is the most celebrated example, but similar stories underlie the ritual at Mounychia and even that at Brauron (see **Iphigenia** and **Little Bears**).

The animal with which women are most closely identified in Greek myth is the bear, which figures in the stories of Atalanta, Kephalos, Kallisto, the tradition of Iphigenia known at Brauron, and the stories behind the ritual at Mounychia and the Little Bears at Brauron (see **Bears** and **Little Bears**). Lions are also intimately linked with women. Not only does Homer address Artemis as a lion, but lions are perhaps the most frequently encountered animals in the depiction of the Mistress of Wild Beasts (no. 108, see **Artemis**). Thetis adopted the form of a lion in her struggle with Peleus (nos. 106-108), and "Leaina," meaning "Lion," was a popular name for prostitutes in Classical Athens. A third animal with which women are commonly aligned is the deer. The most familiar tradition is the substitution of a deer for Iphigenia, who had been offered in retribution for the sacred deer her father Agamemnon wrongly killed. One should also keep in mind that Aktaeon, who was fatally punished by Artemis for an offense related to women, was certainly a deer hunter (see **Aktaeon**). A final common point of comparison is the horse, which differs from the above animals in that it was raised in captivity, although it required training to be ridden or driven. In Greek literature young girls are repeatedly compared with fillies which have not yet been subjected to the harness, the implication being that man's domestication of the horse enhanced the animal's usefulness, competence, and even beauty.[1]

So easy is it to understand how women came to be identified with animals that it is very likely that this way of thinking originated in the hunting and gathering phase of human existence. From early times men and women alike were surely awed by a woman's mysterious fertility, her intuitive nurturing skills that likened her to a forest animal, and an apparently instinctive understanding of biological processes that seemed in synchrony with animal life and the annual cycle of vegetation. Moreover, the probable origin of male aggression in mating conflicts accounts for the intimate link between male aggression in hunting, on the one hand, and sexuality and eroticism, on the other (see **Aktaeon**). In Greek thought a woman's bestial side was viewed as the heart of her sexuality and fertility and was accordingly regarded with wonder, respect, anxiety, and fear.

The identification of women with animals finds a particularly vivid expression in the metaphor of courtship as hunting. In a common scene in Classical Greek vase-painting, a male armed with hunting weapons, be they spears or a harpoon, avidly pursues a fleeing maiden as if she were an animal quarry (see **Pursuit Scenes**). The theme of the pursuit is graphically enacted in Peleus' courtship of Thetis, who continuously transformed herself into wild animals, which Peleus wrestled successfully in order to win her as his bride (see **Peleus and Thetis**).

It is important to realize that women did not find distasteful the fact that they were compared to animals pursued as prey. In pursuit scenes women return the gazes of their suitors and even adopt a gesture of acquiescence (see **Gesture and Gaze**, no. 113). At least one pursuit scene was depicted on a wedding vase created especially as a bridal gift (no. 57). The wedding of Peleus and Thetis was considered the quintessential wedding in Greek mythology (nos. 109 and 110). Moreover, bridal scenes on wedding vases presented to the bride as gifts emphasize the romantic ambience of the ritual, even though the verb for marriage means "to tame, to subdue" and the bridegroom's grasp of the bride's wrist was a gesture of abduction and subjugation (see **The Wedding**). It is abundantly clear that in the Classical period the concept of a marriageable maiden as an untamed animal to be domesticated in marriage was a positive image accepted by both male and female.

Despite the broad acceptance of the metaphor of the pursuit, the identification of women with untamed animals was as much one of reproach as of affirmation in the Classical period. The Greek predisposition for antithesis came to identify men with culture and women with its opposite, nature. Women were thought to be subversive of democracy and incapable of remaining socialized to the male-made and male-centered institutions of settled community life.[2] Irrational episodes in male behavior were considered temporary and followed by a return to rational self-control. By contrast, as the penetrated partner, women were thought not to be masters of themselves biologically, and, consequently, were believed to be equally lacking in sexual and moral self-mastery (see **Women and Men**). Women were also thought to indulge in irrational outbursts that were neither of manageable limits nor confined to ordered institutions in the way that war and hunting functioned for men. Aristotle might describe women as characterized by incomplete development, but in the popular imagination a woman was a potential Agave, who might abandon her home and loom to indulge in an explosive frenzy in the mountains that would culminate in the murder of her child (see **Maenads**). Many Greek women must have been compared with the bird-women Sirens, whose irresistible songs lured sailors to their death (see **Sirens**).

Why the metaphor of women as animals was colored by an underlying apprehension and hostility is an age-old question. It is often argued that the polarization of the genders is a proven social strategy, because young boys can be more effectively persuaded to embrace behavior prescribed for manhood if qualities considered its antithesis are ascribed to women. It has also been pointed out that subversion has always been feared from those who have no vested interest in maintaining the status quo, and certainly women living in Greek culture had only a minimal direct stake in the social system.[3] Ancient writers tell us that the sixth-century lawgiver Solon was so sensitive to the ramifications of this inequity that he encouraged the curious and surely late mythical tradition that explained Athenian women's deprivation of civic rights as punishment for their fierce allegiance to Athena.[4] Awareness of the harshness of women's roles in the social order can also be seen in the mythical theme of marriage as a form of sacrifice and in the intense romanticization of the wedding in Classical vase-painting. To keep the issue in perspective, however, one should not forget that the Greeks also realized that their society asked a great deal from young men, and a number of myths and rituals express an analogous sympathy with a youth's transition to manhood.

Nonetheless, a young woman growing to maturity in Classical Athens was the recipient of a confusing message. She was led to believe that her sexual appeal lay in her feral aspect, and her preparation for marriage concentrated on the socialization of this quality. She was also made well aware that her respectability as a grown woman depended upon her submissiveness, which was to be manifested in downcast eyes that bespoke a modesty with overtones of sexual shame (see **Little Bears** and *Aidos* and *Sophrosyne*). If she were lucky, a maturing girl surrounded by these contradictory directives would have learned to achieve the balance that was the guiding tenet of Greek culture. If she were perceptive, she would have come to understand that the total eradication of feral qualities in both men and women was considered neither attainable nor even desirable, and that a tension between the sexes was viewed as inevitable and even appealing. Plato Comicus' charge to a young husband could be taken to be as much a challenge as a warning: "If you relax too much," he remarks, "the wife gets out of control."[5]

1. Anakreon, frag. 78 Gentili. See also Castriota (1992) 53-56.

2. Aristotle, *Politics* 1313b. See Aristotle, *History of Animals* 581b, 10-15, where he emphasizes that girls at puberty require surveillance.

3. Arthur (1984) 24-25.

4. Augustine, *City of God* 18-19. See Castriota (1992) 146.

5. Plato Comicus, 18 K.

BEARS

In Greek thought women are closely identified with bears, a phenomenon all the more remarkable for the fact that bears were extinct in Greece by Classical times and probably long before.[1] In the ancient Greek language the word for bear is feminine. Images of bears have been found in sanctuaries of Artemis, and Pausanias knew of live bear cubs figuring in the festival of Artemis Laphria in Patras.[2] Atalanta is raised by bears, and in some versions of the story of Iphigenia, Artemis substitutes a bear for Iphigenia at the moment of her sacrifice (see **Iphigenia**). Especially interesting are the stories that include a male figure. Kallisto is a beautiful, virginal nymph in Artemis' band, but when she is seduced by Zeus, the angry Artemis transforms her into a bear and either kills her by shooting her with an arrow or allows her to be killed by Hera (see no. 100). In the foundation myth at Brauron, a girl flirts with a bear (see **Little Bears**). In still another tradition, when the hunter Kephalos mates with a bear, the animal immediately takes on the form of a beautiful woman.[3] On some level, the myths clearly tell us, women were equated with bears.

Why women were particularly associated with bears is also not hard to understand. Like a human mother, a nursing sow leans back against a support while cradling a cub at each breast (fig. 1). And, although the male bear at a thousand pounds is an awesome sight, the sow at half the size is usually a more threatening presence. Her legendary defensiveness of her cubs, who remain with her for two or three summers, is such that most injuries to humans come about because a sow has perceived a threat to her young. It is also noteworthy that the process of a sow's hibernation and reproduction closely parallels the Greek view of the earth as a female maternal force, honored as Gaia or Demeter, who initiates the annual cycle of renewal (see **Erichthonios** and **Persephone and Demeter**). Bears hibernate for as long as seven months of the year, during which period the cubs are born and are nursed by their mothers in their dens. In early spring the sow emerges from her den, either with her newborn cubs or with the cubs that were born to her in the winter of the previous year. The sight of a sow coming up out of the earth with her cubs so closely resembles the motif of the female ris-

Fig. 1. Sow nursing cubs. Photo Lynn and Donna Rogers.

Fig. 2. Sow with cubs. Photo by Mark Newman. Courtesy Auscape International.

Fig. 3. Sow emerging from hibernation with cubs. Photo Lynn and Donna Rogers.

committing suicide (the daughters of Erechtheus), in order to assure the survival of the community.

Most interesting are the many Indian traditions that tell of a girl at puberty and a bear so mutually attracted to each other that the girl either changes into a bear or marries a bear and mothers bear cubs.[8] In Ojibwe society the girl at puberty, like her ancient Greek counterpart, was secluded and spoken of as "becoming" a bear.[9] And so deep-seated in Western culture is the conviction, or the evidence, that bears are attracted to fertile human females that even today the United States Forest Service advises menstruating females not to camp in areas where bears might be present.[10]

The Greek myths suggest that a woman's sexual, fertile side is her bear aspect. The childless Kephalos becomes a father when he has intercourse with a bear, and when Kallisto displeases Artemis by losing her virginity, her punishment is to be transformed into the animal that embodies her sexuality. The young girl at Brauron who chose to flirt with a bear apparently recognized no distinction between the nature of her own sexuality and that of the male to which she was drawn, and the bear's response, scratching the girl until it drew blood, has been compared with defloration.[11] Because fertility in a young woman was highly valued in Greek society, it was not the eradication of the bear side of females that the ritual of the Little Bears aimed to accomplish, but rather its socialization through marriage. The metaphor of courtship as the pursuit of a wild animal is a popular subject in Classical vase-painting, and the overtones of domestication in the wedding ritual are well documented (see **Pursuit Scenes** and **The Wedding**). Peleus wrestles with the animal forms of Thetis until she succumbs and assumes the form of a young woman, who becomes his bride (see **Peleus and Thetis**). The imagery in the myth of Kephalos is completely straightforward; when Kephalos has sexual intercourse with a bear, it is transformed into a woman.

ing up out of the earth (Pandora, no. 81), sometimes with a newborn child (Gaia, nos.67-68, 70-72), that the parallel was probably recognized from very early times (fig. 3).

Because the reemergence of the bear in early spring coincides with the rebirth of nature, many hunting societies in North America, Europe, and Siberia have viewed bears as the initiators of the annual cycle of nature's renewal and, therewith, as the mother of all animals.[5] Artemis' identification both with bears and with the Mistress of Wild Beasts argues that this association also existed in early Greek thought, and, indeed, the traditional image of the Mistress of Wild Beasts enclosed by symmetrical animals (p. 303, fig. 1) calls to mind the posture of a nursing sow flanked by her cubs. So remarkably similar, in fact, are the bear traditions in the North American, European, and Siberian hunting societies that scholars generally agree they all stem from a common ancestral source that predated the dispersion of peoples over the Bering Straits and that was widely spread over ancient Europe.[6] We find in these societies, for example, a fervent belief that the killing of a bear is a sacred act that must be carried out with respect and honor and that, after the killing has taken place, the bear spirit must be appeased with gifts. The conviction echoes the foundation stories at Brauron and Mounychia, where Artemis was angry that a sacred bear had been killed and demanded the sacrifice of a maiden in return. In North American Indian tradition a bear hunt has two stages, with a reconnoitering mission to identify the den preceding the moment when the bear is awakened and called out of its den to be killed. Because this two-step process guarantees the death of the bear, the belief arose that the bear offered itself for sacrifice so that human life could continue.[7] The tradition calls to mind the many Greek stories of a young girl willingly offering herself for sacrifice (Iphigenia), and even

1. Note the discovery of an eleventh-century double cremation of a youthful male and female with a bearskin: *BSA* 73 (1980) 30 and Hamilton (1992) 127. On bears, see Aristotle, *History of Animals* 579a 18-30; 594b 5-16; 600a 31-b 13; 6 11b 32.

2. Pausanius 5.11.18; Bevan (1987) 17; Carpenter (1946) 112-13, 117, 162, discusses the possible bear ancestry of Odysseus.

3. Pseudo-Aristotle, *Etymologicum Magnum* 144.26 (s.v. Arkeisios); see Carpenter (1946) 128. Kephalos was also celebrated for killing his wife, Prokris, mistaking her for a wild animal when she followed him on a hunt.

4. See Fair (1990) and Stirling (1993) passim.

5. Rockwell (1991) 6-7, 26, 201. Also Gimbutas (1991) 225-26.

6. Rockwell (1991) 41, 181.

7. Rockwell (1991) 35, 41-42.

8. Rockwell (1991) 17, 95, 116, 123, 126.

9. Rockwell (1991) 16.

10. Rockwell (1991) 125.

11. Lonsdale (1993) 180.

ARTEMIS

Huntress with shafts of gold, she loves archery and the slaying of wild beasts,
thrilling cries and shading woods, and the cities of upright men.

Homeric Hymn to Aphrodite 18

Homer knew Artemis as the *Potnia Theron*, The Mistress of Wild Beasts.[1] That divinity surely had her roots in Paleolithic times as a mother goddess who was revered as the mother of all animals and the provider of needed game to hunters who depended upon it for survival.[2] The close association that Artemis enjoyed with bears in Classical times has suggested to some scholars that this ancient divinity may even have been worshipped in the form of a bear (see **Bears** and **Little Bears**). A descendant of this ancient goddess was surely represented in figurines of about 6000 B.C. that have been found in Çatal Hüyük in southern Anatolia.[3] Here an animal skull is positioned between the legs of a fleshy female as if emerging from her vagina. In Mycenaean times both a "potnia" and Artemis are mentioned on the Linear B tablets, but it is not clear whether the two goddesses are linked at this time or with what qualities Artemis was herself endowed.[4] Certainly by Archaic and Classical times Artemis' realm extended so much beyond the world of woodland hunts that the goddess as we know her must be an amalgam of the Mistress of Wild Beasts with another divinity or divinities.[5]

The Greek poets often extol Artemis in her identity as Mistress of Wild Beasts. In the *Homeric Hymn to Demeter*, Artemis is hailed as the one who "rejoices in arrows" and is the "shooter of arrows," and Aischylos speaks of her role as nurturer of the young of wild animals.[6] The goddess was regarded as a fierce protector of animals too young to be hunted and, at the same time, an enthusiastic hunter who unhesitatingly kills these same animals when they reach maturity. She also has the ability to transform women (Kallisto) and men (Aktaeon) into animals (see **Aktaeon**). She is viewed both as a determined virgin and as the goddess of childbirth, even assisting her own mother Leto to deliver her twin brother Apollo.[7]

In Classical times another side of Artemis is as a supporter of community life and civic institutions. In the *Homeric Hymn to Aphrodite* Artemis is praised as loving the "cities of upright men," and in the *Homeric Hymn to Artemis* she is said upon leaving the hunt to hang up her bow and arrow as she gladly joins the dances of the other divinities on Mt. Olympus.[8] Appropriately, Artemis was honored at the time when young Athenian men entered military service as ephebes. These youths pledged their oath of allegiance to the city-state within the sanctuary of Artemis Agrotera.

It is this broad scope of the goddess' interests, embracing both the hunt and the institutions of civilized life, that accounts for her

Fig. 1. Mistress of Wild Beasts, detail from the François Vase, Florence, Museo Archeologico, inv. no. 4209, ca. 570 B.C. Photograph Hirmer 591.2140.

special identity as a goddess of transitions, who protected young girls as they grew to maturity and embarked upon marriage and motherhood. Little girls were under Artemis' special protection, and votive figurines variously represent little girls or young animals poignantly nestled in the goddess' embrace (no. 94). Just before they reached marriageable age, young girls served Artemis as Little Bears in the goddess's sanctuary at Brauron, and several days before her wedding, a bride would dedicate her toys and a lock of hair to the goddess (see **Little Bears** and **The Wedding**). A young woman would again call upon Artemis during her first childbirth. With the expulsion of the afterbirth, or *lochia*, the young woman would pass from the status of bride, *nymphe*, to that of *gyne*, meaning woman or wife (see **The Wedding**). This culminating moment in a young woman's transition was recognized in an epithet of the goddess, who was known as Artemis Locheia (no. 103). The birth of a child signified the continuity of the community and the young mother's integration into the cycle of generations, and, thus having complet-

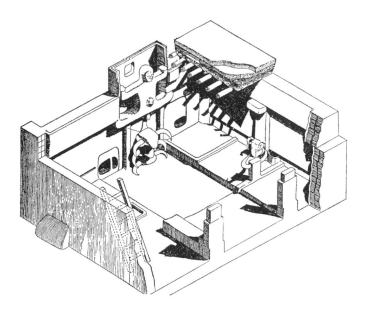

Fig. 2. Shrine from Çatal Hüyük, central Anatolia, with birth-giving goddess above bull heads, seventh millennium B.C. After Gimbutas (1982) 176, fig. 129.

(see **Iphigenia**). Reconciliation of Artemis' ferocity with her benevolence was also achieved in the customs that surrounded childbirth. A young woman in childbirth would call upon the goddess to see her safely through the ordeal, but, in recognition that Artemis could not or would not guarantee her safety, a woman in the agonies of labor would beseech Artemis to send an arrow that would bring her a mercifully swift death.

Artemis' attitude to sexuality could never be described as ambiguous. She protected young girls in their years before puberty, but, once physical maturity had been attained, she was unwilling to delay the inevitable progress towards marriage and motherhood. A virgin herself, she welcomed other virgins into her hunting band and directed the intense energy of their celibacy toward the killing of mature animals, behavior that spotlights hunting's well-attested erotic undercurrents (see **Aktaeon**). Once any of her virginal companions indulged in sexuality, however, Artemis immediately regarded them as prey, a reaction that calls to mind the conventional metaphor equating the hunt with courtship (see **Pursuit Scenes**).

Interestingly enough, Artemis is equally rigid in the case of men.[12] Aktaeon was a successful hunter, but he transgressed boundaries in some manner related to sexuality, whether by aiming for a woman (his aunt) selected by Zeus, by boasting that he was a better hunter than Artemis, or by spying upon Artemis while she was bathing (see **Aktaeon**). As with the punishments of Maira and Kallisto, the angered Artemis caused the hunter to become the prey, and Aktaeon's hounds destroyed him. Another hunter, Adonis, had an equally gruesome experience. Both an unskilled hunter and the offspring of incest, he was gored fatally in the thigh by a boar (no. 61). Both the injured limb and the fact that the animal was a boar lend the wound overtones of castration, and therewith serve as a forceful reminder that the realm Artemis surveyed embraced strict rules that pertained as much to manhood as to maturing females.[13]

ed the transition, the young mother would no longer claim a special tie to a goddess of a world outside civilization and of its margins. The primal experience of childbirth as a biological process rather than one of man-made institutions was probably regarded as a manifestation of a woman's feral side, and thus an appropriate culmination to her transition, comparable to the service of young girls who acted as Little Bears as they prepared to reconcile their animal aspect with their future lives as married women in domestic life.

When Aristotle commented that a young girl's first menstrual period could be compared with the blood-letting of a sacrificial animal, he was referring to an age-old Greek image that equated a physically mature girl with an animal soon to be killed.[9] Virginal maidens such as Maira and Kallisto may have taken part in Artemis' chaste band of huntresses, but once they explored their sexuality, willingly or unwillingly, they became the targets of Artemis' arrows in the manner of young animals old enough to be hunted (no. 100, see **Bears**).[10] In real life the physical maturing of a young girl may have been less vividly experienced but was comparably sobering as a girl eyed with anxiety her approaching marriage, which would mark a simultaneous loss of both childhood and virginity and the proximity of the impending perils of childbirth. The parallel between a girl's marriage and sacrificial death have often been noted, and Artemis' unrelenting adhesion to the program of female maturity must have seemed to some young girls to be as heartless as the arrow the goddess directed at Maira.[11] The need to reconcile the goddess' inexorability with her image as a protecting divinity is evident in such traditions of maiden sacrifice as that of Iphigenia, whose death was demanded by Artemis in atonement for the wrongful death of an animal; at the last minute the goddess rescued the girl by substituting an animal in her place

Fig. 3. Wall painting from Çatal Hüyük temple, seventh millennium B.C. After Gimbutas (1991) 224, fig. 7-1.

1. Homer, *Iliad* 21.470.

2. Burkert (1985) 149.

3. Burkert (1983) 79; Gimbutas (1982) 152, 176; Gimbutas (1991) 224, 255-56.

4. Vernant (1991) 197; see Burkert (1985) 149, who is less certain.

5. For Artemis, see King (1983); Burkert (1985) 149ff, who discusses the masks worn in her cult at Sparta and Archaic depictions of Artemis with a Gorgon's head. See Lloyd-Jones (1983) 87-102; Vernant (1991) 196-255.

6. Aischylos, *Agamemnon* 133-42.

7. Apollodoros, *Bibliotheke* 1.4.1; see Gantz (1993) 97.

8. *Homeric Hymn to Artemis* 15.

9. Aristotle, *History of Animals* 581b 1-2 and *Peri Gynaikeion* 1.6, 72(Littré); King (1983) 120.

10. Homer, *Iliad* 21.483: "Zeus made you a lion to women, to kill any at your pleasure."

11. For Maira, see Pausanias 10.30.5. On the link between marriage and sacrifice, see Burkert (1983) 62-63; Seaford (1994) 306-308.

12. For Melanion, another extreme hunter who rejected women and marriage to live what Vidal-Naquet described as the life of an ephebe manqué, see Aristophanes, *Lysistrata* 781-96; Vidal-Naquet (1981) 119-20.

13. Henderson (1991) 131-32.

The minimal modeling of the stag, its spindly legs, and the conveniently elevated groundline beneath the forelegs suggest that for this area the artist drew his inspiration from vase-painting. By contrast, the figure of Artemis has the sculptural presence of figures from the Nike Temple Parapet. Indeed, the formality of Artemis' pose finds parallels in the sacrificial scenes on the parapet and lends the Kassel relief similar ritualistic overtones. The artist has chosen the moment when the kill is assured and the impending last thrust will be only a symbolic one. The animal has already been pierced by a spear and does not struggle any more. The collapse is irreversible, and the stag's head is perfectly positioned for the *coup de grâce*. Artemis shows no signs of having experienced any difficulty in the conflict, for her billowing drapery signifies only animate activity. In this relief, which was certainly a dedicatory

87

87

VOTIVE RELIEF OF ARTEMIS ELAPHEBOLOS

ca. 410
Kassel, Staatliche Museen Kassel, Antikensammlung, inv. no. SK 41

Marble
H 42 cm., W 30 cm., Th 7 cm.

Publications: M. Bieber, *Die antiken Skulpturen und Bronzen des Königlichen Museum Fridericianum in Kassel* (Marburg 1915) 36, no. 74, pl. 32; G. Bruns, *Die Jägerin Artemis. Studie über den Ursprung ihrer Darstellung* (Borna-Leipzig 1929) 59; Simon (1983) 81, pl. 124,1; *LIMC* II (1984) 653, no. 397, pl. 478 (s.v. Artemis).

Smoothed on the sides and top, rough picked on the underside. Across the top of the scene is a molding. The groundline beneath is rendered as a rocky ledge. The relief is effaced over most of its surface, with sections missing from the upper and lower edges. Completely worn away are Artemis' facial features, parts of her drapery, and the head of the stag.

Over rocky ground Artemis moves to her left, her left leg advanced, the knee bent. She wears sandals and a belted peplos with an overfold that extends to mid-thigh; the open edges are visible down her right side. Her mantle is wrapped around her left upper arm, and the folds billow out behind her back. Behind her waist and legs the swirling ends are completely separate from the folds of her peplos. Her head is in right profile, and the hair is gathered in a knot at the top of the back of her head. Her left arm is extended, the fingers grasping the horns of a stag, whose head is pulled back. Her right arm is brought back behind her, the elbow bent, and her hand holds a spear, the tip of which extends just past her left upper arm and is about to be plunged into the animal's throat. Behind her and parallel to this first spear is a second spear, the tip of which has already entered the base of the animal's neck. The stag is collapsing, and his hind legs have already given way. His front legs scramble upon a rock, the left hoof and the right foreleg pressing against its surface.

offering, Artemis is presented as a goddess who is totally comfortable killing the wild animals that she protected when they were very young. Composed and unhesitant, she inflicts inescapable death upon the stag, whose gracefulness lends him dignity and nobility.

In the early years of Athens' history, at the time when the Attic calendar was taking shape, Artemis Elaphebolos, the hunter of stags, was of such importance that her festival, known as the Elaphebolia, gave its name to the month Elaphebolion. By the Classical period, by contrast, the festival was of minor importance and had been eclipsed by the city Dionysia, dedicated to the god Dionysos. The Kassel relief serves as a reminder to us that, although the festival may have suffered in stature, the cult to the goddess retained enough significance to be honored with this costly dedication.

The drapery dates the relief to the closing decade of the fifth century. At the left side of her waist a tubular fold loops over the belt, forming an angular break, and the enclosed valley is hollowed out as a deep pocket. The fabric lies closely upon the legs, and over the left thigh and between the legs it falls into tubular folds separated by wide, flat valleys. Behind the left knee, two cordlike folds combine to form a single fold that arcs around the back of the lower leg to delineate its contour. The inside contour of the right leg is rather deeply hollowed out, and the central fold of the hem between her legs forms an inflated *omega*. In a few places the grooves of the fabric's valleys are cut directly into the plane of the torso, for example, in the left shoulder, directly beneath the center of her belt, and behind her right knee. Another noteworthy detail is the way the billowing ends of her mantle outside her left thigh are inflated, with much of the swirling underside of the garment visible.

VOTIVE RELIEF WITH ARTEMIS

ca. 400
Berlin, Antikensammlung, Staatliche Museen zu Berlin Preussischer Kulturbesitz, inv. no. SK 941

Attic, from Athens
Marble
H 59 cm., W 43 cm., Th 7.5 cm.

Publications: C. Blümel, *Die Klassisch griechischen Skulpturen der Staatlichen Museen zu Berlin* (Berlin 1966) 71, no. 82, fig. 117; E. Mitropoulou, *Corpus I, Attic Votive Reliefs of the 6th and 5th Centuries B.C.* (Athens 1977) 62-63, no. 122, fig. 173; *LIMC* II (1984) 672, no. 671, pl. 499 (s.v. Artemis).

Reassembled, with a break visible across her neck. The vertical edge behind her and the groundline beneath are intact.

Artemis, identified by her hunting hounds, sits with composure upon a rocky outcropping. Her torso and legs are turned three-quarters to her right; her extended left arm rests on the rock behind her, and her right arm is outstretched in front of her. Her face is in left profile and she gazes ahead of her in the direction indicated by her right arm. She wears a girded peplos and a mantle that is draped across her waist and legs, with the ends brought up beneath her and resting on the rock below her left arm. In front of the rocky seat is a hound in left profile, his forelegs crouching and his head pressed against the ground. Outside her right thigh can be seen the shoulders and torso of another hound in left profile.

The gesture of her left elbow resting on the rocky terrain to her side can be traced back to the figure of Zeus on the east frieze of the Parthenon (p. 249, fig. 2). Introduced into this context, the gesture lends Artemis the same connotations of relaxation, self-assurance, and dignity (see **Gesture and Gaze**). The deity is not, however, completely inactive and, even though seated, does not abandon her role as a hunter. She gesticulates with her right arm, perhaps to give direction to her hounds who are moving in the direction she indicates, and one of them eagerly sniffs the ground in pursuit of a scent. This rocky terrain has a different meaning from that in which Athena is frequently depicted; for the latter goddess, the outcroppings signify the Acropolis with its associations of the political institutions of the polis (see **Athena**). By contrast, Artemis' domain is the rugged landscape of the untamed wilderness and the woodlands (see **Artemis**).

The relief shows clearly influence from the Parthenon beyond the gesture borrowed from Zeus. The drapery scheme is essentially that of the reclining figure M, or Aphrodite, on the east pediment. The folds reveal the breasts, while the girding delineates the waist, and the curving folds over the abdomen emphasize its roundness. The folds of the mantle are wrapped around the thigh to emphasize its contours, and the fabric lies closely over the knee and lower leg

The relief is an interesting example of the way in which the Pheidian style modified and regularized the images of the goddesses. The body is that of a youthful maiden, the mood one of effortlessness and complacency. At the same time, however, the quintessential character of Artemis as a hunter has been curiously accommodated, as from her rocky perch she languidly directs her companions in the hunt.

89

FRAGMENTARY LEKYTHOS WITH ARTEMIS

ca. 480
by the Pan Painter
Basel, Collection of Herbert A. Cahn, inv. no. HC 626a, b

Attic
Clay
2 fragments: 9 cm. x 7.5 cm., 8 cm. x 6.2 cm.

Publication: *LIMC* II (1984) 639, no. 170, pl. 458 (s.v. Artemis).

Two large fragments, broken all around. Missing front of forehead, right arm, and left leg. Beneath the figure is a band of two stopt meanders to right alternating with a saltire square.

Artemis is facing front, her head in left profile. Her left hand holds her bow horizontally out in front of her; her right upper arm is extended away from her body. She wears a chiton beneath a himation that is fastened on her right shoulder and passes beneath her left breast and over her torso; the ends hang to her ankles with swallowtail folds. The lower part of her chiton is decorated with crosses and has a scalloped hem. Her right foot is seen frontally.

Her quiver hangs behind her left shoulder, its side and open flap decorated with volutes. Her long hair is drawn back over her left ear and is gathered in a clasp below her nape; a long curly lock falls forward between her breasts. Her diadem is ornamented with volutes and is surmounted by three upright leaves. She inclines her head downward and gazes down. There is a spiral bracelet on her left wrist.

The Pan Painter has here clothed Artemis in a manner very close to her representation on his lekythos in the Hermitage (no. 90). The crinkly, billowing sleeves of her chiton extend onto her forearm and are enhanced by a series of decorative buttons. Her himation, here fastened over her right shoulder, falls into similar sets of stacked folds, the ends of which form a schematic pattern. Her quiver and diadem are almost identical, and her long hair is similarly gathered by a clasp that is also seen on a lekythos by the Dresden Painter (no. 111). Her bowed head and downward glance also find a parallel in the Hermitage scene. A further point of com-

88

to reveal its forms. Certain details in the drapery are distinctive of late fifth-century Attic sculpture, particularly the way the peplos lying over the left upper thigh falls into flat ribbons with depressed centers. By her left ankle the hem of her mantle takes on the outline of an *omega*.

Certain features distinguish the relief as a superb example of Classical Attic sculpture from the end of the fifth century. The drapery is highly transparent over the right breast, clearly revealing the nipple. The folds of the left armhole are extremely plastic, with the result that they frame her bare torso in deep shadow. At her left hip the tubular folds of her peplos are rendered in high relief and have slightly angular breaks; the folds are separated by deep valleys that are rendered as pockets of shadows. Over the abdomen several valleys are delineated by grooves that have been cut directly into the plane of the torso. Also noteworthy is the clump of folds between her thighs; here the artist has taken an interest in the patterns of the hollowed valleys and the inflated himation hem. Not yet, however, do we see a clear interest in exploring the potential of drapery beyond the confines of the body. Beneath her left arm on the rock, for example, thc folds are rendered in very low relief and with little innovation or animation.

parison is the prominence of her bow, which, like the quiver in the Hermitage scene, reminds the viewer of the more vigorous aspect of her character.

Characteristic of red-figure painting from the early fifth century is the combination of frontal torso and profile breast. Also typical is the rendering of the eye as an elongated oval; the open inner corner looks forward to the Classical eye of the mid-century. In the following decades the protruding chin will also soften.

The Pan Painter's talent for capturing an isolated figure in a quiet, telling moment is also apparent on his lekythos in Cambridge (no. 46).

90

WHITE-GROUND LEKYTHOS WITH ARTEMIS AND SWAN

ca. 490
by the Pan Painter
St. Petersburg, The State Hermitage Museum, inv. no. Б 2363 (B 670)

Attic
Clay
H 37.8 cm., Diam 7.8 cm.

Publications: *ARV²* 557.121 and 1659; *Para* 513; *Add²* 259; G.M.A. Richter, *Attic Red-Figured Vases: A Survey*, rev. ed. (New Haven 1958) 95, fig. 66; A. Peredolskaja, *Krasnofigurinye attischeskie vazy* (Leningrad 1967) 86-87, pl. 62, 63.1; J.D. Beazley, *The Pan Painter* (Mainz 1974) 14, no. 70, pl. 14,1; X. Gorbunova and I. Saverkina, *Greek and Roman Antiquities in the Hermitage* (Leningrad 1975) no. 33; Kurtz (1975) 27, 206, pl. 24.2; Mertens (1977) 207-208, pl. 40.1; Wehgartner (1983) 20-21, n. 4; *LIMC* II (1984) 695, no. 969, pl. 517 (s.v. Artemis); Robertson (1992) 146; *Aus den Schatzkammern Eurasiens* (1993) 192-93, no. 99 (illus.).

Neck mended. The shoulder ornament is in red-figure and includes a band of tongues above palmettes and volutes. Above and below the figural scene is a row of two meanders alternating with a saltire square. Artemis' hair, the ornament on her phiale, the stripe on her mantle, and some of the folds of her chiton are rendered in black glaze; most of the rest of the drawing is in dilute glaze. A coating of white is added to the swan and to the hands, feet, and arms of the goddess.

Artemis stands in right profile, her left foot slightly advanced. Her left elbow is bent, and the left hand, palm upraised and finger extended, supports a phiale. Her right arm is extended to the head of a swan; the right palm is upraised and the fingers are extended. She wears a sleeved chiton beneath a mantle that passes over her left shoulder and upper arm and falls over her torso and thighs in stacked pleats; the hem is edged with a dark stripe. A deerskin is knotted at her throat, and the animal's back, two paws, and the head hang down her back. Behind her shoulder can also be seen a quiver, the flap of which falls behind it. Her head is in right profile, and her hair is drawn back over the ear and falls down to her shoulders, where the ends are gathered by a rectan-

89

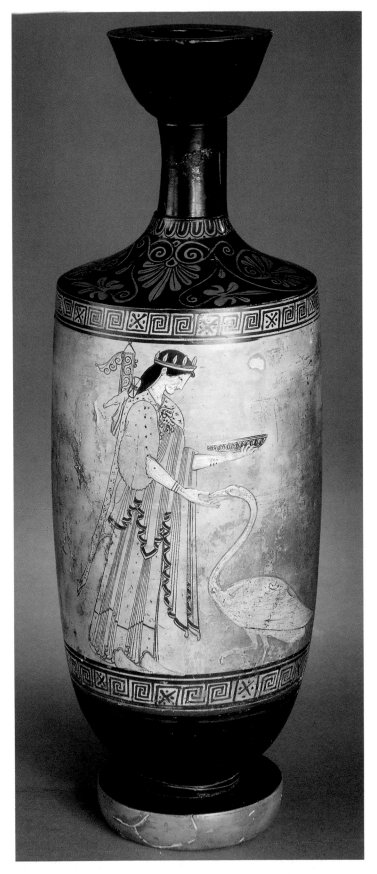

gular clasp that is ornamented with a cross and several horizontal lines across its midsection. She wears a diadem, from which five leaves rise vertically, and a small earring. Her eye is rendered as a narrow oval, closed at the inner corner; her ear is indicated by a series of curves; and her jaw is long and full. She wears a spiral bracelet on each arm, and she is barefoot.

Before her stands a swan in left profile, its right foot raised. The tip of the beak lies just between the goddess's right thigh and fourth finger.

The drawing is superb, as confident and unhesitant as Artemis herself. The undiluted glaze used for her hair, the phiale's ornament, and the zigzag stripe along her mantle's edge balance the dark angularity of the meander borders. The sensitivity to rhythm and design is remarkable; the rounded contours of Artemis' head, right sleeve, and phiale echo the curve and countercurve of the swan's neck and body, and the pattern of her fanned fingers, the tips of which are downturned, complement the stacked pleats of her chiton and mantle folds. The immediacy of the moment, conveyed by the bird's upraised foot, the open cover of the quiver, and the inclination of the folds as Artemis leans forward, heightens the momentary tension as the goddess' fingers approach the bird's head.

Although the scene contains only one human figure, and Artemis is flanked by vast expanses of unadorned background, her imposing presence easily dominates the space. The tip of her quiver, pressing against the upper border, both anchors her firmly and accentuates the way her body leans forward toward the swan. The goddess emanates quiet self-assurance as she gazes at the bird's head and brings her hand to its beak in a practiced gesture that elicits the swan's trust. Despite such expressions of protective affection, however, the Pan Painter has carefully included her quiver and deerskin to remind us of the goddess' less gentle side. The animal's head is concealed from the bird's view, but it is prominently rendered, and the disproportion of the head to the long ears indicates that it belongs to a young fawn. Even the phiale, held just above the bird's head, strikes a disquieting note because it calls to mind the ritual libations with which Artemis was honored before mortals ventured into war and hunting. Behind this seemingly benign depiction of the goddess, therefore, we detect her darker side.

As a bird of the wild, the swan was a denizen of the realm of Artemis. It may enjoy a special link with her through its allusions to the erotic currents that underlie both the goddess' nature and the hunt itself (see **Artemis**). Catherine Johns points out that the swan frequently figures in ancient pornography because, whereas most birds copulate by pressing together two orifices, swans have an intromittent organ that resembles a penis.[1] Probably for this reason the swan carried connotations of virility that are most familiar from the experience of Leda, who was raped by Zeus in the form of a swan.

1. Johns (1982) 108.

90

OINOCHOE WITH ARTEMIS AND FAWN

500-475
by the Dutuit Painter
Paris, Musée du Petit Palais, inv. no. Dut. 327

Attic
Clay
H 30 cm.

Publications: *ARV²* 307.11; *Add²* 212; *CVA* Paris, Palais des Beaux-Arts (Petit Palais), Collection Dutuit (France 15) pl. 19.1-6 and 20.3; A.-B. Follmann, "Die Stellung des Pan-Malers in seiner Zeit," *Wissenschaftliche Zeitschrift der Universität Rostock* 16 (1967) 448, pl. 25.2-3; Boardman (1975) 114, fig. 212; *LIMC* II (1984) 667, no. 618, pl. 495 (s.v. Artemis).

There are palmettes on the handle at the juncture with the mouth. Above the scene is a band of tongues; beneath is a band of two meanders alternating with a saltire square.

Winged Artemis stands in right profile. She is barefoot, and her left foot is advanced. Her left arm is outstretched in front of her, and the left hand clasps the midpoint of her bow, together with an arrow, the tip of which is pointed upward. She extends her right arm downward, placing her outstretched fingers beneath the head of a fawn; her thumb is seen just above its nose. She wears a girded chiton with overfold and has a spiral bracelet on her right wrist. Behind her shoulder is a quiver case, the strap of which passes under her right arm. Her head is inclined downward, and she gazes down toward the fawn. Her hair is bound up in a headwrap, from which the ends protrude at the top of the back of her head.

The spotted fawn stands in left profile, its forefeet just behind Artemis' left foot. Its head is tilted upward, and it looks up at Artemis.

The diminutive size and enormous ears relative to its head tell us that the fawn is very young. It is also very trusting. Although Artemis' fingers do not touch its chin, it responds to her encouragement by lifting its head to gaze up at her, its muzzle framed between her fingers and thumb. The goddess' close proximity to the fawn is also accentuated by the way the animal's ears are enclosed by the back and string of her bow. Similarly, her left foot is placed just beside the fawn's front hooves. By allowing the goddess to circumscribe the fawn's body, the Dutuit Painter reminds us of the degree to which Artemis circumscribes the animal's life as well. For now, however, the menacing bow is at rest, and the arrow's tip points skyward. Until the fawn is fully grown, its safety is assured, and Artemis surrounds it with warmth and protection.

In her identity as Mistress of Wild Beasts (*Potnia Theron*), Artemis appears as a winged deity from the Archaic period (see **Artemis**). In the conventional motif of the *Potnia Theron*, the frontal goddess is flanked by symmetrical animals that are posed heraldically, often as rampant lions. The composition presents the goddess as the controlling authority of animals, with power over them of life or death. On this vase by the Dutuit Painter, the meaning is quite similar; although the benign side of Artemis is in the foreground, the disquieting undercurrents are palpable.

FIGURINE OF ARTEMIS WITH FAWN

early 5th century
Toronto, Royal Ontario Museum, inv. no. 930.101.3

Terracotta
H 14 cm.

Publications: *LIMC* II (1984) 666, no. 586, pl. 492 (s.v. Artemis).

Artemis stands frontally. She is barefoot, and her weight is evenly distributed on both feet, which are slightly apart. Her left hand, at the left side of her waist, steadies the midpoint of the bow in a vertical position. Her right elbow is bent, and her right forearm and hand cradle a fawn, which crouches in right profile; her right fingers curl up around its forelegs. Artemis wears a girded chiton with an overfold that extends to mid-thigh. Her head is frontal, and she gazes ahead of her. Her center-parted hair is drawn back over her ears and falls behind her shoulders in locks that have horizontal ridges and valleys. On top of her head is a tall cylindrical headdress (polos).

The youthfulness of the animal is accentuated by its small scale, gangly build, long ears relative to its head, and tentative crouching pose, with the head pressed against Artemis' right breast. She, in turn, though formally posed and staring straight ahead, embraces the animal affectionately. She is clearly its caretaker, even its nurse. At the same time, however, her prominently positioned bow, so closely juxtaposed to the fawn, alludes to the less benign aspect of her character. We are thus reminded that Artemis is also a hunter and that she delights in the chase, which the fawn must join when it reaches maturity (see **Artemis**).

Dating the origin of the figurine type to the sixth century are such Archaic features as the stiff frontal pose, the vertically stacked pleats between the legs, the hairstyle, and the headdress. By contrast, the Early Classical facial features tell us that the type was reworked in the early fifth century, as koroplasts responded to the continued demand for figurines of Artemis to serve as votive offerings.

92

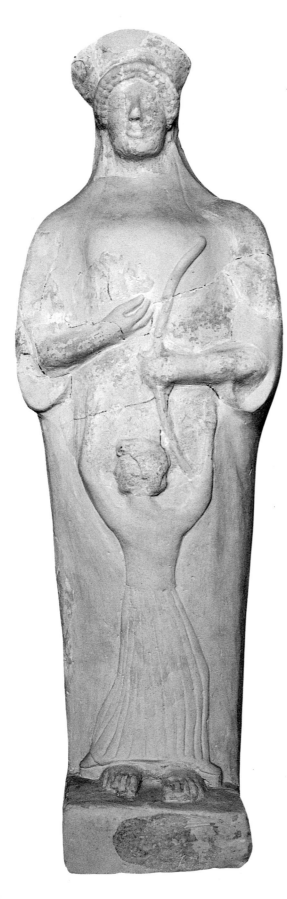

FIGURINE OF ARTEMIS AND YOUNG GIRL

beginning of the 5th century
Athens, National Archaeological Museum, inv. no. 1112

Attic
Terracotta
H 57.5 cm.

Publications: *LIMC* II (1984) 677, no. 723a, pl. 504 (s.v. Artemis).

The breasts, legs, and right hand of Artemis, as well as the figure of the young girl, are extensively restored.

Artemis stands frontally, elbows bent and hands at her waist. Her left hand holds her bow, and the sleeves of her chiton extend over her elbows. Two rows of shell curls frame her forehead in front of a high polos; long locks of hair fall down behind. Standing in front of her is the waist-high figure of a young girl, seen from behind. Her legs are widespread, with her feet straddling those of Artemis, and her arms are upraised to the goddess's waist. The girl's head is in left profile, and she has short curly hair. She wears a garment with a pleated skirt that covers her ankles.

The rigid frontality, the shell curls of the hairstyle, and the high polos indicate that the figurine follows an Archaic type of Artemis; however, the softening of the Archaic smile and the flattening of the cheeks tell us that the type was reworked at the beginning of the fifth century. Koroplasts regularly updated terracotta types by modifying a cast taken in an older mold; an impression from the altered cast would serve as the mold for a new generation of terracottas. With each generation crispness of detail was progressively lost, but the purchasers of terracotta figurines were of modest means and generally found that these images sufficed as inexpensive votive dedications in a sanctuary.

The girl's upraised arms and widespread legs suggest a dancing pose, and we are probably to understand that she is participating in a ritual honoring the goddess. Dances of young girls were common in religious festivals, and dancing surely formed part of the ritual of the Little Bears at Brauron (see **Little Bears**). The position of the girl's body directly against Artemis' skirt and the gesture of her upraised arms, which call to mind those of a child reaching for its mother, emphasize the maternal, protective nature of the goddess' relationship with unmarried girls. Artemis would continue to look over them as they were married and even as they experienced the birth of their first children. Only at the conclusion of that birth would the young mothers be deemed no longer a *nymphe* (or bride), but at last a *gyne* (wife) (see **Artemis**).

A comparison of this figurine with images of Artemis holding young animals of the wild reminds the viewer of the degree to which young girls were equated in Greek thought with untamed animals; in both cases, the young enjoyed Artemis' protection until they were old enough to join the hunt (see **Women as Animals**). However, whereas the goddess' protection was shared equally by young male and female animals, a distinction was made in her relationship with humans. Artemis had no particular link with little boys, although in Athens she was closely associated with ephebes, youths who passed the ages from eighteen to twenty in a form of military service that encompassed a considerable amount of hunting (see **Women and Men**). Each year, new ephebes made sacrifices to Artemis as they took an oath of allegiance to the city-state, undoubtedly also hoping that the goddess would ensure both their success in the hunt and their physical well-being. It is interesting to consider that in Greek thought the goddess' dual roles were accommodated without difficulty; Artemis was protector of both the hunter and the hunted (see **Aktaeon**).

94

94

FIGURINE OF SEATED ARTEMIS WITH GIRL

early 5th century
Munich, Staatliche Antikensammlungen München, inv. no. NI 5240

Terracotta
H 20.1 cm.

Unpublished.

The woman's right foot is broken away. White slip over surface.

A young girl is seated in the lap of Artemis, who sits frontally on a throne, her head facing, and her gaze directed straight ahead. Artemis' legs are slightly separated and her feet, wearing shoes, rest on a small support that is placed on the base of the throne. The sides of the throne are undecorated, and there are no armrests. Artemis' left hand cradles the left buttock of the child, and the goddess's right forearm is brought across the girl's thighs, with the right hand clasping the left side of the girl's left thigh. Artemis wears a garment that reaches the instep of her feet and has sleeves that extend just beneath the elbows. Her mantle is drawn over her head and falls to her shoulders, where the folds blend in with her sleeves. She has bulging eyes, a slight suggestion of an Archaic smile, large disc earrings, and a roll of hair across her hairline.

The girl is seated in left profile in Artemis' lap. She wears a long garment that reaches her ankles and shoes. Her left foot is drawn back, and her left elbow is bent, with the left hand brought to her breast. Her upraised right hand touches the goddess's left breast, as the girl brings her head close to Artemis' nipple. The girl's hair appears to be bound up at the back of her head.

The long dress tells us that the child is a girl, and the quantity of almost identical figurines found in the Sanctuary of Artemis at Brauron indicates that the figurine represents Artemis in her role as caretaker of young girls (see **Artemis**).

The Archaic origin of the figurine type is immediately apparent. The seated goddess, mantle draped over her head, is shown with head and torso rigidly frontal, and legs slightly separated. The Archaic legacy is also apparent in the protruding eyes and the

Archaic smile, which, in the conventional manner, results in a concave area around the mouth.

The stiff formality of the Archaic type is dramatically softened by the addition of the girl, whose later insertion into the type is apparent in the side view, where the girl's lower legs are unrealistically applied on top of the goddess' thighs and knees. Artemis' gesture, by contrast, is skillfully rendered, as she cradles the girl with the familiarity and ease of an experienced mother. Artemis' hands are unusually large, such that they wrap almost totally around the girl's lower torso, communicating protection as well as affection.

The artist has taken pains to show that the girl is not a baby. Should she stand up, she would actually be quite tall, and her slimness relative to her height suggests a rapidly maturing young girl.

Indeed, the way her left leg is drawn back accentuates her lanky form, and the gathering of hair at her nape suggests that she is not far away from adolescence. Because the girl is actually too old to be nursing, her grasp of the goddess' breast and the position of her head close to the nipple are largely symbolic, to express the belief that Artemis watched over a young girl as she passed through childhood, served the goddess as a Little Bear, entered married life, and underwent the birth of her first child (see **Little Bears**). With that birth, the young woman's experience as a *nymphe*, or bride, was completed, and she left behind her special relationship with Artemis. But a mature woman's loyalty to Artemis remained fervent, especially as she came to entrust her own daughters to the goddess' protection.

AKTAEON

The story of the hunter Aktaeon is thought to be one of the earliest of surviving Greek myths, with roots going back to Paleolithic times.[1] Its theme of inversion, the hunter becoming the hunted, is one of the most recurring concepts in Greek thought. The myth was of special interest during the fifth century and was featured in plays by Aischylos (*Toxotides*) and by Phrynichos (*Aktaeon*).

Aktaeon was a superb hunter, inseparable from his hunting hounds, with whom he enjoyed such a close rapport that Hesiod lists the individual names of each dog. In the version of the story known to Hesiod, as well as to the sixth-century lyric poet Stesichoros and the early fifth-century Akousilaos of Argos, Aktaeon angered Zeus by desiring the mortal woman Semele, whom Zeus had selected for himself. Zeus asked Artemis to eliminate Aktaeon, and she immediately did so. Semele became a consort of Zeus and gave birth to the god Dionysos.

Another version was known in the fifth century and is recounted in the *Bacchai* by Euripides, who tells us that Aktaeon was killed by an angry Artemis because he boasted that he was a better hunter than the goddess. An enraged Artemis also figures in a third version of the story that first appears in the poetry of Kallimachos, writing in the third century, but is thought to have been known to Aischylos. Here we learn that Aktaeon was killed because he had gazed upon Artemis when she was naked in her bath in the woods.

The manner of Aktaeon's death is one of the most graphic images in Greek mythology. Two versions were known by the middle of the fifth century. In one Artemis threw a deerskin over Aktaeon's head so that his hounds mistook him for their prey and dismembered him. In the second version, Artemis transformed Aktaeon into a stag, whereupon the hounds, again failing to identify their master, tore him limb from limb.

The final phase of the story was apparently well known from early times. When the frenzy had left the hounds, they roamed in desperation, searching for their master. At last they came to the cave of Cheiron, the wise Centaur (half-horse, half-man) who had originally instructed Aktaeon in the art of hunting. To console the hounds, Cheiron fashioned an image of their master.

Hunting was considered an essential expression of manhood in Greek culture. Hunting was also regarded as the ideal training ground for war, which was closely identified with hunting.[2] A hunter was viewed as a member of civilization who ventured into an uncivilized world where he occupied a liminal status, unlike women for whom the untamed world of nature was thought to be their natural habitat (see **Women as Animals** and **Bears**). Again, unlike women, a hunter left behind him man-made institutions of the city-state to enter the wild by means of another man-made institution, hunting, which was governed by a specific set of rules. Mythical youths such as Achilles and Aktaeon received formal training in how to deal with the wild, and their instructor, Cheiron, reflected in his semi-bestial appearance the foreignness to men of the hunter's realm (see **Peleus and Thetis**). By contrast, a mythical huntress needed no quasi-feral trainer. She either responded to her natural instincts and joined the hunting band of Artemis (Kallisto) or, in the case of Atalanta, received her instruction directly from bears (see **Atalanta**). Ironically, in real life no institutional channels existed by which women could escape the strictures of their lives and the confines of civilization, and it is thought that the opportunity to fill this void accounts for the popularity of Maenadic organizations in historical times (see **Maenads**).

There are elements in the story of Aktaeon that argue compellingly for its extreme antiquity. In one version he actually becomes an animal himself, although transformations to and from animals are more typical of women in Greek myth (see **Peleus and Thetis**, **Bears**, and **Women as Animals**).[3] Especially striking is the violent form of his death by means of dismemberment, which will also be the fate of Aktaeon's first cousin Pentheus at the hands of his mother Agave (see **Maenads**). A third remarkable aspect is the statue of Aktaeon that is fashioned to appease his hounds. Walter Burkert first argued that all these features appear to echo primitive hunting beliefs of a hunting and gathering phase of human society, when a hunter harbored a primal fear that his quarry would turn to become the triumphant predator and that the manner of death envisioned for the prey might rather become the fate of the human pursuer.[4] In a practice documented for traditional societies, and believed to have been observed in the ancient Mediterranean, hunters expiated their guilt from killing an animal by reconstituting its bones, particularly its skull, even draping them with its skin. By showing honor to the victim it was believed that the divinity responsible for supplying animals might continue to provide them or that the spirit of the animal might be assuaged and the hunter might escape its retribution (see **Artemis** and **Bears**). Such fundamental respect for the animal, alive or dead, has continued to characterize hunting into modern times. In the story of Aktaeon, these themes are indirectly expressed. It is not a human's kill of an animal that is the focus of the myth, but rather the dismemberment of a human by an untamed, atavistic element in hounds who are otherwise so well trained that they respond to specific names. Moreover, an image is constructed to console the hounds in the manner of a child's doll; the dogs never apparently become conscious of their deed and consequently suffer no remorse.

Common to all three versions of the story, whether Aktaeon is punished for wanting Semele, for boasting of his hunting superiority, or for gazing at the bathing Artemis, is the theme that Aktaeon has overstepped his boundaries in a context that has sexual overtones. It is probably significant that Aktaeon is invariably described as a deer hunter, because well-trained hounds only attack the quarry they have been schooled to pursue. Deer were always closely associated in Greek thought with both women and Artemis. Moreover, the sexual undercurrents of hunting are well understood and well documented as manifestations of the intimate link between male aggression and male sexuality. As Walter Burkert has discussed, weapons and male sexual organs have traditionally been viewed as interchangeable, and even, or especially, in modern times the same language consistently describes both a weapon's use and male sexual activity.[5] It may be significant that the object of Aktaeon's affection is Semele, his mother's sister, a relationship that was not common and probably not sanctioned in Greek society, although the reverse, a woman marrying her uncle, was routinely practiced. The version of the spying Aktaeon calls to mind the tale of Aktaeon's cousin Pentheus, who goes to the woodlands to spy upon his mother in her maenadic state and is also punished with

dismemberment. It is further interesting to note that in the famous lost painting of the *Nekyia* by Polygnotos in Delphi, Aktaeon was depicted in the Underworld seated beside Maira, a virgin devotee of Artemis and the hunt. When Maira was seduced by Zeus and lost her virginity, Artemis immediately shot down her former hunting companion with an arrow.[6] Transgressions regarding sexuality are not tolerated in the world of Artemis, although, true to her nature as a skilled hunter and the protector of animal life in the wild and of women in childbirth, Artemis always sends a swift death to her victim, and Aktaeon was no exception.

Aktaeon's transgression is also related to that of Melanion, another skilled hunter who was so obsessive in his dedication to hunting that he rejected women and settled community life.[7] His behavior was equally offensive to Artemis; whereas Aktaeon disrupted the balance of the wild, the solitary hunter jeopardizes the survival of the institutions of the city-state, with which Artemis also concerned herself.

Aktaeon's identity as the foremost male hunter of myth was underlined in Greek thought by the identity of his father. Aristaios was a priest who established the annual sacrifice to the "dog," observed when the dog-star Sirius rises in July.[8] It was believed that the ritual precipitated the arrival of the summer winds that alleviated the enervating heat. More distinguished and more problematic was the family of Aktaeon's mother Autonoe, whose sisters Agave and Semele would become the mothers of Pentheus and Dionysos, respectively.

1. Hesiod, *Theogony* 977; Hesiod, *Ehoiai*, frag. 217A MW, also discussed by T. Renner, "A Papyrus Dictionary of Metamorphoses," *HSCP* 82 (1978) 282-87; Stesichoros, frag. 236 *PMG*, mentioned by Pausanias 9.2.3; Akousilaos, frag. 33 *FGrHist*; Apollodoros, *Bibliotheke* 3.4.4; Euripides, *Bacchai* 337-342; Kallimachos, *Hymn* 5.105-118; this is the version made famous by Ovid, *Metamorphoses* 3.138-252; Diodorus Siculus 4.81.3-5; Apollodoros, *Bibliotheke* 3.4.4, tells the story of the image, *eidolon*, most fully.

   See also Gantz (1993) 478-81; L. Guimond, *LIMC* I (1981) 454-69 (s.v. Aktaeon); G. Nagy (1990) 263. For Aischylos' *Toxotides*, see frags. 417-24 in H.J. Mette, *Die Fragmente der Tragödien des Aischylos* (Berlin 1959) 154-56. For the tradition of Artemis' being spied upon, see L.R. Lacey, "Aktaeon and a Lost 'Bath of Artemis'," *JHS* 105 (1990) 26-42, and Arafat (1990) 145.

2. Xenophon, *On Hunting* 12.1. See also Homer, *Iliad* 5.133ff, 8.338ff, 10.360ff, 12.41ff, and 13.102, 198, 470ff. On hunting, see Cartmill (1994) 30, who defines hunting as "deliberate direct violent killing of unrestrained wild (shown to attack humans) animals." See Gilmore (1990) 113-17, who comments that, almost universally in societies that can be observed today, hunting is viewed as nurturing, procreative (in obtaining food), sexual, and a collective effort, and thus analogous to the concept of "executive will."

3. Burkert (1983) 116 cites the analogy with werewolves as a means of ensuring the continuation of the human race by changing the self into a predatory animal.

4. Burkert (1983) 12-23, 111-14.

5. Burkert (1983) 59; see Gilmore (1990) 114-17, who remarks that, among the Kalahari, to be at a loss sexually is "to have no bow."

6. Pausanius 10.30.5. See Gantz (1993) 98.

7. Aristophanes, *Lysistrata* 781-79. See Vidal-Naquet (1981) 114-18; Segal (1991) 84-85; Sutton (1993) 169.

8. Burkert (1983) 110-111.

95 Side B

95 Side A

95

BELL KRATER WITH THE DEATH OF AKTAEON

ca. 440
by the Lykaon Painter
Boston, Museum of Fine Arts, H. L. Pierce Fund, inv. no. 00.346

Attic, "from Vico Equense"
Clay
H 37.8 cm.

Publications: *ARV*² 1045.7; *Para* 444; *Add*² 320; P. Jacobsthal, "Aktaions Tod," *Marburger Jahrbuch für Kunstwissenschaft* 5 (1929) 9-13, fig. 12; Caskey and Beazley (1954) 83-86, no. 110, pl. 62; P. Devambez, "Un cratère à volutes attique," *MonPiot* 55 (1967) 82-83, fig. 5; H. Hoffmann, "Ein neue Amphora des Eucharidesmalers," *Jahrbuch der Hamburger Kunstsammlungen* 12 (1967) 16, 21-22 fig. 15; Webster, *Potter and Patron in Classical Athens* (London 1972) 47-48, pl. 2; Brommer (1973) 474, no. B5; J. Henle, *Greek Myths* (Bloomington and London 1973) 41-42, fig. 25; A. Kossatz-Deissmann, *Dramen des Aischylos auf westgriechischen Vasen, Schriften zur antiken Mythologie* 4 (Mainz 1978) 147-48; *LIMC* I (1981) 462, no. 81, pl. 357 (s.v. Aktaion); Schefold (1981) 141-43, 368, fig. 187; *LIMC* II (1984) 732, no. 1400 (s.v. Artemis); Boardman (1989) fig. 152.

Above the scenes is a band of laurel over a band of egg; beneath, three meanders (stopt) alternate with a cross square. The foot is in two degrees, with the upper degree reserved. Graffito: HE. On Side B a woman runs toward a youth, from whom another woman is fleeing as she looks back at him. Restored on

side A: lower part of Lyssa's hair, neck, and shoulder, as well as her right knee with part of her chiton; Aktaeon's right elbow and part of his upper arm; part of Artemis' left hand and a little of her mantle. Missing: Zeus' right shoulder, breast, stomach, part of the thunderbolt, and the top of the scepter. The inscriptions above the heads of the figures read: ΔΙΟΣ, ΛΥΣΑ, ΑΚΤΑΙΟΝ, ΑΡΤΕΜΙΣ. An inscription over that of Aktaeon reads: ΕΥΑΙΟΝ. Added white on Side A for the groundlines, plants, inscriptions, Zeus' wreath, and his thunderbolt's flame.

Side A: On uneven terrain from which a single stalk grows, Aktaeon fights off his hounds, his booted legs widespread as he tries to brace himself against the assault. His weight is supported by the toes of his left foot and by his right foot, which is pressed against the rocky ledge behind him. His left arm is outstretched and wrapped with his mantle, which covers his left hand; the rest of the mantle is seen behind his right thigh. His right arm is uplifted, and the hand holds two spears, the tips of which are directed toward the ground. His swordbelt passes over his right shoulder, and his scabbard is seen at his left side. Two stag horns rise from Aktaeon's head, and his right ear has the petal form of a stag. His forehead, nose, and cheeks are covered with fur, rendered by brown stippling. He gazes downward at a hound wearing a collar, who leaps in left profile toward the hunter's hand. Another hound is perched in right profile on the rocky ledge, his tail between his legs; he attacks Aktaeon's abdomen. A third hound, also seen in right profile, bites the inside of Aktaeon's left thigh.

Artemis stands quietly just behind the leaping hound. Over her chiton she wears a mantle that is fastened on her left shoulder and edged with a dark stripe. In her left hand she carries her bow, and in her right hand she holds a flaming torch. Her quiver is visible over her left shoulder. Her head is in left profile and her hair is drawn up from the nape in a sphendome. Her head is in left profile, and she gazes at Aktaeon.

On the other side of Aktaeon, Lyssa strides toward him in right profile. She wears high laced boots, and her left leg is outstretched with the foot raised; her arms extend in front of her torso. She wears a short pleated chiton (chitoniskos) beneath a sleeved coat (kandys) that extends to the top of her thighs and is decorated with squares and a dark stripe edging the hem and sleeves. An animal skin is tied around her waist. Her mouth is open, and above her short curly hair rises the head of a dog, seen in right profile. Behind her is Zeus, whose weight is supported by his right leg, with the left foot resting on an elevated rock. His mantle is draped over his left shoulder, with the ends falling over his left forearm; his left hand holds his thunderbolt. His upraised right hand clasps his scepter, and he wears a wreath. He gazes over at Aktaeon.

Zeus and Artemis quietly flank the tumultuous melee, as Lyssa dashes toward the embattled Aktaeon. Zeus' presence, rare in a depiction of Aktaeon's death, tells us that the Lykaon Painter is following the version wherein Zeus ordered Artemis to kill Aktaeon because the hunter eyed the same woman, Semele, to whom the god was attracted (see **Aktaeon** and **Artemis**). As Zeus oversees the massacre with stately calm, Artemis, with equal composure, extends her right hand with a torch, which here probably refers to the lethal intensity of the conflict. Although the verticality of her torch distances the goddess from the furor, her space is, nonetheless, invaded, as air currents disturbed by the fray drive the blowing flames in her direction.

The immediacy of the action is conveyed by Aktaeon's still energetic resistance and by the animation of Lyssa, whose name and extraordinary dog's head refer to madness or rabies. Her roots are to be found in drama, and she is known to have appeared in the *Xantriai* by Aischylos and, later, in the *Herakles* of Euripides.[1] Her open mouth clearly indicates that she is inciting the hounds onward.

This scene and the fragment by the same painter in Oxford (no. 97) are the earliest depictions of Aktaeon in the midst of his metamorphosis into a stag. The painter has accentuated the irony of the hunter's punishment by prominently featuring his boots, which are clearly made of animal skin, most logically deerskin. The horror of Aktaeon's fate is underscored by the drooping tail of one hound and the collared neck of another, which remind the viewer of the partnership and close bonds of loyalty that master and hounds had previously enjoyed.

The superb fragment by the Lykaon Painter in Oxford (no. 97) compares with the Boston scene in that Aktaeon and Artemis are posed similarly, and Aktaeon also wields two spears, surely a manifestation of his lack of preparedness when the sudden metamorphosis and deadly attack began. It is interesting to note that on the Boston vase Aktaeon appears to be oblivious of Artemis, whereas on the Oxford fragment he looks away from the hound he is about to slaughter in order to meet the goddess' gaze, as he acknowledges her supremacy over him as mistress of even of his own hounds.

The Lykaon Painter inscribes the name Euaion on two other vases: a pelike in London, where "kalos" is added, and a bell krater in Naples where a figure inscribed Euaion plays the flute in accompaniment to a dancing flute-girl at a symposium.[2] Although Aischylos had a son, also a tragedian, named Euaion, it is by no means clear that the Lykaon Painter is referring to this individual. It has also been suggested that the inscription may allude to an actor in a performance of the *Toxotides* by Aischylos.[3]

1. Aischylos, frag. 169 Nauck.
2. London, British Museum E 379, red-figure pelike, *ARV²* 1045.3; Heidelberg, white-ground lekythos, *ARV²* 1579; Caskey and Beazley (1954) 85.
3. T. B. L. Webster, *Potter and Patron in Classical Athens* (London 1972) 47-48.

96

AMPHORA WITH ARTEMIS AND AKTAEON

500-480
by the Eucharides Painter
Hamburg, Museum für Kunst und Gewerbe, inv. no. 1966.34

Attic
Clay
H 64 cm., W (at handles) 40 cm., Diam (rim) 29.2 cm.

Publications: *Para* 347, 227.8ter; *Add²* 199, 227.8ter; H. Hoffmann, "Ein neue Amphora des Eucharidesmalers," *Jahrbuch der Hamburger Kunstsammlungen* 12 (1967) 9-34, figs. 1-3, 9-10, 31; Hoffmann, "Erwerbungsbericht des Museums für Kunst und Gewerbe Hamburg 1963-1969," *AA* 1969, 351-53, fig. 37a-c; K. Schauenberg, "Aktaeon in der unteritalischen Vasenmalerei," *JdI* 84 (1969) 29-30, fig. 2; Brommer (1973) 474, no. D6; Boardman (1975) 112, fig. 165; *LIMC* I (1981) 457, no. 27, pl. 350 (s.v. Aktaeon); Schefold (1981) 134, 138, 367, figs. 173, 179-80; E. Simon, "Zeus und Io auf einer Kalpis des Eucharidesmalers," *AA* 1985, 269-73, figs. 50-52; N. Yalouris, "Le mythe d'Io," *Iconographie classique et identités régionales, BCH Suppl.* 14 (1986) 10, no. 10; Carpenter (1991) 45, fig. 78; Frontisi-Ducroux (1991) 113-14, fig. 57.

Intact. Added red for the blood drawn by the three biting hounds.

The amphora is Type A, recognized by the unbroken double curve of the profile, the broad handles whose sides are decorated with an ivy pattern, and the foot comprised of two elements, a flat disc beneath a cylindrical member. Beneath the handles is a palmette. The vertical side of the stepped base is reserved. On Side B is Hermes, Argos, and Io as a cow. Beneath the scenes on both Side A and Side B is a meander pattern.

The figures on Side A are identified by inscriptions as Artemis and Aktaeon (see **Aktaeon**). Artemis moves vigorously forward, her left leg advanced and the knee bent, her right leg well behind her, with the heel raised. She wears a chiton, which has a kolpos and sleeves which reach the middle of her forearm. The neckline is indicated by several concentric lines, and her full, left breast and nipple are seen in profile. Above the belt the fabric is ornamented with groups of three dots. Over her legs her chiton falls into three stacks of pleats. Her mantle passes behind her back, and the ends fall forward over each shoulder to mid-calf. Her head is in right profile, and her hair is gathered up into a knot at the back of her head. She has a narrow, almond-shaped eye, whose iris and pupil are rendered as a glazed dot. She also has a prominently jutting chin.

Her right elbow is bent, and the hand is held at chest-level, palm down, fingers extended. Her left arm is outstretched, and her hand holds her bow and an arrow.

Aktaeon has fallen to his knees, his lower legs and feet all but invisible except for his left foot, which is seen in right profile, with the toes resting on the ground. Hanging behind his shoulders is a spotted deerskin, the underside of which is reserved. Two of the hooves are knotted at his throat, and the other two hang beside his thighs. On his head rests the head of the deer, seen in left profile. Aktaeon's head is also in left profile; he is bearded and the lower edge of his iris is rendered by a line to indicate that the eyeball has rolled upward in the socket. His left hand is at his navel, and his right arm is extended, the fingers hanging limply downward.

Four hounds are visible. One clings to his right thigh and bites into his abdomen. Another hound is perched on Aktaeon's right arm, its jaws entering the outside of his right breast, and a third hound crouches on the left arm, its jaws sinking into the chest at the knot of the deerskin. The last hound, seen in left profile, pounces toward Aktaeon's left side.

96 Side A

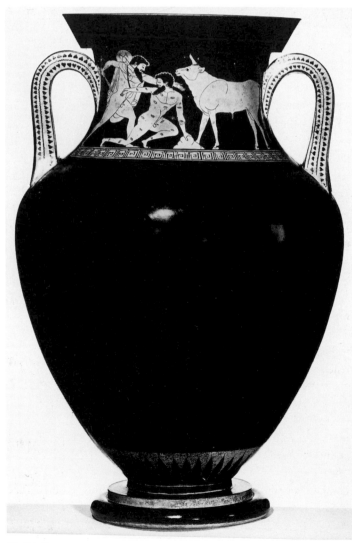

96 Side B

96 Details of Side A

The extraordinary size, exquisite shape, and masterful drawing make the Hamburg amphora one of the finest surviving examples of Greek vase-painting. The broad expanses of black glaze are skillfully balanced by the reserved edge of the base, the reserved background of the handles, and the pattern of the meander border beneath the scene. That the austere contours of the vase and its powerful glazed mass do not overwhelm the figural scenes speaks eloquently for the skill with which the artist has rendered the figures and the composition. Unique among Type A amphorae is the position of figural scenes on the neck alone, without a corresponding scene around the body, and it is possible that the Eucharides Painter was inspired by earlier black-figure amphorae or contemporary kalyx kraters. Cornelia Ewigleben points out that the position of the figural scenes around the neck alone draws our eyes respectfully upward, calling to mind the position of architectural reliefs on a temple entablature.

A date for the amphora not long after the beginning of the fifth century is indicated by a number of details. Artemis still wears the pleated chiton familiar from Late Archaic korai. Foreshortening is minimal, with Aktaeon's left foot revealing some experimentation, as do the heads of the hounds, rendered as if seen from above. Three-quarter views are only hinted at; Aktaeon's torso is almost completely frontal, and the strict profile of Artemis' left breast and nipple is more insistent than realistic. Eyelids are drawn as narrow, continuous ovals, and the ears are rendered as variations on a spiral pattern.

Individual stylistic traits of the Eucharides Painter include the rendering of the mouth as a straight line, the depiction of the ear as

two arcs, the prominence of the breast and nipple, the scalloped hem of the kolpos, and the mantle's edges presented as zigzag ends, the undersides of which are visible.

Aktaeon is not presented here as a man who has been transformed into a stag; instead, a stag skin and mask cover his back and the top of his head. That it is this garment that has deceived the hounds is apparent from their attack. One hound bites the knot of the legs at Aktaeon's throat, and another hound sinks his jaws into the right breast just below the skin edge. Their attack is completely successful, for Aktaeon's eye has rolled back in its socket, and the hand of his outstretched right arm hangs limply. The hunter has lost consciousness and is barely aware, if at all, of Artemis' presence.

The poignancy of the moment is underlined by the irony of the position of the stag's mask, which sits atop Aktaeon's head in the manner of a helmet. But whereas a helmet was its wearer's helpmate and defense, the stag's mask has incited the hounds to destroy their master.

A second subtle comment is offered by the composition of hunter and hounds, who symmetrically flank Aktaeon's frontal torso and widespread arms and legs. The resulting heraldic group would have recalled to ancient viewers familiar Archaic images of the Mistress of Wild Beasts, an identity Artemis had absorbed well before the Classical period (see **Artemis**). The allusion infuses the group of hunter and hounds with the very presence of the goddess.

Artemis' vigorous stride forward communicates the eagerness of her involvement in Aktaeon's punishment, and she brandishes her bow and arrow to emphasize the intensity of her outrage at Aktaeon's transgression. The Eucharides Painter is almost certainly following the version of the myth known to Hesiod and recounted by the painter's contemporary, Aischylos. Zeus, enamored of the mortal Semele, asked Artemis to eliminate Aktaeon as suitor, and Artemis willingly complied, ever predisposed to carry out missions that involved killing. The tradition that Aktaeon was not transformed into a stag but had a stagskin laid upon him was described by the poet Stesichoros, and Herbert Hoffmann points out that this version is most suitable to the stage, whence the Eucharides Painter may have drawn his inspiration.

Although most vases typically have one side on which the figural scene is superior, on this vase Side B is equally well executed. Io, a priestess of Artemis, was beloved by Zeus, but the jealous Hera transformed her into a cow, closely guarded by the many-eyed Argos. Io lived in misery until Zeus sent Hermes to murder Argos, the moment that the Eucharides Painter has chosen to portray. The inscription naming the figures (Hermes, Argos, Kale [the fair]) leaves no doubt that the animal is Io, although the painter has curiously depicted Io as a steer rather than a cow.

The juxtaposition of the death of Argos with that of Aktaeon is undoubtedly intended to present two examples of Zeus' love affairs and the fatal ramifications they hold for the competing suitor (Aktaeon) or the watchful guard (Argos). The scenes also say much about Artemis' subordination to Zeus; she is the agent of his vindictiveness toward Aktaeon and chooses not to interfere with the bovine misery of her priestess Io. Further linking the scenes is the ironic undercurrent of the theme of seeing. As the eyes of the dying men lose focus, the other eyes of Argos gaze helplessly on, and the hounds continue their murderous attack, prompted by a mistaken identification.

97

FRAGMENT OF A KRATER WITH ARTEMIS AND AKTAEON

ca. 440
by the Lykaon Painter
Oxford, Ashmolean Museum, University of Oxford, inv. no. 1890.31

Attic, from Gela
Clay
H 11.7 cm.

Publications: *ARV²* 1046.11; *Add²* 320; *CVA* Oxford, Ashmolean Museum 1 (Great Britain 3) 22, pl. 25.6; P. Jacobsthal, "Aktaions Tod," *Marburger Jahrbuch für Kunstwissenschaft* 5 (1929) 11; Caskey and Beazley (1954) 83, 85; Brommer (1973) 474, no. B6; *LIMC* II (1984) 732, no. 1401, pl. 562 (s.v. Artemis); Arafat (1990) 143-44.

Artemis stands frontally, her left arm at her side. Her right elbow is bent, and the hand holds a lighted torch of which the lower part of the vertical shaft disappears behind a hound's head. Artemis' head is in left profile and she has curly hair around her face and longer locks at her nape, which are gathered in a clasp. She wears a peplos with overfold, a diadem from which three leaves rise vertically, and a spiral bracelet on each wrist.

Artemis gazes downward at the figure of Aktaeon, whose head and upper torso alone are preserved. Aktaeon faces front, turned slightly to his left. His left arm is extended outward, with the hand hidden by the head of a hound, which gazes up in left profile at Aktaeon's face. Parts of two spear shafts and their tips are directed toward the hound's head and were obviously held in Aktaeon's upraised right hand. Aktaeon's head is turned three-quarters toward Artemis and he gazes up at her. He is nude except for a mantle that is draped over his left shoulder and arm; he also wears a swordbelt, and his swordhilt is visible by his left hip. His curly hair is surmounted by two tall, vertical staghorns, and at each temple is a small stag ear. He is beardless, with the beginnings of fuzz along the edge of his right jaw.

It is clear from the horns and ears that Aktaeon has already been transformed into a stag, and it is these features that capture the attention of the hound, who is about to attack its master. The poised spears tell us that Aktaeon still has some vigor remaining within him, but because he does not gaze at the hound, but at Artemis, we can assume that he is now aware of his fate.

In contrast to the tension of the hero and his hound, Artemis stands quietly, gazing with serenity down upon Aktaeon, her mouth slightly open as if she is speaking. The verticality of her torch separates her from him, and only the angled flames, blown by the animation of the struggle, penetrate her world. With no intimation of sympathy or regret, the goddess oversees the destruction of a youth who enjoyed hunting as much as she and who, like her, rejected marriage to pursue a life in the wild. We do not know which version of the story the Lykaon Painter was following and thus whether Aktaeon is being punished because he courted a woman upon whom Zeus had set his sights, because he boasted that he was a better hunter than Artemis, or because he gazed upon Artemis while she was bathing (see **Aktaeon**). What is clear is that despite his youthfulness, which is attested by his incipient beard,

Artemis has decided that he is to be punished without hesitation or mercy.

The position of the spears underlines the irony of Aktaeon's punishment. As a hunter, Aktaeon's identity is to hunt the wild and the unknown, yet now he prepares to turn his spear against his hound, his erstwhile friend and partner. An even more basic irony is that Aktaeon is now being hunted as the prey he used to pursue so avidly.

LITTLE BEARS

Once I was seven, I became an arrephoros. Then at ten I became a grain grinder for the goddess.
After that, wearing [?] a saffron robe, I was a bear at Brauron.
And as a lovely young girl, I once served as a basket bearer, wearing a string of figs.

Aristophanes, *Lysistrata* 641-47 (trans. H. Foley)

The custom by which young girls served as Little Bears in the cult of Artemis is one of the most fascinating aspects of Classical Greek religion. Our evidence for the practice is meager, however, confined to a modest number of literary references and a few vases.[1]

A major sanctuary to Artemis was located at Brauron, a site in Attica near Athens. We know that every four years a group of pre-adolescent girls was selected to live in this sanctuary as Little Bears. We are told that the priestess of the sanctuary was also known as a bear, and that ancient commentators defined the entire ritual, the Arkteia, as "playing the bear" or as a *hieron kunegesion*, a "holy hound hunt." Figuring in the ritual was a *krokotos*, a garment dyed with the orange-yellow saffron herb that was traditionally associated with women and specifically with menstrual ailments (see **The Wedding** and **Athena**). At the conclusion of their period of service, the girls were deemed ready for marriage.

Most of our information about the ritual itself comes from vases that have been found at Brauron, and in other sanctuaries to Artemis at Mounychia, Eleusis, the sanctuary of Artemis Aristoboule on the Athenian Acropolis, and the Cave of the Nymphs in Athens. Young girls, identified by their long hair and short stature, are seen running in the presence of what must be priestesses, and amid various appurtenances such as baskets, branches, altars, and palm trees. Sometimes the girls are nude, but occasionally they wear short tunics, and the variation indicates that changes in clothing played a part in the ritual. The suggestion is reinforced in the *Lysistrata* where a woman proudly remarks that she either "wore" or "shed" the *krokotos* during the Arkteia.[2]

The meaning of the ritual is to be sought in the foundation story of the Arkteia, although we cannot be sure whether the story originated as a later explanation for a long-practiced ritual or whether the ritual was constructed in partial enactment of an age-old story. We are told that there once existed a tame male bear which lived in the sanctuary at Brauron. One day a young girl teased the bear, which thereupon scratched her, drawing blood. Several boys who were with the girl immediately killed the bear, but Artemis was so angered that a sacred bear living in her sanctuary should be murdered she ordained that henceforth young girls should serve her as Little Bears.[3]

The story shares some familiar points with the story of Agamemnon and Iphigenia (see **Iphigenia**). Agamemnon was said to have killed a deer in a sanctuary of Artemis, and in atonement was obligated to sacrifice his daughter Iphigenia. She, however, was rescued on the sacrificial altar when Artemis substituted an animal in her place. In versions connected with Aulis, the animal Agamemnon killed was a deer, and Artemis substituted a deer. In the variant known at Brauron, the substituted animal was a bear.[4] A closely related tradition told of the inadvertent slaying of a female bear that wandered into the sanctuary of Artemis at Mounychia (see **Bears**). When the goddess sent a pestilence as an expression of her outrage, the priest Embaros promised to atone for the sacrilege by sacrificing his own daughter to Artemis, with the understanding that his family would henceforth receive the priesthood in perpetuity. But Embaros did not sacrifice his daughter to Artemis, rather substituting a goat, which he dressed up in his daughter's clothes.[5]

The mythical traditions of Agamemnon and Embaros share with the story of the Arkteia a common theme: an animal dear to Artemis is hunted down by a male and the sacrifice of an unmarried girl is demanded by the goddess in retribution. In the ritual at Brauron, however, the girls are not killed, nor is an animal of the type that was wrongly killed substituted in their place; instead, the girls are regarded as a form of the animal that was slain. Perhaps the most significant difference among the traditions is that in the story behind the Arkteia the entire episode is initiated by a girl when she teases a bear. Steven Lonsdale has pointed out that the word typically translated as "teasing" is conventionally found in contexts with strong sexual overtones, where the word implies titillation and arousal (see **Bears**).[6] That the girl flirted with the bear indicates that she was instinctively drawn to his ursine masculinity, and Lonsdale has even suggested that the scratches the girl received should be equated with defloration.[7] It would seem that Artemis' demand for young girls in service to her was prompted by her disapproval of the young girl's premature exploration of her sexuality, a familiar anxiety in Greek myth (see **Erichthonios** and **Danae**). Given the well-attested evidence that the "bearish" side of a girl was identified with her sexuality, it seems that the purpose of the Arkteia was to reconcile the "bearish" nature of a maturing girl with the role a married woman would assume in settled community life.

As the goddess of transitions, Artemis did not abandon the girl at the threshold of her puberty but rather eased her passage into her adult role as mother and wife (see **Artemis**). The running that was so prominent a part of the Arkteia ritual has traditionally been identified as a foot race of the type that figured in puberty rituals for Hera at Olympia, as well as in the myth of Atalanta (see **Atalanta**). Thomas Scanlon, however, points out that in the vase scenes the girls are often depicted with their forearms extended and hands cupped in the manner of paws (nos. 98-99).[8] Moreover, on a fragmentary kalyx krater the girls appear to flee from a bear, apparently in alarm (no. 99). Scanlon suggests that the girls did literally "act the bear" by pretending to be bears in flight from a pursuing bear. He points out that the girls' ritual expression of fright would be compatible with the component of fear that underlies many rituals of transition. Scanlon's argument is compelling. We know that the denouement of the Arkteia was an acknowledgment of the girls' readiness for marriage; consequently, the preceding race or pursuit must have enabled the girls to attain that state. A ritual chase would act out the well-known metaphor whereby the male pursuit of the female functioned as a socializing device, with the capture of the female the equivalent of domestication (see **Pursuit Scenes**).

Dancing is so much a part of girls' roles in ancient Greek religious festivals that the Arkteia probably also contained a dancing component that was linked with bears. It is interesting to note that tamed bears were kept in sanctuaries as late as Pausanias' time,[9] and the custom was possibly observed in the Classical period. Bears in the wild have been observed to move in a manner that has been described as dancing,[10] and dancing bears are still encountered in touristic settings in modern Turkey. The idea that Little Bears might have danced as bears in the Arkteia is not far-fetched.

As a ritual for young girls before marriage, the Little Bears of Brauron parallel the Arrephoroi, the young girls who served Athena on the Acropolis in Athens (see **The Plynteria and Arrephoroi**). In each ritual young girls lived away from their homes in the precincts of the goddess, and the Arrephoroi served for a period as long as eight to nine months. Although the transition to adulthood was symbolized by the prescribed actions of the ritual, it is likely that as great or greater an impact upon the participants came about

through their lengthy absence from home in the care of priestesses, who probably imbued the girls with mythical and ritualistic guidance appropriate to their future roles. For these girls the lengthy period of service probably did accelerate the process of socialization symbolized by the rituals.

1. On the Arkteia in general see Sourvinou-Inwood (1988). Aristophanes, *Frogs* 307-308 mentions the saffron robe.
2. Sourvinou-Inwood (1988) esp. 128; see Hamilton (1992) 125.
3. *Suda* (s.v. Arktos) ed. A. Adler, 361; Hesychius, *Hypothesis* 25; scholia to *Lysistrata* 645. See Parke (1987) 215.
4. Lloyd-Jones (1983) 93-94. Phanodemus (*FGrHist* 325 F 14) said that a bear was substituted. Tzetzes said that Iphigenia was changed into a bear.
5. Pausanias the Atticist, frag. e 35 (Erbse); Burkert (1992) 73; Parke (1987) 211.
6. Lonsdale (1993) 183.
7. Lonsdale (1993) 180.
8. Scanlon (1990) 73-120.
9. Pausanius 5.11.18.
10. Rockwell (1991) 147.

98

FRAGMENTARY KRATER WITH LITTLE BEARS

430-420
Basel, Collection of Herbert A. Cahn, inv. no. HC 501

Attic
Clay
3 fragments: 39 x 13.5 cm., 14.5 x 5.5 cm., 25 x 11.5 cm.

Publications: L. Kahil, "Autour de l'Artemis Attique," *AntK* 8 (1965) 20-33; L. Kahil, "L'Artemis de Brauron: rites et mystère," *AntK* 20 (1977) 86-98, pls. 18-20; L. Kahil, "Mythological Repertoire of Brauron," in *Ancient Greek Art and Iconography*, W. Moon, ed. (Madison 1983) 237-38; Simon (1983) 83-87, fig. 10a-b, pl. 25.1-2; *LIMC* II (1984) 262, no. 631k (s.v. Apollon); ibid., 700, no. 1034, pl. 526 (s.v. Artemis); H. Rühfel, *Kinderleben im klassischen Athen: Bilder auf klassischen Vasen, Kulturgeschichte der antiken Welt* 19 (Mainz 1984) 102-105, figs. 58-60; Keuls (1985a) 312-15, figs. 277, 279; Sourvinou-Inwood, *Studies in Girls' Transitions* (1988) 39-46, pls. 1-2, reviewed by E. Keuls, *AJA* 94 (1990) 695; K. Dowden, *Death and the Maiden: Girls' Initiation Rites in Greek Mythology* (New York 1989) 27-32; R. Hamilton, "Alkman and the Athenian Arkteia," *Hesperia* 58 (1989) 453, 461-63, 466-67, nos. 31-32; T. Scanlon, "Race or Chase at the Arkteia of Attica?" *Nikephoros* 3 (1990) 85-89, 113-16, nos. 17-19, pls. 6-8; M. Miller, "The *Ependytes* in Classical Athens," *Hesperia* 58 (1989) 325 n. 58; Lissarrague (1992) 188-89, fig. 31; L.B. Zaidman, "Pandora's Daughters and Rituals in Grecian Cities," in Pantel (1992) 343; Lonsdale (1993) 188-90, fig. 22; Serwint (1993) 415 n. 64; Fantham et al. (1994b) 85, fig. 3.4.

Part of the curving rim is preserved.

In front of a palm tree is a girl in right profile, her long hair falling past the short sleeve of a garment that reaches to her knees. Turning toward her is a woman in three-quarter left profile, her mantle covering her body and draped over her left shoulder and arm. Her head is in left profile, and her hair is drawn up into a bun at the back of her head. Her right hand rests on the shoulder of the young girl. Behind this woman, a girl runs in right profile with her arms outstretched in front of her. She wears a short garment to mid-thigh; locks fall in front of her ear and longer locks fall onto her shoulders. The next figure is a woman who stands before an altar, the top of which takes the form of an Ionic volute. Over her chiton she wears a himation that passes over her left shoulder and upper arm; in each hand she holds a branch; her right arm is lowered, her left upraised. Her head is in right profile and her hair is wrapped by a taenia and gathered into a bunch at the back of her head. Behind the altar is a little girl in a garment with rounded neckline; her head is in left profile and her long hair falls down onto her shoulders; her left arm is extended out to the side. Next to her is a facing woman who supports with both hands a basket. Over a chiton, she wears a himation that passes over her left shoulder and upper arm. To her left a small girl with long hair to her shoulders runs in right profile toward a palm tree. On the other side of the tree, four girls are running away in right profile. They wear short, unbelted garments that extend to mid-thigh, and they have long hair to their shoulders. Both arms of one of the girls are extended.

98   Montage of fragments from two sides of the krater.

99 Above and below, fragments showing the Little Bears running from a bear; in the lower frieze, hounds chasing a fawn.

100 Fragment showing the bear-headed Kallisto with a deer.

98 Detail showing the Little Bears beginning to run, with older women overseeing the ritual. The edge of an altar can be seen in front of the woman holding branches.

FRAGMENTARY KRATER
WITH LITTLE BEARS

430-420
Basel, Collection of Herbert A. Cahn, inv. no. HC 502

Attic
Clay
4 fragments: 20 x 15.5 cm., 10 x 6 cm., 12.5 x 7.3 cm., 20.5 x 22 cm.

Publications: see no. 98 above.

Most of three nude girls and part of a fourth are running in left profile; they have long hair down their back and two of the girls hold wreaths out in front of them. A much smaller nude girl runs behind them, her left hand at her waist, her right arm extended out in front of her. Her wavy hair frames her face and forms large curls around her jawline and nape. Behind her is a palm tree on rocky terrain. Beyond is another palm tree behind the torso of an animal, which is in right profile and which resembles a bear; the head is raised and has rounded, upright ears and a high forehead. Four females are running away from the animal. Closest to it is a female whose head is turned back in left profile. Her left arm is extended out to the side, and her hair is gathered up at the back of her head and wrapped several times with a taenia. Ahead of her are two nude girls, and the legs of a third, running in right profile, their arms extended out in front of them, a wreath in their lowered left hands. One of the girls has long hair down her back; the other has shorter hair. Beneath the scene is a band of lotus and palmette above a narrow frieze with four running hounds preceded by a fawn. Beneath is a narrow band of zigzags.

Neither the assignment of the fragments to either krater (nos. 98 or 99) nor the order of the fragments is absolutely certain.

The small, running girls with short tunics and long hair seen on no. 98 compare closely with those found on fragmentary krateriskoi in the sanctuary to Artemis at Brauron, as well as in her sanctuaries in Mounychia and on the Acropolis in Athens. It is generally agreed that the figures represent the Little Bears, those prepubescent girls who performed service to Artemis at Brauron in preparation for marriage (see **Little Bears**). Christiane Sourvinou-Inwood has shown that the palm tree locates the ritual in the sanctuary of the goddess, because Artemis and Apollo were traditionally believed to have been born to Leto on the island of Delos beside a palm tree.[1]

On both nos. 98 and 99, the girls appear to be of different sizes, and their age has been variously calculated from five to ten years of age, an estimate which our literary testimony neither corroborates nor refutes. Older attendants with baskets and branches are obviously coordinating and regulating the activity, which has usually been described as a race, in conformation with other known pre-marriage rituals for girls. Thomas Scanlon, however, points out that not all of the girls are running, a fact that might imply a staggered start, and that two of the girls appear to run with their arms stretched out before them. He suggests that the activity is that of a chase, in which the girls behave according to the ancient definition of the ritual of the Little Bears, whereby girls were said to "play the bear."[2] His theory would explain why the maiden in front of the bear in no. 99 looks back with apparent fright at the bear behind her. In the actual ritual one of the girls could have acted the bear, and it is not impossible that a tame bear actually lived in the sanctuary. It is probably significant that the maiden immediately in front of the bear seems to be more mature than her companions, because her hair is carefully tied up in an adult hairstyle and she does not adopt the stylized gesture of the long-haired girls. Perhaps she is closest to "graduating" from this ritual and consequently occupies the position of greatest symbolic danger nearest the bear.

The role of nudity and clothing in the ritual of the Little Bears has been much discussed. Obviously, girls shed and donned clothes but when and in what order is unknown. Also unclear is the role of the famous *krokotos*, the orange-yellow garment that was dyed with saffron obtained from the crocus and that we know figured prominently in the ritual. Because at the conclusion of their service as Little Bears the girls were deemed ready for marriage, it is logical to assume that at that time they assumed long garments suitable to a marriageable maiden, in contrast with the short tunics that are worn by the youngest participants seen on the vases. That the garment of the marriageable girls was the *krokotos* is logical for several reasons.[3] In Greek culture saffron was traditionally used as a medication for menstrual ailments, and the gathering of saffron by women was a sufficiently meaningful activity that it was the subject of a Mycenaean fresco on Thera, where the representation appears to have quasi-ritualistic overtones (see p. 240, figs. 1-2, and **Textiles**). Most significantly, the bride wore a veil that was saffron colored on her wedding day (see **The Wedding**). It is even possible that the peplos given to Athena at the Panathenaia was saffron-colored (see **Athena**).

Scanlon has pointed out the parallel between the fleeing Little Bears on no. 99 and the hunting scene beneath them, where a fawn is the quarry of the hounds. The correlation of courtship with hunting is well attested in Greek thought, as is the comparison of a girl at puberty with a sacrificial animal (see **Pursuit Scenes**, **Women as Animals**, and **Iphigenia**).

1. Sourvinou-Inwood (1991) 99-143.

2. Scanlon (1990) 73-120.

3. See Barber (1991) 232. Saffron comes from the stamen of the *Crocus stavius*. See Euripides, *Hecuba* 466-74, for the peplos of Athena; Barber (1992) 116; Barber (1994) 115. See also Lonsdale (1993) 177. For Iphigenia and the saffron garment, see **Iphigenia**.

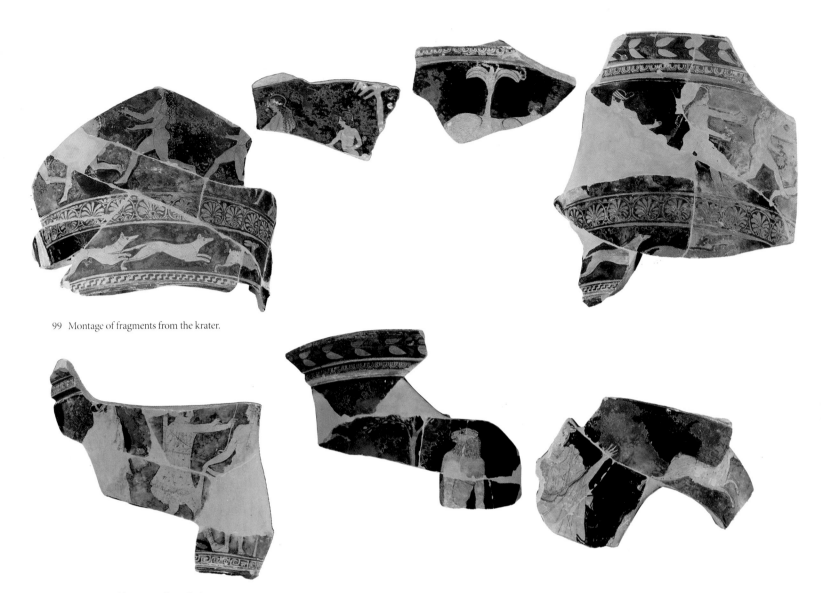

99 Montage of fragments from the krater.

100 Montage of fragments from the krater.

100

FRAGMENTARY KRATER WITH ARTEMIS AND KALLISTO

430-420
Basel, Collection of Herbert A. Cahn, inv. no. HC 503

Attic
Clay
3 fragments: 23 x 15.2 cm., 24 x 15 cm., 17.5 x 13 cm.

Publications: see no. 98 above.

Surviving are part of the upper border with a laurel pattern (right) over a dotted egg pattern. Beneath the scene is a band of meander.

A woman stands in right profile, her left hand raised to her shoulder. Her hair is wrapped in a taenia and gathered up into a bun at the back of her head, and over this is draped her mantle, which she fingers with her raised left hand. In front of her Artemis strides forward with her left leg advanced, both arms extended forward as she prepares to draw back her bow and shoot an arrow. She wears a pleated chiton that extends to the knee; over this she wears a belted tunic that has a fringed hem and is decorated with crosses and circles and, over the breasts, with a galloping horse in right profile. She also wears boots, and over her shoulder is a quiver. Her head is in right profile and her hair is drawn up in a sakkos, from which a curl escapes to fall in front of her right ear. In front of her a man, his upper torso nude, stands almost frontally, his head turned back to Artemis in left profile. His extended right hand holds a sash, which passes horizontally behind his back; the other end must have been held by his left hand. He has the beginnings of a beard down his left jaw, and he wears a laurel wreath.

In another part of the scene we see the forepart of a deer beside a laurel tree with leafy branches. On the other side of the tree is a male figure with the body of a nude man and the head of a bear. The head is turned back in left profile and has a boxy muzzle, large eyes, rounded ears, and a furry neck. The body turns to his left and leans slightly in that direction; his arms hang at his side.

To the left of this figure, a female faces front. Her body is that of a woman, but her head is that of a bear, with petal ears and large eyes. She wears a chiton that has a rounded neckline, and a mantle that is brought forward over her left shoulder and passes behind her back, with the ends drawn over in front of her body to fall over the crook of her left elbow; a dark stripe edges the mantle edge. She also wears a necklace with a round pendant. Her left arm is bent with the forearm raised and the palm frontal, the fingers widespread. To her left, and on the level of her shoulder, a deer seen in right profile bounds away.

Artemis is clearly hunting, but the question is what (see **Artemis**). Deer bound away in flight, but the bear-headed woman also sees herself at risk, and it is very likely that she is Kallisto.[1] Once a beautiful, virginal nymph in Artemis' hunting band, Kallisto was formerly resplendent in her necklace and elegant garment with its low-cut neckline. Her beauty, however, caught the eye of Zeus, and, whether through force or seduction, she engaged in a dalliance with him. When Artemis discovered that one of her nymphs had lost her virginity, the furious goddess cast Kallisto out of the hunting retinue. Traditions differ as to whether Artemis or Hera changed Kallisto into a bear, but it is absolutely clear that the bear-maiden died when Artemis shot her down (see **Bears**). One version of the story tells us that Artemis killed Kallisto deliberately, but elsewhere we hear that Hera tricked Artemis into shooting her former companion. Kallisto's son by Zeus was named Arcas, and he survived to become the founding ancestor of the people of Arcadia. It is surely the bear-headed Arcas who stands beside his terrified mother in this scene. She gazes outward at the viewer with the frontal face that traditionally depicted a mask, a deceased person, an inanimate image (Pandora, see no. 80), or a marginal figure (see Hermes in no.82). Arcas looks back to Artemis, fully conscious of what will be his mother's fate.

The deer in the field to the side of Kallisto probably alludes to another side of this complex goddess, who displayed compassion as easily as she did ruthlessness. Artemis would save Iphigenia from sacrifice by substituting a deer in the girl's place (see **Iphigenia** and **Women as Animals**). In this scene, however, the deer escapes while Kallisto dies; as with the fate of Aktaeon, Artemis is never accommodating when the rules of the hunt are breached (see **Aktaeon**).

The woman behind Artemis fingers her veil in the manner of a married woman (see **Gesture and Gaze** and **The Wedding**). She must be Leto, joining her twin children, Artemis and Apollo. Her happy family gathering forms a sober contrast to the less fortunate, ursine mother and son, who are soon to be separated.

1. For Kallisto, see Carpenter (1946) 120; Pausanias 4.11.3, for the descendants of Arcas; Hesiod, frag. 163 MW; Euripides, *Helen* 375-78; Pausanias 10.31.10. Aischylos wrote a (lost) play entitled *Kallisto*; see Gantz (1993) 98, 725-28.

IPHIGENIA

Iphigenia was a parthenos (a physically mature but unmarried girl) and the daughter of King Agamemnon, who had been appointed leader of the Greek fleet in the Trojan War. When the ships prepared to depart from Aulis, favorable winds failed to appear, and the seer Teiresias announced that the goddess Artemis was angry. In some versions the goddess is angry because Agamemnon killed a sacred deer in Artemis' precinct, but elsewhere it is said that Agamemnon had boasted that he was a better hunter than Artemis. Teiresias declared that Artemis could be appeased only by the sacrifice of Iphigenia, and Agamemnon acceded to the demand. He summoned Iphigenia and her mother Clytemnestra to Aulis on the pretext that he had arranged for his daughter's marriage, which was now to take place. Only as Iphigenia was being led to the altar did she realize the deceit. In some versions of the story she resisted to her death, but, as Mary Lefkowitz discusses in this volume, Euripides presents an Iphigenia who goes to her death willingly with the conviction that her death is a patriotic deed that will assure the survival of the Greek expedition. In some versions of the story Iphigenia died on the altar, but in others she was rescued at the last minute by Artemis, who substituted an animal, whether a deer, a goat, or a bear, in her place. The versions vary as to whether the Greeks recognized the substitution. Iphigenia became a priestess of Artemis in her sanctuary in Tauris, and Artemis decreed that henceforth the clothes of a woman who survived childbirth would be offered to Artemis in gratitude and the clothes of a woman who died giving birth would be dedicated to Iphigenia.[1]

Clytemnestra bitterly resented the death of her daughter and cited this deed as justification for taking Aegisthus as a lover and for murdering Agamemnon upon his return home after the Trojan defeat. That second death triggered another, as Orestes, Iphigenia's brother, killed his mother in revenge for Agamemnon's death. Orestes was hounded by the fearsome female tormentors, the Erinyes, until Athena finally broke the cycle by declaring Orestes absolved.

The death of a parthenos is a recurring theme in Greek mythology. Erigone kills herself upon discovering her father's murder, and Polyxena is murdered on the tomb of Achilles at Troy when a seer declared that the ghost of Achilles demanded her as the bride he would never have on earth. The daughters of King Erechtheus of Athens were said to have willingly given up their lives after a seer implied that their deaths could save the city during the attack by Eumolpos of Eleusis. Some of these maidens resist death vigorously. Among the others, a few accept their fates and others volunteer their lives, and the emphasis upon acquiescence to the point of suicide is probably related to the belief that sacrificial animals must go willingly to their deaths.[2]

Hugh Lloyd-Jones argued that the origins of the theme of the parthenos' death probably lie in the actual sacrifice of a maiden sometime in the distant past, and many scholars now agree that human sacrifice was practiced on Crete and Cyprus as late as the second millennium B.C.[3] Human sacrifice has been variously explained. According to the guiding principle of sacrifice, one gives up something in the expectation that one will receive back from the gods a gift worthy of the sacrifice.[4] Thus in hunting or its equivalency, war, where the killing of game or of human adversaries is desired, the sacrifice of a human life might be deemed appropriate. It has also been pointed out that the practice of human sacrifice could well have initially arisen as a pragmatic solution to a desperate situation, when an animal predator was fended off by appeasing it with a member of the group. On analogy with other traditional societies, it is also possible that the ancestors of the Greeks believed that the gift of a human spirit could release one of an animal; by extension, the human spirit could actually be envisioned as inhabiting an animal body, in the manner in which an animal appears on the sacrificial altar in the place of Iphigenia. The substitution in the story of an animal for Iphigenia may represent a subsequent phase in the history of sacrifice, just as Prometheus' wrapping of the bones within the fat must also explain a historical sequence.

Why the victim of sacrifice should be a maiden is another question. The pervasive analogy in Greek thought between young women and wild animals could certainly be one explanation. Given the erotic overtones of hunting and its particular link with celibacy, the closing off of sexual gratification represented by the sacrifice of a parthenos would be in keeping with an expectation that the gods would respond by granting in its place the sexual gratification of a kill (see **Artemis** and **Aktaeon**).[5] One could also argue that an unmarried but physically mature girl is the ultimate embodiment of supreme and untapped fecundity, and thus the ideal sacrificial victim if one hopes to obtain a life in return. From a sociobiologi-

cal point of view, it has been argued that an unmarried maiden was the most dispensable element in a society.[6] She was not yet a mother, nor yet the wife of a man who would perceive his loss as an insult to himself, in the manner that Achilles' anger over the appropriation of Briseis as his share of the battle spoils sparks the *Iliad's* framework of conflict. A particularly desirable young woman could also have fallen into the category of "first fruits," which are given up voluntarily by a community in order to eliminate the possibility of a destructive competition within the society over who would win the prize; alternately, she could have been selected as a scapegoat, a designation for which both the valued and the loathed were eligible.[7] One should also keep in mind the likelihood that, in the era in which maiden sacrifice might have first been introduced, female murder might already have been a familiar notion through the practice of exposing unwanted baby girls. Still observed in Classical times, exposure was surely a custom of great antiquity.

The choice of a maiden as the object of sacrifice in very early times could also have been related to the image of a bride as a sacrificial victim.[8] The concept was surely age-old by the Classical era, when Aristotle compares the blood shed by a woman during her first menstrual period with the blood of a slaughtered animal.[9] Both Aischylos and Douris (no. 101) liken Iphigenia to a bride, and the equation is not difficult to understand.[10] Soon after puberty a young bride left behind her childhood and family home to enter a new life fraught with virtual strangers amid the real possibility that she could soon die in childbirth (see **The Wedding** and **Persephone and Demeter**). Because a girl's marriage was arranged by her father, a reluctant bride could liken her fate to sacrifice at her father's hands, and it is quite likely that many an unwilling ancient bride compared her father with Agamemnon. That this betrayal would be especially bitter is suggested by the strong thread in Greek thought that views a father-daughter relationship as a special bond. Athena is the prototypical example, but there are many others, such as Antigone, the loving daughter of Oedipus. The explanation for the strength of this bond is thought to be the agonistic nature of Greek society, in which a father's interaction with his son was always clouded by a competitive tension that was absent in his relationship with his daughter.[11]

The link between Artemis and Iphigenia is especially close. As in the stories of Embaros and the origin of the ritual of the Little Bears, Artemis demands a maiden's sacrifice and then shows special favor to the victim (see **Little Bears**). The identification of Iphigenia with a wild animal (bear or deer), the fact that Artemis appoints her as a priestess in the goddess' cult, and the goddess' decree that Iphigenia was to be the recipient of clothes dedicated by woman who died in childbirth has suggested to a number of scholars that Iphigenia, like Atalanta, is a form of Artemis herself (see **Women as Animals** and **Atalanta**).[12] The association of Iphigenia with women dying in childbirth further suggests that the deaths of those women were viewed as a form of sacrifice for the community's survival, leading Vernant to observe that marriage was to a woman what war was to a man.[13] The major difference between a male and female death for the benefit of society was that a man expected to acquire eternal fame through his own death, whereas it was assumed that a woman who died in childbirth would go unnamed and uncelebrated outside the confines of her family (see **Women and Men**). Euripides focuses on the difference in his characterization of Iphigenia, who willingly agrees to die for the well-being of the Greek fleet and remarks that by dying for the cause of the Trojan War she knows that she will receive glory after her death.[14] Her statement implies that only by means of this form of death will she win the honor accorded a man; only through sacrifice could a woman approximate the reward society bestowed upon a man's heroism. The correlation of the parthenos with the male was elsewhere explored in Greek thought (see **Amazons**).

1. For Iphigenia, Sophokles *Elektra* 566-72; Euripides, *Iphigenia in Tauris* 17-24; Pindar, *Pythian* 11.22-23; Pausanius 1.43.1 = Hesiod frag. 23b MW; Herodotos 4.103. Nothing survives of the Aischylean play *Iphigenia*. See also Gantz (1993) 98-99, 582-87, 686-87; Lloyd-Jones (1983) 87-102; Burkert (1985) 149ff; Armstrong (1985).

2. Tyrrell (1991) 78-79. For Erechtheus, see Gantz (1993) 242. For Polyxena, see Gantz (1993) 658-59.

3. On human sacrifice on Crete, see the summary in Hughes (1991) 13-17, 38. For Cyprus, see Burkert (1985) 192, who notes that Achilles killed twelve Trojans at Patroklos' funeral; Lloyd-Jones (1983) 89; Morris (1992b) 165 (infant sacrifice in the late Bronze Age).

4. Burkert (1983) 36-59; Burkert (1979) 73.

5. Burkert (1985) 267; Burkert (1983) 60-67; See also Girard (1972), esp. 18, who speaks of sacrifice as a manner of ending a cycle of violence; another theory is that a death could function to unite a society in guilt, obligation. See Dowden (1989) 199-201, who comments that Persephone was Demeter's Iphigenia.

6. Kuper (1994) 136-48.

7. Burkert (1985) 84; Burkert (1979) 74.

8. Seaford (1994), 306-308; Loraux (1987) 35. She notes (p. 41) that with the sword thrust the maiden loses her virginity.

9. Aristotle, *History of Animals* 581b 1-2 and *Peri Gynaikeion* 1.6, 72 (Littré); King (1983) 120.

10. Armstrong (1985) 1-12; Foley (1982) 168.

11. Strauss (1993) 13-14 and 66-71.

12. For the identification of Artemis with Iphigenia, see Burkert (1985) 200ff; Lloyd-Jones (1983) 95. For the identification of Iphigenia with Hekate, see Pausanius 1.43.1 and Gantz (1993) 583, 686.

13. Vernant (1974) 23.

14. Euripides, *Iphigenia at Aulis* 1376-90.

WHITE-GROUND LEKYTHOS WITH THE SACRIFICE OF IPHIGENIA

500-490
by Douris
Palermo, Museo Archeologico Regionale di Palermo, inv. no. NI 1886

Attic, from the Sanctuary of Demeter Malophoros at Selinus
Clay
H 32.9 cm., Diam 11.7 cm.

Publications: *ARV²* 446.266; *Add²* 241; E. Gábrici, "Il Santuario della Malophoros," *Monumenti antichi* 32 (1927) 331-36, fig. 142, pl. 94; E. Boehringer, *AA* 1929, 151, fig. 53; P. Marconi, *Il Museo Nazionale di Palermo* (Rome 1936) pl. 60.1-2; Brommer (1973) 529, no. B1; Kurtz (1975) 29-30, 140, 200, pl. 10.1; Mertens (1977) 206, pl. 39.3; Roberts (1978) 185, pl. 104.3; L. Kahil, "La déesse Artémis: mythologie et iconographie," in *Greece and Italy in the Classical World. Acta of the XIth International Congress of Classical Archaeology, London, 3-9 September 1978* (London 1979) 82; H.P. Foley, "Marriage and Sacrifice in Euripides' *Iphigeneia in Aulis*," *Arethusa* 15 (1982) 168-73; L. Kahil, "Mythological Repertoire of Brauron," in *Ancient Greek Art and Iconography*, W. Moon, ed. (Madison 1983) 238; Jenkins (1983) 141, fig. 2; M.L. Cunningham, "Aeschylus, *Agamemnon* 231-247," *BICS* 31 (1984) 9-12, fig. 1; Armstrong and Ratchford (1985) 1-12; F. Jouan, "Autour du sacrifice d'Iphigénie," in *Texte et Image. Actes du Colloque International de Chantilly 13-15 octobre 1982* (Paris 1984) 65, fig. 2; A. Prag, *The Oresteia, Iconographic and Orphic Tradition* (Warminster 1985) 61, 149, no. H2, pl. 39a-c; Sourvinou-Inwood (1985) 126; *LIMC* V (1990) 709-10, no. 3, pl. 466 (s.v. Iphigenia); Carpenter (1991) 200, fig. 299; Gantz (1993) 584; Buitron-Oliver (1995) 13, 18, 32, 52, 64, 75 no. 46, 96, pl. 30.

Mended from many pieces with large areas restored, including foot, neck, mouth, and handle. On the shoulder are palmettes; a band of two meanders alternating with a checker square is above and below the scene.

Iphigenia stands with her left leg advanced, her right foot on the ground. Her head is inclined and her gaze is directed downward. She wears a transparent chiton on which traces of yellow survive and through which the inner contours of her legs are clearly visible. Her right hand at her hip lifts folds of her chiton, which fall in stacked pleats. Over her shoulders she wears a mantle decorated with stars, the ends of which fall in points to each knee. A short veil passes over the back of her head, such that the long locks of her hair emerge from underneath the veil to fall down her back. The pointed ends of the veil fall along the right side of her neck to her breast, and the fingers of her upraised left hand lift folds of the veil above her left shoulder. She wears a spiral bracelet on her left wrist and a diadem with meander decoration. Her name is inscribed in the field in front of her.

Striding before Iphigenia is her father Agamemnon. He turns back toward her, his weight on his left foot, his right foot behind him. He wears a cuirass with pteryges that extend to the lower edge of his short tunic, the pleats of which are also visible beneath his shoulder lappets. His mantle is draped behind his back with the ends falling forward over each upper arm. His greaves are visible on his left leg and right knee, and he is barefoot. His face, seen in three-quarter left profile, is largely concealed by his crested helmet, which protrudes into the band of meander above the scene; the cheekpieces are raised and the visor is lowered. He has a mustache and beard and his eyes are directed downward. Three long coiled locks of hair emerge from beneath the bowl of his helmet and fall over his left shoulder. His right arm, largely missing, was stretched out toward Iphigenia, and his right hand grasps folds of her mantle

330

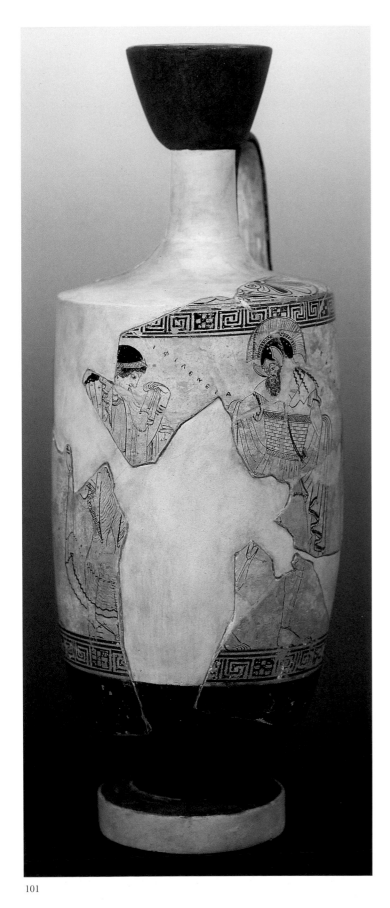

101

just beneath her left forearm. In his left hand he holds a sword, the blade of which is seen above an altar, of which only the uppermost part is visible, in the shape of an Ionic volute. In the field behind his crest are the letters EYKE. Above the altar can be made out the letters AP.

Standing behind Iphigenia is a man whose legs are in right profile, with the weight evenly distributed between them. He is barefoot, but wears greaves, and his short tunic emerges from beneath his cuirass. The blade of his sword is visible in front of his right thigh, the point directed toward Iphigenia. Between him and the palm tree that lies just in front of Agamemnon, there is space for another figure, but no hint as to his or her identity.

Everything about Iphigenia's demeanor suggests that she is unaware of the danger ahead (see **Iphigenia**). Douris is clearly following the version of the myth familiar to the painter's contemporary, Aischylos. In the *Agamemnon* Iphigenia is deceived by her father into believing that she has been summoned by him for her wedding to Achilles. There is no note of anxiety in her composure as her right hand daintily clasps the folds of her chiton, which Douris has painted yellow in allusion to the saffron (yellow-orange) colored garment in which Aischylos clothed Iphigenia, itself a deliberate echo of the traditional color of the bridal veil (see **The Wedding**).[1] Iphigenia's head is demurely inclined in the prescribed *aidos*, or modesty, of a young maiden, and the fingers of her left hand lift the folds of her veil in the traditional gesture of the bride, who unveils her face for her new husband (see **Aidos and Sophrosyne**, **The Wedding**, and **Gesture and Gaze**). Iphigenia appears trustful of her father's grasp of her mantle, unaware of the drawn sword in his left hand, as well as of the second sword directed menacingly at her from behind. The palm tree under the handle, which signifies Artemis' sanctuary, reminds the viewer that the goddess has demanded Iphigenia in sacrifice. In some versions of the story Iphigenia is saved when the goddess substitutes an animal for her, but Aischylos mentions no rescue of Iphigenia, leading us to believed that she was, in fact, killed by her father.

Douris intensifies the poignancy of this moment by likening the procession with Iphigenia to the traditional bridal procession. The bride was led to the bridegroom's home by her new husband, who grasped the bride's left wrist in a gesture symbolic of domination. Greeting the couple at their new home was the groom's mother holding two torches, and behind the bride followed her mother, who also held two torches (see **The Wedding**). In Douris' version of the ritual, a sword replaces the double torches. Moreover, Agamemnon's grasp of Iphigenia's garment just beneath her left arm correlates him with the bridegroom in an equation that would seem to strengthen thc erotic undercurrents some scholars have observed in Agamemnon's relationship with his daughter. The concealment of Agamemnon's face behind the mask of his helmet heightens the scene's intimations of violence. Agamemnon's downward glance is also significant; unlike the bridegroom's gaze, which at this moment is traditionally directed at the bride's face, Agamemnon chooses to look away, with a different kind of shame from the *aidos* of his daughter.

The bridal overtones of Iphigenia's sacrifice and of Douris' rendering of the procession are even further heightened by the artist's decision to paint the scene on a white-ground lekythos, which was traditionally a funerary gift. Perhaps a preference for the tradition of Iphigenia's rescue prompted its dedication in a sanctuary of Persephone, who enjoyed an annual reprieve from her own deathly marriage.

1. Aischylos, *Agamemnon* 239.

101

102

FRAGMENTARY LOUTROPHOROS WITH BRIDAL PROCESSION

440–430
by the Naples Painter
(attribution by John H. Oakley)
Munich, Staatliche Antikensammlungen München, inv. no. NI 9493

Attic
Clay
H 25.7 cm.

Unpublished.

Broken above and below. Mended from several pieces, with sections missing from the figural scene. Above the scene is a band of egg and dart; below the scene is a band of meander (right) alternating with a dotted cross square.

The bridegroom leads his bride in the bridal procession. He stands frontally, his head turned back in left profile. His mantle is wrapped around his waist, with the ends brought forward over his left shoulder. The fingers of his left hand clasp the edges of his mantle in front of his chest; his right hand grasps the left wrist of the bride. Around his head he wears a taenia, to which two rows of leaves are attached, and he gazes back into her face. She stands in three-quarter right profile, her head in right profile and inclined. She wears a belted chiton that is ornamented across the neckline with a row of dots between pairs of parallel lines. The chiton has an overfold to mid-thigh. She also wears a necklace and a disc earring that hangs below her earlobe. Her diadem is ornamented with a band of zigzag and is surmounted by three or four leaves. A veil passes over the top of her head and falls down over each shoulder to her thigh; in back the folds hang down as far as the lower legs. Her right elbow is bent and the fingers are extended, palm inward. She gazes up from lowered eyelids toward the groom's eyes.

Behind the bride stands a woman in a belted peplos with overfold, a black band around the lower hem. Her hair is wrapped with a taenia. Her left hand steadies the bride's right upper arm; the fingers of her right hand are about to straighten the bride's veil at her nape. On the other side of the groom is a woman who steps forward in three-quarter left profile, her right leg advanced, and the heel of her left foot raised. Her head is in left profile, and she gazes ahead of her at the couple. She wears a peplos that has a broad panel at the neckline, and a necklace with pendant beads. A wide band is brought across

102 Side A

102 Side A-B

102 Side B

102 Side B-A

the top of her head and around the locks of hair that are drawn up at her nape. In each hand she holds a torch, and she gazes ahead of her. Behind her stands a woman whose mantle is wrapped around her body, covering her left arm; she holds an alabastron in her upraised right hand. A sash hangs in the field beside a woman who extends her right hand, holding a kalathos, to a man who leans on a walking stick. His right elbow is bent and the hand, covered by his mantle, rests on his right hip. Behind him are two women, facing each other. One of them extends her right hand, which holds a sash, to the other woman, whose torso and arms are wrapped in her mantle.

The scene presents the salient features of the wedding ritual (see **The Wedding**). The gesture by which the bridegroom grasps the bride's left wrist is the traditional one of domination, as the groom prepares to lead the bride to the home of his parents (see **Gesture and Gaze**). At the same time as he prepares to move forward, however, he turns around to look back into her face, in allusion to the moment of the bride's unveiling (the *anakalypteria*), when husband and wife gazed upon each other for the first time (see **The Wedding**). Ancient commentators described the moment as one of "seeing" (*opteria*), but here it is the bridegroom who does most of the looking, as he stares eagerly into her face. Meanwhile, the bride continues to bow her head in the conventional female display of modesty, or *aidos*, but reveals her curiosity by gazing as far upward into his face as the inclination of her head allows (see *Aidos and Sophrosyne*). The prominence of the bride's belt is a deliberate reference to the impending consummation of the marriage; so prominent was the bride's belt in the wedding ceremony that the phrase "loosening the belt" served as a euphemism for sexual intercourse.

Standing behind the bride is the *nympheutria*, the woman who assists the bride, first in donning the bridal garments, and then, as here, in the unveiling. The woman with the torches behind the bridegroom must be the groom's mother, who traditionally held two torches as she awaited the arrival of the bridal procession at her home. The other figures in the scene are relatives and guests who bring the conventional wedding gifts of the kalathos (wool basket) and the alabastron, which was a perfume container. The plethora of containers that were traditionally presented to the bride as wedding gifts carried connotations of the bride's fertility (see **Women as Containers** and **Pandora**). The two vessels depicted here are succinct reminders of the two most important aspects of a bride's persona; the perfume vessel alludes to her sexuality, the wool basket to her mastery of the textile arts (see **Textiles**).

Although other painters were more adept than this one in draftsmanship and composition, the Naples Painter here reveals his skill as an observer of social custom. He carefully documents the key elements in the wedding ritual and also captures the moment's mood. The groom's mouth is slightly open, perhaps in wonder or delight as he first glimpses the face of his bride. She, in turn, gesticulates with her right hand in an expression of heightened emotion, probably a combination of excitement, apprehension, and hope.

VOTIVE RELIEF WITH YOUNG MOTHER

ca. 410
New York, Metropolitan Museum of Art, Fletcher Fund, 1924, inv. no. 24.97.92

Marble
H 26.7 cm., W 21.7 cm., Th 4.1 cm.

Publications: G.M.A. Richter, *Handbook of the Greek Collection* (Cambridge 1953) 94, pl. 73c; G.M.A. Richter, *Metropolitan Museum of Art. Catalogue of Greek Sculpture* (Cambridge 1954) 44-45, no. 67, pl. 55b; J. Frel, "Ateliers et sculpteurs attiques fin 5ème - début 4ème siècle," *Eirene* 5 (1966) 83 n. 21; E. Mitropoulou, *Corpus I, Attic Votive Reliefs of the 6th and 5th Centuries B.C.* (Athens 1977) 45, no. 66, fig. 104; S. Pingiatoglou, *Eileithyia* (Würzburg 1981) 140, no. 7.

Broken down right side and across lower edge. Across the top of the scene is a simple molding. Tool marks are visible over the preserved top and left side, as well as the back. There are abrasions over the surface, including the face of the seated woman. The taenia of the goddess was added separately.

A woman is seated on a stool, with her torso and legs turned in three-quarter left profile. The stool is slightly foreshortened, with the distant rear leg shown. Her peplos is fastened only on her left shoulder, with the right breast exposed, and her mantle is draped over her head and across her waist and legs. Her head is also turned in three-quarter left profile and is tilted to her right and inclined downward. The fingers of her left hand rest against the vertical side of her stool; her right hand is held just above her knees, and the fingers appear to gather a fold of drapery. Behind her a woman stands turned to her right. Her right forearm disappears behind the head of the seated woman, and in the crook of her left arm she cradles a tightly swaddled baby. The woman wears a girded peplos with kolpos and overfold extending below the hips. Her mantle is draped over her left shoulder and over her left arm beneath the baby. Her head is in left profile, and over her short hair she wears a taenia. She gazes ahead of her and apparently downward to the seated woman.

Standing in front of the seated woman is the much larger figure of a woman seen in three-quarter right profile, the knee of her advanced left leg relaxed. Her upraised left hand holds the short dowel-shaped handle of a torch; the fingers are curled just beneath a protective horizontal disc that sits beneath the flammable part of the torch. Her right arm hangs beside her right thigh, with the fingers slightly relaxed. She wears a girded peplos with overfold, and her mantle is fastened on her left shoulder, with the folds looping over her left elbow and the ends falling outside her left leg. Her head is in right profile and is inclined slightly downward, such that she appears to be gazing at the seated woman; her short hair was surmounted by a diadem that was added in metal and of which only the holes remain. Beside the right thigh of the standing woman can be seen the left hand of another standing figure of similar scale; the fingers, pointing downward, clasp a slender shaft that probably belongs to a scepter.

103

mother and has draped her mantle's folds over her left forearm in a sympathetic echo of the way the maidservant has created from her mantle a comfortable resting place for the infant.

The primary goddess of childbirth was Artemis (see **Artemis**). In an expression of this aspect of her realm and through assimilation with lesser deities, Artemis was honored with the epithets Artemis Eileithuia ("giving help") and Artemis Locheia ("lochos" technically refers to the afterbirth). Eileithuia was also regarded as a divinity in her own right and it is likely that she is seen here with Artemis Locheia, who had roots in Minoan religion.[1] The scepter would be appropriate to Artemis Locheia; the torch as a less exalted attribute may belong to Eileithuia.

The woman who dedicated this relief as a thank offering had probably followed the traditional custom of dedicating her clothes to Artemis at Brauron. Clothes of women who died giving birth were dedicated to Iphigenia, the priestess of Artemis (see **Iphigenia**). Women dying in an agonizing childbirth did not assume that Artemis could or would save their lives, but they did believe that the goddess might take pity upon them and send a lethal arrow that would quickly end their unendurable suffering.

The handling of the drapery dates the relief to the end of the fifth century. Over the torso of the seated woman the fabric is mostly transparent, clinging closely to her breast, and falling into corded folds, with several valleys indicted by grooves incised into the plane of the torso. Also consistent with a late fifth-century date is the bunching of the drapery folds in the kolpoi of the goddess and the maidservant, as well as the foreshortening of the stool with the indication of its rear leg. The exaggeratedly relaxed hands of both the goddess and of the seated woman carry almost to the level of affectation the casual gestures of Hephaistos and Athena on the Parthenon frieze (pp. 248-49, fig. 1). At the same time, these gestures contrast with the marked intensity of feeling communicated by the exhaustion of the mother and the solicitous support of her companions. The vivid depiction of the new mother's depletion is extraordinary for fifth-century sculpture and looks forward to the emotional explorations of the fourth century and Hellenistic period.

1. For Eileithuia, see Burkert (1985) 26.

A woman has just given birth of a child and prepares to nurse it, her right breast exposed. The distress of the woman is clearly apparent. Her head sags and droops, and she gazes at no one. Her left hand is pressed against the side of the stool, seemingly for physical as well as emotional support, and her right hand seems equally lifeless. The servant with the baby is sympathetic and extends her right arm out toward her mistress. The especially deep overfold and equally voluminous kolpos (where the fabric is pulled over the girding) indicate that the servant is a young girl, wearing an adult garment into which she has not yet fully grown. Because the childbirth has just taken place, we can assume that the maidservant assisted her mistress through the delivery.

The mantle that is draped over the woman's head and that is also seen together with the newborn child on grave reliefs (no. 105) must refer to the *miasma*, or state of contamination, that was believed to attend a woman who had just given birth. The cleansing of both the woman and the house was observed in a ritual that would take place at least three days after the birth. The size of the woman standing beside the mistress and maid indicates that she is a goddess, for whom a torch is an appropriate attribute. She is accompanied by a second figure of the same scale, whose gesture is that of a divinity holding a scepter (see no. 83); thus the relief is certainly a votive dedication to these deities for their assistance in childbirth. The goddess inclines her head attentively toward the

104

GRAVE RELIEF OF MYNNIA

ca. 380-370
Malibu, J. Paul Getty Museum, inv. no. 71.AA.121

Attic
Marble
H 98 cm., W. 44.5 cm., Th 4 cm.

Publications: J. Frel, "An Attic Stele with Epigram," *GRBS* 14 (1973) 173-77; C.C. Vermeule and N. Neuerberg, *Catalogue of the Ancient Art in the J. Paul Getty Museum* (Malibu 1973) no. 11; Clairmont (1976) 101-102, fig. 5; G. Daux, *BCH* 100 (1976) 206-207, fig. 5; ibid., "Notes de lecture," *BCH* 102 (1978) 604 n. 38; J. Frel, "Le Sculpteur des Danseuses," *GettyMusJ* 6-7 (1978-79) 80 n. 10; J. Frel, "Ancient Repairs to Classical Sculptures at Malibu," *GettyMusJ* 12 (1984) 74-75, no. 6; Clairmont, "'It ain't necessarily so' ... Remarks on some gravestones with inscriptions," *Horos* 5 (1987) 53-57, pl. 15; Vierneisel-Schlörb, *Klassische Grabdenkmäler und Votivreliefs* (1988) 48, n. 2; Clairmont (1993) vol. 2, 655-56, no. 2.718.

Mended from three pieces. Missing most of the left side of the stele. Also broken across the top so that the finial is largely missing. Only the lips and nose survive of the seated woman's face.

A woman is seated in three-quarter right profile on a stool with a low cushion. The toes of her bare right foot rest on the edge of a footstool. She wears a chiton beneath a himation that is draped over her head, framing both shoulders, and is brought across her lap, covering most of her legs. Her head is in right profile and is bowed. The fingers of her left hand hold folds of her mantle in front of her left shoulder; her right arm is extended and the hand clasps the right hand of a standing woman, who is turned in three-quarter left profile, her weight on her advanced right foot. She wears a chiton and a himation that frames her right shoulder and passes from beneath her right breast over her left shoulder, with the folds covering her left arm completely and extending to her ankles. Her head is in left profile and is bowed, and her hair is drawn back from her face beneath a taenia, forming a long braid at the nape. She is barefoot. Her left elbow is bent; her right arm extended in the handclasp. Between the figures kneels a small girl, turned to her right. Her left arm is brought in front of her right thigh and her right arm is extended upward, fingers open, toward the seated woman. She wears a sleeved garment, belted beneath the breasts with two shoulder straps attached to the center of the belt. Her head is in left profile; her hair is rolled across her hairline and bound with a fillet. Antae support an epistyle with two lines of inscription:

ΕΝΘΑ [ΔΕ] ΚΕΙΤΑΙ ΜΥΝΝΙΑ ΜΗΤΡΙ ΠΟΘΕΙΝΗ
ΕΥΘΡΟΣΥΝΗ: ΑΡΤΕΜΙΣΙΑΣ ΜΥΝΝΙΑ ΕΥΤΕΛΟ

"Here lies Mynnia to the sorrow of her mother/ Euphrosyne, Artemisias, Mynnia, daughter of Euteles."

In its original state, the second line of the inscription listed only Euphrosyne and Mynnia. These names were in reference to the first line of the inscription which tells us that "Here lies Mynnia to the sorrow of her mother." The figure directly beneath the word "Mynnia" is the standing female who wears her hair in the long locks of a young maiden. She is most logically the daughter, Mynnia, and the seated, full-breasted woman must be the mother Euphrosyne. Studies correlating grave iconography and inscrip-

104

tions have shown that in scenes with a standing and a seated individual, the standing figure is as likely as the seated individual to be the deceased person. It appears that Mynnia lived to reach adolescence, because her breasts are clearly indicated, but she must have died before she married and thus before she had left the care and the home of her mother.

At some point after the relief was completed, the second line of the inscription was emended, adding the name Artemisias and patronymic Eutelo (of Euteles), who was obviously the father. Clairmont reasonably conjectures that the little girl kneeling before Euphrosyne must be the younger daughter Artemisias, and that she must have died only a few years after the relief was completed and thus also before she was old enough to marry. The family added her name to the grave relief so that the stele could honor both daughters.

It is clear from the first line of the inscription that Euphrosyne's grief at the loss of her daughter is as much an object of focus as is Mynnia's death. This quintessentially Greek sentiment, epitomized in the story of Demeter and Persephone, is here given eloquent expression in Euphrosyne's obliviousness to her younger daughter's plea for attention (see **Persephone and Demeter**). The mother's head is bowed, and her left hand grasps the folds of her mantle, not to bring them out in front of her shoulder in the traditional manner of the bride's unveiling, but rather to draw the fabric even closer about her as if to isolate her even farther in her grief (see **Gesture and Gaze** and **The Wedding**).

Euphrosyne's downcast glance, coupled with Artemisias' complete disregard of her older sister, sets Mynnia so much apart from her mother and sister that she no longer seems to belong among the living. Only through her handshake is Mynnia linked with her mother. This gesture was introduced into funerary sculpture in the last two decades of the fifth century, but, perhaps because of its origin in formal agreements between men, the handshake is rarely encountered in depictions of mother and daughter. Here, the handshake is accentuated by the extended arm of the little Artemisias, whose gesture is cleverly adapted from conventional renderings of young children, who stretch out both arms to their nurse or mother (see **Erichthonios** and nos. 6, 13, and 68). Artemisias' single outstretched arm forms a graceful and poignant complement to the handshake of her mother and older sister. At the same time, the immediacy and passion of the straining little sister infuse emotional energy into the restrained farewell of mother and daughter. Indeed, the formality of the handshake contrasts with the informal and understated interaction of Persephone and Demeter in votive reliefs of several decades before (see nos. 83, 84, and 86). There, the subtle body language of the goddesses communicates a deeply felt emotion, which the ritual of the handshake cannot and does not intend to do.

The style of the drapery easily dates the relief in the first decades of the fourth century. Particularly noteworthy is the handling of the rectangular panel of fabric that hangs below Mynnia's left arm.

Whereas her concealed left hand dictates the direction of its folds, the drapery forms an isolated decorative panel, which hangs like a curtain over the body behind it. Also characteristic of this period is the bulky roll of mantle folds which passes over Euphrosyne's lap, its mass accentuated by several deeply grooved valleys. Drapery in contemporary vase-painting has a comparable volume, taking on a life of its own. Finally, one should note the crinkly texture of the chiton over Euphrosyne's breasts, as well as the deep V-shaped folds that articulate a triangular panel between them.

GRAVE RELIEF WITH WOMAN AND MAID

ca. 375-370
Houston, Museum of Fine Arts, Annette Finnigan Collection, inv. no. 37.25

Attic
Marble
H 43.2 cm., W 50.8 cm.

Publications: Hoffmann (1970) 22-23, no. 6; *The Museum of Fine Arts, Houston. A Guide to the Collection* (Houston 1981) no. 15; Vermeule (1981) 108, no. 78; Keuls (1985a) 139-40, fig. 120; Clairmont (1993) vol. 2, 696-97, no. 2.795.

Broken across the waists of both figures. Repaired from several large pieces. Restored are the servant's raised arms and part of her neck.

Two antae support a plain pediment with akroteria; between and overlapping the antae are two females. Seated turned in three-quarter right profile, her hands drawn forward over her thighs, is a woman who wears a chiton and a mantle, which is draped over her head, framing both shoulders. Her hair is drawn back from her face over the ear, and her head is inclined downward, as she gazes down toward her knees. Standing beside her is a woman turned in three-quarter left profile, her hair rolled back from her face and up from her ears and nape. Both her height, equal to that of the seated woman, and the size of her head, which is smaller than that of the seated woman, indicate that this second female is relatively young. Her head is also inclined, and she gazes in the same direction as does her mistress. Over her peplos she wears a mantle, folds of which lie over each shoulder. Her right elbow is bent and the back of her hand is brought to her chin. Her left forearm cradles a child, who is enveloped in fabric to its neck.

The honored figure is obviously the seated woman, who has apparently died while giving birth to the infant. The draping of the mantle over her head surely refers to the *miasma*, the pollution

105

that childbirth brought upon a woman and her house and that was dispersed about three days after the birth by means of a ritual of cleansing. It is not clear whether the baby in the maidservant's arms survived. What is remarkable is the degree to which the newborn infant is ignored, because the eyes of both women are directed downward. If the object of their gaze is a young child standing at its mother's knee, the scene would be accentuating the separation that death brought to mother and child.

The shared interest of mother and maid emphasizes the degree to which the maidservant was an integral part of the intimacy of the mistress' realm. Certainly, the ease with which she holds the baby implies her participation in the delivery (see no. 103). Mistress and maid are still further linked by the gentle rhythm of their tilted heads, which are inclined beyond the demands of the gaze. The inclination expresses the women's modesty, or *aidos*, which is accentuated by the draping of the mantle over the mistress's head in

the manner of a shy bride (see **Aidos and Sophrosyne**). Because *aidos* bears connotations of submission and respect before a higher authority, the artist seems to suggest that the common denominator of simply being women could surmount class distinctions.

A date in the first decades of the fourth century is indicated by the considerable depth of the carving, which is accentuated by the exceedingly low relief with which the sculptor has rendered the distant folds of the seated woman's mantle. Another feature distinctive of this date is the way the drapery falls into a mass of crinkly folds that are not arranged in an easily comprehended overall pattern, but rather respond to differing stresses and tensions, as, for example, in the folds that skirt the inner contour of the mistress' left breast. Also contrasting with drapery of the late fifth century is the greater thickness of the fabric over the maidservant's breasts. Even the section of garment lying over the mistress' torso is no longer transparent.

PURSUIT SCENES

It is not uncommon in Classical vase-painting to encounter a type of scene in which a youth runs after a fleeing maiden. He may be identified by his attributes as a god (Poseidon, nos. 111-113) or a hero (Theseus, no. 121). A weapon may be held in a threatening position or even engaged (see **Amymone and Poseidon**), or the pursuer may hold spears at his side in an inactive position.[1]

Because of the presence in these scenes of weapons used in hunting, the viewer is obviously intended to understand that the pursuit of a woman is being likened to the pursuit of a quarry. The sexual undercurrents of hunting are well known, and in Greek culture the analogy between hunting and courtship finds many expressions, as, for example, in the ritual of young girls who served as Little Bears in the cult of Artemis at Brauron (see **Little Bears**, **Women as Animals**, **Artemis**, and **Aktaeon**).

Subtleties in these scenes show that pursuits are not as straightforward as they initially appear. In many, if not most, examples, the woman turns to look back at her pursuer. The interlocked gazes submit the youth to the irresistible, erotic gaze of the female, which is expounded throughout Greek literature and myth (see **Gesture and Gaze** and **Gorgon**). We are led to conclude that through the power of her gaze the pursued woman is energetically, even with mutual aggressiveness, responding to her pursuer. Sometimes the maiden's gesture reinforces her seeming acceptance of her pursuer, for she may finger her garment in the traditional gesture of the submissive bride (no. 113). She may even extend her arm back to him (no. 111). Such intimations of female acquiescence find affirmation in literature; one thinks of Kreousa in the *Ion* of Euripides, and Eva Stehle has commented on a number of other parallels.[2] In her essay in this volume, Mary Lefkowitz discusses literary passages in which heroines regret, not the fleeting affair with the god that was initiated through rape or seduction, but rather the fact that the god subsequently abandons them to raise their sons alone.

It is also apparent that women as well as men accepted the image of the male pursuit of the female as a metaphor for courtship. On a lebes gamikos (no. 57), which was a type of vase exclusively associated with the wedding and was presented to the bride as a wedding gift, the scene of bridal ritual on the body of the vase has been paired with a pursuit scene on the base. Here the presence of a dolphin identifies the maiden as Thetis and the pursuer as Peleus (see **Peleus and Thetis**). It is interesting to note that although this vase-painter has not hesitated to decorate a wedding vase with a pursuit scene, he has been careful to palliate the tone of the action. Peleus' stance and gesture are far less aggressive than those in most pursuit scenes, as he stretches out his arm as if to open a conversation. The probable explanation is that, whereas a bride would very much want to believe that she was desirable to a bridegroom who was in actuality barely known to her, the fantasy was only palatable if the aggressiveness of the man's approach was substantially softened.

Some pursuit scenes are unambiguously violent to the modern eye. In the lekythos in Zurich (no. 111), Poseidon plunges his trident into Amymone's side below her breast, exactly as if she were a fish he were harpooning. Even if we can explain the action as a metaphor both of courtship and of creating a spring of water, we are left with an image that is soberingly brutal. To what extent vase scenes such as this one encouraged derogatory attitudes to women through desensitization is a fundamental question that goes beyond an analysis of Greek vase-painting to the modern controversy over pornography.

---

1. A full discussion of the scenes is in Sourvinou-Inwood (1987a) 131-53. For the image of the pursuit in lyric poetry of the Archaic period, see Halperin (1990) 137, 202 n. 148.
2. Stehle (1990) 88-125.

PELEUS AND THETIS

Thetis was a daughter of the sea god Nereus, and as a goddess she would normally have found her husband among the other gods. Zeus, however, decreed that Thetis would be the bride of a mortal man, but when Peleus expressed interest, Thetis resisted what she believed to be a match inappropriate to her stature. Peleus persisted with his attentions and soon found himself in a wrestling match with Thetis, who complicated the encounter by transforming herself into a lion, a dolphin, and a snake. Peleus persevered, and finally Thetis could resist no longer. Their wedding was a glorious event (nos. 109-110), and the offspring of their union was the great hero Achilles.[1]

The myth vividly expresses several themes prominent in Greek thought. Courtship was viewed as a literal pursuit, even a combat, and the process, culminating in sexual intercourse, transformed a wild animal-woman into a domesticated wife (see **Pursuit Scenes**, **Women as Animals**, **Bears**, **Little Bears**, and **The Wedding**). Further, a woman's feral aspect was at the heart of her sexual appeal. Peleus continues to pressure Thetis even when she takes on an animal form, just as Atalanta's undomesticated lifestyle as a hunter attracted countless suitors (see **Atalanta**). The childless hunter Kephalos even mated with a bear, which not only was transformed into a beautiful woman but also produced a baby (see **Bears**).

The lion that functions as one of Thetis' animal equivalencies invites consideration. Lions were closely associated with Artemis both in Homer and through the goddess' identity as the Mistress of Wild Beasts (see **Artemis**). Another mythical woman who eventually takes on the form of a lion is Atalanta, who earlier had also engaged in a wrestling encounter with Peleus. Herakles also wrestles with a lion, and the parallel with Peleus suggests that the Nemean Lion is not entirely bestial. It is further noteworthy that Thetis' son Achilles was celebrated as a lion slayer.[2]

Thetis' resistance to Peleus in the form of a wrestling match characterized by metamorphoses is explained by her identity as the daughter of Nereus, god of the sea, and the sea's powers of transformation. She shares with her aunt Metis a cunning that the Greeks likened to a thread that binds the present to its resolution, much as the Fates spin the threads that tie man's destiny. Thus it is Thetis who pilots the Argonauts' ship, navigating its path through the formlessness of the churning sea. Through these associations Thetis was also identified by Euripides and Herodotos with the cuttlefish, which was distinctive for its entwining tentacles and for its ability to take on the shape of the rock to which it clings. The cuttlefish was also admired for its cleverness in emitting an inky blackness through which it could navigate its escape from danger. Of particular interest in reference to Thetis' ultimately unsuccessful encounter with Peleus is the vulnerability of the female cuttlefish while mating, because at this moment the tentacles of the male and female are so inextricably interlaced that the capture of either one of them will bring death to the other.[3]

Similarities among representations of the encounter of Peleus and Thetis indicate a lost artistic prototype, which must be ultimately derived from depictions of Satyrs wrestling with Nymphs in black-figure vase-painting.[4] One apparent feature of the prototype is the avoidance of eye contact in a manner reminiscent of Perseus' strategy in overcoming Medusa, a diametric contrast to the direct gaze of maidens responsive to their pursuers (see **Gorgons** and **Pursuit Scenes**).

Finally, one should note that Thetis' unwilling participation in her courtship with Peleus is an amusing inversion of the familiar pattern of a goddess pursuing a mortal man (see **Eos and Kephalos**). One should also consider that in antiquity the popular imagination probably linked the transformations of Thetis with the conventional view that women were unpredictable, volatile, and violent (see **Women and Men**).

---

1. Homer, *Iliad* 24.59-63 and 24.534-7; Hesiod, *Theogony* 1006-1007; Pindar, *Nemean* 5.34-4. Philodemos, writing in the first century B.C., relates that Thetis rejected Zeus' advances in order to please Hera (*Kypria* frag. 2 *PEG*). Pindar, *Isthmian* 8.26-47, tells us that Zeus granted Thetis to a mortal when he learned from Themis that the son of Thetis would be stronger than his father. The same prediction is mentioned in Aischylos' play, *Prometheus Bound* 755-68. Thetis was also said to have taken the form of fire and other monsters. See Pindar, *Nemean* 3.35-6; Pausanius 5.18.5. See Gantz (1993) 228-32.

2. Pindar, *Nemean* 3.45.

3. For the discussion of Thetis and the cuttlefish, see Detienne (1978a) 133-74.

4. Barringer (1995) 76, 197 no. 148.

106

106 Detail of interior (tondo).
(See also colorplate, p.298)

KYLIX WITH PELEUS AND THETIS

ca. 500
signed by Peithinos
Berlin, Antikensammlung, Staatliche Museen zu Berlin Preussischer
Kulturbesitz, inv. no. F 2279

Attic, from Vulci
Clay
H 13 cm., Diam 34.2 cm.

Publications: *ARV*² 115.2 and 1626; *Para* 332; *Add*² 174; *CVA* Berlin, Antiquarium 2 (Germany 21) pl. 60-61; *CVA* Berlin, Antiquarium 3 (Germany 22) pl. 122.2,6; A. Furtwängler, *Beschreibung der Vasensammlung im Antiquarium* II (Berlin 1885) 556-60; J.C. Hoppin, *A Handbook of Attic Red-Figured Vases*, vol. 2 (Cambridge, MA 1919) 334-35; C. Robert, *Archäologische Hermeneutik. Anleitung zur Deutung klassischer Bildwerke* (Berlin 1919) 149, fig. 119; Pfuhl (1923) 457-58, pl. 136, fig. 417; C. Haspels, "Deux fragments d'une coupe d'Euphronios," *BCH* 54 (1930) 449, no. 28; H. Diepolder, *Griechische Vasen, Antiken aus den Berliner Museen* 6 (Berlin 1947) 39-41, fig. 28; *EAA* VI (1965) 4-5 (s.v. Peithinos); A. Greifenhagen, *Antike Kunstwerke*² (1965) pls. 64-65; J. Henle, *Greek Myths: A Vase Painter's Notebook* (Bloomington and London 1973) 20-21, fig. 12; Krieger (1973) 28-29, 40, 57-58, 60, 68, 84-87, 160, no. 47, pl. 4c; Boardman (1975) 132, fig. 214.1-3; K.J. Dover, *Greek Homosexuality* (London 1978) no. R196; K. Schefold, *Götter- und Heldensagen der Griechen in der spätarchaischen Kunst* (Munich 1978) 190-91, 315, fig. 257; H.A. Shapiro, "Courtship Scenes in Attic Vase-Painting," *AJA* 85 (1981) 136, 143, pl. 26, figs. 7-10; Sutton (1981) 283-84, 287, 307, 343, 390, no. G9; Keuls (1985a) 54-56, 218, 222, figs. 37, 196-197; Staatliche Museen Preussischer Kulturbesitz, *Antikenmuseum Berlin: Die ausgestellten Werke* (Berlin 1988) 112-13, no. 1; Lissarrague (1992) 213-14, fig. 50; Shapiro (1992b) 56-57, fig. 3.2; Staatliche Museen zu Berlin, *Die Antikensammlung im Pergamonmuseum und in Charlottenburg* (Mainz 1992) 271-72, no. 147 (I. Wehgartner); Sutton (1992) 14-15; Gantz (1993) 229.

Around the tondo is a band of meander (left).

A crouching Peleus encircles Thetis with his arms. She stands with her legs in right profile, her torso frontal. Her head is turned back in left profile and is inclined; she looks down. Her left leg is advanced. Her left arm holds folds of drapery beside her left hip; her right arm is extended behind her, with the palm up and the fingers extended. She wears a chiton that is decorated with widely spaced dots and that is belted and has a kolpos; the folds of her skirt fall into several stacks of pleats, one over each leg and another beneath her left hand. The fabric of her sleeves also falls into stacked pleats that extend below her elbows. Her himation is draped behind her back and nape, with the ends brought forward over each shoulder. Her head is inclined downward and she gazes down. Scallop curls edge her hairline, and the locks behind her ears are gathered up beneath a diadem that has a meander pattern; the ends hang down her neck. She also wears a disc earring and spiral bracelet on her left arm. Around her left wrist are the coils of a snake.

Peleus leans forward, his left knee bent, with the heel visible behind Thetis' left foot. His right knee is also bent and the foot is placed behind him, with the heel raised. The coils of a snake encircle his right lower leg, and the snake's head attacks his right ankle, just beneath an anklet. His left arm apparently passes behind Thetis' back, and the forearm is visible in front of her waist. His right arm is bent at the elbow and the hands are joined in a clasp that is rendered as a meander. The coils of a snake pass over his right forearm and loop over his left forearm, with the snake's head directed at his right jaw. He wears a chiton that is also decorated with widely separated dots, and the folds also fall into stacks of pleats, one down his right side and another over the front of his torso. The pleats of his right sleeve resemble those of Thetis, and pleats also hang below his right buttock; emerging from beneath his buttock is the lower half of his scabbard. His head is in right profile and he gazes downward. Locks of hair frame his face, and the ends are brought up from the nape, with the ends hanging freely. The beginnings of a beard are visible on his right jaw. The center of his forehead is attacked by the head of the snake that wraps around Thetis' left wrist. A lion perches on Peleus' back; the right foreleg is raised, and both hind legs crouch on Peleus' right upper arm. The lion's mouth is open and the tongue is extended; the tail loops up behind. Winding around the inside contour of the tondo above Thetis' head is the inscription:

ΠΕΙΘΙΝΟΣ ΕΓΡΑΦΣΕΝ ΑΘΕΝΟΔΟΤΟΣ ΚΑΛΟΣ
("Peithinos painted (this), Athenodotos is fair.").

The underside presents courting scenes in which youths approach young boys and young women. All the youths have only the beginnings of a beard down their right jaw and they wear a himation and sandals. The older youth is consistently placed on the viewer's left, and the himations of the young boys and of the women frame their backs and the back of their heads, with the ends brought forward over each shoulder; several of the young boys wear fillets. On Side A each pair of males is flanked by sponges, strigils, and aryballoi that hang in the background. A youth leans on his walking stick as he gazes downward; behind him is a stool over which a lionskin has been spread. Next to him a youth stands close beside a smaller boy, whose left hand is at his waist, while his right hand is extended toward the older youth's right hand, which holds a round object against his own right thigh. In the next pair a youth and young boy kiss; the youth has brought his arm around the shoulders of the boy and grasps a walking stick in the left hand. The right hand fondles the boy's genitals. The boy's left hand holds a string from which his aryballos dangles, and his right hand grasps the right upper arm of the older youth. In the next pair the youth bends his knees as he brings his penis next to that of the boy; his left arm passes behind the boy's neck and the left hand holds the handle of a walking stick. The right hand is beside the right thigh, fingers extended. The boy's left arm is at his waist and his right hand grasps the upper right arm of the youth. The lips of the figures are about to touch. In the last group on this side the youth presses his right hand against the back of the boy's head, while his left hand rests on the handle of his walking stick. The boy's left hand is at his side; his right hand grasps the youth's right upper arm. Behind the boy is a hound in right profile.

On Side B three youths approach three women. All the women wear a belted chiton beneath a himation that is draped similarly to that of the boys on Side A. In the first pair the youth gazes downward; his body is enveloped by his himation, and his right hand is at his hip; his left hand clasps the shaft of his walking stick. The woman's left hand is at her side; her right hand is uplifted and the fingers are extended, palm out. She looks downward. In the second group the youth looks downward while he places his right hand on his hip; his left hand clasps his walking stick by the shaft. The woman's elbows are bent and her forearms are extended horizontally with the fingers open; those of her right hand are uplifted. She wears a sakkos, and she looks down. In the final group the youth is seen from behind. His left hand is on his hip; his right hand rests on his walking stick. With her right hand the woman lifts folds of her chiton beside her right knee; her left forearm is horizontal and her fingers are extended and raised. She appears to wear a taenia and she gazes down.

To emphasize the degree to which Peleus and Thetis are entwined in their struggle, Peithinos has so interlocked the figures that even the ancient viewer would have needed a moment to distinguish the forms and drapery (see **Peleus and Thetis**). Peleus' left thigh passes behind Thetis' legs, but his left knee and lower leg are not shown and are not easily visualized. The stylization of the composition is especially evident in Peleus' gesture. His torso and his left lower arm are rendered such that for his left upper arm to

pass behind Thetis' back, her torso would have to be of gossamer thinness. The resulting impression is that her form is as ephemeral in the composition as her transformations proved it mutable.

In contrast to the handling of the same subject on the pelike in Paris (no. 107), Thetis reveals only minimal distress in the extended fingers of her right hand. Meanwhile, her left hand calmly gathers her chiton folds in the ladylike, Archaic manner familiar from the Acropolis korai, and her head is gracefully bowed in an expression of the *aidos* that was expected of respectable women (see **Aidos** and **Sophrosyne**). The diminutive lion appears to be more of an emblem than an agent as he assumes a formal stance and ineffectually prowls down Peleus' back. The snakes are more active, and the snake at Peleus' ankle has presciently chosen to attack the one area that will be the point of weakness in Achilles, the son the couple will bear.

The scene in the tondo is one of the most admired of all representations in red-figure vase-painting. The sureness and the fluidity of the draftsmanship are extraordinary, especially the graceful contours of the legs of both figures and the elegant stylization of Thetis' chiton and himation folds. The complicated and angular patterns of the garment folds accentuate the lyrical rhythm of the bowed heads and the detached calm of the expressionless faces. The painter has so skillfully adjusted the composition to the constraints of the tondo that the inclination of Thetis' head effortlessly echoes the curve of the tondo, and the figures show no difficulty in employing as a groundline the curving lower frame. The linearity of the scene, even to the meander motif of Peleus' clasped hands, is in harmony with the encircling band of meander pattern.

Because so many vases represent the wrestling bout between Peleus and Thetis by means of this basic composition, a famous prototype must have served as the common inspiration. In that original work Peleus' interlocked hands must also have been rendered as a meander, because the detail is retained in most of the vase scenes. The way Peleus leans over and wraps his arms around Thetis' waist calls to mind Archaic representations of Satyrs attacking Nymphs, from which this composition is surely ultimately derived.

The theme of the tondo is more fully developed on the underside. In the tondo mythical courtship is a physical struggle, and the female takes the form of an animal (see **Women as Animals** and **Pursuit Scenes**). The underside deals with daily life, but the lionskin and hound are a reminder that the metaphor of the hunt is still applicable. Because the young men on Sides A and B are not only identical in age with each other but also with Peleus, the artist is clearly suggesting an equivalency between three kinds of courtship: with boys, with prostitutes, and with a goddess.

We are immediately aware that each type of courtship calls for a different conduct. The young boys are embraced, kissed, fondled, and regarded directly; moreover, the suspended sponges and oil jugs inform us that the overtures take place in the male exercise ground, the palaestra. The women, on the other hand, are

106 Side A

106 Side B

approached more gingerly, as was the custom in depictions of financial negotiations with hetairai (prostitutes; see nos. 36-38). The men and women are well separated, and there is neither bodily nor eye contact. Noteworthy is the greater aggressiveness of the women relative to the men, because, whereas the arms of the young men are held close to their bodies, the women extend their hands out in front of their torsos, and their fingers are raised and spread, probably to indicate the financial terms of their service. The exchange of money was a critical difference in the courtship of a hetaira versus that of a young boy, who would have been a son of an Athenian citizen, and for whom the receipt of money for sexual favors was absolutely unacceptable (see **Women and Men**). A final important difference between the two types of courtship is that, whereas the women seem amicably disposed to the relationship, the young boys are less overtly responsive. As we know from ancient commentators, custom dictated that boys approached by

older males should express neither encouragement nor pleasure, and, indeed, three of the youths (including the two that are about to be kissed) lay a restraining hand upon their suitor's right arm.

It has often been remarked that the artist's uncommon name, Peithinos, translates as "the persuader," an appellation extraordinarily appropriate to the scenes on this kylix. The underlying theme is, indeed, the varieties of persuasion that can be employed in forging a relationship with a man or woman: Peleus turns to physical force, hetairai respond to attractive financial terms, and young boys are won over with the blandishments of words, embraces, and love tokens. The vase's correlation of myth with daily life provides unambiguous testimony that the Classical Greeks were fully cognizant of the meaning behind the graphic imagery of their mythical metaphors.

343

107

PELIKE
WITH PELEUS AND THETIS

450-425
in the manner of the Leningrad Painter
Paris, Musée du Louvre, Département des Antiquités grecques,
étrusques et romaines, inv. no. G 373

Attic
Clay
H 39 cm., Diam (at mouth) 13 cm.

Publications: *ARV²* 573.9; *Add²* 262; *CVA* Paris, Musée du Louvre 8 (France 12) 28, pl. 40.1-7; E. Pottier, *Vases antiques du Louvre* (Paris 1897-1922) 240; P.V.C. Baur, *Centaurs in Ancient Art* (Berlin 1912) 108, no. 265; Krieger (1973) 30, 70, 80, 176 no. 186; M.P. Baglione, *Il Territorio di Bomarzo, Ricognizioni Archeologiche in Etruria* 2 (Rome 1976) pl. 47.1-4; B. Schiffler, *Die Typologie des Kentauren in der antiken Kunst* (Frankfurt 1976) 261, no. A/Ch 36; *LIMC* III (1986) 239, no. 29, pl. 189 (s.v. Cheiron); Barringer (1995) 76, 197, no. 148, pls. 85-86.

Above the scene is a band of bud pattern; beneath is a band of simple meander flanked by two pairs of two glazed lines. On each handle is a palmette.

On Side A Peleus wrestles with Thetis. She strides forward with her legs widespread, her left leg advanced, the toes of her right foot on the ground behind her. Both arms are raised and extend into the bud pattern above the scene. The hands face the viewer, with the fingers extended and separated. Her head is in left profile, and she gazes straight ahead. She wears a belted chiton, the neckline of which is decorated with a number or parallel lines. The rest of the fabric is ornamented with a pattern of broad and narrow stripes. Her belt bears a series of dots and arcs. Over her chiton she wears a mantle that passes behind her back and over each shoulder; the ends hang down to her knees. Her hair is brought up from the nape and gathered beneath a diadem that broadens at the back of her head; it is decorated with a narrow band of V's. She also wears a beaded necklace and a disc earring.

Peleus leans forward as he wraps his arms around Thetis. His right leg rests on the ground; his left leg disappears behind Thetis' skirt. He is nude, except for a mantle that passes behind his right shoulder and is brought forward over his right upper arm, with the ends falling down his right side. His swordbelt is visible over his right shoulder. His head is in right profile, and he wears a laurel wreath over his long hair, which falls down his back. One lock trails down his right shoulder, and another falls behind his left ear. In front of his ear are the beginnings of a beard. He gazes ahead. Perched on Peleus' back is a panther whose front right paw rests against the nape of Peleus' head, its hind legs supported by Peleus' back. The animal's jaw is pressed against the nape of Peleus' head, and the tail curls upward above his back. In front of Peleus' legs are the winding coils of a snake.

In front of Peleus and Thetis, and running away from them, is a woman whose left leg is advanced; most of her right leg passes behind Thetis' skirt. Her right hand holds in front of her chest a dolphin, seen in right profile. She wears a chiton beneath a short himation that is draped diagonally, passing from her right shoulder beneath her left breast; the ends fall down her right side. Her head is in left profile and her hair is drawn up under a sakkos, whose ends protrude at the back of her head. She also wears a hoop earring and gazes at Thetis. Her left arm is extended out in front of her, and the fingers of her hand pass behind a short tree trunk, before which are a boulder and a coiled

107 Side A

snake, whose raised head is in left profile and is directed back toward Peleus and Thetis.

Behind Peleus is a woman running to her right, her elbows bent and the arms raised, fingers extended. Her head is in right profile and she gazes back at Thetis. She wears a chiton beneath a himation, and her hair is wrapped in a sakkos.

The other side of the vase continues the scene, as other Nereids gather at an altar. As one maiden flees from the altar, another approaches, her right hand grasping the folds of her garment. Her left hand is extended to grasp the right side of a woman whose body and face are frontal. The woman's right arm is raised, with the right palm facing out and the fingers extended; the left arm is partly concealed by Nereus. She wears a chiton beneath a himation brought forward over both shoulders; she also wears a diadem over her long hair. On the other side of the altar a bearded man stands in left profile, his right elbow bent with the right hand raised, fingers open. Over his sleeved garment he wears a mantle that is draped over his left shoulder; his left arm steadies a staff. Seen in front of the man's legs are the equine barrel and hind legs of the Centaur Cheiron, seen in right profile. The forepart of the Centaur is rendered as a bearded man, draped in a mantle that is brought over his left shoulder and across his legs. His left hand holds a pine branch.

107 Detail of Side B

The scene is presented as a continuous action that moves from Side A to Side B. Peleus' attack on Thetis has so terrorized her four sisters that they run to the altar, beside which stand their father Nereus and mother Doris. The sister beside Thetis is so alarmed that she even runs away with the dolphin that was one of Thetis' weapons of transformation. The last figure in the scene, so placed because his presence looks forward to the future, is the Centaur Cheiron. He will be the tutor of Achilles, the son to be born to Peleus and Thetis. Cheiron was a grandfatherly figure to Peleus, and in some ancient accounts Peleus brought his new bride to Cheiron directly after the struggle. The branch Cheiron carries alludes to his wedding gift to Peleus, which Hephaistos fashioned into an ash spear.[1]

Thetis' capitulation seems imminent, as Peleus, whose youthfulness is emphasized by his nascent beard, lurches toward her, his penis close to the back of her thigh. The diminutive panther employs its instinctual strategy of attacking Peleus on the back of his neck, but the snake that rises so threateningly in front of the goddess' skirt has no apparent involvement in the struggle at all. The strongest indication of Thetis' weakening resistance is her demeanor. In contrast to the cool control she exhibits in other scenes of the myth, the goddess is here distraught. Alone of all the figures depicted, her arms are fully extended skyward in terror, even piercing the ornamental border, and she looks across to her sister for support. In this scene Thetis is not a goddess who prefers that her animal aspects do the work of the resistance; she is rather presented as a frightened and helpless maiden desperate for assistance.

The conduct of Thetis' parents is interesting. Her father's upraised hand expresses his mild surprise, but he is clearly unwilling to become involved, probably because he is aware that the deed has been decreed by Zeus. The role of Doris is puzzling, because

frontality in Classical vase-painting is extremely rare, employed for masks, Gorgons, and dying figures (see nos. 80, 82, and 108). Together with her frontal body, her stiffly upraised hand, and her proximity to the altar, she resembles a cult image, like that of Dionysos in scenes of the Lenaia (see no. 124). Her statuarial character is reinforced by the gesture of her daughter, who presses her fingers against her mother's side, in the manner by which a fugitive obtains sanctuary by embracing a cult statue. By contrast, the position of Doris' left foot implies agitated movement.

The artist has a lively imagination, which sometimes exceeds his skill. In order to suggest that the voluminous folds of Thetis' skirt are dishevelled by the wrestling encounter, he interrupts some of the horizontal decorative bands, but with the result that we are presented with a jumbled array of individual sections of drapery. The painter had further difficulty in integrating the different animals into the wrestling match; thus one snake winds futilely in the foreground, while another coils menacingly beside a rock, and the dolphin is held in the Nereid's right hand as if it were a club. Having only limited skill in foreshortening, the painter has rendered the heads of the panther and the two snakes as if seen from above.

It is unclear why the fleeing Nereid with the dolphin should wear the short Ionian himation that had fallen out of fashion after the Archaic period. The answer may lie in the Late Archaic prototypical representation of the struggle. Certainly, the Archaic elements in the scene are compatible with the likening of Doris to a cult image.

1. Philodemos, *Kypria* frag. 3 *PEG*.
2. See Barringer (1991) 152, who suggests that the Nereids in scenes with Peleus and Thetis are not fleeing but dancing during a festival to Artemis in the goddess's sanctuary.

108

108

MELIAN RELIEF
WITH PELEUS AND THETIS

475-450
London, British Museum, inv. no. GR 1864.10-7.133 (Terracotta 615)

Melian, "from Kamiros (Rhodes), grave 172"
Terracotta
H 17 cm., W 16 cm.

Publications: H.B. Walters, *Catalogue of the Terracottas in the Department of Greek and Roman Antiquities, British Museum* (London 1903) 131-32, no. B 363, pl. 19; F. Studniczka, "Neue archaische Marmorskulpturen: Falsches und Echtes," *JdI* 43 (1928) 184, fig. 30; P. Jacobsthal, *Die melischen Reliefs* (Berlin 1931) 23-24, no. 14, pl. 8; B.F. Cook, *Greek and Roman Art in the British Museum* (London 1976) 76-77, fig. 62.

Unbroken. Blue on the groundline; red on Peleus' torso; red-brown on the hair of Peleus and Thetis and the mane of the lion; deep red on the mantle of Thetis and the teeth of the lion; yellow on the body of the lion.

Thetis hastens to her left with her left leg advanced, both knees slightly bent, and the toes of her right foot resting on the ground behind her. Her torso and head are frontal, her legs in right profile. Her left elbow is bent and the fingers rest on the top of her head; her right elbow is also bent and the lower arm disappears behind Peleus' back. She wears a belted chiton with an overfold that extends just below the knees. Her mantle is draped over her left shoulder. Beneath a diadem her hair is center-parted with shell curls across the hairline and longer locks that fall down behind her shoulders.

Peleus strains forward in right profile, both knees bent. His left leg is advanced, with the lower leg concealed by Thetis' garment, and the foot resting solidly on the ground. The toes of his right foot rest on the ground behind

him. His left arm encircles Thetis' waist, and the left hand clasps the right hand, which is brought forward to her thigh. His head is pressed against Thetis' torso, the face directed down, his neck horizontal. He is completely nude.

On the other side of Thetis is a lion in left profile who rises on his left hind leg, the right hind leg pressed against Thetis' left shin. The lion's left front paw rests against Thetis' left thigh, and the right front paw is brought up to the edge of her garment, just outside Peleus' left elbow. The animal's mouth is open.

The relief is of a type of terracotta openwork relief that was made on the island of Melos around the middle of the fifth century. The flat undersides indicate that the reliefs were intended to be affixed to furniture as appliques. A number of examples were exported, and this relief was discovered on Rhodes, together with a mate that depicted the abduction of the hunter Kephalos by the goddess Eos (see **Eos and Kephalos**). The pairing of the scenes provides confirmation that ancient viewers were well aware of mythical parallels and ironies, because this coupling obviously compared the complicated events that ensue when a mortal pursues a goddess and a goddess pursues a mortal.

The composition of this relief is fascinating. The lion heraldically posed at Thetis' side ostensibly refers to one of the many animal manifestations Thetis assumed in order to elude Peleus (see **Peleus and Thetis**). However, the animal's rearing pose immediately calls to mind the age-old motif of the Mistress of Wild Beasts, where the goddess is flanked by symmetrical animals in rampant poses (p. 303, fig. 1). The allusion here to the Mistress of Wild Beasts, who was another and earlier manifestation of Artemis, underlines the associations that Thetis in her undomesticated state shares with Artemis, whom Homer addresses as "a lion to women" (see **Artemis** and **Women as Animals**). The lion also calls to mind Atalanta, who is another close associate of Artemis. Atalanta had her own wrestling encounter with Peleus and was eventually transformed into a lion when her experience as a socialized female proved unsuccessful (see **Atalanta**).

Although Thetis brings her left hand to her head in the traditional female gesture of distress, she does not seem otherwise perturbed, and her lunging stride is in synchrony with that of Peleus. Certain features of the scene, by contrast, strike an uneasy note. Thetis is noticeably taller than Peleus, even though the artist has accentuated her breasts to emphasize her mature female form. Another goddess who is often given exaggerated height is Eos, the counterpart to Thetis on the matching relief (see Eos, no. 131). Moreover, the frontality of Thetis' face conforms to the convention for representing liminal and inanimate figures, as well as masks and Gorgons. It is probably significant that in most depictions of their struggle Peleus does not look directly into Thetis' face; one is reminded of Archaic depictions of Artemis with a Gorgon head (p. 410, fig. 1, see **Gorgons**, nos. 80, 82, and **Gesture and Gaze**). The accretion of these details speaks to a primal and, to Peleus, irresistible force that Thetis possessed in her untamed state.

109

POINTED AMPHORA
WITH PELEUS AND THETIS

ca. 470
by the Copenhagen Painter
New York, Collection of Shelby White and Leon Levy

Attic
Clay
H (total, with stand) 64.1 cm., H (amphora) 59.3 cm.

Publications: D. von Bothmer, *Glories of the Past: Ancient Art from the Shelby White and Leon Levy Collection* (New York, Metropolitan Museum of Art, September 14, 1990-January 27, 1991) 168-71, no. 121; Oakley and Sinos (1993) 36-37, 112-14, figs. 108-111; Shapiro (1994) 102-103, figs. 68-69.

Reassembled. Around the neck is a complex pattern of six palmettes and two lotuses, and at the root of each handle are paired palmettes. On the shoulder is depicted the battle between the Centaurs and Lapiths; the names of the Lapiths are inscribed. Four Greeks, including Kaineus who is being rammed into the ground, and Lapithas, wielding a saber, fight six Centaurs who bear pine trees and boulders. The round shields of Theseus and Perithous have shield aprons. Above the figural scene is a frieze of four meanders (right) alternating with a checker square. Beneath the scene is a band of three meanders (right) alternating with a checker square. The stand has a band of tongues on its lip and a band of addorsed, angled palmettes around the midsection.

All the figures are identified by inscriptions. Peleus turns in three-quarter right profile, his head in right profile. His mantle is brought over his left shoulder and around his waist, legs, and left arm, which is completely concealed. He has long hair, of which two curly locks are brought forward over his left shoulder, and he wears a fillet that has a band of beads above and below. His right hand grasps the right wrist of Thetis who stands in right profile. She wears a chiton beneath a mantle that is brought over both shoulders; her left index finger and thumb hold folds of the drapery in front of her left shoulder. She wears a diadem over her long curly locks.

Behind Thetis stands Artemis in right profile holding two lighted torches in her uplifted hands. She wears a chiton beneath a mantle that is draped over both shoulders. Her long hair is brought up from her nape beneath a diadem. Following her is Apollo, who stands almost frontally, his head turned back in left profile. He wears a chiton with overfold beneath a mantle that is draped over his left shoulder and around his hips and legs, with the ends falling outside his left arm. His right hand rests on his right hip, and his left hand fingers the strings of a kithara. His head is turned back in left profile and he wears a laurel wreath. Facing him and turned in three-quarter right profile is Leto, who wears a chiton beneath a mantle that is draped over both shoulders. She also wears a necklace and sakkos. Her right hand is at her waist; her left hand is raised and holds a flower bud.

Behind Leto stands Semele, turned to her left, a torch in her right hand. She wears a chiton and a mantle, and over her long curly locks she wears a fillet. Her head is in left profile and she gazes at Dionysos, who stands in three-quarter right profile, a thyrsos steadied in his left hand, his right hand beneath a mantle that is draped over a chiton. An ivy wreath sits atop his long curly hair. Behind him Hopla stands almost frontally, head in right profile. Her left hand is upraised, her right hand at her side. She wears a chiton and an himation, and a fillet is wrapped around her long, curly hair.

Behind Hopla are two columns which stand on a platform and support an architrave. Within is most of a bed supported by a leg with an Ionic capital and palmette ornament. The mattress is striped, and the pillow has patterns of horizontal, vertical, and zigzag lines. Standing almost frontally in front of the platform is Philyra, carrying a lighted torch in each hand and wearing a chiton and a mantle that is draped over her left shoulder, covering most of her body. Her head is turned back in left profile, and she wears a taenia over her long hair. Hanging in the field are an alabastron and a ribbon. Between Peleus and the Ionic structure stands Cheiron, in the form of a man from whose buttocks protrudes part of an equine torso. He wears a mantle and a fillet over long, curly hair and carries a lighted torch in each hand.

Peleus leads forth Thetis as his bride by grasping her wrist in the bridegroom's traditional gesture of domination, but instead of taking her left wrist he reaches for her right wrist (see **Peleus and Thetis** and **The Wedding**). The break in convention frees Thetis' left hand to finger her mantle in the age-old gesture of the *anakalypteria*, the unveiling of the bride. This event preceded the bridal procession to the bridegroom's home, but vase-painters occasionally referred to the unveiling, or even seemed to elide the two moments, by depicting the *nympheutria* in the act of adjusting the bride's veil as she sets out in the procession (nos. 23, 24).

The Copenhagen Painter has toyed with convention in other ways as well. Traditionally, the bride's mother, holding two torches, would follow the bridal procession, and the bridegroom's mother, also holding two torches, would greet the couple at the entrance to the bride's new home. Here the torches are carried by Artemis, standing behind the bride, and by the Centaur Cheiron and his mother Philyra, who await the arrival of the bridal procession. The painter is following the version of the myth wherein Peleus brought his new bride to Cheiron's home on Mt. Pelion. Cheiron consistently functioned as a quasi-godfather to Peleus, and even advised Peleus how best to capture Thetis (by not letting go when she underwent transformations into other animals).[1] After Thetis gives birth to Achilles, Cheiron will raise and educate the boy in his wooded home.

The substitution of Artemis for Thetis' mother also alludes to previous stages of the myth. Unlike others of Artemis' proteges, such as Atalanta, Thetis was both a goddess and a denizen of the sea; nonetheless, she was closely affiliated with Artemis who traditionally assisted unmarried maidens in their willing or reluctant transition to married life (see **Artemis** and **Atalanta**). Vase-painters consistently represented Thetis' transformation into a lion, which was closely linked with Artemis (no. 108, see **Women as Animals** and **Bears**).

The Copenhagen Painter's particular interest in the outcome of the wedding is apparent in his inclusion of three groups of parent and child; in addition to Cheiron and Philyra, we find Artemis grouped with Leto and Apollo, while Semele stands next to her son Dionysos. The context underscores the identity of Peleus and Thetis as parents of Achilles and contrasts the fairly benign,

109 Side A-B

109 Side A

109 Side B

immortal existence of Apollo and Dionysos with the unfortunate and short life that will await the progeny of this marriage between a deity and a mortal. The figure of Hopla, whose name bears the literal translation "arms," surely alludes to the famous, but ultimately futile, armor that Thetis would bring her son Achilles during the Trojan War.

The Centauromachy on the amphora's shoulder is also a depiction of a wedding ritual and thus very much connected with the main scene. At the wedding feast celebrating the marriage of Perithous, leader of the Lapiths, to Hippodamia, the Centaurs grew rowdy and precipitated a battle with the Lapiths, who were led by Perithous and his great friend Theseus. The Centaurs grabbed the pine trees and boulders of their native habitat and rammed into the ground the Greek hero Kaineus who could be killed in no other way. The violence contrasts with the apparent harmony of the main scene, but, at the same time, the juxtaposition of the two weddings reminded the ancient viewer of another aspect to the wedding of

Thetis and Peleus. Whereas the Centaurs were invited to Perithous' wedding feast, it was the deliberate or unintentional exclusion of Discord from the wedding feast of Peleus and Thetis that led to the judgment of the Golden Apples and, ultimately, to the Trojan War.

The Centauromachy returns the viewer to the main scene with the reminder of the uncivilized behavior to be expected of Centaurs, at the hands of whose leader, Cheiron, Achilles would receive his youthful education. The match of pupil and teacher was both fitting and ironic, because Achilles could claim a mother whose reluctantly domesticated nature had just been made fully manifest in the course of her unusual courtship. That Achilles must be indoctrinated into the world outside of civilization, which his mother had been coerced into abandoning, says much about the Greek distinction between the nature of women and men. The latter, through such formal institutions as hunting and warfare, were enabled to indulge in, and presumably master, the world beyond

109 Detail of shoulder, Centauromachy scene with Kaineus

the man-made institutions of the city-state; women, by contrast, were instinctively at home in the wild but were not supposed to venture back after marriage. Perhaps to distinguish Cheiron from his uncouth countrymen, Peleus' mentor is depicted with human legs in a manner familiar from black-figure representations of Centaurs. Though more awkward, the resulting form is more human, and John Oakley suggests that Cheiron may also be likened here to the *thuroros*, the man who traditionally guarded the door to the bridal chamber.

The subtlety of the Copenhagen Painter's composition is equalled by the skill of his draftsmanship. Although the shape of the amphora is unusual, the Copenhagen Painter is known to have painted at least one other example, which also bears a Centauromachy on the shoulder.[2]

1. Xenophon, *On Hunting* 1.2; Pindar, *Nemean* 4.57-61; Apollodoros, *Bibliotheke* 1.13.1-3; *LIMC* VII (1994) 251-52; Gantz (1993) 225-31.
2. In a German private collection.

110

KALYX KRATER WITH THE WEDDING OF PELEUS AND THETIS

ca. 430
by the Peleus Painter
Ferrara, Museo Archeologico Nazionale di Ferrara, inv. no. 2893

Attic, from tomb 617, Spina
Clay
H 54.5 cm., Diam 55 cm.

Publications: *ARV²* 1038.1 and 1679; *Para* 443; *Add²* 319; *CVA* Ferrara, Museo Nazionale 1 (Italy 37) pl. 22; *Notizie degli Scavi di antichità* 1 (1876) pl. 117.1 (1180, 123); N. Alfieri, P. Arias, and M. Hirmer, *Spina* (Munich 1958) 56-58, pls. 88-93; S. Aurigemma, *Scavi di Spina. La necropoli di Spina in Valle Trebba* I (Rome 1960) 103-104, pls. 117-23; T. Kraus, *Hekate, Heidelberger Kunstgeschichtliche Abhandlungen* 5 (1960) 93-94; E. Simon, "Zu den Giebeln des Zeustempels von Olympia," *AM* 83 (1968) 149, pl. 51.1; S. Karouzou, "An Underworld Scene of a Black-Figured Lekythos," *JHS* 92 (1972) 69 n. 31; Simon and Hirmer (1976) pl. 194-195; E. Pemberton, "The Name Vase of the Peleus Painter," *JWalt* 36 (1977) 62, 66-67, 69, 71, figs. 1-5; N. Alfieri, *Spina. Museo Archeologico Nazionale di Ferrara* I: *Ceramica* (Bologna 1979) 64, fig. 148; Y. Korshak, "Der Peleusmaler und sein Gefährte, der Hectormaler," *AntK* 23 (1980) 125 n. 4, 126, pl. 29.1; *LIMC* II (1984) 144, no. 1505 (s.v. Aphrodite); ibid., 287, no. 845, pl. 259 (s.v. Apollon); D. Paquette, *L'Instrument de musique dans la céramique de la grèce antique* (Paris 1984) 112-13, no. C20; Boardman (1989) 62, fig. 142; G. Siebert, *LIMC* V (1990) 323, no. 434 (s.v. Hermes); H. Sarian, *LIMC* VI (1992) 993, no. 44 (s.v. Hekate); Oakley and Sinos (1993) 31, 91, fig. 74; F. Berti and G. Guzzo, *Spina. Storia di una città tra Greci ed Etruschi*, Castello Estense (Ferrara, 26 settembre 1993 - 15 maggio l994) 108, 340, no. 798, fig. 88.

Mended from many pieces. Above the scene is a frieze of lyre palmettes on their sides; below is a frieze of addorsed lotus and palmette, running vertically. On the reverse, a winged woman holds a phiale behind a helmeted warrior with spear and shield. He gazes at a bearded man who holds a scepter and an unbearded man who wears a petasos and a mantle and holds two spears.

The wedding chariot, drawn by four horses, is seen in left profile. As three of the horses toss their heads, the lead horse paws the ground as Hermes tries to distract it. He wears a winged cap and sandals, and he holds a caduceus in his right hand. His cloak is fastened on his right shoulder such that the folds cover his torso and most of his left leg.

Standing in the chariot is Thetis, who wears a chiton beneath a peplos with an overfold to the waist. A black band borders both its overfold and the open edges that fall down her left side. Her hair is gathered into a knot at the back of her head, and she wears a diadem and a wedding veil studded with stars. The fabric falls down her back, and the folds can be seen behind her left arm; the fringed edges of the garment lie behind her left thigh. With her right hand, Thetis fingers the folds of her veil just above her right shoulder. Her braceleted left hand, held before her breast, is open with the fingers extended. She stares ahead of her past the nude figure of a winged Eros who flies toward her, arms extended, bearing a wreath.

Peleus stands on the ground behind Thetis, his left foot visible, his right foot presumably stepping into the chariot. In each hand he holds a set of reins, but the right arm and hand, passing behind Thetis, are not shown. His mantle is draped over his left shoulder and upper arm and around his waist and legs. A narrow black border decorates the open edges of the left side of his mantle. His head is turned back in three-quarter right profile, and over his hair, which falls in ringlets below his ears, he wears a taenia tied across his hairline. He

110   Side A

gazes back at Aphrodite, whose upraised right hands are about to place a wreath on his head. She stands with her weight on her left leg and the knee of her advanced right leg relaxed. Her sleeved chiton is studded with stars, and the neckline and the lower edge of her overfold are decorated with a band of beading. Her mantle is draped over her left shoulder and around her hips and legs, with a dark band borders its seams. Her hair is gathered at the back of her head beneath a stephane adorned with a volute pattern and surmounted by four leaves. The fingers of her left hand steady a scepter, which terminates in a flower and which bears a spiraling line around the shaft.

Visible behind the horses' backs is Hekate, who turns in three-quarter right profile toward Thetis, at whom she gazes. She holds a torch in each hand and wears a peplos, with a sakkos over her hair. Between her and Thetis stands Apollo in right profile, gazing at Thetis. He holds a kithara in his left hand and a phiale in his right hand. His long hair, crowned by a wreath, falls down his back in curling ringlets, and his long pleated garment reaches the ground. A mantle frames his back.

Inscriptions identify all the figures: Hermes, Hekate, Apollon, Thetis, P]eleu[s], Aphrodite.

This is the quintessential wedding procession in Greek mythology, the ideal that mortal couples could only hope to emulate (see **The Wedding**). The vehicle for most Greek brides was a mule cart; here Thetis is conveyed in a glorious four-horse chariot. Providing the music for the occasion is Apollo himself, whose prominent position in the center of the scene underscores the harmony that is wished for in this marriage and the one for which this krater may have been a wedding gift.

Many elements of the traditional Greek wedding ritual are depicted in this scene. Thetis wears the bridal veil, with its distinctive fringed edge (no. 56), and her gesture of fingering its folds is that of a bride who, in the moment of unveiling, reveals herself to her husband for the first time. As is typical in wedding scenes, Eros flies toward the bride to signify her sexual attraction to and for her husband.

The deities in attendance on the bridal couple carry rich connotations. Aphrodite, who here presents the bridal wreath to Peleus, is surely intended to recall for the viewer the terrible events that would soon occur at the wedding celebration. The goddess Eris, or Dis-

110 Detail of Side A, with Thetis, Peleus, and Aphrodite

110 Detail over handle with winged woman and Hermes

cord, angry that she had not been invited, would make a sudden appearance, in some versions, to cast an apple inscribed "to the fairest." When the Trojan prince Paris selected Aphrodite as the most beautiful, the insulted Hera and Athena would instigate the Trojan War as their revenge. Among the many catastrophic ramifications of that conflict was the death of Achilles, the son Thetis would bear to Peleus.

As the supreme god of travelers, Hermes leads other mythical brides: Pandora to her new husband (no. 81) and Persephone on her return to her mother (no. 82) (see **Pandora** and **Persephone and Demeter**). The associations attest to Hermes' strong links with the Underworld as a chthonic god, and the connotation is accentuated through his proximity to Hekate, another chthonic deity who travels with Hermes on his mission to recover Persephone (no. 82). John Oakley suggests that her presence here may allude to the short lifespan that would be Achilles' fate. The goddess carries the wedding torches that were traditionally held by the bride's mother and mother-in-law and stands close to Apollo, with whom she is associated through her identification with Artemis.

Certain details in the scene break with conventional bridal depictions and must be significant. The wedding procession moves to the viewer's left, the direction opposite to most movement in Classical vase-painting. It is also interesting that Peleus does not look at his bride but in the opposite direction. Nor does Thetis turn to gaze at him but rather stares distantly into space. So consistently do Thetis and Peleus avoid looking at each other, whether during their wedding (no.109) or during the struggle that preceded it (nos. 106-108), that there must be an explanation, one that may be linked with Thetis' ability to transform herself into wild animals (no. 108). That aspect of the deity's character gave her a close tie to Artemis, who is rendered with a Gorgon's face in Archaic depictions (see **Artemis**).

A final detail that would have been evocative to the ancient viewer is the position of Thetis between Peleus' arms and the reins that he bears in each hand. The ancient viewer would have recalled with irony that Thetis had associations with entwinement; now that the wrestling that comprised their courtship is past, Thetis is the one securely bound.

The Peleus Painter has such a masterful command of line and composition that he is considered one of the most skillful of all Classical vase-painters. He is fully comfortable with a three-quarter view of the torso, but a three-quarter facial view is more difficult for him, and he attempts it only for Peleus. Most of the feet are seen in profile; the foreshortening of Hermes' right foot is more suggested than rendered, and this almost experimental detail is deliberately hidden under the vase handle.

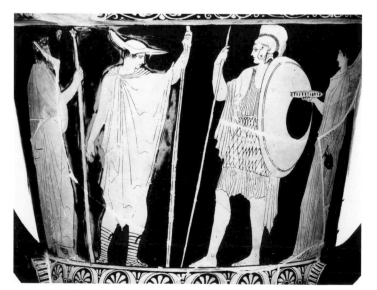

110 Detail of Side B

AMYMONE AND POSEIDON

Amymone was the daughter of King Danaos of Argos, a city-state not far from Attica. In a time of extreme drought, Danaos sent Amymone with her hydria (water jug) to search for water. On her way she was accosted by a Satyr, and when she cried out for help she attracted the attention of Poseidon who pursued her himself. In one version of the story the god won her over as his consort and presented to her the spring of Lerna by striking the rock with his trident. In another version, the god changed her into the spring itself.[1]

The myth, which was viewed in antiquity as the explanation for the origin of the spring of Lerna, deals with a theme familiar from the stories of Persephone and Iphigenia: the young maiden sacrificed to a god for the survival of the community (see **Persephone and Demeter** and **Iphigenia**). The prominence of the hydria accentuates the sexual overtones (see **Women as Containers**). Amymone's father wishes her to fill her hydria, which Poseidon is most eager to do in the form of both semen and water from the Lerna spring. The myth also conforms to the pattern of a god mating with a mortal woman, another example of which is the story of Danae (see **Danae**). Because these myths, like their opposites that involved the pursuit of a mortal man by a goddess, pair an overpowering divinity with a helpless mortal, it has been argued that the stories functioned for both men and women as legitimated fantasies of overwhelming or being overwhelmed (see **Eos and Kephalos**, **Circe**, and no. 61).[2]

To Classical vase-painters the story was appealing because it could be presented as a pursuit, with a fleeing maiden almost within the grasp of a lunging, armed male (see **Pursuit Scenes**). The trident that is the familiar emblem of Poseidon was a weapon used in the hunt of the tunnyfish, the most violent form of fishing. In scenes where the trident is poised to penetrate Amymone, the action suggests both the creation of the spring and sexual intercourse. The scenes are not straightforward renderings of male aggression, however, because painters often injected unambiguous indications that Amymone is responsive and willing. She extends her arm out to Poseidon (no. 111), fingers her garment in the unveiling gesture of the bride (no. 113), and turns the mouth of her hydria suggestively toward him (no. 112, see **The Wedding**). She even turns back to look into Poseidon's eyes, therewith applying the full erotic wattage of her gaze (nos.111-113, see **Gesture and Gaze**). One vase-painter takes the suggestiveness even further, dispensing altogether with the aggressive posture of the trident (no. 114). Although the surviving literary sources for this myth do not explicitly state that Amymone was a willing lover, the traditions surrounding Danae, as well as other mortal maidens with divine pursuers, confirm that some encounters were envisioned by their ancient commentators to be as much mutual arousal as rape (see

Danae). The theme of the sexually responsive virgin is also familiar from the myth of Persephone, the story of Atalanta, and the foundation myth of the ritual of the Little Bears, and it is interesting to note that vases depicting Amymone were found at Brauron (see **Atalanta** and **Little Bears**).[3] In Amymone's case, the sexual connotations of the water and the hydria invite a rationalization for the seduction; in succumbing to Poseidon, Amymone was, in fact, obtaining the water that King Danaos had requested.

The presentation of Amymone's pursuit as seduction over rape eloquently speaks to the manner by which the Greek bride could resolve her emotional dilemma. By social custom a bride was handed over to a groom whom she may not even have met and thus with whom a sexual union was a source of great apprehension. A fantasy of mutual seduction enabled the trauma to be palatable. Vase-painters of the later fifth century particularly respond to this female point of view in their depictions of Amymone's rapprochement with Poseidon, where she is portrayed as a willing bride and where her hydria appears to function as a vessel for her bridal bath (nos. 115-116). This extreme sympathy with the female is in keeping with a general tone in Late Classical vase-painting and has been associated with the renewed appreciation for private over public life, and possibly also with the larger female population in Athens as a result of male deaths in the plague and the Peloponnesian War.

Amymone and her hydria acquire an added dimension of meaning when one considers her lineage. Amymone's sisters, known as the Danaids, were angry that they were compelled to marry their cousins, and so on their wedding night each bride murdered her husband in her bridal bed. As punishment in the Underworld, each sister was compelled in perpetuity to fill with water a vessel that had a hole in the bottom of it. The plight must have been a common one in ancient Greece where filling the water hydria was a woman's task and where many a woman must have compared herself to a Danaid tormented in the Underworld. Giulia Sissa has pointed out that the punishment of the sisters was an apt one, because hydriae that can never be filled up are an appropriate metaphor for the bodies of the Danaids, who resisted intercourse and pregnancy.[4] By contrast, Amymone's intact hydria signifies to Poseidon her sexual availability, and, in scenes where the jug is employed for the bridal bath, the vessel is a harbinger of the pregnancy that would soon produce the Argive hero Nauplion. A tetralogy by Aischylos on the subject of Danaos and his daughters included a satyr play entitled *Amymone*.[5] Because some Classical vase paintings include a Satyr, most scholars agree that the Aischylean satyr play was a major inspiration for this myth's popularity in Classical vase-painting. Aischylos may even have introduced the Satyr into the story.

1. Hesiod frag. 122-129 MW; Euripides, *Phoenician Women* 185-89; Pherekydes, frag. 3F4 *FGrHist*; Apollodoros, *Bibliotheke* 2.1.4-5; Hyginus, *Fabulae* 169, 169a; Pausanius 2.38.2. See Gantz (1993), 204-9; *LIMC* I (1981) s.v. Amymone; A. Greifenhagen, *CVA* Bonn, Akademisches Kunstmuseum 1 (Germany 1) 36; F. Brommer, "Amymone," *AM* 63-64 (1938-39) 173.

   Water is associated with a woman's sexuality. In Homer, bathing in a river was a symbolic way of losing one's virginity (*Iliad* 10.3-8) and in a festival at Kanathos near Nauplion, the statue of Hera was washed in order to recover her virginity (see Burkert [1985] 131ff).

2. Stehle (1990) 88-125.

3. Burn (1987) 52; E. Simon, *LIMC* I (1981) 743, nos. 1 and 2, pl. 597 (s.v. Amymone).

4. Sissa (1990) 153, 162, 171. Keuls (1974) believes that the Danaids were associated with this punishment in Aischylos' *Danaides* and that the punishment was borrowed from Orphic-Dionysian symbolism (Plato, *Republic* 303 d-e) as the lot either of the uninitiated or part of the process of initiation. See 6, 13, 19, 26, 39, 48-50. See also Gantz (1993) 207.

5. Aischylos' tetralogy consisted of three dramas: *Hiketides*, *Aigyptoi*, and *Danaides*, and a satyr play, *Amymone*. The date is not known, but is earlier than the *Persians* of 472.

LEKYTHOS WITH AMYMONE AND POSEIDON

ca. 475
by the Dresden Painter
Zurich, Mr. Hansjürg and Mrs. Franziska Saager

Attic, from Sicily
Clay
H 29 cm.

Publications: *ARV²* 656.15; *Add²* 277; *Münzen und Medaillen Auktion* 11 (1953) 38, no. 340, pl. 22 (A. Brückner); K. Schefold, *Meisterwerke griechischer Kunst* (Basel 1960) 51, 204, no. 223; Kurtz (1975) 85 n. 4, 95, 208, pl. 27.6; Kaempf-Dimitriadou (1979) 26, 98 no. 275; *LIMC* I (1981) 744, no. 17 (s.v. Amymone); Schefold (1981) 253, 373, figs. 360-61; Gantz (1993) 207-208.

Neck broken and repaired, otherwise intact. On the neck is a pattern of lotus and palmette. Above and below the scene is a band of meander.

Poseidon steps forward, his left leg advanced, his torso and head in right profile. He wears a long sleeved garment that has a dotted border around the lower edge. On top of it is a mantle that is fastened on his left shoulder, with the folds covering his torso and thighs. Three long, spiraling ringlets fall forward over his shoulders; the rest of his hair is arranged in wavy locks that extend to his nape. He has a long beard and he gazes straight ahead at Amymone, toward whom his left arm, fingers outstretched, is extended. His right hand holds the shaft of a trident, the central tine of which is about to enter Amymone's right breast.

Amymone moves to her left, her torso frontal with her right breast in left profile. Her right foot is frontal and her head is in left profile. Her right arm is extended horizontally from her shoulder, with the palm up and the fingers open; the index finger barely touches the underside of Poseidon's left forearm. Her left hand clasps the handle of a hydria. She wears a chiton beneath a hima-

111

tion that is fastened on the left shoulder with the folds covering her torso and thighs; the ends of the garment fly out behind her buttocks. Her hair falls in spherical clumps across her hairline and in front of her left ear; the ends are gathered at the nape in a rectangular clasp. She also wears a diadem surmounted by five leaves. She gazes behind her toward Poseidon.

The trident is positioned such that the central tine is about to penetrate Amymone's right nipple (see **Amymone and Poseidon**). To accentuate the violence of the plunging weapon, the artist has clearly indicated her right breast, the only part of her torso that he has delineated. Because a trident was a weapon used to harpoon tunnyfish, its use in this scene presents Amymone as the quarry of a hunt, a prey to be impaled (see **Pursuit Scenes**). The alignment of hunting with courtship was a well known metaphor, and, although a woman was usually the object of the hunt, a man could also be the prey of a woman (see **Eos and Kephalos**).

The thrust of Poseidon's trident refers to the tradition that he created a spring for Amymone by striking a rock. The Dresden Painter has not hesitated to correlate Amymone with that rock, and the result is a violent sexual image. Its tone is offset by the gesture of their arms. Amymone's outstretched arm, with upraised palm and open fingers, is the gesture by which a victim begs for mercy, usually by extending the arm to the opponent's chin, where her hand and gaze are clearly directed. Poseidon's outstretched arm and hand, by contrast, attempt to grasp Amymone, but his gracefully curled fingers sound a softer note, such that his gesture seems lees one of rapacity than of longing.

The implication in the myth that life-giving water is derived from a female source finds a counterpart in the identity of Demeter as the origin of earth's life-sustaining vegetation (see **Persephone and Demeter**). Page Dubois has shown that this way of thinking had extremely early origins and was subsequently superseded in Greek thought by a shift of emphasis onto the male initiative in releasing those resources.[1] The presentation of Poseidon as the agent of the water's release is consistent with the concept that man tills an earth that does not give forth spontaneously. The same image underlies the language of the Classical wedding ritual, whereby the bride's father officially informs the groom that the woman is given over for the "ploughing" of children (see **The Wedding**).

Amymone's full jaw as well as the clumsy foreshortening of her right foot indicate a date in the second quarter of the century. Her rectangular hair clasp is often worn by Artemis (nos.90, 97).

111 Detail

1. DuBois (1988) 49, 57, 59, 68, 147.

112

KALYX KRATER
WITH POSEIDON AND AMYMONE

455-450
by the Achilles Painter
St. Petersburg, The State Hermitage Museum,
inv. no. Б 191 (St. 1535, B 767)

Attic
Clay
H 25.7 cm., Diam 26 cm.

Publications: *ARV*² 991.57 and 1677; *Para* 516; *Add*² 311; K. Schauenberg, "Göttergeliebte auf unteritalischen vasen," *Antike und Abendland* 10 (1961) 84 n. 75, fig. 22; A. Peredolskaja, *Krasnofigurinye attischeskie vazy* (Leningrad 1967) 165-66, no. 189, pl. 130.36.1,3; Kaempf-Dimitriadou (1979) 99, no. 288; *LIMC* I (1981) 744, no. 18, pl. 599 (s.v. Amymone).

Reassembled from several pieces with parts of background restored. Handles reattached.

On Side B a young woman muffled in her mantle approaches a standing man with a walking stick. Above the figures on Side A is an undulating ribbon pattern with dotted triangles in the interstices; beneath the scene two meanders alternate with a cross square.

Amymone flees Poseidon, her body almost frontal, her right leg advanced with the knee bent, her left leg behind her with the heel raised. Her right elbow is bent, and the palm of her right hand is open, the fingers extended. Her left hand holds at her left side the handle of a hydria, the mouth of which is turned toward Poseidon. She wears a chiton, whose folds flare above her left ankle as she hurries away. Her mantle is brought over her right shoulder and upper arm, with the ends brought diagonally across the torso; so closely does one of the scalloped edges echo the curve of her left breast that the mantle appears to reveal to contour of her right breast. Amymone's long hair falls down below her nape, and the locks at her ears are drawn up beneath a diadem, from which

112 Side B

112 Side A

four leaves rise vertically. Her head is in right profile, and she gazes back directly into Poseidon's face.

He follows right behind her, turned in three-quarter left profile. His pose echoes hers, with the left leg advanced and the knee bent, his right leg behind him, with the heel raised. The musculature of his torso is indicated by dilute lines, with some markings that may be for chest hair. His right arm is extended horizontally toward Amymone; his left hand at his left hip holds horizontally the shaft of a trident. His mantle frames his back with the ends brought forward over both shoulders. He has a long beard, and his hair is long, with four curly ringlets falling forward over his shoulders. On his head is a diadem that is thinner than that of Amymone, but from which four identical leaves also rise vertically.

The composition is simple and dramatic. The center of the field is occupied by the trident, which is almost in contact with Amymone's left forearm (see **Amymone and Poseidon**). The ferocity of its tines lends added aggressiveness to Poseidon's outstretched right arm which forms a parallel line just above it. Amymone's right hand is upraised in alarm, as she looks back at the god, whose abundant hair and beard befit his watery world and recall the hairiness of Gaia, who inhabits a similar realm beneath the earth's surface (see **Erichthonios**).

Certain details in this scene of pursuit enrich its meaning (see **Pursuit Scenes**). Amymone's direct gaze back into Poseidon's face indicates her responsiveness to his advance (see nos.111, 113, **Gesture and Gaze**). Moreover, the diadems worn by both figures call to mind the bridegroom's wreath and the bride's diadem (see **The Wedding**). Especially noteworthy is the way the open mouth of the hydria is turned back toward Poseidon, in defiance of conventional laws of motion. The metaphor of a container, and especially a hydria, for a woman's body, calls to mind the fate of Amymone's sisters, who, in punishment for killing their husbands and rejecting married life, were destined to fill perpetually their hydriae in the Underworld (see **Women as Containers**). It appears that Amymone intends that no such fate should befall her.

Still another subtle reference can be found in the figure of Poseidon, whose pose is almost a mirror reversal of the famous statue of Aristogeiton, which was created ca. 477-476. The statue commemorated one of the heroes who killed the tyrants of Athens, preparing the way for Athenian democracy. The motif, with its heroic connotations, became a popular one in vase-painting, and its reuse here was probably intended both to underscore the god's munificence in providing the spring of Lerna and to introduce a note of irony into Poseidon's noble "rescue" of Amymone from the Satyr's pursuits.

The distinctive features of the Aristogeiton pose are the mantle draped over the extended arm and the weapon (a sword) held in the other, lowered arm. On the statue of Aristogeiton the lowered hand is the right one, and, because Poseidon is usually right-handed, the position of the trident in his left hand is puzzling. The reference to the Aristogeiton pose on the lekythos in New York (no.113) demonstrates that, even if an extant artistic tradition positioned Poseidon on the viewer's right, the artist could still have depicted the attacking arm as the right one. Perhaps the intent was to emphasize the trident less as a weapon than as a symbol of the spring of water Poseidon would create for Amymone by striking a rock with his trident. Christiane Sourvinou-Inwood has pointed out that in another type of erotic pursuit scene a youth does not hold his spears upraised for attack, but at his side, with the point directed toward the woman's genitals. Because spears held in this way are less effective as a lethal weapon, the gesture appears to be a purely symbolic one of erotic aggression.[1]

The Achilles Painter is best known for his white-ground lekythoi, where the simple, eloquent compositions he preferred were enhanced by both the medium and the funerary overtones of the vases (nos. 12, 14, and 53). Working in red-figure, the painter was no less elegant in the spareness of his decorative patterns and figural scenes. The succinctness of this composition, with the telling hydria, trident, and arm of Poseidon spotlighted in the center, demonstrates clearly why this artist is viewed as one of the most quintessentially Classical of all Greek vase-painters.

---

1. Sourvinou-Inwood (1987) 131-53.

113

LEKYTHOS
WITH AMYMONE AND POSEIDON

ca. 430-430
by the Phiale Painter
New York, Metropolitan Museum of Art,
Rogers Fund, 1917, inv. no. 17.230.35

Attic, "from Ancona"
Clay
H 45.1 cm., Diam 13.6 cm.

Publications: *ARV²* 1020.100; *Add²* 316; G.M.A. Richter, "Red-Figured Athenian Vases Recently Acquired by the Metropolitan Museum of Art," *AJA* 27 (1923) 283-84, figs. 19-20; Richter and Hall (1936) 154-5, no. 122, pl. 122, 176; Richter, *Attic Red-Figured Vases: A Survey*, rev. ed. (New Haven 1958) 122, fig. 91; H. Walter, *Vom Sinnwandel griechischer Mythen* (Waldsassen/Bayern 1959) 36, fig. 28; Walter, *Griechische Götter* (Munich 1971) 127, fig. 112; Kaempf-Dimitriadou (1979) 27, 99-100, no. 293; *LIMC* I (1981) 744, no. 21 (s.v. Amymone); Keuls (1983a) 214, fig. 14.9; Keuls (1985a) 240, 242, fig. 216; Oakley (1990) 28, 82, no. 100, pl. 79.

Mouth repaired. On the neck is a band of eggs; on the shoulder are three palmettes with scrolls and dots. Above the figural scene is a band of three meanders, alternating right and left, with a cross square; beneath the scene is a band of meander (right). Red for Amymone's wreath and for the stem and berries of Poseidon's wreath.

113 (See also detail, p. 14)

Poseidon strides forward, his right hand holding the trident. His left leg is extended well in front of his right. He is seen from behind and is nude except for his mantle, which is draped over his left shoulder and arm, concealing his left hand. He wears a laurel wreath over his wavy hair, which extends to his nape. Amymone moves away from him in three-quarter left profile, turning her head back in right profile to gaze into his eyes. The toes of her left foot rest on the ground behind her. She wears a peplos that has an overfold, edged with a stripe, to her waist; across her lower hem is a wide black band from which rise a row of short, vertical lines. Her right hand holds the handle of her hydria by her side; the fingers of her left hand clasp the folds of her peplos above her left shoulder. Her long hair is gathered back at the nape, with a spiral ringlet falling forward over her right shoulder. She also wears a pendant earring, a pendant necklace, and a wreath.

Poseidon rushes after Amymone, holding aloft his trident, which was a weapon used to harpoon the tunnyfish (see **Amymone and Poseidon**). The legs of both figures are widespread, and the folds of Amymone's peplos billow out behind her left ankle and left hip. Poseidon has almost overtaken her, his left leg passing behind her left calf, and the folds of his mantle swing out to bridge the distance between them. His completely draped left hand mitigates the intimacy of their proximity and partially distances her from his nudity. The tines of his trident are almost in contact with Amymone's left arm.

Although Amymone is running away, her gaze and gesture undermine the sincerity of her resistance. She turns her head completely around to meet Poseidon's glance, in the manner in which bride and groom looked at each other at the moment of the bride's unveiling, an expression of the Greek belief that the meeting of glances was the moment of greatest mutual attraction and erotic arousal (see **The Wedding** and **Gesture and Gaze**). Amymone confirms the parallel with wedding ritual by lifting the folds of her garment in the traditional gesture of the *anakalypsis*, when the bride signals her acceptance of, and submission to, her husband by participating in her own unveiling. The bridal wreaths that Poseidon and Amymone wear further underscore their analogy to a bride and groom. As in other scenes of pursuit, Poseidon's advance on Amymone is here a metaphor for courtship that would culminate, if not precisely in marriage, then in sexual consortium (see **Pursuit Scenes**).

Poseidon's threatening pose is related to the water Amymone sought, because ancient sources tell us that the god created a spring for Amymone by striking the rock with his trident. By introducing that tradition into the pursuit scene, the Phiale Painter has drastically heightened its violence and intensified the erotic connotations of the hunt. The close proximity of the tines to Amymone's arm enhance the sexual tension, as do Amymone's gesture and gaze, which communicate her willingness to be seduced. Other vase-painters explicitly depict the weapon's penetration (no. 111).

The Phiale Painter, also represented here by nos. 66, 78, and 125, is one of the finest Attic vase-painters working in the middle of the fifth century. Distinguished by graceful drawing, delicate gestures, and meaningful glances, the painter is especially comfortable in the world of women, and he consistently renders his subjects with dignity and grandeur.

114

PELIKE
WITH POSEIDON AND AMYMONE

ca. 450
by the Painter of the Birth of Athena
Rome, Museo Nazionale di Villa Giulia, inv. no. 20846

Attic, "from the tomba dei Vasi Greci, Cerveteri"
Clay
H 45 cm., Diam 33 cm.

Publications: *ARV*² 494.2; *Add*² 250; G. Ricci, *Monumenti Antichi* 42 (1955) 288-94, pl. 5, figs. 47a, 48b; Kaempf-Dimitriadou (1979) 24, 27, 95 no. 234, 99 no. 281, pl. 18.6-7; *LIMC* I (1981) 744, no. 20a (s.v. Amymone); *LIMC* II (1984) 131, no. 1381a, pl. 136 (s.v. Aphrodite).

Mended from many pieces with small restorations in the area of the hydria, of the skirt of the woman in front of Amymone, and in the torso and legs of the standing man at the far edge. Above the scenes is a band of slanting addorsed palmettes; beneath is a band of two meanders alternating with a cross square.

On Side B a bearded male stretches out his right hand to a maiden's genitals. She reaches out her arm, seemingly in protest, but does not make contact with his arm. Her right elbow is bent and her hand is uplifted, and she gazes directly back at him. Two flanking women move away in agitation, and a standing man raises his hand in exclamation.

On Side A Amymone moves to her left, with her weight on her advanced left leg. Her left arm holds the handle of her hydria, and her right arm is bent at the elbow with the hand in front of her breasts, the thumb raised, the fingers extended. Her head is turned back in left profile and is inclined downward, and she gazes in the direction of Poseidon's waist. Her hair is bound up with ribbons, their curly ends falling about her face. She wears a girded peplos, bracelets on both wrists, and is barefoot.

Poseidon strides beside her, seen in three-quarter right profile, with his weight on his advanced left leg. He is nude except for folds of his mantle that

114 Side A

114 Side B

fall forward over his left shoulder, the ends framing his torso and left leg. His left arm passes behind Amymone's back and his hand clasps her left shoulder, his fingers almost entirely resting on the folds of her peplos. His lowered right hand holds the handle of his trident, which rests lightly in his curled fingers, with his thumb steadying the top of the shaft. He has a beard and mustache and wears a leafy crown over hair that is bunched at the back of his head, with a long lock falling over his chest. He stares directly at Amymone. His chest is covered with tufts of hair, rendered as concentric circles. More tufts cover his abdomen, and a fuzzy line extends from his navel to his genitals. His pubic hair is also indicated.

Behind Poseidon Eros flies toward Poseidon, both arms outstretched. Behind Eros stands a woman, whose right hand fingers the folds of her garment by her thigh, while the fingers of her left hand hold a flower by her shoulder. In front of Amymone a woman moves away with both hands uplifted in agitation, as she gazes directly behind her at Amymone and Poseidon. Standing at the far edge is a bearded man in left profile, his right hand steadying a scepter that is placed vertically on the ground in front of him.

Unlike the previous vases, here Amymone is not in danger of being struck by the trident, and thus any reference to the forthcoming spring of water is of secondary focus (see **Amymone and Poseidon**). The accent here is on sexuality, and the painter suggests that Amymone's resistance is now changing to acquiescence. Particularly striking are her exaggeratedly inclined head and gaze. This is not the tilted head of *aidos*, or modesty, but sheer wonderment at Poseidon's masculinity, which the painter has rendered as exuberant hairiness, a feature normally characterizing the uncouth or the bestial, such as the Papposilenos, the elderly male who was half-horse or half-goat (see **Aidos** and **Sophrosyne**). In this scene the emphasis on the body hair must be for shock value, and the strategy seems to have been quite successful with Amymone. Her open, but not raised, right hand communicates a fullness of emotion; its stillness contrasts with the raised hands of the woman beside Amymone, whose gesture is the conventional one of fear and agitation.

The tension between Poseidon and Amymone that the painter has suggested by means of her gaze and gesture is further developed in the rest of their forms. Poseidon's trident and left foot aggressively invade Amymone's space, but her right elbow is protected from direct contact with his shoulder by the folds of his mantle which cover his arm. Moreover, his left hand rests on her peplos folds, not on the flesh itself. The painter has skillfully captured the moment when the seduction is not yet complete, although the denouement is abundantly clear to both the participants and the viewer. Amymone is about to capitulate, even though her female companion is shocked, and even though Amymone is well aware that her father would disapprove. His conservative patriarchal values are well communicated by the verticality of his scepter and posture at the far side of the scene.

So eager was this painter to suggest the intensity and mutuality of the erotic attraction between Poseidon and Amymone that he inserted into the scene elements that do not appear in the almost identical representation found on another pelike from the same tomb.[1] Present on this pelike and not on its counterpart is Eros, who will be a familiar presence in wedding scenes of the second half of the century where he signifies a mutual attraction between bride and groom (see **The Wedding**). A second difference is the position here of Poseidon's left hand on Amymone's shoulder. On the other vase the figures are not physically linked and the intimacy is, consequently, less marked. A final point of contrast between the two vases is the folds of Amymone's garment, which lie quietly around her ankles to indicate that she is no longer running. By contrast, on the other vase, the skirt blows back behind her ankles to signify that she is resisting with flight. All three modifications from the mate, which was probably the earlier vase, function here to intensify the sexual impulses drawing Poseidon and Amymone together.

The same theme of seduction is addressed on Side B. Here the pursuit is still in progress, although the linked gazes and the maiden's ineffectual gesture tell us that her resistance is half-hearted and will be short-lived.

1. *LIMC* I (1981) 744, no. 20,b (s.v. Amymone).

115

SQUAT LEKYTHOS WITH AMYMONE AND POSEIDON

ca. 400
in the manner of the Meidias Painter
New Haven, Yale University Art Gallery,
Gift of Rebecca Darlington Stoddard, inv. no. 1913.152

Attic
Clay
Restored H 20.3 cm., Diam 12 cm.

Publications: *ARV²* 1325.53; *Add²* 364; P. Baur, *Catalogue of the Rebecca Darlington Stoddard Collection of Greek and Italian Vases in Yale University* (New Haven 1922) 102-103, no. 152, pl. 11; Burke and Pollitt (1975) 75-76, no. 61; Kaempf-Dimitriadou (1979) 29, 56, 101, no. 300, pl. 20.3-4; *LIMC* I (1981) 747 no. 68, pl. 604 (s.v. Amymone); Burn (1987) 50-52, 112 no. MM83; S. Matheson, *Greek Vases: A Guide to the Yale Collection* New Haven 1988) 36-37.

Assembled from many pieces with large areas missing from scene. Mouth and handle restored. Band of tongues around the neck. On the shoulder is a chain of palmettes above a reserve line. Beneath the scene is an egg pattern. Below the handle is a vertical group of palmette and acanthus ornament on volutes, flanked by tendrils with spirals, buds, and a pair of enclosed palmettes. White on Amymone's chiton. Relief, once gilded, for Poseidon's wreath and for the berries on the laurel bushes.

On rocky terrain Poseidon stands frontally, his left leg relaxed. His left hand rests on his left hip; his upraised right hand supports vertically the shaft of his

Behind the bushes is a woman seated on a rock and turned in three-quarter left profile, her head turned back in right profile. She wears a belted chiton and a himation that bears a cross pattern and that is draped over her legs. The fingers of her right hand lift folds of her chiton above her right shoulder; her lowered left hand holds the tip of her scepter, which is pointed downward. Her hair is drawn up at the back of the crown into a bun tied with a ribbon. She also wears a necklace and sandals. In front of her left thigh is a chest, decorated with spirals, and in front of her feet is a laurel bush.

Poseidon stands next to the seated Amymone while Aphrodite and Poseidon's wife, Amphitrite, look on. The pursuit long past, Amymone no longer resists, but sits peacefully at the side of the god. He gazes at her as he stands confidently, his trident aggressively positioned so close to her that part of the shaft disappears behind her legs. Both the hydria and her seated position, which looks forward to fourth century and Hellenistic renderings of Nymphs beside their springs, suggest that she is here seated beside the spring Poseidon created for her (see **Amymone and Poseidon**).

The rocky landscape acquires the amorous overtones of an idyllic garden with the presence of Aphrodite, who is seated, and the hare, which was a frequent gift among lovers. There is, in fact, much in the scene that suggests a wedding, including the chest, which was a traditional wedding gift (see **Women as Containers** and **The Wedding**). To the ancient viewer, Amymone's hydria would also have called to mind the custom by which the bride bathed in spring water before the wedding. That we should not take the scene too literally as a wedding is indicated by the presence of Poseidon's wife Amphitrite, who is, however, in an amicable mood. She stands behind Poseidon and fingers her garment in the gesture of the *anakalypteria*, or unveiling, whereby a bride unveils herself to her husband as an expression of sexual submission to him. The gesture was particularly associated with Hera, the wife of Zeus, and so its inclusion here in the figures of both Amphitrite and Aphrodite establishes a conciliatory atmosphere. The lekythos may, in fact, have been a wedding gift, with the scene intended as a celebration of the happy denouement of courtship. No Athenian bride would have been dismayed by the presence of both wife and mistress, for no Athenian husband allowed marriage to curtail his sexual adventures; Demosthenes declares that a man seeks a wife to look after his home and children, a concubine for the care of his body, and a mistress for his pleasure (see **Women and Men**).[1]

The artist painted in the circle of the Meidias Painter, with whom he shared a fondness for pretty scenes devoid of action and intense feeling. Fabric is richly ornamented, transparent, and clings closely to the breasts. Figures are depicted at different levels to suggest a rocky terrain, which is enlivened by plants, and interaction is primarily through charged glances. The figure of Poseidon is ultimately based on a statuary prototype.

1. Demosthenes 59.22.

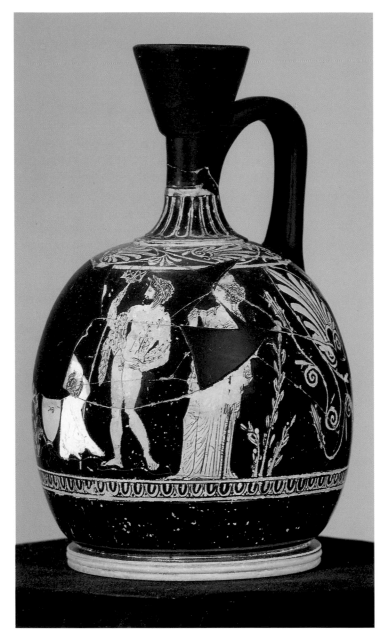

115

trident. He is nude except for his mantle, which is decorated with crosses and which passes behind his back and is brought around his torso to pass over his upper arms; one end is brought forward over his left shoulder, and the other end falls below his right elbow. He is bearded and wears a laurel wreath.

To his left and standing in the foreground is a woman who is seen in left profile, her right knee relaxed. She wears a chiton beneath a himation, which is fastened on her right shoulder; the spiral border across its hem is visible behind her left hip. Above her right shoulder the fingers of her left hand lift the edge of the mantle. Her head is in left profile, and she wears a diadem. Behind her is a laurel bush.

On the other side of Poseidon are the draped legs of a female seated in right profile, her ankles crossed. The shaft of Poseidon's trident passes behind her legs, with the butt visible beneath her feet. To her right is a hydria on the raised rocky terrain. In her lap is a tyle (a circular pad used by women when carrying a load on the head). Behind her are two laurel bushes and a hare.

HYDRIA
WITH POSEIDON AND AMYMONE

ca. 400
by the Meleager Painter
New York, Metropolitan Museum of Art,
Fletcher Fund, 1956, inv. no. 56.171.56

Attic, "from near Naples"
Clay
H 43.6 cm.

Publications: *ARV²* 1412.46 and 1693; *Add²* 374; M. Milne, "Three Attic Red-Figured Vases in New York," *AJA* 66 (1962) 306, pl. 82.5; R. Folsom, *Attic Red-Figured Pottery* (Park Ridge 1976) pl. 59; A.D. Trendall, "Poseidon and Amymone on an Apulian Pelike," *Festschrift für Frank Brommer* (Mainz 1977) 282 n. 4; *LIMC* I (1981) 747, no. 60, pl. 603 (s.v. Amymone); Schefold (1981) 255, fig. 365.

Around the lip is a tongue pattern. Around the neck is a lotus and palmette pattern above tendrils. Beneath the scene on Side A is a band of four meanders alternating with a checker square.

In the center of the composition are Poseidon, seated on his mantle, and Amymone, standing beside her hydria. Poseidon is turned in three-quarter right profile, and his left hand steadies his scepter or staff; his right hand is at his waist. He wears a sleeveless tunic that is richly ornamented and bears along its lower border a band of sea animals. He also wears elaborate boots. His head is in right profile and he wears a diadem upon curly locks extending down his neck. He gazes across to Amymone who turns toward him, her left leg relaxed. She wears a peplos that bears decorative patterns similar to those on Poseidon's garment; bands of sea creatures decorate neckline and hem. Her mantle is draped across her hips and around her left elbow, which rests upon the mouth of her hydria. Her right hand is at her side. Between the couple is the nude winged form of Eros, who is presented as a young boy. He stands on Poseidon's left knee, the relaxed left leg supported only by his toes, which rest on Poseidon's thigh. Eros extends his left arm behind Amymone's right shoulder, and his right arm toward her neckline. His head is in right profile, with curly hair, and he gazes at her.

Beneath these figures is a nude, wreathed Satyr who crawls forward with his left knee advanced, his right hand supporting his body. Over his curly hair he wears a diadem from which several leaves rise vertically. The Satyr's left hand clasps the right knee of a woman who is seated before him, wearing a peplos with a band of sea creatures across the neckline; she, in turn, gazes behind her at a Satyr who darts away to his left, while gazing back at Poseidon and Amymone. Behind the first Satyr is a standing woman who turns to her right while gazing up and back at Poseidon and Amymone. She is dressed identically to her counterpart beside the Satyr, and she holds a taenia in her lowered left hand. Approaching her is a Satyr who steps forward with his left foot uplifted, his left forearm raised with the fingers extended. He is nude except for an animal skin that is draped over his left shoulder. He also wears a wreath decorated with leaves.

Above and behind Poseidon is another Satyr beside Aphrodite, who is turned three-quarters to her right and wears an elaborately embroidered chiton and himation; the figure of Eros is beside her. Above Poseidon and Amymone is a Satyr who emerges from behind a rocky outcropping. Behind and above Amymone is Dionysos, who is seated three-quarters to his left upon his mantle and wears an elaborately decorated tunic and boots. Beside him are a woman and Eros.

Poseidon's vigorous pursuit of Amymone is long past, and the couple is now practically reconciled (see **Amymone and Poseidon**). They relax in the presence of Eros, who is the most animated figure in the group. Enjoying an even greater participation in the scene than he was accorded in depictions of wedding ritual, he thrusts his head close to Amymone's (see **The Wedding**). The energy he devotes to his task suggests that she is not as yet wholly committed to the relationship, and that aloofness is reinforced by the fact that she is standing whereas Poseidon is seated; we are reminded of her lesser, and helpless, status as a mortal. Despite any misgivings on her part, however, the couple seems to be officially linked, and, even if Poseidon's previous commitment to Amphitrite precludes marriage, the two figures are bedecked as bride and groom. Amymone's presentation as a bride lends the hydria connotations of a vessel for the wedding bath, and, indeed, the hydria on which the scene was painted was possibly a wedding gift.

The four Satyrs in the scene undoubtedly refer to the lost Satyr play of Aischylos, in which Amymone was set upon by a Satyr as she searched for water. The maidens with the Satyrs must be woodland Nymphs, whose invariable success in attracting the Satyrs' attentions was a traditional theme in Greek vase-painting. The group's presence implies that Poseidon's pursuit of Amymone was nothing more than harmless, spirited antics, and that any uncomfortable moments in the episode were inconsequential, if not already forgotten.

We should not be surprised that a fourteen-year-old Athenian bride who had been raised in a highly protected family setting would be delighted by a wedding gift that portrayed an already married god in a contented liaison with a maiden whom he had recently terrorized by pursuing like an animal (see **Pursuit Scenes** and **Women as Animals**). The god, moreover, is characterized as of one mind with his attendants, the lustful Satyrs renowned for their unbridled licentiousness. We must remember that on her wedding day an Athenian bride had never been courted, and, indeed, had never had much contact with men at all. It is not surprising that she would be highly receptive to any romantic fantasy that emphasized her desirability.

As leader of the Satyrs, Dionysos can claim a rightful place in this gathering, and since the predominant theme of the scene is coupling we can surely identify as Ariadne the woman seated beside Dionysos. The erotic currents underlying the interaction of Poseidon and Amymone, the Satyrs and Nymphs, and even Dionysos and Ariadne, call for the presence of Aphrodite, who surveys the assemblage accompanied by yet another figure of Eros.

The scene bears many of the characteristics of late fifth-century vase-painting. Figures are disposed over a number of levels and are presented as prettily posed, self-contained individuals who rarely interact with their neighbors beyond a dramatic turn of their heads. Garments are ornately decorated, often bearing, as with the bands of sea creatures, embroidered motifs appropriate to the subject of the scene. Eros, though still a boy, is depicted as younger than

116

116 Detail

116 Detail

he was depicted in earlier decades, and he has proliferated, now appearing several times within a single scene. The easy intimacy of his stance contrasts with the more understated familiarity that he displayed a few decades before (see no. 17). Typical also are the poses and gestures of relaxation. The leaning elbow is a common motif, although here, in contrast to the figure of Aphrodite on the earlier relief (no. 17), Amymone's elbow bears little of her weight

and is predominantly a gesture evocative of leisure and her close association with her hydria (see **Gesture and Gaze**). The general mood is one of lightness and idyllic romance. We sense that in the late fifth century, as the bride romanticized her bridegroom, the families joined by her marriage regarded the wedding festivities as a welcome release from the pressing political and economic concerns that surrounded them.

ATALANTA

By the fifth century two once independent traditions about Atalanta had converged.[1] According to the mythical version from Arcadia, the baby Atalanta had been abandoned in the wilderness, as was the custom with unwanted baby girls. There she was discovered by bears, who raised her and taught her how to hunt. In both the Arcadian and the Boeotian traditions Atalanta grew to adulthood as a superb hunter, so fond of her freedom that she refused to marry. In the Boeotian version we learn that she finally conceded, but agreed to marry only the man who could defeat her in a footrace, with death the punishment for the unsuccessful suitor. Many suitors did lose their lives in the attempt, but one day Hippomenes (or Melanion) presented himself for the race, concealing golden apples that had been given him by Aphrodite. When the race began and Atalanta quickly outsped her opponent, he rolled out first one, then another, and finally, a third golden apple. Each time Atalanta leaned over to pick up an apple, she lost her lead, and when she stooped down to grasp the third apple, Hippomenes raced by her to the finish line and therewith won her as his bride.

The pair did not live happily ever after. According to one tradition, the couple made love in a sanctuary, thereby violating the sacred space and angering the gods. As punishment, Atalanta and Hippomenes were transformed into lions and returned to the wilderness to live. The punishment had an added dimension, because the Greeks believed that lions did not mate with other lions, but only with leopards. Thus Atalanta and her husband were obliged henceforth to live a celibate life.

The role of a bear as Atalanta's foster mother is one of numerous mythical instances in which females are closely identified with, and even transformed into and from bears (see **Bears**). The implication is that Atalanta grows up to be more bear than girl. Not surprisingly, Atalanta's human relatives pressure marriage upon her as a form

of socialization, an echo of the culture's conception of marriage as a taming mechanism for a maturing young woman (see **The Wedding**).

Atalanta's footrace has obvious parallels with the ritual of the Little Bears at Brauron (see **Little Bears**). There, other "untamed" girls, playing the part of bears, took part in a race or chase as part of their preparation for marriage. Footraces were also associated with marriage both in the myth of the Danaids and in the cult of Hera at Olympia, and it is usually assumed that this emphasis upon physical robustness was prompted by concern over the impending rigors of childbirth.[2]

Atalanta's footrace is an ironic variant upon the metaphor of courtship as the pursuit of an animal quarry (see **Pursuit Scenes**). Atalanta the hunter is here pursued as the prey. Moreover, the use of a lure is so well attested in ancient texts on hunting that the apples clearly function as a form of the bait that was regularly used to attract a wild animal.[3] The choice of gold for the lure is easily explained by the belief that golden baubles were irresistible to a woman, so much so that the prospect of the golden wedding finery surely overcame the initial reluctance of many a bride.

Why Atalanta loses the race is the key part of the myth. She does not lose the race because of athletic inadequacy, because she was well out in front of Hippomenes when he rolled out his first apple. It would seem that she loses the race because of her suitor's guile, a trait traditionally considered to be quintessentially female and thus an appropriate foil to the male behavior Atalanta exhibits. Atalanta's maleness is, however, in turn contrasted with her receptivity to the *mala*, a term for a seeded fruit that includes the apple and the quince. At least by the fifth century we know that the *malon* was a slang expression for a woman's breasts.[4] The *malon* was also related to the pomegranate Persephone ate in Hades because a bride traditionally brought a *malon* with her into the bridal chamber (see **The**

Wedding). In that context the *malon* carried the sexual connotations of the pomegranate as a reference to a woman's sexual organs. Thus Atalanta's seduction by the *mala* refers to her biological maturity, which she is unable or unwilling to resist. The myth is very much about the instincts of young girls at puberty, and Atalanta's unsuccessful transition to domesticated life was undoubtedly presented to many a young Greek girl as a warning that a girl who was too wild would not be able to be socialized successfully into the community. The ancient listener would have been acutely aware that only a goddess such as Artemis could successfully cling to celibacy and resist male advances. As a mortal, Atalanta was subject both to society's customs and to biological drives. The myth is a powerful dramatization of the social message that Atalanta could not have both her freedom in the wild and the opportunity to give expression to her sexuality. The story must have had a sobering impact on many young Greek girls.

We must not forget that the myth carries another ironic message about Atalanta's appeal to her suitors. The very untamed aspect of herself that Atalanta was so reluctant to forsake was exactly the quality that the suitors were willing to risk even their lives either to dominate or to make their own (no. 117; see **Women as Animals**). Moreover, just as the celibacy of the virgin huntress, be she Artemis or Atalanta, intensified the erotic impulses of the hunt, both her own and her suitors',[5] Atalanta's subsequent life as a celibate lion in the constant company of her husband constituted a penalty that was quintessentially Greek in its irony.

Atalanta's transformation into a lion calls to mind the close identification Artemis enjoyed with lions and the lion's form that Thetis assumed in her own resistance to a suitor who would become her husband (see **Peleus and Thetis**). The connection is interesting, because a tradition relates that before Atalanta's footrace with Hippomenes she took part in a wrestling match with the hero Peleus as part of the funerary games for the hero Pelias. Atalanta was acquainted with Peleus through their mutual participation in the hunt for the Kalydonian Boar, and she probably came to be paired with him because of her reputation for athletic prowess and his later fame for successfully wrestling with Thetis. The contest differed from that with Thetis in that Atalanta's match was purely a formal competition, and the literary tradition gives us contradictory accounts as to who won, perhaps because for the reputation of either participant a defeat would have been unacceptable.

But if the wrestling match was of secondary interest in the literary tradition, the subject was a popular one with Greek artists. The encounter is regularly portrayed in Archaic vase-painting where, as Anne Ley has shown, Atalanta sometimes has a clear victor's hold but in other instances is being bested by Peleus.[6] She usually wears the *perizoma*, a short, tight-fitting skirt that was identified with barbarians, or non-Greeks, such as Scythians and Amazons.

In the fifth century Greek artists become much more interested in the erotic undercurrents of the encounter. To intensify the impact, painters modernized the locale of the contest, now situat-

ing it in a palaestra, the male exercise grounds where athletic competitions took place. The palaestra was a particularly appropriate choice, because its sexual atmosphere was well known and openly accepted. Men and boys exercised in the nude, and engaged in the overtures that might lead to sexual relationships. Not surprisingly, Classical depictions of the match of Peleus and Atalanta decorate the tondos of male drinking cups (kylikes) that bear on their exterior representations of male athletes also exercising in the palaestra (nos. 118-119). The sexual undercurrents of both subjects are mutually reinforced by means of the juxtaposition.

In Classical depictions of Atalanta and Peleus, vase-painters took pains to emphasize how different Atalanta was from both contemporary Greek men and women. Her body was as muscled as a man, and she scorned female attire and demeanor, even daring to look directly into a man's face, unrestrained by *aidos* (see **Aidos** and **Sophrosyne**). But Atalanta is not to be confused with Greek men, and she continues to wear the foreigner's *perizoma* long after it falls out of use in Greek vase-painting, thereby doubly distinguishing herself by being both barbarian and out of date. Yet while these differences make her an almost comic figure, they do not ignore her sexuality. The Aberdeen Painter eschews the overt implications of the wrestling match itself to focus on the subtle sexual tension in the interaction of the participants before and after the competition (nos. 118-119).

1. Hesiod frags. 72-76 MW; Theokritos, *Idylls* 3.40-42; Ovid, *Metamorphoses* 10.681-704 and *Ars Amatoria* 2.185-192; Hyginus, *Fabulae* 185; Kallimachos, *Hymn* 3.215-224; Apollodoros, *Bibliotheke* 1.9.16 and 3.9.2; Pausanius 5.19.2. See Gantz (1993) 335-39. In connection with the tradition that the Arcadian Atalanta was raised by a bear, it is interesting to note that the Arcadians claimed their descent from Arcas and Kallisto, a woman who was transformed into a bear (see no. 100). See Sourvinou-Inwood (1987a) 145-53. For Melanion, see Vidal-Naquet (1986) 119-20 and **Aktaeon** above.

2. For Hera, see Burkert (1985) 131.

3. Xenophon, *On Hunting* 9.7, recommends capturing the fawn to attract the hind.

4. Henderson (1991) 122, 149; Foster (1899) 39-55. A magical papyrus tells of throwing an enchanted apple in the direction of the love object; see Winkler (1990) 173. Sutton (1981) 324 points out that the custom of throwing a piece of fruit to one's beloved still continues in modern Greek folklore.

5. Atalanta bears so many close similarities with Artemis that she is in a sense a form of Artemis, just as Iphigenia is (see **Iphigenia**).

6. Ley (1990) 44-45.

KALYX KRATER WITH ATALANTA AND HIPPOMENES

ca. 420
by the Dinos Painter
Bologna, Museo Civico Archeologico di Bologna, inv. no. 300

Attic, from Bologna
Clay
H 47 cm., Diam 46.5 cm.

Publications: *ARV²* 1152.7; *Para* 457; *Add²* 336; G. Montanari, *CVA* Bologna, Museo Civico 4 (Italy 27) 16-17, pls. 86-87; C. Robert, *Hermes* 22 (1887) 445-46; B.O. Foster, "Notes on the Symbolism of the Apple in Classical Antiquity," *Harvard Studies in Classical Philology* 10 (1899) 42-43; Pfuhl (1923) 586-87, pl. 230, figs. 578-79; Hahland (1930) 14, pl. 8b; E. Langlotz, *Phidiasprobleme* (Frankfurt 1947) 79, 96, fig. 1; F. Eckstein, "Athletenhauben," *RM* 63 (1956) 92, pl. 43.4; J.D. Beazley, "Some Inscriptions on Vases: VIII," *AJA* 64 (1960) 224; Ginouvès (1962) 83, 117, pl. 23, fig. 68; Durand and Lissarrague (1980) 100; C. Govi and D. Vitali, eds., *Il Museo Civico Archeologico di Bologna* (Bologna 1982) 278; *LIMC* II (1984) 145, no. 1523, pl. 148 (s.v. Aphrodite); ibid., 946, no. 81, pl. 699 (s.v. Atalante); Bérard (1988) 280; Mark (1984) 307 n. 89; Boardman (1989) 96, fig. 179; Ley (1990) 53, 70-71 no. K 23, fig. 19; Sabetai (1993) vol. 1, 38.

Mended from many pieces. On the reverse are three quietly standing men. Above the scene on Side A is a band of alternating upright and inverted palmettes. Beneath the scene is a band of palmette and lotus.

Atalanta and Aphrodite occupy the center of the scene and stand turned away from each other as if oblivious to the other's presence. To our left is Atalanta, who stands on a low rocky slope, with her weight on her right foot, her left leg relaxed and the left toes foreshortened. She is completely nude except for light footwear, a band around the arch and ankle of each foot. Her face and body are shown in three-quarter left profile, and she gazes outward, the direction of her glance seemingly directed partly at the viewer, and partly so that she can catch sight of Hippomenes (Melanion) out of the corner of her eye. Her upraised hands adjust the fabric that ties up her hair; curls tumble around her

117 Side B

117 Side A

face, exposing her left earring. Beside her is a low water basin with stalks beside it.

Aphrodite turns to her left. She stands on slightly higher ground and wears a chiton and a mantle, the folds of which are drawn up over her head, exposing her diadem and earring. She steadies a scepter in her left hand and extends her right hand to accept a small round object, obviously a golden apple, from the right hand of a nude winged Eros who stands on a rock before her, his right foot in profile, the toes of his left foot foreshortened. Aphrodite's inclined head and downcast gaze emphasize her concentrated focus on the handing over of the object, and Eros, his head in left profile and slightly inclined, also studies the transaction. In his extended left hand Eros holds two more apples. Stalks emerge from the rocky groundline above his head. Before the rock on which Eros stands is a pillar on which drapery has been placed. Stalks grow beside its base.

Beside the pillar stands the nude figure of Hippomenes, his weight on his right leg, the toes of his left foot foreshortened. His upraised left hand holds the handle of a scraper above his left shoulder. The fingers of his right hand steady the curved tip in front of his left breast. He has short wavy hair and his head is in left profile as he gazes across at Atalanta.

Beside him are rocks and stalks, and above and behind him we see a seated male figure in three-quarter right profile who rests his right elbow on a rock and turns to gaze back behind him, his face in left profile, his mantle wrapped around his hips and legs, his left hand resting on his lap. He appears to be looking at the male figure above Atalanta's head. A tree is at his left side, and behind it, above the handle, a man steps forward onto uneven rocky ground. He rests his right elbow on his bent right knee, his left hand on his left hip. His mantle is wrapped around his hips and legs, the ends brought forward over his left shoulder.

On the other side of the scene, standing on higher ground to Atalanta's right is a man whose right hand rests on the horizontal handle of a staff and whose body leans against the staff, the toes of the left foot resting on the ground. He wears a mantle around his hips and a wreath over straight hair that falls to his shoulders. His face is in right profile and he gazes in the direction of Atalanta or Hippomenes. Above Atalanta's head the upper torso of a youth rises from behind a rock, his head in left profile, a mantle over his left shoulder, and both arms raised. His head is turned behind him and he exchanges glances with a nude youth who is seated above the handle. This figure, in three-quarter left profile, sits upon his mantle, which frames his back, its ends brought over his left forearm. His left hand rests on his right thigh, and the fingers of his left hand are brought to his face as he gazes behind him. His long straight hair reaches his shoulders. A tree grows at his right side. Behind him is a woman wrapped almost entirely in her mantle, which is brought over her head, exposing curly hair. She leans forward, her left elbow and right hand resting on her raised and bent left knee; the fingers of her left hand are brought up to her chin.

The Dinos Painter has taken up the subject of Atalanta's footrace with Hippomenes (Melanion), but he has chosen not to focus on the race itself, but rather on the pregnant moments before the race begins, when Aphrodite prepares to give over to Hippomenes the golden apples that will precipitate Atalanta's defeat (see **Atalanta**). Although the landscape is rendered as a rocky one, the presence of the washing basin (louterion) and the pilaster indicates that we are in the exercise grounds that were used exclusively by men. Atalanta and Aphrodite share the center of the composition. Standing completely nude before an immediate audience of four men in

117 Detail of Side A

addition to Hippomenes, Atalanta is unfazed and unoblivious. Her alluring pose and unbowed head establish unambiguously that she is enjoying the effect she is producing. This behavior is all the more remarkable when one considers that not only was female nudity restricted to prostitutes in Classical Athens, but for a female to show herself in this open posture, even clothed, was simply unthinkable (see **Gesture and Gaze**). The Dinos Painter has responded enthusiastically to the challenge of rendering a voluptuous and alluring nude female body, but he has achieved mixed results. Atalanta is full-breasted, but below the breasts her torso resembles that of a male, especially in the relatively narrow hips in proportion to her thighs. In deference to the female form, the painter has not added interior lines to indicate abdominal muscles, and he has minimized the projection of the inguinal muscle at the hip, although an interior line indicates its presence at the top of her thigh. A slightly feminine note is struck by the especially low placement of the indentation marking the left side of her waist, with the result that a certain sinuosity is suggested.

In contrast to Atalanta's studied aloofness, Hippomenes is so preoccupied with her that he stares unabashedly at her, unaware of the proximity of the golden apples that will soon secure his victory. He mimics Atalanta's gesture by assuming an equally posed one, holding in a completely unfunctional manner a scraper, which was used by male athletes after they had exercised in order to remove accumulated perspiration and dust, as well as the olive oil that had been rubbed on before competing. Because the race has not yet begun, Hippomenes only toys with the instrument, while Atalanta fiddles with her hair. The position in which he holds the scraper necessitates bringing his right arm completely across his torso, thereby concealing his chest, and therefore provides a marked contrast to the unconventionally exposed breasts of Atalanta. It is clear that both Hippomenes and Atalanta are acting for the benefit of the other, but in this contest Atalanta seems to be the victor.

The juxtaposition of Atalanta with Aphrodite is eloquent, because the painter reminds us of how closely the two women are linked. Both prove irresistible to men, but through different strategies. Atalanta's appeal had heretofore rested on her unconquerable athletic prowess, although the painter is suggesting, and Atalanta herself seems now to be well aware, that her assets also include sheer physical appeal. We are given the intimation that Atalanta's choice of attire, consisting of minimal footwear, earrings, and headwrap, may have been chosen not only for athletic reasons, but also to maximize the competitive potential of all the tools available to her. Meanwhile, Aphrodite, luxuriating in the garments and ornament of the traditional Greek female, is so unsupportive of Atalanta's brazenness that she chooses to ignore it, busying herself with the golden apples that will soon bring Atalanta down the traditional path of womanhood. The artist is reminding us that Aphrodite emerges from this contest the supreme victor, unwilling to permit a mortal female to reject her. In some versions of the myth, Aphrodite will herself transform Atalanta into a lion either for failing to sacrifice to the goddess after marrying Hippomenes or for making love in a sanctuary of the gods. In the face of such divine power, even animosity, Atalanta's athleticism is useless.

117   Details of figures over the handles

The Dinos Painter has given us an unintentional note of irony in his depictions of Aphrodite and Atalanta, because the modern viewer knows what the painter could not: in the decades to come, Aphrodite will come to subscribe to Atalanta's approach to femininity. Hellenistic and Roman images of the nude Aphrodite greatly outnumber clothed versions, as Atalanta's innovative approach to advertising her sexuality came to be accepted as the norm for deities and mythical figures, if not mortals. Here, in a vase painted several decades before the end of the fifth century, the Dinos Painter reveals the Greek artist's nascent fascination with the nude female form.

It cannot be a coincidence that both the Aberdeen Painter (no. 119) and the Dinos Painter illustrate Hippomenes holding the handle and tip of a vertical scraper. Both painters must have been influenced by a common prototype, although obviously they felt free to devise their own variations. It is interesting to note that it would not be before the later fourth century that Greek artists were sufficiently comfortable with the graphic demands of the scraping procedure to render the instrument in use, as Lysippos would do with his Apoxyomenos. Classical vase-painters were content to suggest the action and preferred to concentrate on the scraper's elegant shape.

The male onlookers to the scene include Atalanta's father Schoineos, who leans on his staff. The three youths must be other eager suitors who had been waiting for Hippomenes to be defeated so that they could take their chances with Atalanta. Their shared glances suggest that they have just witnessed Aphrodite's preparation of the apples and now realize that the denouement of this race will be different from that of the preceding ones.

The Dinos Painter's individual style is apparent in his use of thin, dilute lines, usually broken and wavy. He is enthusiastic about extended fingers in almost affected gestures, but he does not execute them very well. His composition, by contrast, is quite successful, with Atalanta nicely silhouetted among figures whose contours echo her own; the diagonals of Schoineos' staff and Aphrodite's scepter provide an articulated frame that isolates and accentuates the recalcitrant athlete and the equally determined goddess.

The Dinos Painter betrays his chronological position within the last decades of the fifth century by the landscape setting and the dispersal of figures over multiple groundlines. Other later fifth-century characteristics are the use of foreshortening, the ease of rendering three-quarter seated poses, and the exchange of meaningful glances in order to allude to the broader narrative and to future events. Particularly interesting is the new, larger size of Eros, who assumes a more important role in this drama than he is conventionally assigned in wedding scenes (see **The Wedding**). The development looks forward to vase-painting of the fourth century.

The Dinos Painter was intrigued with women and particularly with the friction between the constricting conduct prescribed for them and the spirited impulses within them that struggled for expression. The painter addressed scenes of farewell on a bell krater in Syracuse (no. 20) and turned to maenadic ritual on a stamnos in Naples (no. 124).

118 Interior

118

KYLIX
WITH ATALANTA AND PELEUS

475-450
by the Aberdeen Painter
Ferrara, Museo Archeologico Nazionale di Ferrara, inv. no. 1340

Attic, from tomb 991, Spina
Clay
H 10 cm., Diam 25 cm.

Publications: *ARV²* 919.5; G. Riccioni, *Peleo e Atalante* (Rome 1960) fig. 3; Brommer (1973) 316; F. Beck, *Album of Greek Education: The Greeks at School and at Play* (Sydney 1975) fig. 407; *LIMC* II (1984) 947, no. 86, pl. 699 (s.v. Atalante); Ley (1990) 50, 69 no. K 18, fig. 15; *LIMC* VII (1994) 254, no. 30 (s.v. Peleus).

Mended from several pieces. Only the tondo survives. Around the scene is a laurel band between reserved bands. On each side of the underside are the nude legs of male figures who were probably depicted in a palaestra.

Atalanta leans forward in three-quarter left profile, her knees bent, her left foot advanced. Her hands grasp the handle of the pickaxe that was used to turn up and mark the exercise ground of the palaestra. She is nude except for her short garment that wraps tightly around her buttocks and tapers between the legs. It is black except for a reserved band with black dots around the upper and lower edges. Where the contours of the garment lie against the glazed background, they are delineated by a reserved band. Over the top of her head she wears a close-fitting cap, which is ornamented with three circles and which is tied beneath her chin. The profile of her nose is concave and the nose tip is bulbous. She gazes up at Peleus.

He stands before her, his right leg advanced and the knee relaxed. His torso is in three-quarter right profile, and the abdominal muscles are rendered in dilute glaze. His right hand was at his side; his left elbow is bent and the upraised hand gesticulates with the fingers extended. His head is in right profile and has short curly hair. His mouth is open and he looks directly into Atalanta's eyes.

The Aberdeen Painter has chosen to portray the interaction of the competitors in the tense moments before the wrestling competition (see **Atalanta**). Peleus has interrupted Atalanta as she prepares the ground for the encounter. He is the very essence of the youthful Greek athlete: muscular, sleek, and self-confident. By contrast, to the ancient eye Atalanta was nothing short of bizarre: old-fashioned, un-Greek, and decidedly unfeminine. She is larger than Peleus and would, in fact, tower over him if she stood up. She also wears a shorter and even tighter version of a garment (the *perizoma*) that characterized barbarians in black-figure vase-painting of the Archaic period, but which had fallen out of use by Classical times. Moreover, she is given the powerful, triangular thighs of Archaic figures, in contrast to the sleeker physique of the Classically rendered Peleus. Her unorthodox appearance is further underscored by the contrast between the concave contour of her nose and the unbroken, quintessentially Greek, profile of that of Peleus.

Whereas in deference to her femaleness the painter has omitted on her torso the dilute glaze markings that delineate male abdominal musculature, he has, whether deliberately or inadvertently, rendered her breasts in a curious manner, with the upper contours and nipples drawn as concave lines terminating in peaks.

Although the painter intended our eye to be drawn immediately to Atalanta, we soon realize that it is Peleus who dominates the couple's encounter. Atalanta's crouching posture and the ready position of her hands on the pickaxe tell us that she had been actively engaged in her task until interrupted by Peleus, at which point she has raised her head to look at him. He stands calmly before her, but gesticulates so energetically and speaks with such animation that he has captured her attention and, in turn, our respect. The artist seems to be suggesting that this almost comical female athlete, who would pose such an absurd sight in a male palaestra, is here bettered, if not in a wrestling competition, then by the articulate manner of a Greek hero who, unlike Atalanta, was trained to excel in both the physical and the verbal arenas.

119

KYLIX
WITH ATALANTA AND PELEUS

450-430
by the Aberdeen Painter
Rome, Museo Nazionale di Villa Giulia, inv. no. 48234

Attic, "from tomb 430 (Recinto) in Cerveteri"
Clay
H 10.5 cm., W (at handles) 31 cm., Diam 23 cm.

Publications: *ARV²* 919.4; G. Ricci, *Monumenti Antichi* 42 (1955) 1019, fig. 260; *LIMC* II (1984) 947, no. 85, pl. 699 (s.v. Atalante); Ley (1990) 51, 69-70, no. K 20, fig. 17.

Mended from many pieces, with details of Peleus' left shoulder and face effaced. Glaze worn off tops of handles. Encircling the tondo is a band of laurel. Each scene on the underside represents a gathering of three men amid palmettes.

Atalanta is seated on a stone block, almost in left profile. Her legs and knees are placed together with the left foot slightly advanced. Her left elbow and forearm are brought across her torso to rest on her right thigh, such that the left breast is completely concealed. Her right arm is brought over her left forearm and the right hand is placed between the knees. She wears only a close-fitting garment over the buttocks (perizoma). It is decorated with a combination of glazed and reserved bands and dots. Her hair is bound up in a hair covering (sakkos) from which locks escape above her left ear. She looks at Peleus, who stands before her in three quarter-right profile. His right foot is placed in front of his left foot, the toes of which rest on the ground behind him. His left hand holds before his waist the handle of a scraper, the curving tip of which is steadied by the palm of his right hand. He is nude and has short curly hair, and his head is inclined, such that the (missing) eyes must have returned Atalanta's gaze. Behind Peleus are the curved rim and part of the vertical stem of a washing basin; beneath is a triangular object that probably served as a marker for an exercise area.

Peleus prepares to clean himself with a scraper, in the traditional manner of men after exercising. The action signifies that the wrestling match is over (see **Atalanta**). There is no indication of who has won the contest, nor is the painter interested in the competition itself, but rather in the sexual undercurrents of the moment, skillfully communicated by the couple's body language. The washing basin tells us that we are in the palaestra, the exercise grounds exclusively for men. Because washing basins were also associated with bathing women, its presence has erotic overtones.[1]

In many ways Atalanta is presented as the diametric opposite of a conventional female. Her build is no less muscular than that of Peleus, and her exaggeratedly curving back emphasizes the muscularity of her shoulders. Both her tight garment and her powerful thighs are retained from Archaic images of the contest in order to accentuate her foreignness to the mores of fifth-century Athens. Indeed, Atalanta wears no typical female clothing or ornament to enhance or suggest her allure, and her hair is arranged in the most severe of the contemporary hairstyles for women. Moreover, the traditionally downcast glance of modesty, or *aidos*, proper to a Greek female is completely absent; Atalanta gazes directly across to Peleus (see *Aidos* and *Sophrosyne* and **Gesture and Gaze**).

But if her body and gaze break with female convention, they also betray her femaleness. Atalanta is passively seated, initiating no action, and she takes great pains to position herself so that her nearly nude body is not on display. Her hunched shoulders mini-mize her chest, and her left arm is brought completely over her chest to conceal her breasts further. Her legs are pressed together and her hands are protectively crossed over her genitals. Her discomfort reminds us that no respectable woman in Classical Athens entered the male exercise area. The painter implies that both the palaestra and public nudity were foreign realms to any woman, even Atalanta.

Peleus, on the other hand, is thoroughly comfortable with his surroundings and with the nudity that was traditional in the palaestra. He displays his body with self-confidence, stepping forward into Atalanta's space, his right foot overlapping her left foot. Whereas Atalanta's silhouette is closed, his contours create an angular profile as his elbows just out, the left one directed toward her breast. His aggressiveness is by no means hostile. His thighs bend in an almost ingratiating way, his step seems tentative, and his fingers lightly grasp the scraper. He preens and struts and seeks approval. She waits, confident in her athleticism, but, having rejected traditional female demeanor, she is visibly uncomfortable as a female. Regardless of who was the victor in the wrestling contest, the viewer senses that Peleus has the advantage in the aftermath.

Although the scene is simply executed, the painter has successfully captured the awkwardness and energy of the encounter's sexual tension. The subject was obviously a special favorite with him, because he executed an almost identical scene on a kylix in Boston and depicted the prelude to the wrestling match on a kylix in Ferrara (no. 118).[2]

1. Ginouvès (1962) 115-16, discusses Satyrs surprising Nymphs on louteria.
2. Boston, Museum of Fine Arts, inv. no. 03.820; *ARV²* 919, 31; Ley (1990) 51, 69, 325, no. K 19, fig. 16.

119 Interior

Mythical Women as Images of Apprehension

UNTAMED WOMEN

A number of mythical females provide graphic imagery for the fundamental Greek anxiety that women could be domesticated only temporarily or not at all, and that women's basic feral nature would inevitably reassert itself, subverting men and the male-centered institutions of civilized community life.

Some of these females are of semi-bestial form and destroy men by means of their words or their gaze (Sirens, Gorgons). Others have access to superhuman powers of sorcery (Circe) or are goddesses who ultimately emasculate their mortal male lovers (Eos). Others of these mythical women reject any contact with men at all

(Amazons) or resort to the violent murder of a man when rejected or offended (the Thracian Women). Perhaps the most frightening women appear to embrace conventional mores but suddenly, and ostensibly without reason, abandon home and domestic life to kill men and even their own children (Maenads).

The remarkable longevity that these mythical females have enjoyed through the course of Western civilization offers thought-provoking testimony to the enduring primacy of a gnawing suspicion: that the socialization of women to male-centered institutions would ultimately prove unsuccessful—and the results catastrophic.

AMAZONS

> They were considered men for their high courage,
> rather than women for their sex;
> for they seemed to outdo men in their spirit
> more than to be at a disadvantage in their form.
>
> Lysias, 2.4-6 (trans. W.R.M. Lamb)

The Amazons are one of the most evocative and enduring images of Greek mythology.[1] Daughters of Ares, god of war, and the Nymph Harmonia, Amazons lived at the fringes of the known world, in the direction of Thrace or the Caspian Sea. They refused to live in an orthodox society with men and such man-made institutions as marriage, preferring to mate on occasion with men of neighboring communities. While most stories of Amazons tell us that they refused to live with men at all, in one tradition we learn that they invited men to live with them, but only with the understanding that the men would live on terms established by the women.[2] The Amazons raised their children by them-selves and were said to refuse to rear sons. The term "Amazon" was believed to be derived from the words "without a breast," and the literary tradition tells us that Amazons mutilated their right breasts so that they could better draw their bows and hurl their javelins (although no artistic rendering of a one-breasted Amazon is known). Accomplished riders, Amazons were closely identified with horses, and many of their names, such as Hippolyte, have equine roots. The Amazons' close partnership with their horses constitutes a graphic example of the pervasive metaphor that likened unmarried girls to fillies which had not yet endured the harness (see **Women as Animals**).

We are never told about post-menopausal or baby girl Amazons; the only Amazons we ever hear about or see depicted are mature young Amazon women, essentially parthenoi. Their resistance to marriage likens them to Thetis and Atalanta, and their death at the hands of men links them with Iphigenia and other maidens of sacrifice (see **Peleus and Thetis**, **Atalanta**, and **Iphigenia**).

Each of the most prominent Greek heroes had a tumultuous encounter with an Amazon. As one of his arduous labors, Herakles was obligated to obtain the girdle of the Amazonian queen Hippolyte, and so closely in Greek thought was a woman's belt connected with her sexuality that the feat had transparent connotations of sexual conquest.[3] Similarly, Theseus abducted the Amazonian queen Antiope (or Hippolyte) and had a son by her, Hippolytos, for whom, appropriately, integration into the social fabric proved difficult. Achilles encountered Penthesilea on the battlefield of Troy, where she had come to assist the Trojans. According to the celebrated tale of their conflict, as Achilles thrust his spear into Penthesilea in a fatal blow, she looked up at him and he fell in love with her as she lay dying (see **Gesture and Gaze**). These traditions offer parallels for the fusion of eroticism and aggression familiar in pursuit scenes and echo the concept that a potential bride requires taming (see **Pursuit Scenes**). Not all Amazons, however, succumb to male advances. A peninsula in the Black Sea takes its name from the Amazon Sinop, who asked Zeus if she could retain her virginity and was granted her request.

In the decades following the defeat of the Persians in 480, the Athenians came to equate the Persians with the Amazons. The correlation was sparked by the remoteness of the Persian homeland and by the Persian indulgence in luxury, which to the Greek mind was characteristic of female behavior. The comparison with Amazons was considered to be insulting to the Persians, particularly the mythical tale of an Athenian triumph over an attempted Amazonian invasion of Attica.

The Amazons were a popular subject with Greek artists in both the Archaic and the Classical periods, with Classical artists particularly responsive to the erotic undercurrents of the clashes between Greeks and Amazons. On the famous kantharos by Douris in Brussels (no. 120), Herakles plunges his sword into the bared breast of a falling Amazon; on the volute krater by the Niobid Painter in Naples (no. 121), Theseus imitates Achilles by locking glances with the collapsing Amazon he is about to kill.

---

1. Diodorus Siculus 2.45.3; Quintus Smyrnaeus 1.538-810; Plutarch, *Theseus* 26; Hellanikos (of Lesbos) frags. 16-17 (*FGrHist* 3B, 45-6); Hippocratic Treatise, *Airs, Waters, Places*; Diodorus Siculus 2.45.3; Apollodoros, *Bibliotheke* 2.59; Strabo 11.51; Aristophanes, *Lysistrata* 682-80. See Castriota (1992) 53; Dowden (1989), 62; Serwint (1993) 413; Tyrrell (1984); Fantham et al. (1994b) 128-35.
2. Fantham et al. (1994b) 133; Herodotos 4.114.
3. On the girdle, see Barber (1994) 60-62, who discusses Neolithic stringed skirts and their descendants in the form of Serbian fringed aprons.

120

KANTHAROS WITH HERAKLES AND AMAZONS

ca. 490-480
by Douris, signed as potter and painter
Brussels, Musées Royaux d'Art et d'Histoire, inv. no. A 718

Attic
Clay
H 18.2 cm., Diam 15.3 cm.

Publications: *ARV²* 445.256 and 1653; *Para* 521; *Add²* 241; F. Mayence, *CVA* Brussels, Musées Royaux du Cinquantenaire 1 (Belgium 1) III I c, pls. 5-6; Furtwängler and Reichhold (1904-1921) pl. 74.1; Pfuhl (1923) 478, pl. 158, fig. 453; G.M.A. Richter and M.J. Milne, *Shapes and Names of Athenian Vases* (New York 1935) 25-26, fig. 168; Beazley, *Potter and Painter in Ancient Athens* (London 1942) 39-40; D. von Bothmer, *Amazons in Greek Art* (Oxford 1957) 132, no. 10, 139-40, pl. 70.4; M. Wegner, *Duris* (Münster 1968) 57-58, 200-201, fig. 20; Boardman (1975) 137, fig. 298; Simon and Hirmer (1976) 119, pl. 162; *LIMC* I (1981) 592, no. 83, pl. 450 (s.v. Amazones); Keuls (1985a) 45-46, fig. 25; *Mededelingenblad. Vereniging van Vrieden Allard Pierson Museum Amsterdam* 37/38 (1986) 22-23, no. 19, 32, fig. 19a-b (D.L. Scheurleer); Buitron-Oliver (1995) 1, 5, 13, 19-21, 41-42, 63-64, 75-76 no. 48, pl. 32-33.

Mended from several fragments. Missing are fragments from the rim on each side. A thin reserve band runs around the rim, and another below the figural scene forms a groundline for the figures. Added red for the blood, the straps of the gorytoi, and the inscriptions. Dilute brown glaze for Herakles' lion-skin garment and the leather gorytos covers.

Sides A and B are presented as pendant scenes. On Side A Herakles battles four Amazons (see p. 17, fig. 4). In the center of the composition, a bearded Herakles advances in three-quarter left view, his right leg bent and advanced. He extends his right arm forward as he thrusts his sword into the breast of a fallen Amazon. He wears a thin chitoniskos that has stacked pleats on the skirt and short sleeves edged with pleated bands. Over this he wears an elaborate cuirass-like garment fashioned from a lion skin, with the head of the lion worn like a helmet, the forepaws knotted at his throat, and one of the lower paws hanging down in front of his left thigh. He carries a bow in his left hand. Behind the right side of his waist is seen the top of his quiver and bowcase (gorytos), which is slung from a cord around his neck. Behind his back is a small shield. He gazes down at the fallen Amazon.

The Amazon is about to fall on her right side, her right leg extended, her left knee bent with the lower leg drawn back. Her torso is almost frontal and her

120 Detail of Side B

120 Side A (**See also detail, p. 17**)

head is turned back in left profile; she gazes downward. She attempts to draw her sword, clutching the hilt in her right hand and the scabbard in her left. Her chitoniskos is similar to that of Herakles and has a looped neckline and a short apoptygma; the forms of her body beneath are fully indicated, including the nipples. She wears an Attic type of crested helmet with upturned cheekpieces and a forehead piece that mimics curled hair. Her gorytos is slung from a cord that passes over her right shoulder. One lock of hair escapes and falls down the side of her neck. Behind Herakles a crouching Amazon archer in left profile raises her bow in her extended left arm and pulls back the bow-string with her right hand. She kneels on her right knee, her bent left leg planted before her, as she takes aim at Herakles. Her chitonikos, bowcase, and helmet resemble those of her fallen comrade. Behind her an Amazon stands in three-quarter back view as she raises her spear to strike, her bent right arm cocked behind her head; she points her spear directly at Herakles' back. On her lifted left arm she holds a round shield, bearing the emblem of an advancing lioness. On top of her chitoniskos she wears a leather corselet. Behind the falling central Amazon, another Amazon strides in three-quarter right profile, her left leg advanced. In her bent right arm she holds a sword, held alongside her thigh, in front of her genitals; the shield on her left arm is lifted and seen in three-quarter view from the inside. Her chitoniskos is nearly transparent, with the nipples of her breasts clearly visible.

Above the head of Herakles is inscribed:

ΔΟΡΙΣ ΕΓΡΑΦΣΕΝ ΔΟΡΙΣ ΕΠ[ΟΙΣΕΝ]

("Douris painted [this], Douris made [this]").

On Side B a companion of Herakles battles four Amazons in a similar scene. Reading from the viewer's left, an Amazon strides away from the scene in three-quarter left view, her bent right leg advanced. Her torso is twisted frontally as she turns back to view the scene behind her, her head in right profile. Her bent, right arm is raised to hold a battle-axe, which passes horizontally behind her head; in her left hand she holds a bow. Like the other Amazons she wears a transparent chitoniskos with short apoptygma, helmet, and gorytos. Thin drapery lines radiate from her nipples. Behind her an Amazon advances in three-quarter right view, her bent, left leg advanced; in her cocked right arm she holds a spear aimed at the male warrior's abdomen, and on her raised and extended left arm she holds a shield, seen in three-quarter view from the inside. Her chitoniskos is nearly transparent, and not only her nipples, but also her pubes are clearly visible through the garment. Thin lines radiating from the nipples clearly indicate their rounded form. In the center, a bearded warrior lunges to his right, his left leg advanced and his right arm extended, as he thrusts his sword into the breast of an Amazon who falls, both arms still extended above her head. He wears an elaborate cuirass with stylized musculature over his chitoniskos and an Attic-style helmet similar to that worn by the Amazons, but with a smooth forehead piece. He holds a round shield over his left arm, which bears the emblem of a dog. The Amazon before him falls with her torso twisted frontally, her right leg bent under her, and her left leg extended. The transparency of her chitoniskos reveals her breasts and pubes clearly. Her right hand, which grasps a drawn sword, has hit the ground, and her left arm is still strapped into her shield and raised behind her head; the shield is seen from the interior view. Behind the male warrior, an Amazon in three-quarter left view poises to strike him with a club raised in her right hand and cocked behind her head. She leans back, weight on her bent left leg, her right leg advanced. In her left hand she holds a bow.

Inscribed below the rim on the center of Side B:

ΧΑΙΡΕΣΤΡΑΤΟΣ ΚΑΛΟΣ

("Chairestratos is fair").

375

This is a masterpiece of Early Classical Attic pottery by one of its premier painters. The potent eroticism of the images on this vase is unmistakable, in the aggression between male and female on the battlefield, the unconcealed sexuality of the Amazon warriors, and the violent action of the male figure in each scene as he kills his Amazon opponent with a sword-thrust to her breast. As the Greek heroes find themselves outnumbered yet still victorious, their physical and sexual prowess is celebrated in the spirit of a boastful battle-cry.

There are a variety of different traditions about Greeks battling Amazons; the version depicted here is that of Herakles in one the twelve labors he performed for Eurystheus. To obtain the girdle (*zoster*) of Hippolyte, queen of the Amazons, Herakles ventured into the Amazon-controlled lands far to the north. Although the early sources refer to the *zoster* as an insignia of leadership, the sexual connotations of this conquest are obvious (see **Amazons**). It is particularly significant that the vase focuses on the conquest by the Greek heroes while in the Amazons' own territory. Similar dynamics are seen on vases with images of Odysseus and Circe (nos. 132, 133), Perseus and Medusa (nos. 135, 136), and Odysseus and the Sirens (no. 137), all of which focus on the moment of male victory over powerful females, in territory where the females are in control. The message that comes through clearly in all of these images is a sense of celebration that the proper Greek social order, with the hierarchy of male over female, has been established by Greek heroes in foreign lands.

A resplendent Herakles battles four Amazons singlehandedly on Side A of the kantharos, while his companion, who must be Telamon, does the same on Side B. The center of each composition is focused on a male hero killing a falling Amazon with a sword-thrust deep into the breast. For the Greeks this imagery was potently erotic; the bared sword which enters a virgin's breast is tantamount to a sexual conquest. Male Greek heroes are typically killed by a thrust through the ribs, as is threatened for Telamon by the approaching spear-wielding Amazon on Side B.

The poses of the central falling Amazons and the kneeling archer on Side A have striking parallels in the pedimental sculptures from the Temple of Aphaia on Aegina, which date slightly earlier. The scenes on both sides are masterfully balanced compositions of lights and darks, with a tight structure reinforced with strong diagonal elements and a minute, even luxurious, attention to detail. The painter's focus on the breasts, nipples, and pubes of the Amazons' bodies beneath their transparent chitoniskoi adds a heightened tension to the scenes.

This is the only vase that preserves Douris' signature as both potter and painter; there are many vases with Douris' signature as painter, but only one other vase (an aryballos in Athens) is signed by Douris as potter. Most of his vases were made by the potter Python, but the unique shape of this kantharos, with its low foot and flamboyantly curved handles complementing the swell of the body, proves him to have been an innovative potter himself.

The kantharos was a drinking vessel, used in men's symposia, and the *kalos* inscription on Side B adds to the impression that this vase was meant for the male pleasure sphere. It is not surprising that such a triumphant moment of Greek victory over the Amazons, with the men outnumbered by warrior-maidens whose power seems heightened by their potent sexuality, should be seen on a men's drinking cup. The tone of the Brussels kantharos contrasts markedly with a white-ground lekythos on which Douris depicts the sacrifice of Iphigenia in a movingly sensitive and emotional scene, in which the preparations for sacrifice are likened to a bridal procession (see no. 101). Whereas a drinking cup was a man's vessel, lekythoi were used for funerary rituals, usually performed by women. Significantly, the killing of the Amazons parallels Iphigenia's fate: the bared sword in the hands of Agamemnon will soon enter the breast of the sacrificial virgin. The two works, which are approximately contemporary, vividly reveal Douris' intense interest in women, both heroic and tragic, and his innovative exploration of the emotional and sexual undercurrents beneath the surface of well-known, traditional scenes.

The Brussels kantharos predates the association of the mythical Amazons with the enemies of the Greeks, the Persians, which came about after the Persian sack of the Athenian Acropolis in 479 B.C. This association led to the development of a more polarized and antagonistic imagery for Amazons, emphasizing their militancy and aggressiveness (see nos. 121 and 122) in place of the sexuality and vulnerability exhibited here.

CAROL BENSON

121

VOLUTE KRATER
WITH AMAZONS

ca. 460
by the Niobid Painter
Naples, Museo Archeologico Nazionale, inv. no. 2421

Attic, from Ruvo
Clay
H 79.8 cm., Diam 47.5 cm

Publications: *ARV²* 600.13; *Para* 395; H. Schulz, *Die Amazonenvase von Ruvo* (1851); Furtwängler and Reichhold (1904-1921) vol. 1, pls. 26-28, vol. 4, 124-40; B. Schröder, "Mikon und Paionios," *JdI* 29 (1914) 131-32, fig. 6; F. Studniczka, "Zu den Friesplatten vom Ionischen Tempel am Ilissos," *JdI* 31 (1916) 221, fig. 33; W. Klein, "Mikon und Panainos, Mikon und Paionios," *JdI* 33 (1918) 9, fig. 4; Pfuhl (1923) 533-34, 539 pl. 189, fig. 505; T.B.L. Webster, *Der Niobidenmaler, Bilder griechischer Vasen* 8 (Leipzig 1935) 9-10, 14, no. 4, pl. 23; D. von Bothmer, *Amazons in Greek Art* (Oxford 1957) 161, no. 6, 167-68, pl. 74.4; C. Hofkes-Brukker, "Die Liebe von Antiope und Theseus," *BABesch* 41

(1966) 16, fig. 2; K. Schefold, *Die Griechen und ihre Nachbarn, Propyläen Kunstgeschichte* 1 (Berlin 1967) 225, pl. 222; J. Barron, "New Light on Old Walls: Murals of the Theseion," *JHS* 92 (1972) 36-37, pl. 6b-c; *LIMC* I (1981) 859, no. 18 (s.v Antiope II); ibid., 606, no. 298, pl. 479 (s.v. Amazones); J. Boardman, "Herakles, Theseus and Amazons," in Kurtz and Sparkes (1982) 25, pl. 5b; M. Prange, *Der Niobidenmaler und seine Werkstatt: Untersuchungen zu einer Vasenwerkstatt frühklassischer Zeit, Europäischen Hochschulschriften* Reihe 38, Archäologie 25 (Frankfurt 1989) 14, 24, 27-29, 65, 96-98, 183, no. N14, pl. 10; Alroth (1992) 39, fig. 21; Barringer (1995) 197, no. 150.

Around the rim two meanders (right) alternate with a checker square. Beneath is a band of double palmette and volutes above a band of egg. Beneath the scene is a band of angled double palmettes with volutes.

On the neck of Side A, Peleus, in right profile, wrestles with Thetis, who moves to her left, her arms outstretched. A snake writhes along Peleus' back as a manifestation of one of the animal forms into which Thetis is transforming herself in an effort to escape Peleus' clutches. Moving away in front of Thetis are two of her sisters, or Nereids, who flee toward Cheiron, who has human front legs and who holds a pine branch in his left hand. Behind Peleus and Thetis, a second pair of Nereids flee toward a man holding a scepter, who is probably Thetis' father Nereus. He turns to his right to converse with a gesticulating female, who may be Thetis' mother Doris.

On the body of the vase, an Amazon collapses to her left, her right hand extended in a plea for mercy to the chin of her victorious opponent, into whose face she gazes. Her left hand grasps her spear or bow, and she wears a close fitting garment ornamented with bands of zigzag, over which is tied a short skirt. She also wears a helmet and a quiver. Her opponent strides forward, with advanced left knee bent, his eyes returning her glance. His right hand plunges his spear into the Amazon's right shoulder; the spearhead has already sunk into the flesh. He wears a short belted tunic that exposes his right shoulder, and he is also outfitted with helmet, swordbelt, and greaves. His shield is fastened on his left forearm.

A mounted Amazon, seen in left profile, approaches the victorious Greek. Her quiver is visible by her right hip, the end of her bow is seen in front of her shoulder, and the tip of her spear emerges from beneath the head of her horse. In front of her horse's haunch a Greek moves to his left, his head in right profile. His shield, ornamented with a Gorgoneion, protects his left shoulder, and he also wears a helmet and greaves. His opponent is an Amazon outfitted with pelta (curved shield) and spear.

121 Side A

121 Side B

Crouching behind the victorious Greek is a bearded Greek who wears a pilos and holds his spear in his right hand. His shield lies over his left arm, and folds of his mantle are brought forward over both shoulders. Behind him a helmeted Amazon is seen in three-quarter left profile. Holding a spear in her left hand, she draws her sword over her head as she prepares to strike a Greek who crouches before her, a spear in his upraised right hand. In the background is a tree.

In the center of Side B, a two-horse chariot, driven by a figure in a dotted garment, moves in right profile behind a nude youth wearing greaves and a crested helmet. He moves to his left, his spear in his lowered right hand, his shield over his left elbow. In front of him a crouching Amazon is seen from behind, her right, weaponless arm upraised, her shield over her left shoulder. Her opponent is a Greek who strides forward from behind the lead horse, his spear in his upraised right hand. He wears a short belted tunic, a petasos, and a mantle that is draped over his outstretched left arm, the hand of which clasps the Amazon's shield. Following behind the central nude youth is an Amazon who carries a spear in her lowered right hand and another in her raised left hand. Over her close-fitting garment, which is decorated with zigzag bands, she wears a belted tunic. Her hair is gathered at the back of her head and is wrapped several times with a taenia. Behind her and moving away from her is a Greek seen in three-quarter left profile, a sword in his uplifted right hand and his spear in his lowered left hand. Crouching on the ground beneath him is an Amazon, whose mantle, fastened on her right shoulder, conceals most of her body. Her head is seen in right profile, her gaze following the direction of her outstretched left arm.

On the neck of Side B, a youth running in right profile pursues a fleeing maiden. A sunhat (petasos) hangs behind his back and he holds two spears in his lowered right hand.

121 Detail of Side A

Thomas magnificent vase shares so many points of comparison with other Amazonomachies in contemporary vase-painting that a common prototype in wallpainting is usually assumed, probably the celebrated Amazonomachy that was painted on the walls of the Theseion in Athens. Analysis of this vase's relationship to that wallpainting has tended to ignore the brilliant adaptation that the Niobid Painter has achieved, while remaining responsive to the constraints of the vase surface. Particularly noteworthy is the way the exchange of glances between the Greek and Amazon on Side A is reinforced by the angle of his spear, her outstretched arm, and the reins of the Amazon's horse behind them. A second line at a right angle to the first one is established by the right arm of the mounted Amazon; this line is then continued by the lock of hair that trails down the side of the collapsing Amazon's neck, thereby leading our eye down the central seam of the Amazon's garment. An equally adept sensitivity to the balance of dark and light juxtaposes the glazed interior of the Greek's shield with the animated zigzag patterns of the Amazon's garment. The identification of the figures is not absolutely certain.[1] It has been suggested that the Amazon on Side B, who follows as a companion behind the heroically nude Greek, is, or alludes to, Antiope, the Amazon whom Theseus abducted during a youthful escapade. Antiope fought alongside Theseus against her countrywomen, who initiated an unsuccessful invasion in order to avenge the abduction. This allegiance reminds us that the couple would have a son, Hippolytos, who would com-

pletely reject settled community life in order to live as a hunter in the wild. It is interesting to note that in this scene the couple is virtually unchallenged, because the Greek in the petasos has already dispatched the collapsing Amazon.

A more rigorous encounter is presented on Side A, where the victorious Greek must be Theseus. While the Amazon's wound and collapsing posture announce her impending death, the exchange of gazes between her and Theseus is a clear allusion to Achilles, the hero whose achievements served as the model for many of Theseus' feats. Achilles also once fought the Amazons, and it was said that at the moment when he dealt a fatal blow to the Amazonian queen Penthesilea she looked into his eyes with the irresistibly erotic gaze for which women were celebrated, and Achilles fell in love with her as he watched her die (see **Gesture and Gaze**). It is that episode which is echoed here, and the painter has cleverly positioned directly in Theseus' line of vision the Gorgoneion on the shield of the Greek warrior behind the falling Amazon (see **Gorgons**). The Niobid Painter has skillfully heightened the sexual tension between the two figures by the way the Amazon's thumb and forefinger almost clasp Theseus' spear, while his left leg is framed by her bare feet. The figures are further linked by the way the pattern of his upturned cheekpieces complements the ornaments that rise from her helmet's visor, a coquettish detail that is an unmistakable allusion to the ornaments that decorate bridal diadems (nos. 26-27). It is also interesting to note the transparency of Theseus' tunic, as well as those of the other Greeks, with the result that the men's genitals are clearly revealed. Even should this detail have existed in the prototypical wallpainting, it is noteworthy that the Niobid Painter has chosen to retain a feature that is not characteristic of his style.[2]

The alignment of the Amazonomachy with the two scenes on krater's shoulders is clearly deliberate. Above the locked gazes of Greek and Amazon on Side A is a depiction of the wrestling encounter of Peleus and Thetis, another mythical expression of the theme of courtship as conflict (see **Peleus and Thetis**). It is interesting to note that Thetis and Peleus would be the parents of Achilles, who is more explicitly recalled through the presence of Cheiron, who would be the boy's teacher. The correlation of the tempestuous rapprochement of Achilles' parents with an allusion to the hero's own tumultuous relationship with Penthesilea suggests that the wildness Achilles inherited on his mother's side rendered inevitable an attraction to the Amazonian queen.

With similar subtlety the Niobid Painter has correlated the pursuit scene on the shoulder of Side B with the partnership of Antiope and Theseus. Christiane Sourvinou-Inwood has clearly shown that the pursuit scene was a metaphor for courtship, and the sunhat (petasos) was so distinctive an attribute of Theseus that we can surely identify the scene on the shoulder as Theseus in pursuit of one of his many conquests (see **Pursuit Scenes**). The courtship or conquest of an Amazon would require a different strategy, but the abduction of Antiope had a similarly successful resolution.

The alignment of the Amazonomachy with the stories of Peleus' and Theseus' courtships underscores the sexual undercurrents of the Amazons. This emphasis is likely to have been the Niobid Painter's own contribution to the wallpainting tradition, to which he otherwise faithfully adhered. It is well known that, in the decades following the Greek defeat of the Persians, the Amazons were consistently employed as a metaphor for the Persians, the points of comparison being the shared use of the bow and arrow, inhabitation of lands at the fringe of the known world, and an eastern appetite for luxury that was readily equated with the traditional belief in female insatiability. The Niobid Painter's presentation of the Amazonomachy in combination with a pursuit scene and the conflict of Peleus and Thetis returns the spotlight to the sexual tension that underlies these mythical parthenoi. At the same time, however, the Niobid Painter presents the theme in a manner far more benign and bemused than we find on the kantharos by Douris (no. 120) that was painted several decades before.

1. Barron (1972) 37, discusses London, British Museum, inv. no. 99.7-21.5, *ARV*[2] 1052.29, where the defeated Amazon is labeled Andromache, the victorious Greek Theseus.
2. Barron (1972) 37.

122

WHITE-GROUND ALABASTRON WITH AMAZON

ca. 480-470
by the Syriskos Painter
Princeton, The Art Museum, Princeton University,
Museum Purchase, Carl Otto von Kienbusch, Jr., inv. no. y1984-12

Attic
H 14.8 cm., Diam (mouth) 3.5 cm.

Publication: "Acquisitions of the Art Museum, 1984," *Record of the Art Museum, Princeton University* 44.1 (1985) 45.

Restored from fragments, with principal loss on viewer's right side, including lower edge of pelta and right edge of patterned cloak. The top of the wide, flat lip is reserved; black glaze appears around the rim, neck, and upper edge of shoulder. The body of the vase is decorated in white-ground. On the bottom is a narrow black band, separated by a thin reserved band from a solid black rounded tip. At the top of the white-ground body is a wide black band between two narrow bands. On Side B a short tree grows in the center, its slender trunk rendered as a wavy line; to the viewer's right of the tree, on a low stool, rests a crested helmet depicted in left profile.

On Side A an Amazon warrior stands frontally, her arms spread wide. Her head is turned to left profile, and her legs are in right profile and slightly bent. She wears an elaborate patterned costume with long sleeves and trousers, decorated with rows of horizontal dots. Over this is a flaring chitoniskos and a patterned leather cuirass with shoulder flaps. Around her shoulders and hanging down over each arm is a long fringed cloak with broad light and dark embroidered bands. Hanging behind her waist is a large bow-case (gorytos). Her right arm is outstretched, and she holds a battle-axe in her right hand. Her left arm stretches in the opposite direction, and in her hand she grips a crescent-shaped shield (pelta). Her long hair is tied at the nape and streams out behind her left shoulder. Added white for the rows of horizontal dots of patterning on sleeves and trousers; added red on the short chiton and the quiver.

This white-ground alabastron belongs to a large number of similar vessels, all bearing Amazons or Ethiopians with similar costume and Negroid features;[1] one example features an Amazon on one side and an Ethiopian on the other.[2] A tree is usually seen on the reverse, either alone or with variations on the stool shown here. Vessels of this type contained perfumed oils, such as myrrh, which were used for a variety of purposes, from anointing the genitals before sexual activity to preparing a corpse for burial.[3] It is usually assumed that the imagery of the alabastra has been evoked by the Eastern origin of the contents, and, indeed, myrrh was a rare and expensive substance imported from Arabia.[4] Theophrastos tells us that myrrh was harvested by making vertical incisions into the bark of the tree to release the resin, and the wavy lines delineating the tree trunks in the vase depictions are almost certainly referring to those incisions. Theophrastos further tells us that the trees were so valuable that they were guarded by armed Arabians, who, in the

Greek imagination, were thought of as effeminate and of dark complexion.[5] The Amazons and black Ethiopians on the alabastra surely allude to these legendary guardians, an identity reinforced by the at-arms stance of the Princeton Amazon, who has carefully placed close at hand her stool and helmet, emblems of her office.

The strong, militant figure of the Amazon contains many of the same elements seen in other Athenian depictions of Amazons in the period after the Persian wars (see **Amazons** and no. 121). Dressed in the unorthodox and wildly patterned trousered attire also associated with Persians and Scythians (another Eastern warrior tribe), she is armed with bow, arrow, and pelta. Unlike the

modest and restrained figure of a typical Greek woman, whose demeanor is characterized by a closed silhouette and lowered eyes (see **Gesture and Gaze**), the Amazon's stance is powerful and aggressive, and she holds her arms flung wide in an at-the-ready gesture. To the Greek imagination, the Amazons were quintessentially foreign, in a manner that was both threatening and titillating. Because Amazons were believed to live on the fringes of the known world, the Greeks associated them with all of the exotica of the East, and thus Amazons were an ideal choice to represent the militant guardians of the Arabian myrrh trees on alabastra containing imported oils.

CAROL BENSON

1. On the Amazon and Negro alabastra, Neils (1980); Wehgartner (1983) 116-121, 129-131; Sourvinou-Inwood (1991) 106-18.

2. White-ground alabastron from Metaponto, A. San Pietro, *La ceramica a figure nere di San Biagio* (1991) 141. I owe this reference to Dr. Michael Padgett.

3. Perfumed oils used for sexual practices, Aristophanes, *Lysistrata* 938-44; Detienne (1977a) 60-64; Kilmer (1993) 84-85. Myrrh used as a contraceptive, J.M. Riddle, *Contraception and Abortion from the Ancient World to the Renaissance* (Cambridge, Mass. and London 1992) passim, and Riddle et al. (1994) 32. For extensive discussion of the uses and significance of myrrh, see Detienne (1977a) passim.

4. Alabastra containing oil perfumed with myrrh: Sutton (1981) 332-37.

5. Theophrastos, *Plant-Researches* 9.4.3-6; Detienne (1977a) 5-9.

122 Side A

122 Side B

MAENADS

You of this city with its noble towers, people of Thebes, come and behold this prize,
the beast we daughters of Cadmus hunted down,
not with the strap-slung spears of Thessaly nor hunting nets
but with our soft white hands....

Euripides, *Bacchai* 1202-1207 (trans. D. Sutherland)

The Maenads of Greek myth are female followers of Dionysos, god of the wine that sparks their uninhibited dancing and ecstatic trances.[1] In contrast with Nymphs and Silens, who are semi-divine members of Dionysos' retinue, a Maenad was not envisioned as a permanent state of being but rather a mortal woman in a temporary state of madness. The meaning of the Greek term Maenad is mad or raving woman.[2]

In myth Maenads are ordinary mortal women who leave their homes to be initiated into sacred bands (*thiasoi*), induced by wine or the mesmerizing effects of the aulos (flute) and communal dance to give themselves over to unconstrained behavior of an ecstatic, and often violent, nature. Their uncontrolled state is characterized by their ivy-leaf wreaths, animal-skin garments, unrestrained dancing, wild gestures, and their association with wild animals and snakes. Maenads were even said to tear animals apart with their hands and then eat them raw, a practice known as omophagy. After the maenadic trance is over, the women return to their senses and to their everyday lives.

The most celebrated literary appearance of the mythical Maenads is in the *Bacchai* of Euripides, which was first performed in 405 B.C. When Dionysos appears in the city of Thebes, King Pentheus refuses to recognize him as a god and drives him out of the polis. The women of Thebes thereupon leave their homes to follow Dionysos to the mountains. When Pentheus learns of their desertion, he goes after them. First, he spies upon them, and then assumes their dress and manner in order to blend in with the throng. He is, however, spotted by his intoxicated mother Agave, who mistakes him for a wild animal. She calls after the other Theban women, and Pentheus is set upon and torn apart by his frenzied mother and her comrades.

The Maenads of Euripides' *Bacchai* constitute a chilling expression of Greek anxieties about female reversion to the wild and the resultant destabilization of the community. The Theban women abandon the city, their homes, and even, Euripides tells us, the looms which are the symbols of their domesticity (see **Textiles**). Euripides compares the Theban women to fillies who have left the yoke, i.e., reverted to their earlier, unconstrained state (see **Women as Animals**).[4] The women adopt the behavior of hunters but react excessively, like wild animals; Agave even refers to the other Theban women as her fellow hounds, a metaphor that recalls the story of the death of Aktaeon, who was dismembered by his own hounds in a wild frenzy (see **Aktaeon**).[3] The Maenads eat their quarry raw, contrary to Greek custom and violating sacrificial practice. Worst of all, a mother performs the unthinkable, killing, even dismembering, her son. Euripides emphasizes the prominence of the Theban women's families in order to stress the degree to which their mad state endangers the entire structure of the polis. The implication, however, is that all Maenads, all women, have the capability of subverting the natural order of the Greek male-female hierarchy, ignoring the laws and customs of civic life, and threatening Greek society with collapse.

Maenads did not exist only in myth; there is clear evidence that women played the role of Maenads in historical ritual. Perhaps as early as the Classical period there were maenadic associations of women in Athens, Thebes, and Delphi. During the Hellenistic period the Maenads of Miletos were officially recognized and regulated as a women's association by the city, and it is believed that their celebrations took place during the winter months, at which time the women would eat raw meat before leaving the city and going up into the mountains. Here, it is thought, with bare feet and flowing hair, the women would pass the night or nights by torchlight, playing the tympana (cymbals) and flutes.[5]

The official sanction by the polis and the surviving description of maenadic associations indicate that historical Maenads engaged in fairly benign activities, which did include, however, snake-handling and nocturnal wanderings into the mountains. It also appears that membership in the associations carried a certain amount of community prestige, because in Hellenistic Miletos the association's members were well-to-do wives of prominent citizens. These associations apparently served as the only outlet for women to be outside and unrestrained, free of their confinement to their homes and daily roles; the historical maenadic rituals thus represent a socially accepted form of release for women from the strictures of their highly controlled lives.

A scene on a series of so-called "Lenaia" vases from the later fifth century appears to represent a maenadic association of women taking part in a ritual that celebrates the release of women's spirited impulses through the agency of wine (see nos. 124, 125). The scenes feature a temporary cult image of Dionysos placed on a pillar, and a table placed before it with wine jars (stamnoi), ladles, drinking vessels, and food offerings. The women depicted on these vases are mature and matronly, and their actions are marked by solemnity; even as they begin to dance, their demeanor is relatively restrained. A column typically indicates that the setting of the scene is in a sanctuary. On an intriguing example by the Phiale Painter from Warsaw (no. 125), the women's preparations are interrupted by an intimate moment with a baby, whose Satyr ears infuse the scene with a light-hearted humor.

Scholars are divided as to the identification of the Athenian festival depicted. Although a persuasive argument has been made for this to be the Anthesteria, an end-of-winter fertility festival that celebrated the opening of the new wine, the currently prevailing point of view associates the vases with the mid-winter festival of the Lenaia.

We know a great deal about the activities of the Anthesteria, which included a remarkable ritual that clearly reveals the intimate connection between the wine-god, his potent drink, and the fertility of the city. On the third day of the festival, the Basilinna, wife of the city official known as the Archon Basileus, made secret offerings at Dionysos' sanctuary, and entered into a sacred marriage with the god, who was believed for that night to take the form of the Basilinna's husband. A number of vases show the drunken god approaching the open door of the wedding chamber, with the Basilinna waiting inside.[6] Despite the important role of the Basilinna in the ritual, the extensive surviving literary descriptions mention neither a cult idol nor maenadic dances, and for that reason the association of the vases with the Anthesteria must remain tentative.

Much less is known about the Attic festival of the Lenaia, but it appears to have also been associated with wine and fertility; it took place in the Lenaion, a sanctuary in the heart of Athens near the Acropolis.[7] Because the word lenai signified Maenads in the Ionian dialect, it has been argued that the Lenaia was a woman's festival, associated with maenadic rituals. Indeed, a procession and musical contest are explicitly associated with the Lenaia by Aristotle.[8] Scholars have assumed the existence of a cult image of Dionysos Lenaios and have identified it with the one depicted on the vases.

The maternal note sounded by the baby Satyr in the Warsaw scene calls to mind a comment by Diodorus that unmarried maidens were singled out in the Delphic maenadic association as alone eligible to carry the thyrsos.[9] Such allusions to motherhood and maidenhood suggest that the maenadic associations and rituals served a purposeful function in the context of female initiation, marriage, and fertility. Walter Burkert has noted the many links between the cult of Dionysos and that of Hera, who, as the wife of Zeus, is quintessentially associated with marriage.[10] There are further similarities between the female initiation rites of the Heraia at Elis, which involve a race overseen by a group known as the Sixteen Women, and rituals of Dionysos at Sparta.[11]

The connections between maenadic behavior and preparations for marriage and motherhood are strengthened by myths in which episodes of Maenad-like madness are resolved through marriage. The madness of the unmarried daughters of Proitos was brought about both because they resisted Dionysos and because they dishonored the image of Hera. The daughters' madness, which caused them to roam wildly, unclothed, through the countryside, was dispelled after they were chased by Melampus and then married. Similarly, the islanders of Chios believed that their festival of Dionysos originated when the unmarried women went mad, precipitating a conflict within the community that was resolved only by the marriage of the maidens.

The association of maenadic behavior with sexuality, motherhood, and marriage suggests that maenadic rituals evolved as a means of reconciling tensions, explored in the myths, between the constraints imposed upon women by the social code and the perceived natural wildness of women, who were thought to be predisposed to revert to their untamed state. The rituals, in effect, created an outlet through which the women could give productive release to their natural energy and sexuality, and, by extension, their fertility.

An interesting side-light is revealed by the story of Pentheus' encounter with the Theban women, in which maenadic behavior engenders in a man a fatal curiosity about women (see **Women as Containers**), such that Pentheus was lured to dress and act like women. The implication with such cross-dressing is that Maenads compel men not just to convert, but to revert, to female behavior. For this reason, male cross-gender dressing is conventionally recognized as a component of initiation rites to manhood, as the young man imitates an appearance and behavior which must thereafter constitute the diametric opposite of his self-image and demeanor. In the annual rite of the Oscophoria, ephebes, who were young Athenian youths aged eighteen and nineteen, dressed themselves as women.[12] A mythical parallel can be drawn with Achilles; to keep him from his fated death at Troy and, by extension, from the manly feats that would precede that end, his mother Thetis dressed Achilles as a woman and hid him among the women in the court at Skyros.[13]

CAROL BENSON

1. Homer, *Iliad* 22.460; *Homeric Hymn to Demeter* 386; Aischylos, *Eumenides* 25-26 and frag. 382 Radt (1985); Sophokles, *Oedipus the King* 212 and *Antigone* 1122, 1128-29, 1150-52; Euripides, frag. 79 Austin (1968); Euripides, *Bacchai*. See Gantz (1993) 117-18, 142-43. The word bacchante (*bacche* in Greek) is often used interchangeably with Maenad, but it has a slightly different meaning: that of the female worshipper who has experienced religious communion with the god (the male counterpart is *bacchos*).
2. Hedreen (1994) 50; Lonsdale (1993) 82-83, 99-102.
3. Euripides, *Bacchai* 731.
4. Euripides, *Bacchai* 1056-57; Seaford (1994) 309-11.
5. For a cogent recent discussion of the issues involving Maenads, see Hedreen (1994); and earlier, Bremmer (1984); A. Henrichs, "Greek Maenadism from Olympias to Messalina," *Harvard Studies in Classical Philology* 82 (1978) 121-60; A. Henrichs,

"Changing Dionysiac Identities," in *Jewish and Christian Self-Definition* III, ed. B.F. Meyer and E.P. Sanders (London 1982) 137-60, 213-36.

6. These vases were first collected by A. Frickenhaus, *Lanäeanvasen, Berlin Winckelmannsprogramm Archäologischen Gesellschaft zu Berlin* 72 (1912). On the identification as the Anthesteria, see most recently Burkert (1983) 230-38; for a recent summary of the debate about the identification of the festival on this group of vases, see Frontisi-Ducroux (1991) 21-63, and see also Simon (1983) 92-101; Oakley (1990) 35-36; Fantham et al. (1994) 88-90. For vases depicting the ritual involving the Basilinna, see in particular Tarquinia, Museo Nazionale Archeologico, inv. no. RC 4197, *ARV²* 1057.96.

7. The site of the Lenaion sanctuary, which was a large peribolos, has not been identified with certainty, but some of the ancient sources associate it with the Agora; see H. Thompson and R. Wycherley, *The Athenian Agora* XIV (Princeton 1972) 128-29.

8. Aristotle, *Athenian Constitution* 57.1; Simon (1983) 100-101.

9. Diodorus Siculus, 4.3.2-3.

10. Burkert (1985) 222-23.

11. Serwint (1993) 418-419.

12. Simon (1983) 90-91.

13. See Gantz (1993) 577.

KYLIX WITH DIONYSIAN SCENES

ca. 490-480
by Makron, signed by Hieron as potter
Berlin, Antikensammlung, Staatliche Museen zu Berlin Preussischer
Kulturbesitz, inv. no. F 2290

Attic, from Vulci
Clay
H 13 cm., Diam. 33 cm.

Publications: *ARV²* 462.48; *Para* 377; *Add²* 244; A. Greifenhagen, *CVA* Berlin, Antiquarium 2 (Germany 21) pls. 87-89, 128.1,5; A. Furtwängler, *Beschreibung der Vasensammlung im Antikenmuseum* II (Berlin 1885) 581-84; A. Frickenhaus, *Lenäenvasen, Winckelmannsprogramm der Archäologischen Gesellschaft zu Berlin* 72 (1912) no. 11; J.C. Hoppin, *A Handbook of Attic Red-Figured Vases*, vol. 2 (Cambridge, Mass. 1919) 40-41; Pfuhl (1923) 468-69, pl. 152, fig. 438; H. Diepolder, *Griechische Vasen, Antiker aus den Berliner Museen* (Berlin 1947) 38, fig. 25; G.M.A. Richter, *Attic Red-Figured Vases: A Survey*, rev. ed., (New Haven 1958) 81; L. Lawler, *Terpsichore, Dance Perspectives* 13 (Brooklyn 1962) 26 (illus.); L. Lawler, *The Dance in Ancient Greece* (London 1964) 19, 21, 26, fig. 5; Philippaki (1967) xxi; Simon and Hirmer (1976) pl. 169; J.-L. Durand and F. Frontisi-Ducroux, "Idoles, figures, images: autour de Dionysos," *RA* 1982, 84, 93; Simon (1983) 100, pl. 32.2; Keuls (1985a) 360, 363, fig. 299; Simon (1985) 274, 276, 292-93, figs. 264, 282; W.-H. Schuchhardt, et al., *Neue Belser Stilgeschichte 2: Griechische und römische Antike* (Stuttgart and Zurich 1987) 165, figs. 147-48; Staatliche Museen Preussischer Kulturbesitz, *Antikenmuseum Berlin: Die ausgestellten Werke* (Berlin 1988) 124-25, no. 3; E. Keuls, "The Conjugal Side of Maenadism as Revealed by Fifth-Century Monuments," *Praktika tou XII Diethnous Synedriou Klasikes Archaiologias, Athens 4-10 September 1983*, vol. 2 (1988) 99, pl. 19.1-2; Frontisi-Ducroux (1989) 146-48, fig. 206-207; Lissarrague (1992) 190-91, fig. 32; Frontisi-Ducroux (1991) 138-40, 247, no. L 53, fig. 76 a-b; Alroth (1992) 39 n. 42.

Mended from fragments. Below the figures is a narrow reserved band. Dilute glaze for the blonde hair of fifth Maenad on Side A and the third and sixth Maenads on Side B. Added red for the ivy wreaths, ivy branches around the cult statue, grape leaves in the tondo, and blood marks on the altar. In the interior a band of running meander (left) encircles the tondo, which contains a scene with Dionysos and an aulos-playing Satyr. On the left a Satyr in right profile, his right leg advanced and left slightly bent, leans back as he plays the auloi. He has tall, pointed ears and a long, curved tail, and on his feet are soft boots with leather flaps. He is bald on top of his head, and at the back his hair is tied into a small knot; he wears an ivy wreath. As he plays, he gazes up directly into the eyes of Dionysos. The god is much larger in scale, and stoops forward slightly, his right foot advanced. He wears a long-sleeved chiton that is decorated with vertical bands of cross-stitch, and over this is a himation, loosely wrapped. His right hand grasps an upright thyrsos, and his left grips the stalk of a grapevine, which rests on his left shoulder; here it splits into two tendrils, one passing over each shoulder. On his head he wears an ivy-leaf crown.

The activity on the exterior of the vase is centered around the scene at the center of Side A, and from there it circles around the vase. In the center of Side A is an elaborate altar decorated with a palmette crown and a small painted image of a seated figure; next to the altar is placed a cult statue of a bearded Dionysos in right profile. The statue is stiff and has no arms, as if a simple pillar were decorated with a garment and a mask for the head of the god. Ivy branches decorate the statue, and flat discs (cakes?) with holes punched through them have been hung on the branches. The mantle pinned on the statue is very elaborately decorated, with a wide embroidered border with leaping dolphins between ornamental bands; around his neck is a large beaded necklace, and on his head an ivy wreath. Five Maenads dance on this side of the kylix; each wears a thin, belted chiton with long sleeves, a short apoptygma, and long kolpos; the thin pleats of the fabric adhere to the breasts, clearly delineating their contours. On all of the Maenads except the aulos-player, their hair hangs loose, projecting in a thick mass around the head.

From the viewer's left, a Maenad turns in three-quarter left view, as she leans back gesticulating toward the scene behind her. Her left leg is extended forward, and her right leg is bent, supporting her weight. She bends her right arm, holding her hand in front of her chest as if for balance as she pirouettes; her left arm is extended, almost touching the aulos-player behind her. This figure leans forwards in right profile, with her left foot forward. Her hair is caught up in a cap, from which a puff of curls escapes at the back. On the other side of the statue, overlapped by the altar, a third Maenad bends forward in a dancing pose, her right arm extended stiffly downward, and her left arm bent. Her head is bowed. Behind her, a fourth Maenad advances toward the altar. She is seen in three-quarter left view turning back, her weight on her left leg and her right foot kicked up behind her. She turns her head in right profile and extends her left arm behind her. Against her shoulder she rests a thyrsos, supported by her right hand. On the far right, a fifth Maenad bends forward in three-quarter left view, in a dancing pose. Her right arm is bent, and her left arm lifted above her head, her hand bent sharply back toward her ear. Like the third Maenad, her head is bowed.

On Side B six Maenads dance in a frenzied manner, their hair streaming wildly around their heads. Each wears a thin, belted, and sleeved chiton with a short apoptygma and long kolpos, and here too the fabric reveals the breasts by adhering tightly to indicate the rounded forms beneath. From the viewer's left, a first Maenad moves to her left in right profile, her left foot forward, her arms stretched in front of her with a thyrsos in her right hand. A second Maenad in front of her also stands in right profile, and bends forward slightly as she plays the krotales (castanet-like clappers). A third Maenad advances towards them in three-quarter left view, her left leg forward, right leg bent, and her head thrown back in an ecstatic pose. In her right hand she holds a thyrsos, which rests on her shoulder diagonally; in her left hand, stretched out behind her, she supports a miniature fawn. Behind her a fourth Maenad bends over in three-quarter right view, her left leg advanced; against her chest she holds a krater, decorated with ivy leaves, palmettes, and a tiny painted figure. Over her head her right arm bends sharply, her hand touching her head. A fifth Maenad

123 Side A

advances toward her, her left leg pointed out in front of her, her torso twisted as she turns back to look over her shoulder. Behind her head she holds a thyrsos in her right hand; her left arm extends back towards a sixth Maenad. This figure bends forward in right profile, her left leg advanced, and, as she touches her head with her left hand, she reaches forward with her right toward a tall column krater, draped with an ivy-leaf wreath, located under the left handle. Above the krater, on the underside of the left handle, appears the potter Hieron's signature: ΗΙΕΡΟΝ ΕΠΟΙΕΣΕΝ ("Hieron made it").

Around the outside of the kylix, eleven Maenads dance around a cult statue of the god Dionysos beside an altar. Like the depictions on nos. 124 and 125, the Dionysiac realm has again been inextricably fused with the atmosphere of Classical Athens and the festival of the Lenaia (see **Maenads**). What Makron has depicted is both a cult scene and a myth, pursuing the Dionysiac interplay between the historical and the mythical. In situations under the influence of Dionysiac forces, the use of a mask changed the reality of the viewer from the everyday world of Classical Athens to the

realms of imagination and vision. This transformation occurred both in ritual and in Classical drama, which was performed during festivals dedicated to Dionysos. During the ritual of the Lenaia, a mask was hung on a draped pillar to form a temporary cult statue of the god. Through the power of the Dionysiac forces invoked by the ritual, the image became the god, and the women who participated in the ritual dance were transformed into *Lenai*, or Maenads (see **Maenads**).

The Maenads dance, bending and gesturing broadly; some play musical instruments; others hold attributes of their status, including thyrsoi. One Maenad holds a krater; another holds up a tiny fawn. To the Greeks, maenadic behavior was a threat because it gave expression to the wild, uncontrolled side of the female nature, but it was also considered a necessary evil, because it nurtured women's mysterious forces of fertility (see **Women as Containers**).[1] In this moving depiction of the joy of the maenadic dance, with women dancing to please themselves, we find the polar opposite of the behavior normally expected of Athenian women: downcast eyes,

123 Side B

123 Detail of interior (tondo)

restrained postures, and a submissive demeanor (see **Aidos and Sophrosyne** and **Gesture and Gaze**). In contrast, Makron's Maenads represent the very essence of abandoned and unrestrained behavior, in their open and outwardly gesturing poses, the twisting and bending of their bodies, and the positions of their heads flung far back or dipped forward.

As many scholars have noted, the tondos of kylikes often depict a more sobering view of the subject matter treated lightheartedly in the exterior scenes. The user of the kylix would not have viewed the image until the wine had been completely drunk, when, following the spirit of revelry at the symposium, the jocularity of the evening comes to an end with a return to responsibility and serious matters. In the tondo of this kylix, however, a majestic figure of the god Dionysos himself appears with thyrsos and vine, bending forward slightly as he steps forward to the music of an aulos-playing Satyr. With the image of the god now come to life, his power to transform reality into an intoxicating vision is realized before the symposiast's eyes.

Makron decorated all but three of the extant vases with Hieron's signature as potter. He excels in decorative figures, whose linear drapery folds reveal a mastery of patterned effects. On this elaborately decorative kylix, he has created an elegant and expressive vision of the transformative powers of Dionysos, enlivening the exterior with active, dancing Maenads, who convey a musical, rhythmic atmosphere and a boisterous *joie de vivre*.

CAROL BENSON

1. King (1983) 109-111; see also Brumfield (forthcoming).

STAMNOS WITH MAENADS

ca. 420-410
by the Dinos Painter
Naples, Museo Archeologico Nazionale, inv. no. 2419

Attic, "from Nocera de' Pagani." Discovered with a ladle inside.
Clay
H 49 cm., W (at handles) 42 cm.

Publications: *ARV²* 1151.2; *Para* 457; *Add²* 336; H. Heydemann, *Die Vasensammlungen des Museo Nazionale zu Neapel* (Berlin 1872) 292 no. 2419; Furtwängler and Reichhold (1904-1921) vol. 1, 193-95, pls. 36-37; G. Nicole, *Meidias et le style fleuri dans la céramique attique* (Geneva 1908) 122, fig. 30; A. Frickenhaus, *Lanäenvasen, Winckelmannsprogramm der Archäologischen Gesellschaft zu Berlin* 72 (1912) 39, no. 29; Pfuhl (1923) 586, pl. 232, fig. 582; E. Langlotz, *Frühgriechische Bildhauerschulen* (Nuremberg 1927) 21-22, pl. 14i; Hahland (1930) 10, 14-15, pl. 2; L. Deubner, *Attische Feste*, 2nd ed. (Darmstadt 1932) 123-24, pl. 20; H. Thiersch, *Ependytes und Ephod* (Stuttgart 1936) 33-36; Buschor (1940) 220, 230-31, figs. 242-43; Metzger (1951) 23-24, 34; L. Lawler, *Terpsichore, Dance Perspectives* 13 (Brooklyn 1962) 28-29 (illus.); Lawler, *The Dance in Ancient Greece* (London 1964) 76-77, fig. 30; Wegner (1963) 36-37, fig. 15; Philippaki (1967) xviii n. 19, xxi, 135, no. 8; Simon and Hirmer (1976) 145, pls. 212-15; Parke (1977) 106, fig. 36; J.-L. Durand, F. Frontisi-Ducroux, "Idoles, figures, images: autour de Dionysos," *RA* 1982, 94, 96-97. figs. 8-9; Simon (1983) 100; Simon (1985) 275-76, fig. 265; *LIMC* III (1986) 273-74, no. 1 (s.v. Choreia); ibid., 413 no. 10 (s.v. Dione); ibid., 426, no. 33, pl. 298 (s.v. Dionysos); Boardman (1989) 96, fig. 177; M. Miller, "The *Ependytes* in Classical Athens," *Hesperia* 58 (1989) 316, pl. 51b; Frontisi-Ducroux (1991) 21-25, 84-85, 237, no. L 15, fig. 1,19-20; Robertson (1992) 242-43, figs. 246-47; Lonsdale (1993) 101-102, fig. 10a-b.

Around the rim is an egg pattern. Above the scene is a band of tongues. Beneath is a band of three and four meanders (right) alternating with a dotted saltire square.

On Side A four women gather around a frontal and armless image of the wine-god Dionysos, which is mounted on a slender pillar. The face, wearing beard and mustache, stares frontally, wearing a headdress whose steeply sloping sides are surmounted by upright, almost triangular leaves. A large oval attachment, thought to be a cake, flanks each ear. His belted tunic (ependytes) is decorated with rays across neckline and hem, and over the rest of the fabric is a star pattern; the pleated folds of an undergarment are visible beneath. Suspended from the central ornament of the belt is a wreath. Emerging from behind each side of his waist are two long ivy vines, and two more flank each shoulder. The base of the support is flanked by two pairs of stalks.

In front of the image is a table bearing two stamnoi and a ladle, as well as a number of small objects that are indicated in added white and are probably fruit. A woman standing in right profile uses a ladle to fill a skyphos (cup) that she holds in her left hand from one of the stamnoi. She is distinguished from her colleagues by her focused concentration and by the long straight locks that fall down on her shoulders. Like the other figures, she wears a peplos over which a fawnskin has been draped and fastened on the left shoulder. The peplos has two black stripes, which extend from beneath her right arm to her hem. Each woman wears an ivy wreath.

The other three women in the scene are moving forward energetically, the skirts of their garments blowing about their legs, their heads thrown back, and their long locks dishevelled. Behind the woman with the ladle approaches a woman who throws her head back in right profile. Her lowered right hand holds a thyrsos, and another one is held by her left hand above her head. On the other side of the image a woman moves to her right, her head turned back in left profile. Her left hand steadies an upraised tympanum, and the fingers of

124 Side B

124 Side A

her right hand are brought up to the back of her head. The woman behind her moves forward in left profile, head tilted backward. Her left hand holds a flaming torch upright, while her right hand, held above her head, grasps a thrysos, whose flaming end dips behind her shoulders. Inscribed above the woman with the ladle is the name Dione, and above the woman with the tympanum is Mainas.

On Side B a procession of three women moves to their right, behind a leader who plays the flutes and whose attentiveness is underscored by her directed gaze ahead of her. She and her comrades behind her wear ivy wreaths. The women behind her carry the accouterments of the Dionysiac cult: a thrysos and torch; next a tympanon; finally, a thrysos. Each of the following

figures throws her head up and back, but they vary in their choice of hairstyle and garments, which range from a chiton to a peplos, spotted fawnskin, and mantle. Inscribed above the second and third women are the names Choreia and Thaleia.

This celebrated vase belongs to a group of stamnoi that represent women participating in a ritual involving wine and an image of the wine-god Dionysos. The scenes have been variously described as depicting the Anthesteria and the Lenaia (see **Maenads**).

The women are dressed identically and are all bedecked, like the image, with an ivy wreath; however, not one of the women looks directly at the image. The controlled attentiveness and uncurled locks of the woman who ladles the wine contrast dramatically with the abandonment of her comrades, and yet we sense that each figure is acting out a prescribed role in a ritual that obviously combines methodical precision with the exuberance conventionally associated with the Maenads of myth. The obvious continuation of the scene on Side B reinforces the impression that we are witnessing the explicit unfolding of a ritual that celebrated the release of spirited impulses through the agency of wine. It is interesting to note that Pausanias relates a tradition that a Maenad named Choreia formed part of Dionysos' entourage.[1]

The Dinos Painter is fond of the world of women and is an enthusiastic observer of its mores. He represents the changing conventions of departure rituals with both liveliness and dignity (no. 20), and presents with bemused delight the story of Atalanta's drama (no. 117). His garments often bear a pair of stripes running down the right seam, and his agitated folds of drapery are rendered as long, wavy lines with tightly curving tips.

1. Pausanius 2.20.4.

125

STAMNOS WITH WOMEN PREPARING FOR DIONYSIAC RITUAL

ca. 440-435
by the Phiale Painter
Warsaw, The National Museum in Warsaw, inv. no. 142465

Attic
Clay
H 39.8 cm., Diam 31 cm., Diam (at mouth) 22 cm.

Publications: *ARV²* 1019.82; *Para* 441; *Add²* 315; K. Bulas, *CVA* Goluchow, Musée Czartoryski 1 (Poland 1) pl. 26; A. Frickenhaus, *Lenäenvasen, Winckelmannsprogramm der Archäologischen Gesellschaft zu Berlin* 72 (1912) 13, no. 28; Pfuhl (1923) fig. 571; Beazley (1928) 30, 51-53, no. 42, pl. 23; G.M.A. Richter, *Attic Red-Figured Vases: A Survey*, rev. ed. (New Haven 1958) 122; Philippaki (1967) xviii, 137; K. Kerenyi, *Dionysos, Archetypal Image of Indestructible Life* (London 1976) fig. 86a-b; *Quaderni Ticinesi. Numismatica a Antichità Classiche* 5 (1976) 49, fig. 17; A.W. Johnston, *Trademarks on Greek Vases* (Warminster 1979) 111; W. Dobrowolski, *Wazy Greckie* II, *Attycka Ceramika Czerwonofigurowa* (Warsaw 1982) pl. 15; J.-L. Durand and F. Frontisi-Ducroux, "Idoles, figures, images: autour de Dionysos," *RA* 1982, 102-104, fig. 14; M. Daraki, *Dionysos* (Paris 1985) 37, fig. 6; Oakley (1990) 36, 80, no. 82, pl. 62a, 63a-b; Frontisi-Ducroux (1991) 156-59, 251, no. L 66, figs. 94-95; G. Hedreen, "Silens, Nymphs, and Maenads," *JHS* 114 (1994) 57-58, pl. 2a.

Mended from several fragments. Around the rim is an egg pattern; an egg pattern also surrounds the roots of the handles. On the shoulder at the neck is a tongue pattern. Below the scenes is a band consisting of five and six stopt meanders (left) alternating with a blackened and dotted checker square. Around each handle, an elaborate and irregular palmette-tree grows from a stem at the baseline. Added red on the barbiton.

On Side A three women prepare for a ritual involving wine. On the viewer's left, a woman stands in right profile, her left foot slightly advanced. She wears a thin chiton covered by a mantle and a haircovering. The mantle is wrapped around her shoulders and is drawn around her right arm, forming a sling in which she grasps a baby against her waist with both hands. The baby, which has the pointed ears of a Satyr, stretches out both arms toward a woman who turns to her right in three-quarter left view, her right leg relaxed. She is dressed in a fine chiton and a mantle that passes over her left shoulder, behind her back, and is tucked around her waist. Her left hand holds an unstrung barbiton by her side. Her hair is pulled back into a knot, the ends of which fall onto her nape, and on her head is an ivy-leaf crown. She holds out her right hand beneath the baby, who reaches for her. Behind her, a woman in left profile bends over to place a stamnos on a small table with elaborately decorated legs. Her right leg is advanced, her left leg slightly bent. With her left hand she grasps the stamnos firmly by the horizontal handle. She wears a simple, belted peplos pinned at the shoulders, with the pointed ends of the overfold hanging down below her arms. Her hair is tied up at the nape and secured with fillets, and is crowned by an ivy-leaf wreath. Behind her, a slender Doric column identifies the setting as a temple or house.

On Side B three women advance to the viewer's right, each holding implements for the ritual. Proceeding from the viewer's left, a woman in right profile stands with left foot slightly advanced. Her head is bowed forward, and she wears chiton and himation. In her raised left hand she holds a kotyle, and in the left she holds an oinochoe. She wears an ivy-leaf crown. In the center, a woman steps forward in three-quarter right view, her left leg advanced, and her right leg trailing. Her bent right arm is raised above her head in a dancing gesture, and her head is bowed downward in right profile; two ivy leaves project from her crown. In her left hand she holds a kotyle. Leading the group is a woman in three-quarter right view, her left leg advanced and her right leg trailing. As she turns back to gaze at her followers, her head is in left profile, and with both hands she grasps a torch. Like the others, she wears a chiton with a himation wrapped tightly around her; her hair is covered with a cap.

The subject is a unique variation of a scene popular on stamnoi of this date, depicting Maenads or contemporary Athenian women in the roles of Maenads, preparing for a Dionysiac ritual in a sanctuary or courtyard. Their preparations are centered around dedications of cakes and wine, which they set out on a low table. Although many of these vases depict a frontal idol of Dionysos in the center of the scene (no. 124), some omit the idol, as is the case here, although the other elements of the ritual, including the table, stamnos, musical instruments (here a barbiton), and torches, remain the same.

The Attic festival depicted on these stamnoi has been identified as the Lenaia, which reflects the Ionic word *Lenai*, meaning Maenads (see **Maenads**).[1] The scenes appear exclusively on stamnoi, and stamnoi also appear in the depictions, a fact which indicates the significance of the vessels in the ritual and suggests that the vases were made to honor the occasion.

125 Side B

In contrast with the wild, ecstatic Maenads seen on earlier vases (see nos. 123 and 126), scenes on these stamnoi show matronly, respectable women busy with their tasks of preparation before the ritual, juxtaposed with scenes on the reverse which show their companions, now transformed into Maenads, beginning their dance. The power of Dionysos to transform everyday reality into a dream-like, otherworldly existence appears to have taken hold in the transition from Side A to Side B, but on this vase the character of the Maenads' dance is fairly subdued.

The Warsaw stamnos is unique in depicting a scene that allows for an intimate moment between the women participants in the cult and a baby. The poses and gestures of the women and the reaching arms of the baby are typical of Classical scenes of mothers and nurses attending to children (see nos. 6 and 51). The maternal, nurturing side of the participants is stressed for the viewer, an aspect which seems particularly significant for the Dionysian ritual of the Lenaia. Although we do not know the details of the festival ritual, many aspects of Dionysos' cult had marked associations with fertility, and the presence of the baby in this scene emphasizes the strong link elsewhere attested between maenadic behavior and the maternal role (see **Maenads** and **Women as Animals**).

The Phiale Painter was a pupil of the Achilles Painter, and his women in particular have all the grandeur, monumentality, and stately informality of figures on the Parthenon frieze (see pp. 248-

125 Side A

49, fig. 1 and nos. 26, 66, 78, and 113). In addition to his scenes of dignity and solemnity, however, the painter can often be seen to lighten his subject-matter with a playful sense of unreality, mixing Satyrs and Maenads with scenes of daily Athenian life, as in the surprising twist provided by the Satyr's ears on the baby in this Lenaia scene.[2]

CAROL BENSON

1. Simon (1983) 100-101.
2. Oakley (1990a) 36.

126

STAMNOS WITH MAENADS AND THE DEATH OF PENTHEUS

ca. 490-480
by the Berlin Painter
Oxford, Ashmolean Museum, University of Oxford, inv. no. 1912.1165

Attic, from Cerveteri
Clay
H 33.4 cm., Diam 31 cm.

Publications: *ARV²* 208.144; *Para* 343; *Add²* 194; *CVA* Oxford, Ashmolean Museum 1 (Great Britain 3) 18, 21-22, pls. 20.10-12, 25.1-2, 30.5-6; J.D. Beazley, "The Master of the Berlin Amphora," *JHS* 31 (1911) 282, no. 29, pl. 17; H. Philippart, "L'iconographie des 'Bacchants' d'Euripide," *Revue Belge de Philology et d'Histoire* 9 (1930) 65, no. 152; Philippaki (1967) 32-33, no. 5; Robertson (1975) 236, 238, 269, pl. 81c; M.J. Vickers, *Greek Vases* (Oxford 1978) figs. 41-42; Schefold (1981) 182-83, fig. 243; Burn (1987) 77 n. 32; Gantz (1993) 482; *LIMC* VII (1994) 312, no. 42, pl. 258 (s.v. Pentheus).

Restored from fragments; the mouth, handles and most of the neck are modern restorations. Around the neck-joint are two tooled lines. Below the figures is a narrow reserved band. Added red for blood and entrails. Added white for fillet on Pentheus, blood, and ivy wreaths. The composition runs continuously around the vase, with the handles overlapping the figures.

Six figures of Maenads circle the vase in an ecstatic dance, as they hold thyrsoi and the dismembered parts of the body of Pentheus. The Maenads wear a thin chiton and diagonal mantle; their hair is loose, with curls framing the face and streaming onto the shoulders, beneath an ivy crown.

On Side A, reading from the viewer's left, a Maenad moves rapidly to her left, her head thrown back in right profile. Her right hand, which is held behind her, grasps a mass of entrails; her left hand is flung forward. In the center of the scene a Maenad moves to her right. Her outstretched right hand holds a thyrsos; her left hand, held behind her, holds a leg. Her chiton is decorated with dots, and the folds billow up around her ankles. Her head is in left profile as she gazes down. The last figure moves to her right. Her upraised tight hand holds the head of Pentheus, seen in right profile; her left hand, angled to the ground, holds a thyrsos.

On Side B, reading from the viewer's left, a Maenad advances to her left. Her upraised left hand holds a thyrsos behind her head; in her extended right hand she holds an arm. Her head is inclined down. The central figure also moves to her left; her right hand, stretched out behind her, holds an arm; her left arm is extended forward, and the hand holds a thyrsos. The last figure lunges forward; her right hand, held above her head, holds a human leg, from thigh to foot. Her left hand clasps a thyrsos. She gazes downward at a small lion, which is seen in left profile, paws lifted.

The Maenads have dismembered the body of Pentheus, and in their ecstatic trance fling his limbs about (see **Maenads**). The story of the death of Pentheus was one of the most gruesome myths surrounding the uncontrolled, ecstatic behavior of the Maenads in their worship of Dionysos, and one of the most telling regarding Greek anxieties about the consequences of such uncontrolled behavior. The Pentheus myth was especially antithetical to the Greek conception of the woman's role as mother and nurturer, because Agave took part in the death and dismemberment of her own son. This vase antedates Euripides' *Bacchai*, the earliest preserved literary version of the myth,[1] by approximately eighty years but vividly evokes that later narrative. In this chillingly bloody

126 Side A

126 Side A-B

126 Side B

126 Side B-A

scene, youthful Maenads, fully lost in their ecstatic trance, show no awareness of the violence that surrounds them as they gyrate and fling the grisly limbs about. Their heads are bowed or lifted, and their eyes are focused only on an inner vision. The addition of the lion adds a further note of tension to the depiction, reminding the viewer of the violent side of the wildness in women's nature (see **Women as Animals**).

The figures are depicted in such frenzied movement that they seem likely to spin off into the viewer's space, exemplifying perfectly the strengths of the active and decorative poses of this date, ca. 490-480, when the Archaic style was giving way to Classical volume and solidity. On each figure, the hems and drapery folds swing outward to accentuate the direction and speed of her movement.

The Berlin Painter decorated many stamnoi, and the Oxford vase is a superb example of the painter's masterful confidence in contrasting vivid, violently active figures with the tight, stark simplicity of the black-glazed surface of the vase, avoiding the decorative patterning commonly used by other painters to frame the scenes or decorate the shoulder, handles, and rim. Accentuating the power of his figures through expressive silhouettes of stylized elegance, the Berlin Painter succeeds in forging a perfect equilibrium between glazed and reserved areas in an exact aesthetic balance of light and dark.

CAROL BENSON

1. Gantz (1993) 117.

127

WHITE-GROUND PYXIS WITH MAENADS

ca. 460-450
by the Sotheby Painter
Baltimore, Walters Art Gallery, inv. no. 48.2019

Attic
Clay
H (with lid) 19.7 cm., H (without lid) 13.3 cm., Diam 14.5 cm.

Publications: *ARV²* 774-5 1; *Add²* 287; *CVA* Baltimore, Walters Art Gallery 1 (U.S.A. 28) 55-56, pls. 59-60, fig. 18; sale catalogue, Sotheby's (London, December 7, 1920) pl. 1, sale catalogue, Parke-Bernet Galleries, *The Joseph Brummer Collection*, pt. 3 (New York, June 8-9, 1949) 2-3, no. 12, illus.; D.K. Hill, *Fasti archaeologici* 4 (1949) 140-41, no. 1430, fig. 13; Walters Art Gallery, "A Portfolio of New Accessions. Selections from the Brummer Collection," *JWalt* 12 (1949) 66 (illus.); L. Lawler, *Terpsichore, Dance Perspectives* 13 (Brooklyn 1962) 20 (illus); L. Lawler, *The Dance in Ancient Greece* (London 1964) 63-64, fig. 23; Mertens (1977) 137, no. 2; Roberts (1978) 47, no. 8, 54, 58, 204 fig. 5d, pl. 22; Wehgartner (1983) 138, no. 6, 147, pl. IV, 45, 46.2-3; A. Schöne, *Der Thiasos. Eine ikonographische Untersuchung über das Gefolge des Dionysos in der attischen Vasenmalerei des 6. und 5. Jhs. v. Chr.* (Göteborg 1987) 150-151, 155, 301, no. 501.

Intact. The lid is flat on top with a concave lower profile. It has a pomegranate handle with a ray pattern at its base. Around the join is a dotted tongue pattern, followed by a red laurel wreath (left) between reserved bands, a black band, and a band of five stopt meanders (left) alternating with dotted cross square, between two reserved bands. The lower profile of the lid has a ray pattern over a black band. The body of the pyxis is concave, flaring at the keel, and is decorated in white-ground. Above and below the picture field are two black bands. Added clay for wreaths. Golden and brown dilute glazes for most outlines, coloring of fawn, nebris and chiton of fourth Maenad, and chiton of fifth Maenad. Red on wreaths, peplos borders on second and fifth Maenads, mantle border of first Maenad, ivy leaves held by fifth Maenad. White on mantles of first and second Maenads. Brown on mantle of first Maenad, peplos of second. Black on chiton of third Maenad, and on auloi, snakes, and branch.

Five Maenads circle the pyxis, accompanied by a fawn. Beginning at the viewer's left, a Maenad advances in right profile, her right leg forward, the bent left leg trailing behind. She wears a chiton, mantle, and wreath, and plays on a pair of auloi. In front of her a second Maenad in right profile walks forward playing a tympanum. She wears a belted peplos and a wreath over loose curls. Next comes a small fawn in right profile, which gazes at the approaching third Maenad. This figure is shown in back view moving to her left, with both arms outstretched. In her left hand she holds a bearded snake that winds around her arm; in her right are two ivy branches. She wears a belted chiton with a short apoptygma and long kolpos, and a wreath. An upright thyrsos stands between this figure and the fourth Maenad, who advances in three-quarter right profile, her left leg advanced, her head thrown back in a pose of Bacchic ecstacy; her left arm is raised in front of her, and her right arm forms a half-circle behind her head. She wears a chiton with long, open sleeves and long kolpos, covered by an animal-skin garment (nebris) secured by a belt, and a wreath in her curly hair. The fifth Maenad dances in three-quarter right profile, bent forward with her left leg advanced and her right leg bent beneath her. Her arms are outstretched, with a snake in her left hand, wound once around her arm, and two ivy sprigs in her right hand. She wears a belted peplos with a long overfold and a wreath over curly hair.

127

On this graceful vessel made for a woman's toilette, we find the perfect complement between a vase and its decoration. Not only from its shape, but also from chemical traces found inside the vessel, we know that this pyxis was a container for a white cosmetic face-powder.[1] The white-ground decoration of the vessel allowed the artist to experiment more freely with fine lines and colored tints than was possible using the traditional red-figure techniques, and, to a woman using the powder on her face, the correlation with the cosmetic arts would have been obvious.

The technique also heightens the freedom with which the graceful figures dance and move in an atmospheric space. The expan-

siveness of their movement would surely have been a pleasing sight to a young Athenian woman. The affinity a young woman felt with these unconstrained creatures was recognized by the artist, who also revels in a lighthearted mood of pleasure and easy self-indulgence. At the same time, however, it is noteworthy that the Maenads' behavior is more restrained than we see it elsewhere depicted (see no. 126), possibly out of consideration for the demeanor deemed appropriate for respectable Athenian matrons.

127

The shape of the pyxis indicates that it came from the workshop of a group known as the Penthesileans, after a vase-painter who depicted Penthesilea on a kylix in Munich. The Penthesilean workshop was active in Athens for more than fifty years; this pyxis dates to the mid-point of their activity, ca. 460-450 B.C.

CAROL BENSON

1. A material found inside the vessel was identified by laboratory analysis in 1969 as lead carbonate (cerrusite), with a few particles of alpha-quartz. This has been identified as a cosmetic face-powder (*psimythion*). J.H. Oakley, *CVA* Baltimore, Walters Art Gallery 1 (U.S.A. 28) 56.

ORPHEUS AND THE THRACIAN WOMEN

Had I the tongue of Orpheus, O my sire, to charm with song the rocks to follow me,
and witch with eloquence whomsoe'er I would, I had essayed it.

Euripides, *Iphigenia at Aulis* 1211-14 (trans. A.S. Way)

Then one of the women, her tresses streaming in the gentle breeze, cried out,
"See, see, here is the man who scorns us!" and hurled her spear straight at the mouth of Apollo's bard.

Ovid, *Metamorphoses* 11.6-9 (trans. F.J. Miller)

Most modern readers know Orpheus primarily through the story of his journey to the Underworld to bring back his beloved wife Eurydike. According to the most familiar version, the journey ultimately ended in failure, when, unable to control his emotions, Orpheus failed to heed the warning of Hermes and turned back to look at Eurydike before they had safely passed beyond the boundaries to the upper world. Eurydike was forced to return to the Underworld forever, and the grief-stricken Orpheus realized too late that he would never see her again. Yet this powerfully tragic love story, which was also known in alternate versions ending with Eurydike's successful return from the dead, was only one of the many traditions surrounding the famous figure of Orpheus in the Classical period.[1] These reveal surprisingly varied facets of an important and powerful early shaman-like figure, whose songs had magical powers over his listeners and whose poetry revealed secrets of a religious nature to his followers.

Orpheus was said to have been the inventor of song, and his name was linked with those of Homer and Hesiod as the great poets of the distant past.[2] As the singer whose voice charmed every living creature, and moved even the rocks and trees, Orpheus is mentioned in many Classical sources: Simonides wrote of Orpheus charming the birds out of the sky and the fish from the sea; Aischylos contrasted the powers of Orpheus' voice with the ineffectual chorus of Argive elders; in Euripides' *Bacchai*, the chorus extols the power of Orpheus' singing over trees and animals; and in *Iphigenia at Aulis*, Iphigenia says she wished she had the voice of Orpheus, which could even bewitch the rocks.[3] As one of the Argonauts, Orpheus' contribution was through his powers of song; with his knowledge of the heavens he enabled Jason to navigate his course, and, when the ship passed the Sirens, Orpheus' songs drowned out their mesmerizing voices.[4] Writings attributed to him were believed to reveal religious tenets offering a mystical alternative to traditional religion, including belief in an afterlife.[5]

Many Classical sources reflect the ambivalent feelings the Greeks held toward this unusual figure. Unlike more famous Greek heroes such as Herakles and Theseus, Orpheus was not considered brave or manly, and his powers were always viewed with a tinge of suspicion, as if his somewhat effeminate nature made him untrustworthy. The different versions of his exploits reveal that some traditions considered him a magical figure with miraculous powers over man and nature through his voice, describing his singing with the verb *kelein*, to charm or bewitch; others doubted his powers and cast aspersions on his masculinity and effectiveness. The clearest example of this is Plato's reference to the story of Orpheus and Eurydike, where he contrasts Orpheus' cowardice, being unwilling to die for his wife, with Alkestis' strength in dying for her husband Admetus.[6] Orpheus' Thracian origin was continually emphasized; this distant region was thought of as an exotic place where musicians and shaman-like mystics were often said to have originated.[7] Depictions of Orpheus frequently show him wearing high boots and an *alopekis*, an animal-skin cap, which were considered Thracian garb.

This ambivalence toward Orpheus was surely related to mixed reactions to the teachings of the Orphic sect. The religious movement known as Orphism, which traced its origin to the poet, had its roots in the sixth century B.C., and played a significant role in the religious atmosphere of the Classical period. The beliefs of this movement are not well understood because the sources are not only fragmentary, but also allegorical and enigmatic, meant not for the uninitiated but for a small sect of mystical followers. The Orphics believed in purity and asceticism and followed a strict dietary regimen, abstaining from eating meat themselves and from killing animals for sacrifice. They believed in a different cosmological order than that of the traditional Greek pantheon, and by rejecting the religious traditions and rites of the Greek state, which centered around sacrifice, they rejected the Greek political and social structure as well. The Orphics' views on women are not fully revealed in the sources, but the movement was decidedly misogynistic, opposing the pure ideal of the male with the view that women had brought to humankind the disease of birth and death; because women were thought to be impure, they were not allowed to join the sect or any of its activities.[8]

No aspect of the Orpheus myth better reflects the unease of Greek attitudes toward Orpheus than do the myths surrounding his death. Orpheus met a violent death at the hands of Thracian women, whose anger at him mounted until it was out of control, and they took up any implement at hand to beat him with sticks, boulders, axes, spits, even their mortars.[9]

In fifth-century versions of the myth, the women's motives in the brutal killing stemmed from religious as well as sexual friction. In a lost play by Aischylos, referred to by a later writer, Orpheus was said to have been torn apart by Bassarides, maenadic women of Thrace, sent by Dionysos who was angered when Orpheus ceased to worship him.[10] The story is heavily ironic in that women, traditional outsiders in Greek thought who have also been rejected by Orpheus, here defend the existing order of traditional Greek religion, which Orpheus has rejected together with animal sacrifice.

Although the name Bassarides implies that Orpheus was killed by Maenads, the many images on Classical vases which depict this popular scene tell a somewhat different story (see nos. 128 and 129). The women in the majority of these scenes are distinguished by their tattoos, which was believed to be a Thracian custom.[11] Most importantly, they attack Orpheus with a marked deliberateness, not in the throes of the trance or frenzy that traditionally characterized maenadic behavior (see **Maenads**). Although swords and spears are sometimes present, the Thracian women's weapons are largely untraditional ones; Orpheus is killed by a thrust of a spit, with other women bringing boulders, axes, and branches to finish off the job. In some depictions, a woman carries a harpe, a toothed sickle, with which to sever his head.

Especially chilling is the raw violence of the women in these scenes; unlike traditional warfare, in which a system of controls is in place, the women's attack seems both out of control and disproportionately brutal toward their sole, unarmed opponent; they aim not only to kill him, but to crush, dismember, and decapitate him as well.

In many depictions, the spit is given special prominence, thrust into Orpheus' breast as the instrument that causes his death. The act suggests that the women are making Orpheus into a sacrificial animal, in violent reaction to the Orphic rejection of sacrificial ritual, and certainly, too, of Orpheus' rejection of women as inferior creatures, unworthy of joining his sect. The conflict between the ascetic males of the Orphic movement and the women they rejected as impure is embodied in the contrast between the unrestrainable women and the effeminate Orpheus, who tries vainly to ward them off merely with his lyre. The scene reveals a tremendous level of male anxiety about women's innate ferocity and intrinsic lack of self-control.

Post-Classical literary sources offer different explanations for the killing of Orpheus, but all of them adhere to the fundamental theme that the women killed Orpheus in anger at his rejection of them. In one story, the Thracian women are angered when he rejects them in his grief over the loss of his wife Eurydike. In another story, we are told that after his wife's death Orpheus was only interested in pursuing young men, and the women kill him for introducing homosexuality to Thrace. In still another tradition, Konon relates that the Thracian women kill Orpheus either because he hated all women or because he refused to admit them to certain rites.[12]

The tales of Orpheus continue even after his death: the women dismember him and sever his head, but the head continues to have the power to sing, and it floats down the river Hebron and lands on the island of Lesbos, where it functions as an oracle or source of poetic inspiration until Apollo silences this eerie voice.[13] The theme of the vital head, which continues to emit the spoken word after the body's death, is common to a variety of Indo-European traditions, where, as J.F. Nagy has noted, the severed head is consistently related to themes of sexual tension between men and women.[14]

CAROL BENSON

1. The version of the Eurydike myth which is most familiar to modern readers is not fully attested until Virgil, *Georgic* 4.453-503. Linforth (1941) 16-21; Segal (1989) 155-59. See also G. Schwarz, *LIMC* IV (1988) 98-100 (s.v. Eurydike I); L.-A. Touchette, "A New Interpretation of the Orpheus Relief," *AA* 1990, 77-90; Gantz (1993) 722-24. Among the sources that suggest that Orpheus' rescue of Eurydike was successful are Euripides' *Alkestis* (357-62) and Diodorus Siculus (4.25.4). Stories of descent to the Underworld are common in many cultures, and they play a major role in Greek myth, not only for figures such as Orpheus, Dionysos, and Herakles, who attempt to bring loved ones out of Hades, but for fertility figures, as in the myth of Persephone (see no. 82). In the case of Orpheus, the journey was not only to defeat death and rescue Eurydike but also one of knowledge-gathering. After having been to the Under-

world, Orpheus had knowledge no ordinary man could have, having learned the secrets of the cosmological order; Segal (1989) 157. This was also true of the Sirens (see **Sirens**).

2. Aristophanes, *Frogs* 1032 6; Plato, *Apology* 41a; Robbins (1982) 5.

3. Simonides 567 *PMG*; Aischylos, *Agamemnon* 1629-32; Euripides, *Bacchai* 560-64; Euripides, *Iphigenia at Aulis* 1211-14.

4. Apollonios of Rhodes, *Argonautica* 4.891-921.

5. M. Detienne, in M. Eliade, ed., *Encyclopedia of Religion* 11 (1987) 111-14 (s.v. Orpheus).

6. Plato, *Symposium* 179D; see Linforth (1941) 11.6.

7. Orpheus was the son of Oiagros of Thrace according to most of the ancient sources, including Plato, *Symposium* 179d; Apollonios of Rhodes, *Argonautica* 1.23, 4.905; Apollodoros *Bibliotheke* 1.3.2; his mother was the muse Kalliope. Orpheus was called son of Apollo by Pindar, *Pythian* 4.176-177, and Asklepiades *FGrHist* 12F6; and one source gives his mother's name as Polymnia (scholia to Apollonios of Rhodes 1.23). See Linforth (1941) 4-5, 22-26; Gantz (1993) 725. For the Thracian origins of other mystic figures, see Linforth (1941) 28; Segal (1989) 159.

8. Guthrie (1952); Robbins (1982) 13.

9. Robbins (1982) 23 n. 45.

10. Pseudo-Eratosthenes, *Katasterismoi* 24; Linforth (1941) 9-10; Freiert (1991) 40-41; Gantz (1993) 722. Plato also says that Orpheus was slain by women, in his passage on the myth of Er (*Republic* 10.620A). On Orpheus' death, see Guthrie (1952) 32-33, 54-55, 61-62; Freiert (1991) 34-35. The term bassarides means foxes, and is used as a synonym for Thracian bacchantes, who were thought to wear fox-skins.

11. K. Zimmermann, "Tätowierte Thrakerinnen auf griechischen Vasenbildern," *JdI* 95 (1980) 163-196.

12. Phanokles, *Kaloi*, frag. 1 in J.U. Powell, *Collectanea Alexandrina* (Oxford 1925); Konon *FGrHist* 26F1.45; Gantz (1993) 723.

13. Schmidt (1973).

14. Nagy (1990) esp. 216-17.

128

KYLIX WITH ORPHEUS AND THE THRACIAN WOMEN

480-470
by the Painter of Louvre G 265
Cincinnati, Cincinnati Art Museum, Museum Purchase:
John J. Emery, William W. Taylor, Robert S. Dechant, and
Israel and Caroline Wilson Endowments, inv. no. 1979.1

Attic
Clay
H 10.5 cm., Diam 32.5 cm.

Publications: *ARV²* 416.2; *Add²* 234; M. Schmidt, "Der Tod des Orpheus in Vasendarstellungen aus schweizer Sammlungen," *Zur griechischen Kunst: Hansjörg Bloesch zum sechzigsten Geburtstag am 5. Juli 1972, AntK Beiheft* 9 (Bern 1973) 98-99, pl. 33.1-3; *Bulletin of the Cincinnati Art Museum* 11.4 (1980) cover and 32; K. Schefold and F. Jung, *Die Urkönige, Perseus, Bellerophon, Herakles und Theseus in der klassischen und hellenistischen Kunst* (Munich 1988) 82-83, figs. 93-95; Gantz (1993) 724.

Intact. The tondo is framed by a band of meander (left) relieved by three equidistant cross-square panels, one of them beneath the feet of the figures. On the exterior, a reserved band runs below the scene. Added red for blood.

In the tondo two women advance in three-quarter left profile toward an irregular rocky mass that is cut off by the circular frame. The two women are nearly in step, but one advances aggressively forward, while the other leans backward, weighted down by the boulder she carries on her left shoulder, supported by both hands. The woman in front moves forward with her weight on her bent right leg. She wears a thin, pleated chiton and a heavier himation that is drawn over her left shoulder and wrapped around her waist and hips. Her head is turned back in right profile, and her eyes meet those of her companion. Her hair is gathered at the nape and secured by a fillet; one long tendril escapes from behind her disc earring. In her left hand she grasps a long spear which rests against her left shoulder. In her upraised right hand she holds a curving knife (harpe), its blade directed menacingly outward. The word ΚΑΛΕ ("beautiful") appears incongruously in the field, intersected by the curled edge of the knife. The second woman's right leg is advanced, but her body is angled back parallel to the line of her companion's spear. She wears a more elaborate chiton with a long kolpos and a narrow mantle, the ends of which are brought over each shoulder and swing outward with her movement; her skirt also billows out behind her to indicate her rapid movemennt. The front feet of the two women overlap, their back feet exactly in step. Though they appear as a simple vignette of two figures in a V-shaped composition, the intricate structure of their poses, their weapons, and their steady gaze lock them into a ominous dramatic movement.

In the center of Side A, Orpheus collapses against a boulder amidst an attack by four women armed with spears and rocks. He sinks onto his folded left leg, his right leg outstretched in front of him. His head is sunken onto his chest and his eyelid is drooping, beneath disheveled curls. In his upraised left hand he holds his lyre, the plektron dangling near his shoulder. His right arm is outstretched in the traditional gesture of an entreaty for mercy toward the chin of the woman before him. He wears a himation draped loosely around him, revealing his slender bare chest. Blood streams from several wounds: one in his right breast, one between his breasts where the spearhead belonging to the woman behind him has entered, and a third wound in his right side from which a long wavy instrument, perhaps a meat spit, protrudes. Standing in front of Orpheus, her right foot uplifted, is a woman who leans back to support the weight of a boulder on her right shoulder. She wears a thin, crinkled chiton with a long kolpos. Behind her, a woman turns to her left, her head in right profile. Over a sleeved chiton with kolpos, she wears a chlamys (a short cloak usually worn by men), which is fastened on her right shoulder and completely conceals her outstretched left arm. Her upraised left arm prepares to cast a spear. Behind Orpheus a woman leans forward, her left leg advanced, both hands supporting a spear which she thrusts into Orpheus' chest. Over her chiton with kolpos, she wears a chlamys that is fastened on her left shoulder. Following her is a woman who is dressed similarly, two black stripes running down the center of her garment. Her upraised right hand wields a spear, whose tip hovers beside Orpheus' left forearm. The hair of all the women is neatly knotted at the nape, and they wear earrings in the form of double-headed snakes. Under each handle is an irregular boulder.

On Side B five women in various animated poses prepare to join the attack. In the center of the scene a woman moves to her right, advanced right foot raised. Her head is turned back in right profile as she stretches her arm out as if to gesticulate to those behind her, and in her right hand are two spears, held vertically. Over her sleeved chiton she wears a chlamys that is fastened on her right shoulder, covering her left arm except for the hand. Her hair is bound is a sakkos. Behind her a woman rushes in the opposite direction, the heel of her rear right foot raised. In her lowered right hand she carries a double-axe; her outstretched left arm is concealed beneath the folds of her chlamys, which is fastened on her right shoulder; beneath is a sleeved chiton with kolpos. The

128 Side A (**See also colorplate, p. 372**)

hair of this woman is also wrapped in a sakkos. Approaching the central woman from the other side is a hastening woman, turned to her left, the heel of her rear right foot raised. Her outstretched left hand holds a harpe, and the hand of her lowered left arm gesticulates in animation. Her dress and hair covering resemble those of her companions. Behind her two women stand almost stationary, engaged in conversation. One women stands in right profile, wearing a chiton with a kolpos and a sakkos; her left hand steadies a spit on her left shoulder, while her right hand is upraised in gesticulation, as she exchanges glances with a companion whose right hand is raised in animated response. This latter woman holds a double axe in her upraised left hand, and wears a mantle over a chiton; her hair is gathered at the nape with a ringlet trailing down her neck.

The wild women of the scene by Hermonax (no. 129) have here given way to an organized, even efficient, and curiously social event. The pair of women in the tondo move forward with a lively dignity as if to a festive ritual. Their rapport is evident in their complementary strides and friendly conversation, and they brandish their unorthodox paraphernalia in a matter-of-fact and effortless manner. Meanwhile, their fellow Thracians have been so successful in their attack on Orpheus that further assistance is unnecessary. Orpheus succumbs to multiple wounds, and, as his head lolls forward, his right hand is extended in the traditional plea for mercy that is the hallmark of the defeated and dying. On the other side of the handles the artist has given us his vision of typical female bus-

128 Side B

128 Detail of interior (tondo)

129

STAMNOS WITH ORPHEUS AND THE THRACIAN WOMEN

ca. 470
by Hermonax
Paris, Musée du Louvre, Département des Antiquités grecques,
étrusques et romaines, inv. no. G 416

Attic, from Nola
Clay
H 31.2 cm., W (at handles) 33.2 cm., Diam 26.9 cm.

Publications: *ARV²* 484.17 and 1655; *Para* 379; *Add²* 248; *CVA* Paris, Musée du Louvre 3 (France 4) 10, pl. 19.1,4,6-7; *CVA* Paris, Musée du Louvre 4 (France 5) pl. 20.1-2; J.C. Hoppin, *A Handbook of Attic Red-Figured Vases*, vol. 2 (Cambridge, Mass. 1919) 34; Caskey and Beazley (1954) 74, no. 14; N. Weill, *BCH* 86 (1962) 80, fig. 11; F. Schoeller, *Darstellungen des Orpheus in der Antike* (Freiburg 1969) 56-57, 62, pl. 20.3-4, 21.1; Philippaki (1967) 37, no. 3, 39, fig. 2, pl. 24.1; Brommer (1973) 504, no. B8; Boardman (1975) 193, fig. 354; K.J. Dover, *Greek Homosexuality* (London 1978) no. R659; K. Zimmermann, "Tätowierte Thrakerinnen auf griechischen Vasenbildern," *JdI* 95 (1980) 176-77, no. 14, 184, fig. 11a-c; Carpenter (1991) 82, fig. 142; Lissarrague (1992) 225-26, fig. 60; Gantz (1993) 724.

tle, as women rush in opposite directions, while others pause in lively chatter. The only irregular note in this animated gathering is the lethal arsenal the women casually wield.

The popularity of Orpheus' death in fifth-century vase-painting suggests that religious tensions were only part of this subject's appeal (see **Orpheus and the Thracian Women**). The violence of the Thracian women, well in excess of the force needed to destroy the effeminate Orpheus, explores the popular apprehension of women out of control, incapable of self-restraint because of the absence of any inherent self-mastery (see **Women and Men**). The aggressive brutality of the Thracian women goes well beyond the excesses of the Maenads responsible for Pentheus' death (no. 126), because the Thracian women are not under the influence of any Dionysiac ecstasy or trance. The harpe, the sickle-shaped, serrated knife they brandish, is a harbinger of Orpheus' impending decapitation, but it also bears overtones of castration.[1] The presence of the meat spit refers to the animal sacrifices of the Dionysiac rites observed by these women but denounced by Orpheus, who excluded women from his own Orphic religion, with obviously disastrous consequences.

The exceptional composition and draftsmanship of this kylix possess a monumentality suggestive of influence from a major wallpainting. The Cincinnati kylix is the liveliest and most detailed rendering of the death of Orpheus and is delineated by the sure hand of an accomplished draftsman of the Brygan circle.

CAROL BENSON

1. Hesiod, *Theogony* 174-81.

Intact. On the lip is an egg pattern. Above the scene is a band of tongues; beneath is a band of two stopt meanders alternating left and right, separated by a dotted saltire square. The scene encircles the vase without a break at the handles, which overlap two of the figures, partially obscuring them. Added red for blood.

On Side A Orpheus dies at the hands of the Thracian women. He collapses to his left, his left knee and the toes of his extended right leg supporting the weight of his body. The fingers of his left hand reach for the ground but encounter the right foot of a charging woman behind him. Orpheus' right arm is raised above his head, and the hand grasps his lyre. His mantle is draped behind his back, the ends brought forward over his left shoulder and right hip, exposing his genitals. His head is in left profile and his hair falls in two long ringlets on either side of his neck. He gazes upward at a woman who moves aggressively forward in three-quarter right profile, the foot of her advanced left leg pressed against Orpheus' right thigh, the heel of her right foot raised. With both hands she plunges a spit into Orpheus' right breast, and the blood pours down his torso. The billowing folds of her garment and her streaming hair testify to the intensity of her charge. The woman wears a peplos that slips down her left shoulder and has a deep kolpos. The folds are arranged in clusters of narrow pleats separated by broad, flat expanses ornamented with lines of dots. The contours of both breasts are clearly indicated. On each arm is a line of tattooed dots or chevrons. Her wavy hair falls to her shoulders, and her head in right profile.

Behind Orpheus another woman advances in three-quarter left profile, a boulder held with both hands behind her head. Her garment is similar to that of her companion, except that it has a short overfold, beneath which the contours of both breasts are clearly visible. Two ringlets fall forward over each shoulder. At the opposite side of the scene a woman advances to her left, her extended left arm covered by her cloak. Her upraised right hand holds a small boulder; her head is in right profile, and her hair is gathered at her nape.

On Side B three more women rush to join the attack. In the center a woman in three-quarter right view advances to her left, her left leg advanced, her chiton with short overfold and kolpos billowing around her. Her right hand, held behind her, grips a curved knife (harpe), and her left hand is stretched out in

129 Side A

129 Side B

front of her in an expression of haste or agitation. Her long hair is tied at the nape. In front of her a woman springs to her left, a double-axe in her right hand, her mantle wrapped around her extended left arm. Her hair is bound in a roll and secured by a fillet. On the opposite side of the scene a woman in left profile moves forward vigorously, her thin garment streaming out behind her. Her right arm is stretched forward, covered by her chlamys, and her upraised left hand brandishes a spear. Her hair is also bound in a roll, secured by a fillet.

The painter has chosen to present Orpheus and his Thracian opponent, not in a moment when the denouement is as yet undetermined, but rather in an age-old battle format that shows the victor dealing a deadly thrust into the breast of the defeated foe. Here, unconventionally, the victim is the effeminate Orpheus and the conqueror is a violent women with tattooed arms and loose, uncombed hair. The weaponless Orpheus raises his lyre helplessly, obviously at a loss as to how to defend himself. Meanwhile, his blood mingles with his curly ringlets, which are identical to those worn by the woman behind him. The poet's masculinity is further undercut by the contrast between the gracefulness of his collapse and the crude lunge of the attacking woman. The exposure of his

genitals and the accentuation of the women's breasts reinforce the sexual undercurrents of the scene and call to mind the kantharos in Brussels (no. 120), where Herakles delivers a penetrating thrust to the exposed breast of the falling Amazon. In that scene, Herakles is outnumbered by the Amazons but still victorious; here, by contrast, Orpheus is helpless, when, completely alone, he is set upon by a parade of enraged women, who explode at their exclusion from Orpheus'"pure" religion and his rejection of the animal sacrifices of the Dionysiac cult to which these women adhere. The weapon that delivers the lethal blow is most appropriately a spit, an instrument of sacrifice.

The similarity of the figures on Side B to those on the kylix in Cincinnati (no. 128) indicates that both vases were inspired by a monumental narrative prototype. Obviously derived from that prototype was the motif of the woolen cloak draped over the women's outstretched left arm and hand such that the fabric functions as a shield. The parallel with the famous statue of the tyrant-slayer Aristogeiton must be deliberate.

The large scale, unrestrained movement, and loose drawing of Hermonax's scene infuses his figures with an arresting brutality that contrasts markedly with the more delicately rendered and ele gantly composed scene on the Cincinnati kylix.

CAROL BENSON

EOS AND KEPHALOS, EOS AND TITHONOS

Now Dawn rose from her couch from beside lordly Tithonus,
to bring light to immortals and to mortal men....
Homer, *Iliad* 11.1-2 (trans. A.T. Murray)

When a young man well-born and beautiful should die, they euphemistically describe
the dawn funeral procession as the snatching by Day [*Hemera*] not of a dead man,
but through erotic desire for the one who was snatched. Following Homer they say this.
Herakleitos, *Homeric Allegories* (trans. E. Vermeule)

Eos, goddess of the dawn, was notorious among the Greek goddesses for her unabashedly self-satisfying sexuality. She took a variety of mortal lovers, including Kephalos, Tithonos, Orion, and Kleitos, snatching them from the midst of their manly pursuits to become her consorts in the land of the immortals.

The goddess fell in love with Kephalos of Athens when she saw him hunting one morning on the slopes of Mount Hymettos. Kephalos was the son of Hermes and Herse, one of the daughters of Kekrops, and as such was an important figure to the Athenians; he was thought to be the founder of the tribe known as the Kephalidae and the eponym of the Attic deme Kephale.[1] Eos pursued and abducted him, and they had a son, Phaethon, who in turn was abducted by Aphrodite, and became the guardian of her shrine.[2] In late traditions, Kephalos was a personification of daybreak, or the morning star that vanished with the dawn.[3]

In a parallel myth, Eos fell in love with the youth Tithonos of the royal house of Troy; in Homer, the dawn goddess is said to rise each morning from his bed. The children of Eos and Tithonos were Memnon, King of the Ethiopians, and Emathion.[4] The *Homeric Hymn to Aphrodite* tells how Eos loved Tithonos so dearly that she asked Zeus for immortality for Tithonos but forgot to ask for eternal youth as well. As he grew old she continued to care for him, although no longer as a lover, and in the end he became so old and feeble that she shut him in a room where he babbled endlessly; in some versions, the aged Tithonos finally metamorphoses into a cicada.[5]

The story of Tithonos, in particular, speaks vividly to the overwhelming force of the goddess' sexuality, which enervates her male quarry and depletes him of his masculinity (see **Sirens**). The popularity of the myth in Greek thought indicates that the stories of female figures who actively pursue their own pleasures were both arousing and threatening to the Greek imagination (see **Amazons**, **Circe**, and **Medea**). Eva Stehle suggests that stories of the snatching of a youth by a goddess, the counterpart of the numerous myths about rapes of young women by the gods, reflect both male fantasies about being sexually overwhelmed and male anxieties about sexual feelings between mothers and sons and between older women and younger men (see **Pursuit Scenes**).[6] Her interpretation is supported not only by the subject's tremendous popularity in Classical art, but also by the moving parallels in the vase-painting imagery between such depictions as the amorous Eos abducting a youthful Kephalos on the tondo of a kylix in Berlin, (see no. 70) and scenes in which a grieving Eos carries the body of her son Memnon from the Trojan battlefield.[7] Emily Vermeule emphasizes the degree to which the abductions carried out by Eos have overtones of death as well as eroticism. She cites Herakleitos' comment that, at the dawn funerary procession of a beautiful youth, it would traditionally be said that Day (Himeros) had snatched the youth out of sexual desire.[8]

In the artistic tradition, Eos' sexuality and its implied consequences were portrayed as either titillating or poignant, depending on the context. Depictions on vases were numerous, becoming especially popular in the fifth century. It is difficult to distinguish scenes of Eos with Tithonos from those with Kephalos, or to identify any depictions of Orion or Kleitos, but scholars assume that in the scenes on vases where Eos pursues a hunter it is Kephalos, and where she pursues a schoolboy holding a lyre it is Tithonos. On a few vases, however, inscribed names reveal that the vase-painters have identified hunting figures as Tithonos and schoolboys as Kephalos, and we cannot know if this is merely a case of workshop confusion.[9]

On a number of important vases depicting the birth of Erichthonios with elaborate detail, the pursuit of Kephalos by Eos appears as the pendant scene on the reverse or tondo (see nos. 70-72). Although the significance of this relationship between the two themes is not fully clear to the modern viewer, the link might be in the figure of Herse, who plays a role in both. Herse, Kephalos' mother, is also one of the three daughters of Kekrops, who were asked by Athena to guard over the kiste (basket), which contained the baby Erichthonios, but disobeyed by looking into the basket. The pairing of the two scenes suggests an emphasis on the family of Kekrops, the first king of Athens; the contrast between the fate of Herse's son Kephalos and that of the child she failed to care for, Erichthonios, is striking and thought-provoking (see **Erichthonios** and the essay by Alan Shapiro in this volume).

Extremely significant is the fact that monumental sculpture also portrayed the myth. Atop the Stoa Basileios in the Athenian Agora, terracotta akroteria decorated the roofs of its projecting wings; on one side was the group of Eos carrying Kephalos upward to the heavens and on the other Theseus throwing Skiron into the sea. Similarly, marble akroteria on the Temple of Athenians at Delos represented Eos and Kephalos on one side and Boreas abducting Oreithyia on the other, both flanked by Nikai. A fragmentary marble group in the Louvre has also been identified as Eos and Kephalos. Winged creatures were favorite choices for akroteria, and the abductions of both Kephalos and Oreithyia as beloved by the gods were a poetically resonant choice; their prominence on civic architecture suggests that the allusion was heroic as well as sexual.[10]

CAROL BENSON

1. Hesychius (s.v. Kephalidai); J. Toepffer, *Attische Genealogie* (1889) 255.

2. Hesiod, *Theogony* 986-7; Euripides, *Hippolytos* 954-958; Apollodoros, *Bibliotheke* 3.14.3; Hyginus, *Fabulae* 160, 189. Kephalos was a famed hunter, and, like many other Greek heroes, was said to be one of the pupils of Cheiron: Xenophon, *On Hunting* 1.2. See J. Fontenrose, *Orion: The Myth of the Hunter and the Huntress*, University of California publications in Classical studies 23 (Berkeley and Los Angeles 1981) 86-111; Gantz (1993) 36, 238-39, 245-47; and the essay by Andrew Stewart in this volume.

3. A separate tradition exists in which a different figure named Kephalos, who was the son of Deioneus, had a tumultuous marriage with the Athenian huntress Prokris. By the Hellenistic period the two stories had become conflated, and the myth of Eos' abduction was modified to one in which she steals away the youth but cannot make him love her, and to get her revenge she attempts to trick Prokris into appearing to be unfaithful.

    See Gantz (1993) 36, 245-46; the Hellenistic Nikandros is apparently the first to conflate the two figures. Sources for the many versions of the story of Kephalos and Prokris include Pherekydes *FGrHist* 3.34; Apollodoros, *Bibliotheke* 3.15.1; Hyginus, *Fabulae* 189 (contrast 160); Ovid, *Metamorphoses* 7.672-862; Antoninus Liberalis, frag. 41 in E. Martini, ed. *Mythographi Graeci* 2.1 (Leipzig 1806). Another citation in Apollodoros has conflated the two stories in a different configuration: Kephalos marries Prokris, but later Eos falls in love with him and carries him off (*Bibliotheke* 1.9.4).

4. In Homer, Tithonos is the son of Laomedon and brother of Priam: *Iliad* 20.237.

5. Homer, *Iliad* 11.1-2 and *Odyssey* 5.1-2; Hesiod, *Theogony* 984-985; *Homeric Hymn to Aphrodite* 218-38; Mimnermos, frag. 4 West. Hellanikos, writing in the fifth century B.C., is the only Greek source to mention that Tithonos turns into a cicada or grasshopper (*FGrHist* 4F140); the next mention is in late Latin commentators such as Servius; see Gantz (1993) 36-37.

6. E. Stehle, "Sappho's Gaze: Fantasies of a Goddess and Young Man," *differences* 2.1 (1990) 88-125.

7. C. Weiss, *LIMC* III (1986) 783-84, nos. 321-24 (s.v. Eos).

8. E. Vermeule, *Aspects of Death in Early Greek Art and Poetry* (Berkeley and Los Angeles 1979) 163. The connection of Eos with the dead has also been discussed by H. Kenner, "Flügelfrau und Flügeldämon," *ÖJh* 31 (1939) 89-90; J. Thimme, *Griechische Vasen. Bildhefte des Bad. Landesmus.*, 4th ed. (1975) no. 43; C. Isler-Kerényi, in H. Bloesch, *Griechische Vasen der Slg. Hirschmann* (1982) 62-63, no. 30; see also C. Weiss, *LIMC* III (1986) 779 (s.v. Eos). Against this interpretation, however, Kaempf-Dimitriadou pointed out that all references to Eos' abductions suggest that her refuge was in the realm of the gods, not the Underworld; Kaempf-Dimitriadou (1979) 16-21, 62-63, 75 n. 533, 81-86, cat. nos. 57-126. This objection is perhaps too literal for the poetic allusion suggested by the imagery.

9. On the hunter/schoolboy distinction, see most recently Weiss (1986) 776-77; on the confusion in the inscriptions, see J.D. Beazley and L.D. Caskey, *Attic Vase Paintings in the Museum of Fine Arts, Boston* 2 (1954) 37-38; and J. Oakley, "A Calyx-Krater in Virginia by the Nikias Painter with the Birth of Erichthonios," *AntK* 30 (1987) 124.

10. Akroteria of the Stoa Basileios: these were seen and described by Pausanias, 1.3.1. Fragments of the group of Eos and Kephalos have been identified: Athens, Agora Museum, inv. nos. T 1261, T 3317, T 3987; C. Weiss, *LIMC* III (1986) 774-75, no. 282 (s.v. Eos). Akroteria of the Temple of the Athenians on Delos: Delos Museum, inv. nos. A 4279-A 4282; Weiss (1986) 774, no. 280. Fragmentary group in the Louvre: Paris, Louvre, inv. no. MA 859; Weiss (1986) 774, no. 281.

130

STAMNOS
WITH EOS AND TITHONOS

ca. 470
near the Painter of the Florence Stamnoi
Baltimore, Walters Art Gallery, inv. no. 48.2034

Attic
Clay
H 36.6 cm., W (at handles) 36 cm.

Publications: *ARV²* 509, 1657; *CVA* Baltimore, Walters Art Gallery 1 (U.S.A. 28) 21, pl. 26, 27.1, fig. 6.3; Philippaki (1967) 57-58, pl. 30.1-2; Kaempf-Dimitriadou (1979) 62 n. 97, 87 no. 130; *LIMC* III (1986) 765, no. 139 (s.v. Eos).

Intact, except for mended pieces around the mouth. Around the rim is a dotted egg pattern. Above the scene is a band of tongue, and beneath is a band of meander (left). Around each handle are a hanging palmette, double volutes, tendrils, and buds. Added white for inscription, plektron, and cord, and tuning pegs of lyre.

On Side B a woman stands in the center, turning to her left, with her head turned back in right profile. Her right hand rests on her hip; her bent left arm is held close to her body. She wears a chiton, himation, and fillet. Meeting her gaze is a bearded man who stands in right profile. He wears a voluminous himation pulled up around his neck; his left hand protrudes to hold the top of a knotty walking stick. On the other side of the woman a youth stands in left profile. He is also wrapped in a himation, his right hand extending to gesture in front of his chest. His covered left hand clutches a staff against his side.

On Side A Eos runs forward, her legs in right profile with her left leg advanced, her right heel raised. She wears a belted chiton with a long kolpos, and her mantle, edged with a stripe, is drawn forward over each shoulder. Her head is in right profile, and her hair falls in long curls to her shoulder, with short tendrils trailing around her face; a fillet is tied in back with a bow. The fingers of her right hand lift folds of her mantle above her right shoulder, and the hand of her outstretched left arm grasps the neck of a youth who turns his head back in left profile to return her gaze. Long curls frame his face, and his hair is rolled up in back and held in place by a fillet. He also lunges forward, his right, rear heel raised. His mantle is drawn over his left shoulder and passes across his waist and legs. His left forearm is brought across his waist, the fingers extended; his right forearm is raised toward Eos' face, the fingers extended and the palm facing out. His lyre, with the plektron attached by a cord, falls behind

130 Side B

130 Side A

his right thigh. The inscription ΚΑΛΟΣ is written in the space between the torsos of the two figures.

Fleeing away from Eos is a youth seen in three-quarter left profile, his head turned back in right profile. His left foot, the heel raised, passes behind Eos' right leg. His mantle is draped over his left shoulder and around his waist and legs. His left arm is brought to his waist, and his right arm is upraised in front of him in a gesture of alarm. Over his curly hair he wears a fillet.

The lyre identifies the pursued youth as the schoolboy Tithonos, one of several young men whom the goddess Eos was known to have abducted. The fate of Tithonos was particularly memorable for its graphic character. As the recipient of eternal life without eternal youth, his aging body eventually became distasteful to Eos, and she finally locked him away forever out of her sight. Here the painter has suggested that the ultimate disparity in their appearances lies far in the future. In contrast to the rendering of Eos by the Christie Painter (no. 131), the goddess here has approximately the same height as Tithonos. Moreover, the painter has omitted her wings, and, in a further attempt to equalize her with Tithonos, given her the long locks of an adolescent maiden. A note of flirtatiousness is introduced with the gesture of her right hand, which lifts her mantle folds in the manner of a bride unveiling herself for her new husband (see **The Wedding**). Belying these coquettish traits are the goddess's aggressively lunging stride and her firm grip on Tithonos' neck. Not surprisingly, the youth has dropped his lyre in fright and attempts to flee, although his glance back into Eos'

130 Detail of Side A

130 Detail of Side B

eyes suggests that he has already fallen under her spell (see **Gesture and Gaze**). Indeed, her voluminous folds of drapery dominate the scene, and her feet assertively overlap those of both Tithonos and his fleeing companion. As an explicit reversal of the conventional pursuit scene in which a maiden runs away from a following youth, the depiction of an aggressive Eos dominating her youthful male paramour provided ancient viewers with a note of levity, albeit one tempered by an underlying anxiety about the consequences of inverting the existing social order (see **Pursuit Scenes**).

The Walters stamnos is from a small class of seven stamnoi, each with a rounded foot and the same type of ornament, attributed to one workshop. All of the other six stamnoi are by the Aegisthus Painter or a follower, the Painter of the Florence Stamnoi. The ornament on the Walters vase is by the latter's hand, but the figures appear to be by a third (unnamed) artist.

CAROL BENSON

131

BELL KRATER WITH EOS AND KEPHALOS

ca. 440
by the Christie Painter
Baltimore, Baltimore Museum of Art, Bequest of Saidie A. May,
inv. no. 1951.486

Attic
Clay
H 37 cm., Diam 32.5 cm.

Publications: *ARV²* 1048.27; *CVA* Baltimore, Robinson Collection 2 (U.S.A. 6) 32-33, pl. 45; Kaempf-Dimitriadou (1979) 85, no. 110; F. Brommer, *Göttersagen in Vasenlisten* (Marburg 1980) 24, no. 49; E. Reeder Williams, *The Archaeological Collection of the Johns Hopkins University* (Baltimore 1984) 178-79, no. 116 (illus.); *LIMC* III (1986) 762, no. 99 (s.v. Eos).

Mended. Beneath the rim is a laurel wreath, and around the handles are bands of egg pattern. Beneath the scene is a band of two stopt meanders (right) alternating with a dotted saltire square. Added white for the diadem and laurel wreaths on Side A, and for the fillets and the bag's cord on Side B. Depicted on Side B is a palaestra scene with three youths, each wrapped in a himation and wearing a fillet. The central youth leans forward, supported by his staff propped under his left shoulder; his right arm is bent behind him and rests on his hip. In front of him a youth stands in left profile, his right hand gesticulating. The third figure stands in right profile, his right arm resting on a staff. Hanging in the field are a pair of hand weights (halteres) and a bag tied with a cord.

On Side A the winged goddess Eos strides forward vigorously in right profile toward the fleeing Kephalos. Her left leg is advanced, and both arms are stretched forward toward him. She wears a voluminous chiton with an overfold whose hem flares outward to indicate her brisk movement. The belt of her overfold is tied in a bow at the side. Her hair is drawn back into a large bun at her nape, secured by a diadem, whose ornament is rendered in added clay. Her large wings are extended behind her in right profile, and her face is also in right profile as she gazes at Kephalos, whose head is turned back in left profile to return her glance. Inscribed in the field above Eos' left hand: KJΛΛΕ ("beautiful").

Kephalos moves rapidly, his left leg advanced and his right, rear foot overlapping Eos' advanced left foot. His left forearm and hand are upraised in a gesture of alarm; his lowered right hand holds two spears horizontally. His chlamys is fastened on his right shoulder and is edged with a black stripe. A petasos hangs from a cord around his neck, and he also wears sandals. Short curls frame the face beneath a laurel wreath. Behind Eos and moving rapidly away from her is a youth whose dress and pose are a mirror reversal of those of Kephalos.

Eos, the goddess of dawn, who is celebrated for her unabashed sexual self-indulgence, prepares to abduct Kephalos. In Greek myth Eos took a variety of mortal lovers, including Kephalos, Tithonos, Orion, and Kleitos, and scenes of her abductions of Kephalos and Tithonos were especially popular in Attic vase-painting (see **Eos and Kephalos** and no. 130). The youth in this scene

131 Side B

can be identified as Kephalos because he is depicted in the garb of a hunter, with chlamys, petasos, boots, and spears.

The popularity of this myth in Classical vase-painting is easily explained by its inversion of the typical pursuit scene, where a fleeing female is closely followed by a youth, who is often similarly outfitted with chlamys and spears (see **Pursuit Scenes** and no. 121). To the Greek male, the reversal of traditional sexual mores was probably both threatening and titillating. The much greater scale of Eos accentuates her connotations of a mother figure, whose pursuit of youths for sexual pleasure places her in the territory of social taboo and psychological wish-fulfillment.[1] In this scene she looms above Kephalos, her arms extended in a gentle but firm gesture as she reaches out to grab him, and, presumably, to fly away with him. The youthfulness of Kephalos and his companion is underlined by their smaller size, beardlessness, adolescent physiques, and short, curly hair.

Kephalos' gaze backward into Eos' face parallels conventional pursuit scenes, where the fleeing maiden's responsiveness to her pursuer is indicated by her decision to turn upon him the irresistible force of the female gaze, the potency of which was widely celebrated in Greek thought (see **Gesture and Gaze** and **Gorgons**). The fact that Kephalos also turns back to gaze at Eos suggests that the goddess' lure is so irresistible that he cannot help himself, much as Orpheus could not resist the temptation to turn around and gaze at Eurydike (see **Orpheus and the Thracian**

131 Side A

Women). In a manner reminiscent of the Gorgon's countenance, Kephalos and his fleeing companion appear to be frozen into submission by the goddess' stare.

The Christie Painter is often admired for the monumentality of his figures' poses and drapery, which compare well with figures on the Parthenon pediments. The relative simplicity of the painter's compositions is also High Classical in spirit. A telling contrast to the movement of these figures parallel to the picture surface is offered by a depiction of the same subject on a kalyx krater in Richmond, dated ca. 410 (no. 71). There, the graceful, but weightless, figures float within a landscape setting that evokes a three-dimensional recession into space.

CAROL BENSON

1. Stehle (1990) 88-125.

CIRCE

No mythical figures better represent the Greek anxiety about treacherous women than the sorceresses of Greek mythology, Circe and Medea (see **Medea** and the essay by Margot Schmidt in this volume).

In the *Odyssey*, Odysseus tells of coming to the island of Aiaia, which is ruled by the goddess Circe, a sorceress.[1] After scouting the island and spotting Circe's large palace in a distant clearing, Odysseus divides his men into two groups and sends one party to the palace to investigate it, while he himself remains at the ship with the other party. The party which goes ahead first encounters tame lions and wolves around the palace; these will prove to be other men who have preceded them to the sorceress' island, now transformed into beasts. Next they hear the goddess' voice singing sweetly, and glimpse her shape indistinctly through the doorway as she works at her loom. Thus lulled by her apparent domesticity, they all (except their wary leader, Eurylochos) enter her palace at her invitation, and drink the potion she offers them in apparent hospitality. The drink places them under a spell, and with her wand Circe turns the men into swine, and drives them into her pigsties.

The leader returns to Odysseus in great distress; Odysseus hastens unafraid to Circe's palace and meets on his way the god Hermes, dressed as a young man, who offers him an herb, *moly*, which will counteract Circe's magic, and gives him instructions on how to gain the upper hand over the sorceress. Thus when Odysseus enters the palace and Circe repeats her spell, she is caught by surprise that it has no effect; as Hermes instructed him, Odysseus draws his sword as if to kill the goddess and wins her promise that she will not harm him. Then, becoming her lover, he gains the freedom of his men by declaring his unhappiness over their condition, and Circe uses her sorceress' powers to make them stronger, taller, and more handsome than they were before. All are reunited in great joy, and Odysseus lives with Circe as her lover for a period of a year.

When Odysseus and his men make up their minds to leave Circe, she agrees to their departure, saying she does not want to keep Odysseus against his will, and she advises them on how to proceed. She gives them provisions for their journey and sends them on with full instructions on avoiding the deadly obstacles in their way (see **Sirens**).[2]

The story resonates with sexual tensions. All of the human inhabitants of Circe's island are female, and any men who attempt to approach her palace are turned into domesticated animals, whose memories of their origins are erased and who are assigned the role of guarding the island. Because the word for pig in Greek is slang for the female sex organs, Circe's transformation of the men into swine has overtones of emasculation. Also noteworthy is the reverse transformation of the swine into men, because, even though the men's masculinity is ultimately enhanced, a woman is the initiator and controller of the process. Circe's transformation of the swine back into men is an inversion of the common mythical theme of a man who transforms an untamed animal into a woman (see **Women as Animals** and **Bears**).

The story of Circe incorporates other elements familiar in Greek thinking about women: the association of weaving with deception (see **Textiles**); the power of the female voice to persuade and beguile (see **Pandora** and **Sirens**); and female allure as an indistinct, elusive presence. Circe's enchantments have lingered in popular memory; the German verb *bezirzen* means "to lure like a magician," like the Circe of Classical myth.

Depictions of the story of Circe and Odysseus are more common and more varied in the Archaic period than they are in the fifth century (see the essay by Margot Schmidt in this volume). While early depictions show the sorceress as a powerful figure holding a vessel containing her potion and surrounded by transformed creatures, the Classical depictions instead focus on the moment when Odysseus overmasters Circe by drawing his sword. In these images, Circe shrinks back in fear, dropping her bowl and wand in surprise that he is unaffected by her spell; Odysseus advances with a heroic stance, his sword poised in a phallic manner (see nos. 132, 133).

This clear-cut distinction between Archaic and Classical imagery is tremendously revealing. Whereas earlier artists were concerned with illustrating the exotic aspects of Circe's sorcery and her powers over men, the vase-painters of the fifth century instead transform the scene into one of pursuit and sexual dominance (see **Pursuit Scenes**). This new emphasis places the significance of the scene into the context of a morality-tale on the restoration of the proper order, with the male controlling the female, after a temporary situation in which Circe had held power over men. This theme is pervasive in depictions of mythical females in power during the Classical period (see **Amazons**, **Gorgons,** and **Sirens**).

Because Archaic and Classical depictions of Circe often differ in detail from the Homeric version in the *Odyssey*, it seems likely that Odysseus' encounter with the sorceress may also have been popular as a simpler folktale told by nursemaids or around the hearth.[3]

CAROL BENSON

1. Circe and her brother, King Aietes of Colchis, are the offspring of Helios, the sun-god, and Perseis, a daughter of Okeanos; Hesiod, *Theogony* 956-57; Homer, *Odyssey* 10.136-139.

2. Homer, *Odyssey* 10.136-574, 12.1-157,226,268,302. Other sources on Circe include Hesiod, *Theogony* 1011-18; Apollodoros, *Epitome* 7.14-17; Apollonios of Rhodes, *Argonautica* 4.559-61, 4.662-753; Ovid, *Metamorphoses* 14.246-440; Hyginus, *Fabulae* 125. See also Gantz (1993) 34, 703-705, 707, 709-11, 713.

3. Connor (1988) 48-49.

OINOCHOE
WITH CIRCE AND ODYSSEUS

460-450
by the Painter of the Brussels Oinochoai
Paris, Musée du Louvre, Département des Antiquités grecques,
étrusques et romaines, inv. no. G 439

Attic, from Nola
Clay
H 19.4 cm.

Publications: *ARV²* 775.5; *Para* 416; *Add²* 288; E. Pottier, *Vases antiques du Louvre* (Paris 1897-1922) 1109, pl. 144; *EAA* V (1963) 627, fig. 783 (s.v. Oinochoai di Bruxelles, Pittore delle); Touchefeu-Meynier (1968) 94-95, no. 185, pl. 15.2-3; Brommer (1973) 430, no. B2; P. Connor, "The Cup and the Sword: Odysseus Intimidates Circe on a Column-Krater in Sydney," *AA* 1988, 45, no. 2, 46, figs. 6-7; *LIMC* VI (1992) 53, no. 23, pl. 27 (s.v. Kirke); Buitron et al. (1992) 79, 82, 89-90, no. 24.

Restored area between the figures, otherwise intact. A thin reserved band delineates the join of neck to shoulder, and another serves as the groundline below the figures.

Odysseus and Circe are seen on either side of the vase, united by their gestures and gazes into a single scene. A heavy-set Odysseus strides vigorously to his left, his weight on his advanced left leg, his right heel raised. His right arm is tensed and brought back behind his body, and his right hand grasps his sword as if he is about to thrust it forward. His thick chlamys is fastened on his right shoulder, and covers most of his torso and all of his left arm except for his left hand, which emerges at his waist to hold his spear horizontally, the spearhead pointed to the rear, away from Circe. His petasos, or traveler's sunhat, has fallen from his head, indicating that he has just darted forward. His hair and beard are long, scraggly, and unkempt. His face is in left profile, and his eye is open wide, as he meets Circe's gaze.

Circe moves to her right, the diagonal folds of her mantle indicating her rapid movement. Her weight is on her advanced left foot, with her right foot trailing behind as she turns her head in left profile to gaze back at Odysseus. In her left hand she holds a cup (kotyle); her right arm is extended out toward Odysseus and her hand holds up her wand vertically, as if to ward off his advance. The sleeve of her chiton overlaps the folds of her himation, which is brought over her left shoulder, covering most of her torso and legs. Her hair, gathered at the back of her head into a knot, is held in place with a fillet.

132

This type of vase is somewhat more utilitarian than the large kraters and stately stamnoi used on more formal occasions, and its informal asymmetry is enlivened by the animated interaction of the two figures who decorate it.

As on the Warsaw krater (no. 133) the painter has chosen to depict the highly charged moment when Circe realizes that her magic potion is having no effect upon Odysseus. While she holds the drinking cup and futilely waves her wand in alarm, Odysseus, fortified by the magic herb, or *moly*, obtained from Hermes, rushes towards her with sword at the ready. His muscular body and the highly aggressive gesture of his sword arm proclaim a triumphant masculinity that is rendering Circe powerless. The scene is a dramatic contrast to depictions of Circe on vases of the Archaic period, where the sorceress is commonly portrayed as a powerful magician in the act of transforming Odysseus' companions into swine. As Margot Schmidt discusses in her essay in this volume,

132

this painter's decision to depict Circe in defeat demonstrates once again the Classical preoccupation with mythical moments that illustrate the re-establishment of a social order in which male predominates over female (see **Amazons**, **Gorgons**, and **Sirens**).

The simplicity of the scene gives the depiction a lighthearted air and sends an equally simple message: unlike Circe's potion, the wine poured from this vessel will not overpower the senses of the symposiast, but may infuse the imbiber with the same vigor that is guaranteeing Odysseus' triumph.

CAROL BENSON

133

KRATER
WITH CIRCE AND ODYSSEUS

ca. 480
Warsaw, The National Museum in Warsaw, inv. no. 140352

Attic
Clay
H 28.8 cm., Diam (at mouth) 30.7 cm.

Publications: E. Bulanda and K. Bulas, *CVA* Poland, Collections Diverses (Poland 3) IV C, pl. 129.7; J. Orosz, *Eos* 31 (1928) 309-19, pl. 4; Touchefeu-Meynier (1968) 95 no. 186, 119-20; F. Brommer, *Odysseus. Die Taten und Leiden des Helden in antiker Kunst und Literatur* (Darmstadt 1983) 75; P. Connor, "The Cup and the Sword: Odysseus Intimidates Circe on a Column-Krater in Sydney," *AA* 1988, 45, no. 5; F. Canciani, *LIMC* VI (1992) 53, no. 26, pl. 27 (s.v. Kirke).

Intact. Beneath the rim is a laurel wreath between two reserved bands. Around the roots of the handles are bands of egg pattern. Beneath the scene is a band of two stopt meanders (right) alternating with a dotted saltire square. On Side B are three draped men.

On Side A Odysseus draws his sword against Circe while a metamorphosed member of his crew looks on. Odysseus lunges to his left, his advanced left knee bent, his right heel raised. His left arm is extended forward horizontally, and the hand holds his scabbard vertically. His lowered right hand grips his sword, the blade passing just in front of his genitals. He wears a heavy chlamys, pinned on his right shoulder, and laced sandals; a petasos hangs behind his neck. He has a long pointed beard, and his hair forms short curls around his face. His head is in right profile and he gazes in front of him at the fleeing Circe.

Circe runs forward in three-quarter right profile, the flowing folds of her garment and upturned hem of her tunic indicating her rapid pace. Over a pleated undergarment she wears a sleeveless, belted tunic that is ornamented with chevrons and has thick black borders. Her left arm is extended slightly away from her torso, the open palm indicating that she has just dropped the cup (kotyle), which is falling to the ground. Her right arm is stretched back toward Odysseus in a gesture of entreaty or alarm, the fingers extended and palm facing out. Her arm passes behind his left arm, and the billowing folds of her skirt blow up over his lower left leg. Her head is turned back in left profile to meet the gaze of Odysseus, and on her head is a knobbed wool cap.

Behind Odysseus and moving quickly away from him in left profile is a nude male who has a pig's head, which is turned back in right profile; a pig's tail is visible between his legs. The figure's advanced left knee is bent, and his right arm is stretched downward, mirroring the gesture of Circe's left arm.

Circe has just discovered that her magic potion has no effect upon Odysseus who, unbeknownst to her, has received from Hermes the magical antidote known as the *moly*. Circe has now dropped the cup and rushes to escape, but she extends her arm back toward Odysseus' face in a manner that recalls the victim's traditional plea for mercy. But Odysseus does not seem to be in the mood for sympathy, and he brandishes his sword so precisely over his genitals as to leave little doubt of the weapon's metaphorical

133 Side B

133 Side A

connotations. The intensity of his gesture is underscored by the sword's proximity to the porcine sailor, whose cowardly flight confirms the connotations of male effeminacy and female sexuality that swine consistently carried in Greek thought.

Circe's oriental garments refer to her Eastern origin as the daughter of Perseis, an Okeanid. The clothing also reinforces her identity as a woman with magical powers, which were usually ascribed to foreigners, and especially Thracians (see **Orpheus and the Thracian Women**, **Medea**, and **Circe**). Odysseus' pose is clearly an allusion to a famous statue of Aristogeiton, a much-admired Athenian who was honored as a tyrant-slayer and a facilitator of the beginnings of democracy. The equation of Aristogeiton's achievement with the defeat of a powerful woman may serve to elevate Odysseus' triumph, but it also underscores Circe's stature as a formidable opponent.

Indeed, the nature of Odysseus' victory is somewhat ambiguous, because Odysseus will stay on Circe's island for a considerable length of time, his journey homeward suspended as he becomes Circe's lover. The sexual currents between the two figures are already apparent as Odysseus and Circe link gazes, their arms and legs practically in contact with one another (see **Gesture and Gaze**). Directly in their line of vision is the porcine head of the hapless sailor, whose enormous eyes are locked upon Odysseus and Circe in what seems to be a knowing stare, as he witnesses the electrical charge that will precipitate a further delay in the sailors' return to Ithaca.[1]

Comparable depictions of this scene on kraters in Bologna and New York clearly argue for a common prototype.[2] The simplicity of the rendering on the Warsaw krater constitutes a dramatic excerpt of these more elaborate versions and, by virtue of its abbreviated form, is especially powerful.

CAROL BENSON

1. The presence of the creature in the scene in which Odysseus overmasters Circe does not correspond to the Homeric version, in which the metamorphosis of Odysseus' men had already taken place, and the pig-men were penned in the sties; it adds to the narrative richness of the depiction, however, and was a favorite with artists who chose to illustrate this story. See Oakley (1990a), 18; M. Davies, "A Convention of Metamorphosis in Greek Art," *JHS* 106 (1986) 182-3; D. Buitron, in Buitron et al. (1992) 78.

2. Bologna, Museo Civico Archeologico, inv. no. 298, kalyx krater by the Phiale Painter; New York, Metropolitan Museum of Art, inv. no. 41.83, kalyx krater by the Persephone Painter. See Brommer (1983) 74-75.

MEDEA

Unlike her aunt Circe, who worked her magic on a faraway island, Medea carries her family's tradition of treacherous female sorcery into the homelands of the Greeks. Medea is the daughter of Aietes, King of Colchis, and Eidyia, a daughter of Helios, and thus the niece of Circe.[1] Medea enters the life of the Greek hero Jason when he comes to her home with the Argonauts to obtain the Golden Fleece; the two fall in love, in one version under the coaching of Aphrodite, who helps Jason to gain the trust of the Eastern princess in order to succeed at his task. The girl then betrays her own father and countrymen for the Greek hero, as she aids him in overcoming various obstacles and in stealing her father's prize, the Golden Fleece, by charming or killing the snake that guards the tree on which it hangs. She escapes Colchis with Jason, fleeing with him on the Argo, and they eventually reach Jason's home port of Iolkos.

Medea uses her strong magical powers both to help those she loves and, in a cruel and deceitful manner, to harm or kill those she hates. The most vivid episodes involve her ability to rejuvenate living creatures. She achieves this transformation by boiling the dismembered subject in a cauldron, to which she adds an herbal potion; magically, a youthful version of the creature suddenly emerges from the pot (see **Women as Containers**). In several stories, Medea first demonstrates her powers by rejuvenating an old ram, in order to convince a human subject to undergo the spell; she then performs the feat on a man, who emerges from the cauldron as a vigorous youth. In the cyclic epic *Nostoi*, she rejuvenates her husband's father Aison in this manner; Simonides records an episode in which she does the same for Jason himself.[2] In one horrifying tradition, Medea gains a treacherous revenge on her husband's rival Pelias, the King of Iolkos, by convincing his daughters to use this spell to rejuvenate their aging father. She demonstrates the process by rejuvenating the ram in the cauldron but deceitfully withholds her magic potion from them. Thrilled by what they see, the daughters lovingly rush to perform this service for Pelias, killing and dismembering their own father, but without the potion they are unable to bring him back to life.

After the death of Pelias, Jason and Medea flee Iolkos and come to live in Corinth. After residing there for ten years, Jason wearies of Medea and leaves her for Kreousa, daughter of Kreon, Corinth's king. Euripides' play *Medea* gives the fullest Classical account of this part of her story, in which Medea, feeling betrayed and utterly abandoned, gives full vent to her feelings of hatred by using her magical powers to destroy everyone whom Jason loves. In a jealous rage she kills Kreousa and her father by sending Kreousa a poisoned garment as a wedding gift. Medea then kills her two children and flees to Athens in the snake-drawn chariot of Helios. There are variants of the story in which the children are not intentionally killed by Medea, or are killed by the inhabitants of Corinth, but Euripides tells of a very brutal, capricious, and intentional murder of the children at the hand of their mother.[3]

Medea's enduring popularity in ancient Greek thought is undoubtedly due to the fact that her predicament was only a more extreme version of every female's precarious position within Greek society. Like Medea, a wife was always in some sense an outsider to her husband's household, and it was only through her children that she had a strong link to the family. If the children were to die, she would lose the necessary legal link to her husband's family and by custom would return to her father's house. If she could not go back to her father's house, as Medea could not, she would truly be an exile. In Greek society a wife was, therefore, a perpetual outsider like Medea, and, because her intentions and the extent of her powers, especially her sexuality, were unknown and suspect, she could always be regarded as a threat to the established order. Thus, the drastic scenario dramatized by Euripides would not have been incredible to a Classical audience, for whom Medea is the embodiment of, in one scholar's words, "every Athenian's worst nightmare," a foreign wife who deliberately murders her own children, as well as her husband's new wife and father-in-law, using her secret potions and deceitfulness against those whom she wishes to destroy.[4]

Like the story of Circe, Medea's also makes prominent use of such paradigmatic female imagery as textiles (the garment she poisons to kill Kreousa and her father) for deception and guile (see **Textiles**) and emphasizes the capricious nature of women, who cannot be trusted to behave consistently, or to control themselves in the face of powerful emotions such as jealousy.

Depictions of Medea in the Classical period are primarily focused on the tragic story of the daughters of Pelias, which became a popular image in both sculpture and vase-painting.[5] A variation of this scene depicts Medea rejuvenating the ram with Aison or Jason looking on, a scene that represents Medea in a positive light, because she will use her powers to help her husband and father-in-law (see no. 134); a few vases depict a youthful human figure emerging from the cauldron.[6]

CAROL BENSON

1. Hesiod, *Theogony* 961, 992-1002; Pindar, *Olympian* 13.53-54, *Pythian* 4.9, 4.213-250; Pherekydes, *FGrHist* 3F32, 3F105, 3F113; Euripides, *Medea*; Euripides, frag. of *Peli-*

ades (Nauck 550-51); Apollonios of Rhodes, *Argonautika* 1.153, 1.182, 1.219, 3.7ff., 4.410ff.; Apollodoros, *Bibliotheke* 1.9.23-28; Cicero, Pro *Lege Manilia* 22; Diodorus Siculus 4.54; Ovid, *Metamorphoses* 7.9-424 and *Heroides* 6.129-130, 12.113-16; Pausanias 5.18.3, 7.11.2-3; Hyginus, *Fabulae* 23-27. See also Gantz (1993) 190-91, 340-41, 358-73.

3. *Nostoi*, frag. 7 *PEG*; Simonides, frag. 548 *PMG*. For evidence that Medea appeared in a Satyr play (*Trophoi*) by Aischylos, in which she rejuvenates a Satyr in a cauldron, see Simon (1982b) 140, pl. 35a-b.

4. Nugent (1992).

5. H. Meyer, *Medeia und die Peliaden. Eine attische Novelle und ihre Entstehung. Sagenforschung auf archäologischer Grundlage* (Rome 1980); J. Neils, *LIMC* V (1990) 629-38 (s.v. Iason); M. Schmidt, *LIMC* VI (1992) 386-98 (s.v. Medea).

6. *LIMC* V (1990) 634, nos. 58-61 (s.v. Iason).

HYDRIA WITH MEDEA
REJUVENATING THE RAM

ca. 470
by the Copenhagen Painter
London, British Museum, inv. no. E 163

Attic, "from Vulci"
Clay
H 56.2 cm.

Publications: *ARV²* 258.26, 1640; *Add²* 204; *CVA* London, British Museum 5 (Great Britain 7) 10-11, pl. 70; H. Heydemann, *Jason in Kolchis, Hallisches Winckelmannsprogramm* 1886, 19, n. 48; Smith (1896) 148-49; Beazley (1918) 64, fig. 40; J.C. Hoppin, *A Handbook of Attic Red-Figured Vases* (Cambridge, Mass. 1919) vol. 1, 201; Beazley (1928) 80; A.B. Cook, *Zeus: A Study in Ancient Religion* (Cambridge 1914-40) vol. 2, 212, pl. 14; A. Birchall and P.E. Corbett, *Greek Gods and Heroes* (London 1974) fig. 53; Boardman (1975) 113, fig. 200; H. Meyer, *Medeia und die Peliaden, eine attische Novelle und ihre Entstehung* (Rome 1980) pl. 9.2; P. Grimal, *The Dictionary of Classical Mythology* (Oxford 1985) 242; L. Burn, *Greek Myths* (Avon 1990) 62, illus.; *LIMC* V (1990) 634, 637, no. 62, pl. 432 (s.v. Iason); Gantz (1993) 367.

134

Intact. The back of the vase is discolored by fire. Beneath the figures, a strip of stopt meanders (right) in groups of two and three, alternating with cross square with dotted corners. Around the neck is a tongue-pattern; under the handle are two palmettes placed base to base. Added white for the hair and beard of Jason; added red for the flames, the herbal potion, and the inscriptions. Dilute glaze for the shading on the cauldron and the horns of the ram.

On the front of the hydria, Medea rejuvenates the ram, while Jason looks on. Medea stands in right profile, her left foot slightly advanced in front of the right. In her left hand she holds a hemispherical cup; her right arm is extended before her, as she releases a small cloud of her potion of herbs over the head of the ram before her. She wears a thin, pleated chiton and mantle, and on her head a narrow diadem and disc earrings. Her hair is gathered at the nape and

the ends tied into a bundle. She looks not at the ram but across at Jason, meeting his gaze directly. To the right of her head is an inscription with her name: ΜΕΔΕΙΑ.

In the center is a large tripod-cauldron placed over tall flames, rising out of an irregular mass of fuel set below. The rounded bowl of the cauldron has turned dark from the heat, indicated by shading in dilute glaze. Out of the cauldron rises in left profile the foreparts of a ram, drawn with close attention to naturalistic detail, including stippling for the fleece, a curved horn with ridges indicated in dilute glaze, a small, delicate ear, and an expressively rendered eye and curved muzzle. It leaps alertly toward Medea's opened hand, its forelegs raised and its neck lifted vertically. On the right an old man stands in left profile with his right foot slightly advanced, his right arm extended in a gesture of command or speech. He wears a pleated chiton and mantle, and his hair and stippled beard are white to indicate his age. He holds a staff to his side with his left hand. He is labeled with an inscription above his arm: ΙΑΣΟΝ (Jason).

There are several different stories which tell of Medea's magical ability to rejuvenate men. According to some versions, she first demonstrates her power by slaughtering an old ram, chopping its body into pieces, and boiling these in a cauldron, together with a magical potion of herbs. Out of the cauldron a fresh young lamb emerges, and her human subject is thus convinced to undergo this drastic procedure himself. In one version Medea rejuvenates Aison, Jason's father, and in another she rejuvenates Jason himself (see **Medea**).[1] In a parallel story, Medea wreaks a brutal revenge on Pelias, the King of Iolkos who had usurped the throne which was rightfully Jason's. Medea performs the feat of rejuvenating the ram to trick Pelias' daughters into attempting to use the same methods on their father. Instead of sharing her magic with them, however, Medea withholds it, and after the daughters kill and dismember Pelias they find they are incapable of reassembling him and bringing him back to life. Thus the stories surrounding Medea speak as much to her capriciousness and guile as to her magical powers (see the essay by Margot Schmidt essay in this volume).

This famous hydria depicts Medea at the height of her powers as a sorceress, at the very moment when her potions and charms have taken hold over the ram, and it appears resurrected from her cauldron. By labeling the man in the scene as Jason, the Copenhagen Painter alludes to the tradition wherein Medea rejuvenates her husband. To the ancient viewer, familiar with Medea's deceptive nature, the image of the ram and cauldron would also have called to mind the grisly death of Pelias.

The scene has strong parallels with depictions of the other sorceress of Greek myth, Circe, but the contrast between the imagery of the two sorceresses is revealing. Whereas depictions of Circe in the Classical period focus on the moment when Circe drops her bowl and wand as she realizes the impotence of her potion (see nos. 132, 133), here the herbs and spells of Medea bring about a powerful and positive metamorphosis in the ram, and prefigure the rejuvenation of her husband Jason. Thus while Circe yields to Odysseus, who becomes her lover, Medea is here presented as a powerful figure who uses her spells to aid and assist her husband.

The viewer would have, of course, been aware that Jason will soon spurn this foreign-born sorceress and take a new wife; in revenge, Medea will turn her powers against Jason, his new wife's family, and her own children, demonstrating the violence, betrayal, and savagery that was the Greeks' worst nightmare in welcoming a foreign woman into their lands and homes.[2]

The London hydria is one of the Copenhagen Painter's most celebrated masterpieces, with a tight simplicity of line and formal balance between light and dark masses that rival the best work of the Berlin Painter (see nos. 36, 126). The Copenhagen Painter is a superb draftsman who often chose to depict ambitious narrative scenes in a lively, if somewhat stilted, academic manner. By focusing on the aspects of the myth that parallel or prefigure other episodes with more tragic consequences, the artist assumes and exploits the shared knowledge of his intended audience, making this an excellent example of the density to be found in Classical Greek imagery, which often depends on allusion and symbolic references fully comprehended only by those who shared a common cultural background.

Another vase by the same vase-painter, in a lighter mood, is the pointed amphora with Peleus and Thetis (no. 109). A comparison of the two works reveals the painter's preference for stately, isolated figures with very little overlap, resulting in elegant silhouettes and an emphasis on the figures' expressive gestures, and the variety of attributes held in the hands. The striking beauty of the minutely observed ram's head exhibits an outstanding talent for naturalistic rendering.

CAROL BENSON

---

1. Were it not for the inscription, the depiction would be linked with Aison, because the story of Aison's rejuvenation is more common. It has long been noted, however, that the two names are similar enough to have been confused by an scribe; H. Heydemann, *Jason in Kolchis, Hallisches Winckelmannsprogramm* 1886, 19, n. 48.
2. Nugent (1992).

MEDUSA AND THE GORGONS

They had heads coiled about with serpents and great tusks like those of boars,
bronze hands, and golden wings by which they flew.
They turned to stone any who looked at them.

Apollodoros, *Bibiliotheke* 2.4.1-3

Few figures in Greek mythology have received as many and as varied interpretations as Medusa and her two Gorgon sisters, who were distinguished by fangs, snaky hair, and the ability to lithify anyone who gazed at them.[1] We also hear from Pindar of the terrifying sound of their shrill cry.[2]

When Perseus, the son of Danae, grew to manhood, King Polydektes ordered him to obtain the head of Medusa. With the aid of Athena and Hermes, Perseus obtained winged sandals, a cap that would render him invisible, and a pouch in which to place the severed head. Hermes added a curved sickle (harpe) to the hero's armory. Perseus came upon the Gorgons when they were asleep, and according to one tradition Athena guided his hand as he gazed at the reflection of Medusa in his bronze shield. A blow from the harpe decapitated Medusa, and from her neck cavity sprang the winged horse Pegasos, together with Chrysaor, a hero of whom nothing is heard thereafter. Perseus escaped Medusa's pursuing sisters by using his winged sandals and cap of darkness; later, on Seriphos, Perseus used the Gorgon head to turn Polydektes to stone. Perseus then gave Medusa's head to Athena, who affixed it to the middle of her aegis.

Many scholars believe that the Gorgon first existed without a body, as a Gorgoneion, or terrifying mask used to ward off evil, a version of the evil eye. It has been suggested that the body was added for the purpose of enabling Medusa to be killed, not only as a means of explaining the origin of this disembodied terror-head, but also to enact the conflict between man and his fears of a demonic female sexual energy. Indeed, the sexuality of the Gorgon is unmistakable, from the progenitive capacity of her neck cavity, to the snaky locks which have often been compared with pubic hair. The association of a woman's throat and her vagina is well attested in Greek thought (see **Women as Containers**). Moreover, the Gorgoneion bears a strong resemblance to Baubo (a fertility demon associated with female genitals), Demeter, and the ritual of the Thesmophoria (see **Women as Containers**).[3] It is important to note that the Gorgoneion was also associated from early times with the goddess Artemis, in her identity as Mistress of Wild Beasts (fig. 1, and see **Artemis, Peleus and Thetis**).[4]

One of the most provocative, and certainly the most dangerous, features of the Gorgon head was the ability of its gaze to kill men by turning them into stone, and it is probably significant that we never hear of a woman being turned into stone by a Gorgon. Some literary traditions imply that a man was lithified simply by looking into the Gorgon's face; however, as the Richmond representation (no. 135) illustrates, the lethal factor appears to have been the gaze of the Gorgon returning the glance of the beholder. A common theme in Greek myth is looking where one is not supposed to look, although, interestingly enough, the culprits are usually parthenoi, such as Aglauros and Pandora (see **Erichthonios** and **Pandora**). Another common theme in Greek myth is the powerful impact upon a man of a female's gaze, although the woman is generally assumed to be beautiful (see **The Wedding, Pursuit Scenes, Gesture and Gaze**). The inversion, a female gaze powerful through its ugliness, is both an amusing note and the probable explanation for the beautification of the Gorgon head that took place by the middle of the fifth century. Transformed into a calm image of ideal beauty, Medusa's face and her stare emerge as only a more extreme manifestation of a quintessentially female quality.

Fig. 1. Gorgon as Mistress of Wild Beasts, Rhodian Plate from Kameiros, London, British Museum, inv. no. A 748, ca. 630 B.C. Courtesy museum.

Many scholars have offered interpretations of the Gorgon head based on its strong sexual overtones. Allaire Brumfield correlates the Gorgon, who must not be seen, with obscenities, otherwise forbidden words that women uttered during women's rites as a means of sparking the fertility process. Brumfield suggests that both the Gorgon head and the obscenities were related to men's fascination with women and men's simultaneous sense of repulsion, prompted by male awe at women's potentially subversive sexuality.[5] Page DuBois argues along similar lines, proposing that the Gorgon represents male fear of a woman's seemingly self-sufficient sexual and generative capability; she equates lithification with both multiple erections and impotence.[6] Richard Caldwell agrees that the Gorgon represents a castrating female force and suggests Medusa is also the forbidden aspect of a mother's sexuality.[7] Others note that the male qualities evident in the beard with which Gorgons are occasionally depicted indicate an androgynous being, and W.B. Tyrrell proposes that the Gorgon is an image of sexual intercourse.[8] Regardless of the exact associations, the Gorgoneion in the center of Athena's aegis certainly alludes to the sexuality Athena has deliberately forsaken.

Not all interpretations of the Gorgon are sexually linked. Marcel Detienne has noted that, in Homeric passages dealing with the mayhem of battle, the description of a hero's face often resembles that of a Gorgoneion, and the piercing battle cries evoke the Gorgon's shriek. Amid this chaos, Detienne argues, the demon takes possession of the warrior from within, and the confrontation with death freezes the expression as if in death.[9] A further important contribution to the Gorgon's analysis was made by Vernant, who reminds us of the particularly key role that perception played in Greek culture.[10] Vernant points out that what was important was not so much what a man was as how he was seen in other's eyes, because the image those around him reflected back was the manner in which he would, perhaps perpetually, be regarded. In essence, then, the Gorgon's grimace was a response to what the Gorgon saw in the beholder; in looking at the Gorgoneion, we look at ourselves.

Finally, one should note that the lithification of the Gorgon's gaze has been interpreted in broader terms. In his analysis of fairy tales, Bruno Bettelheim suggests that being turned to stone means to be dead to what the world is about, to be oblivious to humanity and to higher values, a condition of being emotionally numb.[11] Bettelheim also points out the longevity of the motifs in the story of Medusa, and, certainly, the birth process of Pegasos and Chrysaor calls to mind the re-emergence of Little Red Riding Hood's grandmother from the neck cavity of the wolf.

1. Hesiod, *Theogony*, 274-83; Pseudo-Hesiod, *Shield of Herakles*, 216-34; Pindar, *Pythian* 10.31-50 and 12.7-21; Euripides, *Ion* 999-1000; Lykophron, 838-46 *PMG*; Apollonios of Rhodes, *Argonautika* 4.1513-1517; Apollodoros, *Bibliotheke* 2.4.2 and 3.120; Diodorus Siculus 3.52.4; Ovid, *Metamorphoses* 4.604-5.249; 6.119-120; Pausanias 2.18.1; Hyginus, *De Astronomica* 2.12 and *Fabulae* 151. See also Gantz (1993) 300-

311; *LIMC* IV (1988) 286 (s.v. Gorgo, Gorgones); *LIMC* VII (1994) 332-33 (s.v. Perseus). As Tyrrell notes (1984) 149 n. 54, Apollodoros' account was mostly based on Pherekydes, but the use of the reflection in the shield was probably a later addition. For the Gorgoneion worn by Athena, see Homer, *Iliad* 5.738; Pausanius 2.21.5.

2. Pindar, *Pythian* 12.19-21.

3. See also the tradition of the Lycians, who were said to raise their skirts and run away at the sight of the Gorgon: Pindar *Olympian* 13.91, with scholia to 1.130; Plutarch, *Moralia* 17.248. See also Zeitlin (1982), who correlates the Gorgon's open mouth with the obscenities uttered at the Thesmorphoria.

4. Burkert (1985) 149.

5. Brumfield (1994).

6. DuBois (1988) 87, 92.

7. Caldwell (1990) 355, 362.

8. Tyrrell (1984) 109. He also suggests that in the birth of Pegasos and Chrysaor from the neck cavity the myth separates the sexual process from the birth process.

9. Detienne (1977b).

10. Vernant (1985).

11. Bettelheim (1975) 77.

135

HYDRIA
WITH PERSEUS AND MEDUSA

ca. 450 B.C.
by the Nausikaa Painter
Richmond, Virginia Museum of Fine Arts,
The Arthur and Margaret Glasgow Fund, inv. no. 62.1.1

Attic
Clay
H 45.5 cm.

Publications: *ARV²* 1683, 48bis; *Para* 452; C. Alexander, "Clay Mirrors of the Age of Gold," *Art News* 61 (1962) 29, 52-53, fig. 6; Alexander, in *Arts in Virginia* 2 (1962) 9; K. Schauenberg, "Zu einer Hydria des Nausikaa-Malers in Richmond," *Kunst in Hessen und am Mittelrhein* 3 (1963) 3-15, fig. 1-3; Virginia Museum of Fine Arts, *Ancient Art in the Virginia Museum* (Richmond 1973) 95, no. 111; J. Floren, *Studien zur Typologie des Gorgoneion* (Westfalen 1977) 180 no. G; Shapiro (1981) 98-99, no. 38; *LIMC* III (1986) 7, no. 20 (s.v. Atlas); *LIMC* IV (1988) 312, no. 299, pl. 183 (s.v. Gorgo, Gorgones); Boardman (1989) 96, fig. 197; Carpenter (1991) 105, fig. 153; Gantz (1993) 307; *LIMC* VII (1994) 338-39, no. 102 (s.v. Perseus).

Mended from fragments, with some restoration on the figures, including the upper edges of Medusa's wings. On the lip is an egg-pattern; at the base of neck is a band with ivy-leaf chain in opposed pairs between two reserved bands. Below the figures is a band of meander (right) alternating at intervals of six and seven with saltire squares. The handles are placed on top of the figural scene, overlapping the figures at the left and right of the composition.

The scene depicts the slaying of Medusa. In the center, on an irregular groundline from which a short tree grows, the Gorgon Medusa is stretched out on her left side. Her frontal face is huge and round and has heavy eyebrows and a large mouth with deeply marked jowls. Her eyes are closed in sleep and her hair is center-parted. She wears a short, belted tunic of thin, pleated material, with short sleeves. Her left arm is curled underneath her, and her right arm is

135

bent and lies across her chest, her elbow pressed against the base of the tree as if for protection. Her right leg rests above her left leg. Her wings are curved above her, closed, and are overlapped by the tree, which has an irregular trunk and four short branches lined with leaves. On the right Perseus advances toward her in left profile. He is bent forward in stealth, his right leg advanced, his left bent beneath him. His right arm is extended and in his right hand he holds the curved harpe (the tip of which has been restored). The leather pouch (kibisis) in which he will place the Gorgon's head hangs from his bent left arm, and he grips one end of it in his left hand. He wears a short, belted tunic. Behind him, Hermes stands frontally. He wears a chlamys pinned on the right shoulder, and a petasos hangs behind his head; in his sharply bent right arm he holds his kerykeion against his chest. His left arm is extended behind him in a gesture of caution or exclamation. His head is in left profile as he gazes at the scene to his right. The left side of the handle overlaps his left leg.

On the other side of the tree and behind Medusa's legs, Athena stands in right profile, extending her right arm as if to direct the action. In her left hand she holds a spear, which rests diagonally against her left shoulder. She wears a chiton and himation, and a tall Corinthian helmet on her head, which overlaps the ornamental band above. Behind her a bearded man sits on a irregular goundline in three-quarter right view, his right arm bent and resting on a curved staff. His left hand is raised in a gesture of surprise or alarm. He wears a sleeveless tunic and a fillet in his hair. His face is in right profile as he gazes at the scene before him.

The hydria depicts the story of Perseus and Medusa with a comparative wealth of narrative detail, including the sleeping Medusa in a landscape setting, seen on only one other Classical example (see no. 136). Her physical connection with the tree emphasizes her vulnerability as she sleeps, and also surely alludes to her association with chthonic forces and with fertility (see **Gorgons**). Perseus advances furtively, as advised by his guides, Hermes and Athena. The goddess does not wear her aegis, as befits the reputed source of her Gorgoneion: when severed from her body, the Gorgon's head will become a potent emblem to ward off evil,

135 Detail

and this device Athena will affix to the center of the aegis as a protective charm.

The sleeping Medusa seen here represents a middle stage between the traditional, monstrous Gorgon familiar from the Archaic period and the beautiful maiden of the later fifth century, who is first seen on the New York pelike (no. 136). As on the slightly later pelike, Medusa here lies upon an irregular groundline, but her face is fully frontal in the traditional manner, and her facial features include the characteristic round, oversize head, huge, grimacing mouth, and deeply furrowed jowls. The frontal face is reserved in Greek art for the monstrous and bestial, for the dying, and for otherworldly and liminal beings (including Hermes Psychopompos in the scene of Persephone's return from the Underworld, no. 82), who were thought to inhabit a special sphere, distinct from the everyday world of men.

Unlike other depictions of the slaying of Medusa, the figures do not avoid looking at her, the implication being that it is not simply the sight of the Gorgon's face which lithifies, but her active gaze at the beholder (see **Gesture and Gaze**). Her latent power is nonetheless emphasized by the large group assembled to overcome her: three deities and a hero against a sleeping, seemingly benign creature. An element of amusement enters the scene, as the figures approach with exaggerated caution the ugly figure who is both maiden and monster.

In his publication of the vase, Karl Schauenberg identified the stately seated figure behind Athena as Atlas, whose presence identifies the geographical locale of the scene as the lands to the far west; an early literary source tells a version of the story in which Perseus encounters Atlas on his way to slay the Gorgon, and is questioned by the Titan about his identity.[1]

From a signed amphora in London we know that this vase-painter's name was Polygnotos, but in order not to confuse him with the other vase-painter of that name, scholars have continued to refer to him as the Nausikaa Painter, after a famous amphora by the same painter in Munich bearing a depiction of Odysseus and Nausikaa. With a taste for narrative stories and imaginative detail, the artist succeeds in endowing his scenes with a lighthearted liveliness.

CAROL BENSON

1. K. Schauenberg, "Zu einer Hydria des Nausikaa-Malers in Richmond," *Kunst in Hessen und am Mittelrhein* 3 (1963) 3-15, figs. 1-3. Gantz (1993) 46, on the version with Perseus and Atlas told by Polyidos, recorded by the scholia on Lykophron (837 *PMG*).

PELIKE
WITH PERSEUS AND MEDUSA

ca. 450-440
by Polygnotos
New York, Metropolitan Museum of Art, Rogers Fund, 1945,
inv. no. 45.11.1

Attic, from South Italy
Clay
H 47.8 cm.

Publications: *ARV²* 1032.55; *Para* 442; *Add²* 318; R. Hampe, "Korfu-Giebel und frühe Perseusbilder," *RM* 60/61 (1935-1936) 298 no. 43, pl. 100; E. Will, "La décollation de Méduse," *RA* 1947, 72; E. Buschor, *Medusa Rondanini* (Stuttgart 1958) pl. 45.1; G.M.A. Richter, *Attic Red-Figured Vases: A Survey*, rev. ed. (New Haven 1958) 128, fig. 96; K. Schauenberg, *Perseus in der Kunst des Altertums* (Bonn 1960) pl. 6.1; T. Karagiorga, *Gorgeie kephale* (Athens 1970) 151, no. I6; J. Henle, *Greek Myths: A Vase Painter's Notebook* (Bloomington and London 1973) 90-91, fig. 43; J. Floren, *Studien zur Typologie des Gorgoneion* (Westfalen 1977) 180, no. E, pl. 16.3; *LIMC* IV (1988) 313, no. 301, pl. 183 (s.v. Gorgo, Gorgones); K. Schefold and F. Jung, *Die Urkönige, Perseus, Bellerophon, Herakles un Theseus un der klassischen und hellenistischen Kunst* (Munich 1988) 103, fig. 126; Boardman (1989) 62, fig. 136; *Götter, Heroen, Herrscher in Lykien* (Vienna 1990) 139, no. 30; Gantz (1993) 307; *LIMC* VII (1994) 339, no. 115 (s.v. Perseus).

Mended from many fragments. Above the scenes between the upper joins of the handles is a short band of palmette chain. Below the scenes is a band consisting of three stopt, broken meanders (right) alternating with a dotted saltire square. Below each handle an elaborate and irregular palmette-tree grows from a stem at the baseline. On Side B are a man and two women; in the center, a bearded man stands in three-quarter right view. He wears a himation wrapped loosely around him, and grasps a scepter with his left hand. As he turns back to gaze at the woman to his right, his torso is twisted frontally, and his right arm is bent behind him, with his right hand resting on his hip. He is identified by inscription as the king Polypeithes. The woman to his right

136 Side A (**See also detail, p. 17**)

136 Side B

stands in right profile, her left arm raised in greeting, and holds a libation bowl (phiale) in her right hand. She wears a chiton and mantle, and a soft cap covers her head; she returns the man's gaze. To the king's right, a woman stands in left profile, a trefoil oinochoe held in her right hand in front of her; she wears chiton, mantle, and soft cap, and her bent, left arm is covered by her mantle.

On Side A Perseus slays the Gorgon Medusa as Athena looks on. In the center, Perseus advances to his left with his head turned back in left profile, his gaze directed at Athena. He stands in three-quarter right view with his left leg sharply bent and lifted, his foot raised and placed on a higher, irregular groundline, and his right leg planted behind him, slightly bent. The musculature of his torso is well defined, although the articulation of the transition to the right shoulder is somewhat awkwardly foreshortened where the right arm crosses his chest. Both arms are extended toward the sleeping figure of Medusa in front of him, his left hand gripping her hair with bent fingers, and with his right hand, which holds a curved, toothed knife (harpe), he prepares to cut off her head. He wears a chlamys pinned beneath his neck, a winged cap from which his long curls protrude, and elaborate winged sandals.

Medusa is stretched out in three-quarter left profile, in a semi-reclining position along an irregular groundline. Her wings are tucked above her head, and reach nearly to the handles; her head is tilted, turned in three-quarter right view, and her cheek is cradled in her left hand. Her eyes are closed in sleep, and her features are those of a fair young maiden. Her torso is frontal, her right arm bent and crossing in front of her chest to hook behind her sharply bent left

arm. She is bent at the waist as if seated, and her legs are stretched out, with her left leg slightly bent and overlapping her bent right leg. She wears a sleeveless, belted tunic with an elaborate patterned panel running down the front and a thick patterned border at the hem. Her long curls hang loose around her face.

Behind Perseus Athena stands turned to her left, her bent left arm raised, holding a staff, and her right arm hanging down by her side, overlapping the palmette ornament behind her. She wears a peplos belted with a cord tied in front, an aegis with curled snakes along the border, a mantle draped over her left shoulder, and a crested helmet on her head. Her head is turned in right profile and she gazes into the eyes of Perseus.

This vase is the earliest known example of Medusa's face transformed from terrifying monster to beautiful woman. Also in a radical departure, her face is depicted in three-quarter view instead of facing frontally, a position that signified to the Greeks monstrosity itself (see no. 135).

Perseus turns his head away as he slips his curved harpe around her neck. As Perseus avoids looking at Medusa, his eyes meet those of his protector Athena, who supports him by the power of her gaze. The intensity of their exchanged glances at such close range underscores the intimacy of their partnership, as it accentuates Perseus' exaggerated efforts to avoid the paralyzing effects of looking into Medusa's face (see **Gorgons** and **Gesture and Gaze**). Athena's strong yet passive figure contrasts markedly with Perseus' active pose and seemingly larger scale. In accordance with the story, Athena's aegis lacks the Gorgoneion, which will later be placed here as an apotropaic device.

The beautifying of Medusa's face drastically alters the mood of the scene. As she sleeps unprotected, she appears believably vulnerable, and the emphasis of the story is thus shifted from one of man against monster to a conflict between a youth and a beautiful maiden, one whose gaze can not only overpower but can kill. This modification not only brings the story of Medusa into the sphere of conventional Greek thinking about the lethal gaze of a beautiful woman but also heightens the sexual overtones of the encounter, especially evident in Perseus' grasp of Medusa's curly locks of hair.

Like the Sirens, whose voices lure men to their death, and Circe and Medea, who use magical arts, Medusa kills men with another intangible weapon, her gaze (see **Sirens**, **Circe**, and **Medea**). And, as in so many Classical depictions of Sirens, Circe, Medea, and

Amazons, Medusa is also represented in the moment of her defeat at the hands of a man (see nos. 120, 121, 132, 133, 134, and 137). The theme of a male's restoration of the sexual and social order is underscored by the vigorous and virile figure of Perseus, who dominates the scene. Just as the gods have aided and advised Odysseus in his travails, so has Perseus benefitted from divine guidance, but here it is significant that it is the intimate bond with Athena that has been the vehicle of his victory.

Polygnotos was a fairly common name in Classical Athens; the painter of this vase is not the same artist as the famous mural painter, Polygnotos of Thasos. Polygnotos the vase-painter was one of the most important of a group of vase-painters active in the mid-fifth century in Athens who demonstrated great facility in using the innovative elements of contemporary painting, including uneven landscape and foreshortening. This painter was particularly skilled at conveying three-dimensional effects through foreshortened views, such as that of Medusa's face, turned at a three-quarter angle as she sleeps.

CAROL BENSON

SIRENS

Whoso in ignorance draws near to them and hears the Sirens' voice,
he nevermore returns, that his wife and little children may stand at his side rejoicing,
but the Sirens beguile him with their clear-toned song.

Homer, *Odyssey* 12.40-44 (trans. A.T. Murray)

And I gave ear unto these Sirens' words, these crafty, knavish, subtle gossip-mongers...

Euripides, *Andromache* 937-38 (trans. A.S. Way)

The story of the Sirens is one of the most familiar and vivid episodes in the *Odyssey*.[1] As Odysseus takes leave of his lover, the sorceress Circe, she warns him to beware of the female Sirens, whose irresistible songs lure men to their death (see **Circe**). The Sirens, Circe says, live on an island, in the midst of a flowery meadow, surrounded by the bones and putrefying flesh of men. Circe tells Odysseus that as he approaches the island the wind will die down and his men will have to row the ship. She advises Odysseus that his sailors' ears must be stopped up with wax, but that he himself may listen to the Sirens' voices, if his men tie him tightly to his mast. Circe does not specifically describe how the Sirens' victims die, but the implication is that men who hear the Sirens' voices and songs become so charmed that they cannot leave the island, but remain with the Sirens until

they die. Odysseus faithfully follows Circe's instructions, and he successfully passes the island without incident.

Circe implies that what is irresistible about the Sirens is their voices, their use of song, and the subject about which they sing. This, we learn in the *Odyssey*, is the honor and glory with which men will be sung of after death as heroes of the Trojan War. Pietro Pucci has noted that almost every expression and formula that make up the Sirens' words is exclusively or almost exclusively drawn from the *Iliad*.[2] Thus, in the midst of his troubled return voyage, as Odysseus struggles with seemingly endless obstructions and near failures that constantly threaten to confirm his helplessness, he is tempted to succumb to tales of the superhuman image with which he will be honored in generations to come. As the piles of unburied and unhonored bones in the Sirens' meadow demonstrate, the enticement had destroyed many men before Odysseus.

What the story says about females finds many echoes throughout Greek thought. The Sirens' irresistibility lies in their voices and words, the erotic potency of which is underscored by the Sirens' domicile in a meadow, which in Greek slang referred to a woman's genitals (see **Gesture and Gaze** and **Persephone and Demeter**).[3] A second important consideration is that the Sirens' voices are lying voices; the Sirens promise Odysseus that, having heard their songs, he will depart from the island as a wiser man. One thinks of the lying words that Hermes instilled in Pandora (see **Pandora**). Also noteworthy is that the Sirens bring death to men through an extreme form of enervation, a technique that calls to mind the stories of Eos who depletes her lover Tithonos, and Medusa, who lithifies men who gaze at her (see **Eos** and **Gorgons**). It is interesting to keep in mind that only a woman, Circe, knows how to evade these temptresses, and Circe is no ordinary woman, but a sorceress who also has the ability to annihilate men through emasculation, by transforming them into animals that carried connotations of effeminacy (see **Circe** and **Medea**). Two further points are worth noting. According to a tradition known in the fifth century and possibly also familiar to Homer, a Siren dies if a man successfully resists her charms; by this zero-sum formula, either a male or a female must die in the encounter.[4] Finally, one should not fail to observe that, whereas the Sirens instantly recognize Odysseus as his ship approaches, they fail to see that Odysseus is tied to the mast and that the sailors' ears are plugged. It is as if the Sirens are lost in the past and do not see what is before them.

The story also tells us much concerning Greek views about men. The Sirens' lure is so powerful that, even though Odysseus knows of their danger, he must be tied down to resist the impulse to approach them. Appropriately, he is lashed to a phallic mast, an image which implies that human masts cannot withstand the Sirens' force. What is especially interesting is that the subject of the Sirens' songs is the eternal glory that was the dream of every Greek male, mortal or mythical. The myth tells us that this temptation, in combination with the Sirens' sexual allure, is so overwhelming that, seduced by his own greatness, blinded by fame, a man suspends good judgment and surrenders. One is reminded of the Athenian law that a man's will could be declared invalid if it could be proven that the deceased had written the will under the influence of a woman.[5]

In the *Odyssey* we are told only that the Sirens are female and that there are two of them. Artists invariably depict the Sirens as bird-headed women, and we frequently encounter these figures on grave stelai, obviously because of the Sirens' association with death (see no. 3).[6] It has been persuasively argued that Greek depictions of Sirens are based upon Egyptian renderings of the *ba*, or soul, which was believed to depart from the deceased's body in the form of a bird-headed woman.[7]

1. For the Sirens see Homer, *Odyssey* 12.39-54, 12.158-200, 23.326; Hesiod, frags. 27, 28 MW; Alkman, Louvre Partheneion 1.96-98 (frag. 30 *PMG*); Simonides, frag. 607 *PMG*; Euripides, *Helen* 167-73; Plato, *Cratylus* 403d; Apollonios of Rhodes, *Argonautica* 4.891 921; Apollodoros, *Bibliotheke* 1.3.4, 1.7.10, 1.9.25 and *Epitome* 7.18-19; Strabo, 1.2.12, 5.4.7, 6.1.1; Ovid, *Metamorphoses* 5.552-562; Pausanias 9.34.3; Hyginus, *Fabulae* 125. See Gantz (1993) 150, 705, 708-709.

2. Pucci (1979); Vernant (1991) 104-105.

3. A. Motte, *Prairies et jardins de la Grèce antique* (Brussels 1973) 50-56, 83-87; Vernant (1991) 104.

4. Lykophron, *Alexandra* 5.712-16; Strabo, 6.1.1; Hyginus, *Fabulae* 141; Servius, *Commentary on Vergil's Aeneid* V, 864; Eusthatius, *Commentary on Homer's Odyssey* 1709, 48. Arafat (1990) 1; Buitron et al. (1992) 131.

5. Plutarch, *Solon* 21.3; Demosthenes 46.14; Aristotle, *Athenian Constitution* 35.2; see essay **Women and Men** in this volume.

6. G. Weicker in W. Roscher, *Ausführliches Lexikon der griechischen und römischen Mythologie* IV (Leipzig 1909-1915) 601-39 (s.v. Seirenen); E. Buschor, *Die Musen des Jenseits* (Munich 1944); H. Sichtermann, *EAA* VII (1966) 341-44 (s.v. Sirene); Touchefeu-Meynier (1968) 145-90, nos. 244-336; J. Pollard, *Birds in Greek Life and Myth* (London 1975) 17, 188-91; K. Schefold, *Götter- und Heldensagen der Griechen in der spätarchaischen Kunst* (Munich 1978) 267-68; D. Woysch-Méautis, *La representation des animaux et des êtres fabuleux sur les monuments funéraires grecs de l'époque archaïque àla fin du IVe siècle av. J.-C.* (Lausanne 1982) 137-40, pls. 62-70; F. Brommer, *Odysseus* (Darmstadt 1983) 83-88; Buitron et al. (1993) 108-124, cat. nos. 34-46. For sirens on Classical mirrors, see L. Keene Congdon, *Caryatid Mirrors of Ancient Greece* (Mainz 1981) 14, 16-17.

7. Vermeule (1979) 75, 131, 137, 169, 201-206.

137

STAMNOS WITH ODYSSEUS AND THE SIRENS

ca. 480
by the Siren Painter
London, British Museum, inv. no. GR 1843.11-3.31 (E 440)

Attic, from Vulci
Clay
H 34.5 cm, W (at handles) 38.1 cm., Diam 28.7 cm.

Publications: *ARV²* 289.1 and 1642; *Para* 355; *Add²* 210; *CVA* London, British Museum 3 (Great Britain 4) 8, pl. 20.1a-d; Smith (1896) 268-69; Pfuhl (1923) 386-87, pl. 172, fig. 479; Philippaki (1967) 98, fig. 5, pl. 36.3; Touchefeu-Meynier (1968) 149-151, no. 250, pl. 24.3; J. Henle, *Greek Myths: A Vase Painter's Notebook* (Bloomington and London 1973) 166-167, fig. 79; Boardman (1975) 113, fig. 184.1-2; Robertson (1975) 218, 241, pl. 85a; Mussche (1982) 119-20, no. 63; D. Woysch-Méautis, *La representation des animaux et des êtres fabuleux sur les monuments funéraires grecs de l'époque archaïque à la fin du IVe siècle av. J.-C.* (Lausanne 1982) 95, fig. 48; Arafat (1990) 1; L. Burn, *Greek Myths* (Avon 1990) cover illus.; *LIMC* V (1990) 425, no. 1 (s.v. Himeros); Carpenter (1991) 235, fig. 346; Buitron et al. (1992) 109-10, 130-31, no. 42; Robertson (1992) 135-36, fig. 138; Gantz (1993) 709; Shapiro (1993) 112-13, 115, 119, 243, no. 53, fig. 63.

137 Side B

Intact. On the shoulder is a tongue pattern over a dotted egg pattern. Beneath the scene is a band of three stopt meanders (left) alternating with a checker square. The scene is framed on each side by a band of net pattern. Added red for the rigging of the ship, wreaths, fillets, and inscriptions. Dilute brown glaze (on Side A) for the shading of the sea, sails, gunwale, and details of the Sirens' feathers, and (on Side B) for the wings of the Erotes and the hare.

On Side B three large winged Erotes fly to their left over a wavy sea. The torso of the lead Eros is frontal, his legs in three-quarter right profile, and his head is turned back in left profile. He holds a sash that is ornamented with a meander pattern and has fringed ends. Inscribed over his head is the word ΗΙΜΕΡΟΣ ("desire"). The middle Eros extends toward the leader a long, slender tendril, and the third Eros flies almost in right profile, his hands supporting a hare. Over the heads of each figure is the word ΚΑΛΟΣ ("handsome").

On Side A the ship of Odysseus passes in left profile between two promontories, upon each of which is perched a Siren. A third Siren plunges headlong from her rocky perch toward the deck of the ship. The sail is furled, and four sailors man the oars, while a fifth sailor holds the rudder. Meanwhile, the wrists of Odysseus are strapped around the mast and his head is tilted upward. In front of him is inscribed his name [Ο]ΛΥΣΕΥΕ, written with the Attic lambda. The Sirens have bodies in the form of birds and heads that are twice the size of the men's heads. Their hair, surmounted by a diadem, is rolled into a bun at the nape, with a single strand escaping in front of each ear. The lips of each Siren are parted in song, but the eyes of the falling Siren are already closed in death. Over the head of the Siren perched above the ship's bow is the name ΗΙΜΕΡΟΠΑ ("voice of desire").

137 Side A

This much beloved vase narrates with lively charm the episode in Book Twelve of the *Odyssey* where Odysseus encounters the famous Sirens. These bird-women lured men to their death by singing of the glory with which men would be celebrated by future generations. Succumbing to the songs, unable to distance themselves from the voices, men would eventually die in the Sirens' meadow amid the mounds of white bones that were the remains of their predecessors. The sorcerer Circe gave Odysseus the secret of how to escape the Sirens' songs: by stopping up his sailors' ears with wax. Odysseus chose not to use the earplugs himself, but instructed his crew to tie him to the mast so that he would not be able to surrender to the songs and turn the ship toward the shore. Here we see him here straining upward to hear the Sirens' songs while, impervious to the sound, the crew rows vigorously ahead, urged on

417

by the helmsman. A single sailor turns around to wonder at his leader's torment, which is so clearly evident in the way Odysseus' chest is thrust outward and his head raised upward to the sky.

The plunging Siren has clearly collapsed in death, a detail that provides our earliest testimony for a tradition that otherwise survives for us only in a post-Classical literary source: if a man successfully resisted the song of the Sirens, one of the Sirens must die.

It is interesting to note that the Siren Painter has chosen to depict not the tense beginning of the encounter when the denouement was yet unresolved, but rather the moment of unambiguous triumph when one of the Sirens plummets headlong onto the deck. The fact that Odysseus' victory has been attained through passive resistance is a diametric inversion of the aggressive approach of the conventional Greek hero but is in keeping with Odysseus' legendary sharp mindedness, obviously the exact trait, with assistance from Circe, required to resist successfully the Sirens' words. Especially noteworthy is the gigantic size of the bird-women relative to the sailors. The Sirens' intimidating scale enhances the magnitude of Odysseus' victory and also implies that an exaggerated scale is necessary to convey adequately the strength of the Sirens' force; we are reminded of the superhuman size of the abducting goddess Eos (see **Eos and Kephalos**). Not surprisingly, the unmistakably phallic mast to which Odysseus has so stiffly bound himself dominates the center of the scene.

A final note is worth pondering. The Sirens do not sing men to their doom with the soft whisperings of lovers (*oaros*), at which women were traditionally thought to excel (see **Gesture and Gaze**). The Sirens rather destroy men by promising what was most fervently desired by all Greek heroes and, by extension, by mortal men—to live on after their death through tales of their glorious achievements. Odysseus and his men required wax and ropes to withstand the fatal temptation of eternal fame.

The winged male figures hovering over the sea on the reverse of the vase offer a marked contrast to the lethal gift proffered by the Sirens, and the juxtaposition of the inscription HIMEPOΣ on Side B with HIMEPOΠA on Side A drives home the correlation. As emblems, even embodiments of sexuality, the Erotes offer the comforting fulfillment of a different kind of desire, but the painter seems to imply that the inadequacy of that temporary satisfaction, when weighed against the Sirens' promises of a grander reward, would always draw men onward to the edges of life and death.

CAROL BENSON

GRAVE RELIEF OF MEGISTO AND ERATOXENOS

ca. 400-390
Houston, The Menil Collection, inv. no. 70-32DJ

Attic
Marble
H 117.8 cm., W 52.4 cm.

Publications: Hoffmann (1970) 18-21, no. 5, fig. 5 a-b; J. Frel and B. Kingsley, "Three Attic Sculpture Workshops of the Early Fourth Century," *GRBS* 11 (1970) 205, no. 24; Clairmont (1993) vol. 1, 415-16, no. 1.695.

Top and side edges preserved. Mended from two pieces, with all three akroteria effaced or broken off. Chipped over surface. Inscribed on the horizontal geison: ΜΕΓΙΣΤΩ ΕΡΑΤΟΞ[Ε]ΝΟΣ.

A woman turns in three-quarter right profile, her right knee relaxed. She wears a chiton beneath a himation that is draped over her head, drawn over her shoulders, and brought across her waist and most of her legs, with the ends passing over her left elbow. Her left forearm is raised, and the fingers of the upraised left hand lightly grasp folds of her mantle just in front of her left shoulder. Her right hand clasps the side of a rabbit that she is handing over to a boy in front of her. Her head is inclined and tilted, and she gazes downward. Her wavy hair is drawn back over the ears and is wrapped several times with a taenia, which passes across her hairline. She wears shoes. The boy is nude and stands in three-quarter left profile, his left knee relaxed, his left arm at his side. His right elbow is bent and most of his right forearm and hand pass behind the hare. He has short curly hair and his head is tilted upward slightly; he appears to gaze at the woman.

Megisto, a well-attested female name, is obviously the boy's mother, and it is likely that she is the deceased, although it is possible that the death of her son Eratoxenos is also being honored. Although his right hand is not shown, we can be confident that the hands of mother and son were united in their clasp of the rabbit, a love token more conventionally encountered in heterosexual and homosexual relationships. The link of the figures' hands, albeit through the animal, calls to mind the handshake of accord and farewell that is often seen in contemporary grave reliefs (see **Gesture and Gaze**).

Megisto's mantle is drawn up over her head, a feature commonly seen on funerary reliefs and probably connotive both of the contamination (*miasma*) of death and the custom of family matrons to drape their mantles over the back of the head when in public. In keeping with the dignified reserve expected of a respectable married woman, Megisto tilts her head downward. The inclination of her head is the conventional means of expressing *aidos*, a modesty with overtones of sexual shame that was customarily communicated through downcast head and eyes (see ***Aidos* and *Sophrosyne***). The nostalgic mood of the early fourth-century grave stelai combines with a tendency toward affectation to account for the exaggerated inclination of her head, as well as its sideways tilt and the mannered gesture of her left hand, of which the gently curling fingers barely grasp the mantle folds. Painted detail would have clarified the direction of her gaze, which is probably focused on her son.

Many elements in the relief look back to the Classical style of the Parthenon. The eyeball lies close under the eyebrow, and the lower eyelids are accentuated as protruding ledges. The cheeks are flat and broad, and the corners of the mouth are slightly downturned in a manner reminiscent of the Parthenon "pout." The drapery, by contrast, exemplifies the fresh directions that characterized sculpture of the first decades of the fourth century. Although the fabric of neither the chiton nor the mantle is transparent, the cloth is thin, and it clings closely to the body. Folds of Megisto's mantle cap her right shoulder, and on top of the shoulder the drapery forms a tight loop before passing over her head. The fabric of her chiton is characterized by deep grooves on her right breast. Her nipples are accentuated and connected by means of a narrow fold of drapery, which is isolated from the surrounding fabric and rendered with angular planes suggesting tension in the cloth. The mantle lies closely over her right leg; noteworthy are the broad expanses uninterrupted by any folds.

There are several reasons for the prominence of women in Attic funerary monuments of the late fifth and early fourth centuries, when a grave relief often functioned as the memorial for an entire family. A woman was traditionally regarded as the heart of her household, and that pre-eminence was enhanced by the renewed appreciation for family life that blossomed in the waning years of the disastrous Peloponnesian War. One should also keep in mind that women were traditionally viewed as closer to the thresholds of life, whether in birth or in death, and thus women assumed a prominent role in funerary ritual and in the tending of the family tombs. Finally, one should remember the deep-seated belief that a mother's grief was always the most profound of all. The story of Persephone and Demeter comes most readily to mind, but, even on a contemporary funerary relief in Malibu, we learn from the inscription that whereas it is Mynnia who has died, the suffering is that of her mother Euphrosyne (no. 104, see **Persephone and Demeter**).

138

ABBREVIATIONS

AA: *Archäologischer Anzeiger*

AAA: *Archaiologika analekta ex Athenon*

Add²: *Beazley Addenda: Additional References to ABV, ARV² & Paralipomena*, second edition, compiled by T. Carpenter (Oxford 1989)

AJA: *American Journal of Archaeology*

AM: *Mitteilungen des Deutschen Archäologischen Instituts, Athenische Abteilung*

AnnArchStorAnt: *Annali del Seminario di studi del mondo classico, Sezione di archeologia e storia antica, Napoli*

AntK: *Antike Kunst*

ArchDelt: *Archaiologikon Deltion*

ArchEph: *Archaiologike Ephemeris*

ARV²: J.D. Beazley, *Attic Red-Figure Vase-Painters*, second edition (Oxford 1963)

ASAtene: *Annuario della Scuola archeologica di Atene e delle Missioni italiane in Oriente*

BCH: *Bulletin de correspondence hellénique*

BICS: *Bulletin of the Institute of Classical Studies of the University of London*

BJb: *Bonner Jahrbücher des Rheinischen Landesmuseums in Bonn und des Vereins von Altertumsfreunden im Rheinlande*

BSA: *The Annual of the British School at Athens*

BWalt: *Bulletin of The Walters Art Gallery*

CEG 1: P.A. Hansen, *Carmina epigraphica graeca saeculorum VIII-V A.CHR.N* (Berlin and New York 1983)

CEG 2: P.A. Hansen, *Carmina epigraphica graeca saeculi IV A.CHR.N* (Berlin and New York 1989)

CVA: *Corpus vasorum antiquorum*

EAA: *Enciclopedia dell'arte antica, classica e orientale*

FGrHist: F. Jacoby, ed., *Die Fragmente der griechischen Historiker* (Leiden 1923-58)

Gentili: B. Gentili, ed., *Anacreon* (Rome 1958)

GettyMusJ: *The J. Paul Getty Museum Journal*

GRBS: *Greek, Roman and Byzantine Studies*

IG: *Inscriptiones graecae*

IstMitt: *Istanbuler Mitteilungen*

JdI: *Jahrbuch des Deutschen Archäologischen Instituts*

JHS: *The Journal of Hellenic Studies*

JWalt: *Journal of The Walters Art Gallery*

Kenyon: F.G. Kenyon, *Hyperidis orationes et fragmenta* (Oxford 1906)

LIMC: *Lexicon Iconographicum Mythologiae Classicae* (Zürich and Munich 1981-)

Lobel-Page: E. Lobel and D.L. Page, *Poetarum Lesbiorum fragmenta* (Oxford 1955)

LSCG: F. Sokolowski, *Lois sacrées des cités grecques* (Paris 1969)

MemLinc: *Memorie. Atti della Accademia nazionale dei Lincei, Classe di scienze morali, storiche e filologiche*

MonPiot: *Monuments et mémoires. Fondation E. Piot*

MW: R. Merkelbach and M.L. West, *Fragmenta Hesiodea* (Oxford 1967)

Nauck: A. Nauck, *Tragicorum Graecorum Fragmenta*, second ed. (Leipzig 1889).

ÖJh: *Jahreshefte des Österreichischen archäologischen Instituts in Wien*

Para: J.D. Beazley, *Paralipomena: Additions to Attic Black-Figure Vase Painters and Attic Red-Figure Vase Painters (Second Edition)* (Oxford 1971)

PEG: A. Bernabé, ed., *Poetarum Epicorum Graecorum 1* (Leipzig 1987)

PMG: D.L. Page, ed., *Poetae Melici Graeci* (Oxford 1962)

RA: *Revue archéologique*

RendPontAcc: *Atti della Pontifica Accademia romana di archeologia. Rendiconti*

RM: *Mitteilungen des Deutschen Archäologischen Instituts, Römische Abteilung*

RVAp: A.D. Trendall and A. Cambitoglou, *The Red-Figured Vases of Apulia* (Oxford 1978-)

Snell *LfrgE*: B. Snell and H.J. Mette, *Lexikon des fruhgriechischen Epos* (Göttingen 1955-)

Tarditi: G. Tarditi, *Archilochus* (Rome 1968)

West: M.L. West, ed. *Iambi et elegi Graeci ante Alexandrum cantati* (Oxford 1971-1972)

Adriani (1971): Adriani, A., et al., *Odeon ed altri monumenti archeologici* (Palermo 1971).

Ahmed (1982): Ahmed, L., "Western Ethnocentrism and Perceptions of the Harem," *Feminist Studies* 8.3 (1982) 521-534.

Aleshire (1989): Aleshire, S.B., *The Athenian Asklepieion. The People, their Dedications and the Inventories* (Amsterdam 1989).

Alroth (1992): Alroth, B., "Changing Modes in the Representation of Cult Images," in *The Iconography of Greek Cult in the Archaic and Classical Periods, Proceedings of the First International Seminor on Ancient Greek Cult, Delphi, 16-18 November 1990* (Athens-Liège 1992) 9-46.

Amundsen and Diers (1969): Amundsen, D. W., and C. J. Diers, "The Age of Menarche in Classical Greece and Rome," *Human Biology* 41 (1969) 124-32.

Andreasen (1984): Andreasen, N.C., *The Broken Brain: The Biological Revolution in Psychiatry* (New York 1984).

Antonaccio (1994): Antonaccio, C.M., *An Archaeology of Ancestors: Hero and Tomb Cult in Early Greece* (Lanham, MD 1994).

Arafat (1990): Arafat, K.W., *Classical Zeus: A Study in Art and Literature* (Oxford 1990).

Armstrong and Ratchford (1985): Armstrong, D., and E.A. Ratchford, "Iphigenia's Veil: Aeschylus, *Agamemnon* 228-48," *BICS* 32 (1985) 1-12.

Arthur (1982): Arthur [Katz], M.B., "Cultural Strategies in Hesiod's *Theogony*: Law, Family, and Society," *Arethusa* 15 (1982) 63-82.

Arthur (1983): Arthur [Katz], M.B., "The Dream of a World Without Women: Poetics and the Circles of Order in the *Theogony* Prooemium," *Arethusa* 16(1983) 97-116.

Arthur (1984): Arthur [Katz], M.B., "Origins of the Western Attitude to Women," in *Women in the Ancient World: The Arethusa Papers*, J. Peradotto and J.P. Sullivan, eds. (Albany 1984) 7-58.

Atallah (1966): Atallah, W., *Adonis dans la littérature et l'art grecs* (Paris 1966).

Austin (1968): Austin, C., ed., *Nova Fragmenta Euripidea in Papyris Reperta*, *Kleine Texte* 187 (Berlin 1968).

Austin (1994): Austin, N., *Helen of Troy and her Shameless Phantom* (Ithaca 1994).

Bakir (1981): Bakir, G., *Sophilos* (Mainz 1981).

Barber (1991): Barber, E.J.W., *Prehistoric Textiles: The Development of Cloth in the Neolithic and Bronze Ages with special reference to the Aegean* (Princeton 1991).

Barber (1992): Barber, E.J.W., "The Peplos of Athena," in *Goddess and Polis: The Panathenaic Festival in Ancient Athens*, J. Neils, ed. (Hanover 1992).

Barber (1994): Barber, E.J.W., *Women's Work: The First 20,000 Years. Women, Cloth, and Society in Early Times* (New York and London 1994).

Barber (forthcoming): Barber, E.J., "On the Origins of the Vily/Rusalki," forthcoming in a Festschrift to Marija Gimbutas.

Barringer (1991): Barringer, J., "Europa and the Nereids: Wedding or Funeral?" *AJA* 95 (1991) 657-667.

Barringer (1995): Barringer, J., *Divine Escorts: Nereids in Archaic and Classical Greek Art* (Ann Arbor 1995).

Barron (1980): Barron, J., "Bakchylides, Theseus, and a Woolly Cloak," *BICS* 27 (1980) 1-8.

Beard (1991): Beard, M., "Adopting an approach, II," in *Looking at Greek Vases*, T. Rasmussen and N. Spivey, eds. (Cambridge 1991) 12-35.

Beazley (1918): Beazley, J.D., *Attic Red-Figured Vases in American Museums* (Cambridge 1918).

Beazley (1928): Beazley, J.D., *Greek Vases in Poland* (Oxford 1928).

Benton (1939): Benton, S., "Excavations in Ithaca, III: The Cave at Polis, II," *BSA* 39 (1938-39) 1-51.

Bérard (1974): Bérard, C., *Anodoi: Essai sur l'imagerie des passages des passages chthoniens*, *BiblHelveticaRom* (Rome 1974).

Bérard (1976a): Bérard, C., "L'impossible femme athlete," *Annali. Sezione di Archeologia e Storia Antica* 8 (1986) 195-202.

Bérard (1976b): Bérard, C., "Le liknon d'Athéna," *AntK* 19 (1976) 101-114.

Bérard (1983): Bérard, C., "Iconographie - Iconologie - Iconologique," *Etude de Lettres* 1983.4, 5-37.

Bérard (1988): Bérard, C., "La chasseresse traquée," *Kanon. Festschrift Ernst Berger* (Basel 1988) 280-284.

Bérard et al. (1989): Bérard, C., et al., *A City of Images: Iconography and Society in Ancient Greece*, trans. D. Lyons (Princeton 1989).

Berger (1990): Berger, E., ed., *Antike Kunstwerk aus der Sammlung Ludwig* 3. *Skulpturen* (Basel 1990).

Bergren (1989): Bergren, A., "The Homeric Hymn to Aphrodite. Tradition and Rhetoric, Praise and Blame," *Classical Antiquity* 8 (1989) 1-41.

Bernal (1987): Bernal, M., *Black Athena: The Afroasiatic Roots of Classical Civilization* I (New Brunswick 1987).

Bernardi (1985): Bernardi, B., *Age Class Systems. Social Institutions and Politics Based on Age* (Cambridge 1985).

Bettelheim (1975): Bettelheim, B., *The Uses of Enchantment: The Meaning and Importance of Fairy Tales* (New York 1975).

Bevan (1987): Bevan, E., "The Goddess Artemis, and the Dedication of Bears in Sanctuaries," *BSA* 82 (1987) 17-21.

Bisel and Angel (1985): Bisel, S.C., and J.L. Angel, "Health and Nutrition in Mycenaean Greece: A Study in Human Skeletal Remains," in *Contributions to Aegean Archaeology: Studies in Honor of William A. MacDonald*, N.C. Wilkie and W.D.E. Coulson, eds.(Minneapolis 1985) 197-210.

Blech (1982): Blech, M., *Studien zum Kranz bei den Griechen* (Berlin 1982).

Boardman (1975): Boardman, J., *Athenian Red Figure Vases. The Archaic Period: A Handbook* (London 1975).

Boardman (1989): Boardman, J., *Athenian Red Figure Vases. The Classical Period: A Handbook* (London 1989).

Boardman (1991): Boardman, J., "The Sixth-Century Potters and Painters of Athens and their Public," in *Looking at Greek Vases*, T. Rasmussen and N. Spivey, eds. (Cambridge 1991) 79-102.

Boardman (1992): Boardman, J., "The Phallos-bird in Archaic and Classical Greek Art," *RA* 1992, 225-242.

Bol (1989): Bol, P., ed., *Forschungen zur Villa Albani. Katalog der antiken Bild-werke* I (Berlin 1989).

Bolen (1994): Bolen, J., *Crossing to Avalon* (New York 1994).

Bott (1957): Bott, E., *Family and Social Network* (London 1957).

Brandt (1932): Brandt, P. [ps. "Hans Licht"], *Sexual Life in Ancient Greece* (London 1932).

Bremmer (1984): Bremmer, J., "Greek Maenadism Reconsidered," *ZPE* 55 (1984) 267-286.

Bremmer (1986): Bremmer, J., ed., *Interpretations of Greek Mythology* (New York 1986).

Bremmer (1987): Bremmer, J., "The Old Women of Ancient Greece," *Sexual Asymmetry: Studies in Ancient Society* (Amsterdam 1987) 191-215.

Bremmer (1994): Bremmer, J., *Greek Religion, Greece and Rome New Surveys in the Classics* 24 (Oxford 1994).

Brommer (1957): Brommer, F., "Attische Könige," in *Charites. Studien zur Altertumswissenschaft*, K. Schauenberg, ed. (Bonn 1957) 152-64.

Brommer (1972): Brommer, F., "Vier mythologische Vasenbilder in Griechenland," *AAA* 5 (1972) 451-62.

Brommer (1973): Brommer, F., *Vasenlisten zur griechischen Heldensage*, third edition (Marburg 1973).

Brommer (1978): Brommer, F., *Hephaistos: Der Schmiedegott in der antiken Kunst* (Mainz am Rhein 1978).

Brommer (1983): Brommer, F., *Odysseus. Die Taten und Leiden der Helden in Antiker Kunst und Literatur* (Darmstadt 1983).

Brouskari (1974): Brouskari, M., *The Acropolis Museum. A Descriptive Catalogue* (Athens 1974).

Brownmiller (1975): Brownmiller, S., *Against Our Will: Men, Women, and Rape* (New York 1975).

Brückner (1907): Brückner, A., "Athenische Hochzeitsgeschencke," *AM* 32 (1907) 79-122.

Brümmer (1985): Brümmer, E., "Griechische Truhenbehälter," *Jdl* 100 (1985) 1-168.

Brulé (1987): Brulé, P., *La fille d'Athènes* (Paris 1987).

Brumfield (1976): Brumfield, A., *The Attic Festivals of Demeter and their Relation to the Agricultural Year* (Diss., University of Pennsylvania 1976).

Brumfield (1991): Brumfield, A., *The Attic Festivals of Demeter and their Relation to the Agricultural Year* (New York 1991).

Brumfield (forthcoming): Brumfield, A., "APORRETA: Verbal and Ritual Obscenity in the Cults of Ancient Women," *The Role of Religion in the Early Greek Polis*, Third International Seminar on Ancient Greek Art, Swedish Institute of Athens, 16-18 October 1992 (Athens forthcoming).

Buitron et al. (1992): Buitron, D., et al., *The Odyssey and Ancient Art: An Epic in Word and Image* (Annandale-on-Hudson, Edith C. Blum Art Institute 1992).

Buitron-Oliver (1995): Buitron-Oliver, D., *Douris. A Master-Painter of Athenian Red-Figure Vases, Forschungen zur antiken Keramik*, Reihe 2, *Kerameus* 9 (Mainz 1995).

Burian (1972): Burian, P., "Supplication and Hero Cult in Sophocles' *Ajax*," *GRBS* 13 (1972) 151-56.

Burke and Pollitt (1975): Burke, S. Matheson, and J.J. Pollitt, *Greek Vases at Yale* (New Haven, Yale University Art Gallery, 1975).

Burkert (1966): Burkert, W., "Kekropidensage und Arrephoria," *Hermes* 94 (1966) 1-25.

Burkert (1979): Burkert, W., *Structure and History in Greek Mythology and Ritual, Sather Classical Lectures* 47 (Berkeley and Los Angeles 1979).

Burkert (1983): Burkert, W., *Homo Necans. The Anthropology of Ancient Greek Sacrificial Ritual and Myth*, trans. P. Bing (Berkeley 1983).

Burkert (1985): Burkert, W., *Greek Religion: Archaic and Classical*, trans. J. Raffan (Cambridge, MA 1985).

Burkert (1986): Burkert, W., "Oedipus and the Greek Oedipus Complex," in *Interpretations of Greek Mythology*, J. Bremmer, ed. (New York 1986) 41-55.

Burkert (1987): Burkert, W., *Ancient Mystery Cults* (Cambridge, MA 1987).

Burkert (1992): Burkert, W., *The Orientalizing Revolution: Near Eastern Influence on Greek Culture in the Early Archaic Age, Revealing Antiquity* 5, trans. W. Burkert and M.E. Pinder (Cambridge, MA 1992).

Burn (1987): Burn, L., *The Meidias Painter* (Oxford 1987).

Burn (1989): Burn, L., "The Art of the State in Late Fifth Century Athens," in *Images of Authority. Festschrift J. Reynolds* (Cambridge 1989) 62-81.

Buschor (1939): Buschor, E., *Grab eines attischen Mädchens* (Munich 1939).

Buschor (1940): Buschor, E., *Griechische Vasen* (Munich 1940).

Buxton (1982): Buxton, R.G.A., *Persuasion in Greek Tragedy: A Study of Peitho* (Cambridge 1982).

Calame (1977): Calame, C., *Les choeurs de jeunes filles en Grèce archaïque, Filologia e critica* 20-21, 2 vols. (Rome 1977).

Caldwell (1990): Caldwell, R., "Psychoanalysis: The Psychoanalytic Interpretation of Greek Myth," in *Approaches to Greek Myth*, L. Edmunds, ed. (Baltimore 1990) 342-387.

Cameron and Kuhrt (1983): Cameron, A., and A. Kuhrt, eds., *Images of Women in Antiquity* (Detroit 1983).

Canciani (1980): Canciani, F., "Circe e Odisseo," in *Tainia. Festschrift für Roland Hampe*, H.A. Cahn and E. Simon, eds. (Mainz 1980) 45-52.

Cantarella (1987): Cantarella, E., *Pandora's Daughters: The role and status of women in Greek and Roman antiquity*, trans. M.B. Fant (Baltimore 1987).

Cantarella (1992): Cantarella, E., *Bisexuality in the Ancient World* (New Haven 1992).

Carpenter (1946): Carpenter, R., *Folk Tale, Fiction and Saga in the Homeric Epics, Sather Classical Lectures* 20 (Berkeley and Los Angeles 1946).

Carpenter (1991): Carpenter, T.H., *Art and Myth in Ancient Greece* (London 1991).

Carrington-Streete (1993): Carrington-Streete, G.P., "Sex, Spirit, and Control: Paul and the Women of Corinth," in *Ritual, Power, and the Body: Historical Perspectives on the Representation of Greek Women*, C.N. Seremetakis, ed. (New York 1993) 95-118.

Carson (1982): Carson, A., "Wedding at Noon in Pindar's Ninth Pythian," *GRBS* 23 (1982) 121-128.

Carson (1990): Carson, A., "Putting Her in Her Place: Woman, Dirt, and Desire," in *Before Sexuality*, D.M. Halperin, J.J. Winkler, and F.I. Zeitlin, eds. (Princeton 1990) 135-69.

Carter (1988): Carter, J.B., "Masks and Poetry in Early Sparta," in *Early Greek Cult Practice. Proceedings of the Fifth International Symposium at the Swedish Institute in Athens, June 1986* (Stockholm 1988) 89-98.

Cartledge (1981): Cartledge, P., "Spartan Wives: Liberation or Licence?" *Classical Quarterly* 31 (1981) 84-105.

Cartmill (1993): Cartmill, M., *A View to Death in the Morning* (Cambridge 1993).

Caskey and Beazley (1931): Caskey. L.D., and J.D. Beazley, *Attic Vase Paintings in the Museum of Fine Arts, Boston*, vol. 1 (London 1931).

Caskey and Beazley (1954): Caskey, L.D., and J.D. Beazley, *Attic Vase Paintings in the Museum of Fine Arts, Boston*, vol. 2 (London 1954).

Cassimatis (1990): Cassimatis, H., "Propos sur le calathos dans la céramique italiote," in *Eumousia. Ceramic and iconographic studies in honour of Alexander Cambitoglou*, J.P. Descoeudres, ed. (Sydney 1990) 195-201.

Castriota (1992): Castriota, D., *Myth, Ethos, and Actuality: Official Art in Fifth-Century B.C. Athens, Wisconsin Studies in Classics* (Madison 1992).

Catling (1976): Catling, H., "New Excavations at the Menelaion, Sparta," in *Neue Forschungen in griechischen Heiligtümern*, U. Jantzen, ed. (Tübingen 1976) 77-90.

Clairmont (1976): Clairmont, C.W., "Studies in Greek Gravestones," *Mélanges d'histoire ancienne et d'archéologie offerts à Paul Collart, Cahiers d'archéologie romande* 5 (Lausanne 1976) 93-98.

Clairmont (1993): Clairmont, C.W., *Classical Attic Tombstones*, 6 vols. (Kilchberg 1993).

Clark (1989): Clark, G., *Women in the Ancient World, Greece and Rome, New Surveys in the Classics* 21 (Oxford 1989).

Clauss and Johnston (forthcoming): Clauss, J.J., and S. Johnston, eds., *Aeetes' Daughter. Essays on Medea in Myth, Art and Literature* (Princeton forthcoming).

Clay (1993): Clay, J.S., *The Politics of Olympos* (Princeton 1989).

Cohen (1989): Cohen, J., '*Be Fertile and Increase, Fill the Earth and Master It': The Ancient and Medieval Career of a Biblical Text* (Ithaca, NY 1989).

Cohen (1991): Cohen, D., *Law, Sexuality, and Society: The Enforcement of Morals in Classical Athens* (Cambridge 1991).

Cohen (1993): Cohen, B., "The Anatomy of Kassandra's Rape: Female Nudity Comes of Age in Greek Art," *Source* 12.2 (1993) 37-46.

Coldstream (1976): Coldstream, J.N., "Hero Cult in the Age of Homer," *JHS* 96 (1976) 8-17.

Cole (1984): Cole, S.G., "Greek Sanctions Against Sexual Assault," *Classical Philology* 79 (1984) 97-113.

Collard (1991): Collard, C., *Euripides: Hecuba* (Warminster 1991).

Connelly (1993): Connelly, J.B., "Narrative and Image in Attic Vase-Painting: Ajax and Cassandra at the Trojan Palladion," in *Narrative and Event in Ancient Art*, P.J. Holliday, ed. (Cambridge 1993) 88-129.

Connor (1988): Connor, P., "The Cup and the Sword: Odysseus Intimidates Circe on a Column-Krater in Sydney," *AA* 1988, 41-53.

Conze (1893-1922): Conze, A., *Die attischen Grabreliefs*, vols. I-IV (Berlin 1893-1922).

Cook (1953): Cook, J.M., "The Cult of Agamemnon at Mycenae," in *Geras A. Keramopoullos* (Athens 1953) 112-18.

Costabile (1991): Costabile, F., ed., *I Ninfei di Locri Epizefiri. Architettura-Culti erotici-Sacralité delle acque* (Soveria Manelli 1991).

Crane (1988): Crane, G., *Calypso: Background and Conventions of the Odyssey* (Frankfurt 1988).

Daube (1977): Daube, D., *The Duty of Procreation* (Edinburgh 1977).

Daux (1972): Daux, G., Stèles funéraires et épigrammes (A propos d'un livre récent)," *BCH* 96 (1972) 503-566.

Davies (1985): Davies, G., "The Significance of the Handshake Motif in Classical Funerary Art," *AJA* 89 (1985) 627-640.

Davies (1986): Davies, M., "A Convention of Metamorphosis in Greek Art," *JHS* 106 (2986) 182-183.

Daxelmüller (1993): Daxelmüller, C., *Zauberpraktiken. Eine Ideengeschichte der Magie* (Zürich 1993).

Dean-Jones (1994): Dean-Jones, L., *Women's Bodies in Classical Greek Science* (Oxford 1994).

deForest (1993): deForest, M., ed., *Women's Power, Men's Game: Essays on Classical Antiquity in Honor of Joy K. King* (Wauconda, IL 1993).

Delivorrias (1978): Delivorrias, A., "Das Original der sitzenden 'Aphrodite-Olympias'," *AM* 93 (1978) 1-23.

Demakopoulou (1988): Demakopoulou, K., ed., *The Mycenaean World. Five Centuries of Early Greek Culture, 1600-1100 B.C.* (Athens 1988).

Detienne (1974): Detienne, M., "Orphée au miel," *Faire le histoire* III, J. Le Goff, P. Nora, eds. (Paris 1974) 56-75.

Detienne (1977a): Detienne, M., *The Gardens of Adonis: Spices in Greek Mythology*, trans. J. Lloyd (Sussex 1977).

Detienne (1977b): Detienne, M., "Le rose de vent," in *Dionysos mis à mort* (Mayence 1977) 99-117.

Detienne (1979): Detienne, M., *Dionysos Slain*, trans. M. and L. Muellner (Baltimore 1979).

Detienne (1989a): Detienne, M., "The Violence of Wellborn Ladies: Women in the Thesmophoria," in Detienne, M., and J.-P. Vernant, *The Cuisine of Sacrifice Among the Greeks*, trans. P. Wissing (Chicago 1989) 129-147.

Detienne (1989b): Detienne, M., *L'Ecriture d'Orphée* (Mayence 1989).

Detienne and Vernant (1978a): Detienne, M., and J.-P. Vernant, *Cunning Intelligence in Greek Culture and Society*, trans. J. Lloyd (Atlantic Highlands, N.J. 1978).

Detienne and Vernant (1978b): Detienne, M., and J.-P. Vernant, "The Orphic Metis and the Cuttle-Fish of Thetis," *Cunning Intelligence in Greek Culture and Society*, trans. J. Lloyd (Atlantic Highlands, N.J. 1978) 133-174.

Detienne and Vernant (1989): Detienne, M., and J.-P. Vernant, *The Cuisine of Sacrifice Among the Greeks*, trans. P. Wissing (Chicago 1989).

Deubner (1925): Deubner, L., "Hochzeit und Opferkorb," *JdI* 40 (1925) 210-223.

Diehl (1964): Diehl, E., *Die Hydria. Formengeschichte und Verwendung im Kult des Altertums* (Mainz 1974).

Dohrn (1957): Dohrn, T., *Attische Plastik vom Tode des Phidias bis zum Wirken der grossen Meister des IV. Jahrhunderts v. Chr.* (Krefeld 1957).

Dontas (1983): Dontas, G., "The True Aglaureion," *Hesperia* 52 (1983) 48-63.

Dougherty (1993): Dougherty, C., "It's Murder to Found a Colony," in *Cultural Poetics in Archaic Greece: Cult, Performance, Politics,* C. Dougherty and L. Kurke, eds. (Cambridge 1993) 178-98.

Doumas (1992): Doumas, C., *The Wall-Paintings of Thera* (Athens 1992).

Dover (1974): Dover, K.J., *Greek Popular Morality in the Time of Plato and Aristotle* (Berkeley and Los Angeles 1974).

Dover (1978): Dover, K.J., *Greek Homosexuality* (London 1978).

Dover (1984): Dover, K.J., "Classical Greek Attitudes to Sexual Behavior," *Women in the Ancient World. The Arethusa Papers,* J. Peradotto and J.P. Sullivan, eds. (Albany 1984) 143-57.

Dover (1993): Dover, K.J., ed., Aristophanes, *Frogs* (Oxford 1993).

Dowden (1989): Dowden, K., *Death and the Maiden: Girls' Initiation Rites in Greek Mythology* (London and New York 1989).

Dubisch (1983): Dubisch, J., "Greek Women: Sacred or Profane," *Journal of Modern Greek Studies* 1 (1983) 185-202.

Dubisch (1986): Dubisch, J., ed., *Gender and Power in Rural Greece* (Princeton 1986).

DuBois (1982): DuBois, P., *Centaurs and Amazons* (Ann Arbor 1982).

DuBois (1988): DuBois, P., *Sewing the Body: Psychoanalysis and Ancient Representations of Women* (Chicago 1988).

DuBois (1993): DuBois, P., "Sewing the Bodies: Metaphors of the Female Body in Ancient Greece", in *Ritual, Power, and the Body: Historical Perspectives on the Representation of Greek Women*, C.N. Seremetakis, ed. (New York 1993) 81-94.

du Boulay (1974): du Boulay, J., *Portrait of a Greek Mountain Village* (Oxford 1974).

Durand and Lissarrague (1980): Durand, J.-L., and F. Lissarrague, "Un lieu d'image? L'espace du loutérion," *Hephaistos* 2 (1980) 89-106.

Durand and Schapp (1989): Durand, J.-L., and A. Schapp, "Sacrifical Slaughter and Initiatory Hunt," in C. Bérard, et al., *A City of Images* (Princeton 1989) 53-70.

Dynes and Donaldson (1992): Dynes, W.R. and Donaldson, S., eds., *Homosexuality in the Ancient World* (New York 1992).

Edmunds (1990): Edmunds, L., ed., *Approaches to Greek Myth* (Baltimore 1990).

Edwards (1984): Edwards, C., "Aphrodite on a Ladder," *Hesperia* 53 (1984) 59-72.

Eilberg-Schwartz (1990): Eilberg Schwartz, H., *The Savage in Judaism: An Anthropology of Israelite Religion and Ancient Judaism* (Bloomington, IN 1990).

Ervin (1958): Ervin, M., "The Sanctuary of Aglauros on the South Slope of the Akropolis and its Destruction in the First Mithridatic War," *Archeion Pontou* 22 (1958) 129-66.

Evelyn-White (1982): Evelyn-White, H.G., *Hesiod, The Homeric Hymns, and Homerica* (Cambridge, MA and London 1914, repr. 1982).

Fair (1990): Fair, J., *The Great American Bear* (Minocqua, WI 1990).

Fairbanks (1914): Fairbanks, A., *Athenian White Lekythoi* II (New York 1914).

Fantham (1975): Fantham, E., "Sex, Status, and Survival in Hellenistic Athens: A Study of Women in New Comedy," *Phoenix* 29 (1975) 44-74.

Fantham et al. (1994a): Fantham, E., H.P. Foley, N.B. Kampen, S.B. Pomeroy, H.A. Shapiro, "Women in Classical Athens: Heroines and Housewives," *Women in the Classical World: Image and Text* (New York and Oxford 1994) 68-127.

Fantham et al. (1994b): Fantham, E., H.P. Foley, N.B. Kampen, S.B. Pomeroy, H.A. Shapiro, "Amazon Women in Control," *Women in the Classical World: Image and Text* (New York and Oxford 1994) 128-135.

Fantham et al. (1994c): Fantham, E., H.P. Foley, N.B. Kampen, S.B. Pomeroy, H.A. Shapiro, "Medicine: The 'Proof' of Anatomy," *Women in the Classical World: Image and Text* (New York and Oxford 1994) 183-205.

Farnell (1921): Farnell, L.R., *Greek Hero-Cults and Ideas of Immortality* (London 1921).

Fehr (1990): Fehr, B., "Entertainers at the *Symposium*: the *Akletoi* in the archaic period," in *Sympotica*, O. Murray, ed. (Oxford 1990) 85-95.

Felten (1984): Felten, F., *Griechische tektonische Friese archaischer und klassischer Zeit* (Salzburg 1984).

Ferrari (1990); Ferrari, G., "Figures of Speech: The Pictures of Aidos," *Metis. Revue d'anthropologie du monde grec ancien* V.1-2 (1990) 185-200.

Fisher (1992): Fisher, N.R.E., *Hybris. A Study in the Values of Honor and Shame in Ancient Greece* (Warminster 1992).

Foley (1981): Foley, H.P., "The Concept of Women in Athenian Drama," in *Reflections of Women in Antiquity*, H. P. Foley, ed. (New York and London 1981) 127-68.

Foley (1982): Foley, H.P., "Marriage and Sacrifice in Euripides' *Iphigenia in Aulis*," *Arethusa* 15 (1982) 159-180.

Foley (1985): Foley, H.P., *Ritual Irony: Poetry and Sacrifice in Euripides* (Ithaca 1985).

Foley (1994): Foley, H.P., ed., *The Homeric Hymn to Demeter* (Princeton 1994).

Forbes-Irving (1990): Forbes Irving, P.M.C., *Metamorphosis in Greek Myths* (Oxford 1990).

Fornara and Samons (1991): Fornara, C.W., and L.J. Samons II, *Athens from Cleisthenes to Pericles* (Berkeley and Los Angeles 1991).

Foster (1899): Foster, B.O., "Notes on the Symbolism of the Apple in Classical Antiquity," *Harvard Studies in Classical Philology* 10 (1899) 39-55.

Foucault (1978): Foucault, M., *The History of Sexuality*, vol. 1, *An Introduction*, trans. R. Hurley (New York 1978).

Foucault (1985): Foucault, M., *The History of Sexuality*, vol. 2, *The Use of Pleasure*, trans. R. Hurley (New York 1985).

Foucault (1986): Foucault, M., *The History of Sexuality*, vol. 3, *The Care of the Self*, trans. R. Hurley (New York 1986).

Foxhall (1989): Foxhall, L., "Household, Gender, and Property in Classical Athens," *Classical Quarterly* 39 (1989) 22-44.

Fraenkel (1950): Fraenkel, E., ed., *Aeschylus, Agamemnon* (Oxford 1950).

Frankfurt et al. (1946): Frankfurt, H., et al., *Before Philosophy: The Intellectual Adventure of Ancient Man* (Chicago 1946).

Frel (1969): Frel, J., *Les sculpteurs attiques anonymes, 430-300* (Prague 1969).

Frel (1973): Frel, J., "An Attic Grave Stele with Epigram," *GRBS* 14 (1973) 173-177.

Frontisi-Ducroux (1989): Frontisi-Ducroux, F., "In the Mirror of the Mask," in C. Bérard et al., *A City of Images*, trans. D. Lyons (Princeton 1989).

Frontisi-Ducroux (1991): Frontisi-Ducroux, F., *Le dieu-masque, une figure du Dionysos d'Athènes* (Paris 1991).

Frontisi-Ducroux (1995): Frontisi-Ducroux, F., *Du masque au visage* (Paris 1995).

Frontisi-Ducroux (forthcoming): Frontisi-Ducroux, F., "Eros, le désir et le regard," in *Sexuality in Ancient Art*, N.B. Kampen, ed. (Cambridge forthcoming).

Furtwängler and Reichhold (1904-1921): Furtwängler, A., and K. Reichhold, *Griechische Vasenmalerei. Auswahl hervorragender Vasenbilder*, Series I-III (Munich 1904-1921).

Gantz (1993): Gantz, T., *Early Greek Myth: A Guide to Literary and Artistic Sources* (Baltimore 1993).

Garland (1984): Garland, R.S.J., "Religious Authority in Archaic and Classical Athens," *BSA* 79 (1984) 75-123.

Garland (1990): Garland, R.S.J., *The Greek Way of Life* (London 1990).

Gauer (1984): Gauer, W., "Was geschieht mit dem Peplos?" *Parthenon-Kongress Basel. Referate und Berichte 4. bis 8. April 1982*, Vol. 1, E. Berger, ed. (Mainz 1984) 220-229.

Gennep (1960): Gennep, L. van, *The Rites of Passage*, trans. M.B. Vizedom and G.L. Caffee (Chicago 1960).

Gerhard (1840-1858): Gerhard, E., *Auserlesene griechische Vasenbilder*, 4 vols. (Berlin 1840-1858).

Gernet (1981): Gernet, L., *The Anthropology of Ancient Greece* (Baltimore 1981).

Gilligan (1982): Gilligan, C., *In A Different Voice* (Cambridge 1982).

Gilligan (1989): Gilligan, C., *Making Connections* (Troy, NY 1989).

Gilligan and Brown (1992): Gilligan, C., and L.M. Brown, *Meeting at the Crossroads: Women's Psychology and Girls' Development* (Cambridge 1992).

Gilly, W., *Antike Vasen und Terrakotten. Oldenburger Stadtmuseum* (Oldenburg 1978).

Gilmore (1990): Gilmore, D., *Manhood in the Making: Cultural Concepts of Masculinity* (New Haven 1990).

Gimbutas (1974): Gimbutas, M., *The Goddesses and Gods of Old Europe* (Berkeley 1974).

Gimbutas (1991): Gimbutas, M., *The Civilization of the Goddess* (San Francisco 1991).

Ginouvès (1962): Ginouvès, R., *Balaneutike. Recherches sur le bain dans l'antiquité grecque*, BEFAR 200 (Paris 1962).

Girard (1972): Girard, R., *Violence and the Sacred* (Baltimore 1972).

Golden (1975): Golden, M.P., and N.H., "Population Policy in Plato and Aristotle: Some Value Issues," *Arethusa* 8 (1975) 345-58.

Goldhill (1994): Goldhill, S., "Representing Democracy: Women at the Great Dionysia," in *Ritual, Finance, Politics. Athenian Democratic Accounts Presented to David Lewis*, R. Osborne and S. Hornblower, eds. (Oxford 1994) 347-369.

Gomme (1925): Gomme, A.W., "The Position of Women in Athens in the Fifth and Fourth Centuries," *CP* 20 (1925) 1-28.

Gomperz (1866): Gomperz, T., *Herkulanische Studien* 2 (Leipzig 1866).

Gordon (1981): Gordon, R.L., ed., *Myth, Religion and Society* (Cambridge 1981).

Gould (1980): Gould, J.P., "Law, Custom and Myth: Aspects of the Social Position of Women in Classical Athens," *JHS* 100 (1980) 38-59.

Graf (1986): Graf, F., "Orpheus: A Poet Among Men," in *Interpretations of Greek Mythology*, J. Bremmer, ed. (New York 1986) 80-106.

Graf (1994): Graf, F., *La Magie dans l'Antiquité Gréco-Romaine* (Paris 1994).

Graf (forthcoming): Graf, F., "Medea, the Enchantress from Afar. Remarks on a Well-known Myth," in *Aeetes' Daughter. Essays on Medea in Myth, Art and Literature*, J.J. Clauss and S. Johnston, eds. (Princeton forthcoming).

Greifenhagen (1957): Greifenhagen, A., *Griechische Eroten* (Berlin 1957).

Greifenhagen (1966): Greifenhagen, A., "Der Tod des Pentheus (Eine Rotfigurige Hydria)," *Berliner Museen. Berichte aus den staatliche Museen der Stiftung Preussischer Kulturbesitz* 16 (1966) II, 2-6.

Grmek (1989): Grmek, M.D., *Diseases in the Ancient World* (Baltimore and London 1989).

Hahland (1930): W. Hahland, *Vasen um Meidias* (Berlin 1930).

Hall (1989): Hall, E., *Inventing the Barbarian: Greek Self-Definition Through Tragedy* (Oxford 1989).

Halperin (1986): Halperin, D.M., "Plato and Erotic Reciprocity," *Classical Antiquity* 5 (1986) 60-80.

Halperin (1990a): Halperin, D.M., "The Democratic Body: Prostitution and Citizenship in Classical Athens," *differences* 2.1 (1990) 1-28.

Halperin (1990b): Halperin, D.M., *One Hundred Years of Homosexuality and Other Essays on Greek Love* (New York and London 1990).

Halperin, Winkler and Zeitlin (1990): Halperin, D.M., J.J. Winkler and F.I. Zeitlin, eds., *Before Sexuality: The Construction of Erotic Experience in the Ancient Greek World* (Princeton 1990).

Hamilton (1992): Hamilton, R., *Choes and Anthesteria* (Ann Arbor 1992).

Hamma (1989): Hamma, K., *The Dechter Collection of Greek Vases*, California State University at San Bernardino (San Bernardino 1989).

Handley and Rea (1957): Handley, E., and J. Rea, *The Telephus of Euripides*, BICS Suppl. 5 (1957).

Handman (1983): Handman, M.-E., *La ruse et la violence* (La Calade, Aix-en-Provence 1983).

Hanson (1990): Hanson, A.E., "The Medical Writers' Woman," in *Before Sexuality*, D.M. Halperin, J.J. Winkler, and F.I. Zeitlin, eds. (Princeton 1990) 309-38.

Hanson (1991): Hanson, A., "Continuity and Change: Three Case Studies in Hippocratic Gynecological Therapy and Theory," in *Women's History and Ancient History*, S. Pomeroy, ed. (Chapel Hill 1991) 73-110.

Hanson (1992): Hanson, A., "Conception, Gestation, and the Origin of Female Nature," *Helios* 19 (1992) 31-71.

Harder (1993): Harder, R.E., *Die Frauenrollle bei Euripides*, Drama Beiheft 1 (Stuttgart 1993).

Harrison (1968): Harrison, A.R.W., *The Law of Athens. The Family and Property* (Oxford 1968).

Harrison (1977a): Harrison, E.B., "Alkamenes' Sculptures for the Hephaisteion, Part I, the Cult Statues," *AJA* 81 (1977) 137-178.

Harrison (1977b): Harrison, E.B., "Alkamenes' Sculptures for the Hephaisteion, Part II, The Base," *AJA* 81 (1977) 265-287.

Harrison (1986): Harrison, E.B., "The Classical High-Relief Frieze from the Athenian Agora," *Archaische und klassische grechische Plastik: Akten des Internationalen Kolloquiums vom 22-25 April 1985*, Vol. 2 (Mainz 1986) 109-117.

Harrison (1988): Harrison, E.B., "Lemnia and Lemnos: Sidelights on a Pheidian Athena," in *Kanon. Festschrift Ernst Berger*, AntK-Beiheft 15, M. Schmidt, ed. (Basel 1988) 101-107.

Haspels (1930): Haspels, C.H.E., "Deux fragments d'une coupe d'Euphronios," *BCH* 54 (1930) 422-451.

Heberdey (1919): Heberdey, R., *Altattische Poros-skulptur* (Vienna 1919).

Heilmeyer (1982): Heilmeyer, W.-D., "Kopierte Klassik," *Praestant Interna. Festschrift für Ulrich Hausmann* (Tübingen 1982) 52-62.

Heinrichs (1978): Heinrichs, A., "Greek Maenadism from Olympos to Messalina," *Harvard Studies in Classical Philology* 82 (1978) 121-160.

Henderson (1991a): Henderson, J., *The Maculate Muse: Obscene Language in Attic Comedy* (New York 1991).

Henderson (1991b): Henderson, J., "Women and the Athenian Dramatic Festivals," *Transactions of the American Philosophical Society* 121 (1991) 133-147.

Henle (1973): Henle, J., *Greek Myths: A Vase Painter's Notebook* (Bloomington and London 1973).

Herington (1955): Herington, C.J., *Athena Parthenos and Athena Polias. A Study in the Religion of Periklean Athens* (Manchester 1955).

Herington (1963): Herington, C.J., "Athena in Athenian Literature and Cult," in *Parthenos and Parthenon, Greece and Rome*, Supplement to Vol. X, G. Hooker, ed. (Oxford 1963) 61-73.

Higgins (1954): Higgins, R., *Catalogue of Terracottas in the British Museum*, Vol. I (London 1954).

Higgins (1980): Higgins, R., *Greek and Roman Jewellery*, second ed. (London 1980).

Hirschon (1983): Hirschon, R.B., "Women, the Aged and Religious Activity: Oppositions and Complementarity in an Urban Locality," *Journal of Modern Greek Studies* 1 (1983) 113-129.

Hoffmann (1970): Hoffmann, H., *Ten Centuries that Shaped the West* (Mainz 1970).

Hoffmann (1977): Hoffmann, H., *Sexual and Asexual Pursuit: A Structural Approach to Greek Vase Painting*, Royal Anthropological Institute of Great Britain and Ireland, Occasional Paper no. 34 (London 1977).

Hoffmann (1985): Hoffmann, G., "Pandora, la jarre et l'espoir," *Etudes rurales* 98-99 (1985) 119-132, reprinted in *Quaderni di storia* 24 (1986) 55-89.

Hoffmann (1994): Hoffmann, H., "The Riddle of the Sphinx: a Case Study in Athenian Immortality Symbolism," in *Classical Greece: Ancient Histories and Modern Archaeologies*, I. Morris, ed. (Cambridge 1994) 71-80.

Holderman (1985): Holderman, E.S., "Le sacerdotesse: requisiti, funzioni, poteri," in *Le donne in Grecia*, ed. G. Arrigoni (Laterza 1985) 299-330.

Hooker (1963): Hooker, E.M., "The Goddess of the Golden Image," in *Parthenos and Parthenon, Greece and Rome*, Supplement to Vol. X, G. Hooker, ed. (Oxford 1963) 17-22.

Hopper (1963): Hopper, R.J., "Athena and the Early Acropolis," in *Parthenos and Parthenon, Greece and Rome*, Supplement to Vol. X, G. Hooker, ed. (Oxford 1963) 1-16.

Hornblower (1991): Hornblower, S., *A Commentary on Thucydides*, Vol. 1, Books I-III (Oxford 1991).

Howard (1990): Howard, S., *Antiquity Restored: Essays on the Afterlife of the Antique* (Vienna 1990).

Howe (1954): Howe, T.P., "The Origin and Function of the Gorgon-Head," *AJA* 58 (1954) 209-221.

Hughes (1991): Hughes, D., *Human Sacrifice in Ancient Greece* (London and New York 1991).

Humphreys (1985): Humphreys, S.C., "Lycurgus of Boutadae: an Athenian Aristocrat," in *The Craft of the Ancient Historian*, J.W. Eadie and J.S. Ober, eds. (Lanham, MD 1985) 199-252.

Humphreys (1986): Humphreys, S.C., "Kinship Patterns in the Athenian Courts," *GRBS* 27 (1986) 57-91.

Humphreys (1993): Humphreys, S.C., *The Family, Women, and Death*, second ed. (Ann Arbor 1993).

Hurwit (1985): Hurwit, J.M., *The Art and Culture of Early Greece* (Ithaca 1985).

Jacobsthal (1927): Jacobsthal, P., *Ornamente griechischer Vasen. Aufnahmen, Beschreibungen und Untersuchungen* (Berlin 1927).

Jenkins (1983): Jenkins, I., "Is there Life After Marriage? A Study of the Abduction Motif in Vase Paintings of the Athenian Wedding Ceremony," *BICS* 30 (1983) 137-145.

Jenkins (1985): Jenkins, I., "The Ambiguity of Greek Textiles," *Arethusa* 18.2 (1985) 109-132.

Jenkins (1989): Jenkins, I., *Adam Buck's Greek Vases, British Museum Occasional Paper No. 75* (London 1989).

Jenkins (1994): Jenkins, I., *The Parthenon Frieze* (London 1994).

Johns (1982): Johns, C., *Sex or Symbol? Erotic Images of Greece and Rome* (London 1982).

Johnson (1991): Johnson, G., *In the Palaces of Memory* (New York 1991).

Joshel (1992): Joshel, S.R., "The Body Female and the Body Politic: Livy's Lucretia and Verginia," in *Pornography and Representation in Greece and Rome*, A. Richlin, ed. (Oxford 1992) 112-30.

Just (1975): Just, R., "Conceptions of Women in Classical Athens," *Journal of the Anthropological Society of Oxford* 6 (1975) 153-170.

Just (1989): Just, R., *Women in Athenian Law and Life* (London and New York 1989).

Kaempf-Dimitriadou (1979): Kaempf-Dimitriadou, S., *Die Liebe der Götter in der attischen Kunst des 5. Jahrhunderts v. Chr., AntK-Beiheft* 11 (Bern 1979).

Kahil (1983): Kahil, L., "Mythological Repertoire of Brauron," *Ancient Greek Art and Iconography*, W. Moon, ed. (Madison 1983) 231-244.

Kallet-Marx (1993): Kallet-Marx, L., "Thucydides 2.45.2 and the Status of War Widows in Periclean Athens," in *Nomodeiktes. Greek Studies in Honor of Martin Ostwald*, R.M. Rosen and J. Farrell, eds. (Ann Arbor 1993) 133-143.

Kardara (1964): Kardara, C., "Glaukopis, The Archaic Naos and the Theme of the Parthenon Frieze," *ArchEph* 1961 (1964) 61-158.

Kardara (1982): Kardara, C., "He Zophoros tou Parthenonos ho Kyrios Mythikos tes Pyren kai to Panellenion Programma tou Perikleous," *ArchEph* 1982, 1-60.

Kauffmann-Samaras (1988): Kauffmann-Samaras, A., "'Mère' et enfant sur les lébetès nuptiaux à figures rouges attiques du V. Jhs. av. J.C.," *Proceedings of the Third Symposium on Ancient Greek and Related Pottery, Copenhagen 1987* (Copenhagen 1988) 286-299.

Kern (1922): Kern, O., *Orphicorum Fragmenta* (Berlin 1922).

Kearns (1989): Kearns, E., *The Heroes of Attica, BICS Suppl.* 57 (London 1989).

Kearns (1990): Kearns, E., "Saving the City," in *The Greek City*, O. Murray et al., eds. (Oxford 1990) 321-344.

Keuls (1974): Keuls, E., *The Water Carriers in Hades: A Study of Catharsis Through Toil in Classical Antiquity* (Amsterdam 1974).

Keuls (1983a): Keuls, E., "Attic Vase-Painting and the Home Textile Industry," *Ancient Greek Art and Iconography*, W. Moon, ed. (Madison 1983) 209-230.

Keuls (1983b): Keuls, E., "The Hetaera and the Housewife: the Splitting of the Female Psyche in Greek Art," *Mededelingen van het Nederlands Instituut te Rome* 9-10 (1983) 23-40.

Keuls (1985a): Keuls, E., *The Reign of the Phallus: Sexual Politics in Ancient Athens* (New York 1985).

Keuls (1985b): Keuls, E., "Patriotic Propaganda and Counter-Cultural Protest in Athens as Evidenced by Vase Painting," in *Ancient Greek and Related Pottery*, H.A.G. Brijder, ed. (Amsterdam 1985).

Kiilerich (1989): Kiilerich, B., "The Olive-Tree Pediment and the Daughters of Kekrops," *AAAH* 7 (1989) 1-21.

Kilmer (1993): Kilmer, M.F., *Greek Erotica on Attic Red-Figure Vases* (London 1993).

King (1983): King, H., "Bound to Bleed: Artemis and Greek Women," in *Images of Women in Antiquity*, A. Cameron and A. Kuhrt, eds. (Detroit 1983) 109-127.

King (1987): King, H., "Sacrificial Blood: The Role of Amnion in Ancient Gynecology," in *Rescuing Creusa: New Methodological Approaches to Women in Antiquity*, M. Skinner, ed., *Helios* 13 (1987) 117-126.

Kirk (1970): Kirk, G.S., *Myth: Its Meaning and Function in Ancient and Other Cultures* (Cambridge 1970).

Kirk (1985): Kirk, G.S., *The Iliad: a Commentary* I (Cambridge 1985).

Kokkorou-Alevra (1988): Kokkorou-Alevra, G., "Ena gnosto-agnosto angeio tou zographou tou Medeia," in *Proceedings of the XII International Congress of Classical Archaeology. Athens 1983*, vol. 2 (1988) 103-114.

Konstan (1990): Konstan, D., "An Anthropology of Euripides' *Kyklops*," in *Nothing to Do With Dionysos?*, J.J. Winkler and F.I. Zeitlin, eds. (Princeton 1990) 207-227.

Korshak (1987): Korshak, Y., *Frontal Faces in Attic Vase Painting* (Chicago 1987).

Krauskopf (1977): Krauskopf, I., "Eine attisch schwarzfigurige Hydria in Heidelberg," *AA* 92 (1977) 13-37.

Krieger (1973): Krieger, X., *Der Kampf zwischen Peleus und Thetis in der griechischen Vasenmalerei, Eine typologische Untersuchung* (Münster 1973).

Kron (1976): Kron, U., *Die zehn attischen Phylenheroen, AM Beiheft* 5 (1976).

Kuper (1994): Kuper, A., *The Chosen Primate* (Cambridge 1994).

Kurtz (1975): Kurtz, D., *Athenian White Lekythoi: Patterns and Painters* (Oxford 1975).

Kurtz and Sparkes (1982): Kurtz, D., and B. Sparkes, eds., *The Eye of Greece. Studies in the Art of Athens* (Cambridge 1982).

Lacey (1968): Lacey, W.K., *The Family in Classical Greece* (London 1968).

Lambert (1993): Lambert, S.D., *The Phratries of Attica* (Ann Arbor 1993).

Laqueur (1990): Laqueur, T., *Making Sex: Body and Gender from the Greeks to Freud* (Cambridge and London 1990).

LaRocca (1973): LaRocca, E., "Una testa femminile nel Museo Nuovo dei Conservatori e l'Afrodite Louvre-Napoli," *ASAtene* n.s. 34-35 (1972-73) 419-450.

Lauter (1985): Lauter, H., *Der Kultplatz auf dem Turkovouni, AM Beiheft* 12 (1985).

Lawton (1993): Lawton, C., "An Attic Document Relief in the Walters Art Gallery," *JWalt* 51 (1993) 1-9.

Leduc (1992): Leduc, C., "Marriage in Ancient Greece," in *A History of Women in the West I: From Ancient Goddesses to Christian Sources*, P.S. Pantel, ed. (Cambridge 1992) 235-294.

Lefkowitz (1981): Lefkowitz, M.R., *Heroines and Hysterics* (London 1981).

Lefkowitz (1986): Lefkowitz, M.R., *Women in Greek Myth* (Baltimore 1986).

Lefkowitz (1987): Lefkowitz, M.R., "The Heroic Women of Greek Epic," *The American Scholar* 56 (1987) 503-518.

Lefkowitz (1993): Lefkowitz, M.R., "Seduction and Rape in Greek Myth," in *Consent and Coercion to Sex and Marriage in Ancient and Medieval Societies*, A. Laiou, ed. (Washington, D.C. 1993) 17-37.

Lefkowitz and Fant (1982): Lefkowitz, M.R., and M.B. Fant, eds., *Women's Life in Greece and Rome: A source book in translation* (Baltimore 1982).

Leipen (1984): Leipen, N., ed., *Glimpses of Excellence. A Selection of Greek Vases and Bronzes from the Elie Borowski Collection* (Totonto 1984).

Lendle (1957): Lendle, O., *Die "Pandorasage" bei Hesiod* (Würzburg 1957).

Lévêque (1988): Lévêque, P., "Pandora ou la terrifiante féminité," *Kernos* 1 (1988) 49-62.

Levine (1987): Levine, D., "Lysistrata and Bacchae: Structure, Genre, and 'Women on Top'," *Helios* 14.1 (1987) 29-38.

Lewis (1955): Lewis, D., "Who was Lysistrata?" *BSA* 50 (1955) 1-12.

Ley (1990): Ley, A., "Atalante - Von der Athletin zur Liebhaberin. Ein Beitrag zum Rezeptionswandel eines mythologischen Themas auf Vasen des 6.-4. Jhs. v.Chr.," *Nikephoros* 3 (1990) 31-72.

Lincoln (1981): Lincoln, B., *Emerging from the Chrysalis* (Oxford 1981).

Lissarrague (1987): Lissarrague, F., *The Aesthetics of the Greek Banquet: Images of Wine and Ritual* (Princeton 1987).

Lissarrague (1990): Lissarrague, F., "The Sexual Life of Satyrs," in *Before Sexuality*, D.M. Halperin, J.J. Winkler, and F.I. Zeitlin, eds. (Princeton 1990) 53-81.

Lissarrague (1992): Lissarrague, F., "Figures of Women," in *A History of Women in the West. I. From Ancient Goddesses to Christian Saints*, P.S. Pantel, ed. (Cambridge, MA and London 1992) 139-229.

Lissarrague (1993): Lissarrague, F., "On the Wildness of Satyrs," in *Masks of Dionysus*, T.H. Carpenter and C.A. Faraone, eds. (Ithaca 1993) 207-220.

Lissarrague (forthcoming): Lissarrague, F., "Identity and Otherness: The Case of Attic Head-Vases and Plastic Sources," forthcoming.

Lloyd (1983): Lloyd, G.E.R., "The Female Sex: Medical Treatment and Biological Theories in the 5th and 4th centuries B.C.," *Science, Folklore and Ideology: Studies in the Life Sciences in Ancient Greece* (Cambridge 1983) 58-111.

Lloyd-Jones (1971): Lloyd-Jones, H., ed., "Appendix," in H.W. Smyth, trans., *Aeschylus, Loeb Classical Library* (Cambridge, MA 1971).

Lloyd-Jones (1983): Lloyd-Jones, P.H.J., "Artemis and Iphigenia," *JHS* 103 (1983) 87-102.

Lloyd-Jones (1990a): Lloyd-Jones, H., *Academic Papers. Greek Comedy, Hellenistic Literature, Greek Religion, and Miscellanea* (Oxford 1990).

Lloyd-Jones (1990b): Lloyd-Jones, H., *Academic Papers. Greek Comedy, Hellenistic Literature, Greek Religion, and Miscellanea*, II: *Greek Epic, Lyric and Tragedy* (Oxford 1990).

Loeb (1979); Loeb, E., *Die Geburt der Götter in der griechischen Kunst der klassischer Zeit* (Jerusalem 1979).

Lonsdale (1993): Lonsdale, S.H., *Dance and Ritual Play in Greek Religion* (Baltimore 1993).

Loraux (1978): Loraux, N., "Sur la race des femmes et quelques-unes de ses tribus," *Arethusa* 11 (1978) 43-87.

Loraux (1987): Loraux, N., *Tragic Ways of Killing a Woman*, trans. A. Forster (Cambridge, MA 1987).

Loraux (1989a): Loraux, N., *Les expériences de Tirésias* (Paris 1989).

Loraux (1989b): Loraux, N., "Le lit, la guerre," in *Les expériences de Tirésias* (Paris 1989) 29-53, 305-17.

Loraux (1989c): Loraux, N., "*Ponos*: Sur quelques difficultés de la peine comme nom du travail," in *Les expériences de Tirésias* (Paris 1989) 54-76.

Loraux (1990): Loraux, N., "Kreousa the Autochthon: A Study of Euripides' Ion," in *Nothing to do with Dionysos?* J.J. Winkler and F.I. Zeitlin, eds. (Princeton 1990) 168-206.

Loraux (1993): Loraux, N., *The Children of Athena*, trans. C. Levine (Princeton 1993).

Maas (1973): Maas, P., "Aeschylus *Agam.* 231ff. Illustrated," in *Kleine Schriften*, W. Buchwald, ed. (Munich 1973) 42.

MacNally (1978): MacNally, S., "The Maenad in Early Greek Art," *Arethusa* 11 (1978) 101-35.

Malti-Douglas (1991): Malti-Douglas, F., *Woman's Body, Woman's Word* (Princeton 1991).

Manakidou (1993): Manakidou, E., "Athenerinnen in schwarz-figurigen Brunnenhausszenen," *Hephaistos* 11-12 (1992-93) 51-91.

Manfrini (1992): Manfrini, Y., "Femmes à la fontaine: réalité et imaginaire," in *L'image en jeu*, C. Bron and E. Kassapoglou, eds., (Lausanne 1992) 127-148.

Mansfield (1985): Mansfield, J.M., *The Robe of Athena and the Panathenaic 'Peplos'* (Diss., University of California at Berkeley 1985).

Manville (1991): Manville, P.B., *The Origins of Citizenship in Ancient Athens* (Princeton 1991).

Marinatos (1984): Marinatos, N., *Art and Religion in Thera* (Athens 1984).

Mark (1984): Mark, I., "The Gods on the East Frieze of the Parthenon," *Hesperia* 53 (1984) 289-342.

Marshall (1911): Marshall, F.H., *Catalogue of the Jewellery, Greek, Etruscan, and Roman, in the Departments of Antiquities, British Museum* (London 1911).

Mayo (1973): Mayo, M.E., "The Gesture of 'Anakalypsis'," *AJA* 77 (1973) 220.

Mayo (1982): Mayo, M.E., *The Art of South Italy. Vases from Magna Graecia* (Richmond, Virginia Museum of Fine Arts 1982).

Meiggs and Lewis (1969): Meiggs, R., and D.M. Lewis, *A Selection of Greek Historical Inscriptions to the End of the Fifth Century B.C.* (Oxford 1969).

Melman (1992): Melman, B., *Women's Orients* (Ann Arbor 1992).

Merkelbach (1972): Merkelbach, R., "Aglauros," *ZPE* 9 (1972) 277-83.

Mertens (1977): Mertens, J., *Attic White-Ground: Its Development on Shapes Other Than Lekythoi* (New York and London 1977).

Metzger (1951): Metzger, H., *Les représentations dans la céramique attique du IVe siècle* (Paris 1951).

Metzger (1965): Metzger, H., *Recherches sur l'imagerie Athénienne* (Paris 1965).

Metzger (1976): Metzger, H., "Athéna soulevant de terre le nouveau-né: du geste au mythe," *Mélanges d'histoire ancienne et d'archéologie offerts à Paul Collart, Cahiers d'archéologie romande* 5 (Lausanne 1976) 295-303.

Meyer (1980): Meyer, H., *Medeia und die Peliaden. Eine attische Novelle und ihre Entstehung. Sagenforschung auf archäologische Grundlage* (Rome 1980).

Mikalson (1991): Mikalson, J., *Honor Thy Gods* (Chapel Hill 1991).

Milne (1939): Milne, M.J., "Kylichnis," *AJA* 43 (1939) 247-254.

Mitten and Doeringer (1967): Mitten, D., and S. Doeringer, *Master Bronzes from the Classical World* (Cambridge, Fogg Art Museum 1967).

Morris (1992a): Morris, I., *Death-Ritual and Social Structure in Classical Antiquity* (Cambridge 1992).

Morris (1992b): Morris, S., *Daidalos and the Origins of Greek Art* (Princeton 1992).

Müller (1913): Müller, F., *Die antiken Odyssee-Illustrationen in ihrer kunsthistorischen Entwicklung* (Berlin 1913).

Murnaghan (1993): Murnaghan, S., "Maternity and Mortality in Homeric Poetry," in *Ritual, Power, and the Body: Historical Perspectives on the Representation of Greek Women*, C.N. Seremetakis, ed., (New York 1993) 35-80, reprinted from *Classical Antiquity* 11.2 (1992) 242-264.

Murray (1990): Murray, O., ed., *Sympotica. A Symposium on the Symposion* (Oxford 1990).

Mussche (1982): Mussche, H.F., ed., *Hommes et Dieux de la Grèce Antique* (Brussels 1982).

Nagy (1979): Nagy, G., *The Best of the Achaeans. Concepts of the Hero in Archaic Greek Poetry* (Baltimore and London 1979).

Nagy (1990a): Nagy, G., *Greek Mythology and Poetics* (Ithaca 1990).

Nagy (1990b): Nagy, J.F., "Hierarchy, Heroes, and Heads: Indo-European Structures in Greek Myth," in *Approaches to Greek Myth*, L. Edmunds, ed. (Baltimore 1990) 200-238.

Neils (1980): Neils, J., "The Group of the Negro Alabastra: A Study in Motif Transferal," *AntK* 23 (1980) 13-23.

Neils (1983): Neils, J., "A Greek Nativity by the Meidias Painter," *BClevMus* 70.7 (1983) 274-89.

Neils (1992a): Neils, J., "The Panathenaia: An Introduction," in *Goddess and Polis: The Panathenaic Festival in Ancient Athens*, J. Neils, ed. (Hanover and Princeton 1992) 13-27.

Neils (1992b): Neils, J., ed., *Goddess and Polis: The Panathenaic Festival in Ancient Athens* (Hanover, Hood Museum of Art and Princeton 1992).

Neumann (1965): Neumann, G., *Gesten und Gebärden in der griechischen Kunst* (Berlin 1965).

Nock (1944): Nock, A.D., "The Cult of Heroes," *Harvard Theological Review* 37 (1944) 141-74, reprinted in *Essays on Religion and the Ancient World*, II, Z. Stewart, ed. (Oxford 1972) 575-602.

Noica (1984): Noica, S., "La boîte de Pandore et l'ambiguité de l'Elpis," *Platon* 36 (1984) 100-24.

North (1966): North, H., *Sophrosyne: Self-Knowledge and Self-Restraint in Greek Literature* (Ithaca 1966).

Nugent (1992): Nugent, G., "Heroes, Heroines and the Wisdom of Myth," audiotape produced by The Teaching Company (Kearneysville 1992).

Oakley (1982a): Oakley, J.H., "The Anakalypteria," *AA* 1982, 113-118.

Oakley (1982b): Oakley, J.H., "A Louvre Fragment Reconsidered: Perseus Becomes Erichthonios," *JHS* 102 (1982) 220-222.

Oakley (1990a): Oakley, J.H., *The Phiale Painter, Forschungen zur antiken Keramik*, Reihe 2, *Kerameus* 8 (Mainz 1990).

Oakley (1990b): Oakley, J.H., "Zwei alte Vasen — Zwei neue Danaebilder," *AA* 1990, 65-70.

Oakley and Sinos (1993): Oakley, J., and R.H. Sinos, *The Wedding in Ancient Athens* (Madison 1993).

Ober (1993): Ober, J., "The Athenian Revolution of 508/7 B.C.E. Violence, Authority, and the Origins of Democracy," in *Cultural Poetics in Archaic Greece: Cult, Performance, Politics*, C. Dougherty and L. Kurke, eds. (Cambridge 1993) 215-32.

Ober and Hedrick (1993): Ober, J., and C.W. Hedrick, eds., *The Birth of Democracy* (Washington, D.C. 1993).

O'Connor-Visser (1987): O'Connor-Visser, E.A.M.E., *Aspects of Human Sacrifice in the Tragedies of Euripides* (Amsterdam 1987).

Osborne (1993): Osborne, R., "Women and Sacrifice in Classical Greece," *Classical Quarterly* 43 (1993) 392-405.

Osborne (1994): Osborne, R., "Looking on — Greek Style. Does the Sculpted Girl Speak to Women Too?" in *Classical Greece. Ancient Histories and Modern Archaeology*, I. Morris, ed. (Cambridge 1994) 81-96.

Osborne (forthcoming): Osborne, R., "Desiring Women on Athenian Pottery," in *Sexuality in Ancient Art*, N.B. Kampen, ed. (Cambridge forthcoming).

Padel (1983): Padel, R., "Women: Model for Possession by Greek Daemons," in *Images of Women in Antiquity*, A. Cameron and A. Kuhrt, eds. (Detroit 1983) 3-19.

Padilla (1993): Padilla, M., Review of R. Hamilton, *Choes and Anthesteria* (Ann Arbor 1992), *AJA* 97 (1993) 578-9.

Page (1941): Page, D.L., *Select Papyri III. Literary Papyri. Poetry* (Cambridge, MA 1941).

Paglia (1994): Paglia, C., *Vamps and Tramps: New Essays* (New York 1994).

Palagia (1992): Palagia, O., *The Pediments of the Parthenon* (Leiden 1992).

Panofsky (1956): Panofsky, D. and E., *Pandora's Box. The Changing Aspects of a Mythical Symbol* (New York 1956).

Pantel (1992a): Pantel, P.S., ed., *A History of Women in the West. I. From Ancient Goddesses to Christian Saints*, trans. A. Goldhammer (Cambridge, MA and London 1992).

Pantel (1992b): Pantel, P.S., *Le cité au banquet* (Rome 1992).

Paradiso (1988): Paradiso, A., "L'agrégation du nouveau-né au foyer familial: les Amphidromies," *Dialogues d'histoire ancienne* 14 (1988) 203-218.

Parke (1977): H.W. Parke, *Festivals of the Athenians* (London 1977).

Parke (1987): Parke, H.W., *Athenische Feste*, G. Hornbostel, trans. and ed. (Mainz 1987).

Parker (1986): Parker, R., "Myths of Early Athens," in *Interpretations of Greek Mythology*, J. Bremmer, ed. (Totowa, NJ 1986) 187-214.

Passman (1993): Passman, K., "Re(de)fining Women: Language and Power in the Homeric Hymn to Demeter," in *Women's Power, Men's Game*, M. deForest, ed. (Wauconda, IL 1993) 54-77.

Patterson (1981): Patterson, C.B., *Pericles' Citizenship Law of 451-50 B.C.* (New York 1981).

Patterson (1990): Patterson, C.B., "Those Athenian Bastards," *Classical Antiquity* 9 (1990) 40-73.

Patterson (1991): Patterson, C., "Marriage and the Married Woman in Athenian Law," in *Women's History and Ancient History*, S. Pomeroy, ed. (Chapel Hill 1991) 48-72.

Payne (1962): Payne, H., *Perachora, The Sanctuaries of Hera Akraia and Limenaia*, vol. II, T. Dunbabin, ed. (Oxford 1962).

Pearson (1907): Pearson, A.C., ed., *Euripides: The Heraclidae* (Cambridge 1907).

Pellizer (1979): Pellizer, E., "Il fodero e la spada. Metis amorosa e ginecofobia nell'episodio di Circe, Od. X 133ss.," *Quaderni Urbinati di Cultura Classica* N.S. 1 (1979) 67-82.

Pemberton (1989a): Pemberton, E., "The *Dexiosis* on Attic Gravestones," *MeditArch* 2 (1989) 45-50.

Pemberton (1989b): Pemberton, E., *The Sanctuary of Demeter and Kore: The Greek Pottery, Corinth XVIII.1* (Princeton 1989).

Pembroke (1967): Pembroke, S., "Women in Charge: The Function of Alternatives in Early Greek Tradition. The Ancient Idea of Matriarchy," *Journal of the Warburg and Courtauld Institutes* 30 (1967) 3-35.

Peschel (1987): Peschel, I., *Die Hetäre bei Symposion und Komos in der attisch-rotfigurigen Vasenmalerei des 6. - 4. Jahrh. v. Chr.* (Frankfurt am Main 1987).

Pfeiffer (1949-53): Pfeiffer, R., ed., *Callimachus*, 2 vols. (Oxford 1949-53).

Pfuhl (1923): Pfuhl, E., *Malerei und Zeichnung der Griechen*, 3 vols. (Munich 1923).

Philippaki (1967): Philippaki, B., *The Attic Stamnos* (Oxford 1967).

Picard (1930): Picard, C., *La vie privée dans la Grèce classique* (Paris 1930).

Pirenne-Delforge (1994): Pirenne-Delforge, V., *L'Aphrodite grecque* (Athens and Liège 1994).

Pomeroy (1975): Pomeroy, S.B., *Goddesses, Whores, Wives, and Slaves: Women in Classical Antiquity* (New York 1975).

Pomeroy (1983): Pomeroy, S.B., "Infanticide in Hellenistic Greece," in *Images of Women in Antiquity*, A. Cameron and A. Kuhrt, eds. (Detroit 1983) 207-219.

Pomeroy (1991): Pomeroy, S.B., ed., *Women's History and Ancient History* (Chapel Hill 1991).

Pomeroy (1994): Pomeroy, S., *Xenophon Oeconomicus: A Social and Historical Commentary* (Oxford 1994).

Popham, et al. (1982): Popham, M., E. Touloupa, and L.H. Sackett, "The Hero of Lefkandi," *Antiquity* 56 (1982) 169-74.

Powell (1906): Powell, B., *Erichthonius and the Three Daughters of Cecrops*, Cornell Studies in Classical Philology 17 (1906).

Powell (1990): Powell, A., ed., *Euripides, Women, and Sexuality* (London 1990).

Prange (1992): Prange, M., "Der Raub der Leukippiden auf einer Vase des Achilleusmalers," *AntK* 35 (1992) 3-17.

Price (1973): Price, T.H., "Hero Cult and Homer," *Historia* 22 (1973) 129-44.

Price (1978): Price, T.H., *Kourotrophos* (Leiden 1978).

Prückner (1968): Prückner, H., *Die Lokrischen Tonreliefs* (Mayence 1968).

Pucci (1977): Pucci, P., *Hesiod and the Language of Poetry* (Baltimore 1977).

Pucci (1979): Pucci, P., "The Song of the Sirens," *Arethusa* 12 (1979) 121-32.

Pugliese Carratelli (1983): Pugliese Carratelli, G., ed., *Megale Hellas* (Milan 1983).

Radt (1977); Radt, S., *Tragicorum Graecorum Fragmenta* 4 (Göttingen 1977).

Radt (1985): Radt, S., *Tragicorum Graecorum Fragmenta* 3, second ed. (Göttingen 1985).

Raeck (1984): Raeck, W., "Zur Erzählweise archaischer und klassischer Mythenbilder," *JdI* 99 (1984) 1-25.

Redfield (1982): Redfield, J., "Notes on the Greek Wedding," *Arethusa* 15 (1982) 181-201.

Rehm (1994): Rehm, R., *Marriage to Death. The Conflation of Wedding and Funeral Rituals in Greek Tragedy* (Princeton 1994).

Reilly (1989): Reilly, J., "Many Brides: 'Mistress and Maid' on Athenian Lekythoi," *Hesperia* 58 (1989) 411-444.

Reinach (1899-1900): Reinach, S., *Répertoire des vases peints grecs et étrusques*, 2 vols. (Paris 1899-1900).

Reinsberg (1989): Reinsberg, C., *Ehe, Hetärentum und Knabenliebe in antiken Griechenland* (Munich 1989).

Richlin (1992): Richlin, A., ed., *Pornography and Representation in Greece and Rome* (New York and Oxford 1992).

Richter (1957): Richter, G.M.A., "Were there Greek Armaria?" in *Hommages à W. Deonna* (Brussels 1957) 418-423.

Richter (1966): Richter, G.M.A., *The Furniture of the Greeks, Etruscans and Romans* (London 1966).

Richter (1971): Richter, D., "The Position of Women in Classical Athens," *CJ* 67 (1971) 1-8.

Richter and Hall (1936): Richter, G.M.A., and L. Hall, *Red-Figured Athenian Vases in the Metropolitan Museum of Art* (New Haven 1936).

Riddle, et al. (1994): Riddle, J.M., J.W. Estes, and J.C. Russell, "Ever Since Eve... Birth Control in the Ancient World," *Archaeology* 47.2 (1994) 29-35.

Ridgway (1992): Ridgway, B.S., "Images of Athena on the Acropolis," *Goddess and Polis: The Panathenaic Festival in Ancient Athens*, J. Neils, ed. (Hanover 1992) 119-142.

Roberts (1978): Roberts, S., *The Attic Pyxis* (Chicago 1978).

Robertson (1975): Robertson, M., *A History of Greek Art* (Cambridge 1975).

Robertson (1981): Robertson, M., *A Shorter History of Greek Art* (Cambridge 1981).

Robertson (1983): Robertson, N., "The Riddle of the Arrhephoria," *Harvard Studies in Classical Philology* 87 (1983) 241-288.

Robertson (1992): Robertson, M., *The Art of Vase-Painting* (Cambridge and New York 1992).

Rockwell (1991): Rickwell, D., *Giving Voice to Bear* (Niwat, CO 1991).

Rosaldo (1974): Rosaldo, M.Z., ed., *Women, Culture, and Society* (Stanford 1974).

Roscalla (1988): Roscalla, F., "La descrizione del sé e altro: api ed alveare da Esiodo a Semonide," *Quaderni urbinati di cultura classica* 29 (1988) 23-47.

Rotundo (1993): Rotundo, E.A., *American Manhood* (New York 1993).

Rudhardt (1982): Rudhardt, J., "De l'inceste dans la mythologie grecque," *Revue Française de Psychanalyse* 46 (1982) 731-63.

Sabetai (1993): Sabetai, V., *The Washing Painter. A Contribution to the Wedding and Genre Iconography in the Second Half of the Fifth Century B.C.* (Diss., University of Cincinnati 1993).

Salapata (1993): Salapata, G., "The Lakonian Hero Reliefs in the Light of the Terracotta Plaques," in *Sculpture from Arcadia and Laconia*, O. Palagia and W.D.E. Coulson, eds. (Oxford 1993).

Saxonhouse (1986): Saxonhouse, A.W., "Myths and the Origin of Cities: Reflection on the Autochthony Theme in Euripides' *Ion*," in *Greek Tragedy and Political Theory*, J.P. Euben, ed. (Berkeley and Los Angeles 1986) 252-73.

Scafuro (1990): Scafuro, A., "Discourses of Sexual Violation in Mythic Accounts and Dramatic Versions of 'The Girl's Tragedy'," *differences* 2.1 (1990) 126-159.

Scanlon (1990): Scanlon, T.F., "Race or Chase at the Arkteia of Attica?" *Nikephoros* 3 (1990) 73-120.

Schäfer (1987): Schäfer, T., "Diphroi und Peplos auf dem Ostfries der Parthenon," *AM* 102 (1987) 185-212.

Schaps (1979): Schaps, D.M., *Economic Rights of Women in Ancient Greece* (Edinburgh 1979).

Schaps (1982): Schaps, D.M., "The Women of Greece in Wartime," *Classical Philology* 77 (1982) 193-213.

Schefold (1978): Schefold, K., *Götter- und Heldensagen der Griechen in der spätarchaischen Kunst* (Munich 1978).

Schefold (1981): Schefold, K., *Die Göttersage in der klassischen und hellenistischen Kunst* (Munich 1981).

Schefold and Jung (1989): Schefold, K. and F. Jung, *Die Sagen von den Argonauten, von Theben und Troia in der klassischen und hellenistischen Zeit* (Munich 1989).

Scheibler (1964): Scheibler, I., "Kothon-Exaleiptron," *JdI* 98 (1964) 72-108.

Scheidweiler (1908): Scheidweiler, F., *Euphorionis Fragmenta* (Bonn 1908).

Schelp (1975): Schelp, J., *Das Kanoun. Der griechische Opferkorb*, Beiträge zur Archäologie 8 (Würzburg 1975).

Schmidt (1968): Schmidt, M., "Die Entdeckung des Erichthonios," *AM* 83 (1968) 200-212.

Schwarz (1985): Schwarz, G., "Hochzeitsbilder der Parthenonzeit: Die Bostoner Loutrophoros und zwei Lekythen des Phialemalers," in *Pro Arte Antiqua. Festschrift für Hedwig Kenner* II (Vienna and Berlin 1985) 319-325.

Seaford (1987): Seaford, R.A.S., "The Tragic Wedding," *JHS* 107 (1987) 106-130.

Seaford (1994): Seaford, R.A.S., *Reciprocity and Ritual. Homer and Tragedy in the Developing City-State* (Oxford 1994).

Sealey (1987): Sealey, R., *The Athenian Republic: Democracy or the Rule of Law?* (University Park, PA and London 1987).

Sealey (1990): Sealey, R., *Women and Law in Classical Greece* (Chapel Hill 1990).

Segal (1984): Segal, C., "Sex Roles and Reversals in Euripides' *Bacchae*," in *Women in the Ancient World. The Arethusa Papers*, J. Peradotto and J.P. Sullivan, eds. (Albany 1984) 195-212.

Segal (1991): Segal, R.A., "Adonis: A Greek Eternal Child," in *Myth and the Polis*, D.C. Pozzi and J.M. Wickersham, eds. (Ithaca and London 1991) 64-85.

Seremetakis (1993a): Seremetakis, C.N., "Durations of Pain: The Antiphony of Death and Women's Power in Southern Greece," in *Ritual, Power, and the Body: Historical Perspectives on the Representation of Greek Women*, C.N. Seremetakis, ed. (New York 1993) 119-150.

Seremetakis (1993b): Seremetakis, C.N., ed., *Ritual, Power, and the Body: Historical Perspectives on the Representation of Greek Women* (New York 1993).

Serwint (1993): Serwint, N., "The Female Athletic Costume at the Heraia and Prenuptial Initiation Rites," *AJA* 97 (1993) 403-422.

Shapiro (1981a): Shapiro, H.A., *Art, Myth and Culture. Greek Vases from Southern Collections* (New Orleans 1981).

Shapiro (1981b): Shapiro, H.A., "Courtship Scenes in Attic Vase-Painting," *AJA* 85 (1981) 133-43.

Shapiro (1986): Shapiro, H.A., "The Attic Deity Basile," *ZPE* 63 (1986) 134-36.

Shapiro (1989): Shapiro, H.A., *Art and Cult under the Tyrants in Athens* (Mainz 1989).

Shapiro (1990a): Shapiro, H.A., "Comings and Goings: The Iconography of Departure and Arrival on Attic Vases," *Metis* 5.1-2 (1990) 113-123.

Shapiro (1990b): Shapiro, H.A., "The Iconography of Erysichthon. Kallimachos and his Sources," in *Akten des XIII. Internationalen Kongresses für klassische Archäologie. Berlin 1988* (Mainz 1990) 529-530.

Shapiro (1991): Shapiro, H.A., "The Iconography of Mourning in Athenian Art," *AJA* 95 (1991) 629-656.

Shapiro (1992a): Shapiro, H.A., "Theseus in Kimonian Athens: the Iconography of Empire," *Mediterranean Historical Review* 7 (1992) 29-49.

Shapiro (1992b): Shapiro, H.A., "Eros in Love: Pederasty and Pornography in Greece," in *Pornography and Representation in Greece and Rome*, A. Richlin, ed. (Oxford 1992) 53-72.

Shapiro (1993): Shapiro, H.A., *Personifications in Greek Art. The Representation of Abstract Concepts, 600-400 B.C.* (Kilchberg 1993).

Shapiro (1994): Shapiro, H.A., *Myth into Art. Poet and Painter in Classical Greece* (London and New York 1994).

Simon (1953): Simon, E., *Opfernde Götter* (Berlin 1953).

Simon (1982a): Simon, E., "Die Mittelszene im Ostfries des Parthenon," *AM* 97 (1982) 127-144.

Simon (1982b): Simon, E., "Satyr-Plays on Vases in the time of Aeschylus," in *The Eye of Greece. Studies in the Art of Athens*, D. Kurtz and B. Sparkes, eds., (Cambridge 1982) 123-148.

Simon (1983): Simon, E., *Festivals of Attica* (Madison 1983).

Simon (1985): Simon, E., *Die Götter der Griechen*, third ed. (Munich 1985).

Simon and Hampe (1959): Simon, E., and R. Hampe, *Griechische Leben im Spielen der Kunst* (Mainz 1959).

Simon and Hirmer (1976): Simon, E., and M. and A. Hirmer, *Die griechischen Vasen* (Munich 1976).

Simon and Hirmer (1981): Simon, E., and M. and A. Hirmer, *Die griechischen Vasen*, 2nd ed. (Munich 1981).

Sissa (1987): Sissa, G., *Le corps virginal* (Paris 1987).

Sissa (1990): Sissa, G., *Greek Virginity*, Revealing Antiquity 3, trans. A. Goldhammer (Cambridge, MA 1990).

Smith (1896): Smith, C.H., *Catalogue of the Greek and Etruscan Vases in the British Museum*, Vol. 3: *Vases of the Finest Period* (London 1896).

Smith (1939): Smith, H.R.W., *Der Lewismaler* (Leipzig 1939).

Snell and Maehler (1975): Snell, B., and H. Maehler, *Pindar*, 4th ed. (Leipzig 1975).

Snodgrass (1988): Snodgrass, A., "The Archaeology of the Hero," *Annali dell' Istituto Orientale di Napoli* 10 (1988) 19-26.

Sommerstein (1994): Sommerstein, A.H., ed., Aristophanes, *Thesmophoriazusae* (Warminster 1994).

Sourvinou-Inwood (1973): Sourvinou-Inwood, C., "The Young Abductor of the Locrian Pinakes," *BICS* 20 (1973) 12-20.

Sourvinou-Inwood (1978): Sourvinou-Inwood, C., "Persephone and Aphro-dite at Locri: A Model for Personality Definitions in Greek Religion," *JHS* 98 (1978) 101-121.

Sourvinou-Inwood (1985): Sourvinou-Inwood, C., "Altars with Palm-Trees, Palm-Trees, and *Parthenoi*," *BICS* 32 (1985) 125-146.

Sourvinou-Inwood (1987a): Sourvinou-Inwood, C., "A Series of Erotic Pursuits: Images and Meanings," *JHS* 107 (1987) 131-153.

Sourvinou-Inwood (1987b): Sourvinou-Inwood, C., "*Antigone* 904-920: A Reading," *Archeologia e storia antica Annali. Istituto Universitario Orientale, Napoli*, Dipartimento del mondo classico e del mediterraneo antico ix-x (1987-1988) 19-35.

Sourvinou-Inwood (1988a): Sourvinou-Inwood, C., "Further Aspects of Polis Religion," *Archeologia e storia antica Annali. Istituto Universitario Orientale, Napoli, Dipartimento del mondo classico e del mediterraneo antico* X (1990) 259-274.

Sourvinou-Inwood (1988b): Sourvinou-Inwood, C., *Studies in Girls' Transitions: Aspects of the Arkteia and Age Representation in Attic Iconography* (Athens 1988).

Sourvinou-Inwood (1990): Sourvinou-Inwood, C., "What is Polis Religion?" in *The Greek City from Homer to Alexander*, O. Murray and S. Price, eds. (Oxford 1990) 295-322.

Sourvinou-Inwood (1991): Sourvinou-Inwood, C., '*Reading' Greek Culture: Texts and Images, Rituals and Myths* (Oxford 1991).

Sourvinou-Inwood (1994): Sourvinou-Inwood, C., "Something to do with Athens: Tragedy and Ritual," in *Ritual, Finance, Politics. Athenian Democratic Accounts Presented to David Lewis*, R. Osborne and S. Hornblower, eds. (Oxford 1994) 269-290.

Sourvinou-Inwood (1995): Sourvinou-Inwood, C., '*Reading' Greek Death* (Oxford 1995).

Sparkes and Talcott (1970): Sparkes, B., and L. Talcott, *The Athenian Agora XII: Black and Plain Pottery* (Princeton 1970).

Stahl (1987): Stahl, M., *Aristokraten und Tyrannen im archaischen Athen* (Stuttgart 1987).

Stecher (1981): Stecher, A., *Inschriftliche Grabgedichte auf Krieger und Athletin. Eine Studie zu griechischen Wertprädikationen* (Innsbruck 1981).

Steedman (1992): Steedman, C., *Past Tenses* (London 1992).

Stehle (1990): Stehle, E., "Sappho's Gaze: Fantasies of a Goddess and Young Man," *differences* 2.1 (1990) 88-125.

Stewart (1990): Stewart, A.F., *Greek Sculpture: An Exploration* (New Haven 1990).

Stewart (forthcoming): Stewart, A.F., "Imag(in)ing the Other: Amazons and Ethnicity in Fifth-Century Athens," *Poetics Today* (forthcoming).

Stirling (1993): Stirling, I., ed., *Bears* (Emmaus, PA 1993).

Strauss (1993): Strauss, B., *Fathers and Sons in Athens* (Princeton 1993).

Sussman (1984): Sussman, L., "Workers and Drones: Labor, Idleness and Gender Definition in Hesiod's Beehive," in *Women in the Ancient World: The Arethusa Papers*, J. Peradotto and J.P. Sullivan, eds. (Albany 1984) 79-94.

Sutton (1981): Sutton, Jr., R.F., *The Interaction Between Men and Women Portrayed on Attic Red-Figure Pottery* (Diss., University of North Carolina at Chapel Hill 1981).

Sutton (1989a): Sutton, Jr., R.F., ed., *Daidalikon: Studies in Memory of Raymond V. Schoder, S.J.* (Wauconda, IL 1989).

Sutton (1989b): Sutton, Jr., R.F., "On the Classical Athenian Wedding: Two Red-Figure Loutrophoroi in Boston," in *Daidalikon: Studies in Memory of Raymond V. Schoder, S.J.*, R.F. Sutton, Jr., ed. (Wauconda, IL 1989) 331-359.

Sutton (1992): Sutton, Jr., R.F., "Pornography and Persuasion on Attic Pottery," in *Pornography and Representation in Greece and Rome*, A. Richlin, ed. (Oxford 1992) 1-35.

Tatar (1987): Tatar, M., *The Hard Facts of the Grimms' Fairy Tales* (Princeton 1987).

Tatar (1992): Tatar, M., *Off with Their Heads* (Princeton 1992).

Tomaselli and Porter (1986): Tomaselli, S., and R. Porter, eds., *Rape* (Oxford 1986).

Touchefeu-Meynier (1961): Touchefeu-Meynier, O., "Ulysse et Circé; notes sur le chant X de l'Odyssée," *REA* 63 (1961) 264-270.

Touchefeu-Meynier (1968): Touchefeu-Meynier, O., *Thèmes odysséens dans l'art antique* (Paris 1968).

Travlos (1971): Travlos, J., *Pictorial Dictionary of Ancient Athens* (New York 1971).

Trendall (1967): Trendall, A.D., *Phlyax Vases*, second ed., *BICS* Suppl. 19 (London 1967).

True and Hamma (1994): True, M., and K. Hamma, *A Passion for Antiquities. Ancient Art from the Collection of Barbara and Lawrence Fleischman* (Malibu, J. Paul Getty Museum, 1994).

Tyrrell (1984): Tyrrell, W.B., *Amazons: A Study in Athenian Mythmaking* (Baltimore 1984).

Tyrrell and Brown (1991): Tyrrell, W.B., and F.S. Brown, *Athenian Myths and Institutions: Words in Action* (New York and Oxford 1991).

Ussher (1992): Ussher, J., *Women's Madness: Misogyny or Mental Illness?* (Amherst 1992).

Valli and Summers (1993): Valli, E., and D. Summers, "Himalayan Caravans," *National Geographic* 184.6 (1993) 5-35.

Van Bremen (1983): Van Bremen, R., "Women and Wealth," in *Images of Women in Antiquity*, A. Cameron and A. Kuhrt, eds. (Detroit 1983) 223-242.

Veith (1965): Veith, I., *Hysteria: The History of a Disease* (Chicago 1965).

Verdenius (1985): Verdenius, W.J., *A Commentary on Hesiod: Works and Days, vv. 1-382* (Leiden 1985).

Vermeule (1979): Vermeule, E., *Aspects of Death in Early Greek Art and Poetry* (Berkeley and Los Angeles 1979).

Vermeule (1981): Vermeule, C.C., *Greek and Roman Sculpture in America. Masterpieces in Public Collections in the United States and Canada* (Berkeley and Los Angeles 1981).

Vernant (1980a): Vernant, J.-P., *Myth and Society in Ancient Greece*, trans. J. Lloyd (London 1980).

Vernant (1980b): Vernant, J.-P., "The Myth of Prometheus in Hesiod," in *Myth and Society in Ancient Greece*, trans. J. Lloyd (London 1980) 168-85.

Vernant (1985): Vernant, J.-P., *La mort dans les yeux* (Évreux 1985).

Vernant (1989): Vernant, J.-P., "At Man's Table: Hesiod's Foundation Myth of Sacrifice," in Detienne, M., and J.-P. Vernant, *The Cuisine of Sacrifice Among the Greeks*, trans. P. Wissing (Chicago 1989) 21-86, 224-37.

Vernant (1991): Vernant, J.-P., *Mortals and Immortals. Collected Essays*, F.I. Zeitlin, ed. (Princeton 1991).

Versnel (1980): Versnel, H.S., "Self-Sacrifice, Compensation and the Anonymous Gods," in *Le Sacrifice dans l'Antiquité*, Entretiens Hardt 27 (Vandoeuvres-Genève 1980) 136-185.

Versnel (1990): Versnel, H.S., "What's Sauce for the Goose is Sauce for the Gander: Myth and Ritual, Old and New," in *Approaches to Greek Myth*, L. Edmunds, ed. (Baltimore 1990) 25-90.

Vidal-Naquet (1968): Vidal-Naquet, P., "Le chasseur noir et l'origine de l'éphébie athénienne," *Annales: Economies, Sociétés, Civilisations* 23 (1968) 947-964.

Vidal-Naquet (1981): Vidal-Naquet, P., "Slavery and the Rule of Women in Tradition, Myth and Utopia," in *Myth, Religion and Society*, R.L. Gordon, ed. (Cambridge 1981) 187-200.

Vidal-Naquet (1986): Vidal-Naquet, P., *The Black Hunter. Forms of Thoought and Forms of Society in the Greek World* (Baltimore and London 1986).

Walbank (1981): Walbank, W.B., "Artemis Bear-Leader," *Classical Quarterly* 31 (1981) 276-281.

Walcot (1978): Walcot, P., "Herodotus on Rape," *Arethusa* 11 (1978) 137-47.

Walcot (1984): Walcot, P., "Greek Attitudes towards Women: The Mythological Evidence," *Greece and Rome* 31 (1984) 37-47.

Wegner (1963): Wegner, M., *Musikgeschichte in Bildern* II: *Musik des Altertums* 4, *Griechenland* (Leipzig 1963).

Wehgartner (1983): Wehgartner, I., *Attisch Weissgrundige Keramik*, Keramikforschungen V (Mainz am Rhein 1983).

Weidauer (1985): Weidauer, L., "Eumolpos und Athen," *AA* 1985, 195-210.

Weidauer and Krauskopf (1992): Weidauer, L., and I. Krauskopf, "Urkönige in Athen und Eleusis," *JdI* 107 (1992) 1-16.

Weill (1966): Weill, N., "Adoniazousai ou les femmes sur le toit," *BCH* 90 (1966) 664-698.

Wells (1975): Wells, C., "Ancient Obstetric Hazards and Female Mortality," *Bulletin of the New York Academy of Medicine* 51 (1975) 1235-49.

West (1966): West, M.L., *Hesiod: Theogony* (Oxford 1966).

West (1978): West, M.L., *Hesiod: Works and Days* (Oxford 1978).

West (1985): West, M.L., *The Hesiodic Catalogue of Women* (Oxford 1985).

Wilkins (1990): Wilkins, J., "The State and the Individual: Euripides' Plays of Voluntary Self-Sacrifice," in *Euripides, Women and Sexuality*, A. Powell, ed. (London 1990) 177-194.

Wilkins (1993): Wilkins, J., *Euripides: Heraclidae* (Oxford 1993).

Williams (1961): Williams, R.T., "An Attic Red-figure Calathos," *AntK* 4 (1961) 27-29.

Williams (1983): Williams, D., "Women on Athenian Vases: Problems of Interpretation," in *Images of Women in Antiquity*, A. Cameron and A. Kuhrt, eds. (Detroit 1983) 92-106.

Williams and Ogden (1994): Williams, D., and J. Ogden, *Greek Gold. Jewellery of the Classical World* (London 1994).

Wilson (1978): Wilson, E.A., *On Human Nature* (Cambridge 1978).

Wilson (1989): Wilson, G., *The Great Sex Divide. A Study of Male-Female Differences* (London 1989).

Winkler (1990a): Winkler, J.J., *The Constraints of Desire. The Anthropology of Sex and Gender in Ancient Greece* (New York 1990).

Winkler (1990b): Winkler, J.J., "Phallos Politikos: Representing the Body Politic in Athens," *differences* 2.1 (1990) 29-45.

Wolters (1930): Wolters, P., "Kirke," *AM* 55 (1930) 209-236.

Zancani-Montuoro (1954): Zancani-Montuoro, P., "Note sui soggetti e sulla tecnica delle tabelle di Locri," *Atti e Memorie della Società Magna Grecia*, N.S. 1 (1954) 71-106.

Zeitlin (1978): Zeitlin, F.I., "The Dynamics of Misogyny: Myth and Mythmaking in the *Oresteia*," *Arethusa* 11 (1978) 149-184.

Zeitlin (1982): Zeitlin, F.I., "Cultic Models of the Female: Rites of Dionysos and Demeter," *Arethusa* 15 (1982) 129-157.

Zeitlin (1985): Zeitlin, F.I., "Playing the Other: Theater, Theatricality, and the Feminine in Greek Drama," *Representations* 11 (1985) 63-94.

Zeitlin (1986): Zeitlin, F.I., "Configurations of Rape in Greek Myth," in *Rape*, S. Tomaselli and R. Porter, eds. (Oxford 1986) 122-51.

Zeitlin (1993): Zeitlin, F.I., "Staging Dionysus between Thebes and Athens," in *Masks of Dionysus*, T. H. Carpenter and C.A. Faraone, eds. (Ithaca 1993) 147-82.

Zeitlin (1994): Zeitlin, F.I., "The Artful Eye: Vision, Ekphrasis and Spectacle in Euripidean Theatre," in *Art and Text in Ancient Greece*, S. Goldhill and R. Osborne, eds. (Cambridge 1994) 138-96.

Zweig (1993): Zweig, B., "The Only Women Who Give Birth to Men," in *Women's Power, Men's Game*, M. deForest, ed. (Wauconda, IL 1993) 32-53.

GLOSSARY

aegis — shaggy or scaly skin with a fringe of snakes and a gorgoneion in the center, often worn by Athena

Agora — marketplace or place of assembly; the central marketplace of Athens

aidos — respectful modesty of demeanor, with strong overtones of sexual shame

akroterion (pl. *akroteria*) — architectural decoration placed at the peaks and corners of a pitched roof

alabastron (pl. *alabastra*) — a small, elongated, cylindrical vessel with a rounded bottom, often containing perfumed oil.

amphora (pl. *amphorae*) — a two-handled jar for containing wine, water or oil

anakalypsis — the gesture whereby the bride fingers her veil in front of her shoulder

anakalypteria — the moment of unveiling in the wedding ceremony

anta (pl. *antae*) — architectural projection which is rectangular in section

arete — excellence

aryballos — a small vase with a rounded bottom and narrow neck, for containing oil

aulos (pl. *auloi*) — a flute-like instrument played with a mouthpiece, often as a pair

chiton — a dress of lightweight fabric

chlamys — a short cloak

chthonic — of or from the earth or the Underworld

deme — a district within Attica

diphros — a chair without a back

engye — the marriage agreement between the groom and the bride's father or kyrios

ephebe — adolescent youth who has entered his two years of military training, between the ages of eighteen and twenty

epikleros — "heiress": a woman whose father dies without male heirs, and who therefore is obligated to marry a relative in her father's family.

Gorgoneion — the disembodied head of the Gorgon, which becomes a device that wards off evil.

gynaikon (also *gynaikonitis*) — the women's quarters of the house

gyne — wife, married woman

hetaira (pl. *hetairai*) — female "companion", or prostitute

himation (pl. *himatia*) — a cloak consisting of a large rectangular cloth, worn draped over the shoulder and wrapped around the body

hydria (pl. *hydriae*) — a water jar with one vertical handle on the back and two horizontal handles on the sides

kalathos — a wool basket with a flaring mouth

kalos — a word meaning "beautiful" or "noble", which when attached to a person's name expresses love or admiration

kalyx krater — a krater with two low handles

kanephoros — an unmarried virgin who functioned as a ritual basket carrier in a religious festival.

kanoun — a basket used for ritual purposes

kantharos — a cup with two vertical handles and a tall foot

kiste — a basket or chest, usually short and cylindrical

kithara — a large stringed instrument resembling the lyre

klismos — a chair with a back

kolpos — the fold of a garment that falls over a belt

kore — unmarried maiden, like a parthenos, sometimes with the connotation of daughter; also a statue of a maiden

kouros — unmarried youth; also a statue of a youth

krater — a large mixing bowl for wine and water, with a wide mouth and a deep belly

kylix (pl. *kylikes*) — a two-handled cup with a broad, shallow bowl, and often a tall foot

kyrios — the head of a family and legal guardian of all women and minors within the household

larnax — box or chest for household storage

lebes gamikos (pl. *lebetes gamikoi*) — "wedding bowl," a deep bowl with a stand

lekythos (pl. *lekythoi*) — a jug with one handle and a narrow neck, often containing oil

liknon — winnowing fan

loutrophoros (pl. *loutrophoroi*) — a tall slender jar with high neck used to carry bathwater for weddings

miasma — pollution or defilement of persons or environments, usually by committing of a crime or contact with the dead

mychos — innermost chamber

naiskos (pl. *naiskoi*) — small shrine with pedimental roof

Nike (pl. *Nikai*) — personification of Victory, a winged female

nymphe — about to be wed, or newly wed, a status that ends with the birth of the first child

oikos (pl. *oikoi*) — household, the family unit

oinochoe (pl. *oinochoai*) — a jug with one handle, used to hold and pour liquids

palaestra — wrestling-school

Panathenaia — the major festival of Athens, celebrated every year, and every fourth year with greater pomp (The Great Panathenaia), on the birthday of Athena.

parthenos — unmarried maiden

pelike — a type of amphora with is greatest width toward its base

peplos — a heavy garment, usually of wool, secured by a pin on each shoulder and worn open on one side or with a belt

petasos — a cap worn by travelers

phiale — a wide, flat bowl without handles or stem, often with a raised central boss, used for ritual libations

phratry — a "brotherhood" or kinship group.

plemochoe — a wide, flat bowl on a high stem, used for unguents and cosmetics

pyxis — a round box used for cosmetics or other small objects

sakkos — a haircovering in the form of a tasseled cap

skyphos — a tall drinking-cup

sophrosyne — discretion, dignity, and moderation of desires

stamnos — a large jar with a short neck and two horizontal handles, used for wine

stele — gravestone; block or slab used as a memorial

stephane — a crown, especially the bridal crown

symposium (pl. *symposia*) — a drinking party

thalamos — treasure chamber and marriage chamber

thymiaterion — incense burner

thyrsos — a fennel-stalk wand ending in a leafy projection like a pinecone, carried by Dionysos and Maenads

volute krater — a krater with two high handles surmounted by volutes

PHOTOGRAPHY CREDITS

THIS BOOK WAS DESIGNED AND COMPOSED BY
ALEX CASTRO
IN MINION AND GILL SANS FONTS
AND WAS PRINTED AND BOUND BY
AMILCARE PIZZI, MILAN